Save the Beatles!

Save the Beatles!
The Rescued Albums: 1970-1982

Rick Prescott

Save the Beatles!
The Rescued Albums: 1970-1982

Copyright © 2020 Lowell H. Prescott.

All rights reserved. No portion of this book may be reproduced in any form without written permission from the author, except as permitted by U.S. copyright law.

This is a work of music criticism. All images are either in the public domain, the copyrighted work of the author, or used for the purpose of criticism under the principles of fair use of copyrighted material as provided for in section 107 of the U.S. copyright law.

Any trademarks remain the property of their owner and are used herein only to review, editorialize and/or describe items related to the trademark holder.

ISBN 978-0-578-68028-6
First Edition, April 2020

For permissions, bulk sales, or other information, please visit:

SaveTheBeatles.com

In Memoriam

Julie Dehn (1940-1991)
who taught me Honor, and the value of asking the right Questions

and

Larry Fleming (1936-2003)
who taught me the essential nature of Details, and that it's all Music

Contents

Prologue xi
Preface xiii
Author's Note xv
Using This Book xix

Part I / Division

1 / Circles 5
2 / Filters 19
3 / Phases 41

Part II / Divination

4 / Tiers 57
5 / Blueprints 67
6 / Structure 77
7 / Façade 89
8 / Proof-of-Concept #1 – *Revolver* 105
9 / Proof-of-Concept #2 – *Magic Myst* 115
10 / Proof-of-Concept #3 – *January* 131
11 / Fusion 145

Part III / Diversion

12 / *Dream* 163
13 / *Beggars in a Gold Mine* 223
14 / *Be Here Now* 269
15 / *Vienna* 323
16 / *Flight* 373
17 / ... Hiatus ... 415
18 / *Wheels, Walls and Waterfalls* 431
19 / *In Spite of All* 465
20 / Coda 503

Appendix

I / Creative Calendar 511
II / Distilled Core Studio Releases 519
III / Catalog of Solo Recordings 535
IV / Certified Sales 565
V / Chart Scoring 571
VI / Beatles Recordings 575
VII / Summary of Rescued Albums 581
Bibliography 583
Song and Album Index 589
About the Author 596

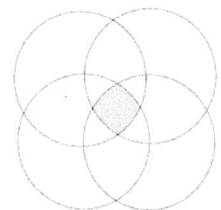

It is not to ring the bell backward
Nor is it an incantation
To summon the spectre of a Rose.

Prologue

"...whenever you listen to too much of the solo stuff, it kind of becomes a drag, you know? But you put 'em next to each other, alright, and they start to elevate each other... and then you can hear it. Huh! It's the Beatles!"

– Dad, *Boyhood* (2014)

Every Beatles fan has done it. You take your favorite songs from the solo Beatles and put them on a single tape, CD or playlist to create a sort of *Frankenstein's Post-Breakup Beatles Album*. I'll never forget hearing Paul's "London Town" on the radio in 1979, followed immediately by George's "Blow Away." The DJ said something like, "Hey! We got your Beatles reunion right here!"

With the advent of YouTube, iTunes, Spotify, Pandora, Tumblr, Blogger, et. al., you can now find an endless supply of such playlists, though they all seem to be variations on a theme. Basically, all of these lists should be titled *My Favorite Greatest Hits of the Former Beatles*. They tend to be made up of the familiar songs from the 70s, collected with only passing regard for style or date or sequence — basically just like *any* greatest hits album: Nice to have together in one place, I suppose, but also not very interesting to anyone but the list's creator.

Some playlists are at least a step up from that. Consider, for example, the so-called *Beatles' Black Album* created by actor Ethan Hawke and referenced by his character in the quote above. Hawke's three discs (his track listings are now widely available) include all of the familiar hits, and he throws in a few album tracks as wild cards along the way. In the words of his character, the music was "carefully found, arranged, and ordered" to get it just right. Another character chimes in: "*Very* arranged and *very* organized, over and over again..."

Even so, he has mixed eras freely, and sequenced in a surprisingly haphazard, if also sometimes overly obvious, way. For example, he clumsily places "Beautiful Boy (Darling Boy)" (John, 1980) between "Bluebird" (Paul, 1973) and "What is Life?" (George, 1970). He opens disc three with John's "Grow Old with Me," then cloyingly follows it with five tracks containing the word "love" in the title. He treats an entire decade of music as if it happened all at once. Frankly, his discs are something of a slog to get through.

There's nothing inherently wrong with these collections. They are fun to make, fun to listen to (up to a point) and no doubt immensely satisfying to their creators. There is no reason to discourage anyone from having fun with Beatles tracks, group or solo. It feels almost like every fan's sacred obligation to explore the question of what it would sound like to put the Beatles back together again.

This book engages in an activity which may seem similar on the surface, but is very different at its core. Here you will find a different methodology, in service to a very different goal. This book explores in great detail what might have happened to the art of the Beatles in the 70s if they had recorded exactly as they did — that is, separately — but then pooled their recordings as dictated by market and creative forces, and applied the same album assembly techniques used to build their classic albums. In other words: What if they had recorded separately, but assembled and released together?

There are reasons to think they could have done such a thing, including the fact that they discussed something along these lines amongst themselves in September of 1969. We also have significant resources at our disposal to figure out how it might have worked, and what the results would have sounded like.

It's a fun pursuit, but also a serious one. It involves detailed analysis of structures from their original albums, as well as a deep dive into how those structures made the most of their materials, and how the artistic processes and decisions worked on both micro and macro levels. It involves new critical analysis of the solo materials, removed from the context of sometimes exasperating solo albums, with an ear toward understanding the music within the post-1970 group dynamic, as well as the shifting popular tastes and evolving music industry.

The idea is not to weave a fantasy narrative, as much fun as that might be, but to consider the artistic and marketing decisions that might have been made by the Beatles' creative team with the music they produced in roughly the first decade after their last group recordings. In the process, we will explore the inherent nature, features and limits of the ever-mysterious Beatle Magic.

The surprising result is a revelation which has been hiding in plain sight all these years. Put simply, the magic of the Beatles *can* be reanimated, and their voices *can* once again elevate one another with powerful — even *thrilling* — results. Music that you know well, and some that you might not, springs to life in seemingly impossible ways. When the creative arcs of the four artists are carefully brought back into sync, it turns out they were in a sort of unseen sync all along. And, when allowed to run its course, this musical thought experiment teaches a shocking but essential lesson that every Beatles fan simply must learn.

Preface

In the fall of 1981, when I arrived for my freshman year at the University of Minnesota, I carried with me exactly one Beatles album, if you can call it that: The "blue" greatest hits package. I did not even own the "red" version, because the family across the street had purchased that one, and we had a deal with them to share the four discs. I did also carry a couple of solo albums, and a handful of cassette mix tapes, including a large segment of a "Beatles A to Z" broadcast taped from radio in the days after Lennon's death. Unfortunately, I only started my tape at "I Feel Fine."

Perhaps more important than the records and tapes, however, was the book I carried and could not put down. *The Beatles: An Illustrated Record*, by Roy Carr and Tony Tyler, was my Beatles bible. Not even six months after its release, my copy was already heavily worn and nearly memorized as I arrived in Minneapolis from my small hometown — where the Ben Franklin was our record store, and their bin had a separation card for the Beatles, but only one sad copy of *Beatles '65* to separate.

One of the first things I discovered about my new home was that the record store in Coffman Union stocked *imports*. That offered the previously unimaginable possibility of owning the Beatles' catalog in the exact configurations that God and the Beatles had originally intended, as trumpeted by Carr & Tyler. (The second thing I discovered was that a whole lot of bin space in that store was given to an up-and-coming local artist named Prince, who eventually obtained large chunks of my disposable income.) It turned out that Beatles imports came into stock only sporadically, and it took nearly the full four years to complete my collection, but eventually I got them all. The Carr & Tyler book served as both shopping list and syllabus to my Beatle studies. In the end, plenty of my college textbooks stayed pristine, while those albums became highly studied acquisitions.

Solo albums were considerably easier to obtain, and I filled my checklist from the Musicland in Dinkytown, and an independent record store down the street known as Positively Fourth Street. Again, the book served as my guide in this wilderness, and I took my time working on my collection. When finances allowed (and between Prince releases), I would purchase an album, and play it over and over until I knew every detail. In some cases I moved on to the next title quickly, but some would keep me entertained for months before I needed a new fix.

Though I knew Carr & Tyler's reviews in advance of hearing the music, I inevitably found that I didn't always agree with them. Their tone began to feel a little too flippant and dismissive. They were harsh toward some music that I liked very much, and raved about things that I found less compelling, even annoying. They were clearly "John fans," and took every opportunity to elevate his work over that of the others. This is understandable given the timing of its publication (spring of 1981), but seriously undermined their credibility as the shock of Lennon's murder faded, and I gradually got to know the actual music.

Like many people my age, with no firsthand memories of the Beatles as a group, it was actually Paul's records which first caught my attention, mainly due to their ubiquity on FM radio. Carr & Tyler, however, savaged much of Paul's solo work, and for reasons I could not understand. It was almost as if his ubiquity was itself a bad thing. The more solo albums I got to know, the more the reviews seemed skewed in perplexing directions. To my uninitiated ears, Paul's work seemed to have a wide range of quality, just like John's, George's, and Ringo's. Each former Beatle had good moments and bad. I would learn later that many critics and fans in the 70s heard the music through the lens of the 60s and the band's breakup. But having been only six years old when the Beatles broke up, and having not heard of any of them until the mid-70s, I had no such lens. I just heard the music, free of all that emotional overhead. I have always considered that to be a very great advantage, and I believe it to be critical to this project.

So, as I got to know the music, I put the book down, and have seldom picked it up since. Despite being grateful to Carr & Tyler for guiding me into the Beatles' musical universe, I learned to trust my own instincts, which have been honed by a formal education in music, five years in radio, ten years in a recording studio producing, arranging and engineering, and decades working as a composer, conductor, and professional vocalist, keyboard player and guitarist.

Through my extensive adventures in music, I became able to hear popular music through the filters of radio and music industry insiders — those generally non-artistic people whose decisions often have oversized artistic impacts. I learned the techniques and importance of properly contextualizing music while producing programs of choral music for public radio. And I came to understand audience expectations first hand by playing bass guitar for years in a Beatles-obsessed band — where we always played whatever song a partying audience member might call out, even if we'd never played it before. In our greatest triumph, we once opened a show for Badfinger, the closest thing I have to a bona fide Beatles connection.

This book is not about me. I offer this background only to give you a sense of where my ideas and opinions come from, and to make it clear that I take this subject very seriously while also hopefully not *too* seriously.

While writing this book, I got a new car that came with a three-month free trial to one of the satellite radio services. Of over 150 channels, only one appealed to me, and so my kids and I listened to *The Beatles Channel* eight days a week for those three months. It reminded me again of how much I love the Beatles' music — group and solo — and how much I want to share that love in a way which hopefully gives other fans, like you, something new to consider.

Author's Note

    This project began with the notion that I would simply create a few playlists, post them on YouTube, and be done. I didn't think of it as anything more than a few days of fun listening and tinkering over a holiday break. I certainly didn't expect to spend over two years researching and writing about this. Indeed, the idea of adding to the large pile of Beatle books already out there would have seemed foolish had I thought of it, and it didn't even cross my mind at first.

    But I quickly realized that, despite having a fair amount of knowledge about the band and the solo artists, I didn't have *enough* information to either fully satisfy my curiosity or to create the best possible finished product. With much of this music being meaningful and even sacrosanct to so many people, including me, attempting what I imagined would require great care and consideration, if only to satisfy myself. Once that principle become obvious, so did my own deficiencies for meeting it. Likewise, after some serious searching, it became apparent that the resources I needed didn't actually exist, at least not quite. That's when it became a book project.

    For example, I felt like I really needed to understand how the Beatles assembled and sequenced their classic albums, not from a fan's perspective, but from the artist's perspective. This would involve much more than simple track lists. I needed to better understand the rhythms and influences (inside and outside) that put pressure on their recording and release schedules. This required a different kind of chronology than is typically available. I wanted to know more about how the group dynamic evolved musically, beyond all of the conventional shorthand, which seems a lot less reliable once you start considering the quality of the sources, and the effects of time. This involved charting things that I had never seen charted before. Most of all, I needed greater clarity on how it worked that the four voices interacted with and elevated each other when they were at their best — both inside the studio and on the finished records. This required closer looks at all of those interactions.

    I recognized that I needed to revisit *all* of the solo records, even those which had languished into obscurity, and especially those I found so unpalatable that I hadn't listened to them in 30 years. I could state from memory the general chronology of each solo career, but needed to know more about how those careers remained intertwined even as the final group recording session faded into memory. I had a vague sense of how the music industry changed in the 70s, but needed more knowledge of the context in which hypothetical Beatles albums would have been assembled and released. This type of deep understanding was essential before I could begin poking and prodding the music to see what it could do.

    After only a short time it dawned on me that I was actually setting out to play a very elaborate version of the same parlor game that Beatles fans have been playing for decades. But I wanted to do it with actual knowledge, and a thorough understanding of the creative processes used by the artists. I realized that, since I would have to assemble the necessary resources myself, and since I had to develop some method of quantifying and channeling the creativity of the Beatles, other fans might like to join the game. Arming people with more Beatle knowledge seems like a noble endeavor, and there would be obvious limits on what I could accomplish by myself. Other fans, armed with the same knowledge, might come to completely different conclusions. That possibility is intriguing, and baked into this project (more in the next section, *Using This Book*).

If we believe that albums are art, then creating new ones — even when doing so as a thought experiment — is an artistic enterprise. The popular solo tracks are pretty well known. What is not known is how a different context can change how they interact with each other, how they can be heard afresh, and how overlooked or under appreciated tracks might *become* essential. That is the charter of this book.

As such, it's important for me to be clear that an essential portion of this book is about how the Beatles assembled their classic albums. Only through understanding that can we move to using those principles on the solo material to assemble albums as they might have. Only through deep understanding of the real world landscape of group and solo music can we make different but *informed* artistic decisions with the solo materials. That makes this a book of music criticism — a connect-the-dots project, if you will — and not a history. You will likely find no new anecdotes or quotes in these pages. Instead, you will find a critical and detailed look at the structure of the classic Beatles albums, new assessments of the music of the solo years, and attempts to marry those two sets of ideas into something special.

In other words, I am not interested in *describing* the music, or retelling the same old stories about how that music came to be, or even labeling tracks "great" or not (though I will, albeit with a different sort of granularity). I am much more interested in *understanding* and *illuminating* the music, because it is my belief that, in order to fully appreciate the solo works of the former Beatles, you simply *must* listen to them next to those of the other former Beatles. When you do, they gain unexpected life — well, *some* of them. That is what I will attempt to show in these pages.

Let me close by underlining something important, and that is to acknowledge how much you already know about the Beatles. I will assume that you are a fan, like me, and you've probably read a whole lot of books about the band, as have I. As such, I don't feel like I have to retell those stories you've already heard many times. When it comes to the Beatles, it seems like every story has been told and retold until we can recite them in our sleep. And when I say, "How Do You Sleep?" you know before I finish speaking what stories I'm talking about.

But if you don't, don't worry. You are still entirely welcome here, and I promise that you'll get everything you need in order to make sense of these ideas, even if sometimes it may be a reference to another book. Basically, I think it's fair to say that *literally millions* of people are *literally experts* on the Beatles, and I want to

Author's Note

acknowledge that you are potentially such a person. In fact, since you are reading this book, there's a decent chance that you could have *written* this book. I want to openly acknowledge that.

Setting aside your level of knowledge, I'm also pretty confident that you, like me, have tried to imagine what might have happened musically if the Beatles had not broken up when and how they did. We've pondered the music they might have made together in the 70s, if only they had found a way around their differences. Even though we know how unlikely that was, given the undulations of vitriol between the various parties, we find ways to set that aside and just wonder: *What if?*

That curiosity is all you really need in order to enjoy what I have put together here. You do not *need* encyclopedic knowledge about the group to enjoy these pages, but it shouldn't be a problem if you have it. I'm going to assume that you know the basics, probably more, and I will retell familiar stories only as absolutely necessary to understand and illustrate these ideas.

Also, you do not need to agree with me, and you probably won't. I accept that, and celebrate it! Ultimately, my goal is just to forge a new path through the first decade of the solo years, and open up new avenues of enjoyment for you, Beatle fan that you already are.

Using This Book

By the time you finish this book, I hope you have a new way to enjoy the recordings made by the former Beatles in the 1970s. To that end, here are some important considerations while reading this book.

First, you will get the most out of this if you actually *listen to the records* to fully understand my comments and ideas. This can mean listening to individual tracks as they are discussed, but more importantly it means actually listening to the new connections between tracks that I will offer. I say this because I believed, at first, that I knew this music well enough to do these thought experiments in my head. Then I tried them and discovered that I was dead wrong. Actually listening to two tracks together is completely different from *imagining* listening to them together. No matter how well you know the solo catalogs, your ears can tell you things that your memory cannot.

So, when I tell you that "Junior's Farm" sits shockingly well next to "What You Got" (chapter 15), I do not want you to take my word for it. Nor do I want you to think about the idea and accept or reject it without actually listening. Through actual listening, and playing around with this music, I learned things and made unexpected discoveries. Tracks I thought I knew well sounded *different* than I remembered. When I pulled at the threads of the solo years, it became clear why that happened, and I want you to share in those revelations. Perhaps you will have new ones of your own. But revelations like I've had cannot be imagined. They must be *heard* and *reproducible*. While reading, plan to get out your turntable! (I suppose you could just fire up YouTube, but how much fun will it be to dust off those old albums?)

Second, I also hope that the listening will make you want to continue the conversation when you finish reading. Since you may disagree — perhaps passionately — with my criticism and artistic suggestions, I want to make it possible for you to respond, and for discussions to develop. Consider this book an invitation to collaborate, rather than something you simply read passively. I am genuinely interested in your ideas.

I also want to make it easy for you to use the resources I have created to either tweak what I have done, or simply scrap it and create your own hypothetical albums, whether based on the principles and techniques established here, or on your own.

All of this, and more, is available at:

SaveTheBeatles.com

With a one-time, free registration, plus verification of your book purchase, you will have unlimited access to enhanced versions of all research materials, including the inevitable corrections and amplifications, and be able to post your own ideas and participate in ongoing discussion.

Most chapters are titled with a single word, as are some sections within the text. On the home page of the site, you can enter that word (for chapters with multi-word titles, use the first word) to be taken directly to the moderated discussion of that section of the book. I moderate all of the comments myself, and read every single submission, responding as appropriate, or just letting the discussion take its course. I moderate to guarantee that every post is worth the time to read for those who have bothered to show up. I genuinely want and appreciate your feedback.

Additionally, through the web site you will have access to the podcast, which introduces each side of each fictional album, as well as other topics related to this project. Please join the project! I look forward to meeting you there.

Conventions

- The **survey period** for this project runs from the release of "Give Peace a Chance" (69-Jul) through *Milk and Honey* (84-Jan). Recordings made before or after this point are not considered.

- Recordings not officially released during the survey period, even if they were released later, are considered to have been **"in the vault."**

- *Album Titles* are italicized.

- **"Song Titles"** are in quotes within bodies of text, but not in track listings.

- **Pseudonymous releases** are defined as projects in which the identity of the participating Beatle was intentionally obscured.

- The silence between tracks is called a **rill**. When mentioned, rills are given in seconds plus decimal parts (not frames). Rills in parentheses indicate a cross-fade, with the first sound of the following track beginning that many seconds before the last sound of the previous track. First and last sounds are defined as any discernible non-silence at the boundary of a fade, be it fade in or out. (Specifying a minimum dB is problematic due to limitations of LPs.) By design, some cross-fades result in portions of tracks not being audible.

- SLS stands for "silly love song."

Save the Beatles!

Part I
Division

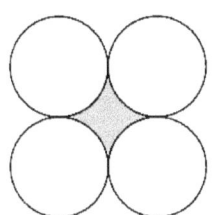

I think, again, of this place,
And of people, not wholly commendable,
Of not immediate kin or kindness,
But of some peculiar genius,
All touched by a common genius,
United in the strife which divided them.

1
Circles

There will be one Beatle there, fine. Two Beatles, great. Three Beatles, fantastic. But the minute the four of them are there...that is when the inexplicable charismatic thing happens, the special magic no one has been able to explain. ...you'll be aware of this inexplicable presence.

— George Martin, quoted by Chris Thomas[1]

As the summer of 1969 faded, the Beatles lurched apart, never to reassemble. Among the final sounds they made together were the epic guitar and drum features for "The End," the unison vocal chant of "Carry That Weight," and the ethereal, timeless, pristine harmonies of "Because." During those heady final days, they also strolled a nearby crosswalk for arguably their most iconic photograph. As final statements go, it is hard to imagine one more confident, successful, and powerful.

For the better part of a decade, the four musicians had moved in tandem, musically and personally, and scaled artistic heights previously unimagined in popular music. But once the final note of *Abbey Road* was in place, each artist, now a superstar in his own right, began forging a new musical path, surrounded by new circumstances and collaborators. Instead of bearing one quarter of the artistic burden, each would now carry that weight alone.

John Lennon began the solo era in earnest[2] by releasing singles and eventually dropping the familiar "Lennon/McCartney" songwriting credit. Ringo Starr took the advice of friends and recorded an album of standards for his mum. George Harrison produced and performed with other acts before pouring his back catalog onto a triple album. Paul McCartney retreated to his farm, and rented a four-track recorder with which to doodle.

In the decade that followed, each former Beatle went on to gradually, and somewhat painfully, develop his own style and identity as a solo artist. Just as they had lurched apart, each now lurched forward, with wildly uneven results. After multiple false starts, Paul routinely topped the charts as a quasi-solo act. The other former Beatles also eventually topped the charts, if less routinely. By 1980, however, both George and Ringo had been dropped by a record company, and neither Ringo nor John had recording contracts of any kind.

---

[1] *The Beatles Recording Sessions*, pg. 174
[2] Experimental and "found sound" recordings are not considered here.

This is not how anyone imagined the solo era would turn out.

To be sure, each former Beatle has made at least *some* great records since leaving the group. Each had at least a couple of big hits. Each made at least one album that is considered a classic all on its own. Some of those albums are positively beloved.

THE HITS: 1970-1983

Solo releases that went to #1 in either the US or UK or both

ALBUMS	Imagine Walls and Bridges* Double Fantasy+	McCartney* Ram^ Red Rose Speedway* Band on the Run Venus and Mars Wings at the Speed of Sound* McCartney II^ Tug of War	All Things Must Pass Living in the Material World*	
SINGLES	"Whatever Gets You thru the Night"* "(Just Like) Starting Over"+ "Woman"^+	"Uncle Albert/Admiral Halsey"* "My Love"* "Band on the Run"* "Listen to What the Man Said"* "Silly Love Songs"* "Mull of Kintyre"^ "With a Little Luck"* "Coming Up"* "Ebony and Ivory" "Say Say Say"* "Pipes of Peace"^	"My Sweet Lord" "Give Me Love (Give Me Peace on Earth)"*	"Photograph"* "You're Sixteen"*

* US only   ^ UK only   + Posthumous

All too many solo releases, however, met a much different fate. Some, nearly unlistenable, were disdained or savaged by critics and fans alike. Others, despite better quality, were virtually ignored, selling poorly and making no discernable impact on the culture or other recording artists. Today, some of these releases are unknown to all but the most die-hard fans.

1 / Circles

The Misses: 1970-1983

Releases that did not make the top ten on either the US or UK charts

	John	Paul	George	Ringo
ALBUMS	Some Time in New York City		Thirty Three & 1/3 George Harrison Somewhere in England Gone Troppo^	Beaucoups of Blues* Ringo's Rotogravure Ringo the 4th^ Bad Boy^ Stop and Smell the Roses* Old Wave^
SINGLES	"Cold Turkey" "Mother"* "Love"* "Woman Is the Nigger of the World"* "Mind Games" "Stand By Me" "Borrowed Time"+ "I'm Steppin' Out" *+	"Back Seat of My Car" "Give Ireland Back to the Irish" "Venus and Mars/Rock Show" "Letting Go" "London Town" "I've Had Enough" "Arrow Through Me" "Getting Closer" "Old Siam Sir" "Tug of War"* "So Bad"	"Ding Dong, Ding Dong" "This Song" "Dark Horse" "You" "Crackerbox Palace" "Blow Away" "Wake Up My Love"*	"Beaucoups of Blues"* "(It's All Down to) Goodnight Vienna" "A Dose of Rock 'n' Roll" "Hey Baby"* "Wrack My Brain"

* Did not appear in the top 40   ^ Did not appear in the top 100   + Posthumous

In the fall of 1969, it would have been inconceivable that the public might hate or ignore or forget an album by a former Beatle. Fifty years later it is the norm, not the exception.

Despite this variability in overall quality and sales, Beatle-related solo records remained highly profitable even as the clinkers started to pile up. From the perspective of EMI/Capitol, breaking up the Beatles looked like it might be something of a windfall, at least initially. Instead of one album per year, they might release four or more. In those early days, singles appeared even more frequently. In 1971, John Lennon told an interviewer, "Between us now, we sell ten times more records than the Beatles did. Individually, if you add them all together, we're doing far better than we were then."[3]

Such a statement really amounts to classic Lennon hyperbole. It simply never was true, and never would be. The public's near-Pavlovian conditioning to buy any Beatles product did not transfer well to the former Beatles, and quickly began to fade, accelerated by the highly uneven quality of the solo records. Eventually the

---

[3] *Beatles Diary*, pg. 41, interview with Michael Parkinson, July 17, 1971.

releases were of interest only to a stable core of fans rather than the public as a whole. To this day, Beatle-related records sell in surprising quantities, but the phenomenon clearly favors re-releases of group material and a handful of better-known solo projects. A large swath of solo material languishes unremembered, or unloved, or both.

Indeed, despite periodic profitability, the sales differences between the classic group albums and the solo releases are stark. The highest-selling[4] solo album, McCartney's *Band on the Run*, is certified at 3.3 million copies — significantly less than the lowest-selling Beatles album, *Let It Be*, certified at 4.1 million.[5] Moreover, the combined certified sales for *all 37* solo albums from 1970 to 1983,[6] just under 30 million, is roughly equal to the reported worldwide sales of *Sgt. Pepper* — or *The White Album* — or *Abbey Road* — or even the greatest hits package known as *1* — take your pick. In the words of Ron Nasty, "Ouch!"

Listening to many of those solo albums can be painful and frustrating. Even when the music is good, there is always something *missing* — and there's no mystery about what that is: It is missing *the other Beatles*. And while it's tempting to blame this single, self-evident factor for all of the vagaries of the solo years, that would be a mistake. Digging deeper, two additional major reasons become apparent — descended from the first, but also distinct from it. Before attempting to rescue any of this music, we must explore these three key factors which contributed to the frustrations of Beatle solo records in the 70s.

Magic

At its simplest, the problem of the solo years is that the recordings could not benefit from the virtuous circle of collaboration, within which all of the group recordings were made. That circle, filled with its own special mystery, is what we tend to call *Beatle Magic* — for lack of anything more explanatory — and *that* is the first and most obvious thing that the solo recordings lack.

That term, "magic," obviously covers a lot of territory, but it amounts to this: Within their virtuous circle, each Beatle had challenged, supported, and cajoled the others into the highest level of writing, performing, and recording. Extremely talented individually, their collective resonance amplified, honed and filtered those talents. Strong competitive instincts also led each of the three principal guitarists/songwriters to try and outdo the others, continually putting upward pressure on

---

[4] See Appendix IV, *Certified Sales*, for more on how sales figures are used in this book.
[5] Before *Revolver* in 1966, UK and US albums had different configurations, muddying the waters for sales figures considerably. It is highly likely, however, that the Beatles sold well over 4 million copies of each and every track from those early albums, just spread across a variety of collections.
[6] This is the survey period for this book, and will be referred to as "the 70s."

1 / CIRCLES

everyone's game. And despite being all personally charming, charm was yet another quality that was amplified when they were together.

After the breakup, each solo artist was without those familiar and essential foils. The other Beatles were simply not there to offer criticism, ideas, or encouragement. They were not there to add their distinctive voices and playing, or to inspire that little extra something in all the other players. They were not there to work a song until it became the best it could be, and thus hold each other to their uniquely high standard. They were not there to diffuse and distribute the burdens of fame and the artistic demands placed upon them.

Outside of their virtuous circle, no individual former Beatle could make up for what had been lost. It isn't that they didn't have enough talent or skill or charm to succeed on their own, but rather that the conditions no longer framed those attributes for best advantage. Weaknesses which had been disguised or mitigated were suddenly revealed. Strengths which had been highlighted or amplified were now left bare. Where the four Beatles had once balanced each other in so many ways, no equivalent was available in the post breakup recordings.

To compound matters, everything they did as solo artists was (and is) inevitably compared to what they had done *before*, something of an impossible standard. Not only could they never be individually what they had been together, but each solo artist struggled to be even *one quarter* of that. Famously greater than the sum of their parts, without each other it was all parts, no sum.

These cracks began to show as soon as they stopped working together. Despite their attempts to put a good face on this, and our own desire to view the solo years in the most favorable light, the hard truth is that for every source of creative stress relieved by the breakup, a bunch more were created. Beyond lawsuits and finances, the basic burdens of a solo career — fronting, writing, recording, promoting — were exponentially greater on each solo artist. None of them was prepared for it in 1970.

Lennon and Harrison mistakenly believed that fans would follow them enthusiastically in new artistic directions — experimental/political and spiritual, respectively. Both started down creative paths which quickly led to their nadirs as recording artists. McCartney appears to have been caught off-guard by even the *thought* of a post-Beatles existence, and was upended personally and creatively when it became a reality. Having thrived in a "group" environment, he would spend the next decade trying to recreate that with other musicians — an utter impossibility. Starr, without the same reserve of creative talent, had made no provisions for a solo career, and was caught chasing musical styles and pursuing non-musical endeavors in the hopes of developing a satisfying second act.

Interestingly, the contract that the Beatles signed with EMI in 1967 actually did imagine a world in which the Beatles recorded separately. It provided specifically that all solo releases would be considered "group" product until 1976. The Beatles themselves, however, made essentially no preparations — either contractual, musical or psychological — for solo careers. Even Harrison, who famously described himself as "not a Beatle anymore" as the group departed Candlestick Park in 1966, appears to have made no serious plans for a solo career until it became a necessity. He would later recall, "I didn't really project into the future. I was just thinking, 'This is going to be such a relief – not to have to go through this madness anymore.'"[7]

Making even small preparations could have eased the transition when the moment came — a moment which was inevitable, even if no one within the virtuous circle truly wanted to think too hard about it. Of course, it is just as likely that preparing for the end might have actually hastened it, undermining the Beatle Magic even as they continued to work together. Ultimately, there is no way to fault them for doing it as they did, despite what we know to have been the consequences.

Still, it's easy to imagine a scenario in which, having acknowledged that they would break up eventually, each Beatle could have tested the waters of a solo career while retaining the group as a backstop. Perhaps, for example, Lennon and Harrison might have made pop recordings instead of experimental recordings as their first solo releases. McCartney might have turned some of his famous demos, such as "Come and Get It" and "Goodbye," into a full-fledged solo release.

In such a world, inevitable failures would have been mitigated while each artist learned the ropes and created a new identity. Call it a "soft breakup," if you will, in which the ultimate result is something more like a fading out of the band era, and a fading in of the solo era. Such an approach might have at least avoided the bad blood and public feuding which developed.

There is certainly also a case to be made that doing it that way would not have made things better. Mistakes might have still been highly embarrassing, and the famous creative tensions might not have been mitigated enough to save the group. Solo careers might have stalled or failed to materialize at all, as was the case with other bands from the same era. Consider that no member of the Rolling Stones, The Who, CSN, the Beach Boys, Led Zeppelin, Pink Floyd, the Moody Blues, the Byrds, Genesis, the Police, or Fleetwood Mac had thriving solo careers concurrent with membership in the group. Perhaps it is not possible.

The more tantalizing outcome, however, is that each Beatle would have had the entire group creative apparatus available to polish those solo releases and avoid the worst mistakes. Even if he wasn't producing the solo Beatles, George Martin might have been available as an editor and critical pair of ears to steer projects toward better artistic outcomes. This, in turn, might have led to a golden era of solo releases which coexisted peacefully with progressively less frequent, but highly-anticipated, group releases.

The lack of preparation for a soft landing meant that the schism, when it came, was sudden and complete, including severing the creative relationship with Martin.

---

[7] *Rolling Stone*, "Remembering Beatles' Final Concert," August 29, 2016, Jordan Runtagh

1 / CIRCLES

As we will see in following chapters, this latter severance may actually have been the most significant aspect, since it led directly to the two other critical ways in which the solo years were ultimately burdened.

Dilution

From the start, each solo recording project began with the need to fill a whole lot more vinyl. On a typical 14-song Beatles album, John and Paul each provided two or three songs, to go along with five or six that started as solo compositions but were finished together. George eventually contributed one track per album side, and Ringo needed no more than one vocal feature — which he generally did not write — and not on every release.

That 14-song standard, used in the UK during the 60s, eventually faded, and pop albums in the 70s typically needed only ten tracks,[8] but now each former Beatle had to provide *all* of them. At the very least that amounted to a *doubling* of past requirements even for Lennon and McCartney — who also no longer had each other to turn to when they got stuck. For Harrison, this amounted to breathing room at first, and burden later. For Starkey, the burden increase is almost literally immeasurable.

This fact alone led to considerable dilution of the material. John Lennon, since he didn't always have 10 great songs available when he started recording an album, filled holes with either substandard originals, quasi-jams or, on some releases, tracks by Yoko. Paul McCartney, despite being the most prolific former Beatle by far, still eventually filled out albums with trifles and novelties such as "links" or tracks by other members of Wings. George Harrison dutifully pounded out enough new material to fill his albums, in the process building his songwriting chops, but also producing a seriously uneven catalog. And Richard Starkey, who authored only two complete songs during his Beatle years, was left to rely on other songwriters or co-writers who frequently let him down. All four eventually resorted to generic filler such as covers and instrumentals.

Just how much of the solo material is either substandard or pure filler is a highly subjective thing. Some fans might reject the notion outright, or severely underestimate how much material could be discarded. Conversely, some might throw out *everything* as obviously inferior to the classic Beatles tracks.

To avoid both instincts and actually quantify the problem, I have listened carefully to 568 solo tracks recorded during the survey period for this project, which runs from "Give Peace a Chance" in July 1969, to *Milk and Honey* in January 1984. That amounts to 456 officially released tracks, plus 112 outtakes, some of which have

---

[8] 30 of the 37 albums in the survey period (1970-1983) have nine to 12 tracks.

since been officially released.[9] I listened to everything both in its original context, the albums or singles on which the music was first released, and also out of context, typically in alphabetical or random order. With each listen, I attempted to put aside my long-held feelings about the music, and tried to hear it as if for the first time.

I also tried to listen with an ear for how each song/track would have sounded to the Beatles' creative braintrust at the time it was recorded. That's obviously a highly speculative endeavor, but it draws on what we know from their actual group releases, what they said about each other's work in the 70s, and the choices each made as a solo artist. It's obviously still guesswork, and certainly subject to debate, but at least it's *informed* guesswork.

What I heard was sometimes very similar to what I had always heard: a robust mixture of qualities, styles, subjects, fashions, successes and failures. I heard evolutions, and the occasional hint of revolutions. Stretching and experimentation became visible, craftsmanship and routinization were revealed, as were lethargy, indifference and sloppiness. I encountered many unexpected reactions when listening this way, and it changed my opinion of a significant number of recordings. Most importantly, through this type of de-contextualized, track-focused listening, it quickly became easy to distinguish between works which were robust, imaginative, and truly worthy of the Beatles name, and those which were not.

This led to the creation of a simple and highly subjective rating scale called *Beatle Quality*, which measures the likelihood that a given track would have met the rigorous content and quality standards that the Beatles always held themselves to. There are three possible outcomes for each track: eligible, not eligible, and provisional. Provisional is used to acknowledge that a song/track *might* have been eligible if the circumstances were just right and it filled a need. For any tracks not marked eligible, I attached a reason for the designation, generally using one or more of the following categories: content, quality, style or filler. (Appendix III, *Distinct Works Catalogs,* contains the complete and detailed outcome of this listening and categorizing, along with some recording information and a thumbnail review for each track.)

By comparing how many tracks received each designation, it becomes possible to see in a broad way the level of dilution which affected the solo years:

---

[9] It does not include 27 tracks found on official releases by John or Paul which are either the work of Yoko Ono or a member of Wings. Unless the former Beatle either wrote, co-wrote, or sang lead, he was essentially serving as a guest musician on someone else's track. Such things would never have been considered for release by the Beatles.

1 / CIRCLES

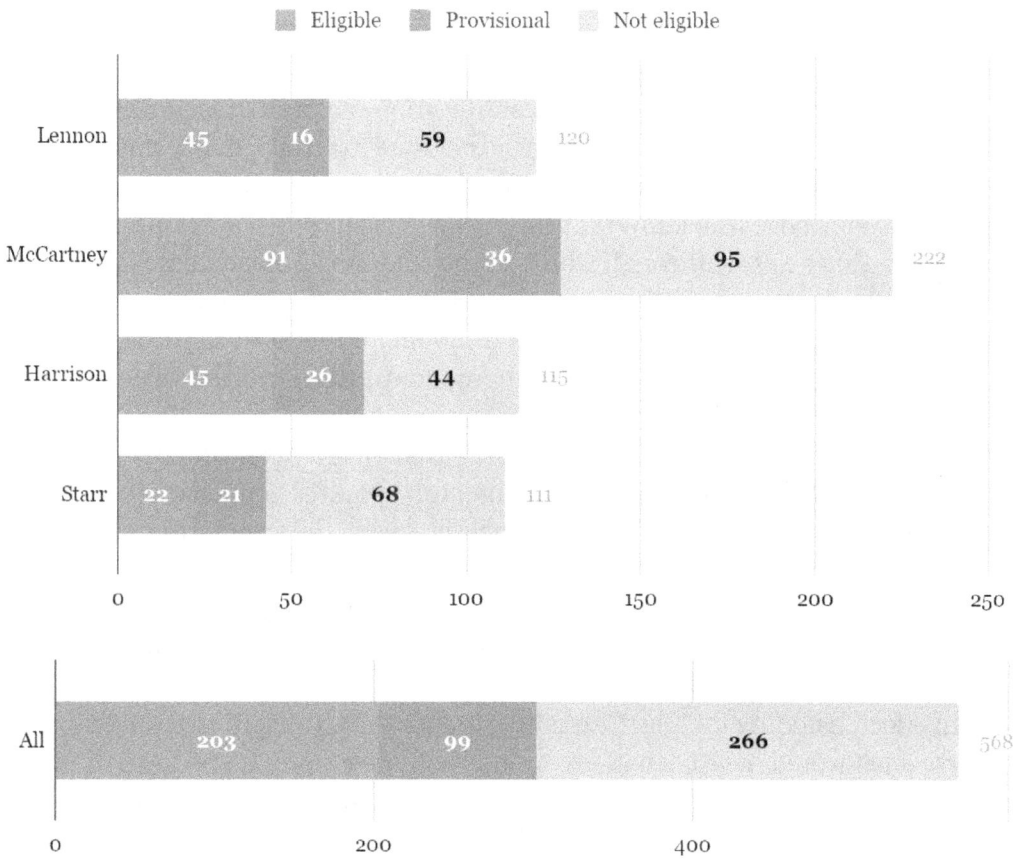

By this admittedly unscientific method, a scant 36% of the available tracks would have been immediately eligible for inclusion on a group project. Conversely, roughly two of every three tracks would have been either questioned or outright rejected by the group if they had been working together.

Though I did not set out with any goal in mind, and did not monitor the totals as I listened, it's hard not to notice that the number of truly great tracks in the band's second decade (203) is roughly equal to the total number of (great) tracks from their first decade (215). Further, they made roughly three times as many albums in the 70s (37) as in the 60s (13), and roughly two-thirds of that, or almost the exact amount as the increase, is not up to the group's original standard. It suggests a practical limit on just how much greatness the Beatles could collectively generate in a given period of time. That was a surprise.

Before moving on, I want to address one objection certain to arise. It is tempting to think that *anything* done by a former Beatle is, by definition, "Beatle quality." How, you might ask, could a song written and played and sung by John Lennon or Paul McCartney *not* be considered "Beatle quality?" Isn't it true that the Beatles could have put anything they wanted onto a Beatles album and called it "Beatle quality?" Didn't they create and define that concept in the first place, and could they not have redefined it in any way they chose?

Of course, they could have. But one assumption central to this project is that the Beatles of the 70s would have maintained the same exacting quality standards that they exhibited in the 60s, even as the music went inevitably in different stylistic directions. For those who know the group catalog inside out, it is a rather simple and instinctive thing to sort through which of the solo music meets that standard and which does not — even if it isn't exactly possible to define the concept of "Beatle quality" any further. Indeed, dilution is a problem for the solo years exactly because some tracks just obviously do not meet the standards the group had carefully established and maintained.

Interestingly, evaluating the solo music based on its "Beatle quality" is very different from listening to it in its actual context. It requires going back to a moment when all that the world knew of Beatle music was what the group had created. There were no solo records, and essentially no disposable or substandard group records. Up until that point, the group had maintained very strict lower limits in terms of song and recording quality, filtering out the lesser material and enhancing even the best material to a higher level of excellence.

In effect, listening for "Beatle quality" is about returning to 1970 and using the filters which would have been in use by fans listening then. At the dawn of the solo era, fans were still conditioned to expect that same high "Beatle quality" from the solo Beatles. Where we are used to the idea that lesser tracks were a regular occurrence, a necessary evil, and an inevitable consequence of the breakup, listeners back then were surprised and deeply disappointed. "Beatle quality" is about listening with raised expectations, so dilution is recognizable as the serious problem it became.

In order to believe that a track like "Aisumasen (I'm Sorry)" might have made it onto a Beatles album, and thus come to redefine "Beatle quality," one must also accept the corresponding belief that the Beatles would have abandoned all of their innate standards, and in effect exited the virtuous circle while marketing it as if it still existed. We won't let them do that. We will, instead, attempt to find a way to maintain the virtuous circle even as it allows for some different working methods. Despite not recording together, they will still hold each other to those original strict standards, and eliminate anything which does not rise to that level.

So we can be sure that Paul, George, Ringo and George Martin would not have let John get away with something as poor as "Aisumasen (I'm Sorry)," and Lennon would have begrudgingly accepted their verdict. To a degree, measuring "Beatle quality" is about listening as George Martin might have: from a stool in Abbey Road studios, with an ear tuned to what the Beatles were capable of, and the clear-eyed ability to say no when something was not up to snuff. Famously, Martin did this again for Paul McCartney on several occasions, and the result was a noticeable uptick in quality for the resulting projects.

Without anyone to say no, or even nudge the individual Beatles back toward the quality standards of the early years, lousy songs got recorded, and lousy records got made. For the fans, each new solo release meant simply putting up with the lousy while waiting for the good. Great musical moments still happened, of course. But now, instead of being concentrated on one release as they had been in the Beatle days, they were scattered far and wide, across multiple releases. You had to buy a whole lot more records, and listen to a whole lot more non-great musical moments, to find the good stuff. The die-hard fans did, and the rest of the world began to tune out, all as a result of this dilution.

Context

A third, less obvious, critical issue joins the lack of Beatle Magic and the dilution of material as an essential explanation for some of the disappointment of the solo years. This is the problem of *inelegant contextualization* — the process by which singles and B-sides are chosen, and tracks are made into albums.

The strange but undeniable truth about the former Beatles is that their best music as solo artists is still very difficult to identify when heard in the way we first heard it — that is, on solo albums of widely varying quality. It's true that *some* of their great music can be identified that way. To be sure, some became highly visible as hits. But not even the hits necessarily represent their *best* music, by any means. Some of the best music is locked in prisons of mediocrity and must be freed. Some great music is obscured by album concepts that are either thin (*Mind Games*), dumb (*Back to the Egg*), bland (*Somewhere in England*), or inexplicable (*Goodnight Vienna*). Some great music is almost literally hidden, either thrown away as space-filling B-sides or tucked into vaults gathering dust.

In short, and somewhat surprisingly, there exists a body of great solo Beatle music from the 70s which is not widely recognized as such. It can be found between the cracks of the better known music, but is essentially "lost" because it was not properly contextualized — that is, not given the best chance to shine. These tracks were counted as "eligible," even if that designation might seem surprising.

These are tracks like Lennon's "What You Got" and "Meat City," McCartney's "Soily" and "Warm and Beautiful," Starr's "Wings" and "Down and Out," and Harrison's "Deep Blue" and the exquisite "Be Here Now." This list is by no means exhaustive. And if you look at those titles and think, "So what?" then the point is made. Each of these tracks, heard in a different context, might have become a classic.

In seeking the best music from the solo Beatles, therefore, it's important to realize that though we start with tracks, we must look *past* individual tracks. Listening to an individual track and saying, "Yeah, that's great," or "Not so much," — in other words, determining its BQ score — is only a starting point, and misses a crucial piece. Since one track can elevate (or drag down) another, finding the absolute best music from the solo years actually means seeking *combinations* of tracks that create something like the virtuous circle found on all of the classic Beatles albums. We're looking for cases where two or more tracks sound *better* together — that is, where the proverbial whole is greater than the sum of its parts. As such, the key to finding the best music of the solo Beatles is to treat tracks as building blocks rather than ends unto themselves.

Examples of this phenomenon abound in the Beatles catalog. "Getting Better" and "Fixing a Hole" are really just serviceable songs, but as a set they lift each other to a new level. "Dear Prudence" can stand on its own just fine, but emerging from the contrails of "Back in the USSR" it gains an indefinable shimmer. Pull any portion out of the long medley on *Abbey Road* and it becomes clear just how slight the material really is. The individual ideas are barely even sketches. It turns out that, once the Beatles got really good at creating individual tracks, they became experts in *aggregation* — with the help of George Martin, of course.

As such, a track with a high BQ that is not generally recognized as great represents a potential opportunity. The question to be asked then is: Could something else from another Beatle gel with this track and make it sound better? Honestly, we can't expect that to happen every time. Some tracks are just terrible, and some are just loners. But in my listening (see above), finding a plausible match happened more often than I would have guessed when I started. It's something like a big game of *Concentration*.

As we will see, George Martin employed specific techniques to make sure that every Beatles track was afforded an opportunity to be heard in its best light. During the solo years, however, after Martin had been excused by all four former Beatles, there was no independent pair of ears to recognize where the strengths of one song might lift another, or conceal its deficits. There was no one to put two songs by different Beatles next to one another in a way which made each sound better than it did alone. Martin was, among many other things, a master at assembling parts of varying quality into unified and satisfying wholes.

Martin learned the important principles behind this aspect of the art during his formative musical education, then developed and honed his techniques over a decade of working with other artists before meeting the Beatles. By carefully and properly placing every track, he did things for the Beatles music which are almost invisible, yet were essential to their success. This represents one of Martin's major, if generally less-appreciated, contributions to the band's success on record. (His techniques will be discussed in detail in Part II).

In the beginning, he applied his techniques to album running orders without consulting the Beatles, who showed no interest and were far too busy to be bothered anyway. He was the expert, they were the neophytes. He was the boss, they were the employees. He was the A&R man, they were the talent. He was the packager, they were the commodity. He knew the industry, they were fans with a toe in the door. He was the teacher, and they were...

Well, the analogy breaks down because they appear not to have been very good students on this subject. One thing which is painfully obvious during the solo years is how little the individual Beatles learned about what Martin had been doing in terms of properly contextualizing their music. It is depressingly rare to find tracks elevating each other on solo albums, and much more common to find them bringing each other down. This is a major difference from what happened in the 60s.

For Harrison and Starkey, this actually shouldn't be much of a surprise. The documentation shows that neither of them was involved in any significant way with the sequencing of any Beatles albums, beyond perhaps giving some ideas to the process, and their approval to the final result. But McCartney and Lennon were deeply involved in the assembly of both *The White Album* and *Abbey Road*. In the case of the former, Lennon, McCartney and Martin spent a famous 24 hour session pulling the pieces together and creating the necessary and memorable connections between tracks. In the case of the latter, the same three artists built the medley together (despite John's later disavowal), and smoothed it to perfection.

But after showing obvious skill with his sequencing of *John Lennon/Plastic Ono Band*, Lennon's later assemblies show none of the subtlety brought to the task by Martin and McCartney. Indeed, of the former Beatles, only McCartney appears to have consistently applied principles descended from lessons Martin was teaching. Paul's careful running orders make significant contributions to the perception of his music in a way that none of the other former Beatles could match, and the choices he made often amplified his gifts as songwriter, arranger, and producer, even when the material was not his best. He did not always get it right, as we will see, but he did much better than his former bandmates.

Therein lies the real tragedy of the Beatles in the 70s. Each of the former Beatles produced both great and terrible records, but it is important to recognize that each of them also threw away songs that, in the right context, might have become classics. The whole decade became something like a fractured version of *The White Album*, only with no editor, no balance, no context, no segues, and worst of all, no strength from unity. They didn't even have the benefit of simple *context*, in which their own individual songs might have sounded better just by being heard next to the best songs from their fellow Fabs.

These are, then, the three primary reasons that the records of the solo era could not match the success of the Beatles: The loss of Beatle Magic, dilution of material, and lack of proper contextualization for the good music they did create. These are certainly not the *only* reasons, but it is for *at least* these reasons that even in their finest post-breakup moments none of the former Beatles ever again reached the creative summit on which they once stood together. There were close calls, and some damn fine records, but nothing again with that same *resonance*.

Frankly, in retrospect it seems unreasonable to have expected that from them individually, severed as they were from such an essential source of strength. But, naïvely, we did expect that, and were duly disappointed — at least to a degree — because each solo Beatle was forced to work with six arms tied behind his back.

2
Filters

When the four were together as the Beatles their creativity had two filters — first of all, each other, and, secondly, [George] Martin. That they should lose both simultaneously made it inevitable that their music might occasionally become self-indulgent and undisciplined — something which happened to all four at one stage or another. Perhaps in many ways it's highly creditable that each accomplished as much as he did during the '70s.

— Bob Woffinden, *The Beatles Apart*

The solo careers of the former Beatles were far too varied and complex to be summarized by any three principles, of course. That's a little like trying to describe a stand of trees from a satellite image. Such a view is not entirely without merit, but makes only a reasonable place to start. You can see the general shape, but will miss more or less all of the nuance.

Though some things went wrong for the former Beatles, plenty of things went right. When things did go wrong, there were many reasons, large and small. Sometimes successes offset failures, and sometimes vice versa. Some things, good and bad, were quickly forgotten, others not so much. Most importantly, perhaps, is to acknowledge that things simply didn't turn out as anyone expected or hoped when the group broke up. Indeed, despite being filled with unique vagaries, each solo career was, in its own way, disappointing.

From our satellite view of the solo Beatles in the 70s, we can see that their recordings exhibit virtually none of the timelessness which characterized the work of the group. The music they made together in the 60s transcended the era, and continues to defy time, seemingly existing outside the confines of tastes and fashion. It somehow finds a new audience in every generation. So much of what they wrote and recorded still sounds every bit as fresh as it did when first released. As a result, the group's catalog retains its commercial value, as well as a surprising degree of cultural relevance. Together, the Beatles soared, and their appeal remains nearly universal.

In contrast, almost everything they recorded separately in the 70s seems hard-wired to the ground of the decade. Not only does it not soar, but it increasingly sounds dated, flat, and anything but timeless. There was precious little transcendence, a distinct lack of freshness. Their ability to rise above the currents of culture and fashion seemingly evaporated with the turn of the decade.

Still, every solo Beatle has, to this day, a robust fanbase. Almost every single solo album has both adherents and detractors. Arguments persist about who had the "greatest" solo career, or made the most "underrated" or "overrated" solo album. "Best" and "worst" lists litter the web, and fans still argue about who was the "genius" of the Beatles — whatever *that* means.

In the process of processing, so much has become blurred. In fact, it has gotten to the point where solo music sometimes gets lumped into collective memory with the group tracks. All too many non-Beatlefans think "Imagine" and "My Sweet Lord" were Beatles records, and "Hey Jude" was by Paul McCartney. For most of the world, there is barely any distinction between the group and solo eras. Beatles were, and always will be, Beatles.

To make more sense of it all, we need to come down from our satellite and take a nominally closer look. In subsequent chapters we will zoom in on the solo music and subject it to great — perhaps even *microscopic* — analysis. But for now, let's come down to, say, treetop level, and fly over each solo career individually. Here we can see some of the themes which led to the vagaries, and get a sense of when and how things when wrong and right.

Each of the following sections begins with a work summary, including a chart of all albums released by the artist during our survey period, which includes all albums from *Sentimental Journey* (1970) to *Milk and Honey* (1984).

The chart contains three elements:

- Approximations of *initial sales* for each album (see Appendix IV, *Certified Sales,* for more information about the use of sales figure in this book)

- A plot of the *chart scores* for each album from both the UK and US (see Appendix V, *Chart Scoring,* for an explanation of this calculation)

- *Quality rank* for each title, indicating best to worst based on critical consensus and conventional wisdom (there will no doubt be quibbles)

In addition, three words are given as the basis for exploring each career in overview. At treetop level, no attempt is made to rummage through all of the underbrush, but merely suss out the big themes, especially those which will be relevant to fusing the music into rescued Beatles albums.

2 / Filters

John Lennon

8 studio albums / 6 non-album tracks / 89 distinct core studio works
Unbridled / Uneven / Conventional

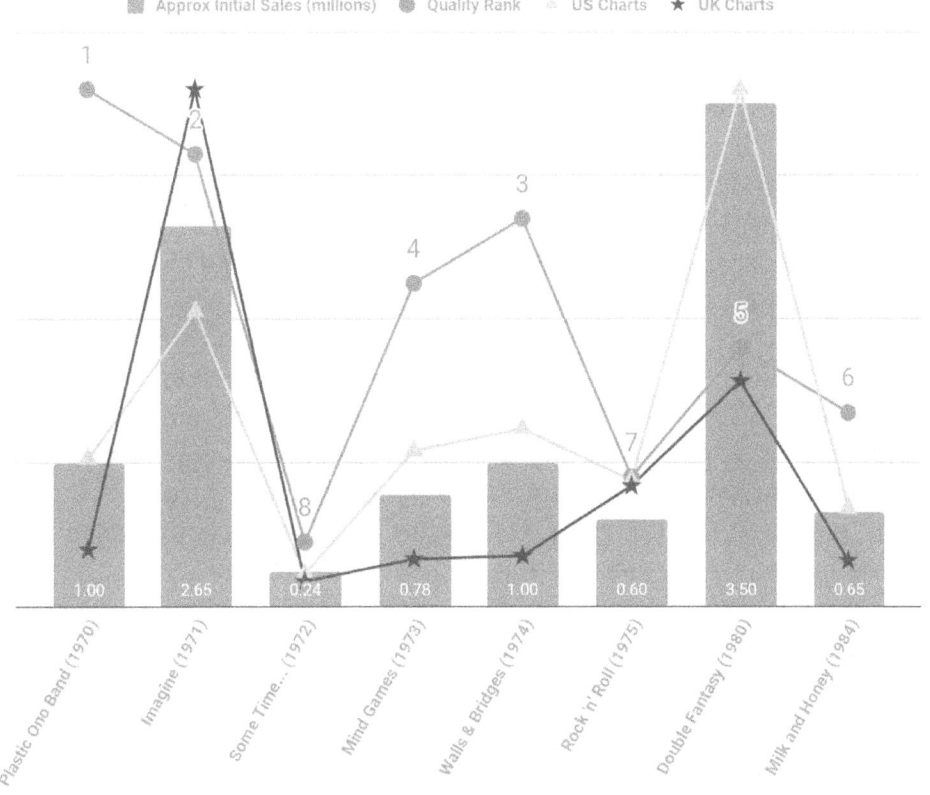

Best	*Plastic Ono Band* (1970)
Better	*Imagine* (1971) *Walls and Bridges* (1974) *Mind Games* (1973)
Worse	*Double Fantasy* (1980) *Milk and Honey* (1984) *Rock 'N' Roll* (1975)
Worst	*Some Time in New York City* (1972)

John Lennon burst out of the Beatles like a sprinter off the starting block. He had a direction, and the need for speed, but surprisingly little fuel. When the race turned out to be a marathon, he quickly ran right into trouble.

With almost no songs stashed in the proverbial vault, he chose to let his muse set the schedule, a decision which eventually came back to haunt him. Where the Beatles had generally used deadlines for focus, Lennon's solo career would careen in mercurial fashion, like a billiard ball on a wobbly table. He popped up here and there, always with a new persona, a new issue, something to sell, and a handful of partially finished songs.

He followed his instincts, and the cultural currents, not really setting down roots until much later. He didn't even stop to put together a new band, but merely picked up players along the way.

Perhaps most significantly, he yoked his future to that of another artist, just as tightly as she yoked her future to his. The merits of this decision will no doubt be debated in perpetuity, but one thing is for certain: Yoko Ono had an oversized impact on the solo music and career trajectory of John Lennon.

In the end, we must sadly admit that his solo years were something of an artistic disappointment, especially given his seminal work as a Beatle. It's hard to recreate what fans might have imagined the future would hold for him in 1970, but whatever it was, they likely did not get it. Only a few of his works proved significant and timeless, but thankfully those were as memorable as many Beatles records. Unfortunately, much of his solo work had little or no cultural impact. Perhaps if he had survived to have a third act things might have been different. But there is no way to know, and speculating about what John Lennon might do next always was, and always will be, a pure guessing game.

Unbridled

The most satisfying art that Lennon made as a solo artist was also his earliest. Like an unbridled horse, he charged into the studio in 1970 and knocked down anything in his way. He poured everything of himself that he could into the music and, for the first time in his career, there was no one there to reign him in.

He then stuck to more or less the same approach for the rest of his career, with generally diminishing returns. Throughout the 70s, he recorded in short bursts, utterly unwilling to labor too long over his recordings. Instead, he sought to capture the sheer force of his performance, an approach which fueled those diminishing returns as the songs became less sharp, and began to gallop around and around the same track.

No producer could have reigned him in because he wouldn't have tolerated it. Phil Spector didn't even try. Jack Douglas didn't even try. Indeed, even deadlines no longer could truly reign him in. He had earned the right to set his own pace and path and paradigm, and appears to have done so without a second thought.

As a result, much of his finished solo music sounds unbridled — a characterization he would no doubt relish. To some, this is what makes Lennon's work in the 70s distinctive. To some, it represents a let down from the exacting standards of the Beatles. To the general record-buying audience, it mattered not at all. When the records were good, the public bought them, but that happened only sporadically. He got surprisingly little special treatment in record stores or radio playlists either for being a former Beatle or for making spontaneous records. The goodwill he had built as a Beatle could not survive a long series of career decisions that the public either didn't understand or didn't like. As a result, his record sales frequently disappointed.

After his death, however, all of that dissipated. What the public generally remembers of John Lennon's solo years — which must be more accurately characterized as duo years — are those several timeless records, the stories of his late life away from the public eye, and the tragic consequences of reentry.

It would be wrong to lament his lack of discipline as a recording artist if it weren't for what we know he could produce when there were reasons to focus. Most people who made music with John said he was one of the greatest rhythm guitarists to play with, and a generous collaborator. Examples of this abound. Many people acknowledge his ability to pull a new song seemingly out of thin air when the occasion demanded ("All You Need is Love"). But without the bridle of the Beatles, he rarely reached that next gear of ingenuity and imagination.

Uneven

Each of John Lennon's solo albums was an adventure in quality control. Great highs often sat directly next to great lows. Fans may differ on which tracks are which, but there is little question that something good was always right around the corner, as was something much less good. Unlike his former compatriots, he did not move in *cycles* of good and bad, but intertwined them almost continually.

As such, none of his solo albums are *entirely* satisfying. Each has skippable tracks, uncomfortable or unsatisfying bits of music which might as well not even be there. Because he did not attempt anything in the way of a large artistic statement on record — nothing approaching a traditional "concept album" — his albums are easy to disassemble, a process which makes the best music easier to extract and appreciate, but lays bare the presence of considerable amounts of lesser material. This is likely the reason that each new Lennon compilation album, made as it is from only the best material, yields a new audience who will have no idea there were ever any lesser tracks.

Interestingly, the relative quality of each track is more dependent on his songwriting than on any other single element of the recording. His vocals rarely disappoint, and he generally surrounded himself with excellent musicians. Though the arrangements periodically could be questioned, and production values were an ongoing concern, his ideas always emerged at center stage. When tracks failed, the song itself was typically the culprit.

Explaining this may require a closer look at his environment. Notably a chameleon and sponge, Lennon routinely absorbed, reflected and amplified whatever was around him. Within the Beatles, these abilities constantly fed the virtuous circle. Outside of the Beatles, and without their singular focus, he appeared more diffuse, more likely to wander and, since he was less likely to be surrounded by excellence, less likely to amplify excellence.

In shorthand, as a solo artist John Lennon wandered in quality because he could, and because no one and nothing offered him the structured environment in which his talents and skills would be nudged continually toward their highest level. The Beatles had been a miracle for him, and it was not repeated.

Conventional

The mantle of "most experimental Beatle" floats between Lennon and McCartney, but which artist led that charge is irrelevant because both experimented and innovated with abandon. Once the group dissolved, however, Lennon appears to have lost that aspect of his creativity. His solo compositions and recordings are utterly conventional, all the way through his reentry in 1980.

The industry may have contributed to that since popular music settled into very clear "lanes" during the 70s. But that same argument could be made about the 60s, when the lanes were even more rigid to begin with. The Beatles continuously crossed over those boundaries, ultimately erasing some of them, blurring or rearranging others, and creating new lanes seemingly at will.

Famously, the novelty of studio wizardry had worn off for Lennon, but it would be wrong to reduce his innovations to mere recording technique. With the Beatles, he also made innovations in the pop form, lyrical content, and instrumentation. He brought about seismic shifts in the position of popular music — and the makers of that music — within the culture, and the ways in which celebrity might be harnessed.

His initial solo work, the sound collages with Ono, suggested that he might be verging on a new era of innovation which, truthfully, not many fans were eager to follow. Few lament the end of that thread, and Lennon may have been deterred there by low sales and harsh reactions. But it would have seemed impossible even then that the volatile and imaginative Lennon would settle into anything approaching conventionality. Yet "conventional" is a regrettably sufficient word to summarize much of his post-Beatles output. The edges of imagination were sanded off. The forms were often stock. His great imagination appears impeded.

2 / Filters

There is nothing in his solo catalog even approaching the intensity of his late Beatles work, and comparing anything he recorded in, say, 1974 to anything from 1969 yields a distinct puzzle: How could these be the same artist? Perhaps it is unfair to lament innovations he did not make, or roads he did not travel, but the 70s were likely poorer for it, as was Lennon's artistic catalog.

The John Lennon of the 70s was not the same artist as the Lennon of the 60s. Key circumstantial differences likely contributed to the shift, not the least of which were the breakup of the Beatles and the marriage to Ono. Beyond these, and the simple advancement of age, lie a great many factors, some of which we will never know. Such is Lennon's complex artistic legacy.

Paul McCartney

12 studio albums / 29 non-album tracks / 167 distinct core studio works
Reinventing / Churning / Selling

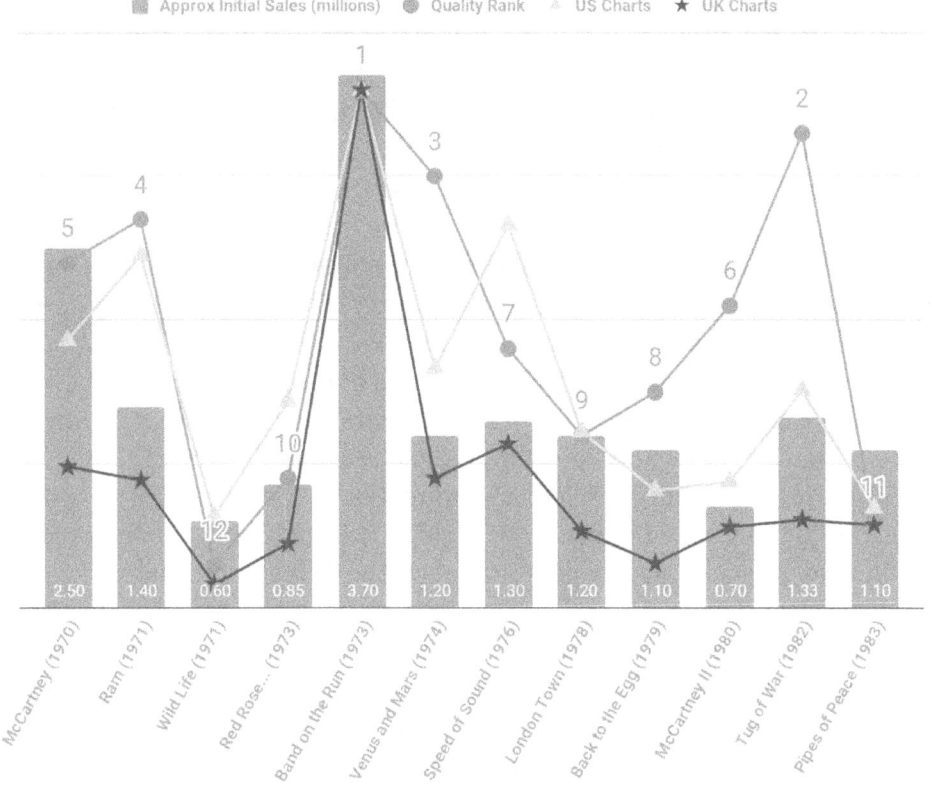

Best	*Band on the Run* (1973) *Tug of War* (1982)
Better	*Venus and Mars* (1975) *Ram* (1971)
YMMV	*McCartney* (1970) *McCartney II* (1980) *Wings at the Speed of Sound* (1976) *Back to the Egg* (1979)
Worse	*London Town* (1978) *Red Rose Speedway* (1972)
Worst	*Pipes of Peace* (1983) *Wild Life* (1971)

 When the Beatles broke up, Paul McCartney effectively crawled in a hole for six months, becoming invisible enough that rumors of his demise actually took root. We know now that he was utterly unprepared for the eventuality of a breakup, had barely even considered the possibility, and sank into a deep depression, from which only resuming work in a new way could extract him.

 After pulling himself together, letting it slip that the group had broken up, and selling a whole lot of copies of his first solo album, he set about trying to force lightning to strike again. Through seven (!!) iterations, Wings would never be the Beatles, but they certainly would be big. At their peak — a year-long world tour in 1975-76 — Wings reestablished McCartney as a household name, and he effectively assumed the mantle of Beatlemania. Now rumors took root of him having been the heart and soul of the Beatles all along, which he did little to quell.

 For those not paying very close attention, that is the entire story — no lousy albums, no singles which did not go to number one, no flailing about to establish a post-Beatles persona, no revolving door on the Wings dressing rooms. Anyone paying attention, however, knows better. Indeed, almost every McCartney triumph is balanced by a misfire of some sort, even as he became by far the most commercially successful former Beatle.

 His superpower, beyond perpetual melodic fertility, may very well have been the ability to shake off whatever happened and just keep making music. Indeed, through sheer determination, he made his best solo music when his chips were down, and success seemed least likely.

2 / FILTERS

Reinventing

After they stopped touring, Paul McCartney had successfully sparked a reinvention of the Beatles with the concept for *Sgt. Pepper*. He had tried again, less successfully, with the *Magical Mystery Tour* film, and later with the *Get Back* project. The long medley on *Abbey Road* might even be considered another attempt at reinvention, and Paul was in the process of pitching still another — the idea that they might go out and play small clubs, unannounced — when John Lennon pronounced him "daft" and quit the band.

Little did Paul know when the Beatles broke up that he was about to become the king of the pop music reboot.

It began with his own sense, during the fall of 1969 and the winter of 1970, that he was being forced by circumstance to essentially start his career over, almost as if from scratch. He did so in fits and starts, and in his early solo days, there were real questions about whether a successful post-Beatles McCartney would ever emerge.

Though it's fair to call his solo career a series of reinventions, he founded it all largely on principles learned with the Beatles. He would be part of a *band*, not a solo act. His band would record and tour, make public appearances and TV specials. It would be like an extension of his family, like some sort of musical commune. And just like the Beatles, he intended it to be a wholly democratic institution, with each member as important as any other to the band's sound and public identity.

Not much of this worked out the way he imagined. Famously, there were perpetually new iterations of Wings, with each successive line-up effectively a reboot of a reboot. The musicians were of widely varying temperaments, styles, and staying power. Stories of Paul's perfectionism and autocratic style were legion. On two occasions, the core of Paul, Linda and Denny Laine were abruptly abandoned by the rest of the band. At other times, members departed before the public even knew their names. There was no way to disguise the fact that every new Wings album featured a new line-up.

Unsurprisingly, Paul's success came despite the faux construct of Wings, built on his fame and prolific songwriting chops. Even there, however, Paul continued to remake himself. Each new album had a new sound to go along with the new names. He continued experimenting with musical styles and lyrical limits. Even as his sound settled firmly into the pop mold, he continued to evolve his own distinct voice. This can be heard most dramatically by comparing *McCartney* to *McCartney II*. Separated by ten years, and despite the same name and face on the cover, the two albums are barely recognizable as coming from the same artist.

To a degree, the reinventions ended in 1983, and Paul settled into a sound he would more or less stick to in succeeding decades, even as he continued moving through a long list of collaborators. Thus, the 70s for Paul McCartney must be seen as a laboratory. He experimented freely, flailed a bit, got his footing, and then found his solo voice, but only through a long series of reinventions.

Churning

In the decade after the breakup, Paul McCartney churned out by far the most songs of any former Beatle — and it isn't even close. But this represented a dramatic shift from when the group was together.

There are 157 songs recorded by the Beatles which are credited to "Lennon/McCartney" or one of its variants.[1] John and Paul each gave at least one interview in which they worked through the entire catalog, creating a sort of "who wrote what" inventory. Their accounts agree far more than they disagree and, when tallied, yield an astonishing statistic: Each wrote exactly 50 of these songs by himself, while the remaining 57 were collaborations ranging from helping each other with finishing touches, to writing "nose-to-nose."[2]

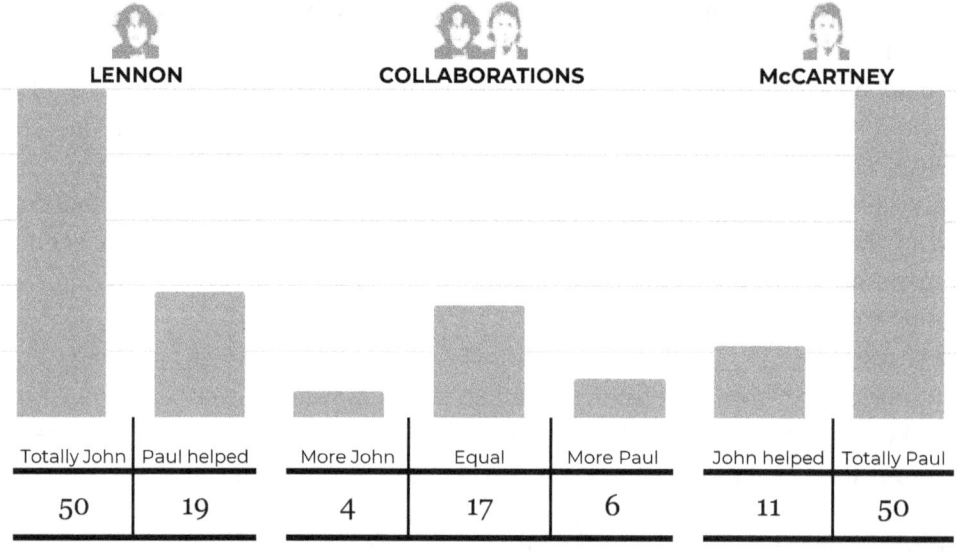

---

[1] "What Goes On" is credited to "Lennon/McCartney/Starkey," while "Flying" and "Dig It" are credited to "Lennon/McCartney/Harrison/Starkey."
[2] The supporting data can be viewed in Appendix VI, *Beatles Recordings*.

2 / FILTERS

It's not clear whether McCartney accelerated his output or had merely been holding back, but in the second decade of their careers, Paul lapped his former partner, 215 to 98.[3]

Of course, quantity is not quality. Like Lennon, not all of McCartney's solo songs are classics. But the simple ability to keep generating new songs at such a pace meant (and continues to mean) that even if the current song isn't a classic, the next one might be. This allowed Paul to keep churning out albums even as critics complained about the quality of the songs, with apparently inevitable new classics born on what seemed like a fairly regular basis.

Selling

McCartney's ability to generate new melodies seemingly at will is legendary. Less noticed, however, is his absolute mastery of the twin crafts of songwriting (a very different discipline from melody-writing) and recording. Words and music and guitars and drums may be the vehicle, but craft is often the driver, and throughout the 70s McCartney consistently demonstrated his commitment to finishing his work well, so that his records would always be positioned to sell well, even if the songs might not be the best.

Though not every McCartney song is a gem, there is hardly a song in his catalog that does not feature a coherent structure, an attractive chord progression, well-formed openings and closings, and satisfying dramatic architecture. Even when his lyrics are nonsensical, they have an inner logic, true rhymes, interesting word play, and some sort of compelling imagery. Likewise, his recordings have always been carefully polished, regardless of the quality of the song, thus elevating even so-so songs into a place where they might be commercially successful.

Among his collaborators in Wings, this perfectionism often became unbearable. Guitarists hired for their prodigious chops found themselves being told exactly how to play a solo. Drummers with unique personal styles were referred to McCartney's performance on record so they might recreate on stage exactly what he played in the studio. In too many cases, tracks presented to the world as band creations were actually the work of a solo Paul.

Thus, Paul's dedication to pure craftsmanship frequently placed a strain on all musicians around him, even as it yielded significant commercial successes. Over and over throughout the 70s (and beyond), Paul positioned all of his work with commerciality in mind, even when art was a simultaneous consideration. As such, it has

---

[3] This includes all songs considered for this project, some of which were not released. 14 of Lennon's 98 are with collaborators, mostly Yoko. 13 of McCartney's 215 are with collaborators other than Linda, mostly Denny Laine. An additional 80 are credited as "McCartney/McCartney," though it has long been acknowledged that this was for royalty reasons only.

always been clear that McCartney does not think of art and commerciality as either/or. He clearly tries to make commercial records, and if art also happens, so be it. Importantly, the reverse could not be said.

The net effect may very well be that he did not produce, in that first decade or since, anything with quite the same obvious artistic heft as *John Lennon/Plastic Ono Band*, even while generating over twice as much music. But that is not to say there isn't a considerable amount of art, and heft, in his catalog.

Art comes in many shapes and sizes, and Paul's art can often be found where it might not be expected. Where the world came to dismiss Paul's work in the 70s as merely a collection of "silly love songs" (hereafter known in this volume by its acronym: SLS), the careful ear recognizes much more. Indeed, the very song which christened that term is an absolute masterpiece of melodic, stylistic, structural, and production craftsmanship. It even works on the meta level of directly addressing critics. That it is not "Mother" is utterly irrelevant.

To say that Paul's output in the 70s is *commercial* might sound something like an insult, but the reality is that creating a commercial sheen required an incredible amount of work, and yielded a wide range of music, with a wide range of meanings and, unfortunately, a wide range of quality. But it's important to note that describing his work as commercial is actually not a comment on its relative artistic value in any way. It would be wrong to assume any sort of mutually exclusive relationship between the two criteria.

Unfortunately, this would have been much easier to see were there not so much actual dross in McCartney's 70s catalog. Instead, however, critics and the public continually pummeled Paul's reputation with well-justified accusations of slightness, and a yielding to the banalities of pop. Though some of this criticism was tied to the perception that he broke up the Beatles, and therefore more harsh than his work deserved, there are also good cases to be made for such assessments — especially when comparing his 70s output to the Beatles. And therein lies the rub: Just like the others, no matter what he might have produced after the Beatles, it would always be *after* the Beatles.

2 / Filters

George Harrison

8 studio albums / 4 non-album tracks / 97 distinct core studio works
Maturing / Sliding / Enlightening

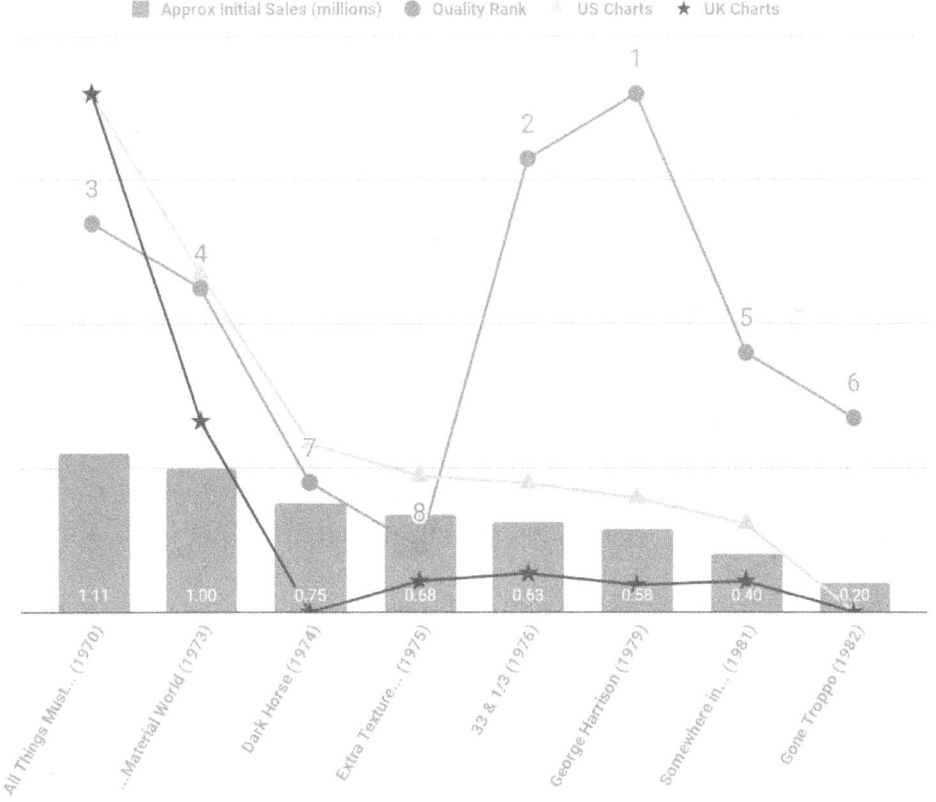

Best	*George Harrison* (1978) *Thirty Three & 1/3* (1976)
Better	*All Things Must Pass* (1970) *Living in the Material World* (1973)
Worse	*Somewhere in England* (1981) *Gone Troppo* (1982)
Worst	*Dark Horse* (1974) *Extra Texture (Read All About It)* (1975)

George Harrison began to emotionally divest from the Beatles about the same time he first heard sitars on the set of *Help!* He was the first of the four to see the emptiness of fame, and by 1966 had found something which meant more to him than any job or band ever could. His spiritual journey inhabited and fueled the rest of his life.

He was famously not present at the meeting when John Lennon announced that he was seeking a "divorce" from the Beatles, but when word reached him, he apparently had no reaction whatsoever. When confronted with questions about the group in early 1970, he blithely declared that they would likely be recording again soon.

This is not to suggest that he wanted that to happen. His non-reaction merely indicates the degree to which he viewed playing guitar with the Beatles as a job, rather than a way of life. Beyond tasting a new spirituality, by the time of the breakup he had also tasted musical freedom, and a different paradigm for recording, by working with a handful of other artists, including Bob Dylan. Those experiences convinced him that it wasn't the music-making he had tired of, merely the Beatles.

Always a junior partner in that endeavor, he started to imagine the freedom to record all of the songs he had stashed away, without having to compete with Lennon and McCartney for precious vinyl real estate, or secure their willingness to play on the records. In Phil Spector, he found the perfect partner-in-crime, someone who not only listened to his demos, but convinced him he could make a massive hit record all by himself.

When it became apparent in 1970 that the Beatles were not going to resume recording any time soon, Harrison realized his dream, and it set him up for a shocking degree of early solo success. Unfortunately, such things are notoriously difficult to maintain or repeat, and his burst out of the solo gate would set expectations for the following decade that he simply could not meet.

Maturing

George Harrison is a rare case of a songwriter who learned his craft entirely in the public eye. The first song he ever wrote, "Don't Bother Me," was heard by countless millions of people, despite being the work of a rank amateur.

His creative maturation is a beautiful thing to explore. It covers early pop classics like "If I Needed Someone," works through an Indian phase which most regarded as curious but tolerable, then touches gold with "While My Guitar Gently Weeps," "Something," and "Here Comes the Sun."

Yet even those classics do not represent Harrison at his most creatively mature. An argument can be made that he didn't reach his absolute peak until "Handle With Care," but a broad look at his entire career finds him actually reaching his final — and very high — plateau around the time of *George Harrison*. This seminal album includes perhaps his most commercial song ever, "Blow Away," along with a host of finely crafted, interesting, and genuinely beautiful songs — a most welcome moment of graduation.

The path was not a straight one. Despite developing the ability to pound out new material as needed, his uninspired songs are considerably less inspired than any by Lennon or McCartney. At his worst, the songs are incomprehensible, and that fact, combined with vocal troubles and a reduction in his recording standards, led to a swift downfall midway through the 70s. By the time Harrison got his feet under him again, his work did not matter anymore to the world of popular music, and his focus on writing trailed off, which is a terrible shame.

Though he learned his craft largely through proximity to Lennon and McCartney, in later years he recorded loving covers of Cole Porter and Hoagy Carmichael, and was quoted professing a new love for some of those *other* influential songwriters of the 20th century. This may have been the final ingredient he needed to reach his songwriting potential. Whatever it was, George Harrison had taken unprecedented opportunity and combined it with diligence and a willingness to make mistakes, and turned himself into another of the 20th century's greats.

Sliding

A phenomenal thing happened when Harrison was no longer yoked to the other Beatles: His guitar-playing changed instantly. Compare anything he played on *All Things Must Pass* to anything of his on *Abbey Road* and he sounds like a completely different guitarist. The slide technique came to dominate his work as a lead guitarist, and it became his signature through the rest of his career.

The change appears to have come about during his time playing with Delaney & Bonnie in December of 1969, thus making it simultaneous with the breakup. This was likely then reinforced by the presence of Pete Drake during the recording sessions the following summer. Drake added distinctive, country-style slide guitar to several tracks on *All Things Must Pass*, and appears to have encouraged and influenced Harrison significantly.

From that point on, much as he had the sitar before, George committed to mastering this new sound, and using it at every opportunity. From a practical standpoint, it meant that his solo work really did not dovetail with his Beatles work at all, in terms of his pure guitar playing. There is a hard line between them, and his style of playing on solo records formed the heart of his personal sound.

Though admirable in his dedication, the net result was a sameness to his arrangements and playing which, though distinctive overall, contributed to the problems of his mid-70s recordings. Though the desire for a clean break is understandable, in some ways the change made his records almost unidentifiable as being from a former Beatle, which inevitably hurt him in the marketplace when the songs themselves were not the best.

Enlightening

No discussion of Harrison's post-Beatles work would be complete without acknowledging that spirituality moved front and center to his art at the moment he no longer played with the Beatles. Whether this was a new personal commitment on his part, or it had been simmering beneath his Beatle façade for a long time is not clear. Obviously, his interest in Indian mysticism became part of the Beatles identity, but some of the language he began to use during his solo career, particularly the word "Lord," would have had no place on a Beatles record.

Indeed his biggest hit ever, "My Sweet Lord," could never have been a Beatles record for at least three reasons. First, it contained the word "Lord" in the title. Second, it built its fadeout on repetitions of the Hare Krishna chant. And third, it would have sounded familiar enough to not make it past their keen editing. Though some may consider this a loss to the Beatles catalog, it is unlikely that John, Paul or George Martin would have seen it that way.

Indeed, as time passed, Harrison's music began to proselytize in a most uncomfortable way. Though fans have always seemed to appreciate George's spiritual identity and focus, they did not always appreciate being preached to on his records. Indeed, his lyrics at times seemed dismissive of those who did not share his beliefs, and/or did not see the value that he placed on spiritual pursuits.

Likewise, his continued fascination with Indian music came to put a barrier between him and the fans. This was particularly true when he engaged his mentor Ravi Shankar to open his *Dark Horse* tour. Fans expecting a rock show, found themselves listening to long sets of Indian music which, though high in quality, did not resonate with his particular western audience. This led him to a period of scolding in his music, which did not enamor him to critics or the public.

Eventually, this less tolerant phase of his music passed, and later songs based on spiritual concepts were considerably more open and gentle. But a certain amount of damage could never be undone, and his solo work was scarred as a result. The time he spent in these doldrums may very well have come at his peak opportunity for success, and the opportunity was missed.

2 / FILTERS

Ringo Starr

9 studio albums / 7 non-album tracks / 103 distinct core studio works
Searching / Splashes / Friends

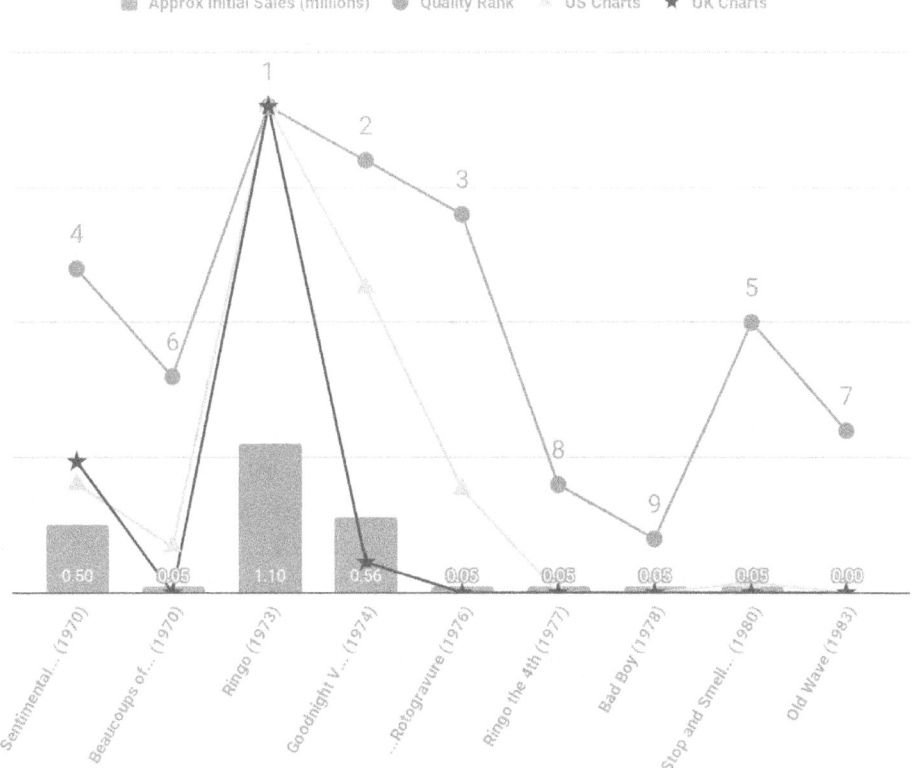

Best	*Ringo* (1973)
Better	*Goodnight Vienna* (1974) *Ringo's Rotogravure* (1976)
Worse	*Sentimental Journey* (1970) *Stop and Smell the Roses* (1981) *Beaucoups of Blues* (1970)
Worst	*Old Wave* (1983) *Ringo the 4th* (1977) *Bad Boy* (1978)

When the Beatles broke up, Richard Starkey was simply out of a job, and while that may sound like a reductionist characterization, it is the literal truth, the musical truth, and the psychological truth. And he knew it.

He had been the last to join the band, long after Lennon, McCartney and Harrison had bonded, and had always been the least secure member of the group, fourth in the pecking order, and for obvious reasons. Recall the story of his tonsillitis, and the ease with which Jimmie Nicol slipped into (and out of) the group. Recall the heartless treatment, and subsequent fall into obscurity, of Pete Best. Recall the days during *The White Album*, when Starkey quit the band, and McCartney simply slid over to the drum kit. In all of these cases, the group swapped drummers literally without missing a beat.

To the outside world, he was an essential part of the greatest band of all time, but he knew the situation from the inside. Though not excluded from contributing ideas, he was generally on the periphery of the group's creative braintrust, simply because he did not have those skills. Recall the days of recording *Sgt. Pepper*, when, by Starkey's own account, he was bored out of his mind most of the time, and passed the hours playing games with Mal Evans and Neil Aspinall off in a corner of the studio.[4] His playing and his voice may have been an essential part of the group sound and chemistry, but where else would that distinctiveness apply? Without the prospect of another group project, Starkey was left in a very bad place. The hardworking Liverpudlian, whose original ambition was to be a hairdresser, was hardly suited to a life of leisure, as would become painfully obvious.

The other Beatles certainly felt protective of him, and that would ultimately prove his salvation — to a degree, for a time.

Searching

The problem for Starkey in the fall of 1969 was that he was the only former Beatle with no real prospects for a second act. There were threads to explore, including vocalist, actor, and general "entertainer," but these were speculative, and not in his fundamental nature. The prospect he faced was that of being a star without an act, in the days before fame itself could be considered an occupation.

So, in the early days after the break-up, he rode his fame, and natural charm, for what it was worth. To his credit, he did explore his options thoroughly, making regular appearances on television, in movies, and as a drummer on some famous records. Most importantly, he maintained good relationships (most of the time) with his former bandmates, gigged whenever possible, and fished around for whatever it meant to be Ringo Starr in a post-Beatles world.

---

[4] This has been told enough times that it even made it into the company-line *Anthology* book, p. 242.

Thus, to talk about Starkey as a *recording artist* in the early 70s seems a bit presumptuous and misplaced. That was only one possibility he explored, to about the same degree as several others, and the results were not encouraging. He was not Paul, who checked all of the boxes for "recording artist" right out of the gate. He was not like John, an Artist in a greater sense, which happened to include recording. And he was not like George, with a cauldron of musical potential bubbling furiously beneath the surface, just waiting to be set loose.

Starkey was, and is, a journeyman — in the best possible sense. His journey through the solo years would have many different stops, and though he would prove very adaptable, nothing would ever "come easy."

Splashes

In all of his record-making, Ringo was entirely at the mercy of the creative people surrounding him. When they were good, as with the Beatles, he had the capacity to rise to it, and provide exactly what was needed. When they were mediocre, uninspired, or overly mercenary, as was too often the case in the 70s, he met them there. He threw his hat in with a lot of idea people along the way, and the quality of the ideas varied widely. In almost every case, the result was exactly as you might predict by looking at the creative names.

With George Martin et. al., Ringo made a warm and aspirational, if awkward, solo album. With Pete Drake, he wandered into the country mainstream. Richard Perry hosted the party that brought about a fleeting return to greatness. With Arif Mardin, he became pure product. With Vini Poncia, he hit a sad nadir of empty musical extrusion. With Russ Ballard and Joe Walsh, things looked up, but by then the die had been cast.

In a very real sense, there is no such thing as a "Ringo Starr record." Starkey did not "make" records so much as *participate* in the making of records. Those around him had much more impact on the finished product, and generally did not know how to best build a project around his unique instrument. His face may have been on the cover, and his voice may have provided the common thread for all the tracks, but he mostly seemed to stand outside of the projects, as if merely trying on the suit rather than wearing it. There is less of the person in the music than the typical pop star, but only because that is not his game.

This is not to say that Starkey was devoid of ideas, or unable to make great records. Obviously, he made a small handful of incredible records. From time to time, his music made great splashes in the waters of pop. The point is more that he never found the right creative team to provide sustained success as a recording artist. Though it seems fair to wonder if such a team ever could have existed, it also seems almost certain that opportunities were missed because it didn't.

Friends

Of all the solo Beatles, Ringo did the most work with famous collaborators. It started with his eponymous hit album, but became the closest thing to a successful formula that he ever had. The list of famous names on Ringo's albums is long and well-known, but his best studio foils were also his first: the other former Beatles.

His best collaborator, by far, was George Harrison. Though there is some mystery in how they wrote (or did not) together, the anecdotes and highly successful outcomes suggest that Starkey generated ideas, and Harrison helped refine them — in a way that fed back into Ringo's own sensibilities. A concrete example can be found in the *Let It Be* film, where the two are briefly seen hammering out "Octopus's Garden," with George obviously helping Ringo locate the chord changes he is imagining. Where other collaborators handed things to Ringo and he performed them, George worked to bring Ringo's ideas to their best possible incarnation, then helped turn them into great records.

Paul McCartney, though famously estranged from the rest of his former bandmates through most of the 70s, did make contributions to three of Ringo's albums, and even invited him to play on *Tug of War* in 1981. Of the former Beatles, his songs were the least successful for Ringo, though the two would share many warm moments in later years.

John Lennon appreciated Ringo as a drummer, enjoyed working with him in the studio, and used him on multiple occasions in the early post-breakup years. In exchange, he gave one track and a couple of ideas to each of Ringo's three mid-decade albums — where styles came and went like grooves in a record. Though Lennon's contributions didn't all hit the mark squarely, they did have the advantage of being *right for Ringo* — something few non-Beatle songwriters accomplished.

What Ringo always needed was collaborators willing to figure out the right way to use his unique attributes. He was unlike any other vocalist, unlike any other drummer, and unlike any other popular personality. As a result, it's probably fair to say that the range of possibilities for him was smaller than many other artists. But when someone took the right approach, which happened more often than not when he worked with other former Beatles, the results could be very special. It just didn't happen very often.

To keep things interesting, Ringo worked with a wide variety of musicians, famous and not, after the Beatles. For the most part, they appear to have had good intentions, but simply could not crack the nut. As such, the resulting records only occasionally show Ringo at his best, and it's not really his fault. In truth, Ringo's voice was often treated by his collaborators as a sort of placeholder — a rare instrument that no one quite knew how to play.

So what would have been right for Ringo? Another band? Sticking with the film career? Semi-retirement? Heading home and becoming the hairdresser he always wanted to be? It is an impossible question to answer. Without songwriting royalties, he couldn't just retire, so the reinventions continued to come. A life of talk shows and career retrospectives is a terrible thing to wish on anyone.

The obvious answer came only many years later, with the creation of the All-Starr Band. Not only are the friends famous, talented, and well-meaning, but they all manage to have fun for adoring crowds wherever they go. They all "make show" and entertain together, highlighting what might have been Ringo's best option all along. If not entirely ideal, it at least casts this former Beatle in a very flattering light.

3
Phases

> *"...whatever we do we are not splitting up the Beatles. This is the Beatles—we don't differentiate." So even though none of the others appeared on ["Yesterday"], it was still The Beatles—that was the creed of the day.*
>
> — George Martin, quoting Brian Epstein[1]

In many ways, we tend to think of the solo era as just another phase in the evolution of the band. Though the former Beatles would all have bristled at this notion, preferring to think of themselves as finally out from under the Beatle mantle, they actually laid the foundation for us to think that way, and reinforced it many times.

To begin with, as referenced in the quote above, "Yesterday" set a precedent they would always maintain that Beatle records did not need to include all four Beatles. At the outset, this was an artistic choice, but beginning with *Revolver*, other factors came into play. Ringo was not needed for "Eleanor Rigby." John was absent for undocumented reasons on "Love You To." Neither John nor George participated in "For No One." And Paul famously left the studio in a huff when it came time to record "She Said She Said" — the first documented occasion when a Beatle would be missing for reasons of personal strife between the bandmates.

Having given themselves permission to complete records in this way, the reasons for being absent eventually multiplied, ranging from not liking the song being recorded, to being supplanted by the songwriter on their instrument, to convalescence after a car accident. Whatever the reasons, fully 28 of their 215 core recordings include less than all four Beatles, and seven include only one.

A parallel precedent was established in their earliest sessions: The Beatles didn't have to play or sing everything themselves — even their own natural instruments. Guest musicians were welcomed, and simply subsumed into the sound. Early uncredited examples include Andy White famously playing drums on "Love Me Do" and "P. S. I love You," and engineer Norman Smith tapping the hi-hat on "Can't Buy Me Love." The band generously began to acknowledge George Martin's regular contributions on *With the Beatles*.

More prominent guest performances began in 1965 when they hired John Scott to add flutes to "You've Got to Hide Your Love Away," and the string players to complete "Yesterday." Though many guests would remain uncredited, those with the

---

[1] *Maximum Volume*, pg. 263

most prominent contributions sometimes did find their names on the album sleeve, such as Anil Bhagwat and Alan Civil on *Revolver*.

The phenomenon shifted, and arguably reached its peak, with Eric Clapton's iconic work on "While My Guitar Gently Weeps." Now a guest was playing an instrument that the Beatles actually played, namely lead guitar, but was invited to add something distinctive to the group's sound from the outside, and was credited for doing so on the sleeve. The same happened with Billy Preston, who also received credit by name in multiple places.

Even if you exclude Martin's 40 guest appearances, and Billy Preston's 12, there are still 60 Beatles tracks which include musical performances by non-Beatles. The precedent was clear: No matter who performed, or didn't, during a Beatles recording session, it was still *a Beatles record.*

It may seem like a giant leap to believe that the group could have simply decided not to record together at all while continuing to release records under the "Beatles" umbrella. In truth, it is barely a leap at all. Indeed, when the group broke up, the recording process changed only slightly.

Since individual Beatles had already been performing solo overdubs on songs for years, the biggest change after the breakup was that they no longer recorded the backing tracks together.[2] Psychologically, this is a significant difference, of course, but in a practical sense, it is relatively small. Their approach to backing tracks had evolved substantially through the years, and as time wore on there were cases where little or nothing was left of the backing track when the recording was completed.

Given the difficulties associated with being in the same studio together, it would have made great sense for the band to decide among themselves that each member could work wherever, however, and with whomever he pleased — just like breaking up — but with the critical difference that the group would come together to sort through everything when the time came to release a new album. Far from revolutionary, this would have been a rather slight *evolutionary* change to their recording technique, comparable in scale to the one they made in allowing McCartney to be the only Beatle on "Yesterday." Such a simple, *intentional*, change could easily have accommodated the group's shifting needs, ranging from logistic, to temperamental, to emotional, to artistic, to stylistic.

This would have amounted to them simply becoming *independent artists* who *fused* their work together — a very natural progression which had been happening informally for quite some time. Indeed, they had laid the groundwork for such a psychological shift all along the way, which becomes clear when you reconsider the actual creative phases that the group went through.

We typically think of the Beatles' career as having three distinct parts: early, middle and late. The delineations are pretty well established and understood. The

---

[2] Greater detail on the Beatles' recording process will be found in forthcoming chapters.

early period is the Fab Four years, from the very beginning through *Help!* The middle period is the psychedelic era, from *Rubber Soul* through *Magical Mystery Tour*. The late period is the fractures and breakup, from "Lady Madonna" through *Let It Be*. These dividing lines are easy enough to recognize that if a new generation of listeners came to the band with no advance knowledge, we can safely assume they would probably end up with exactly the same designations.

Splitting it up this way, however, misses important aspects of how the band's art actually developed. Those typical lines of demarcation create a neat *dramatic* arc, which is easy to understand and absorb, and they work reasonably well along the axes of sound, fashion, influence, general cultural knowledge and musical/lyrical maturity. While these are certainly heavyweight aspects, they are not necessarily the most important ones to understanding the band's creative and artistic evolution.

Other more subtle changes in their circumstances and priorities also brought about three different phases which are equally obvious once pointed out, but tend to be obscured. Partly this is because they do not begin or end at specific moments, but rather overlap, with transitions between that are dissolves rather than jump cuts.

In their nature, these alternate distinctions are actually much more useful because each transition includes both a change in their primary activities, and a realignment of their relationships with each other as artists. Recognizing these alternate phases not only provides a useful frame for understanding the band, it also makes it easier to join the adventure of imagining a considerable expansion to their final phase.

Phase One - Fraternal Show-Makers

In their first phase, which began when the band formed, all of their activities were channeled toward entertaining the audience right in front of them — and having fun doing it. They stood on a stage of some sort, played music for whoever was there, and were either enjoyed or not. If the legends are to believed, most of the time they succeeded in having a lot of fun. The music they played was chosen entirely from the music they had grown up loving: rock and roll records, for the most part, but also some of McCartney's favorite Broadway and Tin Pan Alley standards. As new records came out that they liked, songs were added to the act.

If an audience wanted to hear something specific, they played it. If they didn't know it, they learned it, or bluffed their way through it. Along the way they built a massive catalog of repertoire that they could call on at any moment. Between songs, they learned how to engage in banter with the audience, and perpetrated some legendary on-stage antics. Famously, in Germany, their stage shows went on for hours, and the task at hand was laid out in very plain instructions: "Mach Schau." The Beatles played music, and had fun, and made show — a *lot* of show.

Because they lived together and performed together and hung out together more or less constantly, this is the era when John, Paul and George established the fraternal bond which would unite them for the rest of their lives. In a very real way, the show-making was essentially an extension of their friendship. They came together to play music for fun, became fast friends, had adventures together, played more music, had more fun, became closer friends, had more adventures, and repeated the cycle over and over for five years before the crowds started clamoring for them.

During this time, they famously rejected Pete Best because he simply did not fit into their burgeoning fraternity, and became friends with Ringo, who even from the distance of another band, seemed like someone who could belong.

THE FORMATIVE YEARS

	JAN	FEB	MAR	APR	MAY	JUN	JUL	AUG	SEP	OCT	NOV	DEC
57			+Lennon				+McCartney					
58		+Harrison										
59												
60					+Sutcliffe			+Best	Hamburg I			
61				Hamburg II			-Sutcliffe				+Epstein	
62				Hamburg III	+Martin			-Best +Starr			Hamburg IV	Hamburg V

The emphasis, however, was always on *performing*. At some point, only approximately known, John and Paul each began writing their own songs in earnest, and they also began to collaborate. While some of these songs would find their way into shows, they were mostly novelties, and hardly the meat-and-potatoes of their act. Songs such as "Like Dreamers Do" and "One After 909" were well known by their audiences before the group got famous, but were deemed too rudimentary for use once they began recording in earnest. This is because songwriting during the first phase was really just another adventure, another type of fun, and a footnote to their primary activity as show-makers.

This phase did not end the moment they hit it big. The audiences just got bigger, noisier, and more adoring. Thus the phase lingered, informing their public persona to a decreasing extent for another four years. It is the reason they recorded, released and performed cover songs from their earliest days, and was at the heart of their radio, TV and film personas — arenas in which they continued to make show and have fun just like the old days. It also informed the endless stream of press conferences, their sharp and quick wit having been honed by countless hours responding from the stage to often inebriated audience members.

The phase only gradually faded out, first through a shift in their recording activities. At EMI they recorded 12 covers in 1963, nine in 1964, and three in 1965. For BBC radio, 150 of 244 recorded songs in 1963 were covers (61%), but that dropped to only 27 of 65 (42%) in 1964. Secondly, originals gradually overtook their concert set lists, though traces of this first phase remained in their stage act all the way to the very end, with "Rock and Roll Music" and "Long Tall Sally" still in their set list for the final tour. The first phase finally closed for good when their touring days ended.

In summary, the Beatles' first phase was primarily about show-making, in all its various forms. The relationship between band members was essentially fraternal — brothers in show and adventure. Though the first phase was lengthy, a second phase began to supplant it the moment they set foot in the EMI studios on Abbey Road.

Phase Two - Tandem Performing Songwriters

When George Martin signed the Beatles to a recording contract in 1962, he assumed that he would need to find new material for them in the same way he had for most of his previous artists. He knew that they played mostly covers in their stage act, and the fact that they offered a few original songs for his consideration didn't initially impress him, at least not until they presented their revised arrangement of "Please Please Me."

But when they rejected "How Do You Do It?" and insisted on "Love Me Do" as their debut single, the Beatles began their second phase — defined *not* by the acquisition of a recording contract, success and fame, but by the change in the primary focus of their creative activities. Among the many shifts which took place at that moment, the most artistically significant may have been the psychic shift in John and Paul from *performers* first to *songwriters* first. Almost instantaneously, their songs went from being downtime adventures and occasional novelties on stage to the very focus of their artistic work — and eventually, their brand and income.

Likewise, the group's focus shifted quickly from entertaining live audiences with whatever music was at hand to *writing songs*, making records of *those songs*, and entertaining with *those songs*. Of the many activities which occupied their days, writing and recording got their greatest attention and the bulk of their creative energy. They were still very good at making show, and they still did it for quite a while, but it had become routine for them, and therefore boring. The new thrill was creating original music and lyrics.

The beginning of this phase happened to coincide with the rise of Beatlemania, but was not caused by it. In fact, it appears largely coincidental that John and Paul began to think of themselves as songwriters immediately before signing with EMI. What caused the shift is actually the subject of some mystery, but the most likely explanation is disillusionment and boredom. Though they still drew new stage material from popular records, great songs came along much less frequently than they once had. There was less and less special about the new songs, and it appears that they realized that maybe they could do just as well — or better — writing for themselves. Each had written a few songs, albeit not seriously, and then suddenly it got serious. That seismic shift in thinking seems to have happened sometime in 1962, as they grew tired of the long shows, dreamed of a recording contract, and found new ways to make the most of the time on their hands.

In the first phase, once they had a big enough repertoire and the basics of making show in place, they eclipsed other bands mainly through the sheer force of their personalities, good looks, sound, and energetic stage presence — and *not* specifically what songs they were playing. Indeed, though the Beatles may have had the largest overall repertoire, most semi-professional bands of the era were playing many of the same hit songs as the Beatles. As the second phase faded in, however, songwriting became quickly intertwined with their public identity in a way it never had before, and elevated them even further above their competition. Now they had all of those intangibles on which they had built their following, *plus* great songs *that no one else was playing*.

From their first album release, this aspect of the Beatles' identity was baked right into the publicity, as can be clearly seen in Tony Barrow's liner notes for *Please Please Me*:

> *Their own built-in tunesmith team of John Lennon and Paul McCartney has already tucked away enough self-penned numbers to maintain a steady output of all-original singles from now until 1975! ... The do-it-yourself angle ensures complete originality at all stages of the process.*

In actuality, one part of this hyperbole was true, and the other very much not. While originality was undeniable, a catalog of original songs certainly did not yet exist. Most of the originals on the album hadn't been around for very long, and there were almost none left waiting in the wings for the next release. The Beatles would write most of the new original songs shortly before the next album sessions started, which would become standard operating procedure.

No one needed to know that, of course, and the marketing worked both within the band and beyond. To their credit, the songwriting Beatles, recognizing this aspect as now central to their public personas, always rose to the occasion when a new batch of songs was needed. As such, the identity as songwriters stuck to the Beatles, and those liner notes proved semi-prophetic, even if there wasn't so much as a twinkling of the actual future hits of 1975, "Whatever Gets You Through the Night" or "Listen to What the Man Said," in the minds of Lennon and McCartney back then.

3 / Phases

Because they continued doing shows for almost four more years, vestiges of the first phase continued to fill holes in their sets as they learned their songwriting craft and built their catalog. After all, the concerts were now big business, as were all of the radio and television and press conference appearances. Crowds loved hearing the Beatles sing those oldies, and the band could play them in their sleep. But all of that quickly became a secondary focus of their attention, and such things eventually became odious chores.

In truth, their songs/records were so good, and so fresh, and so popular that the shift was almost beyond their control. Once they decided to commit themselves to that sort of creativity offstage, they found that the public wanted more and more of it onstage. Now originals were welcome — even demanded — in their shows. When they played original music, they were somehow rising above the simple act of putting on a show. Now their *creativity* got the accolades, every bit as much as their appearance, performing and charm. The balance never quite tipped as far as they would have liked, partly because of technical limitations in concert, and partly because of all the screaming, and this certainly fueled their decision to retire from the stage.

Thus the characterization as *performing songwriters* — performance still occupying a lot of their time and public appearances, but songwriting owning the creative focus in private. The shift coincided with trends in the industry, where the singer/songwriter had emerged as an actual category of performer. The Beatles were not singer/songwriters in that earliest sense. Such a label indicated something of a lone wolf, and the Beatles were obvious not "lone" at all. They were songwriters and performers who moved in *tandem* with one another, a characterization which gained strength as George Harrison joined the songwriting party.

That sense of moving in *tandem* is a subtle shift from the process of building fraternal bonds which took place in the first phase. Those bonds remained, and were even strengthened, but subtle shifts occurred in the relationships which changed things significantly. With John and Paul getting constant accolades for songwriting, George and Ringo were relegated to second class Beatle status, at least within the creative braintrust which surrounded the band. Where Paul and John created the songs, George and Ringo focused on how their playing would best support what the others had written. Among other things, the songwriters had much greater clout in the studio.

Eventually, this change would cause significant problems, but at first it was a private matter, since the group moved as one more or less everywhere. The public gradually came to realize that Lennon and McCartney were the songwriters, but it was still all one band. This idea was actually reinforced as Harrison began writing songs. "Beatles music" was just that to the public, regardless of who wrote what (at least within the limits of "favorite Beatle" logic).

In shows, as each Beatle took turns at the microphone singing lead on a song he wrote — or *they* wrote — the audience still saw one group with multiple personalities, one band with multiple aspects, one artist with creative parts that moved in tandem. This essential perception would undergird how the public handled phases yet to come. At this point, however, it was very natural.

On a side note, it's important to remember that the era is *not* characterized specifically by studio innovations. Most of the recordings they made during this phase are very much by-the-book enterprises, distinguished from others on the market only by the voices, distinctive playing, and groundbreaking songwriting. There were certainly incidental innovations, and joy in mixing and matching instrumental sounds, but these aspects were hardly their focus.

Instead, in the second phase we hear in almost every new track the joy of discovering melodies and chord changes and harmonies and shifts in key and time signature. Lennon, McCartney, and eventually Harrison, can be heard finding their compositional voices and enjoying the process. The alternately complex and rudimentary writing is characteristic of songwriters learning their craft by simply doing it over and over. As such, we hear mistakes right alongside major leaps forward. It's notable that one of the most memorable quotes about the group from this era lauds their ability to include the famed "Aeolian cadences." The observation inadvertently highlighted the fact that, as neophytes, Lennon and McCartney had no idea what they were doing, and that was the best possible — and perhaps *only* — way to do what they did.

The second phase is, therefore, marked by the shift from pure show-making to the creation of new songs with which to make the show — from *performance* to *writing*. The fraternal relationship created during the first phase is not erased, but superceded by the way in which they were forced to move in tandem as a four-headed act instead of individuals.

Phase Three - Aligned Studio Auteurs

During a recording session at EMI on October 18, 1964, John Lennon leaned his guitar against Paul McCartney's bass amp and heard a loud buzz of feedback. He and the other Beatles convinced a reluctant George Martin to edit a careful recording of this "found sound" onto the front of their next single, "I Feel Fine." From that small serendipitous seed grew the third phase of the Beatles' career. It would not flower for more than a year, but once it did, songwriting was no longer enough for the nascent studio craftsmen.

Of all the phases, this one seems the most self-evident. The Beatles are perhaps most remembered for the groundbreaking records they created between 1965 and 1969. They had mastered traditional studio techniques quickly, then began an unprecedented period of extending them. This changed the scope and scale of sounds which could appear in a single track, and challenged all other recording artists of the era to do the same.

Beginning with the sessions for *Rubber Soul*, though good new songs kept coming, the Beatles began to think that they could make a great record at out of any idea they could generate. They began combining advances in sound reproduction with the full maturation of their playing and songwriting to yield a laboratory in which even the slightest idea could be extensively explored and just might become a compelling commercial product. The songs became something of a carrier wave on which studio innovation could be delivered.

This characterization is not intended to minimize the quality of the songwriting, but to acknowledge that even a song of lower quality could still be turned into an exciting record by marrying it to new studio technique. An early example of this can be found in "What Goes On," a song which clearly lacks the complexity of other compositions on *Rubber Soul*. It had been passed over in 1963 as sub-standard, but when they got stuck for new material to fill the album, the group resurrected the song and put it through their new filter. Though hardly an innovative recording, the fresh sound brought the song to life, plainly demonstrating the power of pure recording technique.

The phenomenon reached its peak during the heart of their psychedelic era, and is especially obvious in tracks like "Lovely Rita," perhaps the least interesting composition on *Sgt. Pepper*. Had McCartney presented this song to the group even a year earlier it might have been set aside as not good enough. Consider that "Rita" would have sounded decidedly out of place on the same record as either of her sisters, "Michelle" and "Eleanor." But on *Sgt. Pepper*, the combination of vaguely psychedelic imagery and the desire to let studio innovation and craftsmanship do the heavy lifting, made it possible for this very slight song to make the cut.

Since each track ultimately became an adventure unto itself, the quality of the underlying songs — despite still being high — was simply less relevant. In a counterintuitive way, the experiments and advances in studio technique reduced the pressure on their songwriting, and the reduced pressure in turn yielded even higher quality songs. Once again, a virtuous circle ensued, and for the most part, the realization that they *could* use lesser ideas did not routinely result in them *settling* for lesser ideas.

Eventually, the focus on the song would return, and once again recording techniques would be employed merely to make sure each great song was sufficiently realized. This may be the hallmark of *Abbey Road*, where the Beatles' collective songwriting was arguably at its highest point ever.

Interestingly, through the entire phase the working methods were actually not that much different than they always had been. Backing tracks were produced in the same way as always, albeit with higher fidelity and an even stronger sense that they would be significantly augmented by overdubs, and thus didn't need to be quite as polished. As such, the role of the backing track itself gradually began to change as they moved more fully into this phase. What had to this point been a strong foundation on which a finished track could be built began to gradually resemble something more like a skeleton onto which muscle and flesh would gradually be added. Where tracks in the second phase always sounded like a band playing together, tracks in the third phase clearly began to sound more like intentionally assembled collections of performances which created a whole greater than the sum of its parts.

The Beatles themselves recognized this shift almost immediately, and began to complain that they could not play their new records on stage. Indeed, the set list for their final tour famously did not include any songs from *Revolver*, the album they were ostensibly promoting. Even though they could have played them in "second phase" style arrangements, they could not play them like the recordings, and their refusal to even try speaks volumes about the phase shift which was underway.

In some ways, the Beatles began to resemble craftsmen, plying their trade in recording studios, and applying their ever-growing skills to everything they did. But this characterization falls short of describing the level of control and creativity they ultimately exerted. As this phase began they started moving as something of a four-headed *auteur*, collectively exerting complete control over each piece of the art (short of album sequencing, as we will see), and somehow managing to include everyone in the process. In 1965 and 1966, all four Beatles were actively involved in all aspects of these studio creations, even if they didn't play on them. Everyone was present, pitched in with ideas, tried out various things, had a say in the finished sound, etc. Unfortunately, this would not last.

Gradually, each songwriter began to shape the recording of his song, with the ideas of the others being relegated to secondary consideration. Early signs of this shift were when Paul played lead guitar, more and more unsatisfied with what George brought to his songs. As Lennon and McCartney collaborated less on songwriting, each began to dominate the sessions for the song he wrote. And though the presence of all Beatles still regularly resulted in happy accidents, more and more each artist entered sessions with a clear idea of how the finished record should sound. Even when they did not, the system which developed gave the songwriter the final say on the sound, even as other Beatles might still contribute.

From there, it was a rather small step to a very different dynamic, in which each Beatle was essentially a session musician for the songwriter. These were the first seeds of the next phase, and they crept in gradually. For the most part, the era beginning with "Lady Madonna" still mostly required all four Beatles, at least for the backing track, while allowing each songwriter complete freedom to shape the track once the band had laid down the first sounds for it. This led, among other things, to the famous phenomenon described by many engineers of the individual Beatles working simultaneously in different studios, polishing tracks alone that they had begun together.

Thus they were no longer moving in *tandem*, but can better be described as *aligned* toward the same goal — a finished album — even while they worked more and more apart. This alignment was most obvious when it came time to assemble diverse collections of tracks into albums. With everyone's work collected, they began the tedious process of creating running orders and transitions. In a very direct way, at this step they remixed and aligned recordings with one another to create a unified sound that, while not inauthentic, was more of a patchwork than in the days when everyone had participated in everything.

In their last days as a foursome, George Harrison tolerated being McCartney's guitarist while hating every moment of it, but Lennon generally refused to be Harrison's, at times not even showing up. McCartney played on everyone's tracks, but recorded his bass parts late at night, alone. When involved in group sessions, he got frustrated when things didn't sound like he imagined, obtaining a very sticky reputation for perfectionism and bossiness. Ringo was still everybody's drummer, but factions had formed and began to calcify.

The stresses to their alignment were incredible during *Abbey Road*, despite its reputation as a project on which they united for one last time. "Maxwell's Silver Hammer" is often trotted out, with justification, to demonstrate that the four Beatles were still aligned, but that such alignment could not continue under those circumstances. Each Beatle, now an artist on his own, was conflicted about sublimating his artistic impulses to those of the others.

What they did not realize, but might have, is that the fourth way of working together was already available to them. Thus it is with only a slight tweak that we can imagine how a fourth phase might have developed, with the realization that it had been hiding in plain sight all along.

Phase Four - Fused Independent Artists

The fourth phase is hardly pure fantasy, despite never reaching its full potential. It actually describes a slice of 28 tracks in the Beatles' catalog where some combination of less than all four Beatles participated in the recording, which began, as you know, with "Yesterday."

Though these tracks were scattered throughout the later albums, their frequency picked up over time. The critical feature they possess is that many of them could easily have been labeled as *solo tracks*, and even formed the basis for *solo albums*, had anyone wanted that.

Somehow they maintained the unity which Brian Epstein had decreed. The Beatles were not to ever be split up, even as it became more and more clear that they had all outgrown the notion of being a band together. This explains why we must consider them, in this phase, to be *independent*. No longer defined by their fraternal bonds, or moving in tandem, or even being formally aligned with one another, they all began working independently on solo material, but from within the band. That ended with the breakup, of course, but the seeds of what became the solo years clearly took root long before they formally began.

PHASES PLOTTED
Each dot represents one track

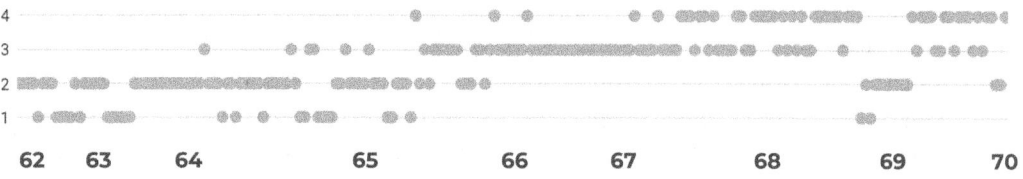

Nonetheless, they continued allowing their work to be *fused* together with that of the others. This is most obvious on *The White Album*, but there are whiffs of it on all albums after *Rubber Soul*. Perhaps the quintessential example would be the way in which George's Indian tracks were fused into the group albums, despite deep reservations from everyone involved. The lesson this example teaches, however, is the potential value of fusion as a process. The Beatles are well-remembered for having included Harrison's trips into unfamiliar musical territory, and in some ways it defines their group identity — despite being entirely the work of a single Beatle. How much worse off would their catalog be if George had resolved to release all of his Indian music as solo records?

This is the phase, already begun long before the breakup, that we would like to expand and reimagine by recasting the solo materials. By looking at the previous three phases, we can clearly see a line that the group might have followed. Instead of abandoning collaboration altogether, they might have simply recognized that their work had fully reached this new level, one in which what they once offered each other in the studio was no longer required or even possible. Such is the nature of superstardom.

Instead, we imagine them as fully mature, but independent, recording artists who might have decided to maintain a *unified* front because of the strength they could still gain from one another, despite not recording in the same studio together anymore. The progression is entirely natural.

There are certainly reasons to think they might have tried such a thing. Not only had they remade their image over and over, and changed their recording style and techniques more or less constantly, but they even discussed a change to their working methods which might have led to something like this in September of 1969. This fact only came to light in 2019, when Mark Lewisohn revealed the existence of a tape recording of a meeting which contained such a discussion.

> *...we hear John suggesting that each of them should bring in songs as candidates for the single. He also proposes a new formula for assembling their next album: four songs apiece from Paul, George and himself, and two from Ringo – 'If he wants them.' John refers to 'the Lennon-and-McCartney myth', clearly indicating that the authorship of their songs, hitherto presented to the public as a sacrosanct partnership, should at last be individually credited.*[3]

The ground-breaking revelation of this conversation changes much of the narrative of September 1969, though it regrettably does not change the outcome. It calls into question whether they really did decide in advance that *Abbey Road* would be their final project together. It definitely suggests that, had the ugliness of early 1970 not destroyed the band's camaraderie, a new path forward could have been on the table. Perhaps it still would have involved going into the studio together, even if on a more limited basis. Perhaps they still would have recorded basic tracks together, but completed each track individually, as had become more and more common.

Or perhaps they would have done exactly as we would like to imagine. Outside musicians could have offloaded some of the "session" work which each Beatle had clearly outgrown, and records made completely separately could be fused onto the same vinyl for release. This would have offered immense creative freedom, constricted only by the possibility that not every finished track would be selected for release. But that potential actually would have been an advantage in disguise, offering an incentive to polish tracks meticulously, making sure they always rose to the typical Beatle standards, while also allowing that leftovers might find a way out on solo releases. This, in turn, could have set the stage for solo careers to begin gradually, while retaining the safety of the group. Arguably, this is what George Harrison really needed all along.

The thought is not entirely pleasant, of course. Special effort would have been needed to manufacture on vinyl the collaboration which was not happening in the studio. The mysterious chemistry would not have been available, but a different type of chemistry might have taken its place, opening up possibilities for growth as a *supergroup* that could never have happened as a simple foursome.

So let us imagine that the Beatles were able to set aside their differences at least enough to consult with one another about once a year, and let the keen ear of George Martin or his proxy, who we will call the "Assembler," cherry pick an album's worth

---

[3] *The Guardian*, September 11, 2019

of tracks from what they had recorded individually. Together, they could have assembled a finished product that everyone could be proud of, perhaps even adding overdubs to each other's recordings to properly "finish" them. The unused material would be queued up for assembly and release as solo albums on whatever schedule worked for everyone.

The result could have been another decade of potentially magical, and strong-selling, Beatles albums. It also could have made it possible for the inevitable solo careers to start more gracefully and organically. Each Beatle would have had more time to become comfortable working on his own, only gradually exerting more independence from the group in a more sustainable fashion.

This may not be exactly the dream we all have dreamed about the Beatles staying together, but it's one we will now set out to explore.

Part II
Divination

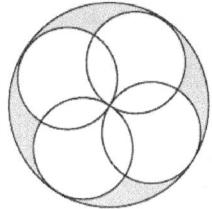

*Since our concern was speech, and speech impelled us
To purify the dialect of the tribe
And urge the mind to aftersight and foresight,
Let me disclose the gifts reserved for age
To set a crown upon your lifetime's effort.*

4
Tiers

Once all the recording is finally complete there is an important task still remaining: all tracks need to be put into a running order (sequencing). This has a significant effect on the way a listener here's a record, particularly for the first time. Imagine starting the Sergeant Pepper *album with "A Day in the Life;" there would be nothing left after the first track.*

— George Martin[1]

The first sound on the first classic Beatles album is . . . a count-off.

The last sound on the last classic Beatles album is . . . a single plucked guitar string — ironically, one which leaves the song unfinished.

Between those two iconic bookends stands a sprawling landscape of music and sound and imagery and culture and fashion and unparalleled artistry. We love it, and most of the time that's enough. At other times, we want to understand it, at least a little, and see if we can figure out just how and why it engaged us and continues to engage us after so many years and countless listens.

George Martin, at least, might discourage us from the endeavor:

I am not sure how much cold-blooded analysis has to do with one's passion for a work of art. It is a bit like falling in love. Do we really care if there is the odd wrinkle here or there? The power to move people, to tears or laughter, to violence or sympathy, is the strongest attribute that any art can have. In this respect, music is the prime mover: its call on the emotions is the most direct of all the arts.[2]

He was describing his initial reaction to "Strawberry Fields Forever," but his point has broader applications. Some elements of artistry can never really be understood, and we should accept that. At its highest levels, such as with the Beatles, art is *mostly* mystery. Like many artists, even the Beatles themselves didn't exactly understand what they had wrought. Every release was the result of hundreds of ideas and decisions — many subconscious, instinctive, and at times even random. Each song, track and album was created *within* a complicated context, and released *into* a

---

[1] *Summer of Love*, pg. 150
[2] Ibid. pg. 13

complicated context. Trying to understand all of that could take a lifetime and still leave us wanting.

Acknowledging this truth is about respecting the art. Thinking too much can render art into a cold, distant, intellectual experiment. Thinking too little, however, leaves potential degrees of appreciation unexplored. The sweet spot in the case of the Beatles is to listen closely, as so many fans actually do, and see if we can catch the echoes of what hides behind the art, in that intricate veil of sound we love.

Specifically, for the current project, we need to distill and understand a little more about the group's techniques and principles of album assembly in order to experiment with extending them. This is both easier than it sounds and harder. On the one hand, we have complete access to everything they did, and an ever-increasing amount of documentation about how and why they did it. The information we need is potentially right there for anyone who seeks it. On the other hand, the thing we're looking for may simply defy description. Even looking straight at it, we may not be able to see it.

I am convinced that we can learn important things, enough to guide us in imagining a new era for the Beatles. Still, nothing is guaranteed. The search is akin to a *divination*, which may or may not reveal the as yet unseen. The best art often guards its secrets well, even when they hide in plain sight.

The artworks in question are the classic Beatles albums, of course. Each is a collection of music which, in some mysterious way, is greater than the sum of its parts. As such, we are interested here in the sum, not the parts. In other words, we want to understand how the tracks were put together, and how they interact to create that distinct whole.

We will use the standard UK catalog because these are the albums assembled directly by the Beatles and/or George Martin. As such, there are ten albums to consider, and though this list will be familiar, there are two essential omissions.

ALBUM	*TITLE* Recorded	Producer	Studio(s)	RELEASE
B03	*Please Please Me* Feb 63	Martin	EMI	63-Mar
B06	*With the Beatles* Jul-Oct 63	Martin	EMI	63-Nov
B11	*A Hard Day's Night* (UK) Jan-Jun 64	Martin	EMI, Pathé Marconi (Paris)	64-Jul
B13	*Beatles for Sale* Aug-Oct 64	Martin	EMI	64-Dec
B16	*Help!* (UK) Feb-Jun 65	Martin	EMI	65-Aug

B18	*Rubber Soul* (UK) Jun-Nov 65	Martin	EMI	65-Dec
B20	*Revolver* (UK) Apr-Jun 66	Martin	EMI	66-Aug
B23	*Sgt. Pepper's Lonely Hearts Club Band* Nov 66 - Apr 67	Martin	EMI, Regent	67-May
B29	*The Beatles* ["The White Album"] May-Oct 68	Martin	EMI, Trident	68-Nov
B33	*Abbey Road* Feb-Aug 69	Martin	EMI, Olympic, Trident	69-Sep

Magical Mystery Tour is excluded because, in its UK incarnation, it is not a full album, and the US version (which ultimately became the official version) was essentially a compilation assembled by marketers, not the Beatles. *Let It Be* is left off because it was assembled by Phil Spector, working partly from specifications given by Allen Klein and Michael Lindsay-Hogg, with little or no input from the Beatles' creative braintrust regarding its final form. Indeed, we will use that album's significant deficiencies to illuminate critical principles present in other albums and utterly missing there (see chapter 10).

Each of these ten albums is a complete artistic statement, one that transcends any track or tracks. These statements, though impossible to extract and summarize, are found in the aggregation of music and words and visual imagery. In each case, songs and ideas and images bounce off of one another, together creating a space in which each piece of music is heard differently than it might be on its own. With or without a central theme, the music forms a unified *set*.

These spaces get progressively more sophisticated, and it's important to note that there is no regression. Each new release is fundamentally different and more complex than the last. In multiple cases the new whole is barely recognizable as continuous from its predecessor. This has caused endless and unresolvable debates about overall "greatness," a blurry distinction which is essentially beside the point. All such comparisons between albums are apples to oranges.

The level of surprise was arguably most noticeable with *Rubber Soul* and *Sgt. Pepper*, but similar sentiments are generally heard in discussions of all the late albums. Each was its own individual revelation.

In the five albums before *Rubber Soul* this transcendence may not be immediately obvious. They appear at a glance to be merely collections of unrelated — or *barely* related — tracks. The two movie soundtracks do have obvious tie-ins to the films, but they collect music that did not actually inform the plots in any significant way, and do not offer any obvious progression in themselves. The other three albums do not even have such a slight thread, but that absence is deceptive. There is much more going on in these apparently simple assemblies than may be obvious at first.

To begin the discussion, however, we must acknowledge that, like all recording artists of their era, the Beatles focused all their energy on *tracks* — or, as they were known in the industry, *sides* — and *not* albums. This is to say that not until a batch of tracks was finished was there much — or any — thought about how they would fit together as a set. The only genuine exception to this is the medley on *Abbey Road*, though even that was only an abstract concept until a test edit, relatively late in the sessions, convinced them it would actually work. Prior to that point, throughout the entirety of the Beatles' career, it would not have occurred to anyone, except perhaps George Martin, to think about the running order of an album until all of the tracks were ready.

Thinking in terms of individual tracks — rather than *collections* of tracks — was just standard operating procedure throughout the industry — and still is, to a degree. Even the complicated recording contract the Beatles signed with EMI in January 1967, which would affect all group and solo releases directly or indirectly through 1976, only obligated them to complete 70 "sides" (tracks) within those nine years. It contained no specific requirement for albums, beyond ensuring EMI's right to release any that they did make.[3]

This is an important point because, over the course of the Beatles' career the recording industry changed dramatically. Tracks went from being the product itself, to merely the *building blocks* of the product. Indeed, led by the Beatles, the pop music recording industry shifted from an economy based mainly on individual tracks sold as singles, to one based on collections of tracks sold as albums. And while that certainly opened up artistic opportunities (which will be discussed anon), the real energy behind the change was that albums had significantly higher profit potential.

While the Beatles certainly transformed the scope and scale of what an individual *track* could be, their greater impact may have been expanding the scope and scale of what an *album* of popular music could be. Yet even in doing so their working methods hardly changed. Though they eventually started projects with the goal of creating some sort of larger and more sustained artistic statement than they had ever created before (well, *some* of them, *some* of the time), they still did the work by recording and polishing individual tracks, only later knitting them together.

It is this foundation upon which we can assemble our rescued, or *fused*, albums, using solo tracks exactly the way they had used group tracks: as building blocks. In short, regardless of how or by whom tracks were recorded, they could be assembled into albums as soon as there were enough available and the schedule dictated. The same could have continued happening in the 70s, if they had only hit on the idea — and overcome some pesky obstacles.

One primary reason this might have worked is that the recording processes used before and after the breakup are remarkably similar. They are also entirely compati-

---

[3] *Northern Songs,* chap. 2

ble with collaboration from a distance. How those processes worked, though pretty well known, is worth briefly recounting here.

From beginning to end, the Beatles' recording process, like that of many other recording artists, started with a song, generally written prior to the session, for which an arrangement was created in the studio. The songwriter taught the song to the group, simultaneously filling in whatever lyrical or musical holes may have still existed, and generating ideas for what instruments and voices might be used in the recording. The order of these steps is not particularly significant, though the general progression followed this description. Eventually, the Beatles did all of these steps with the tape running, creating extensive and fascinating documentation of their creative process.

The foundation for each new recording was the *backing track*, a complete run-through of the song, generally containing only the basic instruments, either without vocals or only a scratch vocal to be replaced later. Additional voices and instruments were then added as *overdubs*, sometimes called *superimpositions*. This process involves listening to the backing track while playing or singing along, and recording the result. When all the desired instruments and vocals had been added, the process of *mixing* created the preferred balance between all of the disparate sounds which had been recorded, while copying the finished product onto a *master tape*.

At almost any point, *editing* could be used to remove or duplicate portions of the track, or replace parts of one performance with another. This could shorten or lengthen a track, or be used for other creative purposes, such when the two different versions of "Strawberry Fields Forever" were famously joined together.

To reiterate, however: No matter how complicated or time-consuming the process, the finished product was *one track*.

Track Workflow

Song ➤ Arrangement ➤ Backing Track ➤ Overdubs ➤ Mixing/Editing ➤ Master

When a track was considered complete, or just complete *enough*, it would be added to a *reel* (sometimes literally, but more often only figuratively) from which releases would be extracted. Releases could be singles, EPs, albums, or something else, but they were always created from the building block of tracks.

Once a track was selected for release, it might undergo a final mix or edit, and then be placed in sequence with other tracks as the finished product. The completed master tape for a project was therefore built from the final versions of each track, generally separated by a length of blank "leader" tape, which indicated where the "rills" (wide spaces, or "bands") should go on the vinyl.

The last step before manufacturing, known as *mastering*, created the physical die from which albums would eventually be stamped. This very delicate process focused, in part, on preventing the needle from skipping while playing the record, and had real implications for how a record would sound on a turntable.

RELEASE WORKFLOW

Track Reel ➤ Final Mixing/Editing ➤ Sequencing ➤ Mastering ➤ Manufacturing

For most of the Beatles' career, the entire process — every step — was overseen and shaped by George Martin. He approved the selection of songs, and the arrangements which were created. He oversaw the recording of the backing track and all overdubs. He sometimes added or removed instruments when the Beatles were not present. He did the mixing personally, and held the reel of finished tracks. Then he selected from the available tracks and assembled the releases before turning them over to a specialist for mastering.

While every step is, in its own way, critical, the one we are most interested in here is the selection of tracks for releases, and the creation of running orders. (In the case of a single, the "running order" is merely the designation of which of two tracks is the A-side, and which is the B-side.)

Martin used very simple and highly subjective criteria for all of these decisions. If it sounded to him (later, to him *and the Beatles*) like it could be a hit, then it went on a single. Of the two songs selected for each single, the one he thought was the strongest would be designated the A-side. Singles were always the first tracks removed from the reel of available tracks. Everything else went onto the albums.

In other words, and somewhat surprisingly, Martin crafted the Beatles albums out of what he thought were the *less commercial tracks*. This is not to say that album tracks were somehow not commercial enough, but rather that, when it came time to assemble an album, what he considered the "cream" had already been skimmed off the top and released, and only the "leftovers" were available.

He would be the first to interject that Beatle leftovers were often better and more interesting than most other bands' cream, but he was also very frank in his assessments of their work, realizing that their tracks came in *tiers of quality*. The top tier always went out as singles. The rest were given very different roles. That discernment and honesty worked to the band's great advantage.

There is a simple reason for this: Conventional wisdom told Martin that singles would succeed or fail based on how they sounded on the radio, where the context in which a song would be heard was entirely out of his control. Album tracks, on the other hand, would be primarily heard next to one another — a very different standard which gave him levers to control how the music was perceived.

The slotting of tracks as singles was therefore part of a desired chain reaction, one that had direct consequences for the albums. It is why many classic Beatles tracks cannot be found on their classic albums. For instance, you will not find "She Loves You" or "I Want to Hold Your Hand" on any Beatles album in Great Britain until the record company began creating compilations. Somewhat shockingly, their classic *albums* did not require their classic *hits* to become classics! Some of their greatest music, which might have made great additions to their albums, had been skimmed off for a different purpose *by design*.

REEL MANAGEMENT

Extracted Tracks	Recorded with, but not used on...
"I Want to Hold Your Hand" / "This Boy"	*With the Beatles*
B-side: "You Can't Do That"	*A Hard Day's Night*
"I Feel Fine" / "She's a Woman"	*Beatles for Sale*
B-sides: "Yes It Is" and "I'm Down"	*Help!*
"Day Tripper" & "We Can Work It Out"	*Rubber Soul*
"Paperback Writer" / "Rain"	*Revolver*
"Penny Lane" & "Strawberry Fields Forever"	*Sgt. Pepper*
"Hello Goodbye"	*Magical Mystery Tour* (EP)
"Hey Jude" / "Revolution"	*The White Album*
B-side: "Don't Let Me Down"	*Let It Be*
"Ballad of John and Yoko" / "Old Brown Shoe"	*Abbey Road*

These decisions collectively represent a primary difference between the UK releases, overseen by Martin, and the US releases, overseen by Dave Dexter.

In addition to the creative reasons, Martin and the Beatles felt that putting singles on albums represented lower value to their paying audience. Capitol did not share that sentiment. In America, record buyers seemed to have no qualms about paying twice for the same music. So Dexter's famous approach was even simpler, and much more mercenary. He simply set out to create the most albums possible from the tracks the Beatles recorded. In addition to using less tracks per album,

Dexter slotted every track he could find onto one album or another, all but ignoring Martin's careful decisions across the Atlantic.[4]

Importantly, it was Martin's savvy selections that made it possible for the Beatles to crack the public consciousness in the first place. Dexter, not particularly a fan of the Beatles from the very beginning, reportedly did not see the potential in any of the early material, but acquiesced in releasing the singles Martin had sent over only after being forced to do so. Had those records, which essentially sparked Beatlemania in America, "I Want to Hold Your Hand" and "She Loves You," not been released as singles, and relegated instead to album tracks, we might not be talking about the group today.

In hindsight, you might argue that these tracks were strong enough to break through no matter how they were released, or that any number of other tracks could have done the same job as singles. And while that is potentially true, it is far from assured, and certainly couldn't have been known when the decisions were made. Every choice was a gamble. The margin of error was greater with the Beatles than most other groups, but no one knew that at the time. A wrong choice — or even a less-than-optimal choice — could have stopped the group's momentum cold. Would "I Saw Her Standing There" or "It Won't Be Long" have caught the public's fancy in the same way? Perhaps, but hindsight tells us that critical choices were made, and they all worked perfectly. This is astonishing.

So the better observation to make is that, without exception, Martin — and, eventually, the Beatles themselves — correctly saw which tracks would stand head and shoulders above the other music on the radio, and which were better heard in context with other Beatles recordings. This fact was key to their early success, though they continued to release stand-alone singles as long as they were a group.

The detailed role played by singles in the popularity of the Beatles is really beyond the scope of our current project. We merely need to note that George Martin made conscious decisions about which tracks went where, and played the market essentially perfectly.

We are interested instead in how those assignments continuously impacted the band's entire album catalog. Conventional wisdom is that the Beatles were a singles band before *Rubber Soul*, and an album band after that. A secondary reading says that with *Rubber Soul* they began a transition to an album band which culminated with *Sgt. Pepper*. But neither of these is strictly accurate. As seen on the chart above, the Beatles were both a singles band and an album band from beginning to end, and at every step assigned tracks to one stream or the other. Our interest lies in how those assignments rippled into making albums.

In one stark example, Martin has written about how *Sgt. Pepper* might have been different if he hadn't removed "Strawberry Fields Forever" and "Penny Lane"

---

[4] Dexter committed other musical atrocities to the Beatles' catalog, not discussed here.

for use as a single. In his speculation, it might have resulted in three other "lesser" tracks being left in the vaults: "Within You Without You," "Lovely Rita," and "When I'm Sixty-Four."[5] Consider that for a moment.

This vivid case represents the leading edge of how we will understand the process Martin used. To him, tracks were clearly like pieces, and albums like puzzles. We will see that he worked with great care and consideration, and a fair amount of cold calculation. Importantly, his decisions were all *artistic* decisions, even when they had important commercial implications.

In America, of course, Martin's great care was largely ignored. Dexter created albums by reshuffling tracks without regard for structure or form. As a result, they are "albums" in format only, and not the artistic sense. Though they obviously sold quite well, even without Martin's innate artistic sense behind them, they are of no use to the current project. Indeed, the early US albums aged badly and have been replaced by Martin's originals in the official canon.

This represents something of a bitter lesson in art: The market often doesn't care in the moment, and a product must succeed in the market to have any chance to age well. Though the George Martin sequences were superior in every way to those released in America, it didn't matter. The source tracks were so good that they just didn't need the extra edge. Eventually, the Beatles gained sufficient leverage to require Capitol to honor their album sequences, one of the key changes which allowed them to progress in their exploration of the form.

In those explorations, however, they wound up giving their music much more than just an extra edge. They were, in fact, defining their music intentionally and with great care. They were using techniques which cast everything in its best light. By exploring how they — mostly George Martin — did it, we can prepare ourselves to bring these same advantages to the deconstructed solo catalogs.

---

[5] *Summer of Love*, pg. 150

5
Blueprints

The product has to be impeccable, technically and artistically. What is more, it must have soul. It must lift the emotions of the listener. It must come from the heart.

— George Martin[1]

When George Martin first proposed that the Beatles make an album of original material after only one really good recording session, he was taking a different type of risk, but with good reason.

After the success of "Please Please Me" I realised that we had to act very fast to get a long-playing album on the market if we were to cash in on what we had already achieved. Because, while a single which sells half a million doesn't reap all that great a reward, half a million albums is big business.[2]

Documentation shows that Martin's decision to make a full album with the Beatles actually came *before* the release of the single, a detail convenient to leave out because his strategy ran directly counter to what EMI typically did with new pop artists. Albums were seen as a product for a much different, older market. When Martin proposed it, there was initial skepticism within EMI that a group like the Beatles could sustain an album of 14 tracks musically, let alone make the more expensive product profitable among their young audience.[3]

Martin intuited otherwise, in large measure because of their personal charisma, and what he had seen on a visit to Liverpool shortly after their initial audition.[4] His first instinct was to record a live album in the Cavern Club to capture the electric atmosphere which surrounded the Beatles there. When this proved logistically impossible, he turned back to studio recording, and pursued it with the same vigor he had always given to all Parlophone artists.

From the beginning, his approach to crafting their albums was equal parts commercial and artistic. He knew from experience that, even with great tracks skimmed

---

[1] *Making Music*, pg. 277
[2] *All You Need is Ears*, pg 130
[3] *Maximum Volume*, pg 109
[4] *All You Need is Ears*, pg 124

off the top and issued as singles, the remainder could be carefully assembled into packages that would yield maximum impact. Additionally, he believed that for an album to compete in the marketplace, a coherent whole had more of a chance than something slapped together.

Martin had honed these instincts for a decade on comedy and novelty records, but his naturally methodical nature would not have allowed a casual approach anyway. His years of musical training, industry experience, and appreciation of classical forms gave him all the tools he needed to do it right. But it is important to note that, without this strategy, the Beatles might always and only have been a "singles" band. Instead, they were set on the path which included albums from the very beginning.

Though Martin is quoted in various places saying that it wasn't until later that track sequencing was treated as part of the art form, the albums themselves argue otherwise. He and EMI hedged their bet on that debut album by including the earlier singles (something they would never do again), but the tracks were utilized carefully in context with the other music. Where a traditional sequence would have put the singles and B-sides up front as the first four tracks on the album, Martin diverged, using them to fill what he perceived as important slots in the overall running order.

Even on that first long-player the tracks were ordered so that the collection would engage listeners at the beginning, keep their attention through the flip of the disc, and send them out with a bang at the end. In many ways he was already employing the same principles and forms used by classical composers, which have much in common with the comedic forms that Martin had helped exemplify with artists like Peter Sellers and Spike Milligan. He also realized quite quickly that, if the Beatles were to remain a *band*, he could not favor one over the others, and would have to play diplomat with the young, competitive, ego-driven artists.

Consider the running order of that famous debut album:

Side A	Side B
1. "I Saw Her Standing There"	1. "Love Me Do"
2. "Misery"	2. "P.S. I Love You"
3. "Anna (Go to Him)"	3. "Baby It's You"
4. "Chains"	4. "Do You Want to Know a Secret"
5. "Boys"	5. "A Taste of Honey"
6. "Ask Me Why"	6. "There's a Place"
7. "Please Please Me"	7. "Twist and Shout"

The layout seems very straightforward, as if just a simple collection of contemporary music by a new band. To a potential buyer looking at the sleeve in a record store, roughly half of the song titles would have been familiar — a definite plus for the record company. The other songs might have seemed intriguing if you paid attention to the various names of band members and songwriters, or read Tony Barrow's breathless liner notes — which was much the same marketing hype as was

5 / Blueprints

found on many albums of the era. Some of those unfamiliar songs actually would have been unfamiliar to even the band's loyal fan base in Liverpool because they were so new.

The album is often described as being made up of the Beatles' stage act, and that is without question the provenance of the covers and several of the originals. These are, after all, echoes of their *Fraternal Show-Makers* phase (see chapter 3). But that characterization significantly understates the sophistication of this release. There is much more going on here than first meets the ear.

To understand just what that much more is, start by considering the following two setlists. The first is from shortly before the famous *Please Please Me* recording session of February 11, 1963, and second is from the following day. Songs which made the album are highlighted.

17-Jan-1963 - Majestic Ballroom, Birkenhead	**12-Feb-1963** - Astoria Ballroom, Oldham
1. *(Unknown)**	1. **I Saw Her Standing There**
2. Shimmy Like Kate	2. Sweet Little Sixteen
3. Whole Lotta Shakin' Goin' On	3. **Chains**
4. **P.S. I Love You**	4. Beautiful Dreamer
5. *(Unknown)**	5. **Misery**
6. **Chains**	6. Hey Good Lookin'
7. **A Taste of Honey**	7. **Love Me Do**
8. **Please Please Me**	8. **Baby It's You**
9. Three Cool Cats	9. Three Cool Cats
10. *(Unknown)**	10. **Please Please Me**
11. **Anna (Go to Him)**	11. Some Other Guy
12. Hey Good Lookin'	12. **Ask Me Why**
13. Hippy Hippy Shake	13. **Roll Over Beethoven**
14. I'm Talking About You	14. **A Taste of Honey**
15. Devil in Her Heart	15. **Boys**
16. Some Other Guy	16. Keep Your Hands Off My Baby
17. **Ask Me Why**	17. **Do You Want to Know a Secret**
18. Roll Over Beethoven	18. From Me to You
19. **Love Me Do**	19. Long Tall Sally (encore)
Album tracks not played: *	***Album tracks not played:***
Misery	*Anna (Go to Him)*
Boys	*P.S. I Love You*
Baby It's You	*There's a Place*
Twist and Shout	*Twist and Shout*

**The three songs listed as unknown were presumably recent originals, since covers and older originals would have been recognized by the fan who created this list. The three most likely titles to fill those spots would therefore have been, "I Saw Her Standing There," "Do You Want to Know a Secret?" and "There's a Place"—though not necessarily in that order. "Hold Me Tight" might also have been in that mix, though it was much older. We can, however, be sure that "Misery" was not among them, since it had not yet been written.*[5]

---

[5] *Many Years from Now*, p. 94

The two setlists are wildly divergent from one another, but *both* are also widely divergent from the album. To say that the album is derived from the stage show suggests, first, a stable and proven setlist which made up most shows at the time and could be tweaked into an album based on success on the stage. A review of other setlists from the same era shows that the Beatles did not have such a thing. They were still playing anything and everything, as the spirit moved them. Further, Martin's characterization suggests that he simply asked the group for a recent set list, pulled out part of it, tweaked it a little bit, and then plunked it down on vinyl, which would have been a quite reasonable approach to take.

But these setlists show definitively that this is not what happened. From descriptions of the session,[6] the Beatles came in with a few songs that they definitely wanted to record, namely their most recent batch of originals, some of which had only just been tried out in concert. These were then augmented by selections from their vast warehouse of covers. The selection of which covers to record is presented as something of an afterthought. The group spent much more time on the originals, and knocked off all the covers in a couple of hours.

In terms of selecting material, Martin was faced with a complicated problem. An album of all covers might have the greatest potential with an audience not already familiar with the group, but he already knew that it wouldn't have satisfied the Beatles, or the new song publishers which he had just helped them acquire. Given that their track record with new material was pretty good (if short) at that point, he was tasked with striking the right balance.

He had to trust his own instincts about whether the new songs were high enough quality, but also about which covers would best show off what the band could do, without stepping on their creativity. He needed a batch of songs that both represented the band well and worked *together*. The exclusion of "Hold Me Tight," and the discussion about "Twist and Shout," both reported in many sources, exemplify this process. Not a part of either setlist, the recording of "Hold Me Tight" ultimately did not satisfy the quality requirements, while "Twist and Shout" struck both the band and Martin as a good choice, despite not being in their current stage show.

Since the Beatles created their own setlists, and George Martin created the album running order, we get an immediate look at how Martin's sensibilities differed from the group's, and how he shaped them in the process of converting their stage show to a salable commodity. We get a glimpse of how his discipline was imposed upon them without stifling them, an incredible accomplishment.

Sequencing an album has at least some things in common with sequencing a show. Start big and end big are two important principles. If there is padding, put it in the middle where no one will notice or remember. Pace yourself, and make sure

---

[6] *The Beatles Recording Sessions*, p. 24 (in addition to many others)

5 / Blueprints

there is variety along the way. Make the best music stand out, and be careful where you place the hits (or, in this era, the *would-be* hits).

Paul's new song, "I Saw Her Standing There," opened both shows and the album, confirming that everyone agreed about its strength. It was even allowed to replace the expected opener, "Please Please Me," which had already been released as a single and would become the album's title track, defying conventional wisdom. Similarly, once "Twist and Shout" had been recorded, it was clear to Martin that that should be the big finish, though the Beatles themselves were not even performing it live at the time (that would change, of course).

The Beatles weren't quite sure what to do with their earlier single, "Love Me Do." In one set it's used to close the show, despite being a pretty lousy closer. Perhaps that is why it was used in the middle of the following show, with another, much more energetic rocker, "Long Tall Sally," closing things out. Martin placed it exactly in the middle of the album, albeit in a place of honor as the side two opener. Again, this was not the typical placement for a hit at that time.

Both shows put "Please Please Me" with "Three Cool Cats." Perhaps this is only incidental, but we do know that they were confident enough in the latter song to have used it in their Decca audition. Whether they proposed it for their debut album is not known, but it's hard to imagine Martin thinking that would be a good display of their abilities. Perhaps he remembered it from the failed demo.

Beyond these simple observations, the only other conclusion to be drawn is that neither setlist exhibits much in the way of discipline or polish. As we know, the group was riding on enthusiastic crowd reaction, which meant they could probably do no wrong. This contrasts vividly, however, with Martin's ultimate track sequence, which is a model of discipline in every way.

To fully understand what is happening on the album, we need to do a little x-ray exploration. Rather than consider it by song title, we will look at other important aspects of each song which will help understand why it may have been placed where it was. For example, consider the following x-ray of *Please Please Me* by song source:

Side A	Side B
1. Original	1. Original (single A-side)
2. Original	2. Original (single B-side)
3. Cover	3. Cover
4. Cover	4. Original ("internal" cover)
5. Cover	5. Cover
6. Original (single B-side)	6. Original
7. Original (single A-side)	7. Cover

We can clearly see that Martin has placed original songs in places of great importance, including the beginning of each side, and the end of side one. We can even suppose that he might have intended the same structure on side two, but wisely swapped some tracks around after realizing the power of "Twist and Shout" to close the album.

We can see that he has used the two previously released singles to bracket the flip of the album, inverting the A and B sides in the first instance so that the better song — the album's title track — could be the last sound on side one. This has the additional benefit of guaranteeing that each side is a complete statement unto itself in the event that the listener only listens to one at a time.

Also clear is that Martin clustered the cover songs in the middle of each side, which we will see later he considered the least important positions. This includes the instance of one Beatle "covering" a song written by the others, featuring the vocalist that Martin considered the weakest of the four at that point. In using this arrangement — originals highly visible, covers used for padding — he has successfully telescoped that this is a band skilled with, and proud of, their original material, and not one which will rely on covers.

It's worth mentioning at this point that covers were a much more frequent inclusion on albums of the 50s and 60s, given that the audiences actually wanted to hear songs that they already knew sung by singers that they liked. This derives, in part, from the great success of the *Hit Parade*, which treated the song as the commodity, not the singer or the recording. The Beatles would change that.

Interestingly, the two sides of the album are almost mirror images of each other, harnessing the beauty of symmetry for entirely instinctive reactions. It's difficult to argue that Martin did this deliberately since he never made any mention of it, nor has anyone else. But whether his symmetrical layout was intentional or not is irrelevant. It placed the music of the Beatles in a very favorable structure which worked on a subconscious level.

Continuing with our x-ray approach, look now at the distribution of vocalists.

Side A	Side B
1. Paul	1. Paul/John
2. John/Paul	2. Paul
3. John	3. John
4. George (+John/Paul)	4. George
5. Ringo	5. Paul
6. John	6. John/Paul
7. John/Paul	7. John

Again we see a striking level of balance, with the sides being as close to full symmetry as possible. No one Beatle is featured over the others, though George is relegated to the middle of each side where his performances will be least noticed, further evidence of a bias which began early, and would persist, to varying degrees, throughout their recording career.

Paul leads off the album, and John closes it. Duet vocals bracket the intermission, though each is paired with tracks which maintain perfect balance. These provide evidence of something Martin says he decided very early, namely that this band would have multiple vocalists, and not be reduced to anyone serving as a "front man." It is with great diplomacy that he has alternated vocalists, making sure that there is never a case of two tracks with the same vocalist back-to-back.

Another measure we might x-ray is the intensity of each song. This is a little harder to quantify. Pure tempo plays a role, but is not necessarily definitive (beats per minute shown in parentheses).

Side A	Side B
1. High (160)	1. Medium (148)
2. Medium (134)	2. Low (134)
3. Low (110)	3. Low (112)
4. Medium (130)	
	4. Medium (124)
5. High (142)	5. Low (102)
6. Low (134)	6. Medium (140)
7. Medium (140)	7. High (124)

Again, symmetry plays a subtle role. The album begins and ends with high intensity ("Twist and Shout" clearly qualifying despite a slower tempo), while the inner capstones are medium. Adjacent to each of those is a complex of three tracks sequenced medium-low-medium, demonstrating Martin's ideas on how to build down from the opener, and up to the closer.

Throughout the assembly, there is a great diversity of intensity. Only once are two tracks with the same intensity next to one another, and this small low intensity cluster is placed in what we will soon discover Martin considers to be the most flexible part of the running order.

Finally, we look at the style of each track, which is something of an extension of intensity, but also impacts perceptions in a slightly different way.

Side A	Side B
1. Rock	1. Pop
2. Pop	2. Ballad
3. Ballad	3. Ballad
4. Pop	
	4. Pop
5. Rock	5. Ballad
6. Ballad	6. Proto-Art
7. Pop	7. Rock

The groupings look somewhat similar to the intensity chart, and we can now see more clearly how this works. Ballads are meticulously placed so that they do not ever bring the album to a halt. The only two ballads found together, "P.S. I Love You" and

"Baby It's You," are actually sufficiently different to sit comfortably adjacent without creating a black hole.

Perhaps it is somewhat shocking to see that there are only three tracks on this debut album that can be clearly classified as "rock." We tend to picture the Beatles in this era as sweating up a storm at lunch time in the Cavern Club, playing nothing but rock-n-roll. Clearly, however, when it came time to put together this album, Martin allowed them to show the side they wanted, and it was a much softer side than we tend to remember from those grainy old movies. It demonstrates that the Beatles were actually masters of pure "pop" music right from the very beginning.

This idea is brought home by one curious track on the album which might have been classified as "pop" but is better to consider in the context of what we know is to come. "There's a Place" contains lyrical content like nothing else on the album, and is by far the most reflective — almost somber, despite a up-tempo beat. Not exactly a ballad, and not exactly pop, I've termed it "proto-art" because it seems to be a template for things that we know Lennon will produce eventually. The problem here, however, is how to contextualize it with all the rest of this simpler, lighter material.

George Martin was nothing if not sensitive to the contents of the lyrics and overall tone of the material, and certainly would have noticed this unicorn, and recognized its need for special treatment. Though there is no documentation of why he placed it where he did, a couple of possibilities seem self-evident.

The first thing to admit is that anywhere it goes could pose a problem. Being so different, it might very well disrupt the flow, and potentially the happy vibe of the album. This is not to call it a "sad" song exactly, but just to admit that it falls in a different class. Thus, the first option open to Martin would have been to "bury" it in the farthest reaches of side two, allowing that the album closer would wipe away any lingering melancholy. The second would be that he merely stuck it in the only spot where no other track could really go. Indeed, anything used to set up "Twist and Shout" would have found itself forgotten very quickly.

But as we will see, Martin had many tricks up his sleeve. He had an instinctive knack for identifying tracks that were important in some way, and always found a spot of honor for them where they would get their due. Rather than wanting to bury this track in a place where it might be less heard, he is far more likely to recognize that the penultimate slot on any album is a place with a unique role. Whatever goes there must work *with* the closer to send the album out in a memorable way.

In this case, obviously "Twist and Shout" was memorable all on its own. But had it been immediately preceded by another high intensity rocker, say "Boys," it would have been diminished, if ever so slightly, by being so close to something similar. Had it been preceded by a pure ballad, say "A Taste of Honey," it would have seemed crass and potentially over-the-top. Martin, a master of contrast, would have recognized these things, and also seen that "There's a Place" was the perfect contrasting idea, with the perfectly complementary music. It creates, and leaves behind, a space in which "Twist and Shout" seems even more exciting, without being too much.

Moreover, it seems possible that George Martin would have seen, in "There's a Place," potential directions the songwriters might go. He already knew that there was something fundamentally different about the Beatles, and would have found "There's a Place" to be a clear cut example of that within their music. There was certainly nothing like it elsewhere in the market. It was too early to be certain, but he could have been hopeful. There would have been no better position on the album to highlight that potential than in the penultimate track, where an idea can subtly linger even if what follows it is completely different.

There are certainly other avenues in which we could explore *Please Please Me*. If you diagram the key signatures, there are clear cases of intentional placement of songs in the same or relative key. There are multiple examples of when the final chord of one song, despite not being the root of the key, perfectly sets up the first chord of what follows. In some ways it's a bit presumptuous to claim that Martin mapped all of these things out intentionally, but not at all presumptuous to think that his instinctive sense of what just felt right may have done that for him. Whether he was intentional about it or not, there it is.

There are similar patterns, connections and rhythms in the sequencing for the next five Beatles albums. For the most part, however, everything up to and including *Rubber Soul* uses the techniques we've considered here, and does not innovate much beyond them. Those assemblies are all masterworks unto themselves, just like the individual tracks. Though Martin claimed that *Rubber Soul* began a new era of album assembly, we don't really see it in evidence until the next album. From *Revolver* on, George Martin and the Beatles began a run of aggregation unlikely to ever be duplicated.

Thankfully, we have a great deal of documentation to support what we can see and hear. So our next step is to delve into these considerably more complex projects and learn the advanced techniques that Martin wants to teach us.

6
Structure

> *The revolutionary new Columbia Long Playing (LP) Microgroove Record plays up to 45 minutes of music on one 12-inch record, or approximately six times as much music as conventional shellac records. After more than a decade of preparation, the world's greatest symphonies, concertos, tone poems and chamber music are now held in their entirety on one album-length record. Available, too, are sparkling collections of lighter music and popular songs, by leading artists.*
>
> — Columbia Record Catalog 1949[1]

Despite all of the detail packed into Mark Lewisohn's indispensable book, *The Beatles Recording Sessions*, there is hardly a word about how tracks were assembled and sequenced into albums. There are a few passing mentions of principles, such as this one from the final *Rubber Soul* mixing session:

> *Three more songs were needed... Balance was everything in 1965; a 13-song album was just not done.[2] Fourteen meant seven songs per side and everything hunky-dory.[3]*

Occasionally, he mentions that it was Martin who made many of the creative decisions until the Beatles became competent, engaged, and available to contribute. Again, for *Rubber Soul*:

> *On 16 November George Martin worked out the LP running order and telephoned it over to Abbey Road. ... "It was the first album to present a new, growing Beatles to the world. For the first time we began to think of albums as art on their own, as complete entities."[4]*

---

[1] Pg. 1; https://archive.org/details/columbiarecordca00unse_0
[2] Actually, the Beatles had already done it once with the 13-song *A Hard Day's Night* soundtrack, and would do it again with the 13-song *Sgt. Pepper*.
[3] *Recording Sessions*, pg. 68
[4] Ibid., pg 68, 69

Even when Lewisohn describes the mammoth 24-hour session which assembled *The White Album*, the subject receives only a relatively few words:

> *Even working in the tried and trusted George Martin formula of opening each side of vinyl with a strong song, and ending it with one difficult to follow, the 31 songs were just too varied and wide-ranging in styles to slip easily into categories. In the end...there was an* approximated *structure, the heavier rock songs...mostly ended up on side C, George Harrison's four songs were spread out one per side, no composer had more than two songs in succession and each side lasted between 20 and 25 minutes. And, as a joke, most of the songs with an animal in the title...were placed together, in succession, on side B.*
>
> *Another decision was to link each successive song, either with a crossfade, a straight edit or simply by matching the dying moment of one with the opening note of the next.* The Beatles, *like* Sgt. Pepper's Lonely Hearts Club Band, *had none of the customary three-second gaps between songs.*[5]

Here we have a clear elucidation of some of the principles we observed at work in the earlier albums. They are worth extracting:

- Each side must open with a "strong" song.
- Each side must end with a song that is "difficult to follow."
- Grouping songs by style or theme or content is appropriate.
- Harrison's (and presumably Starr's) work should be distributed evenly.
- No composer gets more than two songs in a row.
- How songs relate to one another, or not, is artistic territory.
- Balance between sides is important.
- Each side lasts 20 to 25 minutes.

There's actually quite a lot there, but it feels like only a start. For something more elaborate, we can look to Martin's own comments elsewhere. He described some of his basic principles in an article from 1983 (emphasis added).

> *Once all the recording is finally complete there is an important task still remaining: all tracks need to be put into a running order (sequencing). This has a significant effect on the way a listener hears a record, particularly for the first time. Imagine starting the*

---

[5] Ibid., pg. 162

6 / STRUCTURE

> Sgt. Pepper *album with "A Day In The Life;" there would be nothing left after the first track. We must **attract attention in the beginning, sustain interest in the middle, end the first side with a feeling of satisfaction yet leave the listener wanting more**. The second side is similar, although the need for a good opening is not as great as on side one, and **the finale should ideally clinch the whole album with its last notes**.*
>
> *One always tries to have a good number of single tracks in an album and if I had five tracks out of ten that I thought were hits I would probably place them at one, two, five, six and ten to get maximum effect. But, leaving commercial considerations aside, **the flow of the album is by far the most important factor**.*
>
> ***Distances between tracks, too, have to be considered.** Some pieces require a little silence before the following track starts. (Although in Jeff Beck's album* Blow by Blow *I deliberately chose to overlap the tracks with each other, running the album almost like a disc jockey to maintain the pace.)*
>
> *There is a final small consideration. **I try hard to make each side last the same amount of time** — as far as is possible. For one thing, keeping playing time down to **20 minutes per side** gives me a chance to make the record sound louder without distortion. Also, when that album is issued on cassette, an even running time avoids an embarrassing wait at the end of the tape for the "turn over" side to finish running — another commercial consideration.*[6]

Though this is still a rather brief and somewhat generic summary, we get some useful elaboration about techniques he did use with the Beatles.

1. The album opener must "attract attention."
2. The end of side one must provide "satisfaction," yet be less than ultimate.
3. The side two opener plays a role like the album opener, but less restricted.
4. The album closer is the "finale," and must "clinch the whole album."
5. Tracks in the middle of sides need only "sustain interest."
6. Commercial considerations do play a role in sequencing.
7. "Flow" is more important than commercial considerations.
8. Silence between tracks, or lack thereof, is a creative consideration.
9. Album sides should be of roughly equal length.
10. 20 minutes is about the right length for a side.

---

[6] *Making Music*, p. 277

Though referencing the Beatles, he is writing more generally, and roughly ten years after the breakup. For example, his mention of placing singles on albums is a clear break with what he did in the 60s, but accurately reflects how the industry changed in the 70s. Still, this short list of principles is actually quite powerful.

We will consider these concepts as we move forward, but begin with the final one, which was also present in Lewisohn's shorter summary above: *side length*. This consideration derives from the physical medium that would carry the art Martin and the Beatles created — the LP, or long-playing record. As a foundational element, the LP silently dictated important perimeters for the art, in the same way the size and shape of a canvas dictates important aspects of a painting. Martin was exceedingly sensitive to these, despite the fact that they were beyond his or anyone's control.

For example, if the Beatles had been working in the era of 78s, CDs or streaming, they would have been met by a very different set of opportunities and constraints, such as more interruptions, or less, better fidelity, or worse, and different considera-ions on frequency response, mastering, program length, artwork and more. Thus, it matters that they were working in the heart of the LP era. In very real ways the Beatles and George Martin taught the world just what that format could do. And what they accomplished within its constraints has arguably never been exceeded.

To understand how significantly their work was impacted by the format, and how George Martin turned its limitations into advantages, we must quickly review its history, and reckon with how a medium invented to meet commercial needs became a massively influential canvas for the art of popular music. We'll also take this opportunity to define some terms which will be important to our later work.

An Extremely Brief and Incomplete History of the Record Album

The metaphor of "an album of music" has been around since the early days of recorded sound. You may think that the word "album" refers to a 12-inch piece of black vinyl inside a nifty cardboard sleeve, or a shiny, rigid disc in a plastic case with a booklet, or maybe just a folder on your phone. But the idea actually refers to the *collection of music*, rather than to the *medium* on which it is stored and delivered — an important distinction. The "album" is the music, not the format or medium, in the same way that a symphony is the music the orchestra plays, and not the orches-tra itself or the concert hall in which the performance takes place.

In the late 19th century, Thomas Edison's original cylinder format gave way to new formats on flat discs, pioneered by Emile Berliner. These initially came in a range of diameters and playing speeds. By about 1910, the industry had standardized on 10-inch discs, made from brittle shellac, spinning at approximately 78 revolutions per minute (rpm). Where a cylinder had offered only a single, two-minute program, each flat disc had two sides, and could hold about three minutes per side.

6 / STRUCTURE

Despite being a significant advance, two problems were still evident. First, the playing time remained quite limited. Longer pieces of music, such as symphonies, were cumbersome or impossible to record and sell. Second, the manufacturing material meant that discs were easily breakable, a problem exacerbated by the fact that they typically came in a paper sleeve which offered little protection.

Early solutions for the latter led to accommodations for the former. The first "record album" looked much like a photo album, and contained only empty sleeves in which a collection of fragile records could be protected and stored safely on a shelf. Almost simultaneously, record companies realized they could split longer pieces of music onto multiple discs — albeit with frequent interruptions — and bundle them together in that same type of book. Thus was born the metaphor we still use today of an "album" of music.

The first "prepackaged" albums, complete with handsome protective container and multiple discs, were recordings of operas and classical music — that is, long pieces of music split into chunks and spread across multiple sides of multiple discs, and bundled together for sale. In time, collections of popular songs also began to appear in the same form, a perfect match since each side could hold one or two short popular songs. By the 1940s, a typical album consisted of four 10-inch 78 rpm discs bundled together. With roughly five minutes per side, this effectively established the standard album *running time* at about 40 minutes total.

For much of the 30s and 40s, advances in disc technology had happened, but only for the benefit of radio stations. Consumers still had their music interrupted at least every five minutes. Then in 1948, Columbia Records introduced the long-playing record, or *LP*, as the first practical answer to that problem. These 12-inch discs spun at the slower rate of 33⅓ rpm, and featured smaller grooves, increasing the length of each side to roughly 22 minutes, or about 45 minutes per disc. That length was carefully selected through a survey of major musical compositions. Columbia engineers discovered that 96% of all important symphonic works had a performance time of 45 minutes or less.[7]

Unbeknownst to those engineers, they had created a new canvas upon which art might be created, and fixed its size and shape. Running times would be capped at about 45 minutes, just like major classical works, and the music would be interrupted exactly once, at about the halfway point. Each of these features is important to understand, because they are essentially perfect for pop music.

Consider first the mandatory interruption. In the CD and MP3 world, and certainly in the streaming era, it is hard to imagine that there might be anything positive about an interruption in the music. But an enforced interruption at the halfway point of an album does two important things. First, it requires each half of the

---

[7] Martin Mayer, "Fifty Thousand Sides Ago: The First Days of the LP", *High Fidelity Magazine*, January 1958

program to stay within typical human attention spans. Second, it provides a convenient and guaranteed *intermission*, an important structural component in the performing arts.

To the first point, though the average human attention span is somewhat hard to measure, and varies greatly according to content, context and presentation, 22 minutes turns out to be almost perfect for listening to popular music. There is some anecdotal science behind this observation, but also a wide variety of opinions among people who study such things. In truth, we don't really need much science to recognize that 22 minutes is enough time to introduce an idea, explore it, and bring it to some sort of resolution, even if only provisional. This is not to suggest that all pop albums use such an arc, of course, but rather that the format's inherent features make a certain type of art *possible*, while also encouraging artists to use *good practices*. A shorter maximum length would curtail the expressive possibilities, and anything longer risks losing the listener.

To the second point, an intermission creates the welcome perception that the two sides of an album are like separate acts in the same play, separate stanzas in the same poem, separate movements in the same sonata, separate chapters in the same book. Each is perceived as a self-contained unit, that also serves the whole. Though long seen by listeners as a nuisance, the enforced intermission of flipping the disc creates the opportunity for introspection, a moment to breathe, and time to digest what has been heard, while building anticipation for what comes next.

Again, not all albums aspire to, or warrant, such reactions from the listener, but the format not only makes it possible, it provides encouragement to do so. By providing just the right levels of expanse and containment, the LP format supports and encourages a narrative arc, and brings to recorded music principles which all the performing arts have known for centuries: Ideas need space, they need to be chunked, and audiences need a break. The LP has that all built right into the format at basically the perfect levels. This allowed popular music to be commercial and thrive, but also become a mature art form unto itself.

Mastery

The Beatles created their classic albums directly for the LP medium, and the creative team took advantage of the format's features at every turn. For this project, it's an important point because, since the CD format didn't become available until the 80s, any rescued albums we imagine for the 70s would also have been created for LPs. We simply must design them within the constraints of the medium or we will get something very different, indeed.

For example, recall what George Martin wrote about how he would place the best tracks in his running order. Keep in mind that he was writing in 1983, at the exact

6 / STRUCTURE

moment when the LP format was about to give way to CDs. Clearly, he had no idea what was coming and was still, even then, thinking in terms of the LP:

> ...if I had five tracks out of ten that I thought were hits I would probably place them at one, two, five, six and ten to get maximum effect.[8]

For clarity, he is suggesting that "hits" should be placed on an album like this:

Side A	Side B
1. [Hit]	6. [Hit]
2. [Hit]	7.
3.	8.
4.	9.
5. [Hit]	10. [Hit]

This aligns closely with what we saw on *Please Please Me* in the previous chapter. A more typical, less artistically sensitive assembly in that era would put all of the hits first, and work gradually down toward the lesser material. Martin's layout shows that he treats the collection as a whole, rather than a simple queue of tracks marching like soldiers, that a listener may abandon once the quality drops below a certain level.[9] Thus Martin places the best music at the beginning and end of each side, where it gains prominence over everything in between, with the goal of keeping the listener engaged from beginning to end.

We will read more from him on why this is important in the next chapter. For now, however, we can easily tell that he is talking about LPs because positions five and six have literally no significance if the album is designed for CD. Without an enforced intermission — that good old anachronistic flip of the disc — tracks five and six are just part of the body of the album, and there is no place within that body for a track to gain prominence just by virtue of placement.

In other words, what has always looked like an advantage for CDs — namely, the absence of any mandatory interruption or intermission — actually represented the removal of a feature that George Martin and the Beatles consciously used. The change in medium resulted in a change to the art form. Indeed, it brought about the end of the classic album era.

The quintessential example for this particular dynamic can actually be found right in the Beatles catalog. When George Martin programmed "Within You Without You" at the beginning of side two of *Sgt. Pepper*, he did so with the assumption that it would be preceded by the intermission. He made the choice because he saw the

---

[8] *Making Music*, p. 277
[9] Perhaps the producer most notable for using the latter approach would be Phil Spector.

advantage of having time pass after the closing notes of "Being for the Benefit of Mr Kite." The listener needed a moment to process and revel in the novel sound picture. Whether it was a minute, or two, or more, he knew it would be enough time to let one idea fully dissipate before a completely unrelated idea took its place to kick off the second act of Sgt. Pepper's "show."

This was an *artistic* decision, intended to create a specific effect. The two tracks do not particularly complement each other, and Martin was trying to solve the problem of where to program Harrison's creation, which he considered to be a difficult track because it might not fit in with everything else on the album. His solution is simple, brilliant, and harnesses the medium directly.

But when *Sgt. Pepper* was finally released on CD in 1987, the moment so carefully crafted by Martin was simply gone, destroyed by the new format, and replaced by an ironic three seconds of silence.[10] In this case, Martin himself oversaw the remasters and personally acquiesced, but what choice did he have? As a result, a conscious and intentional creative element of the work of art had disappeared, as if a boorish patron had forced Monet to crop out some space between haystacks so the painting would fit over a couch.

For the record, the same exact problem besets the end of "I Want You (She's So Heavy)" and the beginning of "Here Comes the Sun." John Lennon wanted the cold end to lead to silence — lots of it. That anything might ever follow it was not even considered. In that way, side two of *Abbey Road* was plainly intended to be inherently separate from side one, and not a continuation. On LP, that effect was possible. On CD, it is not. Similar problems can be heard in the connection between "Happiness is a Warm Gun" and "Martha My Dear," and from "Long, Long, Long" to "Revolution 1."

The medium dictated what had to be done, and that is exactly the point: Each physical format is a canvas, and silently dictates certain things which impact the art. The Beatles used the LP format because it was all they had available to them, and they made the most of its limitations because they needed to. In the way creative people always do, they turned *limitations* into *advantages*. And since that format would still have been the only option in the 70s, so must we.

So, from that short quote above, and the definitive features of the medium he worked in, we extract one of George Martin's most important foundational ideas about album sequencing. It is decidedly specific to LPs, and in some ways so intertwined with how audiences listened that it feels self-evident. But it must be called out because many listeners likely never noticed the care taken in selecting what went in those positions, and yet it is where Martin started working on each sequence. All other sequencing decisions were descended from those first choices. The basic

---

[10] In its initial release, *Sgt. Pepper* was lauded as the first mainstream pop release not to have the requisite three second gaps, also known as rills, between tracks.

principle is this: The first and last track on the album, along with the first and last track on each side, have special prominence, and therefore special requirements for the music which will be placed there. Though he did not give these positions a name, doing so makes it easier for us to reference and discuss them. Call these...

Pole Tracks

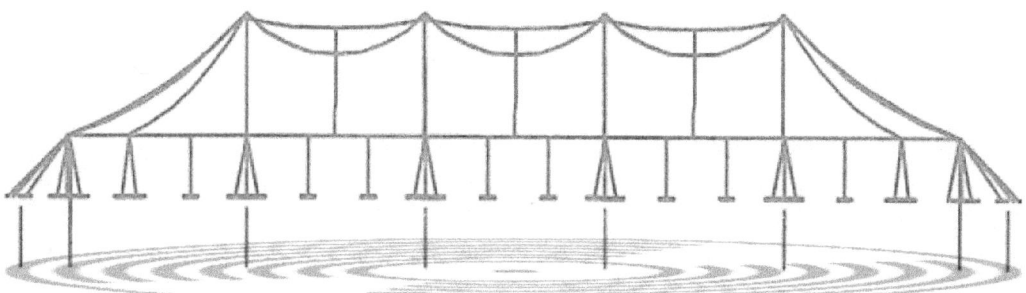

Like the poles of a circus tent, the music placed in structurally significant locations on an album provide important framing for the artistic content. They bracket and enclose all of the music. They are the most likely to be remembered by the listener. They set expectations, tone, and mood. They establish, summarize and complete the album's ideas. They define beginnings and endings.

As set out by Martin, the pole tracks are as follows:

- Hard open, or album opener, first track on side one
- Hard close, or album closer, last track on the last side
- Soft close, last track on any side
- Soft open, first track on any side

Admittedly, it's not hard to understand why these positions might be so important. All art forms that unfold with the passage of time — music, theater, film, dance, comedy, etc. — place special emphasis on the moment a performance begins and the moment it ends. These boundaries signal and facilitate engagement and fulfillment for the audience. They are the most vulnerable moments for the performers, when they ask the audience to make a decision to commit and enter into the art, and again when they hand it off for interpretation at the end. When it works, the beginning is a capture, the end a release. Great care in shaping these moments represents a commitment to the art as a whole.

The first sound a listener hears on the album creates the space in which the rest of the music can be heard. It works the same on a pop album as in a piece of classical music, or theater. The first sound rewards the anticipation built in the audience, or it doesn't. It sets a marker of what is to come, or does not. It works with the final sound to create an arc, allowing the *whole* to leave the audience fully satisfied, or not. It introduces the ideas to be considered, and launches them toward a satisfying conclusion, or it doesn't. The two ideas — beginning and end — either resonate with each other, and what has come between, or they do not. As a result, the entire work of art feels either unified and successful, or not.

This does not mean that pole tracks are necessarily variations on one another, or refer to one another, or even sound alike in any way, though these are all possibilities. It merely means that they work together, often in some instinctive but undefinable way, to communicate with the audience. Even if they are opposites, they are somehow in intentional relationship with each other — or, when that isn't necessary or possible, merely functional. The first and last acts of *The Ed Sullivan Show* did not need anything in common, but each still played a role in satisfying the audience's expectations by virtue of the order they appeared.

The same goes for the four pole tracks on a typical album in the classic LP era. Though these songs/tracks/recordings need not have anything in common, they define the boundaries of the show, and determine whether it meets the expectations held by the audience when they put it on the turntable.

Because the album has a guaranteed intermission, the last sound on side one serves the purpose of bringing the curtain down on the first act. The show is not over, so the music cannot wrap things up too neatly, but the more memorable it is, the more likely anticipation will be maintained until the beginning of the next act. Then the first track on side two works like a junior version of the opener, an entr'acte, which brings the audience back into the space of the music, reintroduces themes, and restarts the action.

The last sound is what the listeners will retain and carry with them after the album is over. In theater, the last scene typically wraps up the plot, resolves any outstanding conflicts, and sends the audience out of the theater satisfied. In classical music, the final movement might involve a recapitulation of the main musical theme, now in a variation which brings about a welcome resolution. In a rock concert, bands typically leave something really big for the very end, something they know will maintain anticipation throughout the show, then wow the crowd and send them out humming and dancing. Comedians carefully pick the first joke to get people laughing, yet generally save the best routine for last.

Even in an album which does not try to create narrative, or have any central concept, the tracks at the outer edge of each side impact how the listener perceives the entire collection. With the right first track, the second track sounds better. With the right final track, the album is remembered better. In other words, any collection of music — indeed any collection of *ideas* — is impacted by the sequence in which it unfolds. In popular music, on the LP format, the pole tracks have an outsized impact on how music is perceived and appreciated. George Martin knew this.

6 / STRUCTURE

As a concrete example, thinking in theatrical terms is a large part of what set *Sgt. Pepper* apart from other albums of its day. The album is framed as a show with two acts, and each side is carefully designed to perpetuate that idea, even though there is no narrative plot. As we will see in the next chapter, this was an illusion very carefully designed by Martin.

Other examples are not nearly so literal. No such theatrical frame envelopes the music on *The White Album*,[11] and yet a sense of motion is maintained by varying the styles, tones, and subjects. These are then bracketed by the strongest, most definitive tracks. Indeed, all of the classic Beatles albums clearly prioritize the pole track positions, placing the absolute best music there.

POLE TRACK INVENTORY

Album	Hard Open	Soft Close	Soft Open	Hard Close
Please Please Me	"I Saw Her Standing There"	**"Please Please Me"**	"Love Me Do"	"Twist and Shout"
With the Beatles	"It Won't Be Long"	"Please Mister Postman"	"Roll Over Beethoven"	"Money"
A Hard Day's Night	**"A Hard Day's Night"**	"Can't Buy Me Love"	"Any Time at All"	"I'll Be Back"
Beatles for Sale	"No Reply"	"Kansas City/Hey…!"	"Eight Days a Week"	"Everybody's…Baby"
Help!	**"Help!"**	"Ticket to Ride"	"Act Naturally"	"Dizzy Miss Lizzy"
Rubber Soul	"Drive My Car"	"Michelle"	"What Goes On"	"Run for Your Life"
Revolver	"Taxman"	"She Said She Said"	"Good Day Sunshine"	"Tomorrow Never…"
Sgt. Pepper	**"Sgt. Pepper's…"**	"…Benefit of Mr Kite!"	"Within You Without You"	"A Day in the Life"
The Beatles	"Back in the USSR"	"Happiness…Warm Gun" "Julia" "Long, Long, Long"	"Martha My Dear" "Birthday" "Revolution 1"	"Good Night"
Abbey Road	"Come Together"	"I Want You (She's So…)"	"Here Comes the Sun"	"The End/Her Majesty"

Album title tracks are shown in bold

Looking at each column as a set, you see that the album openers all have a driving and/or high energy sound. They are all up tempo, and highly accessible. The album closers, in the early years, are typically either high energy rockers, or songs with a sly joke. "I'll Be Back" is actually a note to the fans not to get too worried about the Beatles going away. The placement of "Run for Your Life" is likely due to the presence of the lyric "that's the end." Still, Martin's primary criteria there is that the song is hard to follow, which is borne out on the list.

---

[11] Though, famously, it was considered. The album was provisionally titled *A Doll's House*, after the Ibsen play.

In between the extremes, songs which end sides are a much more varied lot. They range from rockers, to ballads, to pure psychedelia. This indicates that the role of that particular pole position is much more versatile, and must respond to the needs of the other music even more than the outer poles. This is a position for good music which may be hard to categorize, but in some way compels the listener on toward the resumption of the program. They are endings without actually being endings — *provisional endings*, if you will.

Some of the same observations apply to side openers, though there are no ballads in that position. If anything, these are more complicated creations, which could not either begin or end the album, but are uniformly excellent, and able to restart the energy after the intermission. Because they follow *space*, even without a completely clean slate, a wider range of possibilities can be used there.

Saying that the best music is found in the pole tracks is not an indictment of anything placed in between. As Martin mentioned above, flow is more important than anything. The inner tracks may be great, and just not right for the poles. But consider that, for the four classic albums which contain title tracks, those are all found in pole positions, with three of the four being the first song on the album.

The chart clearly shows that, as the Beatles progressed through their career, pole tracks became more complicated, and the range of what could be considered a pole track increased. This is partly a reflection on how good they got, but also the idea that they eventually selected poles more with *artistic intent* than pure commercial or structural intent. When multiple songs were good enough and appropriate enough, the choice became creative, with an ear toward how each option resonated with the other music.

This is exactly where George Martin's ear excelled. Even though his role changed over time, he was still helping decide how to fit everything together when they created the long medley on *Abbey Road*. By then, McCartney had started to pick up on Martin's techniques, and it would serve him very well during his solo career. Lennon also appears to have adopted some of Martin's best ideas, but did not retain them for long. Eventually, his selection of pole tracks was questionable at best. Harrison and Starr, who apparently never had more than a cursory role in sequencing tracks, did not obtain the necessary discernment skills, and this became a major problem during their solo careers.

More on these things will come in the fullness of this project, but the importance of the pole tracks, as dictated by the LP medium, cannot be overstated. As we will see, George Martin made all of his sequencing decisions around what would go in these positions, and he and the Beatles came to understand well their critical role as the support structure on which ever more complicated musical ideas could be hung.

7
Facade

When it came to compiling the album, I tried to edit it together in a very tight format, and in a funny kind of way when I was editing it it almost grew by itself; it took on a life of its own.

— George Martin, regarding *Sgt. Pepper*[1]

When considered in chronological order, it becomes clear that the Beatles mastered the simple album form over their first five albums, coming out of the gate with surprisingly mature albums, due largely to Martin's depth of experience. Then they gave the form a nudge, a kick, and a shove over their next three albums, with their final two representing further explorations and variations on a theme.

Though it's widely acknowledged that the Beatles were pioneers in the overall movement toward albums as whole artistic works, other artists would take what they did and expand on it, ultimately reaching peaks that the Beatles did not. In truth, the Beatles only set the table for more ambitious projects to come. Perhaps their greatest gift to the form is the mere introduction of the idea that there could be such a thing as a "concept album." Though there are earlier examples of such a thing,[2] it wasn't until *Sgt. Pepper* that the world of popular music really started to think in such terms. Suddenly everyone wanted to do segues, eliminate banding, and create synergy between the music and the "look" of the album.

Yet, despite its reputation, *Sgt. Pepper* was more like a critical step toward more ambitious works than an actual realization of it. It introduced the language that many other artists would use, but itself had not much to say. Its success was built partially on the exceptional music, craftsmanship, and synchrony with the cultural moment, but the album reached a whole new level of success largely because of what it caused the audience to *believe* about it — that it was an integrated whole, and somehow greater than the sum of its parts. Obviously, there was at least some truth in this perception — one which endures over 50 years later — but it is instructive to pull at this thread a bit in service to the current project. We need to know *how* it was put together, and *why* that works.

---

[1] *Summer of Love*, pg. 150
[2] Two Franks — Sinatra and Zappa — are credited with earlier examples of concept albums in pop music. Some suggest that Woody Guthrie invented the form in 1940.

To a degree, and from the very beginning, all albums have been "concept" albums. That is obvious if you accept that a "concept" is simply whatever unifies a collection of music — the reason for collecting the recordings together in the first place. Without concepts, no albums. The concept might be as simple as "music by the same composer," "songs by the same singer," or "songs about the same holiday." The concept of the first album ever, in 1909, was "Tchaikovsky's Nutcracker Suite." Even albums without any obvious concept always have one. The sampler disc which came with my first CD player[3] included a seemingly random collection of popular and classical music, but there was still an underlying concept: "This is what digital music sounds like."

In terms of concept, there was an obvious difference between *Sgt. Pepper* and what had come before. If the concept of earlier Beatles albums was, "Here are some songs by the Beatles," *Sgt. Pepper* added a layer which might be summed up as, "Here are some songs by the Beatles pretending to be another band putting on a psychedelic show." The reality, of course, is that this more elaborate concept informed just a small subset of the tracks during the recording process, and even then mostly through style — along with the sense of freedom that the artificial construct gave to the artists — rather than the actual content.

In reality, most of this "concept" was added in the process of assembly. The Beatles had recorded a collection of psychedelic set pieces — individual *tracks*, as always — but carefully assembled them into that famous whole by using essential bracketing material to create the illusion of integration. Even while acknowledging its outsized impact, and obvious status as a classic, this assessment now dominates critical thinking about the Beatles' most famous work, and has in some quarters from the moment of its release. For example, Richard Goldstein, reviewing the album for the *New York Times* in June of 1967, was not taken in:

> *The Beatles have shortened the "banding" between cuts so that one song seems to run into the next. This produces the possibility of a Pop symphony or oratorio, with distinct but related movements. Unfortunately, there is no apparent thematic development in the placing of cuts, except for the effective juxtapositions of opposing musical styles. At best, the songs are only vaguely related.*[4]

George Martin, far from denying this, knew all too well how it had been accomplished, and eventually discussed it openly. One short example:

---

[3] The Technics SL-P2, 1985.
[4] Richard Goldstein, "We Still Need the Beatles, but …", *New York Times*, June 18, 1967

7 / FACADE

> *This reprise just about manages to convince us that we have been listening to a rounded and coherent performance, when we have in fact been listening to a series of little side-shows, each with its own distinct personality.*[5]

Ringo was more succinct, describing the album's tracks, and their relationship to the concept, from within the group:

> *…it was going to be a whole show, but after two tracks everybody started getting fed up and doing their own songs again.*[6]

John Lennon, famously hot and cold about the music of the Beatles, tended to come down cold on the idea that *Sgt. Pepper* had much of a concept:

> *When you get down to it, it was nothing more than an album called* Sgt. Pepper *with the tracks stuck together. …what else is on it musically besides the whole concept of having tracks running into each other?*[7]

And on another occasion:

> Sgt. Pepper *is called the first concept album, but it doesn't go anywhere. All my contributions to the album have absolutely nothing to do with this idea of Sgt. Pepper and his band, but it works, because we said it worked, and that's how the album appeared. But it was not put together as it sounds, except for Sgt. Pepper introducing Billy Shears and the so-called reprise. Every other song could have been on any other album.*[8]

It is important to realize, however, that accepting this fact, and parsing just how they did it, reveals an even more astounding accomplishment than the album gets credit for. With such perilously slight thematic threads, the public perception was largely shaped and fueled by the title track, its remake, a few sound effects, three segues, the absence of silence, four costumes, four moustaches, and a set of iconic photographs.

---

[5] *Summer of Love*, pg. 65
[6] Ibid., pg. 64
[7] *Anthology*, pg. 253
[8] *All We Are Saying*, pg. 197

If *Sgt. Pepper (The Individual Tracks)* was a triumph of imagination and studio innovation and psychedelia, *Sgt. Pepper (The Album)* was a blazing triumph of assembly and packaging.

Fortunately for the current project, George Martin wrote extensively about the making of this album, including full disclosure on how it was assembled with the aim of giving the whole a mythic aura. His 1994 book on the project, *Summer of Love: The Making of Sgt Pepper*, contains the following remarkable, jam-packed — yet still somehow frustratingly succinct — description of how he turned a collection of intriguing but widely disparate tracks, with no apparent linking thread, into a coherent — indeed, brilliant — sequence (emphasis added).

> The running order of the songs on the finished album was pretty much left to me to decide, with the Beatles giving final approval. We had to start with the song that **gave the illusion of a concept**, "Sgt. Pepper's Lonely Hearts Club Band"; that has to be the first track, naturally. The reprise of this song, for the same reason, had to go last — except that the final chord of "A Day in the Life" was so final that it was obvious **nothing else could follow it**. So the reprise of "Sgt. Pepper's Lonely Hearts Club Band" was put back to second to last. That took care of three of our tracks already.
>
> My old precept in the recording business was always "**Make side one strong**," for obvious commercial reasons. Since the last line of "Sgt. Pepper's Lonely Hearts Club Band" introduces the fictional Billy Shears (i.e. one Ringo Starr), "A Little Help From My Friends" had to come immediately after the title track. Four down.
>
> "Lucy in the Sky with Diamonds" was **a great song: it had to go on side one**. It could hardly be more different in atmosphere and mood from "A Little Help From My Friends," so why place it after that? Well, it was because it was so different. It was **a complete change of musical colour**, which was as welcome. It was like saying, "Here's a green show," with the first two tracks, then the lights went down, and suddenly up comes a red show. You wanted a change there; you wanted to hear something really different. The phrase that opens "Lucy" is a great hook, very evocative, and coming here in the running order **it cools the rather hot beginning right down**.
>
> Another principle of mine when assembling an album was always to **go out on a side strongly**, placing the weaker material towards the end but then going out with a bang. With this in mind, "Being for the Benefit of Mr. Kite" ends side one.

7 / FACADE

*The songs that were least interesting had to come before that and after "Lucy." "She's Leaving Home" was a lovely song, but it was a bit downbeat — it didn't exactly shout its optimism — so I decided to place it after the more upbeat but less worthy "Fixing A Hole" and "Getting Better." These were all entirely **subjective judgments**, of course!*

*When it came to "Within You Without You," I could not for the life of me think of anywhere to put it at all. It was so alien, mystical and long. **There was no way it could end a side, nor did it sit comfortably next to anything else on the album.** The self-deprecating laugh George had added at the end of his song gave me a bizarre idea: it could start a side, and I could follow it with a jokey track: "When I'm Sixty-Four."*

*A lot of people like "Lovely Rita," but it was not my favourite song, as I've said, so that one went into **the middle of side two as a bit of padding**. "Good Morning, Good Morning" found its place by virtue of a **happy accident**, when I noticed that the chicken squawk on the end of the song dovetailed, or rather could be made to dovetail, neatly with the sound of the guitar tuning-up that begins the title song's reprise. Finally came the big blockbuster that ends the album. "A Day in the Life": **nothing could come after that** final numbing 42-second chord.*

When we were putting the album together at the end, it struck me that we had such a funny collection of songs, not really related to one another, all disparate numbers...

*If we had not given away "Strawberry Fields Forever" and "Penny Lane" for a double-A-sided single of 1966, but had included them on Pepper, what would we have dropped from the album instead? Maybe "Within You Without You," but that would have broken **the golden rule that George Harrison always had one of his songs on an album**. So it would have to have been "Lovely Rita" and "When I'm Sixty-Four." It's fun to imagine what a re-edited Sgt. Pepper's Lonely Hearts Club Band with those two crackers on it might be like!*

*When it came to compiling the album, I tried to edit it together in a **very tight format**, and in a funny kind of way when I was editing it it almost grew by itself; it **took on a life of its own**.*[9]

---

[9] *Summer of Love*, pp. 148-150

In this extraordinarily breezy passage, Martin conveniently omits any alternatives he may have considered and rejected (which we will get to below), but still makes it clear that there is a fair amount of smoke-and-mirrors at work here. Consider these stunning admissions:

- The "concept" of the album was merely an "illusion."
- There is a hierarchy of material, and that was a driver of decisions.
- He used his own "subjective judgments" (not the band's) to rank the quality of the tracks.
- The better material went on side one absent a reason to put elsewhere.
- There is at least one piece of pure "filler."
- A "downbeat" song had to be disguised.
- Sudden changes of mood were used to solve problems.
- He bowed to certain unwritten band rules, against his artistic judgment.
- He used sequencing to blatantly manipulate the listener's perceptions.
- He used gut instinct in some decisions, intellectual/artistic rigor in others.
- He benefited from a combination of skill and pure luck.

Importantly, these admissions do not diminish the finished work at all, they merely highlight the fact that the album is only greater than the sum of its parts because there was a determination — along with the necessary skill and artistic sense — to make it so. Though he felt that there was a wide variety in the greatness of the individual tracks, he was determined to find exactly the right spot in the running order for each song/track — the place where its assets would be highlighted, and its liabilities either disguised or mitigated.

In considering Martin's techniques, we see two important ways in which he assesses each track that comes along. The first is simply "quality" and basically indicates how good or "strong" he thinks the track is. This is partly a commercial consideration, but not entirely. He admits that it is a subjective call, and provides not much more to go on. Throughout his writings and interviews, Martin labels various songs with phrases like the ones used here, diplomatically ranging from "a great song" to "not my favourite song." Then, when putting them in order, he uses the higher quality tracks to lift any material which he considers not as strong. Thus, stronger tracks have specific places and roles, while weaker tracks — when they cannot be disregarded for some reason — are placed *in relation to* the stronger tracks, rather than in specific positions.

Martin's second way of assessing a track might be called its "character." Though he does not used this word specifically, and it's somewhat broad, the idea is to bring together the intangibles about how a listener will perceive the track — by itself and relative to others — and what impact it can have on the music around it. To say about a track that "nothing else could follow it," is a comment on its character, as is describing it as "evocative," "downbeat," "jokey," or even "green" versus "red." Among other things, he uses these characterizations to establish unexpected but welcome connections:

> *"Within You Without You"...alien, mystical and long...could start a side, and I could follow it with a jokey track: "When I'm Sixty-Four."*

With these basic ideas in mind, it's instructive to actually follow his thought process step by step. I've devised a simple numbering and diagramming system which will be used throughout the rest of this book to follow how tracks get added to running orders. It shows each side of the album as its own box, then lists any tracks which have already been placed so far. Gaps which remain to be filled are shown with an ellipsis. Changes from one listing to the next are shown in bold.

In this way, we see not just the track order, but also which tracks have been placed in logical groupings. Relative locations on side one are 1A through 1Z, and likewise side two is 2A through 2Z.[10] Songs which were intentionally grouped together have consecutive letters. Songs used to fill in gaps have letters not consecutive with those around them, but somewhere in between. Songs remaining to be placed are listed in the right column.

We follow Martin's process in assembling *Sgt. Pepper* by extracting bits from the narrative above.

- *"Sgt. Pepper's Lonely Hearts Club Band"... has to be the first track*

- *The reprise of this song...had to go last*

| 1A. Sgt Pepper's Lonely Hearts Club Band (P)
 ...

 ...
 2Z. Sgt Pepper's Lonely Hearts... (Reprise) (B) | Being for the Benefit of Mr Kite! (J)
 Fixing a Hole (P)
 A Day in the Life (J/P)
 Getting Better (P)
 Good Morning Good Morning (J)
 Lovely Rita (P)
 Lucy in the Sky with Diamonds (J)
 She's Leaving Home (P)
 When I'm Sixty-Four (P)
 With a Little Help... (R)
 Within You Without You (G) |

- *"A Day in the Life"...nothing else could follow it.*

---

[10] Sides sometimes get labeled with letters: Side A, Side B, etc., but that won't work here.

- ...the reprise of "Sgt. Pepper's Lonely Hearts Club Band" was put back to second to last.

- "A Little Help From My Friends" had to come immediately after the title track.

1A. Sgt Pepper's Lonely Hearts Club Band (P)	Being for the Benefit of Mr Kite! (J)
1B. With a Little Help from My Friends (R)	Fixing a Hole (P)
...	Getting Better (P)
	Good Morning Good Morning (J)
	Lovely Rita (P)
...	Lucy in the Sky with Diamonds (J)
2Y. Sgt Pepper's Lonely Hearts... (Reprise) (B)	She's Leaving Home (P)
2Z. A Day in the Life (J/P)	When I'm Sixty-Four (P)
	Within You Without You (G)

- "Lucy in the Sky with Diamonds"...cools the rather hot beginning right down.

- ...go out on a side strongly..."Being for the Benefit of Mr. Kite" ends side one.

1A. Sgt Pepper's Lonely Hearts Club Band (P)	Fixing a Hole (P)
1B. With a Little Help from My Friends (R)	Getting Better (P)
1C. Lucy in the Sky with Diamonds (J)	Good Morning Good Morning (J)
...	Lovely Rita (P)
	She's Leaving Home (P)
1Z. Being for the Benefit of Mr Kite! (J)	When I'm Sixty-Four (P)
	Within You Without You (G)

- "She's Leaving Home" ...after the more upbeat but less worthy "Fixing A Hole" and "Getting Better."[11]

1A. Sgt Pepper's Lonely Hearts Club Band (P)	Being for the Benefit of Mr Kite! (J)
1B. With a Little Help from My Friends (R)	Good Morning Good Morning (J)
1C. Lucy in the Sky with Diamonds (J)	Lovely Rita (P)
1L. Getting Better (P)	When I'm Sixty-Four (P)
1M. Fixing a Hole (P)	Within You Without You (G)
1N. She's Leaving Home (P)	
1Z. Being for the Benefit of Mr Kite! (J)	

---

[11] There is no mention of how the order of these latter two tracks was decided. It will be discussed below.

7 / FACADE

- "Within You Without You" ...it could start a side, and I could follow it with a jokey track: "When I'm Sixty-Four."

- "Good Morning, Good Morning" ...dovetail...title song's reprise.

- "Lovely Rita" ...middle of side two as a bit of padding.

The final running order, with the assembly structure revealed:

1A.	Sgt Pepper's Lonely Hearts Club Band (P)
1B.	With a Little Help from My Friends (R)
1C.	Lucy in the Sky with Diamonds (J)
1L.	Getting Better (P)
1M.	Fixing a Hole (P)
1N.	She's Leaving Home (P)
1Z.	Being for the Benefit of Mr Kite! (J)
2A.	**Within You Without You (G)**
2B.	**When I'm Sixty-Four (P)**
2M.	**Lovely Rita (P)**
2X.	**Good Morning, Good Morning (J)**
2Y.	Sgt Pepper's Lonely Hearts... (Reprise) (B)
2Z.	A Day in the Life (J/P)

Though Martin's narrative was written many years after the fact, and may not represent the actual order in which he made those decisions, we will assume that it does represent something like his progression in decision-making. In truth, it's likely that a great deal of trial and error, based on listening, went into the process which would be difficult to document, and cannot be recreated after the fact.

The ultimate choices are certainly fascinating, but so is the overall progression. In three separate cases Martin starts by deciding beginnings and endings and then proceeding to fill in the middles. It happens first with the album as a whole, and then with each side. This is compatible with all of the descriptions we have of his process, and makes complete sense given the importance he ascribed to the "outer" tracks in a sequence, which we have termed *pole tracks* (see the previous chapter).

To complete each side, he continues the progression from outer to inner. With pole tracks in place, he looks for tracks which can go next to them, either those that come second (followers) or second-to-last (setups). Each of these positions is filled relative to its adjacent pole track, with careful consideration for how that relationship will work. Among other possibilities, tracks which follow openers have the opportunity to extend the mood or create an intentional tone shift. Tracks which precede the closer create a mood which it will either amplify or modify. That makes these two positions especially good for "feature" tracks, those which are distinctive in some way. A track which follows an opener or precedes a closer must not upstage it, and must in some way resonate intentionally with its neighbor.[12]

Thus, on a 14-song album, eight slots are immediately spoken for: four pole slots, and the four slots adjacent to them. The remaining six slots, three per side, are considered infill, and would be places for the weakest tracks in the collection, with the weakest of all going in the middle of side two. That is not to imply that tracks placed in those positions are fundamentally weak, but only weaker in some way than the rest. While this could mean less polished, in the case of the Beatles it is likely to mean more routine and less commercial in some way, though it could also mean just things that didn't fit anywhere else. For example, such tracks tend to more easily stand on their own, and thus have more possible positions than the rest.

Clearly, these are more than just principles, but actually represent a template of sorts, that looks roughly like this:

Side One	Priority	Quality	Character
1A. Hard open	1	Highest	Strong, upbeat, landscape, room, language, tone
1B. Follower	3	↓	Continuation or contrast, feature
...infill...	5	Lower	Various
1Y. Setup	3	↓	Feature
1Z. Soft close	2	High	Strong, hard to follow
Side Two			
2A. Soft open	2	Middle	Distinctive, unique
2B. Follower	4	↓	Continuation or contrast, feature
...infill...	6	Lowest	Various
2Y. Setup	4	↓	Bridge, purposeful, feature
2Z. Hard closer	1	Highest	Strong, final statement, summation, hard to follow

Recognizing the existence of such a template is not intended to imply a paint-by-numbers approach. There is still wide latitude for variation, and the actual music always dictated what went where, and how the principles of the template were implemented or modified for each individual project. But the basic template does show both the relative importance of tracks in the flow of an album, and the path to determining what goes where — a place to start.

Utilizing this template, then, involves frank assessment of the tracks to be included, figuring out which are strong enough for the most important positions, which might fit in feature spots, and which will be used primarily to make connections ("padding," to use Martin's own term). He started by placing a track where he thought it belonged, and then moved it — and everything — around until all parts

---

[12] Recall the issue of "There's a Place," discussed in chapter 5.

had found the best possible home. Some moves became obvious as he went along, while others require a more subtle approach.

As noted, Martin's narrative about the sequencing of *Sgt. Pepper* is incomplete. He leaves out options that he considered but rejected. He also does not provide any real detail about whatever shuffling went into putting the puzzle together. Thankfully, we do find some detail elsewhere which illustrates how Martin assessed his first instincts, then made critical changes to improve the finished product.

Mark Lewisohn reported, in the liner notes for the 1987 CD release, that the first draft of side one ran like this:[13]

1. Sgt. Pepper's Lonely Hearts Club Band (P)
2. With a Little Help from My Friends (R)
3. Being for the Benefit of Mr. Kite! (J)
4. Fixing a Hole (P)
5. Lucy in the Sky with Diamonds (J)
6. Getting Better (P)
7. She's Leaving Home (P)

Significantly, there is a logical progression here, albeit somewhat literal compared to what *Sgt. Pepper* would ultimately become. In this order, the show has a more distinct shape. After an overture ("Sgt. Pepper") and opening number ("Friends"), the lyrics of "Mr. Kite" provide details of the "friends" who we can expect to hear from during the show. "Fixing a Hole" becomes a vaudeville-esque change of pace, perhaps sung by The Hendersons. "Lucy" fixes those holes, now recognized to be "in the sky," with diamonds. Suddenly, things are "Getting Better." But wait! — there's trouble in paradise because "She's Leaving Home."

The narrative arc is obvious, as is the successful invocation of a turn-of-the-century show by a "lonely hearts club" band. Likewise, the fatal flaws of this line-up stand out clearly. With the lengthy and wholly optimistic setup, "She's Leaving Home" cannot help but be experienced as a woefully melodramatic turn, a cliffhanger featuring a beautiful damsel with the back of her hand against her mouth, designed to haunt the audience during the intermission, and bring them back to find out what happened to her.

Notably, the turn from the peak optimism of "Getting Better" to something decidedly pessimistic — from happy chiming guitars to pensive harp arpeggios — is jarring. The balloon is burst just as we've started to enjoy it. There is also a problematic lyrical move from "I used to be cruel to my woman" to "What did we do that was wrong?" The question has already been asked and answered, at least in spirit. In the first song, the problem was in the process of being solved ("I'm changing my scene"),

---

[13] The same alternate line-up is mentioned in *Recording Sessions*, pg. 107.

whereas in the second song it's unexpectedly been replaced by something worse: alienation and despair. In this configuration, "She's Leaving Home" effectively undermines the goodwill that has been built. The show comes to a complete halt, and the last words of side one would have been, "Bye, bye."

In terms of the listener's perception, by ending the side with an unresolved story-song, an expectation is created, namely, that the story will be taken up and resolved in act two. That would have been a reasonable goal, except that it would have been impossible with the material remaining. Perhaps "she" could eventually become "Lovely Rita" or even "blew [her] mind out in a car," or merely live to the ripe old age of 64, but the problems are obvious. "She's Leaving Home" has a strong and unfinished narrative, and nothing else in this collection of songs offers any satisfactory resolution. If too much attention is called to that narrative, there is no assembly of the remaining tracks on side two which could have satisfied those expectations.

The draft line-up reveals that "She's Leaving Home" is actually a *problem track*. In Martin's diplomatic phrasing, "it didn't exactly shout its optimism," but that's only one problem. The deeper and more critical problem is the fact that the song's positioning is limited considerably by its content. Put it in the wrong spot and it will seem dour, saccharine, possibly laughable. Put it in the right spot and this can be disguised. Because it cannot be left off, disguising its liabilities becomes the goal.[14]

Of all the tracks on *Sgt. Pepper*, then, this one requires the most careful attention. By contrast, "A Day in the Life," surely the most complex creation, offers no sequencing problem at all. It simply must go last. There is no second choice. The album's other genuine problem track, "Within You Without You" also turns out to be less trouble because it, too, has only one plausible position. No such obvious choice is available for "She's Leaving Home."

Having identified the problem, Martin went about trying to solve it, and the solution also reveals how a chain reaction is created which ultimately provides a much better line-up for side one.

Realizing that "She's Leaving Home" must not end the side, something must go *after* it. What could that be? What makes a better closer? "Fixing a Hole" ends with a fade, weakly, and is not a strong enough song for a pole position. "Getting Better" ends in a slightly more interesting way, with those optimistic chiming guitars, but that is really a non-ending because they merely trail off, and the song itself isn't really strong enough to end the side. "Lucy" and "Mr. Kite!" are therefore the only real possibilities. Between the two, "Mr. Kite!" has the more memorable final sound, which effectively suggests a curtain coming down, while "Lucy" ends with a simple fade. Clearly, of the two, "Mr. Kite!" make a more suitable and effective side closer.

---

[14] Perhaps this could have been mitigated if Martin had scored it. Just sayin'.

># 7 / FACADE

>1. Sgt. Pepper's Lonely Hearts Club Band (P)
>2. With a Little Help from My Friends (R)
>**3. (...)**
>4. Fixing a Hole (P)
>5. Lucy in the Sky with Diamonds (J)
>6. Getting Better (P)
>7. She's Leaving Home (P)
>**8. Being for the Benefit of Mr. Kite! (J)**

That creates a hole and another problem. Just sliding everything up to fill that gap won't work. The weakness of "Fixing a Hole" is too obvious when following something as strong as "Friends." "Getting Better" might work there, but seems slight, and somewhat redundant. Putting our problem track, "She's Leaving Home," there also doesn't work because it dispels the optimism of "Friends" far too quickly — rather like a sledgehammer, and enough that it would be difficult to recover. The most troublesome qualities of "She's Leaving Home" would be emphasized in that position. "Lucy" suddenly looks like the only answer. It is both strong enough to follow "Friends," and has the advantage of creating a distinct mood change right where one is needed (as noted in Martin's comments).

>1. Sgt. Pepper's Lonely Hearts Club Band (P)
>2. With a Little Help from My Friends (R)
>**3. Lucy in the Sky with Diamonds (J)**
>4. Fixing a Hole (P)
>**5. (...)**
>6. Getting Better (P)
>7. She's Leaving Home (P)
>8. Being for the Benefit of Mr. Kite! (J)

This looks much better already, but again, simply closing the new gap leaves behind the problem of contrast between "Getting Better" and "She's Leaving Home." The obvious solution is to swap the two least consequential tracks on the side to create some distance. "Fixing" provides a soft landing for the optimism of "Getting Better," before the sad story is told. Such a move appears to come with no real penalty because these are the most flexible tracks anyway.

>1. Sgt. Pepper's Lonely Hearts Club Band (P)
>2. With a Little Help from My Friends (R)
>3. Lucy in the Sky with Diamonds (J)
>**4. Getting Better (P)**
>**5. Fixing a Hole (P)**
>6. She's Leaving Home (P)
>7. Being for the Benefit of Mr. Kite! (J)

The resulting sequence is much less literal, which works against the "concept" aspect of the album, but it creates strengths which more than offset that. Those strengths are four-fold, and alluded to above:

1. Strong contrast with "Friends" improves perception of "Lucy."
2. Insulating "She's Leaving Home" disguises its problems, reducing melodrama, casting it as self-contained, without raising expectations.
3. The side ends with a poof of psychedelia, the Beatles at their most playful.
4. Expectations for side two now better match the available material.

As an added benefit, the side's two weakest tracks are tucked together in the middle, where they can buoy each other, and their relative weakness is itself disguised. They become an optimistic core at the center of the side which provides a better lead in to the sad song which follows. Obviously, as many reviewers have noted through the years, not all of the melodrama is removed from "She's Leaving Home." But when followed by a suitable antidote, namely the playfulness and dazzling studio wizardry of "Mr. Kite!" the worst elements are dispelled — i.e. quickly forgotten — for many listeners.

With that first draft line-up, one can imagine a teen listener dissolving into tears at the end of the first side, with thoughts of this poor girl striking out into a lonely world — likely to join the "lonely hearts club" of the album's title — essentially embarking on Eleanor Rigby's life, the ending of which we already know. When that teen turns over the record, she would have immediately faced a deepening of the crisis in George's ode to the pointlessness of life. Is there any recovery from there? It would have been a pit of despair in the middle of what should be a joyous album. Martin's tweaks, which may seem on their face to be mere arbitrary shuffling, are essential to keeping the tone of the album light, playful, and trippily psychedelic.

One quick side note: The original draft better distributes vocalists, alternating more carefully between John and Paul. The revised/final version breaks one of Martin's cardinal rules because it includes three songs in a row written by Paul. Obviously, the Beatles approved this, and so it stands as a useful example of Martin apparently breaking his own rules in the interest of a better flow.

To help illustrate the significance of these sequencing choices, consider a couple of much different albums which might have been created with exactly the same material. Call these "sabotaged" running orders, if you will. Below are just two possibilities. The first emphasizes the isolation which is threaded through the tracks.

7 / FACADE

Lonely Hearts

Side One
1. Sgt. Pepper's Lonely Hearts Club Band (P)
2. Within You Without You (G)
3. Fixing a Hole (P)
4. With a Little Help from My Friends (R)
5. Getting Better (P)
6. Lovely Rita (P)

Side Two
1. Being for the Benefit of Mr. Kite! (J)
2. Sgt. Pepper's Lonely Hearts Club Band (reprise) (B)
3. Good Morning, Good Morning (J)
4. She's Leaving Home (P)
5. Lucy in the Sky with Diamonds (J)
6. When I'm 64 (P)
7. A Day in the Life (J/P)

"Within You Without You" creates a black hole from which the album never recovers. No amount of "fixing" or "help" or "getting better" can do the trick. Even the addition of LSD in the middle of side two doesn't help. By the end, everybody is worse off than when they started! Also, a lot of great music is obscured and would have been forgotten.

The second "sabotage" takes the album's most significant track and builds the theme around it, also drawing out something approaching despair. This album might have been called *A Day in the Life*.

A Day in the Life

Side One
1. Good Morning, Good Morning (J)
2. A Day in the Life (without final stanza or chord) (J/P)
3. She's Leaving Home (P)
4. Being for the Benefit of Mr. Kite! (J)
5. Lucy in the Sky with Diamonds (J)
6. Within You Without You (G)

Side Two
1. When I'm 64 (P)
2. Sgt. Pepper's Lonely Hearts Club Band (P)
3. Fixing a Hole (P)
4. Lovely Rita (P)
5. Getting Better (P)
6. With a Little Help from My Friends (J)
7. A Day in the Life (reprise, final stanza plus chord) (J)

Here we first greet the new day, and then get a preview of what it's going to look like. It doesn't look very hopeful. Somebody leaves home, somebody tries escaping into the sky, and then we're told that it just doesn't matter. By side two, when we start to think there is some hope, the day ends where it began, with pure desolation. Also, a lot of great music is obscured and would have been forgotten.

Despite being the exact same music, either of these running orders would have had a very different cultural effect. Such is the importance of getting the album assembly just right.

What started out as a rather simple exercise on *Please Please Me,* has by the time of *Sgt. Pepper* become a full-on life-or-death thing for the project. Any missteps in the sequencing could have resulted in the album being seen as perplexing, or creepy, or just plain sad.

Fortunate for us, George Martin was giving a master class in album assembly on *Sgt. Pepper,* and we can run with the ideas and priorities and techniques he teaches. As we will see, it isn't really that difficult to follow these steps, to use and modify his template to fit other situations. The most important thing is to listen to the music with track placement in mind. By doing so, everything is given a context in which it can shine. An invisible virtuous circle then carefully surrounds the music, protecting and enhancing it at every turn.

Proof-of-Concept #1

April 1966-June 1966

Revolver

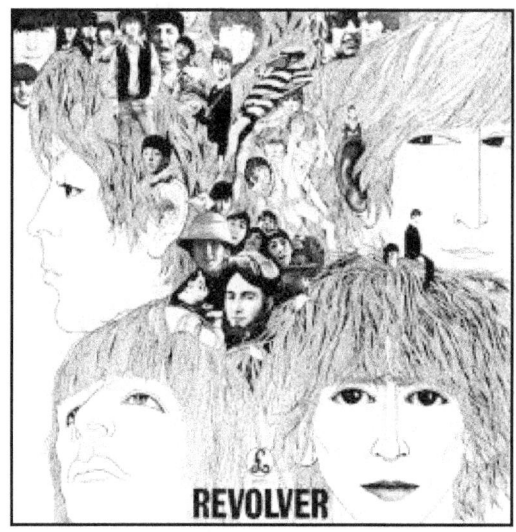

To see if we really understand how George Martin was working when creating album running orders, we will embark on three proof-of-concept projects before entering the Wild West of solo recordings. These are relatively safe projects, the goal of which is just practice, even if the results are interesting in some way.

For the first, we will start with the raw materials Martin had to work with when sequencing *Revolver*, and see if, by applying his principles, we come up with the same running order. Along the way, we may see some of the music a little differently, and hopefully understand why the album came out as it did.

This works as a proof-of-concept because there appears to be no documentation available anywhere describing how or why he made the decisions he did, nor is there any description of how involved the Beatles were. In this era, the Beatles themselves, though engaged in the recording process up to and including the sequencing, had many other things still on their plate, including preparation for their final tour, and all of the burgeoning furor about Lennon's interview with Maureen Cleave. By all accounts, they may have given their input, and even been present when decisions were being made, but left such things up to Martin because they trusted him. Obviously, they approved the finished result.

As we do this, try to forget what you know about the finished album, and travel with Martin through these tracks, exploring how they work individually, how they work together, and how they might best complement one another.

Materials

The songs on *Revolver* are all incredibly familiar now, of course, but they would have sounded decidedly innovative and unusual to anyone hearing them in the summer of 1966. It was obvious to everyone involved that something had changed with the Beatles. Conventional wisdom says drugs played the largest role, and that may well be. But we must also acknowledge that studio capabilities were improving rapidly, the band's playing and writing continued to be refined through sheer experience, and they had a new excitement for recording, having not been in the studio together for nearly six months since the completion of *Rubber Soul*. When the sessions were over, the reel contained these songs (alphabetical for objectivity):

B-110 "And Your Bird Can Sing" (John)
B-108 "Doctor Robert" (John)
B-115 "Eleanor Rigby" (Paul)
B-112 "For No One" (Paul)
B-116 "Good Day Sunshine" (Paul)
B-118 "Got to Get You into My Life" (Paul)
B-117 "Here, There and Everywhere" (Paul)
B-114 "I Want to Tell You" (George)
B-111 "I'm Only Sleeping" (John)
B-105 "Love You To" (George)
~~B-106 "Paperback Writer" (Paul)~~
~~B-107 "Rain" (John)~~
B-120 "She Said She Said" (John)
B-119 "Taxman" (George)
B-109 "Tomorrow Never Knows" (John)
B-113 "Yellow Submarine" (Ringo)

A new single had been required in the spring, and whether by design or circumstance, "Paperback Writer" and "Rain" were removed from this list for that purpose. Additionally, Capitol was finding themselves short of enough tracks to finish *Yesterday and Today*, and convinced Martin to send them three of these tracks in advance: "Doctor Robert," "And Your Bird Can Sing" and "I'm Only Sleeping." Though these were then omitted from the initial US release of *Revolver*, they remained blessedly eligible for the UK version of the album.

Thus, this assembly will attempt to unify a formidable and diverse collection of tracks, arguably the most satisfying and quintessential set the Beatles would ever record. The challenge is to find exactly the right spot for each song, no small task.

Assembly

We start the way we imagine George Martin would have started, namely by looking for potential pole tracks — openers and closers for each side. One such categorization is immediately obvious, and non-negotiable: "Tomorrow Never Knows" simply must end the album. It is arguably the most complex creation here, has the tone of a summation while also sounding like a harbinger of something mysterious which is not found here. The track would have been nearly impossible to follow, easily meeting Martin's fundamental criteria for a closer.

There are four clear candidates with the right energy to open the album:

"And Your Bird Can Sing"	(up tempo, strong hook)
"Good Day Sunshine"	(optimistic, very pop-oriented)
"Got to Get You Into My Life"	(incredibly strong song)
"Taxman"	(count-off, up tempo, catchy, different)

From this list, a few things stand out. "Got to Get You into My Life" is probably the strongest, most versatile track in this list. It could probably fit in *any* of the pole or "feature" slots, including the closer, at least theoretically. That cannot be said about any other track in this collection. Its strength comes with a cost, however, namely that it would be incredibly hard to follow. Anything which comes after it would sound weaker by comparison, if only by virtue of not having the horn section and McCartney's scorching vocals.

That makes it wrong for the opener after all, but still a candidate for the end of side one, where it would send the first half out on a powerful note. Though strong enough to begin side two, the same problem crops up there. In reality, if there were no "Tomorrow Never Knows," this track would be best used as the album closer. As such, it turns out there is only one best spot for "Got to Get You into My Life," and that is immediately before John's closer. Only there does it not upstage what follows. Indeed, it represents a last blast of the conventional, a perfect setup for the decidedly unconventional. Together they create a killer one-two punch to end the album.

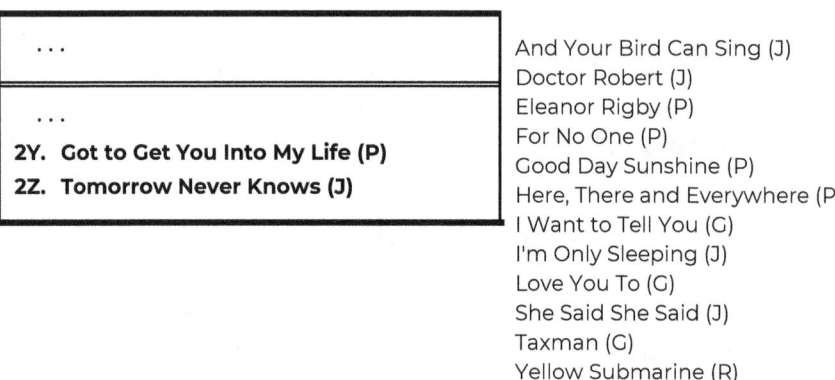

	And Your Bird Can Sing (J)
...	Doctor Robert (J)
	Eleanor Rigby (P)
...	For No One (P)
2Y. Got to Get You Into My Life (P)	Good Day Sunshine (P)
2Z. Tomorrow Never Knows (J)	Here, There and Everywhere (P)
	I Want to Tell You (G)
	I'm Only Sleeping (J)
	Love You To (G)
	She Said She Said (J)
	Taxman (G)
	Yellow Submarine (R)

Despite its happy countenance, "Good Day Sunshine" is a little too loping for the album opener. Its first sound, the pseudo-fade-in piano figure, isn't compelling enough to begin the album either, even if the song would set a nice overall tone. Though still an opener, it really should open side two.

Of the two remaining possibilities, "And Your Bird Can Sing" has some things to recommend it, including a fantastic hook and high energy. But its first sound is decidedly underwhelming, and we know that the Beatles, particularly Lennon, considered it a throwaway. Martin likely agreed, and would have supported it as an opener only if there were nothing better. He likely would have slotted it for somewhere in the middle of side two as, in his word, "padding."

This leaves "Taxman" as the best option. Its crazy countoff makes a great first sound (echoing the start of their first album), and it meets the criteria of being upbeat, catchy, and with a compelling, cheeky lyric. Thus, "Taxman" opens the album, and by asking one simple question, we have programmed four tracks:

	And Your Bird Can Sing (J)
1A. Taxman (G)	Doctor Robert (J)
...	Eleanor Rigby (P)
	For No One (P)
2A. Good Day Sunshine (P)	Here, There and Everywhere (P)
...	I Want to Tell You (G)
2Y. Got to Get You Into My Life (P)	I'm Only Sleeping (J)
2Z. Tomorrow Never Knows (J)	Love You To (G)
	She Said She Said (J)
	Yellow Submarine (R)

At this point, Martin would likely have moved to the flip of the disc, looking for a closer to side one, which is something of a problem. It has to be strong enough, and have the type of ending that brings things to a close while also creating movement into the intermission. Of the remaining tracks, only a couple look truly plausible.

In truth, "Yellow Submarine" would probably have been the first considered, especially given the inevitability that it would be part of the double-A teaser single. It is definitely strong enough, and features a long fade full of goofiness, which is an appropriate way to end a side. Provisionally, it will be given that spot.

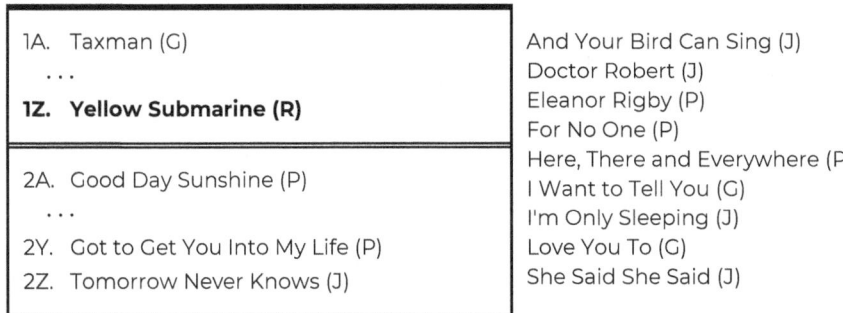

This is perhaps the right moment to note that four of the tracks remaining on the list would have needed special handling in the running order, something Martin would have recognized early. Indeed, two of these would have to be considered "problem" tracks, requiring careful solutions.

Martin would have realized quickly that "Eleanor Rigby" would require special handling. Destined to cause a stir among fans, it was also picked as the teaser single. As such, it would clearly need a place of prominence, most definitely on side one. Obviously not a good album opener, it was likewise wrong to close a side as it might leave too dour a taste. With these things in mind, the natural spot would be as a feature, typically found second on the album. This turns out to work just fine.

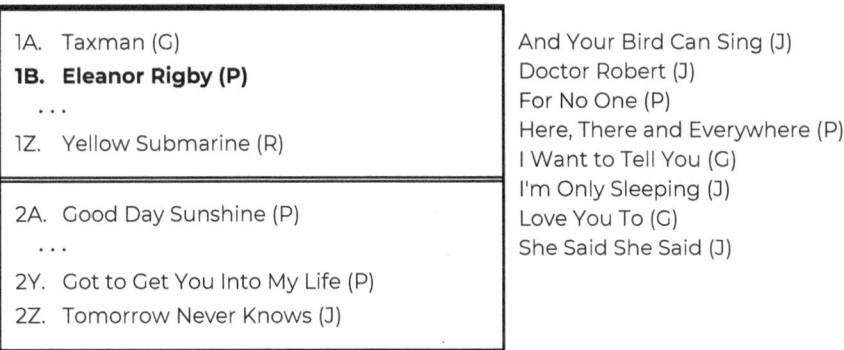

In a different collection of music, "For No One" might also have had the same requirements, but here is it clearly overshadowed by "Eleanor Rigby" for sheer drama. It merely needs to be treated with sensitivity and, given its status as something similar but lesser, Martin would have earmarked this as a side two track. Such is the strength of this collection that "For No One" — an undeniable masterwork — is considered in any way "lesser"! It would be in line to inhabit the corresponding slot on side two except that the side opens with another McCartney track that isn't a very good setup. Something by another Beatle will have to break up that pairing.

The other remaining potential pole track, "And Your Bird Can Sing" is still hanging around, deserving of a spot outside the doldrums of either side. It turns out that inserting John's voice between the two Paul tracks works surprisingly well, allowing both songs their due feature, and solving a problem.

| 1A. Taxman (G) |
| 1B. Eleanor Rigby (P) |
| ... |
| 1Z. Yellow Submarine (R) |
| 2A. Good Day Sunshine (P) |
| **2B. And Your Bird Can Sing (J)** |
| **2C. For No One (P)** |
| ... |
| 2Y. Got to Get You Into My Life (P) |
| 2Z. Tomorrow Never Knows (J) |

Doctor Robert (J)
Here, There and Everywhere (P)
I Want to Tell You (G)
I'm Only Sleeping (J)
Love You To (G)
She Said She Said (J)

The two "problem" tracks, are problems for very different reasons. George Harrison's first Indian track, "Love You To," would certainly be a shock to the Beatles' audience, and have to be placed carefully to give it even a chance at acceptance by listeners. Martin would surely have pegged it initially as a side two track, probably hoping to bury it in the spot where it could have the least detrimental effect on the rest of the album.

But then he would have had to answer the question of how it would be set up and followed. He would not have wanted to weaken the album's ending in any way, and throwing something so foreign that close to the experimental "Tomorrow Never Knows" — which was certainly a gamble in itself — has the potential to be a problem. The dissonance and foreignness of Harrison's song needed to be answered by something consonant and familiar — but *warm*, not *hot*. Given what we know Martin would do with "Within You Without You," he might very well have reasoned that the Indian track needed to be followed by a "jokey" track (his word) — in other words, its polar opposite. That makes "Yellow Submarine," now sitting as the provisional closer to side one, look like the potential key to making "Love You To" palatable. It means moving the song back to side one, and trying something like this:

8 / REVOLVER

1A. Taxman (G)	Doctor Robert (J)
1B. Eleanor Rigby (P)	Here, There and Everywhere (P)
. . .	I Want to Tell You (G)
	I'm Only Sleeping (J)
1Y. Love You To (G)	She Said She Said (J)
1Z. Yellow Submarine (R)	

2A. Good Day Sunshine (P)
2B. And Your Bird Can Sing (J)
2C. For No One (P)
. . .
2Y. Got to Get You Into My Life (P)
2Z. Tomorrow Never Knows (J)

Unfortunately, the same dynamic doesn't really work here. Without the self-deprecating laughter that ends "Within You Without You," the pure novelty track which follows — featuring Ringo's voice and numerous comical elements — comes off as dismissive. As a result, Harrison's record is hung out to dry. The two tracks just don't resonate together, and since no other option immediately appears, "Love You To" remains unsolved for now.

The other problem track is one you might not expect. Considering all that we learned through the sequencing of *Sgt. Pepper*, we still discover a big hole in our knowledge: *Sgt. Pepper*, unlike every other Beatles album, does not contain anything resembling a typical love song — slower in tempo, subdued in tone, romantic, lyrics written in second person, etc. *Revolver*, on the other hand, has one of their all-time best ballads in "Here, There and Everywhere."

There is nothing in George Martin's descriptions of sequencing decisions which addresses specifically what to do with such songs. In reviewing the Beatles catalog itself, for the most part they become the glue in the middle of sides, rather than pole tracks. This is not hard and fast, however. Though there are none which open sides, occasionally he places them at the end. The nature of the song dictates whether that is possible. For example, as mentioned, "I'll Be Back" ends *A Hard Day's Night*, and that placement is justified by the title itself in an era when part of the fun was reassuring fans that the Beatles would "be back" very soon with some new songs. Other examples would be "Michelle," "Julia," and "Long, Long, Long," all of which work because they meet Martin's criteria of being hard to follow.

The lack of such a ballad greatly simplified the sequencing of *Sgt. Pepper*, because such songs must be surrounded by just the right sort of contrasting music to be truly effective and not sound too sweet or sticky — characteristics we know Paul possesses. The closest thing on *Sgt. Pepper* was "She's Leaving Home," and it proved a very sticky problem in the sequencing, one that required special accommodations.

"Here, There and Everywhere" clearly requires a prominent placement, but also both a proper setup, and a proper release. Whatever comes before must leave a clear space for the emotions. Since this track represents the ultimate consonance, that suggests that it be preceded by some sort of dissonance. Whatever follows must then clean away any residual sweetness. Since this track is conventional, that suggests something unconventional. Since this track is deeply emotional, it suggests that both the preceding and following track be in some way less emotional.

Thus it appears that these two problem tracks might just help each other. The dissonance of "Love You To" is nicely offset by the consonance of "Here, There and Everywhere." What's more, this may very well be one of the spots where George Martin would have recognized that a key relationship could help him. "Love You To" ends with a repeated C minor chord[1] which, together with the G major chord at the beginning of "Here, There and Everywhere," creates a musical "Amen" moment which the listener would understand instinctively — not consciously. As such, putting them together represents a very sly solution. It gives George Harrison a special moment when his difficult track would be allowed to mellow in the listener's ear, perfectly balanced and lulled by Paul's gem.

From there, "Yellow Submarine" becomes the palate cleanser, getting the album moving off in a new direction quickly. Between "Love You To" and "Yellow Submarine," Paul's exceptional ballad is perfectly framed.

1A. Taxman (G)	Doctor Robert (J)
1B. Eleanor Rigby (P)	I Want to Tell You (G)
...	I'm Only Sleeping (J)
	She Said She Said (J)
1X. Love You To (G)	
1Y. Here, There and Everywhere (P)	
1Z. Yellow Submarine (R)	

2A. Good Day Sunshine (P)
2B. And Your Bird Can Sing (J)
2C. For No One (P)
...
2Y. Got to Get You Into My Life (P)
2Z. Tomorrow Never Knows (J)

---

[1] The song is not in the key of C minor. In western musical terms, it is what's known as "modal," being built on a scale known as the "Dorian mode." This is a complex enough idea that we won't bother going into it here, but the rock-solid establishment of the foreign-sounding Dorian tonality is one of the reasons that the following track, which returns firmly to a more familiar harmonic language in a relative key, feels so friendly.

8 / REVOLVER

That does, however, raise another problem. "Yellow Submarine" is actually a Paul song. When combined with the side two opener, the trio runs up against Martin's principle that no songwriter should have more than two songs in a row. This simple notion was about keeping things even, and not upsetting any egos. Thus, if side two begins with Paul, side one must end with a different Beatle.

There are now only four tracks remaining on our reel, and only two of those can even be considered to end side one, based on how they end: "She Said She Said" and "I'm Only Sleeping." The latter ends with a backwards guitar break, which might make a reasonable ending, but the overall tone of the track is so sleepy (complete with yawn) that it seems a little risky for that slot. Put simply, "She Said She Said" makes a much better pole track. Everything else slides up, and John gets another feature spot. The album now looks like this:

```
1A.  Taxman (G)                        Doctor Robert (J)
1B.  Eleanor Rigby (P)                 I Want to Tell You (G)
  ...                                  I'm Only Sleeping (J)
1V.  Love You To (G)
1W.  Here, There and Everywhere (P)
1X.  Yellow Submarine (R)
1Z.  She Said She Said (J)

2A.  Good Day Sunshine (P)
2B.  And Your Bird Can Sing (J)
2C.  For No One (P)
  ...
2Y.  Got to Get You Into My Life (P)
2Z.  Tomorrow Never Knows (J)
```

Three tracks remain to fill two gaps. With six songs already on side one, we just need one more there, and it will be whichever one Martin thought was the strongest, recognizing that he always prioritized side one over side two. Since this track will bump up against "Love You To," it can't be George's song. Of the two Lennon songs, "I'm Only Sleeping" is the better choice.

That leaves a decision about how to sequence the other two into the gap on side two. Since that gap is bracketed by two McCartney tracks, that doesn't help make the decision. In the end, this one comes down to a subjective feel for which sounds better next to which. In the end, "Doctor Robert" makes the most sense next to "For No One," and the fade out of "I Want to Tell You" nicely adds strength to the bold beginning of "Got to Get You into My Life."

And with those small final decisions, the album is complete.

1A.	Taxman (G)
1B.	Eleanor Rigby (P)
1F.	**I'm Only Sleeping (J)**
1V.	Love You To (G)
1W.	Here, There and Everywhere (P)
1X.	Yellow Submarine (R)
1Z.	**She Said She Said (J)**

2A.	Good Day Sunshine (P)
2B.	And Your Bird Can Sing (J)
2C.	For No One (P)
2M.	**Doctor Robert (J)**
2N.	**I Want to tell You (G)**
2Y.	Got to Get You Into My Life (P)
2Z.	Tomorrow Never Knows (J)

Discussion

Hey! It came out exactly right! What are the odds? Well, as it turns out, 100%. So let's be clear that the goal here was not to claim some sort of mind-reading trick that revealed the exact steps George Martin took in sequencing *Revolver*. Unless some documentation turns up, those details may never be known.

The only point was to see if his principles provide coherent justifications for the decisions that we know he made, and whether a sublime reverse engineering was possible. Obviously, they do, and it is, and the result to our project is that we can safely use these principles to approximate what Martin might have done with other music. This is in no way absolute, but it is nonetheless a solid foundation.

The letters in the track numbers tell the important story. This album, like all that we will do using Martin's techniques, is built from carefully created sequences, glued together with great skill until a coherent — seemingly inevitable — flow is created. In other words, building blocks become bigger building blocks which then become buildings. The decisions are chunked, and can be evaluated one at a time, making sure that they are always in service to the whole.

Indeed, at each step, the best interest of each track *and the whole* are simultaneously considered, and the picture comes into focus only very slowly, until suddenly... there it is. This is the brilliance of George Martin's techniques.

PROOF-OF-CONCEPT # 2

APRIL 1967–MARCH 1968

Magic Myst

Introduction

Imagine that, while viewing the rushes for *Magical Mystery Tour*, someone in the Beatles' creative braintrust had told Paul, "I don't think this film is a good idea. Let's just put out a new album instead." At that point, they had quite a few tracks in the can, including all of the ones which were slated for the film plus a few more. The question this raises is whether there is another psychedelic masterpiece, a la *Sgt. Pepper*, just waiting to be assembled from parts that were available at that moment.

For our second proof-of-concept project, we will apply George Martin's assembly techniques to this collection of miscellaneous Beatles tracks that were recorded together, but never assembled into a complete album. The object is to get some practice with Martin's guidelines, and see what the attempt tells us about these tracks that might help explain why no such thing ever came about.

Recall that the vinyl releases associated with the film were well-received, but hardly worthy follow-ups to the magnum opus of the previous summer. Both were actually weak compromises.

In the UK, not wanting to gouge their fans or portray the music as on the same plane as *Sgt. Pepper*, the Beatles assembled and issued an innovative six-song double-EP, within a colorful and mysterious package. Despite their best efforts, it was a somewhat underwhelming release. It opened with the title track, but sort of trailed off at the end with "Blue Jay Way," feeling only half-finished.

In the US, marketing instincts prevailed, and a complete album was hobbled together, against the group's wishes. The double-EP's six tracks were placed on side one, and side two was a blank assembly of tracks from recent singles. Despite this dilution — fully six of the 11 tracks had been previously released — the album promptly went to number one.

From an assembly standpoint, it's interesting to note that the US and UK releases use different running orders for the new tracks. In fact, the booklet included with the double EP shows the lyrics in a different order from what was heard on the records. The US release follows the printed booklet, but the whole mess speaks to the disheveled nature of the product.

We will set both pseudo-assemblies aside and start anew.

Materials

For now, let's assume that they would have been aiming for a December 1967 release, at about the same time as the film eventually aired, if maybe a couple of weeks before that in order to make the Christmas gift-giving season. The list of materials available at that point would have looked like this:

9 / MAGIC MYST

B-180	"All Together Now" (Paul)
B-144	"Blue Jay Way" (George)
B-143	"Flying" (All)
B-142	"Fool on the Hill, The" (Paul)
B-138	"Hello, Goodbye" (Paul)
B-139	"I Am the Walrus" (John)
B-182	"It's All Too Much" (George)
B-140	"Magical Mystery Tour" (Paul)
B-179	"Only a Northern Song" (George)
B-141	"Your Mother Should Know" (Paul)

Note that this list does not include "Strawberry Fields Forever" or "Penny Lane" as these had been released nearly a year before. The Beatles were reportedly miffed at Capitol for including those tracks (in mock-stereo, no less) on their *Magical Mystery Tour* album because they had already been in circulation for such a long time. We will also assume that the group would have rejected "All You Need is Love" and "Baby, You're a Rich Man" since both had been released the previous summer. But we will keep these last two in our back pocket, just in case.

Ten songs is a little light for an album, but they do total around 35 minutes, which is directly comparable to *Revolver* and *Rubber Soul* in length, if a little less than *Sgt. Pepper*, which came in at 39 minutes. In those days, however, the number of songs was still the more important metric, at least in the UK.

A problem immediately becomes apparent, however, in the unacceptable imbalance among the voices. Not only is there no Ringo track, but John is relegated to only one new song, plus the group vocal on "Flying." This would simply never work, and argues immediately for pulling in the summer single, which is made up of two Lennon songs. It still gives John only three tracks to Paul's five, which would be placed next to George's bounty of three. This would have been a very atypical imbalance for a Beatles album.

To expand our options, we might consider the two known unreleased titles from the film. "Shirley's Wild Accordion" is a rather pleasant and lively instrumental definitely worth considering. "Jesse's Dream" is a sound collage, and is worth considering since we know the group would ultimately make a move in that direction on their next album. This also suggests that the famously unreleased "Carnival of Light" might have been available for a project like this. Given its unavailability, tossed-off nature, and the objections of both Georges, we'll leave it off the list for now. But we do have access to "You Know My Name (Look Up the Number)," which was in some unfinished state at that point, and perhaps could have been finished. So here is our "back pocket" list:

B-136	"All You Need Is Love" (John)
B-137	"Baby, You're a Rich Man" (John)
	"Jessie's Dream" (collage)
	"Shirley's Wild Accordion" (inst)
B-203	"You Know My Name…" (various)

Combined, it now looks like there might be enough here for an album, and it's quite an eclectic collection. But it probably would still have felt light to the Beatles, who had already decided that some of these tracks should stay in the can. So that would have forced them, and forces us, to postpone the release. Instead of trying for December, they will hold off until March so they can get in at least one more good session. That session, as we know, produced four significant tracks:

B-206	"Across the Universe" (John)
B-181	"Hey Bulldog" (John)
B-146	"Inner Light, The" (George)
B-145	"Lady Madonna" (Paul)

Let's pause here to acknowledge that this is a very odd spot in Beatle history. These four tracks clearly mark the moment that they moved on from psychedelia, perhaps because it has run its course, or perhaps because they had gotten bored, or perhaps because the TV film had been so poorly received. Regardless of the reason, these four tracks form an almost perfect bridge between the excessive studio indulgences of 1967 and the leaner, less precocious, more direct approach they would begin using for *The White Album* a few months later. As such, the music from this later session presents something of a problem to the task of creating a specifically "psychedelic" follow-up to *Sgt. Pepper*. In short, they just aren't quite "psychedelic" enough. We can use them only if they can be made to dovetail with the earlier material. Luckily, at least two of them will.

The full list now consists of about one hour of music in 19 tracks:

B-206	"Across the Universe" (John)
B-180	"All Together Now" (Paul)
B-136	"All You Need Is Love" (John)
B-137	"Baby, You're a Rich Man" (John)
B-144	"Blue Jay Way" (George)
B-143	"Flying" (All)
B-142	"Fool on the Hill, The" (Paul)
B-138	"Hello, Goodbye" (Paul)

9 / MAGIC MYST

B-181	"Hey Bulldog"	(John)
B-139	"I Am the Walrus"	(John)
B-146	"Inner Light, The"	(George)
B-182	"It's All Too Much"	(George)
	"Jessie's Dream"	(collage)
B-145	"Lady Madonna"	(Paul)
B-140	"Magical Mystery Tour"	(Paul)
B-179	"Only a Northern Song"	(George)
	"Shirley's Wild Accordion"	(inst)
B-203	"You Know My Name..."	(various)
B-141	"Your Mother Should Know"	(Paul)

Alas, there is still no Ringo track, and there will be none forthcoming in this era. But, thankfully, at least *some* parity has been restored. John now has five tracks in the list to Paul's six, and George has a remarkable four. Still, even a quick glance at the actual songs suggests that the apparent parity will be difficult to translate to a balanced finished product. Something will have to give.

Assembly

We begin assembly by looking for pole tracks, and can see that "Magical Mystery Tour" is the natural opener. No other options really exist. Potential closers are a little more difficult to identify. "All You Need Is Love" certainly is a possibility, but we will try to avoid it in deference to the Beatles' stated principles about reissues, and its incredibly high visibility as a single. Of the remaining tracks, only a couple really merit consideration, though none is a shoo-in.

"I Am the Walrus" perhaps looks inevitable, as the closest thing in this list to "A Day in the Life." Its tour-de-force nature does make it difficult to follow, but the fadeout is a bit too diffuse to serve as the final sound on the album, and would leave it feeling somewhat unresolved. After all, fans were fresh from that crashing chord at the end of *Sgt. Pepper*, which made it clear that the album was over, but lingered in partial fulfillment of every listener's wish that the album would never end. "Walrus" doesn't have that same effect, sounding more like an incomplete idea as it fades out, with full resolution still to come. Perhaps this could have been changed with a remix, but we cannot work with that possibility here.

"Across the Universe" may be a better choice, even though it ends with a similar fade. Given its mystical properties, the fade makes more sense, as if the song drifts off into the clouds, just as the lyrics evoke. The presence of birds flying away in that earliest version adds to this effect. At the least, it is highly self-contained, with no sense that it requires — or would benefit from — being followed by something else for resolution.[1] But the difficult problem is that it also does not sound of a piece with the rest of the music in this collection. It is, perhaps, too beautiful and — dare I say? — *conventional* in its beauty to sit comfortably with the rest of the experimental material here. Where all of the rest of this music is rather superficial, "Across the Universe" strikes at a much deeper place. Again, this suggests putting it at the very end, but for now we will consider it too foreign to work there, as if the Beatles would have regarded it more as a harbinger of things to come than an addendum to things which have been.

Among Paul's tracks, "Hello, Goodbye" presents itself as very flexible, and has the extended ending which, though also a fade, does at least feel like a conclusion. It might do as a closer. As something of a wild card option, "All Together Now" similarly has a sense of summation, though it might be too slight to take on the hefty role of album closer. Working in its favor is the last sound: the honk of a clown horn.

Clearly, though the closing slot is perhaps the most important, there is no obvious occupant. This alone suggests that we may be swimming in shallow waters here.

This is an important point, in terms of the process we will use later for deconstructing and reconstructing the solo materials: Certain basic criteria in quality, tone and temperament must be met in the music before an album can even be considered. The Beatles, via George Martin for the most part, were incredibly careful about beginnings and endings, and as we have seen, Martin was diligent in minimizing the negative impact of what he perceived as lesser tracks. But even before they could consider assembling an album, they themselves had to be convinced that there was enough quality music on the master reel. Unless they felt confident in that, it was back to the drawing board, where *somebody* always came up with *something*.

This principle may have played into the decision not to make a full album out of this material in the first place. Without the ability to create a coherent whole, it was better not to pretend. Though the double-EP isn't very satisfying, its format suggests that it won't be — right from the moment a buyer pulls it out of the record bin. In this case, the chosen format was used to set expectations carefully, something the US record company could not have cared less about.

The compromise solution for moving forward with here is to set aside both "All You Need" and "Across," then place John's "Walrus" opus in the penultimate spot, followed by a lighter release with "All Together Now." The latter ends with an accelerando, evoking one big party, capped with the aforementioned honk — which, in ending the album, comes off as a small, mischievous nod to the end of "A Day in the Life." It's a little hard to imagine the Beatles stopping there, however, so a short clip from "Shirley's Wild Accordion" will serve as a further wild card coda. The result sounds like a happy send-off to the psychedelic era, with no regrets.

---

[1] This factor also bedeviled its placement on *Let It Be*, and will be addressed more fully in the last proof-of-concept project, found in the next chapter.

9 / MAGIC MYST

1A. Magical Mystery Tour (P)	
...	

...	
2X. I Am the Walrus (J)	
2Y. All Together Now (P)	
2Z. CODA: Shirley's Wild Accordion	

Across the Universe (J)
All You Need Is Love (J)
Baby, You're a Rich Man (J)
Blue Jay Way (G)
Flying (B)
The Fool on the Hill (P)
Hello, Goodbye (P)
Hey Bulldog (J)
The Inner Light (G)
It's All Too Much (G)
Jessie's Dream
Lady Madonna (P)
Only a Northern Song (G)
You Know My Name... (B)
Your Mother Should Know (P)

We turn next to extending the opening, and filling the other two pole tracks.

Both of the actual releases — the UK double-EP and the US album — leave the opener hanging, with essentially no extension. Each follows it with another Paul track, something which was allowed — as long as no more than two songs by the same composer were placed together — but generally avoided whenever possible. In this case, the lack of John contributions probably made that necessary, but neither option is very good. The EP uses "Your Mother Should Know," while the album uses "Fool on the Hill." In the case of the latter, owing to the influence of marketing, this is likely an indicator of which track the record company thought was the second most commercial. The Beatles actually indicate something similar by having "Fool" open the second disc, in effect using it as the equivalent of a double-EP pole track. We can see that priorities were similar on both sides of the Atlantic, but methodologies differed significantly.

In the context of a psychedelic album, it makes much more sense to use one of George's freaky, experimental tracks — even if their quality is somewhat suspect — to extend the opener. The most natural follower to the title track turns out to be "Only a Northern Song," the beginning of which makes for a nice segue from the mysterious final sounds of "Magical Mystery Tour," and the tempo of which maintains its energy. This track was ultimately relegated to *Yellow Submarine*, for obvious reasons, but it works well enough in this spot, mostly because it successfully extends the weirdness, especially in its closing moments. It brings about a one-two punch of pure psychedelia to begin the album.

Looking for an opener to side two, we are led to either "Hello, Goodbye" or "Hey Bulldog." It is tempting to think that "The Inner Light" could also fill that spot, but it has a very different sensibility than "Within You Without You," and putting it there would feel too much like *Sgt. Pepper* — something this track couldn't live up to.

"The Fool on the Hill" might also seem like a possibility, but it is too pensive to properly fill a spot which requires more boldness.

Somewhat arbitrarily then, we will go with "Hey Bulldog," owing primarily to the difficulty in finding a better spot for its powerful riff, which will now make a great, strong statement to open the second act. It can be easily followed by George's "It's All Too Much," which starts with an exclamation from Lennon, but builds into a powerful track that is owed a feature position (even as an edit might be appropriate).

That connection would have become apparent while our Assembler was reviewing these tracks in isolation, as would another. Both the EP and the original album feature "Flying" followed by "Blue Jay Way." On the EP, however, a flip of the disc is required between the two, rather nonsensically breaking up what is otherwise a seamless segue. These are both lesser tracks, and the instrumental must be placed in such a way as to minimize the sense that it is filler. According to George Martin's rules, these probably belong in the middle of side two. But somehow the sequence feels like it really belongs *before* "Hey Bulldog," maybe because the latter feels like a turning of the page. Instead, we will try it in the middle of side one.

Perhaps "Blue Jay Way" could close out the side, but it would do so with a whimper. Basically, the only side closer left now is the versatile "Hello, Goodbye," so it will be slotted there.

1A. Magical Mystery Tour (P)	Across the Universe (J)
1B. Only a Northern Song (G)	All You Need Is Love (J)
. . .	Baby, You're a Rich Man (J)
1M. Flying (B)	The Fool on the Hill (P)
1N. Blue Jay Way (G)	The Inner Light (G)
. . .	Jessie's Dream
1Z. Hello, Goodbye (P)	Lady Madonna (P)
	You Know My Name... (B)
	Your Mother Should Know (P)
2A. Hey Bulldog (J)	
2B. It's All Too Much (G)	
. . .	
2X. I Am the Walrus (J)	
2Y. All Together Now (P)	
2Z. CODA: Shirley's Wild Accordion	

We are left with some holes that need filling, and it is a matter of matching the remaining titles to those holes, hopefully in logical pairings.

If it must be used, McCartney's obligatory music hall number, "Your Mother Should Know," probably belongs on side two, as a counterbalance to the heaviness of the opening. It ends up sounding just fine as a balance to George's chunky rocker.

Including "The Inner Light" would make this the third Beatles album in a row with an overtly Indian track. From their decision to drop it onto the B-side of a single, it seems like the Beatles by this point had moved beyond this as a part of their formula — determined as they were to never succumb to *any* formula. But if we are true to the charter of creating a psychedelic follow-up to *Sgt. Pepper*, it feels like "The Inner Light" must have a place. Its instrumentation yields a much less tranquil sound than its siblings, but the lyric is every bit as graceful. We will slot it into side two to connect "Mother" and "Walrus." The connection actually makes "Walrus" sound even more striking, since the listener's ear is hoping for a return to western sensibility after George's musical travels.

Only one track remains which simply *must* appear on this album, so "The Fool on the Hill" will have to find a place on side one. In both of the original releases, it is used to set up "Flying," and that seems to be a sufficient connection. But that puts us in a position where side one does not yet include a track by Lennon. This would have been unthinkable. Having eliminated "All You Need is Love" and "Across the Universe," we are left with slotting "Baby You're a Rich Man" onto the album, despite the fact that it had already appeared on a B-side. We will justify this by telling the truth: Fans bought that single because of its A-side, and the flip probably got significantly less listens. The Beatles actually did this with "I Am the Walrus," making it the B-side of "Hello, Goodbye," but then also slotting it on the longer release, while the A-side was left off.

This dilemma illustrates well the problems of building a successful running order. The natural next step would be to give in, break the rules, and retrieve "All You Need is Love." But it quickly throws a monkey wrench into all of the sequencing decisions made so far. It would need to be slotted last, as previously mentioned, but would stand there alone, and knock everything else into different, potentially less natural positions. Placing it at the end of side one also seems like a possibility, but it has the potential to feel like an ending, relegating the tracks of side two to the realm of afterthoughts.

Capitol's marketers had no qualms about putting it at the end of their album, without caring how it is set up. In fact, "Baby You're a Rich Man" makes a *terrible* setup, and feels like an interloper on a side of much more substantial music. This is unfortunate because even though it doesn't have the heft of the other tracks, "Baby" is still a fine example of late psychedelia, worthy of better treatment.

The relevant fact here is that "All You Need is Love" is a quintessential *single*. It is self-contained, and strong enough to need nothing around it. Indeed, anything placed around it simultaneously is diminished, and diminishes it. "Baby You're a Rich Man," on the other hand, is a quintessential *album track*. It needs to be contextualized, and though it might not elevate the music around it, it can be elevated by proper placement.

On *Magic Myst*, therefore, we will place "Baby You're a Rich Man" between "Only a Northern Song" and "Fool on the Hill," filling a gap, solving a parity problem (at least partially), and allowing it to be elevated by the music which surrounds it.

Thus, the final hole turns out to not be a hole at all. Despite the fact that the connection was serendipitous, "Hello, Goodbye" turns out to flow naturally from the end of "Blue Jay Way," and there is no hole left in anyone's pocket.

1A.	Magical Mystery Tour (P)	
1B.	Only a Northern Song (G)	
1F.	**Baby You're a Rich Man (J)**	
1G.	**The Fool on the Hill (P)**	
1M.	Flying (B)	
1N.	Blue Jay Way (G)	
1Z.	Hello, Goodbye (P)	
2A.	Hey Bulldog (J)	
2B.	It's All Too Much (G)	
2M.	**Your Mother Should Know (P)**	
2N.	**The Inner Light (G)**	
2X.	I Am the Walrus (J)	
2Y.	All Together Now (P)	
2Z.	CODA: Shirley's Wild Accordion	

Across the Universe (J)
All You Need Is Love (J)
Jessie's Dream
Lady Madonna (P)
You Know My Name... (B)

One final issue also illustrates a critical aspect of assembly. At this point, side two runs right around 23 minutes, while side one runs only 21. The two minute difference could simply be ignored, and might have been, but George Martin and the Beatles would have seen an opportunity, and tried to do something to bring the two sides closer together in length. Martin has specific reasons for doing this (see chapter 5), but it was hardly necessary, especially having reached the magic number of 14 tracks on the album.

Given their propensity for wild card tracks, and the burgeoning interest in sound collages, this feels like a job for "Jessie's Dream." Ninety seconds or so from the end of the track is all that is needed to balance the side lengths, and it can be tacked on to the end of "Hello, Goodbye," like an extended fadeout, without being credited as a separate song. It further reinforces the album's psychedelic charter, and daylights one of the curiosities that otherwise would have remained in the Abbey Road vault.

Two other tracks are left on the original pile, but neither "Lady Madonna" nor "You Know My Name (Look Up the Number)" has any place on the same disc with most of this music. Each would have found other outlets, just as they eventually did.

Magic Myst
Principal Recording: April 1967 - March 1968
Release: March 1968

Side One
1. Magical Mystery Tour (Lennon/McCartney)
2. Only a Northern Song (Harrison)
3. Baby You're a Rich Man (Lennon/McCartney)
4. The Fool on the Hill (Lennon/McCartney)
5. Flying (Lennon/McCartney/Harrison/Starkey)
6. Blue Jay Way (Harrison)
7. Hello, Goodbye (Lennon/McCartney)

Side Two
1. Hey Bulldog (Lennon/McCartney)
2. It's All Too Much (Harrison)
3. Your Mother Should Know (Lennon/McCartney)
4. The Inner Light (Harrison)
5. I Am the Walrus (Lennon/McCartney)
6. All Together Now (Lennon/McCartney)
7. Coda: Shirley's Wild Accordion (Lennon/McCartney)

Make It Yourself
Total Running Time: 45:44

Tk	Rill	Title	Source	Dur
C1-A1	—	Magical Mystery Tour	[1]	2:44
C1-A2	(1.8)	Only a Northern Song	[2]	3:19
C1-A3	(3.1)	Baby You're a Rich Man	[1]	2:55
C1-A4	(2.5)	The Fool on the Hill	[1]	2:56
C1-A5	0.8	Flying	[1]	2:05
C1-A6	(8.6)	Blue Jay Way	[1]	3:51
C1-A7a	0	Hello, Goodbye	[1]	N/A
C1-A7b	*	Jessie's Dream	[U]	4:59

Total: 22:52

Tk	Rill	Title	Source	Dur
C1-B1	—	Hey Bulldog	[3]	3:08
C1-B2	0	It's All Too Much	[3]	6:14
C1-B3	(5.7)	Your Mother Should Know	[1]	2:24
C1-B4	(1.1)	The Inner Light	[4]	2:33
C1-B5	0	I Am the Walrus	[5]	4:32
C1-B6	0	All Together Now	[3]	2:08
C1-B7	*	Shirley's Wild Accordion	[U]	1:52

Total: 22:52

[U] Unreleased (Seek on YouTube)
[1] *Magical Mystery Tour*
[2] Seek the version from *Yellow Submarine Songtrack*
[3] *Yellow Submarine*
[4] *Past Masters, Volume Two*
[5] Seek the 2012 full stereo version

*NOTE: Descriptions of edits and crossfades, with sample audio, are available at **SaveTheBeatles.com**.

Discussion

Having carefully assembled this album as a follow-up to *Sgt. Pepper*, we must engage in *review*: Is it any good? More specifically: Would it have been good enough for the Beatles and George Martin? Would this have been a better use for the material from an abandoned *Magical Mystery Tour* film? Your answer to these questions will depend largely on how attached you are to the original releases, and/or the assembly principles which gave us the classic albums.

9 / Magic Myst

Clearly, there is some dead wood in this forest. George's experimental excesses attempt to conceal the fact that neither his songwriting nor his singing is mature. He has intonation problems, structural problems, and melodic problems in three of his four tracks. The exception, "The Inner Light," while satisfying enough on its own, sounds a little bit uncomfortable next to the other music. There are good arguments to be made for that track being best used as a B-side.

One thing that becomes clear from this assembly it that Paul and John diverged, with John showing signs of fatigue from the psychedelic techniques, and Paul continuing to write to the form. Only with "Lady Madonna" does Paul turn the corner that John had started to turn with "All You Need is Love," where the excesses were beginning to be boiled away (even as their echoes rang on).

John's fatigue obviously extends beyond just psychedelic stylings. His writing here is perfunctory, automatic, uninspired — which he himself admitted. Always restless, he has simply moved on from the 1967 trip, while the rest of the band can be heard running out the string. Had this material actually been collected in this fashion, there is almost no doubt that he would have written more songs, and that would have changed things in ways we cannot imagine. As it is, his voice is uncharacteristically muted, which speaks volumes about this era in the band's narrative.

Magic Myst obviously has no unifying concept, nor does it even suggest that possibility. This would likely have been a disappointment to fans, though certainly not as disappointing as the film actually was. But the dominance of Paul might not have, in itself, been much of a problem. From a fan's perspective, dominance in the group was never an issue as long as they got *something* from their favorite Beatle — only a problem here if yours was Ringo.

Without the film as context, however, there is less of a difference in the perception of these tracks than you might first imagine. In the film, or rather *films* — because you can actually include the *Yellow Submarine* film in this — the songs were not used to advance any narrative. Each was used as a simple set piece in what was essentially a collection of under-developed, intentionally obtuse, psychedelic set pieces. Removed from that very slight context, they don't lose much — if anything.

But they also do not gain very much by being collected in this fashion. Even when segues are smooth and natural, the material itself is so slight as to float away like the album's namesake magic myst — like a fog upon L. A., indeed. Momentum is difficult to create with this collection of tracks, and there is precious little *motion* in the resulting album from beginning to end.

In short, even without the failure of the film, this music was not going to make things right. The best thing the Beatles could have done at this point was probably to lay low, which would have been tough given the pressures surrounding them.

Before moving on, let's look briefly at another possible scenario.

Flying

One final question worth asking is whether the above assembly actually represents the best possible use of all the available music. The answer is simple: It does not. In fact, it is constrained by principles which the Beatles and George Martin had adopted, namely that tracks released as singles do not belong on albums, and balance among the Beatle voices is important. So, without belaboring the point, let's suppose that we decide (or are pressured into deciding) that the two Lennon masterworks we set aside earlier simply *must* go on this album, regardless of temperament or prior release. The list of source materials is therefore unchanged, but the assembly process looks very different.

The album will still start with the same prologue, but then we must choose between two complicated options for the finale. "Across the Universe" would win that battle, based on its overall heft and the presence of the better lyric and a meaningful mysticism, relegating "All You Need is Love" to the end of side one. The goal of properly setting up each track then yields only one preferred option. The spacey noises at the end of "Flying" best sets up "All You Need," even thought it might also seem useful before "Across." There, however, it would make for a weak penultimate album track — something of a blank space when some sort of statement to precede John's would be more in order. In that spot, therefore, we must use "Fool" instead, allowing Paul's song a pensive feature position, where his voice can resonate through proximity to John's, owing also to the fact that the song is simpatico with the ideas that John will give us.

But that boots the album closers chosen above in the first round, which now need new homes. It turns out that "Walrus" can actually extend the opener, moving "Northern" to third. And if we use "Blue Jay" to set up "Flying" (instead of following it), we have only a small gap yet to fill on side one. Either "Your Mother" or "All Together" could fill that gap, and we will use the latter as it is less cloying, and does foreshadow one of Paul's ad libs in "All You Need."

Side two can begin the same way as it did in the other lineup, with the strong statements of "Bulldog" and "Too Much," but then we must deal with remaining tracks that still need homes. The trio we must use is more slight, but the middle of side two is where weaker tracks belong, and this is about the best we can do with what we have. Ultimately, "The Inner Light" serves rather well to set up "Fool," while the remaining two are sequenced somewhat arbitrarily. Thus, in this lineup, the unreleased tracks remain unreleased.

9 / MAGIC MYST

1A. Magical Mystery Tour (P)	Jessie's Dream
1B. I Am the Walrus (J)	Lady Madonna (P)
1C. Only a Northern Song (G)	Shirley's Wild Accordion
1M. All Together Now (P)	You Know My Name... (B)
1X. Blue Jay Way (G)	Your Mother Should Know (P)
1Y. Flying (B)	
1Z. All You Need Is Love (J)	

- 2A. Hey Bulldog (J)
- 2B. It's All Too Much (G)
- 2M. Hello, Goodbye (P)
- 2N. Baby, You're a Rich Man (J)
- 2X. The Inner Light (G)
- 2Y. The Fool on the Hill (P)
- 2Z. Across the Universe (J)

Clearly, this is the better lineup, and comes much closer to the idea of a powerful psychedelic follow-up to *Sgt. Pepper*. But it needs to break some of the self-imposed rules to do so. The Beatles weren't much for rules, of course, but they would have needed to get past George Martin, and this is the biggest sticking point because, even in this better assembly, the finished product might have felt to the world like a pale descendent of its predecessor — unless the packaging provided better framing.

More importantly, the lesson learned here is that assembling an album is less like doing a jigsaw puzzle and more like doing a crossword. In the first, you know what the finished image will look like, and merely need to find the right location for each piece. In the second, you start with clues and empty boxes. Each box serves at least two purposes, and all parts are thoroughly intertwined. Make a mistake in one spot, and it could cost you dearly in another.

Maybe an even better analogy is those little puzzles with sliding numbered tiles, where the goal is to get all the numbers in proper sequence. With each move something else may be bumped to an undesirable spot, and what you are seeking is the magic sequence of moves by which everything falls in the right place.

In George Martin's careful style of sequencing, decisions in one place have ramifications across the entire project, and the game is to suss those out and finesse every portion until it gives the best result. Each decision must serve both the music and the listener — indeed, serving the former is the only way to serve the latter.

Whether those decisions result in the best possible finished product is certainly a subjective matter. In the end, not everyone will agree, but the important takeaway is that the assembler of an album has critical power to influence the listener's perceptions, and that often involves decisions that the casual listener might not even realize had to be made.

Flying

Side One
1. Magical Mystery Tour
2. I Am the Walrus
3. Only a Northern Song
4. All Together Now
5. Blue Jay Way
6. Flying
7. All You Need Is Love

Side Two
1. Hey Bulldog
2. It's All Too Much
3. Hello, Goodbye
4. Baby, You're a Rich Man
5. The Inner Light
6. The Fool on the Hill
7. Across the Universe

Make It Yourself
Total Running Time: 47:48

Tk	Rill	Title	Source	Dur
C1 C2-A1	—	Magical Mystery Tour	[1]	2:44
C2-A2	0	I Am the Walrus	[2]	4:32
C2-A3	0	Only a Northern Song	[3]	3:20
C2-A4	0	All Together Now	[4]	2:06
C2-A5	0	Blue Jay Way	[1]	3:51
C2-A6	0	Flying	[1]	2:13
C2-A7	0	All You Need Is Love	[1]	3:48

Total: 22:37

Tk	Rill	Title	Source	Dur
C2-B1	—	Hey Bulldog	[4]	3:08
C2-B2	0	It's All Too Much	[4]	6:14
C2-B3	(5.8)	Hello, Goodbye	[1]	3:24
C2-B4	0	Baby You're a Rich Man	[1]	2:55
C2-B5	0	The Inner Light	[5]	2:35
C2-B6	2.0	The Fool on the Hill	[1]	2:55
C2-B7	0	Across the Universe	[6]	3:58

Total: 25:11

[1] *Magical Mystery Tour*
[2] Seek the 2012 full stereo version
[3] Seek the version from *Yellow Submarine Songtrack*
[4] *Yellow Submarine*
[5] *Past Masters, Volume Two*
[6] *Past Masters, Volume Two*, original speed restored (104% to D Major)

*NOTE: Descriptions of edits and crossfades, with sample audio, are available at **SaveTheBeatles.com**.

Proof-of-Concept #3

January 1969 – January 1970

January

Introduction

    The Beatles' rehearsals and recording sessions of January 1969 may be the most misunderstood and unfairly maligned in their entire history. While it's undeniable that both the resulting album and film were disappointing, that isn't the fault of the songwriting, or singing, or playing — which are all uniformly excellent. Indeed, many of the finished songs are widely regarded as classics. It isn't the fault of the project's central concept, which even George Martin agreed was "a fantastic idea."[1] It isn't even the fault of the alleged "bad vibes," which people who were there, including Glyn Johns, say have been vastly overstated.

    What is at fault, quite simply, is exceedingly poor assembly. For our third and final proof-of-concept project, we will collect the materials recorded in and around January of 1969 and attempt to apply George Martin's principles of assembly to the one Beatles album he never got to touch. As you might imagine, it turns out that there is a great album still waiting to be found in these tracks, and it will take Martin's techniques to bring it out.

    Famously, the Beatles had set about making an album of them playing *together* like they had in the old days, and that's exactly what they did during the sessions. It worked remarkably well, and the resulting tracks sound like nothing else they had recorded in recent years. Though they initially thought they would rehearse and record the new songs live in front of an audience, that aspect wasn't really required to accomplish the underlying goal.

    Unfortunately, there were actually *two* underlying goals, one held by Paul McCartney and the other held by John Lennon, which were subtly different and caused confusion throughout the project. Where Paul wanted the Beatles to record *like they used to* — i.e. playing together as a band — John wanted the Beatles to record *like they used to* — i.e. without excessive studio "trickery." It's a subtle, but crucial, distinction. To Paul, the project was about renewing camaraderie and rebuilding the old Beatle Magic. To John, the project was about a return to immediacy and "honesty" in recording. Though not exactly incompatible goals, the divergence haunts the project to this day.

    It is what happened *after* the sessions ended, however, that truly doomed the music. Instead of polishing the recordings in mixing, and pushing toward the goal of creating a collection worthy of their name, the Beatles punted. They gave Glyn Johns two shots at doing the job for them, but he was caught between multiple charters —

---

[1] Indeed, it was an echo of his very first idea for recording the band, which did not come to pass, but would have involved transporting recording equipment to the Cavern Club in Liverpool in 1963.

yet another charter imposed the idea of showing the Beatles in the studio, "warts and all" — and assembled albums which met none.

Then they dumped it all on an outside producer who had no business trying to fix a broken Beatles project. Though conventional wisdom has it that Phil Spector "rescued" the *Get Back* project into *Let It Be*, that is obviously a dubious claim because almost all of his creative decisions were exactly wrong. He added inappropriate orchestrations, rushed through unskilled and insensitive mixing, retained unnecessary studio scruff, and sequenced the tracks in the worst way.

Further dooming the album in post-production, graphic designer John Kosh created funereal packaging that — somewhat intentionally — made the project feel like a tombstone.[2] Even the marketing hyperbole on the back cover touting the record as beginning a "new phase" reads like an excuse, doing no favors to the music.

Perhaps worst of all, Michael Lindsay-Hogg and his editing team turned the documentary film into an elegy for a band which had not, in fact, broken up. Indeed, his rough edit of the film, which the group screened together in July of 1969, may have actually helped push them over the edge.

What they might have done instead with the album is what they actually did with two of its singles. Paul McCartney and Glyn Johns polished the rooftop recording of "Get Back" until it shone like a diamond. No one who bought that single would have ever guessed the conditions under which it was recorded. Later, George Martin and the engineers at Abbey Road applied their considerable skills to "Let It Be," retroactively supplying the typical Beatle sheen to a track recorded live in a wild studio still under construction. In each case, the versions released as singles sound nothing like Spector's later, clumsy mixes, and demonstrate that respectability for the individual *Get Back* tracks was only ever a careful remix away.

Better mixes alone, however, would not have resulted in better assembly. For that, we need to engage the artist who knew the Beatles best, and how to get the most out of everything they recorded.

Materials

Though the Beatles famously recorded snippets of many, many songs during the sessions in January 1969, the vast majority were never considered candidates to make the final album. As they jammed, however, the Beatles gradually began to identify songs which were original, complete, and good enough to work on. These nine titles will form the core of our materials list, and are discernible from the set list for the rooftop concert, together with related studio sessions.

---

[2] "Beatles Art Director on Secrets of the 'Abbey Road' Cover" David Browne, *Rolling Stone*, August 9, 2019

In order to guarantee George Harrison a presence on the project, his 12-bar blues original, "For You Blue," was plucked from an earlier session. Alas, no equivalent track exists for Ringo.

The *Get Back* Nine

B-192 "Dig a Pony" (John)
B-189 "Don't Let Me Down" (John)
B-185 "For You Blue" (George)
B-188 "Get Back" (Paul)
B-190 "I've Got a Feeling" (John/Paul)
B-193 "Let It Be" (Paul)
B-187 "The Long and Winding Road" (Paul)
B-191 "One After 909" (John/Paul)
B-194 "Two of Us" (Paul)

Altogether, however, those nine tracks total only about 30 minutes of music — really not enough for a full album in 1969. This problem, compounded at one point by the removal of "Don't Let Me Down" for use as a B-side, beset all attempts to turn the material into a full album, and resulted in the unfortunate addition of obvious padding in each version.

The *Get Back* Scruff

"Dig It"
"Get Back (Reprise)"
"Maggie Mae"
"Rocker"
"Save the Last Dance for Me"
"Teddy Boy" (demo)

Working from Martin's playbook, we will resolve not to use anything which smacks of filler, eliminating all of this scruff from consideration. Further, recognizing that crispness and polish would best serve this particular collection of recordings, Martin would have insisted that this not be some sort of *audio vérité* document of the sessions, but scrubbed to perfection. As such, all of the studio banter would have been removed without hesitation.

Helping things is the fact that the filmmakers eventually identified two additional songs which would be featured in the film, and asked that they also be featured on the album. This adds the significant tracks, "Across the Universe" and "I Me Mine," to the pool.[3] Now, with 11 tracks available, we have about 36 minutes of music — enough in minutes, but still a little light in tracks. The Beatles clearly could have gotten away with this, but two more tracks became available before the album would have been assembled.

---

[3] In this experiment, we are disregarding the proofs-of-concept, *Magic Myst* and *Flying*.

The stellar single "Ballad of John and Yoko," backed with "Old Brown Shoe," was recorded in mid-April 1969, and though neither track was part of the *Get Back* project, they are both simpatico with the tone of the material.

If we wanted to look further, there are many other songs referenced in the movie which might be considered. But this needlessly complicates things. This is enough music, and the right music, for the project which they undertook in January of 1969. So the assembly begins with this list:

  B-150 "Across the Universe" (John)
  B-195 "The Ballad of John and Yoko" (John)
  B-192 "Dig a Pony" (John)
  B-189 "Don't Let Me Down" (John)
  B-185 "For You Blue" (George)
  B-188 "Get Back" (Paul)
  B-212 "I Me Mine" (John)
  B-190 "I've Got a Feeling" (John/Paul)
  B-193 "Let It Be" (Paul)
  B-187 "The Long and Winding Road" (Paul)
  B-197 "Old Brown Shoe" (George)
  B-191 "One After 909" (John/Paul)
  B-194 "Two of Us" (Paul)

Not a bad collection at all, and even a cursory glance at the lyric sheets for these songs reveals a pretty clear theme: comings, goings, movement, travel, pathways, wandering, restlessness, seeking, and even disorientation.

"I'm traveling on that line…"
"I'd hate to miss the train…All these years I've been wandering around…"
"Get back to where you once belonged…"
"You can penetrate any place you go…"
"…so glad you came here…"
"The long and winding road…will never disappear"
"Two of us riding nowhere… Two of us Sunday driving…"
"On our way back home…We're going home."
"You and I have memories longer than the road that stretches out ahead…"
"Caught the early train back to London…"
"They call me on and on… They tumble blindly as they make their way…"

Though certainly not a robust "concept" for an album, it is an important undercurrent running through everything, which might be used in some way as a unifier. Indeed, the month in which the bulk of this album was recorded is named after Janus, the Roman god of doors, transitions and new beginnings.

Assembly

No less than four attempts have been made to turn this material into something worthy of the Beatle brand — five if you count the second disc of *Anthology 3*. None of them really works, and for good reasons.

GET BACK/LET IT BE VERSIONS

Get Back (1) Glyn Johns, May 1969	***Get Back*** (2) Glyn Johns, Jan 1970	***Let It Be*** Phil Spector, May 1970	***Let It Be…Naked*** Paul McCartney, Nov 2003
Side One 1. "One After 909" 2. "Rocker" 3. "Save the Last Dance…" 4. "Don't Let Me Down" 5. "Dig a Pony" 6. "I've Got a Feeling" 7. "Get Back"	**Side One** 1. "One After 909" 2. "Rocker" 3. "Save the Last Dance…" 4. "Don't Let Me Down" 5. "Dig a Pony" 6. "I've Got a Feeling" 7. "Get Back" 8. "Let It Be"	**Side One** 1. "Two of Us" 2. "Dig a Pony" 3. "Across the Universe" 4. "I Me Mine" 5. "Dig It" 6. "Let It Be" 7. "Maggie Mae"	**Side One** 1. "Get Back" 2. "Dig a Pony" 3. "For You Blue" 4. "Long and Winding…" 5. "Two of Us" 6. "I've Got a Feeling"
Side Two 1. "For You Blue" 2. "Teddy Boy" 3. "Two of Us" 4. "Maggie Mae" 5. "Dig It" 6. "Let It Be" 7. "Long and Winding…" 8. "Get Back (Reprise)"	**Side Two** 1. "For You Blue" 2. "Two of Us" 3. "Maggie Mae" 4. "Dig It" 5. "Long and Winding…" 6. "I Me Mine" 7. "Across the Universe" 8. "Get Back (Reprise)"	**Side Two** 1. "I've Got a Feeling" 2. "One After 909" 3. "Long and Winding…" 4. "For You Blue" 5. "Get Back"	**Side Two** 1. "One After 909" 2. "Don't Let Me Down" 3. "I Me Mine" 4. "Across the Universe" 5. "Let It Be"
	Drops: "Teddy Boy" **Adds:** "I Me Mine" "Across the Universe"	**Drops:** "Rocker" "Save the Last Dance…" "Don't Let Me Down"	**Restores:** "Don't Let Me Down" **Drops:** "Dig It" "Maggie Mae"
Running time: 42:26 Music: 28:52 Chatter: 3:35 Filler: 9:59	Running time: 43:58 Music: 33:48 Chatter: 3:47 Filler: 6:23	Running time: 34:42 Music: 32:00 Chatter: 1:21 Filler: 1:21	Running time: 34:58 Music: 34:58 Chatter: — Filler: —

Our Assembler begins by discarding any notion of *audio vérité*. All of the studio chatter will be removed, and these tracks will be polished extensively to sound finished and wholly professional. Care in mixing can mitigate a lot of sins.

This can and would be done with integrity, in the same way the "Get Back" and "Let It Be" singles were polished. No rules about overdubbing or studio "trickery" need to be broken — beyond the degree to which they already were by the Beatles themselves. Remember that the "no overdubs" policy was always somewhat tongue-in-cheek, and broken by the Beatles on multiple tracks.

Second, the running order will adhere to the strict principles George Martin has always used for the Beatles. The curiously disappointing *Let It Be...Naked* demonstrates plainly that merely scrubbing the tracks of Spector's work and remixing them in the same "warts and all" manner does not eliminate the problems. It inadvertently confirms yet again that sequencing matters.

This assembly starts, like all others, with an attempt to locate the proper pole tracks. This isn't really as hard as the project's reputation would suggest. Truth be told, there is only one track in this collection which can reasonably be considered an opener, and Glyn Johns found it: "One After 909." It is upbeat, optimistic, and features strong vocal and instrumental performances from everyone involved. It also features John and Paul singing lead together, which had become a rarity by this point, but is always a delight. The song also has the advantage of provenance, being a remake of a song from their earliest days. It makes a wonderful first sound for the album, better than anything else on the list.

Further, if the album is generally to be about beginnings and endings, openings and closings, and movement from one place to another — which the lyrics strongly suggest — then there could hardly be a better choice of opener than a song about train travel written in their pre-Fab days. It properly sets the stage for the "concept" which will inhabit the album.

Three tracks present themselves as potential album closers. "The Long and Winding Road" has the benefit of sentiment, but would leave a too-sticky feeling here, just as it does at the end of the "blue" greatest hits package. It is definitely good enough to be a pole track, and does contain a sense of closure, so we will slot it instead at the end of side one. "Let It Be" has a strong enough anthemic quality, and does come to a real close (rather than a fade), but isn't especially hard to follow. As the closer of *Let It Be...Naked*, it leaves the album feeling incomplete. But, like many McCartney tracks, "Let It Be" is very versatile, and could work in many different spots in the sequence. We will hold that one out for the time being.

Instead, to close the album properly, we will turn to the one track that *is* difficult to follow, being grand in scope but plaintive in quality, while also arguably the most substantial work on the album. Though perhaps not as obvious a choice for album closer as "A Day in the Life" was, "Across the Universe" has a mystical quality which drifts off dreamily at the end, beautifully symbolizing the ultimate motion — from somewhere to everywhere. The sound of birds taking flight, from the original mix by George Martin, makes the perfect send-off, a realization of all the talk of movement.

Glyn Johns also realized the value of this track, and placed it as the penultimate song on his second version of the album. Regrettably, he followed it with a sloppy "reprise" of "Get Back" that muted its effect, but he at least got partway there. His line-up might have been improved if he had taken a lesson from Martin and moved the reprise to *before* Lennon's powerful closer, as on *Sgt. Pepper*. But that earlier reprise was a tight restatement of the album's central theme, performed in a different fashion. This one is just more of the same. It adds nothing, while also being overly sloppy. It is best left in the can.

As we look for the remaining pole track, the opener for side two, it's worth noting that "I Me Mine" is a classic "problem" track, in that it will require the most careful placement of any song on the album. Wherever it ends up, it will have a large effect on the tracks which surround it, and poor placement will yield undesirable results. This is not to say that it is in some way a "lesser" track, which is clearly not the case, but its sentiments are tricky. It has the potential to sour whatever it follows, and certainly will at least *frame* whatever follows it — unless the following track can serve as a direct response.

In Phil Spector's formulation, "I Me Mine" sours a wasted "Across the Universe" in the dead space at the middle of side one. He then uses a piece of light filler to provide some distance from what follows, which could then be just about anything. We will pick up on something Spector teed up but missed.

If you simply remove "Dig It" from between the two tracks, you discover something miraculous. "Let It Be" is essentially the perfect response to "I Me Mine," while also being in a relative key.[4] The resulting segue makes an incredible moment of heightened tension followed by welcome release. Each track gains strength.

But the problem of how to set up "I Me Mine" remains, and there is no good solution. Since it is strong enough to be a pole track, not right to open the album, and would benefit from some space between it and whatever precedes it, we will slot it in as the opener for side two, with Paul's masterwork in tow. This solves the problem nicely, and also allows some essential space after "The Long and Winding Road."

1A. One After 909 (J/P)	Ballad of John and Yoko (J)
. . .	Dig a Pony (J)
	Don't Let Me Down (J)
1Z. Long and Winding Road (P)	For You Blue (G)
	Get Back (P)
2A. I Me Mine (J)	I've Got a Feeling (J/P)
2B. Let It Be (P)	Old Brown Shoe (G)
. . .	Two of Us (P)
2Z. Across the Universe (J)	

Next, we turn to ways to extend the album opener and set up the two closers.

Only one track is entirely simpatico with the album's opener. "I've Got a Feeling" also features John and Paul singing lead together, albeit in a variation they have never used before: singing two different but intertwined melodies simultaneously.

---

[4] The A minor of "I Me Mine" to the C Major of "Let It Be."

Happily, the track's loose feel makes a nice contrast to the tightness of "One After 909." It also can lead us right to another track which extends the feel, namely Paul's "Get Back" — which happens to be in the same key. The three songs together find the Lennon/McCartney songwriting team at both ends of their joint career, something which was clearly on their mind, based on their choice of cover photo for *Get Back*.

Setting up our selected closer turns out to be more difficult. Nothing jumps out of the list, and it's actually better to move on than try to solve this now.

Properly setting up "The Long and Winding Road" requires some care. Whatever it is must be, at least in some way, the absolute opposite. It cannot be weepy, or even pensive, and also must be faster. This eliminates "Don't Let Me Down" and "Two of Us." It should not be another Paul song, but something at least reasonably close in concept, to avoid a too-jarring transition. Only one track really fits these parameters, and happily it is John's own long and winding travelogue, "The Ballad of John and Yoko," which works very well in that spot.

After the heavy one-two punch that begins side two, something light is in order. Of the remaining tracks, "For You Blue" is the best to fit that bill.

1A. One After 909 (J/P)	Dig a Pony (J)
1B. I've Got a Feeling (J/P)	Don't Let Me Down (J)
1C. Get Back (P)	Old Brown Shoe (G)
. . .	Two of Us (P)
1Y. Ballad of John and Yoko (J)	
1Z. Long and Winding Road (P)	

2A. I Me Mine (J)
2B. Let It Be (P)
2C. For You Blue (G)
. . .
2Z. Across the Universe (J)

This leaves us with two holes in the running order, and four songs with which to fill them. Believe it or not, there are only a couple of ways that these four tracks can be configured that will actually show each in its best light.

"Dig a Pony" can't really be paired very well with either "Two of Us" or "Don't Let Me Down." Frankly, it sounds too random next to either of these, whether before or after. But it sits remarkably well next to "Old Brown Shoe," a song that manages to resonate by virtue of a sort of shared randomness. So we split these four tracks into two pairs:

"Dig a Pony" / "Old Brown Shoe"
"Don't Let Me Down" / "Two of Us"

A quick listen shows that the first of these pairs belongs on side one, and the other on side two. Indeed, though they have been listed alphabetically for consideration, it turns out they are in the perfect order already.

1A.	One After 909 (J/P)
1B.	I've Got a Feeling (J/P)
1C.	Get Back (P)
1M.	**Dig a Pony (J)**
1N.	**Old Brown Shoe (G)**
1Y.	Ballad of John and Yoko (J)
1Z.	Long and Winding Road (P)
2A.	I Me Mine (J)
2B.	Let It Be (P)
2C.	For You Blue (G)
2M.	**Don't Let Me Down (J)**
2N.	**Two of Us (P)**
2Z.	Across the Universe (J)

Despite the way it came together, with some positions filled based on what remained, this running order meets all of Martin's requirements. There is strength and high quality in all of the pole positions. Followers and setups genuinely resonate with their partners. Relatively weaker music is found in the middle of each side, and the overall flow was well-served by each decision. With that, this proves the smoothest and most satisfying assembly of this music yet.

January

Principle Recording: January 1969 - January 1970
Release: February 1970

Side One

1. One After 909 (Lennon/McCartney)
2. I've Got a Feeling (Lennon/McCartney)
3. Get Back (Lennon/McCartney)
4. Dig a Pony (Lennon/McCartney)
5. Old Brown Shoe (Harrison)
6. The Ballad of John and Yoko (Lennon/McCartney)
7. The Long and Winding Road (Lennon/McCartney)

Side Two

1. I Me Mine (Harrison)
2. Let It Be (Lennon/McCartney)
3. For You Blue (Harrison)
4. Don't Let Me Down (Lennon/McCartney)
5. Two of Us (Lennon/McCartney)
6. Across the Universe (Lennon/McCartney)

Make It Yourself

Total Running Time: 42:10

Tk	Rill	Title	Source	Dur
C3-A1	—	One After 909	[1]	2:43
C3-A2	0	I've Got a Feeling	[2]	3:27
C3-A3	0	Get Back	[3]	3:12
C3-A4	2.0	Dig a Pony	[2]	3:34
C3-A5	1.0	Old Brown Shoe	[3]	3:16
C3-A6	1.2	Ballad of John and Yoko	[3]	2:57
C3-A7	1.0	Long and Winding Road	[4]	3:41

Total: 22:53

Tk	Rill	Title	Source	Dur
C3-B1	—	I Me Mine	[2]	2:24
C3-B2	0	Let It Be	[3]	3:50
C3-B3	1.7	For You Blue	[2]	2:26
C3-B4	1.0	Don't Let Me Down	[3]	3:32
C3-B5	0	Two of Us	[2]	3:03
C3-B6	(19.0)	Across the Universe	[5]	3:58

Total: 19:17

[1] *Get Back*, chatter removed
[2] *Let It Be*, chatter removed
[3] *Past Masters, Volume Two*
[4] *Anthology 3*
[5] *Past Masters, Volume Two*, track 13, original speed restored (104% to D Major)

NOTE: Descriptions of edits and crossfades, with sample audio, are available at **SaveTheBeatles.com**.

Discussion

When you listen to the individual tracks recorded by the Beatles in and around January of 1969, *you just can tell* that it should have made a really good album. They tried a new way of working, and it really *worked*. It created yet another new sound for the group — nothing like they had ever sounded before, and yet still wholly *Beatles*. The songs are uniformly very high quality, and there are genuine masterworks present from John, Paul and George.

The travesty of *Let It Be* and all of the other versions, therefore, is that they turn such great material into such lousy albums. When this is the case, you have to look to assembly as the explanation. Beyond the running order, this includes packaging, promotion, photography, and a host of other elements — tangible and intangible. It all conspired to torpedo this project. The Beatles are at fault for letting it happen, but they had different fish to fry.

So they can be excused for thinking that Spector had worked a miracle. Their expectations were so low that almost anything he did would have exceeded them. Lennon actually alluded to this in his famous assessment of the album in his 1970 *Rolling Stone* interview. After declaring that Spector "made something" out of the tapes, he inadvertently revealed his low level of expectation: "When I heard it, I didn't puke." As a result, they simply couldn't see how badly Spector had whiffed.

In contrast, what becomes obvious with a running order based on George Martin's principles, and the prospect of better packaging and promotion, is that there has always been a great album hiding there, waiting to be brought out. *January* allows all of the great work to get its due, and allows the Beatles to be who they wanted to be when they started recording on the project. By removing the veil of bad assembly, we hear just how much fun this album must have been to make, and how much serious thought is hovering just beneath the surface.

The opening trifecta sets a beautiful table. The three songs form a mini-suite that isn't too precious and probably would have even satisfied Lennon. It is three great songs strung together that sound stronger in each other's company than they ever could scattered throughout the album. They feature John and Paul writing together and singing together, and establish clearly that this is not some tossed-off product — which would surely have *disappointed* Lennon, who really wanted to break the mystique. (Yes, he would have been satisfied and disappointed simultaneously.)

When the first rill comes, the Beatles shift gears, and make their way down a fascinatingly long and winding road, four tracks that build in strength, while never sounding too serious. The result is a lift to McCartney's ballad, which otherwise always sounds too weepy. Here its weepiness is mitigated by the jaunty song which sets it up. It feels like an *appropriate* response which resonates well with Lennon's travelogue. The side ends with a wistfulness that, in context, doesn't sound maudlin.

With the flip of the disc, George's micro-masterpiece offers some vitriol, but not without justification. The track would always be hard to swallow, but in other formulations it brings the album to a halt. Here it sets up a tension which is immediately and thoroughly released by Paul's anthem, in a way which acknowledges that the beefs are valid, but that there are other options for response. George's fun 12-bar number then demonstrates a tacit agreement with Paul, one that sounds even more pleasantly light after two heavy pieces.

But then, after all this, the album veers into its most significant territory. "Don't Let Me Down" was completely wasted by relegating it to a B-side. It is a powerful song, performed powerfully by the band on the rooftop, a lament that is as pure as John Lennon ever wrote. When the emotions settle, we find McCartney sidling up alongside him to tell a little story which serves as a reassurance of sorts. In this context, "Two of Us" sounds wistful and sad, while never going too deep into melancholy. Its evocation of remembering and traveling along the road together frees John, allowing "Across the Universe" to shine in a way it never has before. In closing the album, it sounds like a statement for the ages, immune from the usual criticisms. In one way it sounds like a Beatles throwback to an earlier incarnation, and in another it sounds unlike anything else they ever recorded, a feature which is hard to recognize anywhere else it is found.

Because *January* is free of the chatter and scruffiness, it highlights the fact that these tracks sound like *group* tracks, and this album like a *group* album, in a way that even *Abbey Road* does not. There is a very palpable sense throughout of the four Beatles sitting in a studio *together*, face to face, playing and singing simultaneously, pounding out this material, applying their considerable abilities to songs which they may have thought, deep down, might not be worth it. (If they thought that, they were wrong.) They soldier on, incredibly hard-working studio artists that they were, and give their all to the material, which deserves proper contextualization, and comes to life once it gets it.

The effort pays off because of the unique combination of high quality songs and this playing *together* — on the soundstage, in the studio, and on the rooftop. These tracks, when you can listen without all of the heavy subtext found in other incarnations, are a revelation in this regard, and the act of getting this group to play together again is the real fruit of McCartney's original idea, accomplishing John's slightly different goal at the same time. Not only do they rely very little on studio "trickery," they sound like the old camaraderie has truly been reanimated.

George Martin's principles, though hardly foolproof, gives us a window into how the Beatles worked, and how much they had going for them outside of all their talent, intelligence, good looks and charm. What *January* really shows is that learning from Martin is essential to understanding the Beatles, and we can now see that it has the potential to rescue even more difficult collections of music.

11
Fusion

> *If people need the Beatles so much, all they have to do is to buy each [solo] album and make it — put it on tape, track by track, one of me, one of Paul, one of George, one of Ringo, if they really need it that much. Because otherwise the music is just the same only on separate albums. And it's far better music.*
>
> John Lennon, October 25, 1971[1]

Recall the three main issues which haunted the solo Beatle output in the 70s: Lack of Beatle Magic, dilution and contextualization. The first of those is utterly beyond repair since the four Beatles never played together again. Indeed, they were never again even in the same room. We cannot retroactively sprinkle Beatle Magic onto individual tracks, like pepper onto a salad.

Maybe someday someone will invent an algorithm that allows us to hear what solo George might have played on "My Love," or how Paul's bass and backup vocals might have lifted "Imagine" to yet another level. Or maybe similar software could give us Ringo drumming on "This Guitar (Can't Keep from Crying)," or John writing a saving counterpoint for "Morse Moose and the Grey Goose." If that were to happen, it would certainly be fascinating, but not in any way a reanimation of the group's special chemistry. That is gone. Forever.

Amazingly, however, we *can* address the other two deficiencies, and in doing so, potentially generate a *new* type of Beatle Magic. We can remove the dilution altogether, by just dropping the tracks which are not of sufficient *Beatle Quality*. We can also create better contextualizations by learning and applying the techniques that George Martin used for album assembly. In this way, we have the potential to genuinely reanimate the interplay at a meta level, allowing them to elevate one another from afar, and avoiding the need to get them back together in the studio.

As noted at the outset, the rescued Beatles albums, or what might be better called *fused* albums, are actually hiding in plain sight. This is not a new idea. Many fans — perhaps *most* — have thought this at one point or another. But finding and rescuing them is not nearly as simple as throwing the greatest hits, or even just your favorite tracks, together. Go ahead and do that for your own personal listening pleasure, but it is a far cry from considering and applying the techniques and sensibilities used by

---

[1] *The Beatles Tapes from the David Wigg Interviews*

George Martin and the Beatles to try and divine a glimpse of what *they* might have done. For that, much more is needed.

Obviously, a glimpse is all we can hope for. We can never know for sure what they might have done. There are too many variables, and *we* are not *them*. Since predicting the Beatles in the 60s would have confounded anyone who tried, it's reasonable to assume the same about the 70s. They certainly would have surprised us, and it's impossible to discern surprises they never thought up.

There is, however, a reasonably good chance that even if they had been collaborating on some level, the imagined Beatles of the 70s would have written many of the same songs that the former Beatles actually did. Certainly not all. Some were born out of difficulties they wouldn't have had, and would disappear from a slightly altered narrative. Likewise, different circumstances would no doubt have brought about other songs which, in the real world, didn't get written. But we will assume, for the most part, that the songs they actually wrote would likely still have been written, and probably on roughly the same schedule. That's all we have to work with.

As far as putting them together into albums, once again we can only speculate. But we can use close observation, along with the existing documentation as enumerated in the previous chapters, to help us learn their techniques and make an *educated guess* at what they might have done. We should get something which can give us at least a hint, and maybe more. While, at heart, this is mostly just a fun guessing game, it is much more fun when you learn everything you can from what they actually did, and *try to think like them*. Impossible? Yes, of course. Worthy of our time? Indeed, yes.

Narrative

In order for us to imagine that the Beatles might have continued working together in 1970, we also have to imagine that something changed. The parameters and sequence of the breakup are well-known, and most observers agree that a moment of no return was reached only when Paul announced the schism on April 10, 1970. Before that, the rift was private, and potentially still resolvable. After that, all were hardened into their corners.

Not that there wasn't still hope, even then. Both George Harrison and George Martin were quoted later as saying the Beatles were expected to record together again very soon. John Lennon was famous for recanting past statements and decisions, even those that were harsh and seemed absolute. But Paul's announcement resulted in a media frenzy, despondency among the fanbase, and a variety of emotions among the band members, including relief. Once out of the bottle, that genie could not be recalled or reigned.

11 / FUSION

In order to establish our slightly altered narrative, all we really need is a small change or two around then. Ringo had already been recording his album of standards, so someone would have had to talk him out of releasing it — advisable for multiple reasons. Paul would have had to agree to withhold his solo album as well while something was worked out. Maybe a slightly different wording from George on the letter Ringo delivered on March 31, or a different choice of words by Ringo himself, could have accomplished this. Maybe if Paul had just been in a different mood that morning.

No one could have talked John out of releasing his "instant" singles, but what if he had credited "Give Peace a Chance," "Cold Turkey" and/or "Instant Karma!" to the Beatles? That certainly would have established the critical precedent. Even though the line-up of musicians had expanded, such a move would have declared to the world that the Beatles were still in business, but had entered a new era.

Rather than spinning out some elaborate fiction about how all this could have happened, we will merely assume that somehow it did. Somehow all were convinced to engage in a "cooling off" period of some sort, running from October of 1969 through the summer of 1970. During this time each Beatle could pursue solo recording however he liked, but agreed not to say, or do, or release anything which might cause a permanent schism or public panic. This would have had to include scuttling the *Let It Be* film.[2] The future of the band could then be decided calmly, and plans made on how to proceed.

So, by the summer of 1970, all parties would have calmed down and presumably seen the advantages of pooling their resources. Instead of multiple albums of widely varying quality, they would have agreed to try another way of working together.

Assembler

A few things would have been necessary before everyone agreed to try making "fused" albums. First and foremost, all four Beatles would have had to be convinced that their artistic integrity would have been protected. They would have needed to know that, no matter how this new type of album was created, the music would come first, and the same artistic standards as always would apply.

Moreover, since the Beatles themselves were highly competitive, and not always altruistically motivated, they would have recognized the need to hire someone impartial, with high standards, exceptional artistry, and who all of them could trust, to oversee the process. The group would still have input, of course, and need to approve the finished product, but instead of fighting with one another over which

---

[2] At the time of this writing (April 2020), Peter Jackson's *The Beatles Get Back* is still months away from release. But imagine if the footage had been edited back then with more focus on the joy in the sessions. It might have actually saved the band.

tracks would make the album and whose would go where, they would give this responsibility — and *trust* — to one person.

If you think this is too big a leap, remember that the group had done this many times before. Not only had they entrusted George Martin with their finished product from the very beginning, they also trusted Phil Spector to create their final release entirely unsupervised. What we are imagining, therefore, is a close cousin to the process which produced *Let It Be*, with piles of solo recordings replacing the piles of group recordings.

In a very similar manner, they would be handing that large batch of uncurated recordings to a trusted collaborator who, despite not being at the sessions, would sort, assess, and assemble them into something releasable.

Enter the Assembler. Obviously, in the best possible case this would have been George Martin. He was notorious for calling out the sub-standard material, and allowing only the very best to get through. He also knew how to sweeten arrangements when necessary, play the right instrument himself, commission remixes, edit out extraneous bits, and most importantly, how to sequence tracks for best effect. This would have been key to uniting such varied tracks into a coherent whole, while giving every individual artist the chance to shine.

Martin also just plain understood what made for a great Beatles record. After all, it was he who had taught them how to make those records, and it was he who reinforced again and again the need for excellence that they all shared. They came to resent his watchful eye, but this is exactly what would have made him the perfect arbiter of the solo tracks.

Most importantly, he was perhaps the only person in the world who had any chance of commanding the respect and trust of the Beatles in creative matters. Recall that when he produced *Tug of War*, he famously became the first person in over a decade to tell Paul that some of his songs weren't good enough, and sent him back to make revisions and/or write some new ones.

So, in the same way they went back to him after the *Get Back* sessions, we can imagine the Beatles going back to George Martin yet again sometime in 1970, and asking him to assume this new role, promising to give him complete creative freedom, abide by his decisions, and not interfere.

Unfortunately, Martin might have turned them down. He famously started tiring of working with the Beatles around 1968, fed up with all the stress and drama, and feeling unneeded. Though he returned for *Abbey Road*, he reportedly felt he was done with them when it was finished. (How wrong he was!) Beyond that, he had a burgeoning business of his own in AIR, and was able to cherry-pick his projects. He may not have wanted or needed the trouble.

Though we could probably come up with other candidates, say Abbey Road engineers, trusted associates within Apple, or even outside producers or artists, the actual person doesn't really matter. In fact, it would be presumptuous to put any made-up running orders into someone else's mouth. So rather than name anyone, we will simply assume that someone suitable would have been found and accepted the job. We will call this person The Assembler.

We will, however, insist that this person was well-studied in the principles and techniques that Martin used — if not an actual protégé, at least an admirer.[3]

The Assembler would have had three primary roles. The first would be to listen carefully to all of the music which got made, and select only that which matched the standards of the band and the goal of the project. Second, he would take all of the identified materials and stitch them together into a finished product suitable for release under the Beatles name. Third, he would have to keep the peace with his artists, satisfying their wide-ranging demands, making them sound as good as possible, and occasionally assuaging dented egos. This would not have been a job for the faint of heart.

Agreements

The mention of superstar egos highlights the need for some parameters around which all decisions will be made. We will presume that, after someone somewhere had suggested the idea of creating conjoined releases, and all Beatles had agreed to the idea in principle, and an Assembler had been engaged, a period of negotiation would have established the ins and outs of the process.

This starts with formally defining their relationship to that Assembler to guarantee that the process used to create the albums would be fair and fruitful. Though we imagine that Assembler would have absolute authority on things like selecting and ordering tracks, he would still be bound by whatever agreements were needed between the individual Beatles, with all projects subject to their final approval. The first set of agreements sets the stage for this.

Fusion Agreement #1 - Process

(a) Releases are scheduled by the Assembler, in consultation with the record company and the Beatles.

(b) The Assembler selects and orders the tracks.

---

[3] Obviously, for all intents and purposes in this book, that means the Assembler is me. But I will try hard to channel what is known about Martin's principles, and not my own — even though I basically learned mine by listening to records he created. Keep in mind that you can have a go at it yourself at SaveTheBeatles.com!

(c) Each Beatle has veto power over the inclusion of any specific track, but not over placement within the running order.

(d) The finished product requires unanimous group approval.

The next most obvious agreement would have to be around parity. It seems likely that, before agreeing to participate, George Harrison would have rightfully demanded that he receive songwriting representation equal to whatever John and Paul got. He had clearly earned that right, and we will assume that this would have been granted. Likewise, John and Paul would have wanted to make sure that no songwriter became overly dominant. As an aside, we assume that the Lennon/McCartney writing credit would have been retired after *Abbey Road*, and only used in the event that they actually wrote a song together.

Ringo might not have insisted on any specific representation, but it's reasonable to imagine that while John, Paul and George were getting such a commitment, one would have been extended to him as well.[4] In his case, it is merely a commitment that his voice will be heard on each album, and not a specific allotment of tracks, or songwriting representation.

Thus we start with a blueprint for each 14-song album: At least four tracks each for John, Paul and George, and at least one for Ringo. Admittedly, this does leave one track up for grabs, and that might have been a subject for further conversation. If they had considered switching to 10-song albums at this point, it would have gotten even easier: 3+3+3+1. No matter, the idea of maintaining the proper balance would have been important and made very clear.

Fusion Agreement #2 - Balance

(a) All four Beatles must be heard as vocalists on every release.

(b) No more than two tracks from the same composer/vocalist may be heard in succession.

(c) Every attempt will be made by the Assembler to ensure that Lennon, McCartney and Harrison have equal composer/vocalist representation on each album.

(d) In the event that equal representation is not possible, the Assembler makes the final decision.

---

[4] This was also suggested by their phone meeting in September 1969.

11 / FUSION

We can be sure that, in an imagined world where tracks were being recorded solo and aggregated for release, there would have been jockeying and lobbying among the Beatles for or against certain tracks, themes, segues, placement, etc. They would have been competing directly for things like the album opener, closer, teaser single, and the like, trying to convince the Assembler of this or that.

In other words, they would not have been as dispassionate about the materials as they were about *Get Back/Let It Be*. In that case they simply handed over the master tapes to an outsider and washed their hands of it. Here they would very much have had a vested interest in making sure the work they had done got the proper respect and an appropriate placement. One can imagine this being a whole new source of stress for the band, and that is why we must make sure that our Assembler is firmly established as the ultimate arbiter on such things, with absolute control over accepting, rejecting, remixing, editing, and even requesting remakes if necessary.

This could certainly lead to a Beatle not getting his way, something they probably would have chafed at. So we can even imagine that they might have started to game the system, and perhaps not put forward the very best of what they recorded, slyly saving things for potential solo releases. So another agreement that would have been made is that the Assembler got to hear *everything* that was recorded, and had final approval on the overall sound of each track that was selected. This reduces the chance to cheat, and improves the chance of the finished product sounding united.

Fusion Agreement #3 - Materials

(a) At least one Beatle must appear on each track.

(b) Lead vocals may be by Beatles only. No guest lead vocalists.

(c) The Assembler has the right to hear all recordings made.

(d) The Assembler will approve all final mixes, and has the right to edit tracks, remix tracks, do additional production, and request alterations or remakes, as necessary.

(e) The Assembler is free to combine multiple tracks into sequences using segues, crossfades, edits or other means.

In exchange for agreeing to these terms, all of the Beatles get the right to put out solo releases as they please, with the schedule subject to approval by Apple to avoid collisions in the marketplace. They will also get access to the Assembler, if they like, as a collaborator on creating those. They also can do whatever solo outside projects they like — including creating their own bands and playing live shows — without getting any approval. There would likely have also been agreements about packaging and publicity and compilation albums, none of which need to be considered here.

What we are imagining is that they would have worked out the most important things, in the interest of doing what was best for the Beatle brand. Admittedly, this level of cooperation is hard to picture in that era, but if it had happened, the possibilities for more great music stagger the mind.

Next, we turn from what the Beatles would have done to make this possible, to what must be done here, in the current project, to properly imagine the fused albums. The basic process is simple: Listen carefully, choose carefully, and assemble carefully. But a few things must be in place to make this possible.

Fusion Eras

Like every other recording act, the Beatles had deadlines set by the market, the record company, and circumstance. For example, they always tried to have something available at Christmas because sales were always higher then. They had a general sense of when a new single was due based on whether the previous one was still getting airplay. Releases sometimes had to be coordinated with movie premieres or concert tours. In some cases, they just had enough material ready and that was a good enough reason to put it out.

In the case of the solo Beatles, they were no longer coordinating recording sessions or release dates with one another. Since all of their solo releases were on Apple Records until 1976, a certain amount of passive cooperation existed, as well as nudges from EMI/Capitol, but the will of a Beatle was generally enough to get something released whenever it suited him, regardless of potential conflicts. As such, there are many examples of the former Beatles coexisting with, and sometimes stepping on, one another in the marketplace during the 70s.

Indeed, when you plot their recording activities and releases on a calendar (see Appendix I, *Creative Calendar*), certain rhythms stand out. More often than not, all four former Beatles finished recording projects within a few months of one another, at least until Lennon exempted himself. This allows their solo output to be grouped and considered in chunks:

1970	*Sentimental Journey* *McCartney* *Beaucoups of Blues* *All Things Must Pass* *John Lennon/Plastic Ono Band*	Ringo Paul Ringo George John
1971/72	*Ram* *Imagine* *Wild Life* *Some Time in New York City*	Paul John Paul John

11 / FUSION

1973	*Red Rose Speedway* *Living in the Material World* *Mind Games* *Ringo* *Band on the Run*	Paul George John Ringo Paul
1974/75	*Walls and Bridges* *Goodnight Vienna* *Dark Horse* *Rock 'n' Roll* *Venus and Mars* *Extra Texture (Read All About It)*	John Ringo George John Paul George
1976/77	*Wings at the Speed of Sound* *Ringo's Rotogravure* *Thirty Three and 1/3* *Ringo the 4th*	Paul Ringo George Ringo
1978/79	*London Town* *Bad Boy* *George Harrison* *Back to the Egg*	Paul Ringo George Paul
1980/81	*McCartney II* *Double Fantasy* *Somewhere in England* *Stop and Smell the Roses*	Paul John George Ringo
1982/83	*Tug of War* *Gone Troppo* *Old Wave* *Pipes of Peace* *Milk and Honey*	Paul George Ringo Paul John

In theory, each of these periods *might* result in a fused album. But as enumerated in the agreements above, the Assembler sets the release schedule subject to market needs *and* the availability of enough good music from all four Beatles. As you can see, this raises problems in some of those periods.

For example, some segments run a bit thin, and some are way out of balance. In fact, all but one of these groupings contains two albums by the same artist. Where we might be able to handle thinness from Ringo, we certainly could not from any of the others.

Obviously, the Assembler will consider more than just the albums. All singles and B-sides, along with selected unreleased tracks, will be available, so the picture is more nuanced than that list indicates. Additionally, rather than consider tracks by their release date, it is better to consider them by the date they were completed, which we will call the *availability date.*

Given the vast amount of literature on the recording activities of the former Beatles, finding availability dates is relatively easy for many tracks. There are still holes in that information, of course, especially as recording sessions moved into home studios where documentation may be private, or not exist at all. Indeed, for Lennon's contributions during his Dakota years, some decisions will rely on sketchy hearsay about the timing of his demos. Fortunately, the dates really only matter if a track falls near the cutoff between the designated eras, or if there is a need to correct imbalances, or account for quality issues.

The official eras the Assembler will use, therefore, are built around a period of *principle recording*, with a fixed cutoff date, followed by an imagined *release date*. These reflect the real world recording activities of the former Beatles, merged with presumed market expectations. Those expectations derive, in part, from the patterns of release that the Beatles actually used in the 60s.

For each era, therefore, we will attempt to imagine the Assembler in a studio with a big stack of tapes submitted by these four rock-n-roll icons, with the mandate to turn those tapes into a finished product that is artistically satisfying — and *saleable*, though no one will actually say that out loud. Keep in mind that it isn't enough to make a *good* album. It must be another *classic*.

The applicable recording eras will be discussed in detail in each album chapter. A concise summary can be found at the end of Appendix I, *Creative Calendar*.

Listening

The process begins with the Assembler merely *listening*. Keep in mind that this is listening to *tracks*, not *albums*. The Assembler has no foreknowledge of what the solo Beatle might have done with any of the music, or how it would be received by the public and critics. The Assembler is not deconstructing existing albums looking for music to use, but hearing everything in isolation. Thus, it is essential to set aside everything we know about how things transpired in the real world after the music was recorded. It must be as if the Assembler is hearing everything for the first time, with no preconceived notions.

This includes ignoring knowledge of what became a single, a hit, or simply disappeared into the morass of the solo Beatle graveyard. It also involves ignoring contemporaneous reviews and all received wisdom about the quality of the music. Every track must get the benefit of the doubt, but also be ruthlessly assessed to determine which songs and recordings are good enough — and appropriate enough — to make the cut.

We are imagining that our Assembler would have been capable of doing these things, and entrusted with that responsibility — without interference — by the Beatles. We will further assume that the Assembler could justify all decisions, and satisfy the recording artists with those explanations.

The process of listening and rating the solo music has already been described in chapter 1. Recall that this yielded a *Beatle Quality* (BQ) rating for each and every track that the solo Beatles released in the 70s, and only tracks deemed *eligible* or *provisional* will be considered for group albums. Not all will make it.

11 / FUSION

Assembly

The process of assembly will yield a running order for the album, along with a list of segues, crossfades, edits, remixes, or other "punch list" items which would have required attention before final release. It will also yield a title for the album, and a rudimentary conception for the artwork, which can have a great impact on how the project would be perceived out in the world. The Assembler would certainly engage the Beatles on the packaging, with their sensibilities much more important in that regard than his.

Each of these parts has a few little guidelines to go with it, which are based on some sort of research and documentation (see the accompanying chart), along with a healthy helping of creativity by the Assembler and the Beatles.

Album titles would be based around whatever central idea the Assembler used to create each album. Looking back at the classic Beatles albums, we find that only about half had a title track — meaning the album was named after one of the songs it contained. The rest used abstract concepts, or just a compelling turn of phrase. To minimize confusion in the current project, album titles which were used for real world solo albums are ineligible here.

Surprisingly, only about half of the classic albums feature a **group photo** on the front cover. While we tend to remember *Let It Be* for the symbolism of not including a group photo, the approach goes all the way back to *A Hard Day's Night*, when the individual Beatles are pictured in separate rows of thumbnails. Because of this, and the fact that there are no group photos available from the 70s, it's assumed that there would have been no such expectation from fans, and the album art would have evolved accordingly.

An assumption has been made that the Beatles would have maintained their desire to have **14 tracks** on each album, even as the industry moved toward longer tracks and less per release. This is consistent with their goal of providing exceptional value to fans, as well as the presence of lots of music to choose from.

Album lengths will typically follow the guidelines George Martin used, which harnessed the parameters of the LP format. This means that all albums are designed for the LP medium, with roughly 20-25 minutes per side. This acknowledges that, even as longer programs became possible, the Beatles would generally have demurred out of respect for typical attention spans.

Other, smaller guidelines will be discussed as they are implemented.

Classic Album Overview

RLS	VITALS		SONGWRITING CREDIT				LEAD VOCAL [a]				PACKAGE		POLE TKS	
	Tks	Len (min)				Other					Title song	Group Cover photo	Side 1	Side 2
	14	33	8	-	-	6	7	5	2	1	Y	Y	P..J	P..J
	14	32	7	1	-	6	7	3	3	1	N	Y	J..J	G..J
	13	30	13	-	-	-	9	4	1	-	Y	N	J..P	J..J
	14	34	8	-	-	6	9	5	1	1	N	Y	J..P	J..G
	14	34	10	2	-	2	6	5	2	1	Y	N	J..J	R..J
	14	36	12	2	1[b]	-	7	6	3	1	N	Y	P..P	R..J
	14	35	11	3	-	-	5	5	3	1	N	?	G..J	P..J
	13	40	12	1	-	-	5	8	2	1	Y	Y	P..J	G..J
	6[c]	19	5	2	1	-	1	3	1	-	Y	?	N/A	
	17	46	14	2	1	-	6	8	2	1	N	N	P..J	P..J
	13	47	11	2	-	-	5	4	2	1			P..G	J..R
	4[d]	15	2	2	-	-	1	1	2	-	Y	N	N/A	
	14[e]	47	14	2	1	-	6	8	3	1	N	Y	J..J	G..P
	12	35	9	3	1	1	5	5	2	0	Y	N	P..J	P..P

a. Some tracks have multiple lead vocalists.
b. "What Goes On" is credited to Lennon/McCartney/Starr.
c. Double-EP version
d. New tracks only
e. In three instances, two songs were recorded as a single track.

Album Chapter Overview

Each of the chapters in the next section describes one rescued/fused Beatles album. It covers all of the music which was made during that specific era, in addition to general historical information, and the process used to select and sequence the tracks. These chapters are divided into discreet sections, some of which focus on historical information, while others focus on creative or imagined things. Each section is described here to make clear which is which. (Prototypes for each section were also seen in the preceding proof-of-concept chapters.)

The **Title Page** contains the project name, principle recording and presumed release date. It also shows a visual representation of the solo releases which were mined to create the fused album, and a rough conception of the album's packaging.

A page of real world **Quotes** gives a sense of how each former Beatle was feeling about the prospect for more collaboration between them during the period.

A **Chronology** aggregates selected real world events which impacted the creation of music during the period.

The chapter's **Introduction** reviews the broad context in which the project would be created, creating the frame into which the concept of a fused album can be imagined. As applicable, it reviews where the previous imagined project left off, and dovetails real world events with those being imagined.

The **Recording** section gives a brief narrative of the actual recording activities undertaken by the former Beatles during the period in question. This is intended only as a refresher, and does not attempt to be comprehensive in any way. Many other resources are available to those who want further detailed historical information about the creation of solo recordings. The goal of this section is to give a summary, enough to understand the context in which each Beatle was recording.

Next, all of the **Materials** which will be available to build the album are considered. This section is pure criticism, assessing recordings and offering justification for why music has been included or excluded. It also focuses on how the Assembler might have reacted to the tracks while they were being created, before any public reaction was available.

These "materials" sections begin with an **Overview,** which discusses whatever relationships the recordings of the individual artists have to one another, followed by **a section for each Beatle**, with reviews of significant projects and music. Not every track is necessarily covered in the narrative, but each is given at least a "thumbnail review" in the list of materials. The individual sections are sequenced chronologically, according to when each former Beatle released new material.

The next section focuses on the actual **Assembly** of the album. This details the application of George Martin's principles to the music which has been selected. Options are considered, and decisions justified. Diagrams are provided of how the sequencing proceeded, with the result being a finished track line-up and any other details required by the process. A final section gives information on how to **Make It Yourself**, including which track versions to use, time between tracks, which edits apply, and more.

Since each album has an imagined **Release** date, the next section reviews the music scene at that moment. The first part reviews significant albums which had been released since the last imagined meta-Beatles album, and the second looks at the top ten chart at the time of actual release. This section attempts to give a sense of what was happening in music, which could have impacted the reception of a new Beatles album.

Finally, a **Discussion** of the album looks at its contents, and offers some assessment of how the album sounds as a whole, and how it might have fit into the overall Beatles narrative. It also attempts to imagine how critics and the public might have reacted, as well as any lasting changes to the reputation of the group brought about by the release.

These chapters deal in historical fact as much as possible, attempting to suggest only broadly how an altered narrative might have looked. As such, though the project is one large fantasy, it involves much more. For clarity, here is a list of the sections in each chapter, along with the primary role each plays.

CHAPTER SECTIONS

Name	Type
Chronology	*History*
Quotes	*History*
Introduction	*Narrative*
Recording	*History*
Materials	*Criticism*
Assembly	*Creative*
Release	*Analysis*
Discussion	*Analysis*

Despite being based on history, to truly appreciate the fused Beatles albums, and the process by which they will be created, you will need to totally forget about some of the solo albums. This will seem hard at first. You will want to say, "What about this track?" or "What happens to that album?" You may find that your favorite track doesn't transfer to a group album. For example, you will not find "Band on the Run"

11 / FUSION

or "Power to the People" or "My Sweet Lord" on any of these rescued albums — and for good reasons. If anything, that is one lesson of this project.

Perhaps it could go without saying that the magic of the Beatles was not about the individual voices, but rather the interplay between them. During the 60s, that happened whenever they were in the same place together. We are trying to explore the interplay between their voices through the music they made as individuals, and determine if a similar, but distinct type of magic can be sparked for the era in which they were not ever in the same place together.

The lesson learned by considering the solo recordings in this way is that *the interplay still happened* — unseen, unassembled, dormant — and remains available to us even though it did not see daylight at the time. Think of it as sort of like a great soufflé that never got made. The raw ingredients were used to make dishes that were less savory, but we have the opportunity to disentangle those ingredients and try again — to unbake those bad dishes and start over using a better recipe.

This may sound like a bold claim, but it really should come as no surprise. Beatle magic cannot be explained, and its depths continue to be plumbed and revealed over 50 years after John, Paul, George and Ringo last played together. There are many different types of resonance, and here we are not setting out to *create* new resonance, but merely *reveal* that which has always existed, if unseen.

Perhaps trying to rekindle the Beatle Magic in this way seems like a fool's errand. But let's be fools. In our best case, we divert the former Beatles from paths better left untrod. We abscond with them to a place where the virtuous circle is restored — by a means that all could abide. We convince them there are depths yet to plumb, and that the hidden Music calls.

Part III
Diversion

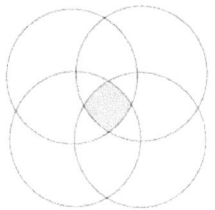

*History may be servitude,
History may be freedom. See, now they vanish,
The faces and places,
    with the self which, as it could, loved them,
To become renewed, transfigured,
    in another pattern.*

Fusion Era #1

October 1969 - October 1970

Dream

12 / DREAM

"We've got to a point where we can see each other quite clearly. And by allowing each other to be each other, we can become the Beatles again."

– George Harrison, April 1969

"What's happened now is that each of us has become very strong individuals in our own right."

– Paul McCartney, April 1970

"I've no idea if the Beatles will work together again, or not. I never really have. It was always open... It could be a rebirth or death. We'll see what it is. It'll probably be a rebirth."

– John Lennon, May 1970

"We did have some musical differences and we'd have to overcome them."

– Ringo Starr, July 1970

Chronology

1969

Abbey Road completed	**AUG**	Mary McCartney born
Sign new recording contract Lose control of Northern Songs *Abbey Road* released	**SEP**	Performs live in Toronto Requests "divorce" from Beatles Records "Cold Turkey" Hospitalized for stress

...Fusion Era #1 Begins Here...

Yoko suffers miscarriage "Cold Turkey" released Recording with Blind Faith	**OCT**	Arranges "Stardust" for Ringo Begins recording *Sentimental Journey*
Returns MBE	**NOV**	
Peace for Christmas concert Begins recording *McCartney*	**DEC**	Delaney & Bonnie tour (10 shows, 5 nights) Performs with John at *Peace for Christmas* *The Magic Christian* (film) premieres

1970

Final "group" session ("I Me Mine") "Instant Karma!" recorded/released *Bag One* lithographs seized by police	**JAN**	Tapes *Laugh-In* (TV) appearance Producing Doris Troy (*Doris Troy*) Producing Billy Preston (*Encouraging Words*)
Top of the Pops (TV)	**FEB**	*Laugh-In* (TV) appearance airs
Phil Spector begins work on *Let It Be* *Sentimental Journey* released Begins recording "It Don't Come Easy"	**MAR**	Threatens Ringo with bodily harm over letter from the other Beatles denying early release of *McCartney*

12 / DREAM

Final overdub session (orchestra and choir for *Let It Be*)			Attends final overdub session
Calls John to say he is quitting the band *McCartney* released Reveals breakup	**APR**		Wins *Bag One* lithograph case Begins "primal scream" therapy
			Writes / jams / records with Bob Dylan
Let It Be (album) released *Let It Be* (film) premieres, (no Beatles attending)	**MAY**		Recording with Howlin' Wolf Quoted: Beatle split "not permanent" Begins recording *All Things Must Pass*
Recording with Eric Clapton	**JUN**		Records *Beaucoups of Blues* in Nashville
Louise Harrison (mother) dies	**JUL**		Cynthia Lennon remarries
Apple press office closes	**AUG**		Yoko suffers miscarriage
Completes "primal scream" therapy Begins recording *John Lennon/Plastic Ono Band*	**SEP**		*Beaucoups of Blues* released Records "Early 1970" (with George, and perhaps John)
Finishes recording *John Lennon/Plastic Ono Band*	**OCT**		Shoots performance for *Cilla* (TV) Records "Early 1970" with GH (and JL?)

Introduction

At Christmas of 1970, you could have purchased five very different Beatle-related solo albums as gifts for your favorite Beatle fan. That's a lot of music to sort through. How would you decide? Just go with your favorite Beatle? Trust the reviewers? Buy the album for the single you liked on the radio? The one with the coolest cover? Buy them all — at a significant cost?

What if, instead, there had been a double album by the Beatles available that Christmas? Would you have cared that it was recorded differently?

Indeed, you might not have realized that anything was different. This first *real* fused Beatles album would have felt warm and familiar in some places, and yet different enough in others to tell you that something new was afoot. But that much had been true for *all* Beatles albums. The Beatles of the 70s would have been *expected* to sound different from the Beatles of the 60s.

The album most certainly would have sold in the many millions — likely more than the combined sales of those five solo albums.[1] Even if it didn't, by some weird chance, outsell them, it would have trounced them all artistically. The individual former Beatles said many times in interviews that money could not motivate them to stay together or reunite, but the music might. So, despite their *Anthology*-era reversal on that, the argument for creating this album isn't really about record sales. It's about the fact that the combined album actually produces a better representation of who the four artists were, individually and collectively, at that moment.

Even in our slightly altered narrative, this album would have been assembled at a very tense moment, and the participation of all parties would have been difficult to obtain. Yet it is an undeniable fact that, despite what was happening *between* the band members, all four Beatles made plenty of music in the 12 months following the completion of *Abbey Road* — a total of seven full platters of 12-inch vinyl. There were more than enough finished recordings for multiple projects, solo and group.

If this collection of recordings had been handed to our Assembler for curation, he would have been forgiven for tossing up his hands in dismay. But once he started listening and culling, he would have quickly realized that there was actually far too much great material here to fit on a single album. Indeed, it would once again take a double album just to accommodate the great stuff. And unlike its double-album predecessor from 1968, the filler could have been kept out completely, with plenty of *usable* songs still available for solo projects when all was said and done.

Entering this world of music is a little like following Alice into the rabbit hole or, as the Beatles themselves once imagined, stepping into Nora's multilayered

---

[1] Reportedly somewhere around 5 million altogether. See Appendix IV, *Certified Sales*, for more on how sales numbers are calculated and used in this book.

dollhouse. There are certainly many curiosities, unexpected twists, and a general sense of disorientation. Frightening moments coexist with the comic and absurd. But when you finally emerge, a mysterious sense of something special — a sense of wonder — hangs in the air.

Recording
October 1969 - October 1970

◉ Studio Recording   ◀ Concert(s)   ◯ Single Release

Shortly after John Lennon's private revelation that he was quitting the band, which came on September 20, 1969, Richard Starkey became the first Beatle to officially begin work on a non-experimental solo album. Encouraged by his bandmates to have a go at a collection of standards, he engaged George Martin to oversee the project. Martin, in turn, recruited a veritable who's-who of arrangers — Quincy Jones, Maurice Gibb, Elmer Bernstein, Klaus Voorman and even Paul McCartney — to create a vehicle for the Beatle most likely to need a little help from . . . the experts. When released the following March, *Sentimental Journey* became the first proper solo studio album from a former Beatle.

It sold quickly at first, on the strength of Ringo's name alone, but made only a fleeting appearance on the charts. Sales of the lightly-promoted album plummeted as fans realized that the it bore little in common with Beatles records. It became very clear, perhaps even during the sessions, that this was not the right path for Ringo's solo career.

Paul McCartney, meanwhile, began recording in secret at his home studio, sketching out new tunes, revisiting old ones, and playing all the instruments on what were essentially elaborate demos. Eventually, he took his tapes to proper studios for finishing, and assembled them into his solo debut, *McCartney*. Despite some very fine music and significant sales, the album was overshadowed by the accompanying self-interview which revealed the group's split.

The early part of 1970 saw the Threetles meet to finish *Let It Be*, but also had George recording with both John ("Instant Karma!) and Ringo ("It Don't Come Easy"). In the case of the latter, the session appears to have cemented a bond between the two musicians which would bear significant fruit in the coming decade. When finally released in 1971, "It Don't Come Easy" was a significant hit, suggesting a solution to the riddle of just how Ringo's career should proceed, albeit one that wouldn't be pursued for another two years.

Almost simultaneous to the breakup reveal, Harrison began six months of sessions with Phil Spector, recording what would become *All Things Must Pass*. Perhaps most notable about the project is that it was largely made up of songs which had been rejected by the Lennon/McCartney/Martin braintrust. In the initial, legendary planning session for his new album, George demoed literally dozens of worthy songs, from which the album's contents were chosen. The resulting triple album was a massive success, suggesting that George's voice, having now emerged from the shadow of his bandmates, might dominate the airwaves in a way that it never had before. Unfortunately, it was not to be.

While playing on George's sessions, Ringo became acquainted with Pete Drake, a veteran country session musician. The resulting friendship led him to Nashville in late June of 1970 to record an album of country songs with a long-established group of session musicians. Purportedly written in a week, and recorded over just a couple of days, *Beaucoups of Blues* became Ringo's second album of 1970. Stylistically, it was completely removed from his first album, and thus served as something of a second marketing experiment in the process of determining just what would work for the former Beatle with the least marketable skills. It was not a success. Again, a potential avenue for Ringo's solo career had come to a dead end.

Toward the end of the summer of 1970, John Lennon borrowed Ringo, Klaus Voorman, and Phil Spector from Harrison's sessions to hastily record his first proper studio solo album. He had written a collection of emotionally raw songs as a result of undergoing primal scream therapy earlier in the year. The resulting album, *John Lennon/Plastic Ono Band*, would likewise be raw, sparse, and filled with Lennon's distinctive angst. It would ultimately stand as an artistic triumph, a monument to Lennon's courage and vulnerability as a writer and performer.

But there were problems. Preorders for the album were strong, but the finished product did not connect well with the typical Beatles audience, who were already pining for a reunion. John's declaration in "God" that he didn't "believe in Beatles," was especially painful for the fans. Sales stalled quickly, and many copies of the album would be returned from retail outlets to distributors after languishing unsold. The disappointing commercial results for his most intimate, revelatory and powerful music would chasten Lennon throughout the rest of his solo career. He never attempted anything this deeply personal again.

By the end of this period, all four solo careers had been launched, though they were bruised by very mixed sales results, fallout over the breakup, and even one notorious copyright infringement lawsuit. All things passed, but all was not well.

Materials
81 tracks: 27 eligible, 6 provisional

Overview

Working together, the Beatles often produced a great deal of finished music in a very small amount of time, so it should be no surprise that they could create even more when working separately, without all the rancor. But there was no other year in their entire collective careers when they released anywhere *near* this much material — 87 tracks in 1970, if you include *Let It Be*.[2] That alone is an astounding, and generally underappreciated, feat for musicians who were also quarreling, both in person and through lawyers, while their business landscape was in complete chaos. Things got very rough, and these four people turned to making music for solace — or at least *distraction*.

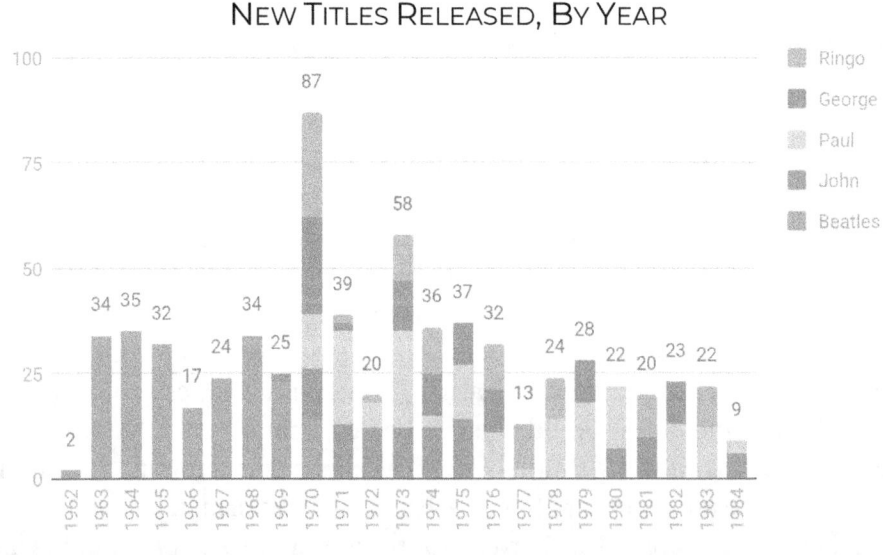

New Titles Released, By Year

---

[2] This does count the two versions of "Let it Be" separately.

12 / DREAM

Admittedly, not all of this music was *recorded* in 1970, but the vast majority actually was. Despite all the music the group had made and recorded together over the previous few years, there was simply no precedent for such an outburst.

Oddly, the tables were turned in terms of quantity. Ringo, who in the entire Beatles catalog had only 11 lead vocals to his name, released a total of 25 tracks in 1970. George, accustomed to being allotted roughly one track per album side, nearly doubled his entire career output in one fell swoop: 28 lead vocals with the Beatles, 23 tracks (19 with vocals) on *All Things Must Pass*. By comparison, Paul and John, who each released "only" a single disc, had barely half as much new music as their former bandmates — 25 tracks to 48. And when you eliminate everything which is purely filler, it gets even more lopsided.

Putting it all together, this massive tapestry of solo tracks runs over 4¼ hours *in released form*. Another hour or so of unreleased songs, mainly by George, had received at least some studio time and might have been available for consideration in the fall of 1970. This robust trove of recorded material contains both great highs and incredible lows. But unlike the sprawling tedium of the *Get Back* session tapes, full of wandering out-of-tune jams that never coalesced into releasable material, all of the new sprawl was at least finished into "releasable" form. And a fair amount was genuinely *great*.

The Beatles had already released one album in 1970, and so it's reasonable to wonder whether they would have needed or wanted, in our slightly altered narrative, to release a second album — let alone a double. But given their dissatisfaction with the overall quality of *Let It Be*, and the availability of so much new music, we are going to assume that they would have wanted to clear the air quickly, get as much as they could of what they recorded to the public, while also meeting the deadline to capture holiday sales. Even if the individual Beatles did not care about this, many of the business people around them would have. If there was any whiff of a new album, there would certainly have been great, albeit probably unspoken, pressure to get it done in time to reap the highest sales, which was always during the holidays.

Presumably, our Assembler would have been listening to potential contributions as they were completed, so some material would have been ruled in or out along the way, not necessarily with the knowledge of the Beatle who recorded it. The sequencing would have been done in one massive session in November 1970.

As suggested in the previous chapter, both Paul and Ringo would have had to agree to forgo releases (*McCartney* and *Sentimental Journey*, respectively) in deference to the potential for a group project later in the year. We are assuming that someone could have said the right words to make that happen. Conversely, by the time they were recording, both George and John would have known that a Beatles project was likely going to happen, and not have needed any further convincing to delay or withhold release. In such a scenario, we can imagine George recording enough to make sure that he can also release a solo album later, created from tracks which don't get on the group album.

We are also going to assume, for reasons enumerated below, that no one would have tried to stop Ringo from releasing *Beaucoups of Blues*, since it offered no material that the Beatles could use. Perhaps it wouldn't have been made at all. If it was, it could have been released in September, just as it was in the real world, or maybe the following spring, and with roughly the same results.

So, what would our Assembler have made of this first, unruly batch of solo recordings? A few things are rather obvious.

First, much of this music sounds at least compatible with what the Beatles have recorded in the recent past, despite the four artists having gone in five different creative directions (counting Ringo twice). It's important to realize that this isn't really a problem to the concept of fused albums because the evolution of the Beatles sound was never *gradual*. Each new Beatles album, starting with *Rubber Soul* in 1965, had sounded starkly different from its predecessor — up to, and including, *Let It Be*. In that way, the new sounds would likely have been welcomed by fans as merely the next evolutionary stage in the band's sound. The fans had even been subtly prepared for such an eventuality by the presence of Eric Clapton (and others) on *The Beatles*, and Billy Preston on *Abbey Road* and much of *Let It Be*.

But there is a thin line between "group" and "solo" in the character of the music — a line which cannot be crossed. We definitely can see, in these tracks, the individual artists diverging: Paul toward his farm and family; John toward his demons and politics; George toward his spirituality and disillusionment; and Ringo toward pure performance. Both John and Paul were also moving toward new spouses and the prospect of children. In these moves, we also see some difficult and potentially troublesome aspects of each artist unleashed in the music of 1970, namely George's anger, Ringo's disorientation, John's desperation, and Paul's detachment. Only by carefully selecting in and around the deepest valleys, can a project be put together which respects the individual artists, with all of their tendencies present, but is still the Beatles.

It's not that certain roads must be avoided on a Beatles album. They had always been trailblazers both in the music and lyrics. But our Assembler would have needed to craft the new album using these volatile ingredients without letting them compete to overwhelm each other. This is inherently the task of imagining the fused albums: To find the right combination of the important subjects the Beatles are writing and singing about, while also allowing each individual voice to have both the space, support, and spotlight that it deserves. To a degree, our Assembler is also charged at times with saving the Beatles from themselves. Only in doing so can they actually still be the Beatles — that is, an artistic unit greater than the sum of its parts.

The stylistic differences in the recordings certainly must be carefully considered.

Harrison and Phil Spector have filled every metaphorical crevice of the tape with sound, starkly contrasting with both McCartney and Lennon, who have stripped everything back to a bare minimum. Both approaches have strengths and weaknesses, but they are not inherently incompatible, especially considering that each artist has selected a recording style which suits the content of the songs. The same can be said for both of Ringo's projects — that the recording style matches the contents — despite the problems this poses for a group project.

Significantly, it is Ringo's projects, despite the speed with which they came together, that demonstrate the type of attention to detail which had characterized all of the Beatle records to that point. *Sentimental Journey* benefits significantly from the presence of George Martin at the helm. He makes sure that every track meets a certain standard of polish, even if the ideas within the arrangements can be questioned. The Nashville album is likewise built on the solid foundation laid by a crack group of seasoned studio musicians. These well-established session pros knew how to churn out releasable material almost as fast as they could play it, and the tracks would have fit in quite credibly among other country music of the era — if only that had been the actual target audience.

The polish on *All Things Must Pass* is very different, almost claustrophobic. One cannot help but wonder just what transgressions Spector's overproduction has buried in the mixes. To whatever degree he actually "produced" Lennon's album, it is clear that precision was not a criteria for him, compounded by the fact that John famously prioritized passion over accuracy. Together, Lennon and Spector may have produced the most intense album that a solo Beatle would ever make, but it is also the sloppiest, by far.

It may be fair to ask whether you could ever have both intensity and accuracy, but the Beatles themselves demonstrated that possibility on multiple occasions — at least partly a function of Paul and John playing tug of war. Our Assembler would have had to tread lightly, but also enforce a certain level of excellence that was part of the Beatles brand. This likely would have taken the form of some judicious editing of John's tracks, or perhaps an overdub or remix here or there, to mitigate some of the most obvious mistakes. McCartney's tracks do not have any such quality issues, probably due to the fact that they were mostly sketches to begin with, but also due to Paul's almost obsessive need to produce clean records, even if without a mixing board! But then, Paul does not typically traffick in *passion* as his stock in trade.

These tensions of sensibility between the individual Beatles, which had previously fueled their recording sessions together, had by 1970 gotten to the point where they were barriers rather than fuel. This is exactly where the concept of a "fused" album can step in as potential savior. Instead of finding these issues *within* recordings, with individual musicians yielding to each other in ways they no longer find comfortable, the same conversations can be had in a macro or meta way *between* the tracks. At least that is the potential which our Assembler would be trying to find in this ungainly conglomeration of music.

John Lennon
13 tracks: 8 eligible, 3 provisional

Sources

L03		"Instant Karma!" / "Who Has Seen the Wind?" R: Jan 70 P: Spector		S: EMI	70-Feb
L04		*John Lennon/Plastic Ono Band* R: Sep-Oct 70 P: Lennon/Ono/Spector		S: EMI, Ascot Sound	70-Dec
		(Unreleased)			

Tracks

God (Lennon)	L04-10, +R, 70-Oct
≈ (Content) Big ideas, big emotions, big words, big music. It doesn't get much bigger than this one.	
Hold On (Lennon)	L04-02, +R, 70-Oct
✓ A warm blanket of self-comfort, wrapped in simple and beautiful music, and a cookie.	
I Found Out (Lennon)	L04-03, +R, 70-Oct
≈ (Content) Primal pain channeled into guitar licks, this really works. Music is original, significant.	
Instant Karma! (Lennon)	L03-01, +G, 70-Jan
✓ Jaunty and catchy but overrated. The lyric is cynical, cold, and the music nothing special.	
Isolation (Lennon)	L04-05, +R, 70-Oct
✓ A "primal" track, it brings its title emotion to life. Effective painting in words and sound.	
Long Lost John (Lennon)	L04, 70-Oct
⊘ (Style/Demo) Rockabilly, and not without potential. Something of a cliché in its unfinished form.	
Look at Me (Lennon)	L04-09, 70-Oct
✓ Feels like a rerun somehow, and the least successful track on the album.	
Love (Lennon)	L04-07, 70-Oct
✓ Fantastic ballad, in which a small sound creates a big emotional space.	
Mother (Lennon)	L04-01, +R, 70-Oct
≈ (Content) JL bares it all. Among his most powerful art ever. Pain felt, transmitted, but not dispelled.	
My Mummy's Dead (Lennon)	L04-11, 70-Oct
⊘ (Content/Style) The instinct is understandable, but as codas go, this is too melodramatic. TMI.	
Remember (Lennon)	L04-06, +R, 70-Oct
✓ Sloppy track, and the song is not quite tamed. But who cares?	
Well Well Well (Lennon)	L04-08, +R, 70-Oct
✓ Primal screams run amok. Not bad, but could have used an edit.	
Working Class Hero (Lennon)	L04-04, +R, 70-Oct
✓ Chilling and pointed, efficient and honest, this is Lennon at his absolute best.	

Though John began his solo career first, he was the last to release his debut album of new studio material. When he did finally start recording solo material in earnest, every track was essential. This would be true throughout his solo career. He left hardly any studio outtakes, and there was very little material that he demoed but did not adapt and finish — at least until he retreated to the Dakota. For the purposes of creating fused Beatles albums, this means that every track he did release will have to be considered carefully, and there will be instances where almost all of his output must be accommodated. This is one such project.

Even after all these years, *John Lennon/Plastic Ono Band* is an easy album to appreciate, but a difficult album to enjoy. As arguably Lennon's best solo album, the *power* of the work is undeniable, and it is rightly considered a classic. But listening to this music can be emotionally fraught. Whenever I think of the album, and consider listening to it, I have a visceral negative reaction because of the emotional work involved and the toll that I know it will take — on me, the listener. As the tolling bells and opening track signal, this is not a record to put on the turntable lightly. John's primal pain is so immediate and amazingly portrayed that I feel simultaneously like a confidante, a voyeur, and an intruder.

But if listening intently is difficult, I also cannot bear listening at a distance, such as in the background while doing something else. To do so would feel disrespectful toward what the artist has accomplished. So I just don't listen to this album, and I think I am not alone in that approach. Can an album that makes you not want to listen to it be deemed a success? In commercial terms, maybe not. In artistic terms, well, it's another matter.

The shorthand description of *Plastic Ono Band* is that it's John's "primal scream album," but like all shorthand descriptions, that is completely insufficient. Primal screams are only one element of this album, given that only three tracks contain anything which might be termed an actual "primal scream." What's more, it appears that John has intentionally tried to space these out in his sequencing. There appears to be a very intentional pattern of highly intense tracks surrounded by less intensity. More on this below.

Much larger than the presence of screaming is the overall effect of the music: Listening to these songs always results in returning psychologically both to John's painful personal tragedies, and to perhaps the most painful era in Beatles history — an unpleasant prospect on almost any day. To his eternal credit, John focused on, and lived, his pain, and poured it onto multitrack tape to create art. When I do listen, I always experience a distinct sense of awe at an artist whose work can reanimate so palpably such swirling emotions. That makes this album simultaneously a shockingly durable artistic statement, and painfully dated. While listening to his emotions so graphically expressed, it is almost impossible to remember that anything else happened after these recording sessions. This music has the ability to both turn back the clock, and then freeze it.

This immediacy was a tough commercial sell,[3] and would also have been a tough sell to the other Beatles and our Assembler. A primary problem, from a marketing standpoint, is the lack of anything resembling a hit single. John couldn't have cared less, of course, and that doesn't detract from the art, but it's hard to sell a record on reputation alone. John's name certainly opened the door for this record, and the anticipation was very high, but then word of mouth took over. Without even a concert tour, something really needs to be accessible and playable on the radio to keep an album — especially one this complex — in the public's imagination. Nothing here matches that description.

That is one way in which including this music as part of a Beatles project actually *helps* it. Any tracks which made that leap would have been heard by millions more people, way more than who have actually heard them. They also would have had a durability, and therefore a much greater and more lasting impact. Ironically, John's disillusionment with the deification of the Beatles could have meant much more had it been heard on a Beatles record.

With other Beatles providing the necessary promotional pieces, there would have been no downside to letting John plumb his personal depths, without the pressure to make it overly commercial. Having proven over and over that he could write hits essentially on demand, he has earned the right to do something different. Ringo's presence notwithstanding, it remains a terrible shame that he was left to chase his demons on record without the benefit of all of his Beatles creative foils — at least one of which shared his sentiments about the group.

John's "commercial" contribution to a group project, therefore, would have had to be "Instant Karma!" Its relationship to a fused album in the fall of 1970 would have been similar to the relationship of the "Get Back" single and the *Let It Be* album. It would have been released well in advance, thought of as something of a teaser single, but from a project still on the drawing board. Adding it to the group project is essentially a no-brainer because it sounds Beatle-y, and sold *very* well. There would have been no question.

A secondary problem with the *Plastic Ono Band* material is the risk that John's desolate intensity would not sit well next to the other new recordings turned in by Ringo, George and Paul. When considered in isolation, some of John's tracks seem

---

[3] Murrells reports in *Million Selling Records* (pg. 310) that the album had advanced orders of 2.5 million, but it definitely did not sell that many. As of 2020, it has not been certified platinum, with estimates of worldwide sales running just under one million.

like black holes from which nothing could ever escape. The other Beatles and the Assembler might have felt that it was all too much for a fused album that they hoped would also be very commercial, even as it ushered in a new era for the group. Alternately, John might have feared that his intended intensity would be overly diluted by placement next to tracks by Paul or, God forbid, George (whose songwriting John famously could not abide).

JOHN LENNON/PLASTIC ONO BAND STRUCTURE

Title	Style	Tone	Function
1. "Mother"	gospel variant	primal	tension
2. "Hold On"	ballad	relaxed	release
3. "I Found Out"	rock	primal	tension
4. "Working Class Hero"	ballad	intense	both, simultaneous
5. "Isolation"	gospel/ballad hybrid	multiple	alternating
1. "Remember"	rock	driving	tension
2. "Love"	ballad	relaxed	release
3. "Well Well Well"	rock	primal	tension
4. "Look at Me"	ballad	relaxed	release
5. "God"	gospel variant	multiple	alternating
6. "My Mummy's Dead"	nursery rhyme	detached	coda, vacant

Those fears, however, lead right to the second advantage of combining his work with that of the others, and it has to do with tension and release. The alternation between these two states is part of the recipe for a strong album, and for strong music in general. Indeed, this idea is embedded in all music, and other artistic media, and the Beatles traded on it routinely throughout their career.

In that regard, we should note that John has sequenced his album just about as well as possible, given the materials he had to work with. He basically alternates between tracks which bring tension or potentially offer release, sometimes finding elements of each within a single track.

Unfortunately, even the tracks he has used to provide release contain a component of despair which prevents them from fully discharging their purpose. Even when he sings, "it's gonna be alright," the listener can't help but wonder whether he really believes it. It feels more like a façade of hopefulness over a deeper sense of something dark. The familiar undercurrent of Beatle optimism is utterly missing. This will ultimately give *Dream* its essential pathos.

As an artist, Lennon certainly has the right to this approach. He was, after all, in the process of trying to undermine the hagiography which had grown up around the band. Making desolate music seems, at first, to be a fine way to accomplish that.

But when you put these tracks next to those of the other former Beatles in this era, you get a much more complex and satisfying accomplishment of the same task. John was not the only former Beatle trading in desolation in 1970. Paul writes of loneliness ("Man We Was Lonely"), George writes of darkness ("Beware of Darkness"), and Ringo trades largely in despair on many tracks on *Beaucoups of Blues*. This unity of emotion has the potential for great power. In assembling the fused album, finding this power and magnifying it will be a primary objective.

To that end, as stated above, almost everything John recorded for his album must at least be considered for the group project, but this is where some things get very sticky.

The two "mother" songs are perhaps the most problematic. The demo of "My Mummy's Dead" would not have been considered. "Mother" would have to be considered, but only used if a suitable place in the running order could be found. That is pretty hard to imagine because in some ways the song feels just too personal for a group effort. It would almost literally stop the show no matter where on a Beatles album it appeared. John's use of the song as an opener is a nod to the importance of the subject matter in his personal journey, as well as an acknowledgement of the power in the recording. On his album, it sets a tone that (intentionally) colors everything which comes after it, almost to the point where it is the whole artistic statement in microcosm.

All of this makes "Mother" the one song on *Plastic Ono Band* most likely to be diminished by placing it on a group album. "Julia" had worked on *The White Album* because it is beautiful, simple, understated, and the angst is suggested by, but subsumed into, John's slinky guitars. The same cannot be said for "Mother," which descends majestically into crashing piano chords and primal screams that leave a scorched earth of grief behind. Indeed, as we saw in his sequencing, the primal screams heard here are so intense that the rest would have to be carefully spaced throughout the album to prevent them from being overwhelming. Even then, it turned out to be too much for most of the audience. On this opening track, nothing could be done to reduce their impact, and trying to do such a thing would be a crime against the art anyway. The best way to handle this track with regard to an imagined Beatles album may be to just leave it off.

Arguably the most complicated track on the album, "God" is universally hailed as one of John's masterworks, but it presents a unique set of problems when considered in the context of a Beatles project. The final section amounts to a classic example of John's penchant for self-conscious list songs.[4] The obvious problem arises when he goes all the way to declaring disbelief in "Beatles." This would have been a tough sell, especially when followed immediately by the "dream is over" segment. It forces us to ask whether this track has any chance of finding a place on a rescued Beatles album.

Perhaps a better question to ask about "God," however, is whether it would have been written at all if there was a prospect for a new Beatles album in late 1970. Would John have felt so free to create his long list of disbelief if not for the pain he was suffering at the time? Or might the list have been subtly different? Might a reduction in animosity have led to a different lyrical resolution in the song? These are obviously questions which cannot be answered, but we will assume for this project that it would have been written just as it was. Since our slightly altered narrative requires only a small shift from events in the real world, there are good reasons to think John would have felt this way no matter what.

Given these assumptions, the real reason it feels eligible for this project is that John was very plain in interviews of the era that by "dream" he meant the 1960s, which *included* the 60s-era Beatles, but was not *limited to* the Beatles. In December of 1970, when the song was still very fresh, and the emotions very immediate, Lennon explained it to Jann Wenner this way:

> ...Beatles was the final thing because it's like I no longer believe in myth, and Beatles is another myth. I don't believe in it. The dream's over. I'm not just talking about The Beatles is over, I'm talking about the generation thing. The dream's over, and I have personally got to get down to so-called reality.[5]

As such, a disbelief in "Beatles" isn't necessarily an indictment of the group, or the group dynamic, or McCartney, or anything *within*, but rather the role the band has played, its relationship to the audience, and the many things which have been ascribed to it throughout the culture. A disbelief in the myth of the Beatles actually *requires* a redefinition of the group and its relationship to the world — which could,

---

[4] "List songs" became a staple of popular music in the early 20th century. Essentially, the lyrics are built around a long list of items which might be related, or unrelated, or somehow make sense (or intentionally not) together. One classic list song in popular music is Billy Joel's "We Didn't Start the Fire." "Glass Onion" and "Dig It" are earlier examples by the Beatles, while "Give Peace a Chance," "Let 'Em In" and "Cook of the House" are examples from the solo era. Broadway composer and lyricist Stephen Sondheim has suggested that list songs, despite their apparent complexity and cleverness to the listener's ear, are actually among the easiest to write, and therefore represent something of a cheat. As such they are not well regarded among songwriters.

[5] *Lennon Remembers*, pg. 11

but need not, imply a disbanding of the group. John is essentially saying that what the Beatles *were* is over, and the time has come for something new. Any fused Beatles album created at this point would have sent that message loud and clear, making the inclusion of "God" seem, upon reflection, almost a necessity.

Thinking of it in that way, the song can be seen as something of a charter for what might come next, while also being a pronouncement of death for what has gone before. In this way it extends a familiar idea — burying the "old" Beatles — that the group first referenced on the cover of *Sgt. Pepper*. The fans, however, could be forgiven for quaking upon hearing such lyrics on a Beatles album, which is definitely something to consider.

All of this leads to the reason to keep it eligible for a group project, despite the liabilities: It is provocative and emotional without being irrational. It is a very good song, and the meaning of the lyrics, far from being certain, is worthy of consideration by all who hear it. Contextualizing it next to the work of the other Beatles gives the meaning a different shade from what it had on *John Lennon/Plastic Ono Band*, to be sure, but the added complexity, ambiguity and provocation is very much in keeping with what John expressed that he had always wanted for the group.

Again, whether it would actually work on the album will be a difficult question for our Assembler. As you will hear, "God" ultimately serves as the linchpin of the album's theme, all of its glorious provocation intact.

The remaining tracks on *John Lennon/Plastic Ono Band* tend to get overshadowed by the very powerful music at the beginning and end, as well as by "Working Class Hero" in the middle. All but two of these will be on the rescued album, and will be discussed in greater detail when it comes to the assembly, later in this chapter.

As mentioned, John will ultimately produce much less music than his former bandmates, but any hope of making up the disparity with outtakes will be frustrated. To both his credit and detriment, Lennon was an artist who wanted to use every scrap of idea for something. As such, there are very few other demos out there from this period, and no real studio outtakes which could have been seriously considered for a group album. An early recording of "I'm the Greatest" shows the song as not yet quite ripe, and thus not really eligible. His playful medley of "Honey Don't/Matchbox/Don't Be Cruel" recorded during the *John Lennon/Plastic Ono Band* sessions was clearly for personal enjoyment only, though, thanks to YouTube, anyone can enjoy it now.

One final, sad reminder: Lennon was famous for plucking new songs out of thin air when he needed to. Many sources describe both John and Paul as only starting to write new material when a deadline loomed. It is therefore easy to imagine him creating additional material for a Beatles project if there had been one. Alas, such songs were never written and must remain a subject for our imaginations.

Ringo Starr
29 tracks: 4 eligible, 2 provisional

Sources

S01	*Sentimental Journey* R: Oct 69 - Mar 70 P: Martin	S: Various (7)	70-Mar
S02	*Beaucoups of Blues* R: Jun 70 P: Drake	S: Music City (Nashville)	70-Sep
S03	~~"Beaucoups of Blues"~~ / "Coochy Coochy" R: Jun 70 P: Drake	S: Music City (Nashville)	70-Oct
S04	"It Don't Come Easy" / "Early 1970" R: Mar-Oct 70 P: A: Harrison, B: Starr	S: Trident, EMI	71-Apr
	(Unreleased)		

Tracks

$15 Draw (Pickard) — S02-07, 70-Jun
⊘ (Style/Quality) Story song. Ringo's a guitar player now? Vocal deep in reverb. Cheap product.

Beaucoups of Blues (Rabin) — S02-01, 70-Jun
⊘ (Style/Quality) Straining at the top of his range, uncharacteristic, BVs and dobro are hardcore country

Blue, Turning Grey Over You (Razaf/Waller) — S01-07, 70-Feb
⊘ (Style) Big band really swings. RS double-tracked vocal can't keep up. Not right for him.

Bye Bye Blackbird (Dixon/Henderson) — S01-04, 70-Mar
⊘ (Quality/Style) Back porch banjo. Awkward segue to big band. RS is probably dancing. Also awkward.

Coochy-Coochy (Starkey) — S03-02, 70-Jun
✓ A one-chord jam, but sounds like they were having fun. It's Ringo-quirky in many ways.

Dream (Mercer) — S01-09, 70-Feb
✓ A standard that actually fits Ringo's voice and emotional range, in a very nice arrangement.

Early 1970 (Starkey) — S04-02, +JG, 70-Oct
≈ (Content/Quality) Sweet sentiments, and simple. Hopeful. But not "Beatle quality" writing.

Fastest Growing Heartache in the West (Kingston/Dycus) — S02-03, 70-Jun
⊘ (Style/Quality) Fiddle and steel, but set very high for Ringo's voice.

Have I Told You Lately That I Love You? (Wiseman) — S01-11, 70-Feb
⊘ (Style/Quality) Just add go-go dancers and comic takes for the camera. Dreadful.

I Wouldn't Have You Any Other Way (Howard) — S02-09, 70-Jun
⊘ (Style/Quality) Slow dance, complete with tickled ivories and female duet voice. Un-Ringo.

I'd Be Talking All the Time (Howard/Kingston) — S02-06, 70-Jun
⊘ (Style/Quality) "Ringo'd be talkin' all the time"

	I'm a Fool to Care (Daffan)	S01-05, 70-Feb
	✓ Voorman has disavowed it, but this is a very nice arrangement, and RS sounds great.	
	It Don't Come Easy (Starkey)	S04-01, +G, 70-Mar
	✓ Among Ringo's best ever. A great start that regrettably didn't set the pattern.	
	Let the Rest of the World Go By (Ball/Brennan)	S01-12, 70-Feb
	⊘ (Quality) Likable in some ways, but sounds horribly dated. RS sings harmony!	
	Loser's Lounge (Pierce)	S02-10, 70-Jun
	⊘ (Style/Quality) Very straight country song, and very wrong for Ringo. He has nothing for it.	
	Love Don't Last Long (Howard)	S02-02, 70-Jun
	⊘ (Style/Quality) Vocal tremolo, sad story, formulaic, key change.	
	Love Is a Many Splendoured Thing (Fain/Webster)	S01-08, 70-Mar
	⊘ (Style) A nice arrangement for just about anyone else. RS is buried in a chorus of 60s clichés.	
	Nashville Freakout (Drake/Starkey/et. al. (+15))	S02, 70-Jun
	⊘ (Filler) Probably was fun to record, but nothing really to it.	
	Night and Day (Porter)	S01-02, 69-Oct
	≈ (Quality) Starts with promise, but vocal limitations are evident immediately. Band is fantastic.	
	Sentimental Journey (Green/Brown/Homer)	S01-01, 70-Mar
	⊘ (Quality) Sounds like a joke, like it might break into something cool at any second. Doesn't. A total mess.	
	Silent Homecoming (Pickard)	S02-12, 70-Jun
	⊘ (Style/Quality) Another sad story song. Timely, but has aged poorly. Melody is too much for RS.	
	Stardust (Carmichael/Parish)	S01-06, 69-Nov
	⊘ (Quality) RS strains to tame the melody. Instrumental flourishes tend to go over the top. Too much.	
	Waiting (Howard)	S02-11, 70-Jun
	⊘ (Style/Quality) Why is Ringo singing this? Wrong for his voice, image, talents, persona. Bad idea.	
	Whispering Grass (Don't Tell the Trees) (Fisher/Fisher)	S01-03, 70-Mar
	⊘ (Quality) RS vocal is actually charming, but the busy string arrangement piles on the sap.	
	Wine, Women and Loud Happy Songs (Kingston)	S02-08, 70-Jun
	⊘ (Style/Quality) Might work if Ringo were some sort of loser. But he's not, and this song is just bad for him.	
	Wishing Book, The (Adcock)	S02, 70-Jun
	⊘ (Style/Quality) Much like the rest of the album, it's just wrong for Ringo.	
	Without Her (Pickard)	S02-04, 70-Jun
	⊘ (Style/Quality) Kind of sounds like The Monkees	
	Woman of the Night (Pickard)	S02-05, 70-Jun
	⊘ (Style/Quality) Again very high, story song.	
	You Always Hurt the One You Love (Roberts/Fisher)	S01-10, 70-Mar
	⊘ (Style) Great potential disappears into a pure cheese arrangement. But don't blame the great band!	

When people talk about the early post-breakup era in Beatles history, George Harrison's burst of creativity tends to be the headline, overlooking the fact that Ringo made two complete — and *completely different* — albums within six months of each other. Unfortunately, both of Ringo's efforts are basically novelty records, of very little interest to anyone, and they were disappointing in many ways. This *should* have alerted the other Beatles that there was potential trouble brewing out in solo album land — if that were not yet apparent — but they were too busy squabbling.

Sentimental Journey has an earnest hopefulness that almost saves it, descended no doubt from Ringo's fondness for songs he remembered singing as a child. But it was not the right material for his first solo recording, and the idea just didn't work. Despite George Martin's insistence on high quality recordings, the overall "cheese" factor is just too high. Many parts of this album come across as the soundtrack to a variety show that never got made — thankfully. Even when trying to listen through 1969 ears, the songs themselves were already mostly clichés. The arrangements, though competent and sometimes imaginative (with grating exceptions), can't save the tracks, and also can't seem to figure out how to work around Ringo's liabilities. A crooner he is not.

This is not to say that Starkey's voice is *bad*, of course. It is *highly distinctive* — a good thing — but also *range limited*, in both pitch and expression. The first thing that anyone producing Ringo must accept is the responsibility to use his voice only in a way which shows off its best qualities. When you consider the 11 Beatles recordings which featured Ringo as lead singer, you can see that the group recognized his limitations, and resolved not to bump up against them. This is relatively easy to do on that scale, and the strategy produced only winners for him in the Beatles. When he requires 10 to 12 songs in a row on the same album, it is much more difficult. Regrettably, this has been proven over and over in his solo career.

RINGO'S ELEVEN[6]

Song	Album
"Boys"	*Please Please Me*
"I Wanna Be Your Man"	*With the Beatles*
"Matchbox"	*Long Tall Sally* (EP)
"Honey Don't"	*Beatles for Sale*
"Act Naturally"	*Help!*
"What Goes On"	*Rubber Soul*
"Yellow Submarine"	*Revolver*
"With a Little Help from My Friends"	*Sgt. Pepper*
"Don't Pass Me By"	*The White Album*
"Good Night"	*The White Album*
"Octopus's Garden"	*Abbey Road*

---

[6] Starkey is also generally credited with co-lead vocals on "Flying" and "Carry That Weight," though his voice is subsumed into the mix as part of a whole group sound.

In those early days of his solo career, and at various other points along the way, it was felt that Ringo's immense and undeniable charm was the primary saleable commodity, so a certain amount of clunkiness in his vocals could be excused. *Sentimental Journey* trades on this idea directly. But even a cursory listening reveals that while his vocals had been fine in small doses, they are problematic as the focal point for a whole album. The presence of his singing voice had been very important to the classic Beatles albums,[7] but it was problematic at center-stage due to the limits of his upper vocal range,[8] dubious accuracy with pitch overall, and his limited expressive abilities. Arguably, this would be a problem throughout his solo career.

Fortunately, there are tracks on this album with redeeming, even Beatle-y, qualities. The two songs which the Assembler and all three other Beatles would have considered accepting into a new album project, "I'm a Fool to Care" and "Dream," have the benefit of solidly unsentimental arrangements, made by people intimately familiar with the group, Klaus Voorman and George Martin, respectively. Both melodies have a smallish range, and have been carefully set in the heart of Ringo's vocal range, requiring no vocal stretching at all. The subject matter picks up on aspects of his vocal inflections, making both tracks sound like a natural fit for him temperamentally, much in the manner of "Good Night."

These two tracks also succeed because the songs themselves had not yet turned into moldy oldies when the album was made.[9] Such cannot be said for most of the others, especially the title track, with its inexplicable use of a talk box for the solo, and the very unfortunate, banjo-based "Bye, Bye, Blackbird" — complete with simulated tap dancing — arguably the two most grating arrangements on the album.

The other arrangements are all either beyond Ringo's abilities, or not worthy of him. The big band arrangement of "Night and Day," commissioned from Count Basie but credited to one of his arrangers, Chico O'Farrill, swings nicely and is among the best on the album. But Ringo's vocal falters, and just cannot do it justice. Still, it is good enough to keep on our provisional list. A similar criticism applies to other

---

[7] *A Hard Day's Night, Magical Mystery Tour*, and *Let It Be* were without Ringo's lead vocals, as is the entire catalog of songs found only on singles. All were the poorer for it.

[8] Geoff Emerick told the story of the other Beatles gathering close around Ringo to give him enough courage to hit the final note of "With a Little Help from My Friends." The note in question is the E above middle C, which is described by Emerick as a near impossible task for Starkey. But a quick survey shows that Ringo has not only hit this note many times before and after, but also gone even higher without any special difficulty — at least no more difficulty than he has with pitch in general. His actual vocal range would have to be classified as baritone, and with a full two octaves evident across his catalog, he may actually have the largest vocal range of any of the four Beatles. That said, range and pitch accuracy are two very different things.

[9] Indeed, these two songs, despite being stalwarts of the Tin Pan Alley era, remain to this day among the least over-exposed relative to the rest of that catalog. Putting them on a Beatles album would have no doubt changed that.

arrangements, like "Whispering Grass" and "Blue, Turning Grey Over You," which are competent but cannot offset a weak vocal performance, and would have been wrong for a group project.

Among the unworthy arrangements, Quincy Jones turns in an instantly-dated arrangement of, "Love is a Many Splendoured Thing," which solves the lead vocalist issue by burying Ringo in a chorus of backup singers, and manages to sound like it belongs in an episode of *The Partridge Family*. Similarly dated is, "You Always Hurt the One You Love," which might have been better for Sonny and Cher. Elmer Bernstein's dreadful, "Have I Told You Lately That I Love You?" contains orchestral stabs and comical inserts perfectly placed for double-takes and visual gags, reminiscent of something more appropriate for *Laugh-In*. "Let the Rest of the World Go By" tries to evoke "Good Night," but manages to merely summarize all of the other clichés and bad decisions found in this collection.

You might think that the third track with a Beatles connection, "Stardust," arranged by McCartney and nearly selected as the title track, would be a shoo-in for a 1970 fused Beatles album, but it is overly cheesy, as if Paul felt that hamming up the arrangement would help the singer. The familiar-but-slippery and rangey melody is far beyond Starkey's abilities, and the arrangement comes off as incredibly condescending, as if to say, "We all know this is cheesy, so let's cheese it up real good." As such, it is very difficult to get through without cringing. Though we have to assume that Paul would have lobbied for including this track on a group album, there's no way it belongs next to the other new Beatles recordings. Our Assembler would have rejected it quickly and emphatically. That it got through onto Ringo's record may actually speak to how low the expectations were for the project in the first place, despite the elaborate nature of the production.

But the two good tracks really have some life in them, and can be used on the Beatles album to provide a necessary counterbalance to the rampant intensity of the John and George contributions, and the subdued nature of Paul's. They can be used as release points, being less serious, less intense, and more easily digestible, allowing them to work as counterpoint and palette-cleansers next to more complex works. This is the role Ringo's tracks always served on Beatles albums, and these can do the same thing here. These two tracks have Ringo sounding the most comfortable and like himself, a very important consideration. It is also a relief to bring forward at least *some* of this material, which Ringo clearly cherished.

Beaucoups of Blues, alas, has no such redeeming tracks. Though the album supposedly has apologists among the fan base, they are few and far between. This is an incredibly unfortunate collection, probably the most awkward album that any former Beatle would ever make.

There is little consolation in acknowledging that everyone's heart was in the right place. A listener is left to wonder if anyone involved had ever heard a Beatles record.

As suggested above, this album may have been inevitable as a marketing experiment. But the artistic idea, perhaps also inevitable given Ringo's tastes, is really terrible. The songs cast him as a sort of balladeer, telling generally forlorn stories about sad, random people ("Eleanor Rigby" with a twang). Despite the obvious excellence of the musicians, the album's execution is serviceable but uninspired — at least by Beatles standards. It is mainstream market product, not Beatle Brand. Despite the claim that the songs were written specifically for Ringo, they seem not customized at all to his actual performing style — which might not have improved things anyway. The overall lasting impression is that the session musicians essentially made a "session" album with Ringo serving as the guest vocalist, in the same way they might have done with any number of other, largely interchangeable country vocalists of the era. The finished product is as far removed from the work of the Beatles as might be imagined.

It's important to note, however, that the material isn't *inherently* bad. Though in no way groundbreaking, this is a perfectly serviceable country album. Compare it to contemporaneous country albums such as Bobby Bare's *This is Bare Country*, or *Skid Row Joe: Down in the Alley* by Porter Wagoner. The songs are, in many ways, interchangeable.

The Jordanaires, true country royalty by then, lend their distinctive, classic backup vocals that many people — even rock-n-roll fans — appreciated. But their presence tells you all you need to know about the album relative to the Beatles: It is cut from an entirely different piece of cloth.

Ringo's singing doesn't even sound like the Ringo we know and love from the very recent "Octopus's Garden." In what sounds like an attempt to add expressiveness, he sings somewhat like a man who has lost his dog. His voice lacks power and confidence. His singing comes off as plaintive and homely, without even the benefit of double-tracking to disguise his pitch issues. He treads very gingerly on songs which push in many different ways beyond his typical material. Indeed, the whole project might have been more successful with a genuine country voice, such as Willie Nelson or Conway Twitty. It was all just plain wrong for a guy from Liverpool.

As such, none of the finished tracks are of a style or quality that the Beatles would have accepted. The playing, though competent and stylish for country music at the time, is workmanlike — especially when compared to the work of his former bandmates. The production is banal and absolutely by-the-book — especially when compared to everything the Beatles recorded after *Help!*. Nothing here would be elevated or better contextualized next to the tracks produced by the other former Beatles. Indeed, this project may have seemed like a good idea, but it wasn't. No one likely would have tried to talk Ringo out of releasing this, maybe they should have.

12 / DREAM

Albums like this are the worst kind of career filler, and in the real world, it almost killed Starkey's solo career before it started. It would take the whiff of a Beatle reunion three years later to wash away the stain of this unfortunate album.

The lone saving grace from the sessions is Starkey's only songwriting contribution — the one-chord, semi-jam, "Coochy Coochy," thrown away on the B-side of a single that no one heard. Surprisingly, this track actually sounds something like the other Beatles music of the era, and fits nicely on the rescued album, though our Assembler would probably have insisted on some additional editing. Given its simplicity and rambling nature, it  might be tempting to classify this as filler, but it is infectious, quirky, and a considerable step up from something like "Don't Pass Me By." Its primary attraction is that it doesn't aspire to be anything more than it is. It's just pure Ringo, having some fun singing, blessedly double-tracked. He sounds relaxed, and there are none of the vocal or emotional challenges which revealed his considerable limitations on the two albums.

Rounding out Ringo's work in this era is the single, "It Don't Come Easy." Though in the real world it was not released until later, much of the recording had been completed by the fall of 1970, and it fits stylistically with the rest of the material in this era. There is little doubt that this track would have been polished and completed for inclusion on a Beatles album if there had been one in  late 1970, especially given the significant presence of George Harrison.

This song actually answers the question of what was missing from the other two Ringo solo projects. Here Ringo is singing music written by someone who knew his voice and his strengths very well, in a style descended from the Beatles, and with gigantic commercial potential — which it actually did realize. This is one of Ringo's best ever solo tracks, and it sits very nicely with the work of the other Beatles. It also highlights the folly of Ringo's two real-world album projects.

The single was backed with "Early 1970," an incredibly interesting track, and one which must be considered for inclusion because of its provenance. Three of the Beatles would probably have lobbied for it (possibly because they played on it, although John's involvement remains unconfirmed), but Paul would have most likely exercised his veto because the lyrics cleary take a (gentle) swipe at him. I don't think the Assembler would have wanted this on the album anyway, given that its clunky simplicity is just not a match for the sophistication of the material the other Beatles were recording at the time. It would have stuck out terribly if inserted among the much better material available for the album. Still, it's a little piece of fun which might have emerged, with a slight edit of the lyrics, as a Beatles B-side.

So, what would have happened to Ringo's two solo albums if the Beatles had been collaborating? There were enough leftover tracks to complete and release *Sentimental Journey* even if two tracks were repurposed to the Beatles project, but it probably would have been best to leave it unreleased — except perhaps to Ringo's mum, for whom it was actually made. Or perhaps it could have been saved for later in his career, when it might have made more sense. *Beaucoups of Blues* could easily still have been released, perhaps on its original schedule or a few months later in early 1971, so as not to compete with the group project. As a test of the country market for Ringo, it still would have failed. Perhaps, with a fused Beatles album hovering around on the schedule, it wouldn't even have been made. And if it had, cooler heads might have tossed this material into the ether, where even bootleggers probably would have taken a pass.

Paul McCartney
16 tracks: 8 eligible, no provisional

Sources

M01	*McCartney* R: Dec 69 - Feb 70 P: McCartney		S: Home, Morgan, EMI	70-Apr
	(Unreleased)			

Tracks

Don't Cry Baby (McCartney) ⊘ (Filler) Instrumental of "Oo You"	M01, 70-Jan
Every Night (McCartney) ✓ An instant classic. Great musical idea, and nice lyric.	M01-04, 70-Feb
Hot as Sun/Glasses (McCartney) ⊘ (Filler) A doodle.	M01-05, 70-Jan
Junk (McCartney) ✓ Cloying, but simple — in a generally good way.	M01-06, 70-Jan
Kreen - Akrore (McCartney) ⊘ (Filler) Paul can drum. He can really drum. Questionable way to end the album.	M01-13, 70-Feb
Lovely Linda, The (McCartney) ⊘ (Filler) A pleasant stub. Appropriate way to transition from group to solo.	M01-01, 70-Jan
Man We Was Lonely (McCartney) ✓ Alternately cheesy and profound. Bad chorus spoils good verses.	M01-07, 70-Feb
Maybe I'm Amazed (McCartney) ✓ One of Paul's all-time great love songs. And this recording is definitive.	M01-12, 70-Feb
Momma Miss America (McCartney) ⊘ (Filler) Template for many forgettable B-sides to come.	M01-09, 70-Jan

12 / DREAM

	Oo You (McCartney)	M01-08, 70-Jan
	✓ Template for the "solo rocker." Nice riff, but feels somehow hollow.	
	Singalong Junk (McCartney)	M01-11, 70-Feb
	⊘ (Filler) Pleasant filler. Less cloying without lyrics, but aimless.	
	Suicide (McCartney)	M01, 70-Jan
	⊘ (Style/Quality) Music hall, with strange lyric, diffuse melody, weird word accents, a curiosity only.	
	Sunshine Sometime (McCartney)	M03, 70-Oct
	✓ Simply and lovely, giving the impression of a morning in Scotland.	
	Teddy Boy (McCartney)	M01-10, 70-Jan
	✓ Classic or misfire? A story song with only sketchy story. Carefully written.	
	That Would Be Something (McCartney)	M01-02, 70-Jan
	✓ Only a one-line lyric, yet it's enough. The simple riff works.	
	Valentine Day (McCartney)	M01-03, 70-Jan
	⊘ (Filler) A fine instrumental, but probably could have been a nice song.	

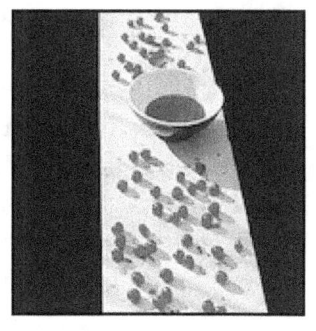

Paul McCartney's solo debut is fascinating in its slightness and complexity, its maddening vacancy yet simple charm, its unfinished feel which overall reads as gentle elegance. Ultimately, it is a genuinely satisfying record — just barely. Likable, but disappointing. It feels incomplete, but also somehow just right. Very vexing.

The album is populated by five songs which represent complete ideas, four of which must be acknowledged as McCartney masterworks. Two of the other songs are only partially completed but still engaging, while the remaining six, though fine displays of McCartney's musicianship, must be considered basically filler. That is a hard designation to apply because any of these ideas could have probably become fine songs ("Singalong Junk" actually did), but in their present form they come off as basically Paul just noodling around — albeit interestingly.

On a breezy, 33-minute album, it works out to 11 minutes which have gone down as some of Paul's best-ever solo tracks, 8½ minutes that are serviceable at best, and 13½ minutes that are interesting and pleasant but somewhat maddening in their perpetual state of unrealized potential.[10] Given that breakdown, the only way this album succeeds is as a triumph of sequencing — and it is very much that. More on that in a moment.

Our task here, of course, is to tear it into its component parts, and mine it for material which could go on a rescued Beatles album. Some such material is readily apparent, and the question becomes where to draw the line between sufficiently finished tracks and those which are too sketchy. Had there been a Beatles album,

---

[10] By contrast, the first two platters of George's magnum opus contain only one track which can be plainly characterized as filler — the second version of "Isn't It a Pity" — which comes to five minutes out of 75.

Paul might have fleshed some of these out, but that potential doesn't help us while looking back like this.

Surprisingly, the thinness of some of these tracks only becomes apparent when you extract them from Paul's running order and/or set them next to anything from this era by John, George or Ringo. The lesser tracks actually sound noticeably weaker — the *opposite* of what a fused Beatles album should accomplish! Listening alphabetically, for example, makes it easy to see just how little there is here to work with. Yet *McCartney* is an album which manages to be more than the sum of its parts, rendering even the best tracks as somewhat forlorn when removed from the album's context. You have to give Paul credit for turning this collection of notions into a classic.

But the net result, when broken back into its component parts, is that Paul's contribution to an imagined Beatles album seems muted by comparison to the others, which is an accurate reflection of his production during this period. The case can be made that the other Beatles would have been happy at this development, given their lingering resentment over his recent domination of the band.

The five tracks on *McCartney* which actually feel reasonably finished are formidable, indeed. "Maybe I'm Amazed" is justifiably recognized as one of Paul's masterworks, and despite many fine live performances of the song in these latter years, the version on *McCartney* is clearly definitive. Paul's vocal uncharacteristically reveals his emotions as his melody hovers above the descending chord progression, only gradually yielding to it. It captures not just the spirit of the idea and the plaintive emotions behind it, but the spirit of the moment in history when his vulnerability — yes, I'm using the v-word in reference to Paul McCartney! — was at its peak. The bombast required later for arena performances always takes that vulnerability away, which probably feels more comfortable for Paul, but diminishes the song by no small measure. One wishes he would only ever sing it in clubs, alone at the piano, in low light.

Similarly, "Every Night," "Junk" and "Teddy Boy" are Paul at his best. Unlike "Maybe I'm Amazed," however, these three songs had been offered to the Beatles during the *Get Back* sessions. Paul has created clean readings of these songs for his solo album, while perhaps imagining something more elaborate had the group agreed to take them up later. In other words, the recordings of these songs on *McCartney* offer evidence to support the idea that some of these tracks may have actually been intended as demos first. The fifth song in this category is "Man We Was Lonely," which begins with a clichéd chorus that marks it as a potential throwaway, but shifts into a verse which is fully realized, and highly engaging.

Those five songs are so diverse in style and content that they really shouldn't sit very well next to one another on the same album. And even when taken as a whole, they come nowhere near a complete and coherent artistic statement. Paul has masterfully sequenced the tracks so that each significant song is surrounded by something less significant, and transitional.

The diversity is never apparent because each significant song is allowed to breathe, being both preceded and followed by something less substantial, serving effectively as the best kind of palette-cleansers.[11] It works both as a method of contextualizing the gems, and as a very clever stretching of material. His sequencing suggests that he thought "That Would Be Something" and "Oo You" also held stand-alone value, but despite some charm, neither is actually a complete song — though this only becomes apparent when you remove them from the context he has given them, another testament to his assembly. In context they both sound more substantial because of what precedes and follows them, but each of these songs needs another verse, and maybe a bridge, to feel complete. This is why they must be considered as semi-filler: songs which, if selected, would then have been finished properly — or perhaps paired with a compatible snippet from Lennon.

McCartney Structure

Title	Type	Status
1. "The Lovely Linda"	vocal	sketch
2. "That Would Be Something"	vocal	incomplete
3. "Valentine Day"	instrumental	sketch
4. "Every Night"	vocal	complete
5. "Hot as Sun/Glasses"	instrumental	sketch
6. "Junk"	vocal	complete
7. "Man We Was Lonely"	vocal	complete
1. "Oo You"	vocal	incomplete
2. "Momma Miss America"	instrumental	sketch
3. "Teddy Boy"	vocal	complete
4. "Singalong Junk"	instrumental	complete
5. "Maybe I'm Amazed"	vocal	complete
6. "Kreen – Akrore"	instrumental	complete

The remaining instrumental tracks would never have been considered for a Beatles album, and so become orphans in this process. Of those, the closing track,

---

[11] John does almost exactly the same thing on *Plastic Ono Band* (see analysis above), though the effect there is not as pronounced due to the overall intensity of the album. *McCartney* has no such issue. Here, it works beautifully.

"Kreen-Akrore" is the most compelling. But Ringo was right when he said that drum solos are boring, and no amount of "ahs" can disguise that this track is basically a long drum solo. McCartney's chops were never in question, and he shows them off extensively both here and on the other instrumental tracks, but had these been finished into real songs, it is at least possible to imagine them as something much more memorable. As they are, out of the album's context they come off as a guy just blowing off some steam.[12]

Knowing what we do about Paul's working methods and acknowledged perfectionism, one has to wonder whether he ever intended to release these tracks at all. The stories told about this era make the *McCartney* album look almost like a bluff that got called. If your volatile, hyperbolic, drug-addled, primal screaming partner has declared "divorce," what better way to put pressure on him than to threaten a solo release that would send the whole world into a tizzy? When Ringo arrived at Paul's house on March 31, 1970, to deliver a letter from the other Beatles brusquely denying Paul's request for an early release on this album, Paul may have been surprised, expecting the message to be something more like, "Let's not do anything hasty. Let's talk about this. We can work it out. Don't release your album until we've had a chance to figure this all out." It is certainly a point where a better alternate reality could have emerged.

When the response turned out instead to be a very cold rebuff, Paul may have found his bluff called, and needed to go forward with an album that even he knew was rather slight. The letter may have sounded to Paul more like a dare: "Go ahead and do it. We won't stop you from releasing this shit. If this is what a solo McCartney sounds like, we've got nothing to fear. Good luck out there." That would certainly add fuel to the explanation for his uncharacteristic and surprisingly ungracious response to Ringo.[13]

I do not know of any documentary evidence to specifically support this idea, but with only 11 minutes of actually completed songs on this album — essentially a solo EP stretched precariously into an LP — the question must be asked. It's hard to believe that McCartney would have preferred to start his solo career with such a slight collection. Were he serious about making a releasable album in late 1969, it would have made more sense for it to be on a much larger scale, say the scale of *Ram*. This is even more likely the case when you consider the scale of Ringo's first solo release, of which Paul was keenly aware, and to which he contributed.

Regardless of why he did it the way he did, the album sold very well, and is still highly regarded by many. It is something of a quirky classic. Paul basically took four very fine finished songs, added a couple of sketches, filled it out with instrumentals,

---

[12] See Steve Miller's "My Dark Hour" for a contemporary, far more satisfying example.
[13] For those unfamiliar with the end of the story, Paul raged and fumed and basically threw the messenger — Ringo — off his property.

sequenced it all with great care, and called it an album. The message he appears to have been sending to the other Beatles is, "Look what I can do all by myself. With almost no effort. With my *demos!* I'll bury you all, if it comes to that." Remember, things were pretty nasty in this era. It brought out the worst in everyone involved.

Considering it as an artistic statement, in its very unusual moment of time, *McCartney* had an odd effect. It could push a listener either further *into* Paul's corner, or further *away* from it, and the line between is very thin. Is it a simple sketch about a man's happy life, or a calculated and grating look-at-what-I-can-do moment of showing off? Is it enough to justify its price and success, or some sort of tricky rip-off? Is it intentionally spare or merely unfinished? Tear the album into its individual tracks and you can clearly see the glass as either one-third-full or two-thirds-empty, depending on your opinion of the artist. If Paul was your favorite Beatle, this album probably sounded great, and you could easily forgive some of the filler. If you were more inclined toward one of the others, you probably could see only the exact opposite. The unfortunate convergence of album and breakup, which Paul crassly/shrewdly used for publicity, did not help things. Later generations of Beatles fans, if they know this album at all, will likely know it more for the notoriety of signalling the breakup, and perhaps for the photo on the back cover, than for "Momma Miss America."

In the slightly altered reality we are imagining, in which there is no debut album called *McCartney*, the best tracks have found their way onto a Beatles release, and the rest, if they existed at all, would probably only surface as throwaway bootlegs. That says a lot about this material.

A few outtakes from the era really must be considered in order just to fill Paul's quota on the new double-album. As will always be the case with Paul, plenty of options are available. Both "Suicide" and "Womenkind" (sometimes listed as "Women Kind" or "Woman Kind") are music hall clunkers which deserved the abandonment they got. But the very lovely "Sunshine Sometime" rises to a much different level. Though it would not have fit well stylistically on *McCartney*, it has a next-generation Beatle-y quality which foreshadows much easy listening pop music which would be made (by Paul and many others) in the following decade. The slight lyric is still more developed than much of what got onto the *McCartney* album, and it earns a place in consideration for the new Beatles album.[14]

"Indeed I Do" is really just a sketch, but a simple and lovely one. It has a Buddy Holly/Everly Brothers feel, and is sung on the demo in simple duet with Linda,

---

[14] Dating the lyrics and vocal for "Sunshine Sometime" is a little difficult. They may not have existed in 1970. Since we can't know for sure one way or another, I'm going to assume that the whole song would have been available then, even if it wasn't actually recorded that way in the real world. This falls into the category of songs that probably would have gotten finished and recorded if a Beatles project were in the offing.

whose pitch approximations are easy to forgive here. The song may have become the foundation for Paul's much later, and much more substantial, "On the Wings of a Nightingale," given to the Everly Brothers. In 1970, it was not yet ready.

"1882" bears a fair amount of scrutiny, and represents a reasonably substantial early solo work for Paul. He has performed it live, but did not release an official recording until 2018, despite including it in the first draft of *Red Rose Speedway*. The story told in the song is potentially interesting, if somewhat over long, but the whole thing plays out in such an extended fashion (over six minutes) that it has less than its possible impact. It is hard to imagine the post-*Abbey Road* Beatles or our Assembler having any interest in this lumbering and somewhat aimless track, rendering it irrelevant to the rescued album.

One quick note: Paul recorded "Another Day" and started work on *Ram* in the fall of 1970, possibly in time for some tracks to be considered for this project. Though using some of these early tracks might have allowed Paul a less muted presence on the current project, between Paul's perfectionism and the stylistic differences, all of this material is best considered with the next fused Beatles era.

George Harrison
23 tracks: 7 eligible, 1 provisional

Sources

H01	*All Things Must Pass* R: May-Oct 70 P: Harrison/Spector S: EMI, Trident, Apple	70-Nov

Tracks

	All Things Must Pass (Harrison) ✓ Sloppy recording of a great song. The feel sells it, as did the news around it.	H01-14, +R, 70-Oct
	Apple Scruffs (Harrison) ⊘ (Quality) Respectful? Possibly. Its simplicity is both vice and virtue. What's hidden matters.	H01-11, 70-Oct
	Art of Dying (Harrison) ✓ Great riff, and part of the real power of this era. Confident and inspired writing.	H01-16, 70-Oct
	Awaiting on You All (Harrison) ⊘ (Content) Really joy-filled track. Another statement of what GH has in the tank — i.e. a lot.	H01-13, 70-Oct
	Ballad of Sir Frankie Crisp (Let It Roll) (Harrison) ⊘ (Quality) Good idea for a song, but not fully realized. Structural problems get in the way.	H01-12, 70-Oct
	Behind That Locked Door (Harrison) ✓ Country, but in a sweet way. Nice lazy feel has a warmth in its lyric and arrangement.	H01-07, 70-Oct
	Beware of Darkness (Harrison) ⊘ (Quality) Unfortunately eery in sound and structure. This is simply a misfire.	H01-10, +R, 70-Oct
	Hear Me Lord (Harrison) ⊘ (Quality) "Lord" language notwithstanding, this track feels preachy from its bones. Unattractive.	H01-18, 70-Oct

12 / DREAM

	I Dig Love (Harrison) ✓ Flawed but fixable. Needs an edit to tame it, which is not a small thing. Playful at least.	H01-15, +R, 70-Oct
	I Remember Jeep (Harrison) ⊘ (Filler) A jam which can be safely ignored, unless you are among the few who are totally into that.	H01-22, 70-Oct
	I'd Have You Anytime (Harrison/Dylan) ≈ (Style/Quality) Lousy song, and GH does nothing to improve it. Ponderous and boring.	H01-01, 70-Oct
	If Not for You (Dylan) ⊘ (Style/Quality) Sticks out as a mismatch of song and artist. Comes off as wimpy pop-rock.	H01-06, +R, 70-Oct
	Isn't It a Pity (Version One) (Harrison) ⊘ (Content) GH rewrites "Hey Jude," but the impact is muted by overlong and over-dramatic reading.	H01-04, +R, 70-Oct
	Isn't It a Pity (Version Two) (Harrison) ⊘ (Filler) One version was more than enough. This is regrettable filler.	H01-17, +R, 70-Oct
	It's Johnny's Birthday (Martin/Coulter/Harrison) ✓ Whimsical and full of good energy.	H01-20, 70-Oct
	Let It Down (Harrison) ✓ As powerful as GH ever got, this is a cry and a shout and a deep breath. On fire.	H01-08, 70-Oct
	My Sweet Lord (Harrison) ⊘ (Content) Derivative but infectious. The chanted Hare Krishna language can be off putting.	H01-02, +R, 70-Oct
	Out of the Blue (Harrison) ⊘ (Filler) Jams are generally boring, and this is no exception.	H01-19, 70-Oct
	Plug Me In (Harrison) ⊘ (Filler) Another boring jam. Pure filler.	H01-21, 70-Oct
	Run of the Mill (Harrison) ⊘ (Quality) A song which never settled. Not bad, exactly, but always feels unfinished.	H01-09, 70-Oct
	Thanks for the Pepperoni (Harrison) ⊘ (Filler) Great chops, but who cares? This is a waste of vinyl.	H01-23, 70-Oct
	Wah-Wah (Harrison) ⊘ (Content) Powerful guitar image. Full arrangement, yet not cluttered. A fine piece of work.	H01-03, +R, 70-Oct
	What Is Life (Harrison) ✓ Clearly a "statement" song, and one of GH's masterworks.	H01-05, 70-Oct

George Harrison poured everything he had into *All Things Must Pass*, yet even in creating this massive collection he did not clear his vaults of the original material which had been stacking up. Nonetheless, there was enough good stuff that the world saw a Beatle emerging from the shadows of The Beatles — or, more accurately, Harrison emerging from the shadow of Lennon and McCartney.

This is an understandable reaction. After hearing only 22 Harrison originals up to this point, including the instant classics, "Something" and "Here Comes the Sun," the arrival of 16 more at once must have seemed like an unimaginable bounty to those who held him as their favorite Beatle. Many listeners also apparently heard the potential in Harrison's voice to lead the next decade of music in the way the Beatles had led the previous — the little brother of the 60s maturing into the visionary of the 70s. All of this, along with the irresistibly catchy single, "My Sweet Lord," guaranteed that *All Things Must Pass* would sell well, even with a high retail price.

Additionally, the palpable catharsis baked into these tracks certainly accounts for some of the rave reviews that the album got. George writes and sings and plays with great emotion throughout this project, and draws out fine performances from all of his collaborators. Indeed, the release of the painful marginalization he has felt is palpable almost at the level of *John Lennon/Plastic Ono Band*, albeit expressed in a very different way.

This new form of expression, however, also raises some issues. Specifically, three new aspects of his work appear on this album that George has never displayed before. The first, proselytizing, would be the bane of a large swath of his solo output. The second, anger, heard generally in nascent form here, would get much worse before it got better. The third, disillusionment, would become his stock in trade, the most palatable of the three. The fans appeared to ignore (or at least excuse) the first, while resonating with the second. They shared with George at least *some* anger over the events of the recent Beatle past. The third aspect, disillusionment, was becoming widespread as the 60s came to a close, and forms one of the great themes of music in the 70s. In this regard, George was indeed something of a leader.

Beyond these three aspects, a close look at the songwriting yields distinct evidence that Harrison has progressed, but also distinct examples in which he has not. Some of the material is robust and satisfying, and some is thin or forced. Despite what *All Things Must Pass* is generally given credit for proving, George wouldn't become a reliably competent songwriter for several more years, truly coming into his own only about the time that solo Beatles lost their relevance.

Still, George's debut is widely considered a classic, an assessment generally applied, notably, to the aggregate — which includes the classic cover image, and the emotions that swirled around and beyond the recordings themselves. For our project, we must consider these tracks individually, separate from the whole, and that's when the problems become very apparent. Some of this material is frightfully thin, overly strident, and occasionally harsh. It moves George down a theological path which will color (pollute?) too much of his 70s output. This is not "happy" Beatle music, which though not inherently a bad thing, can be tiring. Some of the songs are entirely disposable, and at least some of the writing is clichéd, banal, or just plain clunky.

Indeed, even after its success, it is unlikely that John and Paul and George Martin would have considered this material the testament to George's songwriting skills that the public did. While it is tempting to say that their reactions would have been just another example of stepping on George as a "junior" Beatle, it's important to remember that they were, in fact, *very good editors* of one another, despite documented blind spots. They definitely missed some great songs, but they also helpfully stepped on some real clunkers, for which we can be grateful.

It's important to acknowledge these things because we need to view this album, like all the others, from the perspective of the other Beatles and our Assembler, who would have been mining George's explosion of work for tracks which could go on a group project. This doesn't necessarily mean only "happy" Beatle tracks, but it does mean fully realized ideas which are compelling, engaging, and of a high enough quality. Identifying the tracks which meet these criteria is the task of our Assembler, and it is made easier by the fact that it would not have been rudimentary demos being considered, but fully realized tracks. This would have worked in George's favor because the songs in his "explosion" sounded plain on the demos, but are ultimately well-realized on the album.

I have to admit that my reaction to this album is deeply affected by the fact that I only came to know it as a second generation Beatles fan. Even after repeated listenings, I still find myself perplexed that this collection is so highly regarded among fans. While not a *bad* album really, it seems uneven, disheveled, and highly padded to my latter day ears. There are some fine songs, but also some which would not be missed if they had been left off. The sequencing seems basically random. The use of harmonicas and pedal steel guitars is off-putting — an unwelcome tilt toward country music. The religious language, though heartfelt, is simplistic and discomfiting. While some of the lyrics seem perceptive, graceful and timeless, others seem petty, banal, overly evangelistic, or simply inscrutable. Some of this music makes my heart beat faster, some leaves me cold, and some always makes me cringe.

It is clear that I cannot hear this album the way it would have been heard when it was released. In one sense, this makes it easier to be objective about the music. In another, it's impossible to understand the emotions which would have accompanied most listenings in 1970. I'm not sure whether that puts me at an advantage or disadvantage.

Ultimately, the love for this album was likely as much an outpouring of love for the artist himself as he finally came into his own. After the painful public breakup, and after what the other solo Beatles had released, there was a great deal of desire among the fans to feel good again about something — *anything* — Beatle-related. No other solo album by the former Fabs could become such a repository, for a variety of reasons. The fans just wanted something they could love, and George provided enough music that everyone could find at least *something*.

When breaking the album into its component parts, it becomes clear that these tracks are neither enhanced nor diminished by removing them from the album's sequencing. Where both Paul and John used sequencing to lift their material, George and Phil Spector have made no apparent move to do so. This should hardly be a surprise, given that George had no experience in that process himself. He was never more than peripherally involved in sequencing Beatles albums, and Spector was famous for dismissing the whole album format as, "two hits and ten pieces of junk."

Spector's sensibility was always toward singles, and so he treated every track without regard to how it might be heard in a collection, and every collection as merely an arbitrary assemblance of unrelated recordings. He made tracks that were utterly self-contained — a fine skill in itself, and a great thing in a world dominated by singles. But the world of singles had begun to fade (some would say had already disappeared) by 1970. Not taking advantage of sequencing opportunities to improve an album represents at least a missed opportunity, and borders on dereliction of duty. This approach is very easy to hear in the tracks of *All Things Must Pass* because listening to them alphabetically doesn't change the overall impact, beyond the advantage of hearing the iconic title track first.

That said, there are clearly opportunities for better sequencing which were not utilized. For example, Harrison and Spector open with perhaps the worst choice possible, "I'd Have You Anytime." The track is sleepy, banal, and nowhere near one of the best in the collection, all of which run counter to George Martin's criteria for an opener. Similarly, the second disc opens with the clunky, ominous, and overly self-important "Beware of Darkness," a track hardly deserving of such prominence, and perhaps best left off the album entirely. Likewise, the pleading and overly repetitive closer, "Hear Me Lord," leaves the secular listener with something of a bitter aftertaste. Simply put, there were better choices available for these and other spots. This is a case where a lack of good sequencing didn't mortally wound the strong tracks, which are sufficiently self-contained, but better sequencing could have improved the perception of everything, if not entirely mitigated the worst of it.

For our purposes here, this means that nothing is lost by breaking the album into its component parts and using them to build a fused Beatles album. *All Things Must Pass*, it must be admitted, is an album largely made of spare parts to begin with, built as it is from Beatle rejects (which is not meant pejoratively).

As such, when considering the individual tracks, some decisions are obvious for the Assembler. The second version of "Isn't It a Pity," for example represents pure filler — blessedly the only such instance on the first two discs.

The third disc, however, is almost entirely filler, and all of the jams would also have been set aside. This is not to say that jams of any sort should automatically be rejected. But even the best jams typically fare poorly over multiple listenings, making them skippable very quickly. It is the rare jam which captures something so magical that it justifies such high visibility.

That said, the likelihood that some sort of jam might have eventually appeared on a fused Beatles album is certainly greater than zero. John included jams (in some cases labeled as "songs" by Yoko) on *Live Peace in Toronto* and *Some Time in New*

York City. The Beatles had seriously considered the 12-bar jam known as "Rocker" for *Let It Be*, and had recorded others at various points. But any such material would have represented a career low, and the Assembler will not let that happen.

Four tracks are ineligible because they contain problematic material, even though they are among the most interesting in the collection. "Wah-Wah" is a rocket of a track, so much so that there are several points in the middle when it feels like it's about to implode. Spector's wall-of-sound fits this song well, and George's backup singing is absolutely outstanding. Still, it feels like one that the Beatles might not have been offered, or they would have rejected for its angry tone and musical wanderings. Though the riff is magnificent, the song's chord progression lurches around in that distinctive way that only Harrison can do — and *will* do many times over the course of his solo career. Lyrically, it also walks something of a line that, while not overly critical, could be read as at least ungrateful. It comes too close to that line for the Beatles and the Assembler.

"Awaiting on You All" is a similarly fantastic track, again with the wall-of-sound appropriately applied. It's also a rare track on *All Things Must Pass* that is exactly the right length, and needs no editing. In the end, however, it also sounds like a very "solo" track — lyrics notwithstanding. It has a catchy hook and upbeat feeling which contrasts with much of the rest of the album, but lyrics which would have been something of a minefield for the other Beatles.

"Isn't It a Pity" had been famously rejected by the Beatles before and, despite conventional wisdom to the contrary, with very good reason. It is repetitive, unimaginative, and generally maudlin. It is a sad song which comes off more as *self-pity* than anything else. Further, the recordings on this album reveal that it was clearly an attempt by George to create something on the scale of "Hey Jude," but the result is not satisfying, even in its final polished form.

The Assembler would have boldly excluded "My Sweet Lord" without even a moment's hesitation. This is not to suggest anything negative about it other than that the Beatles would never have been able to get behind it. They would have rejected the overtly religious lyrical theme, the "hare krishna" language, and quite possibly would have detected the song's derivative nature.

Six songs would have been rejected as just not high enough in overall quality. These just aren't very good songs, even when they are modestly interesting. "Hear Me Lord" and "Beware of Darkness" are George at his most unattractively preachy, and the latter song is also built on a shaky chord structure. "Apple Scruffs" again features George's amazing and under-appreciated backup vocals, but the song is barely a jot. "Run of the Mill" has some interesting rhythmic turns, but always feels like an idea which is not fully realized. The song never quite gets off the ground, and ends by basically stepping off the chord carousel it has been on, without really resolving sufficiently. "The Ballad of Frankie Crisp (Let It Roll)" has an interesting lyric, but musically is another case of an idea not fully realized, wandering off into a tonal wilderness in search of something it can hang its hat on. In some ways it plays like George's attempt at writing his own "Being for the Benefit of Mr. Kite," but not quite getting a strong enough musical idea to support the text.

The two collaborations with Bob Dylan occupy a sort of netherworld between not good enough and necessary to include. Like so many superstar collaborations, which seem to have great potential on paper, this one sort of fizzles. Perhaps it is out of deference to Dylan, but George has the least amount of personality on these tracks, and they are both banal and uninteresting. Indeed, a case can be made that they are simply too *boring* for a Beatles album.

The recording of "If Not for You" sounds so different from everything else on this album that it sticks out by a mile when it appears, like a song meant for a different time and space altogether, which it was. "I'd Have You Anytime" is the better track, but in addition to being wrong as an album opener, it feels more like MOR[15] than should appear in the work of a former Beatle not named McCartney.

That said, "I'd Have You Anytime" remains eligible for inclusion on the group project — provisionally — under the assumption that George would have lobbied hard for at least one of the Dylan-related tracks. Had that happened, the other Beatles would have perked up at the idea of having Dylan's name on their record. And since the track isn't completely without merit, the Assembler would have looked for a place it could fit. Note that such lobbying isn't prohibited by the agreements the Beatles would have made with the Assembler, but need not be honored.

Happily, what remains after these eliminations is a bevy of very fine songs that are not too soloistic, and at least not harsh toward the group, even if they do reference (sometimes obliquely) the tension and breakup. Those songs would have been happily welcomed into the group project by the Assembler, and be enough to make up George's newly-earned allocation.

Great riffs power both "What Is Life" and "Art of Dying," pointing the direction in which George's songwriting should (and would) be headed. In both cases, he takes serious lyrics and sets them to catchy — and relatively simple — music, which would always be the hallmark of George's best solo work.

The country waltz, "Behind That Locked Door," represents a beautifully gentle release of the stresses built up elsewhere on the album. Unfortunately, this is hard to hear because it is dropped into the wasteland on side two where there is nothing it can release. Ideally, this song would be preceded by something intense to make the contrast more obvious and purposeful. It would make a good track to end a side.

Instead, in George's running order, it is followed by one of the songs which might better have gone before it. "Let It Down" is perhaps the best song on the album, combining as it does a powerful opening statement with gentle offsets. It is clearly a

---

[15] MOR stands for "Middle of the road," a radio format which came of age in the 1970s.

case where nothing in the demo, which had been offered to the Beatles, would have given anyone an idea of the power the song could have. Thankfully, Spector's realization is ideal and not overblown. It finds the drama, and the softer side, and knits them into a classic track.

In a similar fashion, the album's title track had been offered, but not impressed anyone in the Beatles camp, and represents another opportunity missed for lack of imagination. Since we have access to early attempts by the group to record "All Things Must Pass," we can see clearly that they just didn't get it, possibly because of the emotional punch it packed, and possibly because they were biased against George's songwriting abilities.

It is hard to imagine anyone passing up the finished version. In fact, it's easier to imagine the Assembler actually selecting this as the title track for the group album, though not without reparations to the main riff, which is heard in three different permutations — a regrettable mistake which should have been corrected.

The two remaining tracks in consideration show George at his most playful. These would have been irresistible to the Assembler. "I Dig Love" is a happy jot, albeit in need of some serious editing to straighten out its structure. And "It's Johnny's Birthday," weirdly wasted between two jams on the third disc, has the feel of a quirky wildcard, which may be needed among all of the other serious music.

Beyond the album tracks, there are a host of songs demoed in that era which either got finished later or didn't get properly recorded at all. Because George chose to finish these songs for *All Things Must Pass*, and mining them proves sufficient for his contribution to the group, the rest will wait for another time.

With so much of *All Things Must Pass* rejected by the Assembler, the logical assumption is that George would have regrouped and assembled these leftovers into his debut (non-experimental) solo album in 1971. Somewhat surprisingly, these tracks sound very different from those which make it to the group album, and together they make a fine set that demonstrates George's growing range of artistic impulses, and would have allowed him still to establish his own identity in the marketplace. Significantly, it would have included the smash single, "My Sweet Lord," which would also have been the title track. Assisted by the Assembler in implementing George Martin's principles, the line-up could have looked like this:

My Sweet Lord

Side One
1. Awaiting on You All
2. Ballad of Sir Frankie Crisp (Let It Roll)
3. Run of the Mill
4. Isn't It a Pity
5. My Sweet Lord

Side Two
1. Wah-Wah
2. I Live for You
3. Beware of Darkness
4. Apple Scruffs
5. Hear Me Lord

This would have best been a single album, but perhaps the jams could still have been given away as a bonus of sorts, turning it into an ersatz double. This lineup continues to omit the painfully conventional "If Not for You," which is just a failed track, replacing it with the more worthy outtake, "I Live for You."

The primary advantage of a collection like this would have been an early success that did not necessarily set up expectations he would not be able to meet. In other words, while still clearly part of the Beatles, his solo album represents a toe in the water of a separate career — and a very successful one at that. *My Sweet Lord* would certainly have sold quite well, while still only *setting the stage* for what George might do. In this way, the learning curve of a solo career could have been less steep, and perhaps a better foundation laid for creative success.

Assembly

33 tracks: 27 eligible, 6 provisional

	≈ God	L04-10, +R, 70-Oct
	✓ Hold On	L04-02, +R, 70-Oct
	≈ I Found Out	L04-03, +R, 70-Oct
	✓ Instant Karma!	L03-01, +G, 70-Jan
	✓ Isolation	L04-05, +R, 70-Oct
☥	✓ Look at Me	L04-09, 70-Oct
	✓ Love	L04-07, 70-Oct
	≈ Mother	L04-01, +R, 70-Oct
	✓ Remember	L04-06, +R, 70-Oct
	✓ Well Well Well	L04-08, +R, 70-Oct
	✓ Working Class Hero	L04-04, 70-Oct
	✓ Coochy-Coochy	S03-02, 70-Jun
	✓ Dream	S01-09, 70-Feb
	≈ Early 1970	S04-02, +JG, 70-Oct
	✓ I'm a Fool to Care	S01-05, 70-Feb
	✓ It Don't Come Easy	S04-01, +G, 70-Mar
	≈ Night and Day	S01-02, 69-Oct
	✓ Every Night	M01-04, 70-Feb
	✓ Junk	M01-06, 70-Jan
	✓ Man We Was Lonely	M01-07, 70-Feb
☥	✓ Maybe I'm Amazed	M01-12, 70-Feb
	✓ Oo You	M01-08, 70-Jan
	✓ Sunshine Sometime	M03, 70-Oct
	✓ Teddy Boy	M01-10, 70-Jan
	✓ That Would Be Something	M01-02, 70-Jan

✓	All Things Must Pass	H01-14, +R, 70-Oct
✓	Art of Dying	H01-16, 70-Oct
✓	Behind That Locked Door	H01-07, 70-Oct
✓	I Dig Love	H01-15, +R, 70-Oct
≈	I'd Have You Anytime	H01-01, 70-Oct
✓	It's Johnny's Birthday	H01-20, 70-Oct
✓	Let It Down	H01-08, 70-Oct
✓	What Is Life	H01-05, 70-Oct

Looking at that highly complex collection of music, it's clear from the start that the challenge for our Assembler is significant. One might wonder if it is even possible to find underlying themes, and then select and sequence the tracks in such a way as to minimize, or maybe even *utilize*, the disparity in sound. Spector's production on George's album has the distinct potential to sound jarring next to the spareness of John and Paul's tracks. Paul's sketches were so few and so slight that they would have to be carefully spread across the sides to minimize the apparent falloff from the majesty of *Abbey Road*. John's tracks, each a complete statement, but overwhelming in the aggregate, need to be given sufficient release and breathing room, which basically means spacing them as far apart as possible.

The first decision is easy: There is no way it will all fit onto one album. There is more than enough for a double, with *no* filler. And there appears to be a pretty even distribution among the artists, definitely close enough to meet the new parity requirements. Aiming for a double album of 28 tracks, that would mean eight each for Paul, George and John, plus four for Ringo. So at least the assembly starts from abundance and balance — a very good place, though obviously some things will not make the final cut. The first task: find pole tracks.

Very few options are available to open the album. Though it may seem tempting to go with "All Things Must Pass," it would not set the right tone. The song sounds like a summation — the end of a process rather than the beginning of one. Still, "All Things Must Pass" is strong enough to fill a pole position, and actually belongs at the beginning of a different side. Instead, another of George's tracks gets the call.

"What Is Life" looks like an album opener right away, with a great and simple riff, plus very high commercial potential (which it partially realized as a single). It starts the album with a big question, but also with very positive energy, and becomes only the second time Harrison opens a Beatles album — which seems entirely appropriate to the new era the group is entering.

In the listening, another track immediately resonated with "What Is Life," and can serve as an extender. Paul's great song "Every Night" never really got to shine on his own album, but it is in the same key, with a different but compatible musical figure, also highly commercial, and one of the overall stronger Paul tracks in this collection. It extends the opening mood, while also changing it just enough to be interesting. The two songs complement each other as if it were intentional.

Yet a third song leaped out of the listening to round this into an opening trio. John's "Hold On" continues in the same key, but with a different take. As a lighter ballad, it provides a shift in mood right where one is needed, yielding a mini-suite that doesn't sound like something so precious. Indeed, it sounds like the three principle songwriters in the group doing what they do best — writing great songs, complementing one another, and demonstrating well how the work of one Beatle can make a beautiful foil for another.

| 1A. What Is Life (G) |
| 1B. Every Night (P) |
| 1C. Hold On (J) |
| ... |
| ... |
| ... |
| ... |

All Things Must Pass (G)
Art of Dying (G)
Behind That Locked Door (G)
Coochy-Coochy (R)
Dream (R)
≈ Early 1970 (R)
≈ God (J)
I Dig Love (G)
≈ I Found Out (J)
≈ I'd Have You Anytime (G)
I'm a Fool to Care (R)
Instant Karma! (J)
Isolation (J)
It Don't Come Easy (R)
It's Johnny's Birthday (G)
Junk (P)
Let It Down (G)
Look at Me (J)
Love (J)
Man We Was Lonely (P)
Maybe I'm Amazed (P)
≈ Mother (J)
Oo You (P)
≈ Night and Day (R)
Remember (J)
Sunshine Sometime (P)
Teddy Boy (P)
That Would Be Something (P)
Well Well Well (J)
Working Class Hero (J)

At the other end of the album, a destination is necessary. Once again, there are very few options for the album closer. Remember that the goal is to find something summative, and difficult to follow. Again, "All Things Must Pass" looks possible, but again it leaves the wrong tone. It might be mistaken as the last word on the future of the group, something no one would have wanted just yet.

12 / DREAM

Additionally, it isn't really all that difficult to follow. The listening reveals that the end of "All Things" works beautifully with the fade-in opening of Paul's masterwork, "Maybe I'm Amazed." Specifically, Paul's opening piano figure feels like exactly the transition necessary to get from George's riff to Paul's first verse — again, as if they were designed to fit together that way. The two tracks also feel temperamentally kindred, in that Paul's love song seems the perfect balance to George's beautiful fatalism.

At this point, the Assembler would have made a somewhat arbitrary decision that this pairing would open side four, sensing the beginning of a conversation which might become some sort of meditation on the state of the Beatles.

Though John has often provided closers to Beatles albums, a quick scan of his tracks here shows all of them unresolved in some way. None has that ultimate quality of "A Day in the Life," "Tomorrow Never Knows," or even "Twist and Shout." Perhaps the only possibility is "Instant Karma!" with its long repeated final chorus containing repetitions of "We all shine on…" But the song isn't quite big enough to serve that role. In fact, with its opening countoff, it more likely belongs at the beginning of a side. So it will be placed at the head of side two, and the Assembler will insist on using the unfaded version, allowing it to connect directly with something else.

Recalling the end of *The White Album*, Ringo's "Dream" might seem like a possible album closer here. It concludes with dreamy chords and this very reassuring final couplet:

> *Things never are as bad as they seem,*
> *So dream, dream, dream.*

That very lyric, and the song's overall subject matter, suggests a connection to one of our obvious problem tracks. Perhaps some sort of one-two punch can be assembled to end the album.

John's "God" is only a provisional option on the track list, mostly because of its lyrics. To anyone hearing this track for the first time in the summer of 1970, it would have seemed almost impossible that any Beatles album could ever contain the lyric, "I don't believe in Beatles." But as we have seen, there are nuances within the subtext which make things possible that might not seem so at first.

Continuing with the idea of making side four of this album about the state of the band itself, and seeing that we already have George and Paul's voices present, an opportunity to place "God" opens up. Where John's final section is about the dream being over, could there be a better response than Ringo's?

George: All things must pass away.
          ...
Paul: Maybe I'm a lonely man
          Who's in the middle of something
          That he doesn't really understand.
          ...
John: And so, dear friend
          You'll just have to carry on.
          The dream is over.
          ...
Ringo: Dream, when you're feeling blue,
          Dream, that's the thing to do.

Beyond the sympathetic lyrics, and sympathetic tones of the songs, Ringo's voice itself offers balance and comfort and resolution to John's gentle resignation, even as it highlights a different aspect of the idea the two songs share in common. The alignment becomes obvious, justifiable, and irresistible — at least to the Assembler. Admittedly, resistance may have been John's reaction, but it is well known that he had days when the dream — whatever that meant to him — was over, and other days when it might have been, in some small way, still alive. It seems at least possible that he would have embraced such a pairing, in the same spirit as being both "in" and "out" during "Revolution."

A small problem arises in that putting the end of "God" right against the beginning of "Dream" does not quite work. There needs to be a pause of some sort for John's closing lyric to hang in the air before the listener's ear is ready for Ringo to offer a counterpoint. Perhaps the right amount of silence is enough, but this will remain an issue for consideration.

Even after putting these two songs together, this formidable one-two punch doesn't quite work to close the album. Both songs are a little too sleepy and reflective. It also feels too much like something the Beatles had done before.

A late key change in George Martin's arrangement of "Dream" makes another connection possible. The beginning of Harrison's "Let It Down" aligns perfectly with the end of "Dream," and emerges like a volcano from Ringo's song. With its crashing guitar figures, closing sentiment of "Let your love flow and astound me," and long fade, it sends the album out on a most powerful note. The Assembler would have made two small edits to reduce some of the dead space, after which the track would be a tight and formidable closer — the first time George has closed an album since *Beatles for Sale*.

At this point, it looks like an ending sequence has been created, with other tracks placed in the process.

12 / DREAM

1A. What Is Life (G)	Art of Dying (G)
1B. Every Night (P)	Behind That Locked Door (G)
1C. Hold On (J)	Coochy-Coochy (R)
...	≈ Early 1970 (R)
	I Dig Love (G)
	≈ I Found Out (J)
2A. Instant Karma! (J)	≈ I'd Have You Anytime (G)
...	I'm a Fool to Care (R)
	Isolation (J)
	It Don't Come Easy (R)
...	It's Johnny's Birthday (G)
	Junk (P)
4A. All Things Must Pass (G)	Look at Me (J)
4B. Maybe I'm Amazed (P)	Love (J)
...	Man We Was Lonely (P)
4X. ≈ God (J)	≈ Mother (J)
4Y. Dream (R)	Oo You (P)
4Z. Let It Down (G) [Edit]	≈ Night and Day (R)
	Remember (J)
	Sunshine Sometime (P)
	Teddy Boy (P)
	That Would Be Something (P)
	Well Well Well (J)
	Working Class Hero (J)

Half of the pole tracks are in place, and some of the most complicated aspects of the running order have been solved. The search for another track to open a side leads right to Ringo's hit, "It Don't Come Easy," which will be slotted to open side three. The three remaining side closers, however, will be much more complicated.

As with "God," John's tracks all appear to be the most difficult to follow, even as they don't really work to close sides. One obvious exception to this is "Working Class Hero." On John's solo album, the song is immediately followed by "Isolation," which is too similar, and robs "Working Class Hero" of a degree of power by feeling like a weaker continuation. If separated, each of these tracks has immense power, but together they weaken each other. The reality is that nothing can follow "Working Class Hero" without seeming lesser — no matter how good it is. As such, John's masterwork simply must end a side, with the intermission serving as the space into which it can reverberate for as long as the listener likes.

Perhaps even more complicated for this particular track, however, is the need for a proper lead-in. Nothing by Paul or Ringo has the necessary gravitas, which leaves George to fill the role, and some quick listening reveals that "The Art of Dying" makes the perfect setup for "Working Class Hero."

Despite being one of George's great songs, it leaves something of a dark aftertaste on its own. That is actually mitigated nicely by putting something even more bleak after it. Though addressing a similar subject (the pathway of life), it does so in a very different, but sonically compatible way. Spector's wall-of-sound production generates an almost claustrophobic space, affording "Working Class Here" the ability to sound even more spare and barren than it already does. George's song feels like a bridge across a dark and scary chasm, and when you get to the other side, John is standing there, alone with his guitar. Not happy Beatle music, obviously, but incredibly powerful. That the two tracks are in the same key merely seals the deal.

Since we already know that this sequence won't end the album, we also know that some other song will follow it — whenever the listener finally gets up and flips the disc. Whatever begins the next side must also be carefully considered, and it turns out that only "All Things Must Pass" represents a plausible option, meaning the George/John sequence goes at the end of side three. When the indeterminate, presumably long pause after "Working Class Hero" finally lifts, George's anthem is there for some sort of reassurance from a distance. Yet again, two tracks by ostensibly solo Beatles complement each other wonderfully. Indeed, in this configuration George sounds like he has used John's ideas as a starting point.

| 3Y. Art of Dying (G) |
| 3Z. Working Class Hero (J) |
| 4A. All Things Must Pass (G) |

Moving on, "Remember" feels like a potential side closer, ending as it does with an escalating vocal line followed by an explosion. In a way, it echoes the ending of *Abbey Road*'s side one. In this case, however, the explosion feels more like an unanswered question. It creates not a space for contemplation, but an opening begging to be filled. Were the silence to linger, the listener might feel like something very bad had happened. On John's album, that silence is broken by the reassuring fade-in piano which opens "Love" — not a bad transition at all, and perhaps the most successful on his album.

The Assembler is certainly allowed two consecutive songs by the same Beatle, but the combination isn't quite right in this context. After some listening, the proper response to the explosion appears to be the sound of a euphonium. Klaus Voorman's playful and swinging setting of "I'm a Fool to Care" represents a welcome counterpoint to John's four-in-the-bar driving intensity. It picks up on John's subtle playfulness, extends it through Ringo's relaxed and understated vocal, then carries it all the way to a drum fill button on the end — the perfect way to close a side. Again, Ringo provides the right response to John's intensity. This will end side one.

Another intense track by John, "Well Well Well" contains some powerful primal screams, but ends with a chuckle from the screamer. Again, this would have to be a candidate to end a side, but can't do so without some sort of response. George's beautiful and reassuring "Behind That Locked Door" steps into that space to make the proper connection. Once more, George's lyric seems to be responding directly to John's. This pairing will end side two, and therefore the first half of the double album. All pole tracks are now in place.

1A. What Is Life (G) 1B. Every Night (P) 1C. Hold On (J) ... **1Y. Remember (J)** **1Z. I'm a Fool to Care (R)**	Coochy-Coochy (R) ≈ Early 1970 (R) I Dig Love (G) ≈ I Found Out (J) ≈ I'd Have You Anytime (G) Isolation (J) It's Johnny's Birthday (G) Junk (P) Look at Me (J) Love (J) Man We Was Lonely (P) ≈ Mother (J) Oo You (P) ≈ Night and Day (R) Sunshine Sometime (P) Teddy Boy (P) That Would Be Something (P)
2A. Instant Karma! (J) ... **2Y. Well Well Well (J)** **2Z. Behind That Locked Door (G)**	
3A. It Don't Come Easy (R) ... **3Y. Art of Dying (G)** **3Z. Working Class Hero (J)**	
4A. All Things Must Pass (G) 4B. Maybe I'm Amazed (P) ... 4X. ≈ God (J) 4Y. Dream (R) 4Z. Let It Down (G) [Edit]	

The Assembler must now turn to filling gaps in each side. With side four already having its own theme of sorts, it makes some sense to look at the other three sides and see if anything stands out which might lead to the right tracks still on the list.

The music of side three has something of a harrowing unity. Two songs on our list seem to resonate with what's already there: John's "Isolation," and Paul's "Man We Was Lonely" — two very different treatments of the same subject. Lyrically, either would make a natural extension of Ringo's opening lament. In a stroke of luck, the latter emerges quite naturally from "It Don't Come Easy," and the former works nicely as the third in a "life is tough" cluster. Together, they do, however, create something of a downward slope.

> 3A. It Don't Come Easy (R)
> **3E. Man We Was Lonely (P)**
> **3F. Isolation (J)**
> . . .
> 3Y. Art of Dying (G)
> 3Z. Working Class Hero (J)

Indeed, the beginning and the end of side three are now so dark that something needs to break it all up, lest there be a black hole three quarters of the way through the album. Several possibilities remain on the list, but they all could play different roles elsewhere. So we will move on, and return later to this gap.

The side two tracks have no apparent underlying connections. Working from the beginning, we find that either "Sunshine Sometime" or "I'll Have You Anytime" sound good following "Instant Karma!" The necessary nudge is provided by the fact that this is the only slot anywhere on the album that the Dylan collaboration sounds at all good. If it must be on the album, it simply must go here, where its mellow aloofness sounds like an answer to John's more demanding pop grittiness. Since we are assuming that all four Beatles would have wanted Dylan's name on their record, this is where it will go. Following it immediately with "Sunshine Sometime" provides a smooth return to a more Beatle-y sound, clearing the air nicely.

With all of the side two songs running a bit long, it looks like only one more title is necessary. The side still contains no track by Ringo, but neither "Coochy-Coochy" nor "Night and Day" can sufficiently bridge the gap between "Sunshine Sometime" and "Well Well Well." Again, a smaller gap is retained and we move on.

At this point, there are a few tracks remaining on the list that we know will need to be placed. It might be better to work in the other direction — that is, pick a track, and find a slot for it.

Paul's "Teddy Boy" is among the most substantial left on the list, but feels like a problem track in search of a solution. It doesn't really sound like anything else on this album, and doesn't have much to say which resonates with other lyrics. Its storytelling is somewhat murky. One possible outcome is to just leave it off. After all, it had already been rejected by the Beatles once.

But the finished version is a self-contained nugget that is certainly worthy of inclusion on a group album. After all, when the Beatles rejected it, it wasn't even finished yet. The Assembler would have recognized its value, but realized it would stand alone no matter where it was placed. It has to be sort of tucked in somewhere when a break is needed. Such tracks are necessary to every running order, and realizing that this is such a track frees the Assembler from trying to do anything more elaborate with it.

Of the remaining gaps, only side one looks plausible. It doesn't really work coming out of "Hold On," but makes a reasonable breather right before returning to something heavy by John. Thus, "Teddy Boy" goes right before "Remember."

George also has a stand-alone track left on the list, and a quick listen confirms that "I Dig Love" — with an appropriate edit to fix its structure — can fill the gap between "Hold On" and "Teddy Boy." Side one is thus balanced and complete.

1A.	What Is Life (G)	
1B.	Every Night (P)	
1C.	Hold On (J)	
1M.	**I Dig Love (G) [Edit]**	
1T.	**Teddy Boy (P)**	
1Y.	Remember (J)	
1Z.	I'm a Fool to Care (R)	
2A.	Instant Karma! (J)	
2E.	**≈ I'd Have You Anytime (G)**	
2F.	**Sunshine Sometime (P)**	
	...	
2Y.	Well Well Well (J)	
2Z.	Behind That Locked Door (G)	
3A.	It Don't Come Easy (R)	
3E.	**Man We Was Lonely (P)**	
3F.	**Isolation (J)**	
	...	
3Y.	Art of Dying (G)	
3Z.	Working Class Hero (J)	
4A.	All Things Must Pass (G)	
4B.	Maybe I'm Amazed (P)	
	...	
4X.	≈ God (J)	
4Y.	Dream (R)	
4Z.	Let It Down (G) [Edit]	

Coochy-Coochy (R)
≈ Early 1970 (R)
≈ I Found Out (J)
It's Johnny's Birthday (G)
Junk (P)
Look at Me (J)
Love (J)
≈ Mother (J)
Oo You (P)
≈ Night and Day (R)
That Would Be Something (P)

Since it appears there really is no room for a third big band track anywhere on the album, and "Early 1970" was never really a serious contender, Ringo's fourth entry will have to be "Coochy-Coochy." As mentioned, it does not fit in the gap on side two, and it would also be wrong for side four. But temperamentally it slides nicely into side three as part of the black-hole-buster.

In terms of balance, it does mean two tracks from Ringo on side three, with none yet on side two, but the Assembler will be able to justify that pretty easily since it still results in four tracks for the drummer on a four-sided album. A bigger problem is that side three only contains one track each from Paul and George, and being only one song short, something will be out of balance here.

The answer comes in the fact that George is featured prominently on Ringo's opener, including having ghost-co-written it. Though that doesn't *technically* count toward his allotment, it is enough to break the tie. The final slot goes to Paul.

Working backwards, the best track to lead into "Art of Dying" is Ringo's casual "Coochy-Coochy," and the best of Paul's remaining tracks to lead into that is the slick guitar riff stretched into a track, "Oo You." It is then mere good fortune that the cold end of "Isolation" works very well with Paul's drumming intro to "Oo You."

Somewhere along the way, the Assembler would have realized that John's "Love" and Paul's "Junk" feel like two sides of the same coin, and would be utterly natural working together to fill the gap on side four. John's piano fade-in emerges most naturally from the end of "Maybe I'm Amazed," and if the track were ended at his final piano chord (setting aside the fade-in coda), Paul's cold opening to "Junk" essentially extends John's song. Here is a case where moving directly from John's tender but clear-eyed sentiments to Paul's tender but misty-eyed imagery strengthens both tracks. We don't have the luxury of turning them into one song, but it's not out of the question that *they* might have.

When the sequence ends, the opening piano chords of "God" appear in a space which welcomes them warmly — a return from sentiment to something harder. By connecting these tracks, John and Paul each provide something that the other doesn't have here, and all of this music sounds better for it. In a sure sign of divine providence, the excised coda of "Love" makes the perfect spacer between the ending of "God" and the beginning of "Dream."

For balance reasons, the remaining gap on side two must go to Paul, and "That Would Be Something" is all of his that remains. Thankfully, it fills the spot appropriately, though it does bring about the first instance on the entire album of the same songwriter appearing twice in a row. As this technically does not break any rules, the Assembler will accept it as a necessary concession to the music.

One more concession awaits, however. Remaining on the list is George's fun and Beatle-y "It's Johnny's Birthday," written as a gift for John Lennon on his 30th birthday. Since the album was being prepared right around that very occasion, and with the same milestone in the air for all of the Beatles, it seems reasonable to imagine that someone would have slipped the track onto the end of side four as a wildcard coda. In truth, it feels like the perfect touch to cap off this magnum opus, while also bringing the album into perfect balance: Eight tracks each for John, Paul and George, with four for Ringo.

1A. What Is Life (G)	≈ Early 1970 (R)
1B. Every Night (P)	≈ I Found Out (J)
1C. Hold On (J)	Look at Me (J)
1M. I Dig Love (G) [Edit]	≈ Mother (J)
1T. Teddy Boy (P)	≈ Night and Day (R)
1Y. Remember (J)	
1Z. I'm a Fool to Care (R)	

2A. Instant Karma! (J)
2E. ≈ I'd Have You Anytime (G)
2F. Sunshine Sometime (P)
2M. That Would Be Something (P)
2Y. Well Well Well (J)
2Z. Behind That Locked Door (G)

3A. It Don't Come Easy (R)
3E. Man We Was Lonely (P)
3F. Isolation (J)
3M. Oo You (P)
3N. Coochy-Coochy (R)
3Y. Art of Dying (G)
3Z. Working Class Hero (J)

4A. All Things Must Pass (G)
4B. Maybe I'm Amazed (P)
4M. Love (J) [Edit]
4N. Junk (P)
4W. ≈ God (J)
4X. Dream (R)
4Y. Let It Down (G) [Edit]
4Z. CODA: It's Johnny's Birthday (G)

The Assembler has left five tracks on the available list. Four of these were only provisional to begin with, and no explanation would be necessary. Among these, perhaps the most disappointing is "Mother," though it is clear from a survey of the finished album that there is no spot where it could have gone that it wouldn't have been out of place. Also left behind is "Look at Me," by far John's thinnest composition in this collection, which is simply the odd track out in terms of balance.

But it is striking that the best of all the music made by the former Beatles in and around 1970 almost perfectly fills a double album. It highlights how dilution began to creep in from the very beginning of the solo era, and how eliminating it — in effect *distilling* what the solo Beatles recorded — creates an oversize statement which is still just the right size for the moment.

SAVE THE BEATLES!

Dream

(Double album)
Principal Recording: October 1969 - October 1970
Release: December 1970

Side One
1. What Is Life (Harrison)
2. Every Night (McCartney)
3. Hold On (Lennon)
4. I Dig Love (Harrison)
5. Teddy Boy (McCartney)
6. Remember (Lennon)
7. I'm a Fool to Care (Daffan, arr. Voorman)

Side Two
1. Instant Karma! (Lennon)
2. I'd Have You Any Time (Harrison/Dylan)
3. Sunshine Sometime (McCartney)
4. That Would Be Something (McCartney)
5. Well Well Well (Lennon)
6. Behind That Locked Door (Harrison)

Side Three
1. It Don't Come Easy (Starkey)
2. Man We Was Lonely (McCartney)
3. Isolation (Lennon)
4. Oo You (McCartney)
5. Coochy Coochy (Starkey)
6. Art of Dying (Harrison)
7. Working Class Hero (Lennon)

Side Four
1. All Things Must Pass (Harrison)
2. Maybe I'm Amazed (McCartney)
3. Love (Lennon)
4. Junk (McCartney)
5. God (Lennon)
6. Dream (Mercer, arr. Martin)
7. Let It Down (Harrison)
8. It's Johnny's Birthday (Martin/Coulter/Harrison)

12 / DREAM

Make It Yourself

Total Running Time: 1:31:06

Tk	Rill	Title	Source	Dur
F1-A1	—	What Is Life	[1]	4:18
F1-A2	(1.5)	Every Night	[2]	2:27
F1-A3	(3.0)	Hold On	[3]	1:47
F1-A4	(2.6)	I Dig Love [Edit]	[1]	3:56
F1-A5	2.0	Teddy Boy	[2]	2:22
F1-A6	0.5	Remember	[3]	4:32
F1-A7	0	I'm a Fool to Care	[4]	2:38
			Total:	22:02
F1-B1	—	Instant Karma! [Long version, no fade]	[5]	3:33
F1-B2	0.7	I'd Have You Anytime	[1]	2:54
F1-B3	0	Sunshine Sometime [Vocal version]	[U]	3:15
F1-B4	1.2	That Would Be Something	[2]	2:37
F1-B5	1.0	Well Well Well	[3]	5:56
F1-B6	0	Behind That Locked Door	[1]	3:20
			Total:	21:38
F1-C1	—	It Don't Come Easy	[6, bonus]	2:58
F1-C2	(1.7)	Man We Was Lonely	[2]	2:57
F1-C3	1.5	Isolation	[3]	2:49
F1-C4	(1.0)	Oo You	[2]	2:48
F1-C5	0	Coochy-Coochy	[7, bonus]	4:34
F1-C6	(7.8)	Art of Dying	[1]	3:35
F1-C7	(1.0)	Working Class Hero	[3]	3:47
			Total:	23:30
F1-D1	—	All Things Must Pass	[1]	3:38
F1-D2	(4.0)	Maybe I'm Amazed	[2]	3:45
F1-D3	(25.5)	Love [Edit]	[3]	2:20
F1-D4	0	Junk	[2]	1:54
F1-D5a	1.0	God	[3]	N/A
F1-D5b	(8.8)	Love (Reprise) [Edit]	[3]	4:36
F1-D6	0	Dream	[4]	2:40
F1-D7	0	Let It Down [Edit]	[1]	4:09
F1-D8	0	It's Johnny's Birthday	[1]	0:50
			Total:	23:56

[U] Unreleased (Seek on YouTube)
[1] *All Things Must Pass*
[2] *McCartney*
[3] *John Lennon/Plastic Ono Band*
[4] *Sentimental Journey*
[5] Seek the official video version
[6] *Ringo*
[7] *Beaucoups of Blues*

NOTE: Descriptions of edits and crossfades, with sample audio, are available at **SaveTheBeatles.com**.

Release
December 1970

Most Popular Albums
January - November 1970

US		UK	
The Beatles	Let It Be	Andy Williams	Greatest Hits
Chicago	***Chicago II***	The Beatles	Let It Be
CCR	Cosmo's Factory	Black Sabbath	Black Sabbath
CCR	Willy and the Poorboys	CSNY	Deja Vu
CSNY	Deja Vu	Deep Purple	Deep Purple in Rock
James Taylor	Sweet Baby James	James Taylor	Sweet Baby James
Led Zeppelin	Led Zeppelin II	Led Zeppelin	Led Zeppelin II
Led Zeppelin	Led Zeppelin III	Led Zeppelin	Led Zeppelin III
Neil Young	After the Gold Rush	Original Soundtrack	Easy Rider
Paul McCartney	McCartney	Original Soundtrack	Paint Your Wagon
Santana	Abraxas	Paul McCartney	McCartney
Simon & Garfunkel	Bridge Over Troubled...	The Rolling Stones	Let It Bleed
Soundtrack	Woodstock	**Simon & Garfunkel**	***Bridge Over ...***
Tom Jones	Live in Las Vegas	Tom Jones	Live in Las Vegas
The Who	Live at Leeds	Various Artists	Motown Vol 3

Most popular album in bold

It's clear from this list that the 60s were fading — but not yet gone. Familiar names from the old decade mingle with names that will define the new decade. Since two of the biggest acts here had just disbanded, this list looks a lot like the turning of the page that this era became.

Stylistically, there is no clear direction. The early edges of the soft rock movement are here, as are some of the early heavy metal sounds. Both styles — hard and soft — were in transitional periods, not yet mature.

In many ways, the Beatles dominated 1970 just as they had most years in the previous decade. Many acts seen here can trace their roots to something in the Beatles' catalog, portents of the schisms to come.

Topping the Charts
December 1970

US			UK	
Santana	Abraxas	1	Led Zeppelin	Led Zeppelin III
Carpenters	Close To You	2	Andy Williams	Greatest Hits
Led Zeppelin	Led Zeppelin III	3	Various Artists	Motown Vol 4
James Taylor	Sweet Baby James	4	Emerson Lake Palmer	Emerson Lake Palmer
The Jackson 5	Third Album	5	Simon and Garfunkel	Bridge Over...
Sly & The Family Stone	Greatest Hits	6	Bob Dylan	New Morning
Bob Dylan	New Morning	7	Led Zeppelin	Led Zeppelin II
Stephen Stills	Stephen Stills	8	Deep Purple	Deep Purple In Rock
CCR	Cosmo's Factory	9	Andy Williams	Can't Help Falling...
Various Artists	Jesus Christ Superstar	10	Nana Mouskouri	Over And Over

12 / Dream

The Beatles were still at number one with *Abbey Road* in January of 1970, and only dropped out of the top ten a few weeks before the release of *Let It Be*. Then they occupied number one for most of May and June with their soundtrack album, which was still in the top 40 as late as October of 1970. *Dream* would have been released at exactly the moment that the public was conditioned to expect a new album.

George Harrison and John Lennon released solo albums at exactly that moment, and each would be in the top ten within a couple of weeks. Setting aside the quality of the music, the timing alone set them up for success — George obviously benefitting more than John and, for that moment at least, assuming the mantle of Beatlemania. That success lends support to the idea that the first fused Beatles album, in replacing *All Things Must Pass* and *John Lennon/Plastic Ono Band*, would have enjoyed similar chart success, at least matching the group's previous two releases, and likely besting either of those solo releases — which are erased from our slightly altered narrative.

In the weeks to come, *Dream* would have been competing primarily with Simon and Garfunkel's magnum opus, the pop stylings of The Carpenters, and one of the heirs apparent, Led Zeppelin. In this context it's hard to imagine anything less than total chart dominance for a Beatles double album, regardless of how it was put together. We can imagine the Beatles either downplaying or highlighting the change in working methods, but it's hard to imagine either marketing approach having much impact on sales, given the quality of the result. The fans would have quickly moved past the lower quality of *Let It Be*, and been decidedly relieved after a year of rumors about the band's imminent demise.

Discussion

It feels safe to say that any album released by the Beatles at Christmas of 1970 would have been greeted with a bit of relief, and a bit of trepidation — at least to the degree that the public was aware of the change in working methods. We assume that the album credits would have been transparent, but even if they weren't, the industry would have taken note, as would the media, of the fact that the Beatles had scattered, never entered a studio together, yet still managed to make a new album.

Perhaps this would have led to a backlash of some sort, a collective cry of "faux Beatles." More likely, however, the music would have triumphed. Once these discs were on turntables, the value of the finished result would be clear. This would have been a majestic album.

Most critics, once they got over their understandable skepticism, would have hailed it as a new Beatles for a new decade. Paul's relative retreat in dominance would have been noted, but George's surge would have been the headline. On *Dream*, Harrison sounds confident, capable, and even visionary. Indeed, it is his increased presence which might have been seen as the biggest change to the overall sound — though critics would likely also have seen it as a natural next step after his contributions on *Abbey Road*.

John Lennon's stripped down sound would also have been noted and welcomed. The intensity of his carefully framed contributions would have been regarded as a source of strength, even as, like Paul, he seems to have retreated in overall influence. Ringo's four tracks would have received warm notices.

The record-buying public would have made sure the album was a great success. Undaunted by a slightly higher retail price — as demonstrated by *All Things Must Pass* in the real world — the album would have topped the charts quickly, and easily sold in the millions.

Inevitable comparisons to *The White Album* would have been favorable, and not in the sense of lifting one over the other, but merely acknowledging how utterly different they were. There would have been no surprise that *Dream* sounded nothing like any other Beatles album before it, but a growing awe that they could still find something new to offer.

As always, naysayers would have nitpicked. Some might have complained that no single track included all four Beatles, and that everything sounded just a little bit different. They might have claimed that the public was being sold a bill of goods, but be hard pressed to point out something on the album which was less than stellar.

If anything, close listeners would have noted that *Dream* had production elements in common with *The White Album*, such as subsets of Beatles, but a more intentional and finished sound overall. Where the earlier album was a model of studio playfulness and controlled chaos, the new double is bursting at the seams with fully-formed and fully-realized songs and recordings. Emotions are still raw in places, especially on John's tracks, but we hear the Beatles maturing before our ears, and nothing here sounds like a sketch — even those tracks from Paul which actually *were* sketches.

The effect of putting these ostensibly solo tracks together is to once again offer a sprawling landscape of music, but one which derives from freedom rather than constriction. Since each Beatle could record as he liked, the resulting sound of each track more directly reflects the artist. Yet, somewhat paradoxically, this studio divergence sounds like strength when all of that freedom is aggregated. The result is that the album would have sounded like something totally new. No one would have mistaken it for a sequel to *Abbey Road*.

Some voice somewhere would no doubt have encouraged them to "just break up already," while another would have lauded their ability to recover after *Let It Be*. Some critic would probably have recognized that *Dream* represented an evolution of their work not unlike those that the band had undergone before, while another might have lamented that they had "jumped the shark," using whatever metaphor would have worked in that era.[16]

Regardless of the diversity of reactions, however, it would have been hard for any critic to deny that the music is like all other Beatles projects in being infused with strong emotions — including joy. This is considerably less obvious when listening to the four Beatles as solo artists during this period. John's album is so desolate, and George's so bloated and uneven, and Paul's so maddeningly minimal, and Ringo's two albums both so off the beaten path, that any joy is muted and distant. Cherry-picking from among them, and setting the four voices again next to one another — even while not minimizing the complex negative emotions — yields a result which is only slightly less dramatic, but fully reveals the unexpected levels of joy hidden in the solo projects.

This is an important point because placing this palette of strong emotions together in one collection elevates everything. Paul's best sketches sound even more like the classics that they are. Ringo's standards sound classy and warm versus gimmicky. George's stridency is not even noticed. Most importantly, and contrary to what you might expect, John's voice is not muted or diluted. His tracks still peel the wallpaper with angst, and yet never get to the point where a listener is pushed into the corner of revulsion or alienation or sadness.

There is an argument to be made that John would have *preferred* revulsion, or at least *discomfort*, and had tried to infuse his album with pain that would infect the listener. But the counter-argument is that John's discomfort is more palpably *felt* by the listener when it is surrounded by music which allows it to take aim, hit its mark squarely, and then retreat. When John's voice is the only one on the album, the overall effect on the listener is exhaustion. With other voices, and especially with the right setups and releases, the listener is drawn deeper into the emotions. (There is an argument to be made that Lennon wouldn't have *cared* how a listener reacted. But that would require a far too simplistic regard for who John Lennon was.)

Even today, hearing this familiar music in a new configuration for the first time, there is revelation to be found. Hearing songs from this tender period in relief against one another highlights the complications they faced as individuals while all crossing, or preparing to cross, the 30-year-old mark — appropriately noted by the light-hearted coda. That means there is a great deal of love, family, and, perhaps not surprisingly, angst and loneliness, all of which is amplified by allowing their reactions to bump into each other.

As often happens with maturity, spirituality takes on enhanced significance, and here George's new spirituality undergirds everything without overwhelming it. Paul's contributions are the slightest, and John's the heaviest, but when heard together, a balancing point becomes discernible, allowing each Beatle to contextualize his

---

[16] The Fonz would not actually jump a shark until September 20, 1977.

brethren and make them sound better. Ringo provides simplicity — the *lack* of complication — in welcome proportion.[17] In the end, that's really what made the group work in the first place, and it's on frequent display here. By collecting and editing this music, it becomes one part reaction to what has gone before, including some contempt, and one part dreaming about what might be, hence the title.

More importantly, every single track sounds better in this context than it did on its source album or single. The Beatles truly do elevate each other here, just by *proximity* to one another. That it didn't involve them being in the same studio at the same time is its own revelation.

---

[17] Ringo plays or sings on at least 10 of the album's 28 tracks, and it may actually be more since session documentation for George's album is somewhat sketchy.

FUSION ERA #2

NOVEMBER 1970-SEPTEMBER 1971

Beggars in a Gold Mine

13/ BEGGARS IN A GOLD MINE

> "My own view is that all four of us together could even yet work out everything satisfactorily."
>
> – Ringo Starr, February 1971

> "I think this whole episode [lawsuit] shows how a disagreement could be worked out so that we all benefitted."
>
> – George Harrison, February 1971

> "We always thought of ourselves as Beatles, whether we recorded singly or in twos or threes."
>
> – John Lennon, February 1971

> "...that's how the Beatles got to be... You were very much a Beatle in your own eyes, and to an extent we all still are."
>
> – Paul McCartney, April 1971

13 / BEGGARS IN A GOLD MINE

Chronology
1970

All Things Must Pass released	**NOV**	Lee Starkey born
Christmas Album released to fan club *A Hard Day's Night* (film) TV premiere Files lawsuit to dissolve the Beatles	**DEC**	Sits for interview with Jann Wenner for *Rolling Stone* magazine *John Lennon/Plastic Ono Band* released With Ono, produces/directs two films: *Up Your Legs Forever* and *Fly*

1971

First proceedings in dissolution lawsuit Records "Power to the People" Part 1 of Wenner interview published	**JAN**	Auditions and recording for *Ram* "My Sweet Lord" single released
Making *200 Motels* (film) "Beatles might yet stay together as a group" Part 2 of Wenner interview published	**FEB**	Recording with Ronnie Spector "Another Day" released
Sued by Bright Tunes over "My Sweet Lord" "Power to the People" released	**MAR**	Receiver appointed for Beatles finances JGR throw bricks through Paul's window Win Grammy for *Let It Be* (album) Accepts Grammy award
Win Oscar for *Let It Be* (soundtrack) Quncy Jones accepts on their behalf	**APR**	"It Don't Come Easy" released Tapes segment for *Cilla* (TV)
Ram released	**MAY**	Producing Badfinger (*Straight Up*)
Recording *Imagine* Plays with Frank Zappa at Fillmore East Oversees recording of *Thrillington*	**JUN**	Plays on *Imagine* Making *Blindman* (film) Tapes segment for *Cilla* (TV)
Records/releases "Bangla Desh" Announces benefit concert, holds rehearsals *Help!* (film) TV premiere	**JUL**	Finishes recording *Imagine* Making *Imagine* (film) Invites Denny Laine to join band
Performs at *The Concert for Bangladesh* Recording *Wild Life*	**AUG**	Performs at *The Concert for Bangladesh* Leaves UK for the last time
Making *Imagine* (film) *Dick Cavett Show* (TV) *Imagine* released Records "Back Off Boogaloo"	**SEP**	Stella McCartney born Apple Studio opens

13 / Beggars in a Gold Mine

Introduction

After the presumed (essentially guaranteed) success of a first real fused album, we are left with a series of pressing questions: Would the Beatles be willing to work together this way again? How would this type of collaboration affect the business dealings? Would such projects heal old wounds, make things worse, or change nothing? Would they replace solo albums, or somehow coexist with them? Would the fans keep coming back to future releases like this with the same enthusiasm?

These are all unanswerable questions, of course. But for our purposes here, we will make a couple of assumptions. First, the fans would have been relieved and pleased and spent money with an abandon approximating previous group releases. Second, the record company would have been happy with the flowing cash, easing some of the business stresses.

Third, within the band, some tensions would have been relieved, but others might have arisen. The studio sparring would have been avoided by simply working with other musicians. For the moment, Paul would have been satisfied to work on his own, but as the one who most enjoyed being a Beatle in the studio, that satisfaction would not (and in fact, did not) last long. John would have enjoyed the freedom from pressures and expectations that hovered over group sessions, but likely also been frustrated that some of his work — including at least one masterwork — didn't see the light of day. George would have been delighted not to be a session musician for Paul — despite having adopted that role with a number of other artists, including the two other former Beatles, during this era. More importantly, he would have been happy that his songs received the respect they deserved. Ringo would have been relieved to still have a standing gig, but also started to recognize the need to diversify since so many Beatle-related sessions were now using other drummers. Given less pressure, though, he might have avoided his worst missteps of the era.

In 1971, the reality of bona fide solo albums would have become an issue. Three of the four Beatles would have had significant material left off of *Dream*. Though embryonic solo projects had been trickling out since 1968, the new and obvious abundance of music would have created an unproductive glut on the market if all four artists released at will, competing head-to-head with one another and the group — which we know because it actually happened. In addition to working out procedures for creating the new group albums, this would have been the time when managing the release schedule became an ongoing issue. We can easily imagine the old theme of inter-group competition emerging with new variations.

Still, a new paradigm might also have emerged, whereby solo releases were slotted in the first nine months of the year, with a group project being the goal for the major holiday sales season. Indeed, the first of these might have been the imagined *My Sweet Lord* album made from George's leftovers (see the previous chapter). Such a schedule would not be too far from what George Martin and Brian Epstein had concocted as a schedule in the very beginning. Remember, even in our slightly altered world, solo releases would have been considered group releases in a contractual sense until 1976. The Beatles simply would have had greater options — which, if managed properly, could have led to significant increases in sales. Timing and marketing would have become the new game.

Suffice it to say that *Dream* would have served as a proof-of-concept — a smash success, no less — and by the middle of 1971, all parties would have seen the advantage of the meta-Beatles approach, even if they bristled somewhat at the particulars. Once again we can imagine a new Beatles album for Christmas, though creating that album would have required delicately working around some unprecedented complications.

Perhaps the biggest wrinkle is that George Harrison, after a smattering of sessions early in the year, all but disappeared into the Bangladesh project. Even if the Beatles were still collaborating on some level, we have no reason to think he would have taken a different approach to the humanitarian crisis. He reacted as he would have under any circumstances: with compassion and commitment.

In the real world, the result was a great concert, a highly successful live album and film, and the firm establishment of all-star benefit concerts as a mechanism for advocacy and fundraising. George was on a roll, and we can assume that all of this would carry over into our slightly altered reality. But where real world events effectively ended that roll, the creation of another Beatles album might have made it possible for him to avoid that. He might have had the recuperative time he needed, while the band took some of the pressure off him.

Intriguingly, George invited all three of his former bandmates to perform at the concert, but only Ringo accepted. If the Beatles had still been collaborating on any level, George would have had more leverage, and a Beatles reunion on stage in August of 1971 could have changed the narrative considerably. Unfortunately, we cannot work with that potential. Nor can we work with the possibility that George might have been drawn back from the charity work long enough to produce a new track or two for a group album. His representation on the project might have been the most complicated to acquire, and even run the risk of retreat — at least temporarily — on his hard-won right to have equal songwriting representation with Paul and John.

One important difference this new type of collaboration could have brought about is a reduction in the public sniping between John and Paul, which took place throughout 1971. We will assume that, with détente enforced through the new approach, even if these tensions were not completely avoided, they might have either been kept from the public sphere, or played out in tracks right next to each other on the same album — thus muted, to a degree. Perhaps Lennon would either not have given his famous interview to Jann Wenner, or would have pulled some of his punches in deference to the group's continued activities (the effects of heroin notwithstanding). The music might still have held coded messages, but the public need not have known. This shift results in at least one recording lost, but "How Do You Sleep?" has always been a stain on Lennon's catalog which would have been better avoided anyway.

In this period, Paul McCartney established the pattern of producing significantly more work than any of his former bandmates. As a result, we find Paul with enough new music to dominate any Beatles project if he chose, but the other Beatles would not have let him do that, and our mythical Assembler won't either. Indeed, it's John who will be dominant here. Paul will also make some important contributions, but much of his work will still emerge on solo albums. In truth, given the quantity of recorded material available, Paul's real world albums require only slight modifications to accommodate our fantasy extractions. By contrast, John creates only enough polished material for his contribution to the group album, with hardly anything left over — again establishing a pattern which will endure.

Even without Paul's lawsuit to dissolve the business relationship, which we erase from our altered world, some sort of lean period was probably inevitable after the musical verbosity of the previous year. From this point forward there would always have been whispered questions about whether the group should just hang it up. We will not let them do that, however, because *Beggars in a Gold Mine*, though resembling nothing like the sprawling breadth of its predecessor, and nothing like any of the real world albums, is still a significant improvement over the patchwork of uneven releases it could have supplanted. This is something of a miracle.

In the real world of Beatles history, this period is remembered mostly for the legal struggles of the former bandmates, the public feuding, and George's all-star concert. In our imagined and slightly altered reality, it could have yielded the group's sophomore fused album in place of lawyers and feuds. Everyone knows the reputation of sophomore projects, but that will be avoided in spectacular fashion here. Though at first it looks like pulling together scraps, and doing so would have been an especially delicate task for our Assembler, when all is said and done, the album is complex, rewarding, and still sounds like the Beatles — albeit with a new energy. *Beggars in a Gold Mine* will still have greatness baked into its grooves, which is all we can ask.

SAVE THE BEATLES!

Recording
October 1970 - September 1971

⊛ Studio Recording   ◀ Concert(s)   ◎ Single Release

		JAN	FEB	MAR	APR	MAY	JUN	JUL	AUG	SEP	OCT	NOV	DEC
70	J										⊛	⊛	
71	J			⊛	◎		⊛	⊛◀	⊛◎		img		
	P		⊛	⊛◎			img		⊛				img
	G			⊛				⊛	⊛◎	◀			img
	R					◎			◀	⊛			

After the overflowing bounty of new music in 1970, things changed considerably. In addition to being a time of terrible stress, or perhaps because of it, the output of the solo Beatles reflected a return to the former status quo in terms of pure quantity. John and Paul each had new albums — indeed, Paul actually had two, plus a non-album single. Ringo had only one lonesome — but very good — recording to release, having given most of his energy to film work. But George…

George Harrison continued some casual recording of his own material, but much of his work in early 1971 was in the producer's chair, working on tracks by Ronnie Spector, Badfinger, Doris Troy, Billy Preston, and others. But his year — and career — took a hard turn when his mentor, Ravi Shankar, made him aware of the great humanitarian crisis taking place in Bangladesh.

Harrison immediately turned his energies away from recording, and gave them instead to raising funds for those in desperate need. He did record a benefit single, "Bangla Desh," which preceded the benefit concert, but this would be his last studio release for nearly two years.

By the end of 1970, Paul McCartney was well into the recording of his second solo album, *Ram*, along with a big bunch of tracks which would populate his albums for years to come. Indeed, he recorded so much during this period that tracks would still be trickling out over 30 years later.[1]

---

[1] "A Love for You" was begun during this era, and finally emerged on a film soundtrack in 2003! Even after all that time, it required only some minor additional production and a remix. This is but one extreme example. Many others are possible, and it's not out of the question that even more from this period will eventually see official release.

13 / Beggars in a Gold Mine

Having accepted that the Beatles would not be recording together any time in the foreseeable future, and not interested in playing all of the instruments by himself again, McCartney held covert auditions in New York for new sidemen. The musicians he hired, not yet to be known as "Wings," were uniformly excellent, but one thing was non-negotiable: at least one rank amateur would be among them. Linda McCartney would be a member of the band and also Paul's new musical collaborator. She would learn to play keyboard on the fly, and endure a great deal of "coaching" from her husband when recording vocals (mostly backup). Paul was undeterred. This decision affected a new sound for his records, something he deeply desired, though that's not why he did it. He wanted the camaraderie of his new wife, and his family, wherever he went. And though the band members, and many fans, would not always appreciate it, this decision would have a deep impact on his recordings for decades.

The sessions for *Ram* took place in studios not used before by Beatles, and with new engineers. Most of the recording was done in New York, with mixing in Los Angeles, and the first fruit was a single, "Another Day." The record became a modest hit, and was generally well-received, if considered a bit slight compared to his Beatles output. The album, however, met with generally harsh reviews, even as its first single, "Uncle Albert/Admiral Halsey," topped the US charts. Two other singles did not fare nearly as well, and suddenly the trajectory of Paul's solo career began to tip downward. It would not be pointing up again any time soon.

Even as *Ram* faded, Paul remained determined to make good on his growing desire to form a new band as the core of his post-Beatles identity. In the summer of 1971, he added a second important musical foil in guitarist/vocalist/songwriter Denny Laine, and spent two weeks at Abbey Road studios hastily recording a new batch of original songs. Unfortunately, this collection of material would be arguably the worst in McCartney's career, and the low quality of the songs was only the first problem. Taking a page from John Lennon's playbook, Paul wanted to record quickly and with a sense of spontaneity, capturing a "feel" instead of striving for perfection. As a result, over half of the tracks on *Wild Life* would be comprised of first takes, a fact that reviewers noticed and scalded. The intentional underproduction did not have the desired effect, and *Wild Life* sold poorly.

Indeed, both of McCartney's 1971 albums were received with an unfamiliar undercurrent of hostility by critics, and neither album sold anywhere near as much as a Beatles album would have. Some of this was reaction to Paul's legal strategies rather than to the music itself. But where *Ram* has since found many defenders, *Wild Life* remains among the most vilified solo releases by any former Beatle. The lasting impact of this one-two punch of poorly-received albums would be disillusionment among fans and lowered expectations for future McCartney projects.

John Lennon was almost too busy with advocacy work and artistic "happenings" in 1971 to record new music. Much like Harrison, he essentially put his recording career on the back burner while he sought after ways to use his celebrity to advance a social agenda. Still, he did have some song ideas.

Another one-off session in early 1971 yielded a new protest anthem, "Power to the People," as well as first passes at some of the material which would become *Imagine*. When he finally had enough material for a full album, much like McCartney had done, Lennon quickly assembled a band and headed into the studio for a very short round of sessions. This time, Lennon's band actually included George Harrison, at least for a few days. Among other things, their collaboration notably yielded the scorched earth message to Paul known as "How Do You Sleep?" which fanned the flames of a very public feud between the two former Beatles that lasted for months.

Unlike Paul, however, John's hastily-assembled 1971 album, *Imagine*, would be much more warmly received, largely due to its title track, which quickly became cultural shorthand for idealism. Critical reactions were somewhat more guarded. Though generally positive, some critics preferred the harder edge of the album's predecessor, and some noted that outside of the title track and the McCartney thrashing, the other songs were rather dull. Despite these issues, the album sold much better than John's debut, and is widely considered a classic.

Late in the year, John and Yoko recorded yet another of the timeless anthems which would come to define Lennon's post-Beatles career. "Happy Xmas (War is Over)" gives a strong summation of what was on Lennon's mind in 1971, further supporting the idea that his recording career was something of an afterthought, and only to be used as a tool for other purposes. But that fact makes it even more remarkable that, of the scant recordings he did in 1971, two are among the most beloved tracks ever recorded by a former Beatle.

Ringo Starr spent most of 1971 focusing on his burgeoning acting career. His only release was the Harrison collaboration, "It Don't Come Easy," which was already over a year old. His only new recording in 1971 would also be with Harrison, who co-wrote and produced, "Back Off Boogaloo," though it would go unreleased until the following spring.

The highest profile Beatle-related release in this era may very well have been *The Concert for Bangladesh*, another triple album which Harrison worked on for months. Though it provides no material which might have been used by the Beatles, it is one of the elephants in the room in this era around which any new group release would have had to maneuver, resulting in quite a challenge for the Assembler, had there been a project to assemble.

Materials

Overview
72 tracks: 26 eligible, 16 provisional

In this era, Lennon famously asserted that he thought the split had actually strengthened the work of the former bandmates. "I think we're much better than we ever were when we were together," he claimed.[2] But listening objectively, the solo music of 1971 demonstrates rather plainly that none of the former Beatles had found a comfortable solo voice yet. What they produced bounces around in style, temperament, and quality. This is important because it is descended from the fading afterglow of both the classic Beatles years and the first burst of solo freedom.

If there's any overarching theme to the results, it's that all four former Beatles exhibited large swings in their output. Ringo and George both swung from unexpected musical verbosity to near silence. Paul swung from working totally alone to actively cultivating new ongoing collaborators and new ways of doing things. John swung from starkness to sweetness, but also from revelation to obfuscation. Both John and Paul also swung from positivity to negativity, at least to some degree, a most un-Beatle-like development.

Collectively, their sounds and priorities continued to diverge, but there is still a lingering sense that each can elevate the others, despite the fact that they probably didn't want to.

Paul McCartney
39 tracks: 13 eligible, 7 provisional
Bracketed tracks are considered in a different era

Sources

M02		"Another Day" / "Oh Woman, Oh Why" R: Oct-Nov 70 P: McCartney		S: Columbia (NY)	71-Feb
M03		*Ram* R: Oct 70 - Mar 71 P: McCartney/McCartney		S: Columbia (NY) +2	71-May
M04		*Wild Life* R: Jul-Aug 71 P: McCartney/McCartney		S: EMI	71-Dec
M06		["Mary Had a Little Lamb"] / "Little Woman Love" R: Nov 71 - Mar 72 P: McCartney/McCartney		S: Columbia (NY)	72-May
M09		*Red Rose Speedway* (3 tracks considered) R: Mar-Dec 72 P: McCartney		S: Various (6)	73-Apr

---

[2] Alan Smith, "At Home With The Lennons, Part 2," *New Musical Express*, August 7, 1971.

M10	["Live and Let Die"] / "I Lie Around"			73-Jun
	R: Oct 72	P: A: Martin; B: McCartney	S: A: AIR; B: Various	

(Unreleased)

Tracks

1882 (McCartney)		M09, 70-Dec
≈ (Style) Long, elaborate, dark story song. Equally fascinating and tedious. Studio version best.		
3 Legs (McCartney)		M03-02, 70-Oct
⊘ (Content) Sending a message, music and lyrics are pointed, good.		
African Yeah Yeah (McCartney/McCartney)		M04, 71-Aug
⊘ (Filler) Weed-fueled nonsense. Is this fun? You decide.		
Another Day (McCartney/McCartney)		M02-01, 70-Oct
✓ One of Paul's "lonely" characters. Slight but catchy. Successful pop.		
Back Seat of My Car, The (McCartney)		M03-12, 71-Jan
✓ Structured and significant, sounds like act two of a movie. Very good.		
Big Barn Bed (McCartney/McCartney)		M09-01, 71-Mar
✓ Catchy, uptempo pop. Builds nicely, but settles into annoying repetition.		
Bip Bop (McCartney/McCartney)		M04-02, 71-Aug
⊘ (Quality) A hopelessly cutesy "baby" song.		
Bip Bop (Link) (McCartney/McCartney)		M04-07, 71-Aug
⊘ (Filler) Unnecessary, but harmless — even though it "reprises" a lousy song.		
Blackpool (McCartney)		M03, 71-Aug
≈ (Filler/Quality) Blues, with a back-to-roots feel, but the lyric is pretty lousy.		
Dear Boy (McCartney/McCartney)		M03-04, 71-Mar
⊘ (Content) Ambitious, and well-formed. Vocal work is all excellent.		
Dear Friend (McCartney/McCartney)		M04-09, 71-Aug
⊘ (Content/Quality) Weepy. Repetitive. Needs a good edit. Should have been a B-side.		
Eat at Home (McCartney/McCartney)		M03-09, 70-Oct
≈ (Content) Inoffensive, but borders on filler. Built on simple pleasures, but not one.		
Get on the Right Thing (McCartney/McCartney)		M09-03, 70-Oct
✓ Nice structured pop, but labored. Takes a long time to get to not much point.		
Great Cock and Seagull Race (McCartney)		M03, 71-Feb
⊘ (Filler) 12-bar fun. Instrumental excellence, to be sure, but really nothing to see here.		
Heart of the Country (McCartney/McCartney)		M03-07, 70-Nov
✓ Earnest but cloying. In context, feels derivative and twee. Still a pretty good song.		
Hey Diddle (McCartney/McCartney)		M03, 70-Oct
✓ Walks a fine line between catchy and annoying, but the craft is strong and this works.		
I Am Your Singer (McCartney/McCartney)		M04-06, 71-Aug
⊘ (Quality) Weak idea. Tortured melody. Rough duet. Weird arrangement.		
I Lie Around (McCartney/McCartney)		M10-02, 71-Mar
✓ Goofy but fun. Designed to sound lazy, but isn't. Deserves an album slot.		
Indeed I Do (McCartney/McCartney)		M04, 71-Aug
⊘ (Unfinished) Simple enough jot with potential unrealized. Similar to "On the Wings of a Nightingale"		

13 / BEGGARS IN A GOLD MINE

Little Lamb Dragonfly (McCartney/McCartney)		M09-05, 71-Mar
✓ Quirky, structured, interesting. Inscrutable lyric, but nice payoff.		
Little Woman Love (McCartney/McCartney)		M06-02, 70-Nov
✓ This is McCartney firing on all cylinders. A great, lost track.		
Long Haired Lady (McCartney/McCartney)		M03-10, 70-Oct
✓ A "big" song, but not fully realized. Alternates between moody and silly.		
Love for You, A (McCartney)		M03, 70-Oct
✓ Unusual vocal probably doomed release, but it's a poppy, catchy song. Very slight.		
Love Is Strange (Baker/Vanderpool/Smith)		M04-03, 71-Aug
⊘ (Filler) Weird choice for a cover, and not interesting at all. Straight reading.		
Monkberry Moon Delight (McCartney/McCartney)		M03-08, 70-Nov
⊘ (Quality) Pushing for something new, but this is not it. Bad song. Bad record.		
Mumbo (McCartney/McCartney)		M04-01, 71-Aug
⊘ (Quality) Brutal vocal. Everything forced. Unlistenable.		
Mumbo (Link) (McCartney/McCartney)		M04-10, 71-Aug
⊘ (Filler) Another pointless "reprise." Not bad, but not helpful.		
Now Hear This Song of Mine (McCartney)		M03, 71-Feb
⊘ (Filler) Likely no more than sung refrains, there's nothing here.		
Oh Woman, Oh Why (McCartney)		M02-02, 70-Nov
⊘ (Content) Truly unfortunate. One of Paul's "stains."		
Ram On (McCartney)		M03-03, 71-Feb
≈ (Quality) A stub. Pleasant enough, but insufficient for the "concept" of an album.		
Ram On (Reprise) (McCartney)		M03-11, 71-Feb
≈ (Filler) No new ideas. A reprise of nothingness.		
Rode All Night (McCartney)		M03, 70-Oct
≈ (Filler) Raucous drum and guitar jam, occasional vocal improv. Potentially useful with edit.		
Smile Away (McCartney)		M03-06, 70-Nov
⊘ (Quality) Forced. Bad lyrics. Cliché. Another "stain."		
Some People Never Know (McCartney/McCartney)		M04-05, 71-Aug
✓ Simple idea, but ineffective. Obvious, automatic, banal. LM vocal distracts.		
Tomorrow (McCartney/McCartney)		M04-08, 71-Aug
⊘ (Quality) Shoddy song. Never mention in the same breath with precursor. Sketchy vox.		
Too Many People (McCartney)		M03-01, 70-Nov
⊘ (Content) Feud-starter, but structured, and actually a fine song.		
Uncle Albert/Admiral Halsey (McCartney/McCartney)		M03-05, 71-Jan
✓ Three-parter. Cinematic, but plot-free. Quirky but catchy. Playful, fun.		
When the Wind Is Blowing (McCartney/McCartney)		M04, 70-Dec
≈ (Unfinished) Quiet, gentle vibe, but largely wordless vocal leaves it incomplete.		
Wild Life (McCartney/McCartney)		* M04-04, 71-Aug
⊘ (Quality) Plodding, overlong, nothing to catch or hold the ear. Dumb lyric. Bad vocal.		

This time, in a strong sign of things to come, it is Paul who has the most recordings from which to choose. Unfortunately, like Ringo before him, one entire album is completely unusable, while the other yields only a few select treats. Given the quantity of outtakes, it's tempting to think some unreleased tracks might make up the difference, but that isn't the case. As will become the norm, portions of Paul's contributions will be taken from stand-alone singles, which brightens things nicely.

Ram, though now considered a classic, proves complicated to unpack and use on a Beatles project for two reasons. The first is content, and the second is technical.

To the first, the album contains the initial salvos in what would become some very public feuding. Paul is at his most cutting with some of these tracks. Indeed, this is the most angry material he will ever release as a solo artist. Never before or since has he ventured into such direct criticism of his former partners, sending harsh coded messages that he knew they would decode instantly, without caring whether anyone else — i.e. every fan everywhere — might also figure it out.

Our Assembler would have been forced to set aside anything that John perceived as an attack, whether rightfully or not. This dooms "Too Many People," "3 Legs," and "Dear Boy" — the latter in error since Paul has made it clear it was directed at Linda's first husband. These simply could not have been considered, and might not have even been presented for consideration in the first place.

Also in the category of content issues, and uncharacteristic for Paul, is the presence of truly lousy songs, likely a by-product of needing to fill an album all by himself — our familiar dilution problem. Even when he is not directly expressing Beatles-related anger, he has written angry lyrics and sings them in an angry voice over substandard music. This is most obvious on "Smile Away" and "Monkberry Moon Delight," two songs not typically considered related to the Beatles situation. Our Assembler would surely have rejected both, along with "Eat at Home," as insufficient in quality — relegating all three to the scrap heap.

But like his first solo album, the tracks which do get carried forward to the Beatles project are true classics. "Uncle Albert/Admiral Halsey," despite being almost pure confection, retains a cinematic breadth and interesting structure that makes it a McCartney classic (thanks, in part, to George Martin's uncredited orchestration).[3] It is clearly a case of Paul throwing together a few unfinished ideas and creating a "suite," something he had done before, and would do again often — though rarely with this level of ease and success. When Paul's unfinished ideas were combined with John's, the result was often a finished product greater than the sum of its parts, but he will not be able to accomplish this feat on his own quite so easily. On this particular track, he does.

"Back Seat of My Car" reads almost like a bookend, despite telling the middle portion of a completely different story. It's interesting to wonder what the beginning

---

[3] A deconstruction of the recording session published by *Mix* in 2004 notes that the track is comprised of 12 discrete sections.

and end of that story might sound like, and if telling that story might have made a better album. Perhaps it would have started with "Two of Us" and ended with "Rode All Night." Then again, perhaps this is actually best left to the imagination. The unreleased, and perplexing, "1882" is an example of a case where Paul told the whole story, and we might have been better served by him telling a little less. The track remains provisionally eligible only because Paul would probably have lobbied for it.

"Heart of the Country" sounds like vintage McCartney, somewhat obviously descended from "Mother Nature's Son." In a different context it might be just fine. But coming in the middle of this very uneven album, it sounds too clever, and just a little too self-satisfied for its own good. Still, its Beatle-esque qualities will keep it eligible for use on a group project.

Similarly, "Long Haired Lady" is complex enough, and of a high enough quality, that it must also be considered. The brass score (also by Martin), lends the song a grandness it may not quite deserve. It sounds something like a precursor of the medley on *Red Rose Speedway*, and features a long, repeated section over the fade which may have actually been a first pass at creating a climax for the album.

The title track and its reprise are likely too slight for inclusion on a Beatles project. One can certainly imagine Paul pitching this to the group as a framework for the new album, but there's basically nothing to it beyond the visual image (on the album cover) and the novelty of a ukulele. By this point, the whole idea of a "reprise" begins to look more like a cheap tactic to make it seem like the collection has a larger theme when really it does not. We all agreed to overlook that on *Sgt. Pepper*, but here it is ridiculously thin, and no one is being fooled. Even Paul seems a little chagrined about using it.

In trying to put the best of these tracks together with the work of the other Beatles in this period, our Assembler will find an unprecedented technical issue: The tracks on *Ram* have a distinctly different sonic quality from all previous Beatle-related releases. Indeed, *Ram* sounds different from anything Paul has ever released.

This was intentional, of course, as Paul sought to distance himself from all things Beatle — or at least appear to be doing so. The result infects not only his singing and playing, but every part of the recording, most notably the mixing. Many parts of *Ram* are slathered with long reverb, and have a muddiness and occasional harshness not typical to his previous work. Of all McCartney's solo works, *Ram* is the one which might most benefit from a complete remix, rather than just a remaster.

The Assembler can work with this, of course, and mitigate the differences with the other solo Beatles by carefully selecting and contextualizing the tracks on the group album. There might also have been some selective remixing at EMI in preparation for using any of these tracks, with the goal of bringing the sound back into more familiar Beatle territory.

All in all, *Ram* genuinely sounds like a classic today. Contemporary reviewers dismissed all of the attention to detail, and the fact that it creates its own little world to inhabit, focusing on the soap opera saga found in the most provocative lyrics. But this album somehow does manage to be greater than the sum of its parts, a real accomplishment when you consider how slight some of these parts are. *Ram* simply shouldn't be as good as it is.

McCartney's second album of the period, *Wild Life*, from which we might hope to extract a song or two, proves impossible to use. Each and every one of these tracks is bad all on its own, each in a slightly different way, and together they create an unholy 12 inches of vinyl.

The album was supposedly sequenced in the same order as it was recorded, generally a bad idea. In this case, it results in the bitter taste of "Mumbo" carrying all the way through the album, polluting tracks to the bitter end. The misguided sequencing results in a progression that moves from faster, lighter and wilder to slower, more tamed and introspective, ending in ponderous. When listening to it as released, one gets the sense that maybe just reordering the tracks would improve things, but this is not the case. These tracks are all lousy, and there is no sequence which can hide that.

So when considering the collection as a whole, it's tempting to say that Paul was just trying too hard, and that is about the best explanation anyone can offer. The core ideas — musical and lyrical — for "Mumbo," "Bip Bop," "Wild Life," "I Am Your Singer," and "Tomorrow" simply cannot support complete songs. These would all have been better left as stubs, perhaps thrown away in a medley or "suite" — or never released at all. One can imagine a world in which *Wild Life* stayed in the can, and gradually grew a reputation as some sort of great, lost McCartney album. That might have been a better fate.

The cover of "Love is Strange," arguably the best song on the album, feels like filler (as latter day covers almost always do), but more importantly suggests the possibility that Paul might have imagined releasing this track, and perhaps the whole album, *anonymously*. The vocal arrangement carefully buries Paul's voice, in what sounds like a conscious attempt to disguise his presence.

Similarly, all across side one of this disc, Paul uses vocal techniques we have never heard from him before. His shouting on "Mumbo" and "Wild Life" are distant cousins of his "Little Richard" voice, different enough to indicate that he was trying to find something new, but in no way good. Points for the attempt, but it does not work. He also manages a previously unheard "flat" voice on "Bip Bop," cementing the notion that Paul worked very hard here to get out of his various Beatle personas. Again, he is to be commended for the effort, but it falls completely flat.

"Dear Friend," certainly the most significant track on the album, presents two problems, neither of which is mitigated by Paul's genuine vulnerability. First, it's a lousy song — slow, ponderous, with an uncharacteristically clunky melody that takes Paul way out of his comfortable range both vocally and emotionally. And second, the tone of the performance is so positively weepy that the song's whole theme is undermined. The sound of Paul basically begging for some form of reconciliation makes for a truly terrible album closer, and would have fared no better in any other slot on the album. If this had to be released at all, it might have worked better as a space-filling B-side, where it could have accomplished the task of communicating with Lennon, but then disappeared, as unloved and forgotten as dreck like "Oh Woman, Oh Why."

The only track on *Wild Life* potentially worth bringing forward is the similarly slight "Some People Never Know." It is the only idea on the album worth turning into a complete song, though our Assembler would have insisted on some editing, and a reduction in volume of Linda's pitch-challenged co-lead vocal.

Through the years, Linda's vocals have led to so much discussion that it feels like a subject that has been beaten to death. The upshot is this: Singing in tune is *not* a requirement for pop musicians. It never was, and certainly still is not with the advent of autotune. The ability to sing in tune is just a nice bonus. Also, being a *natural, polished* and *confident* singer, like Paul, is not a requirement. If it were, there are many voices which might never have been heard — starting with George Harrison and Ringo Starr — and the universe of popular music would be much poorer for it.

But two critical pieces of being a pop singer are *uniqueness* and *distinctiveness*. In the case of the former, a voice which *sounds like no other* is potentially of great value. In the case of the latter, a voice which contains *instantly recognizable personality* is of similar value. On these two intertwined metrics, Linda scores very highly.[4] Even more than Paul's voice, the presence of Linda's voice is part of the formula which made Paul's music in the 70s sound distinct from his work in the 60s. Whether she wanted to or not, Linda provided one of those little things which set Paul's new band apart from his old band.

That said, she acquitted herself sufficiently on most occasions, the aforementioned "Some People Never Know" being an obvious exception — another sign that the project was rushed. Across the rest of his catalog, Paul's insistence on getting things right ensures that very little blatantly out-of-tune singing is heard.[5]

Paul has admitted in interviews that he worked Linda very hard to make that happen. She no doubt had to do many takes, and many punch-ins, on her vocals

---

[4] As, of course, does Yoko Ono. Unfortunately, Ono's voice also has something of a fingernails-on-a-blackboard quality which many listeners simply cannot get past.

[5] Linda's abilities are perhaps on greatest display in the tight harmonies that she and Paul sang with Eric Stewart on *Tug of War*. Her voice is clearly audible, and clearly in tune. The backup vocals on that album are one of its chief delights.

before Paul was satisfied. That's one of the great things about working in a recording studio — which completely disappears on a concert stage. Linda's natural vocal abilities were always likely to be a liability in concert, where it can be difficult or impossible to hear yourself over everything else. As such, it isn't really fair to isolate any one singer's vocals from a live recording, as happened with Linda in 1990. Even the absolute best singers can sound terrible under such trying circumstances. The Beatles themselves often sound horrible on concert recordings made at the height of Beatlemania. But in the studio, where everything is isolated, Linda was largely able to meet the demands Paul placed upon her, and he should be credited for making those demands.

That said, giving her a featured vocal was never the best idea. As with Ringo before her, Paul had enough musical sense to limit the demands on her, for the most part. Where some might fault Paul for putting her in the band at all, it's better to appreciate that Paul, determined to have her there, didn't just set aside his standards. He figured out a way to make it work, despite the limitations of her natural abilities. As such, the sad truth is that Linda's overall effect on Paul's musical output was significantly less harmful than Yoko's effect on John's — despite the fact that both voices contain uniqueness and distinctiveness.

Given the somewhat slim pickings on the two albums, it will have to be music released only on singles that will round out Paul's contributions to the new group album. "Another Day" is a fine piece of pop songwriting that sold well and fits temperamentally with the other solo Beatle tracks of the era. "Little Woman Love" is also from this period, despite not being released until much later. It was thrown away as the B-side of "Mary Had a Little Lamb," a clear case of Paul making the wrong choice for the A-side. It's a fun track with a catchy sound, again fitting nicely with the rest of the new album's music.

The aforementioned outtake, "A Love for You," was also recorded around this time and would have been considered for this album. On the track, Paul experiments with a somewhat breathless vocal style he would never use again. It works, mostly, and the song is pure pop. The track is perhaps known more for the many times it has been remixed and *almost* released.

The one outtake which proves irresistible is "Rode All Night." Unedited, it constitutes about eight minutes of Paul playing (approximately) 12-bar blues and improvising a sketchy lyric over drummer Denny Seiwell's fantastic thrashing. The energy is electric and contagious, even if there's not much of a song there. While there's no way the Beatles would give up nearly nine minutes of an album to a jam like this, it stays on the provisional list with the idea that it might be edited somehow

13 / Beggars in a Gold Mine

and available to fill a slot if necessary.

With only a small amount of the material Paul created during this period good enough to go on a Beatles project, Paul's contribution will once again be somewhat muted compared to the classic Beatle days. But it was inevitable that Paul would create way more music than a group project could handle, making it obvious, even from this early point, that having a healthy solo career — and maybe even a second band — would be a necessity for Paul, if only to give him an outlet for all of his ideas.

John Lennon
16 tracks: 7 eligible, 1 provisional

Sources

L05	"Power to the People" / ~~"Open Your Box"; "Touch Me"~~ R: Jan-Feb 71 P: Lennon/Ono/Spector S: Ascot Sound				71-Mar
L06	*Imagine* R: Feb-Jul 71 P: Lennon/Ono/Spector S: EMI, Ascot +1				71-Sep
	(Pseudonymous release)				
	(Unreleased)				

Tracks

Crippled Inside (Lennon) ≈ (Quality/Content) Clichéd and flip, this is a blunt JL working in tired folk forms.	L06-02, +G, 71-Jul
Do the Oz (Lennon/Ono) (Issued as "Elastic Oz Band") ⊘ (Filler) Serviceable instrumental, but Yoko's vocals will drive away most ears.	L, 71-May
Gimme Some Truth (Lennon) ✓ A successful blend of anger and cleverness.	L06-06, +G, 71-Jul
God Save Us (Lennon/Ono) ⊘ (Quality/Content) Thin politics over thin music. It made no political or artistic impact.	L, 71-May
How Do You Sleep? (Lennon) ⊘ (Content) Cheap shots and overplayed insults result in a blood stain on JL's catalog.	L06-08, +G, 71-Jul
How? (Lennon) ✓ Fantastic original music with a heartfelt, searching lyric. Best in show.	L06-09, 71-Jul
I Don't Want to Be a Soldier (Lennon) ⊘ (Quality/Content) Sloppy and unfinished, it is loved more for what a listener imagines it to be.	L06-05, +G, 71-Jul
Imagine (Lennon) ✓ A triumph of inspiration over craft. Great ideas render an otherwise dull track timeless.	L06-01, 71-Jul
It's So Hard (Lennon) ✓ Bluesy feel, unusual vocal, distinct sound. Underrated and very successful.	L06-04, 71-Jul
Jealous Guy (Lennon) ✓ Protesting too much, this reads like an excuse, and fails to convince. Whistling.	L06-03, 71-Jul

Oh My Love (Lennon/Ono)   L06-07, +G, 71-Jul
✓ A weepy love song that's just the right amount of weepy. GH guitar is beautiful.

Oh Yoko! (Lennon)   L06-10, 71-Jul
⊘ (Content) Light and fun, but built around a lyric that is far too specific. Ultimately, it annoys.

Power to the People (Lennon)   L05-01, 71-Feb
✓ Tough political statement. Politics aside, it is a powerful, funky, very big track.

Sally and Billy (Lennon)   L, 70-Nov
⊘ (Demo) Intriguing, with potential, but not usable as is.

San Francisco Bay Blues (Fuller)   L06, 71-Jul
⊘ (Demo) A lark, just for fun.

Well (Baby Please Don't Go) (Traditional)   L06, 71-Feb
⊘ (Quality) Heavy and slow, this really lumbers. Great take — vocal and band — but just for fun.

John Lennon characterized the recording and assembly of *Imagine* this way: "It took me nine days to make this album and ten to make the last one. So I'm getting faster. There are ten tracks on it. I had more, but Phil [Spector] suddenly said that I had no more room, so we stopped."[6]

At the least, this places John and Paul at opposite ends of the perfectionist spectrum. Perhaps the coldest response one could give would be to say, "It shows." Unfortunately, that is also the appropriate critical response.

The songs sound unfinished, rushed. The arrangements are pedestrian, rushed. The playing is sloppy, rushed. The production is a mess, rushed. The orchestrations by New York arranger Torrie Zito are thin and shrill, and had been rushed. Despite John's wishful comments about having been "happy" when it was recorded, *Imagine* sounds more like its cover image looks: faded, monochrome, uneven, unfinished, unpolished, unvarnished, unhappy.

Yet, of course, it's a classic. It sold very well, and is certainly *remembered* well, largely on the strength of its title track. But it is a better album in memory and emotion than it is on a turntable. It just never lives up to the potential heard in its best tracks, no matter how much one wants to like it. We seem to love the *idea* of this album — in the way we often love the *idea* of John Lennon — rather than the *actual* album and its *actual* music. If we are being honest, this album feels more like a single . . . with nine B-sides. Only the faithful likely made it much past the opener on subsequent listenings.

The problems, while apparent in the album as released, become even more stark when breaking it into its component parts. Though there's not much to the assembly, there appears to be some strength in simple aggregation. To a degree, this music is all of a piece in that similar themes float throughout, and there is a unity to the

---

[6] From *Imagine John Yoko*: imaginejohnyoko.com/recording-the-imagine-album

sound — i.e. a similar sonic quality throughout, in much the same way that Paul's contemporary album had a unified sound. In this way, and others, *Imagine* is rather simpatico with *Ram*, despite the very different roads they took to completion.

Listening to the tracks as parts, however, reveals some surprising negatives. Not only are the songs not John's sharpest, the production is not Phil Spector's sharpest. The fading remnants of the "wall of sound" are paper thin, more like a motel than a bank vault. Though not bad, exactly, there just isn't much to it. With only a couple of exceptions, the sound is utterly *conventional*. We can cut them some slack because they were working in a studio that was still being built around them, but the banality of the sound seems to be more about lack of imagination than lack of technical capabilities. For example, though the home studio fidelity is uniformly great, the utter lack of backup vocals on the entire album is completely mystifying. No vocal isolation booth, perhaps?

The strangest thing may be that Lennon's voice, which is well known to have the fantastic ability to stand starkly in front of the instrumental background, is too often subsumed creamily into the mixes like another violin ("Crippled Inside," "Gimme Some Truth," "How" and "I Don't Want to Be a Soldier"). The edges are sanded off his vocal performances, if not the content.

Indeed, when we dig into the songs as the Assembler would have, we find some striking confirmation for Lennon's assertion that *Imagine* was just "...'Working Class Hero' with sugar on it..."[7] A veneer of sweetness conceals — dishonestly — Lennon's anger, despair, disillusionment, and an unhealthy, almost sycophantic devotion to his spouse. (Is it any wonder that Ono curated a massively — and somewhat absurdly — extended version of this album for release in 2018?[8])

Lennon sings in docile tones about strident subjects, things that really require stronger vocal performances, and considerably more focused production. His singing is uncharacteristically uncoupled from the subject matter. The bouncy "Crippled Inside" maintains a docile tone while spewing a scathing lyric, capturing in its broad net so many things to hate. "Gimme Some Truth" likewise uses catchy music to condemn everything in its path, with Lennon begging for some nebulous, essentially meaningless *something* — "truth" — while setting himself up as the sole arbiter of what that might be.

"Jealous Guy," stands out as a prime example of this dishonesty. John coos regret, as his tone and the music (the unfortunately orphaned "Child of Nature") attempt to paper over the real possibility that he is referring to some sort of actual emotional or physical violence, of which we know John to have been eminently capable:

---

[7] Letter from John Lennon published in *Melody Maker*, December 4, 1971.
[8] In fairness, most latter day "special editions" feature an element of absurd excess.

I began to lose control
I didn't mean to hurt you
I'm sorry that I made you cry
Oh my, I didn't want to hurt you
I'm just a jealous guy

Worst of all, however, may be the use of slinky, slow, seductive blues, augmented with orchestral niceties, to tear mercilessly into a friend-turned-foe. "How Do You Sleep?," one of the most unfortunate tracks in Lennon's entire catalog, may have given the album the extra push it needed to catch the public's attention, turning the airwaves into a Beatles-themed soap opera, but it leaves a sour taste to this day, being dishonest in both lyric and music. No matter whose side of the business dispute you are on, there is no justifying the wholly misplaced cheap shots found in these lyrics. While some of the other songs can make it through to a Beatles project, this one simply cannot — a true shame, because with different lyrics, it might have been a classic.

Better things can be found when the songs turn introspective. The chunky "It's So Hard" is more or less harmless, despite falling into Lennon's "suicide" lane with the repeated refrain, "Sometimes I feel like going down." Also in that lane is "How?," which manages to sound hopeful even as John again laments, "Sometimes I feel I've had enough."

Throughout the album John turns the phrase "oh no" into "Ono" in a cloying PDA, but the actual love songs he includes are among the album's best tracks. "Oh Yoko!" provides a peppy, harmonica-laced conclusion, but would be categorically rejected by the Beatles and the Assembler since it includes multiple repetitions of her name. Frankly, John's need to sing her name over and over is grating, to say the least — and the same would be true even if he had used a different name. Both "Oh Cynthia!" and "Oh May Pang!" would have worked just fine as replacement lyrics, but would have produced a song every bit as grating. Back in the day, Harrison had talked Lennon into changing "Maharishi" to "Sexy Sadie," but apparently couldn't offer the same service here. It's a shame that some alternative couldn't have been found, because the song is otherwise highly commercial.

The other "oh" song, "Oh My Love," is as tender a ballad as John would ever write. His lyrics and singing are as supple as George's guitar, and together there is a whiff of the old Beatle magic.

Oh, what if George Martin had produced *Imagine*? That thought experiment is seductive because this collection — which *should* be great, but is not — really needed a good editor. Martin might not have been able to prevent all of the missteps, but he certainly would have provided Lennon with exactly what these songs needed: discipline, polish, aspiration. And he probably wouldn't have let Lennon stop at ten tracks because there was "no more room." He would have insisted on a few more so that there were options, and a chance to pick the absolute best.

Whatever Spector's actual role in these sessions, he appears not to have had the desire or ability to act in the best interest of his artist. He did not reign in Lennon's most unfortunate instincts, and may have stoked them — along with Ono and Allen Klein, both of whom reportedly contributed snide lyrics to "How Do You Sleep?"

Our Assembler would have quickly rejected some of this material, starting with "I Don't Want to Be a Soldier." Despite its powerful subject matter and provenance, i.e. George Harrison's presence, the record is effectively just a jam, with John trying to make his lyrics work to licks that haven't quite been finalized. The band lumbers along, making chord changes *approximately* where they might have gone on a finished version, but never quite locking in the way the song deserves. Indeed, this could have been a very fine piece of work, but it is sloppy, unfinished, and almost unbearable to listen to as a result. Our Assembler may have tried to send John back for a remake, to which Lennon probably would have responded with middle finger raised. There is really no choice but to exclude it.

The title track, of course, would have become the center of Lennon's contribution to a group project, even as its presence might complicate the assembly by overshadowing pretty much everything else. It is a great example of the powers at John Lennon's command when he chose to wield them. Simple, positive music with a simple, positive lyric can, in fact, change the world. And therein lies the lesson of the *Imagine* album: The positive messages can become timeless, while the negative messages can only haunt.

John's thundering non-album single, "Power to the People," will certainly be available for consideration on the fused album. Though it sounds like a cliché to latter day ears, it would not have at the time. Catchy and driving, it highlights the best of what Lennon can do as a singer and songwriter — great hook, great chorus, great vocal — and also the best of what Spector can do as producer — a crisp, distinctive sound, just big enough to  make you think that maybe the whole world is singing along. It makes quite a contrast to the tracks on *Imagine*, started at the same time, which lack the same resoluteness of purpose and confident vibe. John's music and performance are perfectly aligned with his lyrics and intent, which is why "Power to the People" displays so clearly the power of John Lennon.

George Harrison
15 tracks: 5 eligible, 7 provisional

Sources

H02		"Bangla Desh" / "Deep Blue" R: Jul 71 P: Harrison/Spector		S: Record Plant West (LA)	71-Jul
		(Unreleased)			

Tracks

Bangla Desh (Harrison) — H02-01, +R, 71-Jul
⊘ (Quality) Unfortunately a truly lousy song, with its heart in the right place.

Cosmic Empire (Harrison) — H01, 70-May
≈ (Demo) A great, catchy, upbeat, lost song. Would definitely be considered if completed.

Deep Blue (Harrison) — H02-02, 71-Jul
✓ GH mourns his mother with grace and dignity. A hidden gem.

Dehradun (Harrison) — H01, 70-May
✓ Anthemic in feel, it would have been great to hear this fully realized.

Down to the River (Harrison) — H01, 70-Jun
⊘ (Quality) Blues just for fun — and it is fun. No doubt meant for a private reel, and best left there.

Everybody, Nobody (Harrison) — H01, 70-May
≈ (Demo) Ballad with great potential, might be used as is.

Going Down to Golders Green (Harrison) — H01, +R?, 70-May
✓ Whimsical, if derivative, 8-bar fun. Fully realized and worth considering. GH sounds good.

I Don't Want to Do It (Dylan) — H01, 70-May
≈ (Demo) A catchy lament. Another lost potential classic.

I Live for You (Harrison) — H01, 70-Jun
✓ Very simple, straightforward, fully formed, with a solid lyric. Nice song and track.

I'll Still Love You (Harrison) — H01, 70-Oct
✓ Great song, but no complete GH recording to use. We will use Ringo's version later.

Mother Divine (Harrison) — H01, 70-May
≈ (Demo) Potential anthemic qualities, but not much more than a sketch.

Nowhere to Go (Dylan/Harrison) — H01, 70-May
≈ (Demo/Content) Tortured chord progression. Embodies its title, and goes nowhere. "Beatle Jeff/Ted"

Om Hare Om (Gopala Krishna) (Harrison) — H01, 70-Jun
⊘ (Style) Not usable by the group, but good enough (with a better vocal) for a GH solo album.

Tell Me What Has Happened to You (Harrison) — H01, 70-May
≈ (Demo/Quality) A sketch with some potential, but not fully formed.

Window, Window (Harrison) — H01, 70-May
≈ (Demo/Quality) Jaunty waltz. Lyric isn't quite refined. Imagery is a little diffuse.

As mentioned above, George's work on the benefit concert precluded him from much recording during this period. A more cynical reading might say that he had used all the good stuff he had on *All Things Must Pass*, and didn't really have any new songs worth recording. That, however, would be proven almost completely wrong as demos for songs he left off of his triple album started to trickle out. Some of the songs he left in the can would go on to make memorable appearances on later albums, but even among those that did not, a few gems can be found.

Before turning to the would-be's, let's consider the actually-were's, which can be dispatched pretty quickly. George's lone release during this period, the single "Bangla Desh," is not eligible for inclusion for quality and content reasons. It just isn't Beatle material, and very few fans can probably hum any part of this song.

Its B-side, on the other hand, is the very compelling "Deep Blue," written about his mother's final illness. It's a jaunty piece of work, the light music running in direct contrast to the heavy lyrics. Unlike Lennon, however, Harrison's vocal does not try to disguise anything. His sorrow is barely, but understandably concealed. It was a true shame that this fine song, which prominently features George's burgeoning slide guitar capabilities, got thrown away on the back of a lousy single. This has album track written all over it.

One track, however, is not enough to fill the quota he had been promised on the fused albums. George will expect four tracks on the album, so we owe him the courtesy of digging through the archives to see if his quota can be filled for this period from there.

One rather famous outtake from *All Things Must Pass* was the completed track "I Live for You," which clearly would have been available and appropriate for a group project. Among the compelling demos is "Dehradun," a song which appears to never have been properly recorded, though the demo is more robust than the others.[9] It has the quality of movement, and provides a neat lyrical idea which resonates with subjects that seem to have been floating around in the Beatle air during this period:

> *See them move along the road in search of life divine...*
> *Beggars in a gold mine*

It is an uncharacteristically gentle (for the era) nudge toward spirituality, which resonates especially well with both Lennon's "Imagine" and McCartney's "Back Seat of My Car." As such, "Dehradun" easily makes the short list for consideration.

Some demos sound like they might have required significant development before they could have been considered for inclusion. Thus, the fate of songs like "Cosmic

---

[9] The song is also famously referenced in the *Anthology* documentary, with George describing it as one that he never recorded, and playing a snippet on ukulele, which Paul and Ringo join rather self-consciously.

Empire," "Mother Divine," and "Tell Me What Has Happened to You," is left in limbo. We cannot say for sure that they would not have been developed, but likewise we probably can't use them to get an idea of what a hypothetical Beatles album might have sounded like at this particular moment.

Two demos, however, have the potential to be brought into the project unaltered. In the first, "Going Down to Golders Green," George channels both his love for 8-bar blues and his disdain for the trappings of wealth. It is a charming track, reminiscent of a stripped down "For You Blue," with George channeling Elvis on his vocal, and Scotty Moore on his guitar. The other Beatles would have eaten this up.

The other demo-turned-potential-master, "Everybody, Nobody" could not be more different. Ultimately something of a desolate song, the recording features George's plaintive vocal over a single strummed acoustic guitar, and needs absolutely no additional adornment. Indeed, to Spector-ize this lovely and simple song would have been a crime. It will come through on the provisional list only because it was intended as a demo.

Assuming all of these four fit the themes developed in the album, George's quota can be met, and we can get the glimpse we seek of the Beatles in 1971.

You may feel some sentiment to include music from the concert album in this project. In the best case scenario, a Beatles reunion would have happened at the concert, and they might have played one or more new tracks which could have been used. Alas, that must remain a fantasy because nothing performed at the concert would have been appropriate for a hypothetical Beatles album. Everything there had already been released in studio versions, meaning that project would have had to remain entirely separate, which is just as well.

Keep in mind, however, that George's presence in the meta-Beatles will come not just from his own tracks, but from his presence on John and Ringo's tracks. That could amount to a very substantial contribution to the album, depending on how it all shakes out. As you may already have figured out from the title of this chapter, one major contribution is already assured: George will get the honor of having one of his lyrics become the project's title.

13 / BEGGARS IN A GOLD MINE

Ringo Starr
2 tracks: 1 eligible, 1 provisional

Sources

| S05 | "Back Off Boogaloo" / "Blindman" R: Aug-Sep 71   P: A: Harrison, B: Starr/Voorman   S: Apple | 72-Mar |

Tracks

Back Off Boogaloo (Starkey) — S05-01, +G, 71-Sep
✓ (Content) A great song. The recording is likewise fantastic, just the right level of density.

Blindman (Starkey) — S05-02, 71-Aug
≈ (Quality) A true oddity, but very Ringo. The record really captures his unique quality. A quirky gem.

Like George, Ringo has produced very little to consider during this period. Unlike George, however, it will only take one good track to fulfill his quota of songs on the album, and that will come in the form of a collaboration between the two, "Back Off Boogaloo."

Conventional wisdom has it that this song was seen as Ringo's swipe at McCartney, and part of the "feuding" era, but Ringo has always insisted otherwise. If Paul had objected to the track, it would not have been eligible, just like John's "How Do You Sleep?" But we will assume that, if convincing was necessary, it would have happened. The track is simply too catchy to leave behind, and all would have recognized that. The presence of Harrison as producer, instrumentalist, and likely co-writer seals the deal.

The single's B-side, "Blindman," is certainly interesting — another case where Ringo's most interesting records are the quirky one-offs. Strange sounds, and inscrutable lyrics aside, it is a catchy tune. Still, it turns out to be just too slight for the Beatles.

If there is anything in the can by Ringo from this era it has not surfaced. This is no surprise since he was focused on making movies at the time, but it does mean that, without "Back Off Boogaloo," there may have been no Ringo on any group album in 1971. Bullet dodged.

SAVE THE BEATLES!

Assembly
42 tracks: 26 eligible, 16 provisional

≈ 1882	M09, 70-Dec
✓ Another Day	M02-01, 70-Oct
✓ Back Seat of My Car	M03-12, 71-Jan
✓ Big Barn Bed	M09-01, 71-Mar
≈ Blackpool	M03, 71-Aug
≈ Eat at Home	M03-09, 70-Oct
✓ Get on the Right Thing	M09-03, 70-Oct
✓ Heart of the Country	M03-07, 70-Nov
✓ Hey Diddle	M03, 70-Oct
✓ I Lie Around	M10-02, 71-Mar
✓ Little Lamb Dragonfly	M09-05, 71-Mar
✓ Little Woman Love	M06-02, 70-Nov
✓ Long Haired Lady	M03-10, 70-Oct
✓ Love for You, A	M03, 70-Oct
≈ Ram On	M03-03, 71-Feb
≈ Ram On (Reprise)	M03-11, 71-Feb
≈ Rode All Night	M03, 70-Oct
✓ Some People Never Know	M04-05, 71-Aug
✓ Uncle Albert/Admiral Halsey	M03-05, 71-Jan
≈ When the Wind Is Blowing	M04, 70-Dec
≈ Crippled Inside	L06-02, +G, 71-Jul
✓ Gimme Some Truth	L06-06, +G, 71-Jul
✓ How?	L06-09, 71-Jul
✓ Imagine	L06-01, 71-Jul
✓ It's So Hard	L06-04, 71-Jul
✓ Jealous Guy	L06-03, 71-Jul
✓ Oh My Love	L06-07, +G, 71-Jul
✓ Power to the People	L05-01, 71-Feb

13 / Beggars in a Gold Mine

≈ Cosmic Empire		H01, 70-May
✓ Deep Blue		H02-02, 71-Jul
✓ Dehradun		H01, 70-May
≈ Everybody, Nobody		H01, 70-May
≈ I Don't Want to Do It		H01, 70-May
✓ Going Down to Golders Green		H01, +R?, 70-May
✓ I Live for You		H01, 70-Jun
✓ I'll Still Love You		H01, 70-Oct
≈ Mother Divine		H01, 70-May
≈ Nowhere to Go		H01, 70-May
≈ Tell Me What Has Happened to You		H01, 70-May
≈ Window, Window		H01, 70-May
≈ Blindman		S05-02, 71-Aug
✓ Back Off Boogaloo		S05-01, +G, 71-Sep

    Once again the assembly starts with a bounty of tracks, and the notion that maybe this should be another double album. But unlike the previous project, imbalances are immediately apparent.

    A double album would require eight tracks each from John, Paul and George. That works fine for Paul, obviously, but it's a little close for John, who would need all of his tracks to find appropriate spots — a potentially tall task. More problematic is that George's quota would have to dig pretty deeply into his provisional tracks, most of which are demos.

    The designation as "provisional" means that the track *could* work, but has caveats that must be carefully considered. Use too many alternates, and you might have a much less satisfying finished product. These must be used only to solve problems, be placed very carefully, and must not *sound like alternates* when the assembly is complete. That places an effective limit on how many can be used without creating a house of cards. In the case of a double album, there is a much greater chance that lesser material will be *perceived* as filler, which must be avoided.

    We also have a problem with Ringo, who has only one really good track available. His other three slots, and maybe two or three of George's allocation, would need to be filled by someone else, and only Paul has that many available. Such a choice could lead to a double album widely imbalanced toward Paul, which no one, not even the Assembler, would have allowed.

    One possibility might be to reach back for something left over from the previous era, but that doesn't look like a good option for either George or Ringo. George didn't really have much usable material left over, and likely would have released it all on a solo album. Had the Beatles been collaborating, maybe Ringo and George would have gotten together and finished a few new tracks, but we can't work with that.

The use of archival tracks — those passed over on previous projects — will always be a possibility, though one the Assembler will try to avoid. As with most pop music, recordings generally have a short shelf life, and artists like the Beatles were always focused on what they were going *right now*. The past didn't matter.

The simpler answer is to make this project the best single disc possible, and let the rest of these tracks trickle into solo projects, which their authors would probably have preferred anyway.

With that decision made, we will thin the list of tracks a bit. With everything collected into one place, it becomes clear that some of Paul's options really have no chance of making the album, and likewise some of George's demos. In context, Ringo's provisional track also looks out of place. If the Assembler gets stuck, any of these could still be called back into service, but for now, the following are removed from eligibility before we even begin:

- ≈ 1882 (P)
- ≈ Blackpool (P)
- ≈ Blindman (R)
- ≈ Cosmic Empire (G)
- ≈ Eat at Home (P)
- Hey Diddle (P)
- ≈ I Don't Want to Do It (G)
- I Lie Around (P)
- I'll Still Love You (G)
- Love for You, A (P)
- ≈ Mother Divine (G)
- ≈ Nowhere to Go (G)
- ≈ Ram On (P)
- ≈ Ram On (Reprise)
- Some People Never... (P)
- ≈ Tell Me What...to You (G)
- ≈ When the Wind... (P)
- ≈ Window, Window (G)

After reviewing this freshly trimmed list, the Assembler will start with a couple of basic assumptions which seem obvious, each of which will have serious ramifications for the finished project, mostly because they turn out to be completely wrong.

The first of those assumptions is that the most powerful tracks, which happen to both be from John, "Imagine" and "Power to the People," would open and close the album. Which one would go in which place would have to be determined, but under the basic rules, these would seem preordained for those two spots.

Each of these tracks, however, has a very long tail, and would color everything else. For example, if "Imagine" opens the album, as it did John's solo album, what could follow it? Where do you go from one of the most powerful tracks any solo Beatle would ever record? Anything which followed it would sound light.

So, obviously, that means it must go last, with *nothing* following it. Problem solved, right? Well, it turns out to have a rather weak, cold ending when heard in context at the very end. Though the final lyric is profound, John's circle of chords feels overly exposed and just sort of seems to stop. The result is that it feels wrong as the final sound on an album, which is simply a function of the context. In other words, the ending is actually fine for the *song*, but just not right for an *album*, where it saps the track of some of its strengths.

13 / Beggars in a Gold Mine

The Assembler's first realization is that "Imagine" cannot go in either outer pole position. It may turn out to work at one of the inner poles, but it may be better used in a feature spot, where its impact can be fully realized. For now, however, placing "Imagine" will have to wait.

The opening of "Power to the People" seems like it would make the perfect first sound for the album. But exactly the same problem presents itself: What could follow it? In this case, it is not the pure greatness of the track which is overwhelming, but the force of its sound and message. John's track sounds like a demand, and nothing else on the eligible list is anywhere near as focused and insistent. All would sound wan by comparison.

So, again, maybe it should go at the end. But there, it washes away anything else that the album might have contained. It essentially hijacks the proceedings, inserts itself as a new paradigm, and then is off to the races. As a final sound, it would potentially leave the listener mystified that the album's finale sounded so far removed from everything which came before.

The same exact issues would haunt the proceedings if "Power to the People" were placed in either of the inner pole track positions. It just sounds so different from anything else on the list. So the unexpected realization is that "Power to the People" is simply too self-contained to be on *any* album. It is a quintessential stand-alone single, and must be left as such. It cannot be tamed, and should not be tamed. It has enough power to stand on its own, and it must.

So the natural next turn is to Paul's strongest tracks, with the assumption that they will certainly fill those important pole positions. Unfortunately, "Uncle Albert/Admiral Halsey" starts with an apology ("We're so sorry…"), making it dicey as either an album opener or closer. Do the Beatles need to apologize for anything? "Back Seat of My Car," Paul's closer from *Ram*, does not work at all as an opener, and also leaves the listener unsatisfied as a closer, ending as it does with a quick fade while the track sounds like it still has more to give.

Turning to George, we finally find something which will work. The quirky "Dehradun" comes in under the radar, feeling somewhat slight for a pole track. But it definitely has the feel of a summation, with a contagious refrain that has the potential to grow in volume, while having just as much impact in a whisper. The lyric resonates well with the other music from this era.

> *Many roads can take you there, many different ways*
> *One direction takes you years, another takes you days…Dehradun*
>
> *Many people on the roads looking at the sights*
> *Many others with their troubles looking for their rights…Dehradun*
>
> *See them move along the road in search of life divine*
> *Beggars in a gold mine…Dehradun*

We can assume that the Assembler would have seen to it that this song got a more elaborate recording — or the demo at least some polish — and thereby would have discovered its natural anthemic quality (versus the forced nature of "Isn't It a Pity"). Indeed, one can imagine the number of voices multiplying on each successive chorus until the sound is stadium-sized, then retreating back to George's hushed solo voice for the final chorus. Though tempting to dismiss "Dehradun" as too small or too strange, this is a familiar case of George's demo being merely a pebble-sized starting point. Even in demo form, however, the song will make a memorable close to this album.

To open the album, nothing else from Lennon appears to be a candidate. McCartney offers "Get on the Right Thing" and "Big Barn Bed." Both sound at least a little like openers, with strong opening figures and long introductions, but neither has anything approaching high enough BQ to open a Beatles album. They are both ultimately throwaways. McCartney will eventually use the latter to open the slimmed down *Red Rose Speedway*, and it will mark the collection from its beginning as very slight, indeed.

"Another Day" also looks like a possibility, but placing it up front will highlight its weakest aspect — the sort of run-of-the-mill story it tells of a rather uninteresting character. Musically, it could work, but like the others, it just doesn't have enough weight to be the first sound on a Beatles album.

None of George's tracks sound like openers, but Ringo's "Back Off Boogaloo" starts with a drum figure, followed by George's guitar. That might work. Still, it would have seemed to the Assembler like more of a side two opener.

It begins to appear as if the only track with enough heft to open the album would be "Uncle Albert/Admiral Halsey." Despite the presence of an apology, it is not unprecedented for a Beatles album to start with a cold vocal. Indeed, they did it no less than three times on the classic albums.[1] More importantly, the cinematic nature of the song moves past the opening pretty quickly. And it does have the quality of being among the very best tracks on the album, meeting one of George Martin's primary criteria for an opener.

With all of this in mind, the only option to get this assembly moving is to slot a few tracks as best guesses and see what can be made of them. So the Assembler assigns pole tracks as follows and sort of hopes for the best.

---

[1] All three times it was John whose voice opened the albums. "It Won't Be Long" opened *With the Beatles*, "No Reply" opened *Beatles for Sale*, and the title track opened *Help!*

13 / Beggars in a Gold Mine

1A. Uncle Albert/Admiral Halsey (P)	Another Day (P)
. . .	Back Seat of My Car (P)
1Z. Imagine (J)	Big Barn Bed (P)
	≈ Crippled Inside (J)
	Deep Blue (G)
2A. Back Off Boogaloo (R)	≈ Everybody, Nobody (G)
. . .	Get on the Right Thing (P)
2Z. Dehradun (G)	Gimme Some Truth (J)
	Going Down...Golders Green (G)
	Heart of the Country (P)
	How? (J)
	I Live for You (G)
	It's So Hard (J)
	Jealous Guy (J)
	Little Lamb Dragonfly (P)
	Little Woman Love (P)
	Long Haired Lady (P)
	Oh My Love (J)
	~~Power to the People (J)~~
	≈ Rode All Night (P)

On *Ram*, "Uncle Albert" ends with a crossfade into "Smile Away." We won't use the latter track, but the nature of the guitar part suggests a connection to the opening of Lennon's "It's So Hard." The two songs turn out to sit well together.

"Back Off Boogaloo" seems to be temperamentally compatible with "Gimme Some Truth." Each is a refutation, but Ringo's more laid back admonishment seems to set up John's and prepare listeners for his harder edge, which actually then sounds a little less harsh, and a little more justified, after Ringo.

McCartney's "Back Seat of My Car" obviously belongs on side two, and its frenzied guitar ending yields nicely to George's simple strumming.

"Imagine," however, is still an orphan. Though closing out side one does seem like a reasonable place for it, there is nothing which sets it up sufficiently. About the best the Assembler can do is try something with contrast, allowing John's piano-heavy track to sound more meaningful. For now, that contrast will come from George's "Deep Blue," though it hardly feels like an ultimate solution.

1A. **Uncle Albert/Admiral Halsey (P)**	Another Day (P)
1B. **It's So Hard (J)**	Big Barn Bed (P)
...	≈ Crippled Inside (J)
1Y. **Deep Blue (G)**	≈ Everybody, Nobody (G)
1Z. **Imagine (J)**	Get on the Right Thing (P)
	Going Down...Golders Green (G)
	Heart of the Country (P)
2A. **Back Off Boogaloo (R)**	How? (J)
2B. **Gimme Some Truth (J)**	I Live for You (G)
...	Jealous Guy (J)
	Little Lamb Dragonfly (P)
2Y. **Back Seat of My Car (P)**	Little Woman Love (P)
2Z. **Dehradun (G)**	Long Haired Lady (P)
	Oh My Love (J)
	≈ Rode All Night (P)

Despite some progress, the best thing about this lineup is that it reveals an important thing: "Imagine" does not belong at the end of side one. Not only is it difficult to set up in that spot, but when followed by an entire side of music, it is effectively lost in the shuffle. This wasn't obvious with only pole tracks in place, but with a little bit more shape to the album it jumps right out.

Thus a large problem in this assembly is solved. For maximum impact, "Imagine" must be placed in the second-to-last spot on the album. It cannot be last because it leaves too inconclusive a sound, but it cannot really be any farther forward in the running order, or it risks a lower impact. It realizes its best potential in this feature slot.

The question remains of what can properly set it up, but here is where a stroke of good luck intervenes. The simplicity of its piano opening suggests that something relatively complex should precede it, allowing it to gain strength from contrast. But complexity alone would not be enough. There also must be some *distance*. By happenstance, "The Back Seat of My Car" is already there to provide just the right level of complexity and distance. The guitar figures of its closing section, combined with a feeling of incompleteness, leaves just the right space in which to hear the opening piano chords of "Imagine."

So the Assembler simply slides "Imagine" in between the two final tracks from the previous list and a great sequence falls into place unexpectedly. The angst of Paul's road-based masterwork ("Speed along the highway...we believe that we can't be wrong..."), indirectly sets up the idealism and hopefulness of John's masterwork ("You may say I'm a dreamer..."), which is then given a proper release by George's simple and dry-eyed summation ("See them move along the road in search of life divine..."). Fortunately, all of the musical connections work as well.

Given the weight of "Imagine" in Beatle lore, this may be the most unlikely sequence on any of the fused albums, but it works amazingly well. The album comes to fruition with driving and drama and dreaming. Three Beatles elevate each other's

13 / Beggars in a Gold Mine

work by simple proximity. Best of all, sequencing decisions can now aim toward this very satisfying conclusion.

With the side one closer (and "Deep Blue") available again, John's unanswered questions in "How?" seem like an important antecedent that should be introduced before the flip of the disc. Not that side two will answer them, exactly, but that placing them in the listener's mind will give greater depth to what is to come.

By this point, the Assembler would have noticed that Paul's "Another Day" is in the same key as "How?" and is about much the same subject. Paul's song is a third person account of the same disenchantment that John explores in the first person. Fortunately, the contrasting musical styles dovetail nicely, with the final steel flourish on Paul's track perfectly setting up John's cold open.

Even better, John's "Jealous Guy," also in the same key, makes a remarkable setup for Paul's character. In fact, without getting cloying or too spot on, John's apology for heinous acts of jealousy creates the perfect subtext for "Another Day" and elevates it significantly. Paul's character is no longer without a backstory, and her routine daily acts take on a new meaning as she decides how to respond.

1A. Uncle Albert/Admiral Halsey (P)		Big Barn Bed (P)
1B. It's So Hard (J)		≈ Crippled Inside (J)
. . .		**Deep Blue (G)**
1X. Jealous Guy (J)		≈ Everybody, Nobody (G)
1Y. Another Day (P)		Get on the Right Thing (P)
1Z. How? (J)		Going Down...Golders Green (G)
		Heart of the Country (P)
		I Live for You (G)
2A. Back Off Boogaloo (R)		Little Lamb Dragonfly (P)
2B. Gimme Some Truth (J)		Little Woman Love (P)
. . .		Long Haired Lady (P)
2X. Back Seat of My Car (P)		Oh My Love (J)
2Y. Imagine (J)		≈ Rode All Night (P)
2Z. Dehradun (G)		

Looking at this lineup now, something surprising stands out: The opening sequences are clearly in the wrong places. Each works, but now it's obvious which should set up which side. Simply swapping them fixes this nicely.

Paul's apology, which really would never have served as a proper album opener anyway, can be heard for what it is: a piece of a story, and not a message from the artist. The admonishments by Ringo and John open the album, which isn't ideal, but is good enough for now. As we will see, side one will actually get two different pole tracks before this assembly is complete.

1A. Back Off Boogaloo (R) **1B.** Gimme Some Truth (J) . . . 1X. Jealous Guy (J) 1Y. Another Day (P) 1Z. How? (J)	Big Barn Bed (P) ≈ Crippled Inside (J) Deep Blue (G) ≈ Everybody, Nobody (G) Get on the Right Thing (P) Going Down…Golders Green (G) Heart of the Country (P) I Live for You (G)
2A. Uncle Albert/Admiral Halsey (P) **2B.** It's So Hard (J) . . . 2X. Back Seat of My Car (P) 2Y. Imagine (J) 2Z. Dehradun (G)	Little Lamb Dragonfly (P) Little Woman Love (P) Long Haired Lady (P) Oh My Love (J) ≈ Rode All Night (P)

Moving on to side two, "It's So Hard" ends with John singing, "Sometimes I feel like going down." This suggests a connection to one of George's eligible demos, and "Going Down to Golders Green" feels like a tongue-in-cheek response that lightens Lennon's load, and would have pleased him.

In looking for something to bump up against the opening guitar figure in "Back Seat of My Car," we find "Oh My Love," in which George plays a not dissimilar guitar figure, in a very similar timbre. John's tender love song then, in a parallel to side one, gives subtext to Paul's characters, who are clearly leaving a scene where their love is forbidden.

This type of contextualization is rather atypical of the Beatles, of course. When they have told stories in the past, they tend to have been self-contained. See: "Eleanor Rigby" and "The Continuing Story of Bungalow Bill" as only two of many possible examples. This assembly must be careful, therefore, not to impose too much on these songs or how they interact with one another. Luckily, these connections are not overt. In neither of these sequences is it that a John song directly references a Paul song, or vice versa. Rather, these connections are identified just to aid in the assembly and maybe create subconscious contexts in which each song can be heard in elevated form, even if the listener never makes the conscious connection. If these were cases of obvious connections, the Assembler would be obliged not to make them. As it is, however, these justifications will remain out of public view, merely being mechanisms by which the songs are assembled for maximum elevation, and not examples of long-form, or multi-song, storytelling.

The last bridge to make on side two, from "Golders Green" to "Oh My Love," requires a very light touch. Though the album's ending is not exactly heavy, this is the point in the show where we need a piece of craftwork that continues the mood, but need not add anything significant. To that end, "Little Woman Love" will be slotted. It is compatible with both tracks, and closes the gap nicely.

13 / Beggars in a Gold Mine

1A. Back Off Boogaloo (R)	
1B. Gimme Some Truth (J)	
...	
1X. Jealous Guy (J)	
1Y. Another Day (P)	
1Z. How? (J)	

2A. Uncle Albert/Admiral Halsey (P)	
2B. It's So Hard (J)	
2C. Going Down to Golders Green (G)	
2M. Little Woman Love (P)	
2W. Oh My Love (J)	
2X. Back Seat of My Car (P)	
2Y. Imagine (J)	
2Z. Dehradun (G)	

Big Barn Bed (P)
≈ Crippled Inside (J)
Deep Blue (G)
≈ Everybody, Nobody (G)
Get on the Right Thing (P)
Heart of the Country (P)
I Live for You (G)
Little Lamb Dragonfly (P)
Long Haired Lady (P)
≈ Rode All Night (P)

Side one needs slightly more refinement. Neither the opener or closer is absolutely perfect. They are good, but could be better. With some good George tracks still not slotted, and his contributions a little low, the Assembler will take a track and look for a spot.

The first of these is "Deep Blue," which is too good to leave off the album. Neither an opener for the album nor a closer for side one, it will have to fit into the gap. Surprisingly, it provides a very fine bridge between John's "Gimme Some Truth" (featuring George's own blistering guitar work), and the ballad, "Jealous Guy." It turns out to be enough to close that gap all by itself.

From here, any additions will either break up sequences already created, or maybe extend a side. Though already at 14 tracks, the album is obviously not quite done yet. There remains important work.

Of all the tracks remaining, "Everybody, Nobody" stands out as very sympathetic with this collection of music. Though only listed as a provisional possibility, in the context of the album as it already stands, the song feels worthy to include as something spare, plaintive, meaningful, and rather unexpected. Even in demo form, with its mournful guitar figure, which both opens and closes the track, it sounds like it might be a better closer for the side than that flip of John's fingers (or it is Nicky's?) on the piano. And when placed immediately after that, it turns out that "Everybody, Nobody" is an indirect, but very sophisticated response to John's existential questions in "How?" George's track, with some reparative editing, thus becomes the last sound before the flip of the disc.

Obviously, however, something is still not quite right. The album's opener would be Ringo's drum rolls on "Back Off Boogaloo" — not bad, exactly, but a little underpowered for a Beatles album which would surely have been anticipated as a major event in the music world. We also have to admit another problem in that Paul has only one song on the first side, despite being represented roughly well enough on the album as a whole. Not only would fans have been disappointed, Paul would have insisted on an adjustment.

Among the Paul tracks remaining is the blistering improvisation, "Rode All Night." It is rough around the edges, not even as formalized as "I Don't Wanna Be a Soldier," but the energy in the drumming, guitar-playing, and singing is palpable and contagious. It certainly isn't worth nine minutes of the album, but it was brought forward in the first place with the idea that it might be edited down to, say, its best two minutes.

The "aha" moment for the Assembler comes with the realization that "Rode All Night" and "Back Off Boogaloo" are in the same key, and the cold ending of the former aligns perfectly with the drum figure which opens the latter. Thus it becomes a sort of prologue, bolstering Ringo's track, which becomes the de facto opener after all. Together they make for a very satisfying first sound and great, energetic sendoff to the album.

1A.	**≈ Rode All Night (P) [Edit]**	
1B.	Back Off Boogaloo (R)	
1C.	Gimme Some Truth (J)	
1M.	**Deep Blue (G)**	
1W.	Jealous Guy (J)	
1X.	Another Day (P)	
1Y.	How? (J)	
1Z.	**≈ Everybody, Nobody (G)**	
2A.	Uncle Albert/Admiral Halsey (P)	
2B.	It's So Hard (J)	
2C.	Going Down to Golders Green (G)	
2M.	Little Woman Love (P)	
2W.	Oh My Love (J)	
2X.	Back Seat of My Car (P)	
2Y.	Imagine (J)	
2Z.	Dehradun (G)	

~~≈ 1882 (P)~~
Big Barn Bed (P)
~~≈ Blackpool (P)~~
~~≈ Blindman (R)~~
~~≈ Cosmic Empire (G)~~
≈ Crippled Inside (J)
~~≈ Eat at Home (P)~~
Get on the Right Thing (P)
Heart of the Country (P)
~~Hey Diddle (P)~~
~~≈ I Don't Want to Do It (G)~~
~~I Lie Around (P)~~
I Live for You (G)
~~I'll Still Love You (G)~~
Little Lamb Dragonfly (P)
Long Haired Lady (P)
~~Love for You, A (P)~~
~~≈ Mother Divine (G)~~
~~≈ Nowhere to Go (G)~~
~~Power to the People (J)~~
~~≈ Ram On (P)~~
~~≈ Ram On (Reprise)~~
~~Some People Never... (P)~~
~~≈ Tell Me What...to You (G)~~
~~≈ When the Wind... (P)~~
~~≈ Window, Window (G)~~

13 / Beggars in a Gold Mine

With all of the spare tracks visible, it becomes clear that, though there might be other ways to assemble this, nothing essential has been left off the album, with the possible exception of "Power to the People" — removed for a very good reason. The second tier of quality would include Paul's "Heart of the Country," and George's "I Live for You," neither of which feels right with the tracks that actually *need* to go on the album. The four big productions from Paul are clearly in the third tier: "Big Barn Bed," "Get on the Right Thing," "Little Lamb Dragonfly," and "Long Haired Lady." From there, it's all downhill.

Admittedly, the finished album is slightly imbalanced, which might have raised questions. Given the large quantity of tracks available from Paul, an explanation will be needed for why he has five — and only two on side one — to John's six. Much easier to explain is why George has four, and Ringo only one.

The answer is no more complicated than this: That's just the way it worked out. Recall that the Assembler has the right to determine the final balance, with only the commitment to keep it as close to the ideals as possible. In this case, George's activities explain one part, and the music itself explains the other.

Perhaps it seems once again reasonable to revisit the question of whether this could or should have been a double, but the answer has not changed. Any selection of 14 more tracks would have brought some of the banality of the solo releases into a group project designed to disguise or eliminate it. It will always be better to leave good music off than to extend the collection with filler. That is at the heart of reducing dilution, and thus at the heart of creating fused albums in the first place.

The Assembler will happily answer all criticisms, especially because, as this album turned out, the decisions paid off nicely.

Save the Beatles!

Beggars in a Gold Mine

Principal Recording: November 1970 - September 1971
Release: November 1971

Side One
1. PROLOGUE: Rode All Night (McCartney)
2. Back Off Boogaloo (Starkey)
3. Gimme Some Truth (Lennon)
4. Deep Blue (Harrison)
5. Jealous Guy (Lennon)
6. Another Day (McCartney*)
7. How? (Lennon)
8. Everybody, Nobody (Harrison)

Side Two
1. Uncle Albert/Admiral Halsey (McCartney*)
2. It's So Hard (Lennon)
3. Going Down to Golders Green (Harrison)
4. Little Woman Love (McCartney*)
5. Oh My Love (Lennon**)
6. The Back Seat of My Car (McCartney)
7. Imagine (Lennon**)
8. Dehradun (Harrison)

* Originally "McCartney/McCartney"
** Posthumously revised to "Lennon/Ono"

13/Beggars in a Gold Mine

Make It Yourself
Total Running Time: 51:18

Tk	Rill	Title	Source	Dur
F2-A1	—	Rode All Night [Edit]	[1, bonus]	1:40
F2-A2	(10.0)	Back Off Boogaloo	[2, bonus]	3:14
F2-A3	0	Gimme Some Truth	[3]	3:10
F2-A4	0	Deep Blue	[4, bonus]	3:38
F2-A5	(2.5)	Jealous Guy	[3]	4:11
F2-A6	0	Another Day	[1]	3:39
F2-A7	(1.3)	How?	[3]	3:39
F2-A8	0	Everybody, Nobody [Edit]	[U]	2:41

Total: 25:54

Tk	Rill	Title	Source	Dur
F2-B1	—	Uncle Albert/Admiral Halsey	[1]	4:54
F2-B2	0	It's So Hard	[3]	2:24
F2-B3	1.0	Going Down to Golders Green	[U]	2:20
F2-B4	0	Little Woman Love	[5, bonus]	2:06
F2-B5	0.4	Oh My Love	[3]	2:40
F2-B6	(1.3)	Back Seat of My Car, The	[1]	4:27
F2-B7	1.5	Imagine	[3]	3:03
F2-B8	1.5	Dehradun [Edit]	[U]	3:27

Total: 25:24

[U] Unreleased (Seek on Youtube)
[1] *Ram*
[2] *Goodnight Vienna*, avoid all remakes
[3] *Imagine*
[4] *Living in the Material World*
[5] *Wild Life*

NOTE: Descriptions of edits and crossfades, with sample audio, are available at:

SaveTheBeatles.com

Release
November 1971

Most Popular Albums
December 1970 - October 1971

US		UK	
Three Dog Night	*Golden Bisquits*	Andy Williams	*Can't Help Falling...*
Carole King	***Tapestry***	Andy Williams	*Home Lovin' Man*
Carpenters	*Carpenters*	Carole King	*Tapestry*
Carpenters	*Close to You*	Emerson, Lake & Palmer	*Emerson, Lake &...*
Cat Stevens	*Tea for the Tillerman*	Frank Sinatra	*Greatest Hits Vol 2*
George Harrison	*All Things Must Pass*	George Harrison	*All Things Must Pass*
James Taylor	*Mud Slide Slim and...*	Groundhogs	*Split*
Janis Joplin	*Pearl*	James Taylor	*Mud Slide Slim and...*
Jethro Tull	*Aqualung*	**John Lennon**	***Imagine***
The Partridge Family	*Partridge Family Album*	Paul & Linda McCartney	*Ram*
Paul & Linda McCartney	*Ram*	Rod Stewart	*Every Picture Tells...*
Rod Stewart	*Every Picture Tells...*	The Rolling Stones	*Sticky Fingers*
The Rolling Stones	*Sticky Fingers*	Various Artists	*Motown Vol 5*
Sly & The Family Stone	*Greatest Hits*	Various Artists	*Motown Vol 6*
Various Artists	*Jesus Christ Superstar*	Yes	*The Yes Album*

Most popular album in bold

In this era, the next generation of singer-songwriters moved into prominence with seminal albums by Carole King, Cat Stevens and James Taylor, and a significant move toward superstardom for Elton John — whose first two albums just missed the eligibility requirements for these lists. Major solo acts like Janis Joplin and Rod Stewart (with Marvin Gaye just off the list) are balanced against bands without superstars like Chicago, Yes, Creedence Clearwater Revival, Jethro Tull and Three Dog Night. Meanwhile, a few juggernaut holdovers from the 60s continued making an impact.

Notably, three former Beatles appear here, cementing the group's popularity, even after being splintered. In our slightly altered universe, this popularity, including the immense success of John's solo album in England, would presumably have transferred to the group album. Our narrative still allows George and Paul to have slightly modified solo albums in this period, with the presumption that they would have been timed not to disrupt sales of the group project. As such, it's hard to guess how they might have done in the wake of the *Beggars in a Gold Mine*, though it is clear that the public was still clamoring for Beatles — presumably in any form.

13 / Beggars in a Gold Mine

Topping the Charts
November 1971

US			UK	
Soundtrack	*Shaft*	1	Rod Stewart	*Every Picture Tells...*
Santana	*Santana III*	2	John Lennon	*Imagine*
Rod Stewart	*Every Picture Tells...*	3	Various Artists	*Hot Hits 7*
John Lennon	*Imagine*	4	T Rex	*Electric Warrior*
Carole King	*Tapestry*	5	Various Artists	*Motown Vol 6*
Cat Stevens	*Teaser and the Firecat*	6	Simon and Garfunkel	*Bridge Over...*
Carpenters	*Carpenters*	7	Carole King	*Tapestry*
The Moody Blues	*Every Good Boy...*	8	James Taylor	*Mud Slide Slim and...*
Paul/Linda McCartney	*Ram*	9	Cat Stevens	*Teaser and the Firecat*
The Who	*Who's Next*	10	Various Artists	*...100 Best Tunes*

With another year gone by, and rumors of breakup still ebbing and flowing, it seems reasonable to expect that a group album would have been greeted with relief, and entered the charts near the top, as always. Nothing on either of these charts appears strong enough to have stood in the way of the Beatles.

Bridge Over Troubled Water continued to show remarkable longevity, but was nearing the end of its run, and many of these other albums would likely have seen similar results even if the Beatles had entered the fray at this moment. In other words, it seems unlikely that the presence of a Beatles album would have suppressed the success of anything here.

Perhaps the only albums which stood to lose would have been the hit compilations being sold in the UK. In themselves, such projects — which consistently did remarkably well — argue for the success of a fused Beatles album in the UK, suggesting that buyers might have been indifferent to the change in working methods, so long as filler was kept to a minimum.

Discussion

Despite being only a single album, *Beggars in a Gold Mine* somehow manages to demonstrate a whole new degree of scope and breadth for the Beatles. Emotions are running high, from McCartney's drum thrashing and cinematic storytelling to Lennon's vitriol and romance to Harrison's deep losses and spiritual quest. Even Starr sounds uncharacteristically fiery on the album's de facto opener. Almost everything here sounds fresh, and unlike anything the group had done before.

Noticeably, these Beatles are wearing a new level of maturity, while still lapping the field of popular music as usual. It's undeniable that nothing else on the market sounds like this album, which itself sounds nothing like the releases from which its parts were collected.

Though subtly dominated by Lennon, with six tracks to McCartney's five and Harrison's four, the voices sound well balanced, even unified. Reviewers would certainly have noticed that Paul was taking a more elaborate, even cinematic approach to his tracks, while Lennon was staying within well-worn lanes. That divergence would have been recognized for what it was: maturity. There is no reason to think that the four Beatles would have grown in the same manner, and every reason to believe that they would have asserted different personalities in their records just as they inevitably would have in their very public lives.

The unity comes from similar themes threaded throughout. Disillusionment, restlessness, and the passage of time all factor in multiple tracks, giving the album a somewhat sad feel overall, even as it still has an optimistic Beatlesque heart. John's "How?" becomes the poster track for the questions, and his anthemic "Imagine" offers his — and here, also the Beatles' — idealistic answers.

There are similar balances for George and Paul. People stuck in a perpetual roundabout in "Everybody, Nobody" are later learning, in "Dehradun," that the road is all that's real, and the gold is all around for anyone willing to see it. Paul's restless all night ride which opens the album whistles with an uncertainty that is finally addressed in a parallel, now defiant, ride in "The Back Seat of My Car."

That movement by individual Beatles is amplified by their proximity on the same vinyl. The opening four songs set up the issues very clearly, making noise about what is wrong, and missing, and possible. The next four combine for a more quiet unified statement about everyday emptiness. Side one is both individual tracks and a unified suite, which no doubt would have been recognized, and both pleased and irritated both John and Paul.

If side one could be heard as a setup, then side two is a payoff far greater than anyone might have expected from the conjoined Beatles. Two cinematic masterpieces from Paul combine with timeless anthems by John and George to offer a response, and a path, and hope.

It would no doubt have surprised many that the Beatles, now in their 10th year of recording, could still create a multilayered masterpiece which sounds unlike anything they've done before, reflects their own maturation, and even yields big time hits. In the real world, no less than four of these tracks were significant hits, and that would have kept this album on the public's radar for quite some time.

If it hadn't already been noticed, fans would by now have begun wondering whether the four Beatles would ever actually play together again. Some reviewers might have faulted the meta-Beatles approach as yielding too much divergence between the voices, and some fans would have feared that the new technique meant the imminent coming of the end.

These would become persistent themes, but the Beatles would have confounded those fears with releases like this, revealing that they still knew what they were

13 / BEGGARS IN A GOLD MINE

doing, and they were still doing it together, even if they did not assemble as each other's session men anymore.

Since this would have been the second conjoined album, a sophomore slump might have seemed inevitable, but was neatly avoided. Still, solo albums would also have started to appear around this time, but their success or lack thereof, artistically or commercially, would have been mere footnotes. If it hadn't already been firmly established with *Dream*, it certainly would have been with *Beggars in a Gold Mine*: The group projects would still be the flagship of the brand, and they would continue to be formidable, allowing solo dinghies to come and go at will, while the mothership continued to sail proudly.

Fusion Era #3

October 1971-November 1973

Be Here Now

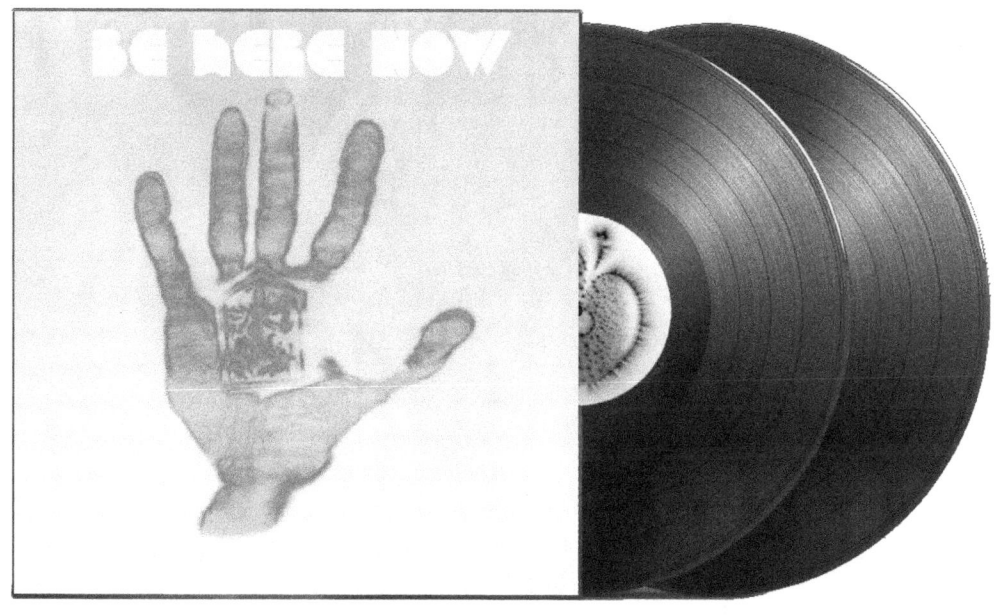

14 / Be Here Now

So yes, it's quite possible about the Beatles working as a unit, because I might play on George's or Ringo's if they wanted my style of playing."

— John Lennon, February 1972

"It doesn't seem right that it should or could end [where it did]!"

— George Harrison, April 1973

"In a way there's been some collaboration already and I think that kind of thing might happen more often. I'm happy to play with the other three and I'm sure they are too if it is physically possible..."

— Paul McCartney, April 1973

"...we're still tied to each other..."

— Ringo Starr, December 1973

Chronology

1971

Records "Happy Xmas (War Is Over)"		OCT	Announces that band will be called Wings
200 Motels (film) premieres Blindman (film) premieres		NOV	Dick Cavett Show (TV)
"Happy Xmas (War Is Over)" released (US) Performs at rally for John Sinclair Performs for Attica State benefit Kyoko Cox last seen		DEC	Wild Life released David Frost Show (TV)

1972

Concert for Bangladesh (album) released		JAN	David Frost Show (TV)
"Give Ireland Back to the Irish" released Wings University Tour (11 shows)		FEB	Co-hosting Mike Douglas Show (TV, 5 days) US visa expires
"Back Off Boogaloo" released Directing Born to Boogie (film) Wins Grammy for "Uncle Albert/Admiral Halsey"		MAR	Concert for Bangladesh (film) premieres Official fan club closes
Glyn Johns quits Red Rose Speedway		APR	"Woman is the Nigger of the World" released
Dick Cavett Show (TV)		MAY	"Mary Had a Little Lamb" released
Meets Elvis after a show		JUN	Some Time in New York City released
Wings Over Europe tour (8 shows)		JUL	
Wings Over Europe tour (17 shows) Recording with Cilla Black		AUG	One to One concerts (2 shows) Making Son of Dracula (film)
Jerry Lewis Telethon (TV)		SEP	Police raid farm, find cannabis
Making That'll Be the Day (film)		OCT	Recording Living in the Material World
Tommy released (two tracks feature Ringo)		NOV	"Hi, Hi, Hi" released
One to One (film) aired in US Imagine (film) aired in US		DEC	Born to Boogie (film) premieres David Frost Show (TV)

1973

The original Cavern Club in Liverpool closes	**FEB**	Begins work on *James Paul McCartney* (TV)
Records "I'm the Greatest" with J & G	**MAR**	Allan Klein's contract not renewed
Yoko OK to stay in US, John to be deported		Bootleg *Alpha Omega* appears
Wins Grammy for *Concert for Bangladesh*		Concert for *James Paul McCartney* (TV)
		"My Love" released
That'll Be the Day (film) premieres	**APR**	*James Paul McCartney* (TV) airs
Moves to the Dakota		*"Red"* and *"Blue"* retrospectives released
Announces creation of Nutopia		
Red Rose Speedway released	**MAY**	"Give Me Love (Give Me Peace on Earth)" released
Wings 1973 UK Tour (17 shows)		
"Live and Let Die" released	**JUN**	*Living in the Material World* released
Wings 1973 UK Tour (4 shows)	**JUL**	Pays £1M in taxes on Bangladesh concert
Premiere of *Live and Let Die* (film)		
McCullough and Siewell quit Wings	**AUG**	Star Club in Hamburg tapes surface
Travels to Lagos for recording sessions		
Returns from Lagos	**SEP**	Buys Tittenhurst Park mansion from John
"Photograph" released	**OCT**	"Helen Wheels" released
Splits from Yoko, "Lost Weekend" begins		Recording with Ronnie Wood
Recording *Rock 'n' Roll*		
Ringo released	**NOV**	*Mind Games* released

Introduction

Even in our imagined and slightly altered reality, 1973 would have been the tenth anniversary of the Beatles breaking in America. This means that, even if the group was collaborating on some level, the bootleggers would still have brought out the unauthorized compilations for the anniversary if the group didn't. There would have been no choice but to match them.

As we know, that's exactly what happened, and it meant that, like it or not, the solo Beatles spent this era making music in the long shadows of their former selves even more directly than usual. Though the proposition of this ghostly competition was probably quite daunting, the end result was almost entirely positive on many levels. The two official double album retrospectives ("red" and "blue") sold like the old days, banishing the bootleggers, and all of the solo projects of the era got positive bumps as a result.

Since there was clearly not enough new music for a group album in 1972, we will assume that the retrospectives, or something very similar, would have been part of the altered landscape late in the year to fill that gap. Since we can safely assume they would have sold just as well then, perhaps even better, and filled everyone's coffers nicely, it's fair to wonder what motivation the Beatles might have had to come together again for another group project. The answer is surprisingly simple: They all *hated* nostalgia.

None of the Beatles ever wanted to coast on — or even be reminded of — what had gone before. They discarded it, discounted it, dismissed it, almost as if they wished it had never happened. John Lennon, particularly, expressed disdain for all the work of the past. It all sounded "old" to him, and even "dishonest." Only what he was doing *right now* held any value to him.[1] The others were all quoted with variations on, "We aren't dead yet!" If nothing else, they all wanted to move on. In an irony that would not have been lost on a real life Sergeant Pepper, they were unwilling to be harnessed as objects of gauzy nostalgia.

But the overwhelming success of the greatest hits albums might have brought them together for that specific reason: to create a sufficiently forceful response. They needed to say to the world, "Forget all that. We have. Look what we're saying and doing today." Competing with themselves, they would have wanted to outsell those compilations just to prove they could.

Harrison, who got the closest to the retrospectives, also penned the most pure response in his elegant and moving song, "Be Here Now." Regrettably, it got buried in the middle of an unfortunately disposable solo album. Extracting this particular

---

[1] This is an incredibly important point to remember when interpreting anything Lennon said in interviews about his past work. He often hated it just because it wasn't *now*.

song and reassigning it to the group gives it the power to sum up plainly and gracefully how all four Beatles felt:

> *Remember, Now, Be Here Now*
> *As it's not like it was before.*
> *The past, was, Be Here Now*
> *And it's not what it was before—it was*

What fans may not realize is that all four former Beatles recorded such responses, but they were scattered and diluted over multiple solo projects. And those responses were not harsh, or simplistic, or angry, or even particularly dismissive. Indeed, they were tinged with wisdom.

That said, they did a whole lot of grousing in interviews around this time, even as the music they made showed them maturing, and regarding their history with slightly more nuance. Heard separately, there are only hints of this reckoning on the solo releases. You can hear nods toward the fun of the past in a lyric here, a track there, a vocal inflection, a guitar lick, a distinctive pair of hands on a keyboard or fingerboard, the return of an old collaborator, or one distinctive voice hovering behind another.

Rather than trying too hard to separate themselves from the past, as they had largely been doing since *Abbey Road*, their collective musical reaction, if assembled, allows that those years shaped them (and us), and that there was value — *selective* value — to be found there. They never *said* this in so many words, but their music always said more than their spoken words, and definitely does so here.

Had they chosen to continue the meta-Beatles approach — and, based on their presumed success with it, we have no reason to think they would not have — this reckoning with, and newfound calmness about, the past would have been distilled, and the whole world would have heard something remarkable. Part of our assumption in this exercise is that, at every turn, the four principle artists would have found ways to satisfy two distinct desires: balancing the need to advance solo careers with the nagging sense that the Beatles still had something to give as a unit.

Creating a collective vinyl response to the reanimation of the old days could have fulfilled the latter goal in elegant fashion, being unsentimental, touched with humor, and only passingly self-referential — avoiding a trap that snared John Lennon on multiple occasions, and would do the same to all three surviving Beatles at various points. The earlier triumphs, while once again appreciated, could have been firmly pressed back into the archives, and gently superseded by a collection of highly sophisticated, modern recordings that acknowledge where the Beatles have been, while also demonstrating an ongoing, evolving relevance.

But another primary motivator for coming together would likely have been a return to the safety of the unit after decidedly perilous adventures out in SoloLand. The desire for those familiar comforts would have been balanced against a few lingering wounds from the previous fused release.

George would have been ready to reclaim a full return to parity with John and Paul, while John might still be smarting from having some of his tracks orphaned on past projects. Ringo was clearly seeking a return to his Beatle roots in 1973, and would likely have participated gladly, perhaps even instigating this project. Paul, who had continued ploddingly making new records in the hope of finding his old swagger, would likely have relished the opportunity to use the group as an avenue to release some of his growing backlog. Unfortunately, until a major breakthrough in the fall of 1973, even the best of Paul's new tracks were still among the slightest he would ever produce, mandating careful selection and placement by our Assembler.

The finished product would have been their third, and final — and arguably *greatest* — double album, another massive masterpiece that likely would have outsold even the retrospective packages. George Harrison provides not only the title track, but sensibilities which set the overall tone, framing the work of the others, in order to highlight where the Beatles had been, and where they were at that moment.

In 1973, the Beatles would have needed to break the spell — again — and the best way to do that was by making even *greater* music. Not an easy task, of course. As always, when scattered across lonely solo albums, the greatness can be hard to hear. But if compiled together, the great music of 1973 would sound like no other Beatles record before or after, offering greatness in an entirely new way.

Recording
September 1972 - November 1973

⊕ Studio recording ◯ Single release ✈ Touring

In the months before this era began, John's "Happy Xmas (War is Over)" had been released in the US and garnered goodwill from many corners.[2] But John would quickly find that goodwill short-lived as his next project would be the recipient of some of the harshest reviews in Beatle history.

Some Time in New York City, recorded in early 1972, featured bluntly political songs, written and performed by Lennon and Ono as a duo backed by a local band. Reviewers savaged the project, much as they had Paul's *Wild Life*, for self-indulgence, banality, and an overabundance of clichés. As a double album with a high retail price, it also sold very poorly, jeopardizing a royalty increase contractually due to the Beatles. Lennon was stung by the harsh reaction, and did not record again for over a year.

Despite the critical thrashing of *Wild Life*, McCartney pressed forward with Wings, releasing two singles and hitting the road in the summer of 1972. The first of those singles, "Give Ireland Back to the Irish," sold tepidly despite being banned by

---

[2] A royalty dispute delayed its UK release by about a year.

the BBC. The other, "Mary Had a Little Lamb" was seen as a response to the earlier ban, though Paul insisted that he was merely writing for children. A third single, "Hi, Hi, Hi," — curiously coupled as a double-A with the likable throwaway "C Moon" — would become Wings' first real hit in December of 1972, this time benefitting nicely from BBC censorship.

By that time, sessions were underway for the second Wings album, *Red Rose Speedway*, which Paul initially intended as a double. That ambition may very well have been in response to the fact that both George and John had already released multi-disc sets, and even Yoko Ono was about to get into the act with *Approximately Infinite Universe*. Somewhat astonishingly, McCartney would be the one turned away by the record company, which felt there was not enough good material to justify the increased cost — a criticism which, with the benefit of hindsight, might have applied to all of these multi-disc releases. Both versions of *Red Rose Speedway* were built largely out of scattered ideas and spare parts from previous projects, with the rejected longer version including both concert recordings and features for other members of Wings.

George Harrison spent the first half of 1972 tending to remaining fallout from the Bangladesh concerts. In addition to wending his way through a morass of financial entanglements, he prepared the movie version of the concert, which was finally released in July of 1973. Shortly thereafter, he returned to the studio to begin another solo album. The result, *Living in the Material World*, would be a successful follow-up to his solo debut, if not quite as widely heralded.

In late 1972, work began in earnest on the "red" and "blue" Beatles retrospectives, initially conceived to accompany Neil Aspinall's documentary film about the band.[3] The timing of the album was accelerated to answer the illicit release of *The Beatles Alpha Omega*, a bootleg 4-disc set which appeared in early 1973. Only Harrison participated at all in the creation of the group's official retrospective, and only to a very limited extent. Most of the track selection was done by Allen Klein, with predictably haphazard results.[4]

Record buyers did not seem to care. Though the bootlegs caught people's attention, the official versions sold in quantities comparable to the original classic albums, and Beatles were everywhere in the summer of 1973. The group's rising tide even lifted all the solo boats. *The Beatles (1967-1970)* (aka "blue") hit number one on the Billboard album chart on May 26, 1973, with its twin, *The Beatles (1962-1966)* (aka "red") sitting at number three. For the next three weeks, *Red Rose Speedway* occupied the top spot. And immediately following that, *Living in the Material World*

---

[3] After many false starts, the film eventually formed the basis for the *Anthology* series.
[4] Release of these albums was somewhat mysteriously held up until Klein's contract with the Beatles expired, thus denying him royalty participation.

held down number one for five consecutive weeks. Both *Mind Games* and *Ringo* would also benefit significantly later in the year.

Right in the middle of it all, McCartney returned to the charts with the theme song for a James Bond movie, "Live and Let Die." In addition to selling well, and being widely hailed as his best solo single yet, the record featured the distinctive fingerprint of George Martin, who was engaged as producer and orchestrator. As a result, the track featured an entirely different sound, more reminiscent of the Beatles, and far removed from anything else McCartney released in this era.

Ringo Starr, after becoming a very visible performer in 1972, had finally returned to recording late in the year, and famously corralled all three of his former bandmates to assist. He even managed to get two of them into the same studio with him in March of 1973. Release of *Ringo* was perfectly timed to the moment when the compilations had reached saturation and the public was once again searching for something new by whatever combination of the Fabs they could get. The album went all the way to number two on the Billboard charts, and Ringo's collaboration with George, "Photograph," topped the singles chart, becoming an instant classic.

John Lennon did not record again until late summer 1973, eventually producing an album about as far removed from its predecessor as possible. Critics accepted *Mind Games* as a welcome return from Lennon's political forays, and compared it favorably to *Imagine*. The damage done by *Some Time in New York* was at least dispelled, if not entirely mitigated, and *Mind Games* was considered a success, despite stalling on the charts at — wait for it — number nine.

Lennon immediately turned his attention to resolving the copyright infringement lawsuit over "Come Together" by recording an album of rock and roll classics. Again, and for the final time, Spector was producing, but the sessions were beset by problems, occurring as they did at the start of John's "lost weekend." Not only was Spector more mercurial than ever, he eventually made off with the tapes of the sessions, and disappeared into convalescence after nearly being killed in a car accident. The project didn't get very far before being shelved indefinitely.

As this era came to a close, Paul was brimming with newly-restored swagger only to see Wings all but disintegrate. On the eve of sessions for their next project, two members quit, leaving the McCartneys and Denny Laine to fill in all the gaps themselves. The resulting album, *Band on the Run*, partially recorded in Lagos, Nigeria, would be regarded as a solo masterwork, with a long and lucrative run on the charts, and canonization as arguably the best ever solo Beatle album.

14 / Be Here Now

Materials

Overview
86 tracks: 33 eligible, 20 provisional

All in all, this is arguably the most successful period, artistically and commercially, ever experienced collectively by the solo Beatles. Indeed, both Paul and Ringo recorded their best and most successful albums during this window, while George and John each turned in solid, if not definitive, work. Each former Beatle sounds confident on his album, and each produces robust and accessible music. At no other time would they all be in such positive territory simultaneously.

Being finally free of Allen Klein certainly helped, as did the warm reception received by the retrospectives, and the settling of some legal disputes. Almost all of their recordings at this moment sound like an exhale of relief, a lightening of the load, a shaking off of recent tensions. Conciliatory words were finally flowing between the Beatles.

The emotional height of the era probably came when Ringo, John and George met to record "I'm the Greatest." A complex masterwork, the song serves as a centerpiece of the era and bittersweet reminder of what Lennon can do. It comprises a catchy, nuanced and multi-layered, three-and-a-half-minute summation of, and reflection on, who the Beatles were — to themselves. The record also reanimated the old Beatle Magic to a surprising degree. If only Paul had been in town...

Similar reflective and summative themes float throughout the solo songs at this time, including McCartney's misty and mercurial lyrics to "Band on the Run," Harrison's fragile "Who Can See It," and Lennon's pensive "You Are Here" — which feels like a gentle answer to what will become the title track of this fused album. Ringo and George even team-up to canonize this moment of cloud-clearing on "Sunshine Life for Me (Sail Away Raymond)."

Tellingly, however, the mere presence of all four Beatles on the same piece of vinyl generated an electricity something like the old days, giving support to the central theme we are working with here: The Beatles were always stronger together, even if not in the same way they had been strong together in earlier years. In the music and the atmosphere, that is the underlying theme of this era, which will be driven home by distilling their solo works into a unified statement.

Save the Beatles!

John Lennon
26 tracks: 8 eligible, 4 provisional

Sources

L07		"Happy Xmas (War Is Over)" / ~~"Listen, the Snow is Falling"~~ R: Oct 71 P: Lennon/Ono/Spector S: Record Plant (NY)			71-Dec
L08		*Some Time in New York City* R: Feb-Mar 72 P: Lennon/Ono/Spector S: Record Plant (NY)			72-Jun
L09		*Mind Games* R: Jul-Aug 73 P: Lennon S: Record Plant (NY)			73-Oct
		(Unreleased)			

Tracks

Aisumasen (I'm Sorry) (Lennon)   L09-03, 73-Aug
 ⊘ (Quality) Impossibly boring.

Angela (Lennon/Ono)   L08-09, 72-Mar
 ⊘ (Quality) Another duet that really shows how poorly these voices go together.

Attica State (Lennon/Ono)   L08-03, 72-Mar
 ⊘ (Quality) Heartfelt garbage. Song and track are terrible.

Aü (live) (Lennon/Ono)   L08-14, 71-Jun
 ⊘ (Filler) Raise your hand if you listened to this all the way through at least once... Liar!

Bring on the Lucie (Freda Peeple) (Lennon)   L09-05, 73-Aug
 ≈ (Content) Simple, almost simplistic. Passing lyric issues, but overall positive vibe.

Cold Turkey (live) (Lennon)   L08-10, +G, 69-Dec
 ⊘ (Filler) Lousy recording of a lousy, sluggish, overlong performance. Mushy jam.

Happy Xmas (War Is Over) (Lennon/Ono)   L07-01, 71-Oct
 ⊘ (Content) Timeless — in a good way. The only duet with Yoko that actually works.

I Know (I Know) (Lennon)   L09-10, 73-Aug
 ✓ Rather plain song. The recording is clean, if conventional.

Intuition (Lennon)   L09-07, 73-Aug
 ✓ Uncharacteristically jaunty. Pure pop, but covering well-worn territory. Fine for what it is.

Jamrag (live) (Lennon/Ono)   L08-12, 71-Jun
 ⊘ (Filler) Out of tune. Wandering. Boring. Noisy. Yoko. Seriously: I want these five minutes back.

John Sinclair (Lennon)   L08-08, 72-Mar
 ⊘ (Quality) From the back porch somewhere. Poor lyrics, instantly dated. "Got ta, got ta, got ta, got ta..."

Luck of the Irish, The (Lennon/Ono)   L08-07, 72-Mar
 ⊘ (Quality) Sounds like a jot that filled a hole. Lyrics are trite and unpleasant.

Meat City (Lennon)   L09-12, 73-Aug
 ✓ An overlooked classic. Slick and cool, in the best way. Seek the remix, which clears things up.

Mind Games (Lennon)   L09-01, 73-Aug
 ✓ Repetitive, circular, somewhat thin, but somehow a classic. A place you want to spend time.

14 / BE HERE NOW

New York City (Lennon)		L08-05, 72-Mar
⊘ (Quality) As homages to a favorite city go, this sucks. Banal in the worst possible way.		
Nutopian International Anthem (Lennon)		L09-06, 73-Aug
≈ (Content) Silly, but maybe he could have talked the others into it.		
One Day (At a Time) (Lennon)		L09-04, 73-Aug
✓ Original, but so wifty that it all but floats away. Musical cotton candy — sticky.		
Only People (Lennon)		L09-09, 73-Aug
✓ Would-be anthem has virtually no heft. Routinized passion.		
Out the Blue (Lennon)		L09-08, 73-Aug
✓ Not bad, exactly, but rewriting himself. Harrison-esque chord wandering.		
Rock 'N' Roll People (Lennon)		L09, 73-Aug
≈ (Quality) Not inherently a bad song, but JL has troubles with the melody. Can't commit. A rare problem.		
Scumbag (live) (Lennon/Ono/Zappa)		L08-13, 71-Jun
⊘ (Filler) I think you had to be in the band to appreciate this one.		
Sunday Bloody Sunday (Lennon/Ono)		L08-06, 72-Mar
⊘ (Quality) Strident, and well-intentioned, but over the top. Two notches too big.		
Tight A$ (Lennon)		L09-02, 73-Aug
≈ (Quality) Spicy enough, if a bit repetitive.		
Well (Baby Please Don't Go) (live) (Ward)		L08-11, 71-Jun
⊘ (Filler) Sounds mean-spirited, angry. Very chunky beat, slow. Band takes time to figure it out...		
Woman Is the Nigger of the World (Lennon/Ono)		L08-01, 72-Mar
⊘ (Content) Powerful, but built on a squishy metaphor. The idea does not outweigh the offensive term.		
You Are Here (Lennon)		L09-11, 73-Aug
✓ Gentle, sweet, and new musical territory for John. Simplicity is an asset here. Nice steelwork.		

John Lennon began working on his follow-up to *Imagine* almost immediately after its release, deciding to throw himself, and his art, in with politics. For the first time — setting aside the experimental projects — he also decided that the new album would be a full collaboration with Yoko. At the suggestion of a friend, he enlisted Elephant's Memory to play on the sessions, and he recalled Phil Spector to produce.

All of these were bad decisions. Very, very bad. *All* of them. Every single one.

The resulting album, *Some Time in New York City*, had virtually no fans when it was released, and it sold very poorly. To this day it retains every bit of the bitter taste it had in 1972. Perhaps it is unnecessary to rehash the deficiencies of this album, especially because of where it falls in our "fusion era" narrative: No part of it would have been offered or accepted for consideration on a Beatles release. Even in our slightly altered world, this would have been a solo (well, duo) release, and it would have failed just as completely.

Our Assembler would have, as always, listened with an ear for whether any of the material was redeemable — perhaps just a tweak, edit, remix or remake away from consideration on the next Beatles project. He would have looked for material which was salvageable by putting it in a different context, but found nothing. The songs are all clichés — musically and lyrically. In addition, the lyrics are strident, unimaginative, and would have been utterly forgettable even as a press release.

Some latter day reviewers suggest that the song "New York City" has some value to Lennon's catalog as a passionate love letter to his adopted home, but a listener may find it difficult to get past the opening lyric: "Standing on a corn-o, just me and Yoko Orn-o..." It only gets worse from there — like an evil twin to "The Ballad of John and Yoko." The name checks are positively unbearable. Lennon's vocal is terrible. The band is supremely undistinguished.

In a snippet of studio chatter, Yoko says, "Male chauvinist pig engineer," to which John replies, "Right on, sister." The exchange, no doubt included for levity, is shorthand for almost everything wrong with the album. This project was of a moment, but it was a clichéd and shallow reaction to that moment, tossed off as if a mere mention of a problem could represent a move toward some sort of resolution. John famously flitted from cause to cause, and this album sounds more like a testament to his fleeting attention span than to the causes which captured it.

The material was not carefully considered, or carefully crafted, and Lennon's strong opinions were certainly not wrought into anything approaching art. It touched on universal issues, things very much worthy of consideration and discussion, but it did so in the worst possible way: through specific instances whose details were poorly, and not widely understood, and were quickly forgotten. This guaranteed a short shelf life for themes which really deserve something better. The good intentions of the artists notwithstanding, the whole thing barely rises above banal sloganising, and amounts to making "bad things are bad"-style references to the political problems of the day.

Moreover, everything was tied directly to that specific moment, one which had passed by the time the record was released — perhaps even by the time the amps were cool after the recording sessions. Where John had once trafficked in timeless ideas, or at least ideas not tied to any particular time, this album makes the mistake of tying itself to issues that wouldn't remain relevant even for the relatively long attention spans of the era.

What makes it especially hard to bear is that John had previously shown himself capable of rending political discomfort into genuine art. "Revolution" and its variants address similarly contemporary issues, but do so with an eye toward the universal concepts which underlie them. One can imagine a version of this album that still would resonate years later, but only if the strangling references to "Angela" and "John Sinclair" had been set aside for the universal aspects of their respective plights. We know John could do this, which makes the work on *Some Time in New York City* seem ill-considered, shoddy and lazy.

On this album John's songwriting has finally sunk to Yoko's level — rather than him bringing her up to his abilities. He is said to have felt envy for her prolific songwriting in those days, but that envy would have been severely misplaced. Her songs are terrible — the best of them being worse than even John's worst by almost any metric. As always, Yoko's songwriting is the work of a well-meaning amateur.[5] But John's melodies here are also banal and clichéd, just like his chord progressions and lyrics.

This issue is regrettably present on the teaser single, "Woman is the Nigger of the World," the one track that non-fans might remember from this project. Considering this track, almost outsized enough to overshadow everything else on the album, is a delicate problem. Though generally held to be some sort of breakthrough, it is less a seminal statement on the plight of women than the more mercenary act of harnessing another "issue" for a commercial enterprise. The record is more "notorious" than "classic." It had almost no lasting impact — commercial or social — including on John's own reported personal behavior. His "lost weekend," complete with an arranged paramour, was still to come.

To the song itself, John's use of the N-word in the title, which he intended to be shocking, confuses rather than clarifies his point, and there were reverberations as a result from the African American community. It is, at best, a clumsy, fuzzy metaphor. He had to repeatedly explain that he was using the word as a stand-in for any oppressed subgroup of people, but the very need to explain it confirms that it was an ill-considered choice. Even when fully understood, the image tends to induce cringing.

Perhaps more disappointing is the fact that the title was the most provocative part of the song. The rest of the lyrics, a sadly accurate litany of the ways in which women are routinely marginalized, feels more like a list song built from John's own long-standing misogyny. It leads only to the weak calls to action of "do something" and "scream about it." John appears to have been self-aware enough to recognize his personal need for atonement, and most likely saw the song in this context. But the mere existence of this song is woefully insufficient penance.

The single makes reasonable use of Spector's "wall of sound," a technique which serves primarily to bury details — a blessing in this particular case. But he still accepted a truly terrible sax solo, which basically spins around for a few bars and then peters out when the instrumentalist runs out of ideas. Again Spector misses the opportunity to shape the recording by accentuating drama where the song needs it.

---

[5] Her songs often remind me of the very young George Harrison — in addition to many, many amateur singer/songwriters I have recorded. Every songwriter has their embarrassing early songs. Some songwriters never get past that phase. But most do it in relative privacy. Both Harrison and Ono made their youthful songwriting mistakes in a very bright spotlight. Sadly, only one evolved into a fine songwriter.

While the overall sound is competent, the sameness of the track from start to finish misses an opportunity to make the recording something special. It is another case of a collaborator failing to elevate John's material. The track is just plain boring at times. It's not fair, however, to blame Spector for the problems in songwriting. He just missed the chance to take a little of the edge off.

The song is significant enough to require consideration for a group release, but when assembling *Be Here Now*, the Beatles and our Assembler would have rejected it as too far over the edge. Perhaps it's more likely that John would not have even offered it, expecting such a rejection, and retaining it as more of a Lennono song anyway. Interestingly, it is a large enough piece of work to categorize with "Cold Turkey" and "Power to the People" as songs just too big for *any* album. All three of these are quintessential *singles*, something of a lost art form in the era.[6] John is alone among the former Beatles to create anything like that, and it is a testament to the sheer power of his will, charisma and his natural abilities at the *craft* of songwriting.[7] That this song does not succeed artistically may be beside the point.

Similar issues in content and production plague the entire album. The backing band is competent but boring. Spector's production is often just good enough, teetering right on the edge of incompetence. All of the mixes are muddy and cluttered — the "wall of sound" more often sounding like a pile of rubble. The final mixes are thick in a way that renders the instruments as a clump — which worked well for AM radio in the 60s, but not here.

Individual songs have individual problems, but they are all of a piece. On "Sunday Bloody Sunday" John's vocal, though passionate, sounds like he knows just how bad this material really is. "John Sinclair" features the annoying repetition of the words "got ta," as if more repetitions will emphasise the sentiment. The annoying slide guitar (likely played by John) makes very clear just how good George Harrison is with the instrument. "Luck of the Irish" is an incredibly terrible song — hackneyed, mean-spirited lyrics set to a nursery-class tune, simplistic in the extreme. No matter how bad the political situation, or heartfelt the sentiments, this song is a stain on Lennon's catalog.[8] Even "Angela," perhaps the most palatable music on the album, is still full of easy, cheap shots, and banal rhymes.

The Assembler, who we presume would have had exceptional diplomatic skills in dealing with delicate egos, would probably have politely handed these tapes back to John without comment, and John would have had them released anyway.

---

[6] The form would be revived only after physical discs were retired as the primary distribution method of popular music. We can only wish that John had survived into the era of MP3s and streaming, when he might have once again thrived as a singles artist.

[7] Paul released plenty of non-album singles, but none of those tracks (with the possible exception of "Mull of Kintyre") were left off albums because they were too big. In the solo era, John's big songs were always bigger than Paul's big songs.

[8] McCartney's corresponding "protest" song is likewise a stain on his catalog.

Unfortunately, chances are good that the public would have reacted just as they actually did, ignoring this collection and quickly moving on.

In direct contrast to all this dreck was "Happy Xmas (War is Over)," an anthem for the ages, even despite — or perhaps because of — its overt simplicity and somewhat treacly façade. Spector acquits himself nicely on the production by going just far enough, and John and Yoko have created music worthy of its lyrics, and vice versa. For our purposes here, however, it is of no consequence. It would have been released as a Johnandyoko single even in the alternate world. Perhaps more significantly, and most in contrast to the album being worked on simultaneously, it demonstrates the value of using timeless ideas if one must trade in greeting card level sentimentality. Of John's solo catalog, this is likely the most played single track, showing up like clockwork on mainstream radio each December.

Almost 18 months passed between the last session for *Some Time in New York City* and the first for its follow-up. Thankfully, *Mind Games* is about as far removed from its predecessor as possible. The bar band has been jettisoned, as have the politics, Spector, and Yoko. Things could only get better, right?

In many ways they do. The songs are at least more original and easier to enjoy. There are a couple of classics, and the overall tone is decidedly less time-locked. The title track returns Lennon to his playful use of language and an optimistic tone, while the album closer, "Meat City," shows Lennon as a rocker in a very modern sense. This type of chunk-rock actually contains the genuine vitality that would be lacking in *Rock 'n' Roll*, recorded almost concurrently.

Lennon gives fans some pure pop in "Intuition" and "You Are Here," both of which are pleasant confections. The latter neatly avoids going down a more esoteric path. Even his politics are now served in more palatable pop form. "Only People" is catchy and peppy, and serves a simple, timeless (if somewhat simplistic) message. "Bring on the Lucie (Freda People)" manages to be almost a send-up of his own former stridency, while still having a little nip of admonishment.

His love songs suddenly sound more universal and less specific. "One Day (at a Time)" serves love inside pop, while "Out the Blue" serves it with a UFO — just the sort of happy quirk we've longed for from Lennon ever since "Come Together." We even get a little sex in "Tight A$," a track which always sounds like a rewrite of something, but rolls quite pleasantly.

There are problems, however. The production remains a murky mess. Like Spector, Lennon famously always thought in mono, and wasn't particularly engaged in this era by the minutia of the recording and mixing process, as we have already seen. His ear for the finished product was never as carefully tuned as McCartney's, and it shows — especially on this album and its two immediate successors. When this album was fully remixed for reissue in 2002, a whole new world of detail was revealed in every single track, allowing lyrics to be much better understood, and instruments to truly sing as an ensemble.

Some fans objected to the remixing as some sort of desecration of John's work. As a result, the next re-release of *Mind Games*, in 2010, was simply a remastering of the original mixes, as if the remix had never happened. This is a true shame, since the remixed album was better in almost every way possible, and allowed the songs and recordings to truly shine — without sounding too drastically different from the original.[9] The effect was akin to the removal of a layer of varnish from a treasured painting. Remixing is one of the services the Assembler would have provided (or required), and here is a case in point. The original mixes did a disservice to John's music, and the Assembler would have detected and disallowed that.

Also somewhat problematic is Lennon's wholesale return to writing in his typical "lanes." His regrettable penchant for apologia has two examples here in the completely unlistenable "Aisumasen (I'm Sorry)" and the less weepy but still overwrought "I Know (I Know)." The former is often mentioned among Lennon's worst ever solo tracks, and for good reason. It is an unbearably ponderous 4:45, built from seemingly random chord changes with no hook or release to speak of. As such, it is barely a song at all. Another troubling lane is represented by "Intuition," which, though offering a happy façade, contains the by now requisite mention of suicide.

Other lanes are less fraught, and we happily welcome back the "peace" lane in "Only People," and less stridency in his "politics" lane, as mentioned. You could probably also count the "Nutopian International Anthem" in one of these two lanes, if you like, though it could also be classified as "mischievous, well-meaning, Fluxus-descended nonsense." As mentioned, the "love" lane is sufficiently well represented on *Mind Games*.

Perhaps most reassuring is a track like "Meat City," which closes the album with a blast of something that seems to come truly "out the blue." There is hardly anything else like it in his entire catalog, and the album goes out on an unexpectedly joy-filled mystery ride. Such bursts of genuine creativity are a clear sign that he still has something left in the tank, but they have become rare. Indeed, the album as a whole leaves the listener with the sense that something is impeding him. Conventional wisdom says that Yoko was that something, at least to a degree, but depression, disillusionment, fame, fatigue, drugs, lawsuits, taxes, and immigration must also be considered.

Indeed, the major problem with the album is how familiar the territory is that we are asked to walk with him. Despite some catchy new music, and a much less

---

[9] No one was wrong, however, to hate the revisionist videos.

strident approach, there is a familiarity which hangs over the project and mutes its overall effect. Most of what Lennon offers on *Mind Games*, which might also be called *Son of Imagine*, mines the same emotional territory he has since *The White Album* — or even earlier — when what the listener generally hopes for from Lennon is something new to think about.

In this case, he started the project still smarting from the reaction to *Some Time in New York City*, and sought retreat to a safe harbor. If you count the mixed reaction to *Plastic Ono Band*, two offerings of "something new" had now been rejected, making his retreat into familiar territory on this album completely understandable. But John would never escape this trap in his solo work.

Thankfully, there is plenty of great-enough material to work with here for the group project. The challenge with contextualizing this batch of tracks is to take work that is good but not ground-breaking, and expose its inherent creativity. The other Beatles and the Assembler should be able to do this nicely.

Paul McCartney
37 tracks: 13 eligible (3 withheld), 8 provisional (4 withheld)
Bracketed tracks are considered in a different era

Sources

M05		"Give Ireland Back to the Irish" / "Give Ireland... (Version)" R: Feb 72 P: McCartney/McCartney S: EMI	72-Feb
M06		"Mary Had a Little Lamb" / ["Little Woman Love"] R: Nov 71 - Mar 72 P: McCartney/McCartney S: Columbia (NY)	72-May
M07		"C Moon" & "Hi, Hi, Hi" R: Nov 72 P: McCartney S: Various	72-Dec
M08		"~~My Love~~" / "The Mess (live)" R: Mar 72 - Aug 73 P: McCartney S: A: EMI, B: The Hague	73-Mar
M09		*Red Rose Speedway* (9 tracks) R: Mar-Dec 72 P: McCartney S: Various (6)	73-Apr
M10		"Live and Let Die" / ["I Lie Around"] R: Oct 72 P: A: Martin; B: McCartney S: A: AIR; B: Various	73-Jun
M11		"Helen Wheels" / "Country Dreamer" R: Aug-Sep 73 P: McCartney S: EMI (Lagos), ARC (Lagos)	73-Oct
M12		*Band on the Run* R: Aug-Oct 73 P: McCartney S: EMI (Lagos), ARC (Lagos) +2	73-Dec
M13		"~~Band on the Run~~" / "Zoo Gang" R: Apr 73 P: McCartney S: EMI	74-Jun
		(Pseudonymous release)	
		(Unreleased)	

SAVE THE BEATLES!

Tracks
◆ *Eligible or provisional but withheld for solo project*

	4th of July (McCartney/McCartney)	M, 73-Mar
	⊘ (Quality) Forced writing. Vaguely incoherent lyric. Chord progression and melody sound tortured.	
	Band on the Run (McCartney/McCartney)	M12-01, 73-Oct
	✓◆ Another three-parter. Great imaginary landscape. Sounds wide and worthy.	
	Best Friend (McCartney)	M09, 72-Aug
	⊘ (Quality) Somewhat generic blues. Skates along without much character or shape. A throwback.	
	Bluebird (McCartney/McCartney)	M12-03, 73-Oct
	✓ Non-silly love song. Mysterious and well-formed. Perfect instrumentation.	
	Bridge on the River Suite (McCartney/McCartney) (Issued as "The Country Hams")	M, 72-Oct
	⊘ (Filler) Soundtrack-like, this sounds mostly like the lost B-side of "Live and Let Die"	
	C Moon (McCartney/McCartney)	M07-01, 72-Nov
	≈ (Quality) Likable enough, but slight in the extreme.	
	Country Dreamer (McCartney/McCartney)	M11-02, 72-Sep
	⊘ (Style/Quality) Lazy writing. Clichéd words and music. Nice steel playing, but very misplaced.	
	Give Ireland Back to the Irish (McCartney/McCartney)	M05-01, 72-Feb
	⊘ (Content/Quality) Politics aside, this is a terrible record.	
	Give Ireland Back to the Irish (Version) (McCartney/McCartney)	M05-02, 72-Feb
	⊘ (Filler) The instrumental version is better because no bad lyrics.	
	Hands of Love (McCartney/McCartney)	M09-11, 72-Oct
	✓ The only good part of the medley. A nice pure pop song. Linda BVs out of tune.	
	Helen Wheels (McCartney/McCartney)	M11-01, 73-Sep
	✓ Another great post-Beatles rocker. Quirky but rock solid.	
	Hi, Hi, Hi (McCartney/McCartney)	M07-02, 72-Nov
	✓ Cheeky and catchy. A very slight confection.	
	Hold Me Tight (McCartney/McCartney)	M09-09, 72-Sep
	⊘ (Quality) Pure purgatory SLS. Terrible lyric. Goes around in circles to nowhere.	
	Jazz Street (McCartney)	M09, 72-Nov
	⊘ (Filler) Another typical "link" track.	
	Jet (McCartney/McCartney)	M12-02, 73-Oct
	✓◆ Great pop with rock echoes. Paul's vox and guitars are fantastic.	
	Lazy Dynamite (McCartney/McCartney)	M09-10, 72-Sep
	⊘ (Filler) Turn of phrase becomes lousy stub of a song. Harmonica? Really?	
	Let Me Roll It (McCartney/McCartney)	M12-05, 73-Oct
	≈ (Content) With or without subtext, a solid song, great riff, strong vocal, nice arrangement.	
	Live and Let Die (McCartney/McCartney)	M10-01, 72-Oct
	✓ Forceful and confident. Large scale. The first real portent of hope.	
	Loup (1st Indian on the Moon) (McCartney/McCartney)	M09-08, 72-Mar
	⊘ (Filler) Pointless filler. Kills the album dead. Belongs on a B-side, not as album track.	
	Mama's Little Girl (McCartney/McCartney)	M09, 72-Mar
	✓ A bit too cute, but simple, classic Macca.	
	Mamunia (McCartney/McCartney)	M12-06, 73-Sep
	≈◆ (Quality) Somehow overcomes its leaning toward vapidness.	

○	**Mary Had a Little Lamb** (McCartney/McCartney) ⊘ (Content/Style) Intentions aside, this is a terrible record.	M06-01, 72-Mar
	Mess I'm In, The (McCartney/McCartney) ✓ One of Paul's great post-Beatles rockers. Wasted in live version on a B-side.	M09, 72-Mar
○	**Mess, The (live)** (McCartney/McCartney) ⊘ (Live) A staple of the live show, this rocker sounds fine live, but better in the studio.	M08-02, 72-Aug
	Mrs. Vandebilt (McCartney/McCartney) ≈◆ (Quality) Slight but manages to sound important through strong structure.	M12-04, 73-Oct
	My Love (McCartney/McCartney) ✓ Sappy MOR, but catchy, if template driven. Skilled writing. The original SLS.	M09-02, 73-Jan
	Night Out (McCartney) ✓ A rare sketch with real force, probably due to the guitars and driving beat. A good one.	M09, 72-Sep
	Nineteen Hundred and Eighty-Five (McCartney/McCartney) ≈◆ (Quality) Very odd song. Lyric is weak, but the intensity saves it. It rolls well.	M12-09, 73-Oct
	No Words (McCartney/Laine) ≈◆ (Quality) Forgettable, but not unlikeable. Feels like part of the "story."	M12-07, 73-Oct
	One More Kiss (McCartney/McCartney) ✓ Music hall. Quaint and skilled writing. Has a place, but maybe not here.	M09-04, 72-Dec
	Picasso's Last Words (Drink to Me) (McCartney/McCartney) ✓◆ Not the greatest song, but the legend elevates it. Works well with reprise.	M12-08, 73-Oct
	Power Cut (McCartney/McCartney) ⊘ (Quality) Forced writing. Not entirely bad, but not a whole idea. Forgettable.	M09-12, 72-Oct
	Single Pigeon (McCartney/McCartney) ⊘ (Quality) Forced writing. Weak idea padded. Very slight for the amount of effort.	M09-06, 72-Mar
	Thank You Darling (McCartney) ⊘ (Quality/Filler) Weak rewrite of "Heart and Soul" — with kazoos.	M09, 72-Dec
	Tragedy (Nelson/Burch) ≈ (Filler) Casual cover. Nice enough, but improved when rewritten as "Band on the Run."	M09, 72-Mar
	When the Night (McCartney/McCartney) ≈ (Quality) Germ of a good song, but never pays off. Endless call-response very annoying.	M09-07, 72-Mar
○	**Zoo Gang** (McCartney/McCartney) ⊘ (Filler) Just a sketch, and not very interesting.	M13-02, 73-Apr

Note: *"Seaside Woman" is from this era but not considered because it was neither written, co-written, nor sung by Paul.*

As will become more and more true over time, McCartney here bests the field in terms of the pure *quantity* of new music available. The quality is also, all things considered, generally higher than that of the other former Fabs, though wildly inconsistent. This is mainly because it is in this period that Paul finally figures out how to actually be a solo artist, despite still trying to do it as part of a theoretical "band." It's certainly not a straight line. The whiplash of twists and turns in this period is hard to overstate. But eventually, something clicks.

This is perhaps the right place to remind ourselves that the first *four* albums Paul released after the end of the Beatles were significantly below the quality standard he had set with the group. That is an astonishing statistic, and it is a minor miracle that the record company did not give up on him along the way.

Red Rose Speedway, the last of these four, summarizes the problems of the first three, while also adding to the pile. From its inexplicable title and inexplicable cover image to its inexplicable closing medley, and "secret" braille message to Stevie Wonder, *Red Rose Speedway* inhabits a very odd spot in McCartney's canon.

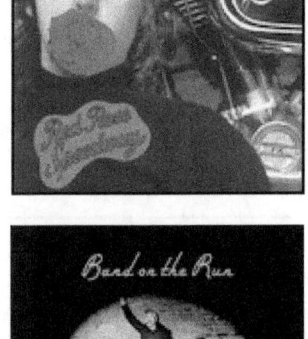

Perhaps the best way to understand it, however, is to compare it to its immediate successor, the redoubtable *Band on the Run*. Given that these were made in quick succession, the main question has to be: What does the later album have that is missing from the earlier one?

Part of that answer is easy: Better songs. But only *some* of the songs are actually better. In fact, a couple of the songs in the middle of *Band on the Run* are right out of the same mold as those on *Red Rose Speedway*. This would have to include "Mamunia," "Mrs. Vandebilt" and "No Words." It should raise no controversy to say that these three songs are comparable in raw quality to "Big Barn Bed," "Get on the Right Thing" and "When the Night." And we might appropriately wonder if "Nineteen Hundred and Eighty-Five" is really all that much better than, say, "Little Lamb Dragonfly."

Direct comparison is always tough because such assessments are wholly subjective, but there is little question that most people perceive the tracks — or perhaps the *aggregation* of tracks — on one album as somehow fundamentally better than those on the other.

Indeed, on *Red Rose Speedway*, there are no songs as great as "Jet," "Bluebird," or "Band on the Run." There is nothing quite as smooth as "Let Me Roll It," or as steeped in lore as "Picasso's Last Words (Drink to Me)." Likewise, there is nothing on *Band on the Run* as energy-sapping as "Loup (1st Indian on the Moon)," as ponderously overlong as the side two medley, or as embarrassing as "Single Pigeon." If we chart the song quality, we get a rough measure of the difference between the actual contents of the albums.

HIGHER QUALITY

	↗ Band on the Run
	↗ Jet
	↗ Bluebird
My Love	↔ Let Me Roll It
One More Kiss	↔ Picasso's Last Words (Drink to Me)
Little Lamb Dragonfly	↔ Mrs. Vandebilt
Big Barn Bed	↔ Nineteen Hundred and Eighty-Five
Get on the Right Thing	↔ Mamunia
When the Night	↔ No Words
Medley ↙	
Single Pigeon ↙	
Loup (1st Indian on the Moon) ↙	

LOWER QUALITY

Interestingly, the three outliers on each end of the scale have superficial things in common. "Band on the Run," for example, is actually a "medley" of three separate ideas, connected with the same aspirations as the earlier unsuccessful medley. The difference is that the individual parts of "Band on the Run" are inherently more interesting, resonate well with each other, collectively tell a story (sort of), and are glued together with much greater skill.[10] They simply elevate each other, and that is a magical thing. Whenever Paul gets this mechanism right, the results are memorable.

The other two commonalities are more fun: As avian species go, bluebirds make better subjects than pigeons, and jets make for way better trips than weed-fueled moonshots.

The real surprise in the comparison is just how much quality overlap there is between the two albums. These are obviously subjective rankings, and your mileage may vary.[11] But let's say this is close enough to determine that differences in pure song quality explain only about half of the difference in listener perception between the two albums. Clearly, something else is at work.

As always, we turn to the assembly for answers, and it provides quite a few.

When thinking of assembly, we tend to consider the placement of the individual tracks first, but there is a much larger factor at work with *Band on the Run*. In one particularly crucial decision, Paul has returned to the formula which served him so well in the past: The project includes a memorable and compelling cover image.

---

[10] Compare the "Lazy Dynamite/Hands of Love" segue to the one between "...if we ever get out of here." and "The rain exploded..." The musical problem is similar, as is the technique used to solve it, but the latter solution is orders of magnitude more satisfying.

[11] To hear them for best objectivity, listen in alphabetical or random order.

Indeed, this cover is one of only two or three in McCartney's 70s catalog which does not look either ill-conceived or like a hasty afterthought.

The power of this image, carefully-posed figures frozen against a wall in the beam of a searchlight — cannot be overstated. It sets expectations from the moment the album is in a buyer's hands — and even before, through advertising. It creates a robust context for the music long before the needle touches the vinyl. The image actually suggests a story all by itself, without too much specificity, in the same way Paul's lyrics often do, as in the case of the title track. When the very first sounds on the album match the cover image, a virtuous circle is established in which the photo contextualizes the music, and the music lives up to that contextualization. Mysteriously, even the lesser music on the album seems somehow relevant to the cover image, and the simple but compelling sketch of a story it implies.

It will sound reductive to say this, but once Paul added the brief reprise of the title track to the end of the album, he had realized once again the complete formula which first fell into place with *Sgt. Pepper*. Images and music merged, and the perception of a concept — slight as it may be — miraculously appeared. *Band on the Run* is not a concept album, but it sure seems like one. This is to McCartney's great credit as an assembler. Put simply: Assembly matters.

The music on *Red Rose Speedway* may not be the greatest, but it isn't *that much* worse than *Band on the Run*. It simply has none of the advantages good assembly might have provided. No compelling cover image. No concept, or even a whiff of one. No virtuous circle between the packaging and the music. No virtuous circle among the music itself. Each part of the album seems to serve only itself, and there isn't even a simple resonance between the various parts.

Interestingly, the exact same thing can be said of the double album version of *Red Rose Speedway*. Both versions appear to be blank collections of unrelated tracks. It is difficult to argue that the longer version would have sounded better, or done any better in the market, or be remembered any differently from the one we actually got. It is a little more showy, a little more varied, and a little more balanced between band members, but none of that makes it measurably better.

The recording process explains part of this, since the entire project started as a housecleaning of sorts. Demos for many of the *Red Rose Speedway* songs can be found co-mingling with those that wound up on his two previous LPs. At least half of the songs were more than a year old when the album was released. Ideas and whole tracks left over from *Ram* were brought out and tweaked. Recordings took place both well before and well after the sessions for *Wild Life*.

It's difficult to maintain much consistency of tone when recording this way. Contrast *Red Rose Speedway*'s sessions, spread across more than two years, with those of *Band on the Run*, which were completed in a brisk and focused two months. This accounts for the relative unity of sound on the latter, and the inevitable disunity of sound on the former. A lot can be done in mixing, but the passage of time matters. A lot of life happened between the start and finish of *Red Rose Speedway*, and as a result, some things were baked into the tracks which could not be mixed out.

As a whole, however, the recordings on *Red Rose Speedway* are far more ambitious and polished than much of what had come before it. They also have roughly the same amount of polish as those on the album which followed. The difference on *Red Rose Speedway* is that McCartney sounds like he is really *trying*, when his earlier efforts seem like either intentionally *not* trying, or at least not *admitting* to trying. On *Red Rose Speedway*, Paul appears to be aiming very carefully, but still widely missing his mark. In contrast, *Band on the Run* features only do, no try.

Where *McCartney* was earnest but sketchy, and *Ram* was visceral but awkward, and *Wild Life* was unbridled but inauthentic, *Red Rose Speedway* is crisp but vacant. The progression shows just how desperate Paul was to find a solo voice. *Band on the Run* solves that, being loose, confident and sounding completely effortless, a key component to its commercial and artistic success.

From our Assembler's point of view, the outtakes and singles which were recorded along with *Red Rose Speedway* are of more interest than just about anything that made the actual album. Only "Hands of Love" and the hit, "My Love," will be brought forward for consideration, and the former feels pretty light when compared to what other Beatles will bring to the table.

The love song, however, is significant as something of an inevitable anomaly. Though there is precedent for Paul to write a sugary love song, there is no real precedent for the particular style of "My Love." Contrary to conventional wisdom, there is no straight line to "My Love" from say "Yesterday" or "I Will" or even "The Long and Winding Road" (which comes closest). A turn of thinking was required, as well as a release of some past technique.

Significantly, "My Love" was the last song completed for the album, clearly the result of increasing comfort in his solo skin. In terms of confidence, it is of a piece with "One More Kiss," the second-to-last song completed, and harbinger of what would come next. Indeed, "My Love" became a template for much of Paul's later writing. As such, it actually represents a clear moment when Paul finds his next act and joins the MOR field in full force, where he would ultimately find great success, if also some loss of credibility.

To understand what changed, consider this list of Paul's major love ballads:[12]

---

[12] I am here excluding anything which is either not a ballad, not a direct expression of love by the singer, or to which John Lennon contributed significantly.

1962 - "P.S. I Love You"
1964 - "And I Love Her"
1964 - "I'll Follow the Sun"
1965 - "Yesterday"
1965 - "Michelle"
1966 - "Here, There and Everywhere"
1968 - "I Will"
1969 - "The Long and Winding Road"
1970 - "Maybe I'm Amazed"
1973 - "My Love"

First, notice that this is a much shorter list than you probably imagined. Despite the conventional wisdom that Paul wrote "silly love songs" (SLS) throughout his career, he didn't really begin to rely on the form until *after* "My Love," perhaps because it became a smash success. Though Paul did sing ballads like "A Taste of Honey" and "Till There Was You," he didn't write them, and they were inserted into the Beatles catalog primarily because they had been popular back in their club days.

Second, notice that most of these cannot be fairly called "silly" love songs. There is nothing frivolous about anything on this list until, arguably, "My Love."

Third, "My Love" bears little in common with its predecessors. It is not a rewrite of an earlier song, or a regurgitation of tropes he has mined in the past. As he did throughout his career, Paul struck out in a new direction, though he was clearly influenced by a shift in popular music toward "soft rock."

"My Love" is very much in keeping with other songs topping the charts in those days. Contemporary hits included "Killing Me Softly" by Roberta Flack, "Touch Me in the Morning" by Diana Ross, "Clair" by Gilbert O'Sullivan, and crooner Perry Como's "And I Love You So." Several years of highly successful ballads by the Carpenters probably also did not escape his notice. Basically, Paul synthesized a new voice for himself by moving right into the popular styles of the day. Perhaps it was inevitable that he would eventually do so, but that doesn't make the moment any easier to digest.

This may actually be why the song was greeted with such derision from diehard Beatles fans even as it topped the charts. Rather than Paul leading, as he had done for so long, he was clearly following the pack, even if he was doing it in his own voice. In other words, there is no question that "My Love" is something original, and very much a Paul McCartney song, even as it must also be admitted that it is *derivative* of other music in the marketplace.

His handlers at the label were probably quite satisfied with this turn of events, but it is fair to ask whether Paul ever again was a leader of tastes rather than a follower. The Assembler will be happy to consider "My Love" for the group album, recognizing it as a fine piece of work, compatible with the Beatle brand, and something that they hadn't really done before. With proper surroundings, fans might not have even noticed its more sappy characteristics.

From *Band on the Run*, the Assembler will have to talk Paul into setting a couple of songs aside for the group project. As a whole artistic statement, it feels wrong to rob from such a great album. But "Bluebird" and "Let Me Roll It" have simply too much to offer the group, and could certainly be replaced in Paul's album lineup with minimal disruption (perhaps "Mine for Me" for "Bluebird" and "Tragedy" for "Let Me Roll It"). The structure of *Band on the Run* could remain completely intact, but its bounty spread around. "Let Me Roll It" is often considered a response to John Lennon, a closing of the famous feud, but it is so gentle that the Assembler will not worry about a veto from John, whose opinion of the track became clear when he respectfully quoted it in "Beef Jerky."

To accommodate the dynamic at work here, the Assembler will, for the first time, give a solo Beatle the right to withhold music from consideration by the group. This means that great songs like "Band on the Run" and "Jet" will not be considered because we assume that Paul would not have wanted them to be — unless they got their proper due.

This may seem anathema to fans who rightfully believe these are among Paul's greatest tracks in the 70s, and think they would be perfect on a Beatles album. We all can imagine a slightly different version of that cover photo with four of the frozen figures being Beatles — a very attractive idea. But had Paul's title song and "concept" come to frame a Beatles album, it seems more likely that a tug of war for the heart of the project might have ensued. These particular ideas would have been simply wrong for the group in 1973.

The reality is that these powerful tracks elevate each other in Paul's assembly, and would have had to be transplanted in large chunks onto a Beatles album to retain that. Such chunks would clearly have overwhelmed a Beatles album, turning it into a de facto McCartney solo album that just happens to feature other Beatles. That's a very different thing from a fused album — more like *Ringo* than *Revolver*.

In our imagined process, where balance between Beatle voices is critical, the days would have been long gone when one Beatle could drive the project in the way these tracks would have. Indeed, the Assembler's primary job is to keep things within certain specific parameters. Paul's epic begs to be the title track, and that decision would have guided every other subsequent decision. Where in 1967 the result of Paul introducing such an overarching theme was elevation, here it would be more like domination.

"Band on the Run" by itself is big enough to put a firm frame around any music placed on the same album with it, which would have necessarily displaced work by the others. In part, this is because the actual music we have to work with from John,

George and Ringo was made without any apparent knowledge of Paul's idea. We can certainly imagine a different scenario in which Paul presented the idea for *Band on the Run* to the others, along with a demo of the song and sketch of the cover photo, and challenged them to fill in the blanks. That's an album every fan would probably love to hear. Despite being an interesting idea, however, we can't work with it. We just don't know either how they would have reacted or what music they might have created if they had taken up the challenge. Perhaps John would have repeated his earlier assessment that Paul was "daft." Or perhaps he would have written the absolute perfect song to complement it.

Instead, our Assembler will recognize *Band on the Run* as a breakout moment for Paul as a solo artist, and know the importance of such a thing. Thus, even in our slightly altered narrative, Paul's magnum opus would have appeared very similar to the way we know it.

Though this may be hard to swallow, consider that Paul offers a great many tracks to choose from outside of the album. Among Paul's singles from this era, "Hi, Hi, Hi" seems a natural for a group project, along with "Helen Wheels" (which would then not have been added to the album in America) and "Live and Let Die." In the case of the latter, it is not only the presence of George Martin which marks this as a potential group track. The overall scope in both songwriting and record-making is so different from any of Paul's contemporary solo projects that it only makes sense to see what it sounds like next to work by the other Beatles, which both McCartney and Martin might have championed.

Our Assembler can also use some great outtakes, including the pounding "Night Out," and the much smaller "Mama's Little Girl," which comes in as a fully-formed McCartney gem, your reaction to which will depend on your feelings about such precious material. Though the live version of "The Mess" would not be eligible, a contemporary studio version certainly would.

The underlying issue is that Paul was generating so much more music than his erstwhile bandmates that using it all would result in him dominating the band in a way that would not have been tolerated. As such, the Assembler must, from this point forward, pick and choose very carefully from what Paul creates. He will be looking for music that rises to *Beatle Quality*, of course, ignoring the worst of Paul's mistakes like "Give Ireland Back to the Irish" and "Mary Had a Little Lamb," while seeking that which resonates best with the work of the others. Of necessity, good — even *classic* — tracks will be left behind as a result.

This process would have become the "secret sauce" by which Beatles albums were created — a conscious decision about what constituted "solo" versus "group" material, and recognition that group projects were even more becoming a puzzle to be solved. The bare quality of the songs is just not enough information because of how the music would have to be assembled. As such, the Assembler would have had to prioritize *resonance* over simple *quality* — which, above a certain threshold, doesn't matter. That is a delicate and highly subjective matter, but it is fortunate that Paul has created so much music to consider. The net result is positive both for the solo artist and the fused Beatles — the best of all possible (imagined) worlds.

George Harrison
12 tracks: 4 eligible, 5 provisional

Sources

H03	~~"Give Me Love (Give Me Peace on Earth)"~~ / "Miss O'Dell" R: Oct 72 - Mar 73 P: Harrison S: Apple, FPSHOT	73-May
H04	*Living in the Material World* R: Oct 72 - Mar 73 P: Harrison (Spector) S: EMI, Apple, FPSHOT	73-May

Tracks

	Be Here Now (Harrison) ✓ A gem. Gentle, introspective, calm, pointed, beautiful.	H04-08, 73-Mar
	Day the World Gets 'Round, The (Harrison) ≈ (Content/Quality) Not a bad idea, but something missing. Preachy.	H04-10, +R, 73-Mar
	Don't Let Me Wait Too Long (Harrison) ✓ Great record. Should have been a single. One idea short of classic.	H04-04, +R, 73-Mar
	Give Me Love (Give Me Peace on Earth) (Harrison) ✓ A plaintive plea, but hopeful. Catchy and welcoming.	H04-01, 73-Mar
	Light That Has Lighted the World, The (Harrison) ⊘ (Content/Quality) Heartfelt, but grating. Palpably sad, but not a great song.	H04-03, 73-Mar
	Living in the Material World (Harrison) ≈ (Quality/Content) Galloping beat quickly gets annoying. Strident vocal.	H04-06, +R, 73-Mar
	Lord Loves the One (That Loves the Lord), The (Harrison) ⊘ (Content) Music is a mixed bag, but lyrics really kill the potential good vibe.	H04-07, 73-Mar
	Miss O'Dell (Harrison) ≈ (Quality) Mostly inside jokes and laughter. Sloppy, but has some charm.	H03-02, 73-Feb
	Sue Me, Sue You Blues (Harrison) ≈ (Content) Inventive and jaunty. Bad vibes transmuted without anger.	H04-02, 73-Mar

✋	**That Is All** (Harrison)	H04-11, 73-Mar
	≈ (Quality) Weepy. Preachy. Reedy. GH voice set badly.	
✋	**Try Some, Buy Some** (Harrison)	H04-09, 73-Mar
	✓ Ambitious (Beatle-y) scale. Mostly works, despite reedy vocal.	
✋	**Who Can See It** (Harrison)	H04-05, 73-Mar
	⊘ (Quality/Content) Almost great, but awkward. GH vocal is weak in upper range.	

Knowing what George Harrison had just accomplished through his charitable efforts and the ensuing financial madness, and also knowing what's ahead in his catalog, one feels the need to shower some affection on *Living in the Material World*. And there are indeed some fine tracks.

But George's descent into shaming his audience had begun, and the weepiness only hinted at in "Isn't a Pity" has started to blossom. More importantly, even the good music on this album is either buried beneath a pervading sense of self-pity, or as unassuming and nearly invisible as a flower growing among the weeds.

Still, an important truth about George's solo career can be understood by listening to this album: There is such a thing as too much George. His vocal range is small, and when he tries to stretch it on the higher end, his voice becomes reedy and strident and weak, no matter what he is singing. Further, his emotional range as a singer is likewise frightfully small. The differences in performance style between, for instance, "Don't Let Me Wait Too Long" and "That Is All" — two very different songs — is almost nil.

The production of this album tries to make up the difference in various ways, from elaborate backup singers to a wide palette of guitar sounds. But at the heart of each track is George's vocal, and it sets the tone, like it or not. The biggest problem with *Living in the Material World* may very well be that there is nothing to break up the sameness of George's voice — a telling piece of support for the idea of Beatles working together from a distance to elevate one another. If nothing else, it would break up the sameness.

His songwriting is, unfortunately, a contributing factor to this dilemma. Though increasingly varied and maturing, it has an unsettled quality. Phrases do not go where the ear expects, and rhythms often feel off balance. Some of this is, no doubt, intentional, yet the effect created is of songs based on sketchy musical ideas, or that are either unfinished or at least unpolished.

The central problem, really, is about piling on. Each song seems to compound the problems of the others, rather than relieving or at least offsetting them. As a result, this album becomes something of a slog to get through, even though some of the music is quite good.

When that happens, we look to the sequencing for an explanation, but that doesn't necessarily offer a solution here. These songs are somewhat interchangeable, and the difference between best and worst is frustratingly small. Trying to create a workable resequence runs into problems quickly because three songs, "Who Can See It," "The Day the World Gets Round," and "That is All" are effectively the same song written three slightly different ways. And a case can be made that "The Light That Has Lighted the World" also belongs in this group.

Further, in an emotional sense, these songs are also simply variations on a theme. That fact might suggest placing them together in a suite of sorts, where they could potentially elevate each other, while also distinguishing one from the other through proximity. But that is not the effect which happens. Together, they amplify the weaknesses of each other rather than the strengths, which argues for dropping the least of them and finding something else.

A couple of the tracks are on the borderline of consideration, the first being "Who Can See It," a clunky but sincere piece of writing that feels important, but also rather disposable. It contains a sentiment that we want to embrace because it so inhabits Harrison's approach to his solo career, and indeed all of life after the Beatles. It would have been tough to consider for the group project because it feels perpetually unfinished, as if the musical ideas haven't really been worked out yet.

The album's greatest track may very well be one of the best ever solo Beatle recordings, but "Be Here Now" is buried in the dead zone of side two. It follows the most unfortunate "The Lord Loves the One (That Loves the Lord)" — a track so distasteful that the casual listener is forgiven for lifting the needle off the record and walking away from the album. What should be George's centerpiece for the album is completely lost, sounding like a mere variation on the banal mystical/religious themes espoused elsewhere on the record. Pulling it out from the morass, which happens right away when listening to the tracks alphabetically, makes it clear that it is one of George's lost masterworks. It succeeds beautifully as a suitably gentle rejoinder to anyone who longs for reanimation of the past, the perfect answer to the swarming of the public over the Beatles retrospectives.

At this point, it's worth saying that the idea of reanimating the past is not central to the ideas of this book. Our charter is much more about daylighting overlooked great music by putting it next to much better songs where it can shine. In other words, the rescued Beatles albums are in no way about somehow reliving the glory days, but rather making new ones by uncovering greatness which in one way or another went unheard at the time. "Be Here Now" perfectly embodies that sentiment, and has the advantage of containing the trademark Beatle greatness, as expressed for a new era. It has the potential to give context to the music of the other solo Beatles, drawing out the fact that they all shared this sentiment, and wrote about it, if only indirectly.

Living in the Material World is a good — not great — album. It barely provides enough material for George's contribution to the group's double album, though the material it does provide clearly sets the tone and frames everything else in a way which does not overwhelm it. With nothing much in the way of outtakes from George in this era, that — plus his significant collaborations on which Ringo sings lead — will have to be enough. In the end, the goals that George appears to have had for this solo album will end up being more effectively accomplished by taking the best of what he recorded and bouncing it off the work of the other Beatles, the exact goal of our rescue project.

Ringo Starr
11 tracks: 8 eligible, 3 provisional

Sources

S06		"~~Photograph~~" / "Down and Out" R: Oct 72 - Jul 73 P: Harrison/Perry		S: B: Apple or FPSHOT	73-Sep
S07		*Ringo* R: Mar-Jul 73 P: Perry		S: Various (7)	73-Nov

Tracks

	Devil Woman (Starkey/Poncia) ✓ Well suited to Ringo's style, voice, and drumming. Just having a fun time.	S07-09, 73-Jul
	Down and Out (Starkey) ✓ Great song, wasted on a B-side. GH guitar is most welcome. Nice production, too.	S06-02, +G, 72-Nov
	Have You Seen My Baby (Newman) ≈ (Quality) Spirited arrangement and playing lifts a pretty plain song.	S07-02, 73-Jul
	I'm the Greatest (Lennon) ✓ Ringo sings this better than John could have. May be his best-ever track — says something.	S07-01, +JG, 73-Jul
	Oh My My (Starkey/Poncia) ✓ One of Ringo's likeable, classic novelties. Not a viable, long-term career strategy, though.	S07-06, 73-Jul
	Photograph (Starkey/Harrison) ✓ Other candidate for "best Ringo track ever." Catchy, upbeat, well-formed.	S07-03, +G, 73-Jul
	Six O'Clock (McCartney/McCartney) ≈ (Quality) Nice when Beatles work together again, but this is a non-event. Song is lousy.	S07-08, +P, 73-Jul
	Step Lightly (Starkey) ✓ Great low-key groove. Perfect fit — voice, tone, content. A straight success. Ugh, tap dancing.	S07-07, 73-Jul
	Sunshine Life for Me (Sail Away Raymond) (Harrison) ✓ A great track. Simple and fun. GH and RS always make a great team.	S07-04, +G, 73-Jul
	You and Me (Babe) (Harrison/Evans) ✓ In context, this really works. Outside, it sounds a little dumb. Still, likeable all around.	S07-10, +G, 73-Jul
	You're Sixteen (Sherman/Sherman) ≈ (Filler) A simple and fun cover. Nobody is trying too hard, and it just works.	S07-05, +P, 73-Jul

Sometimes an album is just so full of positive vibes that the question of whether it's any good is answered before the music even starts. Such is the case with *Ringo*, assembled as the only real post-Beatles cooperative effort by the four principles. This album is great without even listening to it.

As such, thinking too hard about the contents is not advised. Ringo didn't just gather the former Beatles, he got a whole bunch of feel-good types to write and play and sing and produce his return to popular music after a nearly three-year absence. The album has, perhaps, the sunniest disposition of any post-breakup effort, all the way up to the present day.

Its creation also utilized a process very close to what we are imagining with the meta-Beatles project. Ringo essentially convinced his mates to record separately but release together — even going so far as to ship tapes overseas for overdubs. All participants gave something close to their best on individual tracks, and then the album emerged as an assembly of those efforts. It's too bad that George Martin wasn't invited to the party because who knows what little idea or refinement he might have added to top this off.

The essential problem, if there is one, is that there's not much *album* in this album. It's a collection of individual tracks, all of which are great on their own, without ever becoming that *something bigger* that actual Beatles albums always became. It's an arguable point whether anything bigger could have been created through better sequencing, or whether that is even worth considering. Ostensibly, the idea is that the tracks all represent a show — a la *Sgt. Pepper* — yet only the opener and closer do anything to even approximately delineate that "concept" in the music. The iconic cover image certainly sets that expectation nicely, but the sequencing must always serve the *music* first, which is the only way that the music can then properly serve a larger *concept*. In other words, it is not a chicken-egg question; music always comes first.

The reality, therefore, is that even with the opener, closer and cover image working together, these tracks never coalesce into anything other than "a collection of songs sung by Ringo Starr." In this case, that's definitely enough, but this error, which has minimal immediate consequences, would propagate through the rest of Ringo's recordings with devastating effect. The reason is simple: In his later catalog, the individual tracks were just never as good as these, and could not make the necessary impact on their own.

For example, having learned George Martin's principles, we have to question whether starting the album with "I'm the Greatest" is really the best idea. It is certainly the most consequential song on the album, and the one most likely to appeal to buyers of the LP, but using it as a pole track to open the album runs the distinct risk of making everything that comes after sound lesser in some way. That does not happen here, thankfully, but there is a much better opener available which could have allowed the impact of the semi-reunion track to be even more powerful.

That more obvious opener was also the album's greatest hit, "Photograph." Instead of rendering following tracks lesser in some way, it would have set an even better table for the party which follows. Lennon's track could have become the featured extender, with McCartney's track sliding in as the change of pace.

The question with a lineup like that would be how to follow three Beatles tracks with anything else. But there is plenty here which could change and even heighten the mood. "You're Sixteen" is well-placed at the end of side one, and "You and Me (Babe)" is the only possible album closer, given its narration. But "Sunshine Life for Me (Sail Away Raymond)" is too good to waste in the middle of a side. It should have led off side two. The rest then slot in rather simply.

1A.	Photograph
1B.	I'm the Greatest
1C.	Six O'Clock
1Y.	Devil Woman
1Z.	You're Sixteen
2A.	Sunshine Life for Me (Sail Away Raymond)
2B.	Step Lightly
2M.	Have You Seen My Baby
2Y.	Oh My My
2Z.	You and Me (Babe)

An important thing to note here is that three of the four pole tracks are by George Harrison — a testament to his abundance of creativity. Unfortunately, his own releases were never quite this free of worry and unwelcome intent.

Of course, a more intentional assembly would risk upsetting the overwhelming party atmosphere, and obviously, we couldn't have that. But it really doesn't. In fact, it would have sharpened it. This is a party album — literally: It is the recording of a big party which happened in various recording studios over a few months. And though we know now that it began a period of time which would be extraordinarily difficult personally for three of the four former Beatles, none of that crept into the recordings, which are uniformly joy-filled and, each in its own way, *exciting*. Thinking too much doesn't enter in. A revised assembly just amps everything up, allowing an even higher climb into classic status.

Since this is just a party, there isn't really a significant lyric anywhere beyond the opener. In that way, this album hearkens back to the pre-*Rubber Soul* days more than many other Beatles-related projects — including *Get Back/Let It Be*. The only thematic idea is to sing a few songs and have a few laughs. That purity was certainly a welcome thing in 1973, but may also explain why the album hasn't had quite the legs of heftier projects like *Band on the Run* or *Imagine*.

Indeed, the individual *pieces* which make up this "album" have had much longer legs than the album itself. It's still possible to hear "You're Sixteen" occasionally in the supermarket, even after cultural changes have rendered its lyrics problematic. Similarly, "Oh My My" and "Photograph" have aged well and become mainstays on oldies radio. Ringo's solo career is often summed up by referring to songs on this album, which is certainly his most successful, both creatively and financially.

Our Assembler would have had a field day with some of this material. John's track is an obvious lift, as are two of the three George tracks. Paul's contribution will be brought forward for consideration, but it is the least of the collaborations. Unlike some of the other solo projects in this era, *Ringo* feels like it is ripe for the picking. What would have remained could have been combined with tracks from the next album (which also will be picked clean of Beatle-related tracks) and form a very nice party album of its own.

If this seems disrespectful to Ringo, keep in mind that we might be assuming that he initiated the meta-Beatles recording project in this era, and would have been recording with just such contributions in mind. If that were the case, he might have seen anything left over as gravy, and the seeds of a potential solo project later.

In the album's closer, Ringo sings, "Give us a smile if you liked the show," a George Harrison lyric which really sums up the whole point of the project. Much of this goodwill will transfer to the group project, and even be elevated in the process.

In the real world, *Ringo* was arguably the closest the group ever got to reuniting. Here were all four Beatles on the same disc, even if John's appearance is fleeting, and Paul's contributions are forgettable. As a result, the album established a template for Ringo's future albums and, coupled with the overall increase in media exposure, also created a lasting public persona for Ringo as the life of the party.

Assembly
46 tracks: 30 eligible, 16 provisional

≈	Bring on the Lucie (Freda Peeple)	L09-05, 73-Aug
✓	I Know (I Know)	L09-10, 73-Aug
✓	Intuition	L09-07, 73-Aug
✓	Meat City	L09-12, 73-Aug
✓	Mind Games	L09-01, 73-Aug
≈	Nutopian International Anthem	L09-06, 73-Aug
✓	One Day (At a Time)	L09-04, 73-Aug
✓	Only People	L09-09, 73-Aug
✓	Out the Blue	L09-08, 73-Aug
≈	Rock 'N' Roll People	L09, 73-Aug
≈	Tight A$	L09-02, 73-Aug
✓	You Are Here	L09-11, 73-Aug
✓	Bluebird	M12-03, 73-Oct
≈	C Moon	M07-01, 72-Nov
✓	Hands of Love	M09-11, 72-Oct
✓	Helen Wheels	M11-01, 73-Sep
✓	Hi, Hi, Hi	M07-02, 72-Nov
≈	Let Me Roll It	M12-05, 73-Oct
✓	Live and Let Die	M10-01, 72-Oct
✓	Mama's Little Girl	M09, 72-Mar
✓	Mess I'm In, The	M09, 72-Mar
✓	My Love	M09-02, 73-Jan
✓	Night Out	M09, 72-Sep
✓	One More Kiss	M09-04, 72-Dec
≈	Tragedy	M09, 72-Mar
≈	When the Night	M09-07, 72-Mar
✓	Be Here Now	H04-08, 73-Mar
≈	Day the World Gets 'Round, The	H04-10, +R, 73-Mar
✓	Don't Let Me Wait Too Long	H04-04, +R, 73-Mar
✓	Give Me Love (Give Me Peace...	H04-01, 73-Mar
≈	Miss O'Dell	H03-02, 73-Feb
≈	Living in the Material World	H04-06, +R, 73-Mar

14 / Be Here Now

≈ Sue Me, Sue You Blues	H04-02, 73-Mar
≈ That Is All	H04-11, 73-Mar
✓ Try Some, Buy Some	H04-09, 73-Mar
✓ Devil Woman	S07-09, 73-Jul
✓ Down and Out	S06-02, +G, 72-Nov
≈ Have You Seen My Baby	S07-02, 73-Jul
✓ I'm the Greatest	S07-01, +JG, 73-Jul
✓ Oh My My	S07-06, 73-Jul
✓ Photograph	S07-03, +G, 73-Jul
≈ Six O'Clock	S07-08, +P, 73-Jul
✓ Step Lightly	S07-07, 73-Jul
✓ Sunshine Life for Me (Sail Away...	S07-04, +G, 73-Jul
✓ You and Me (Babe)	S07-10, +G, 73-Jul
≈ You're Sixteen	S07-05, +P, 73-Jul

The assembly of this album starts with twin realizations. The first is that there is obviously enough here for a well-balanced, filler-free double album. The second is that, as suggested above, in "Be Here Now" George has written the most important statement that a former Beatle could make at this point in their history, one that all would have agreed should be central. His gentle and almost hypnotic song simply must be the title track. All other decisions descend from these starters.

Before beginning, we will do as before and eliminate some tracks which clearly do not belong, now that the list has been compiled. Among these are a few covers, and some that just don't look good enough anymore in this context:

≈ C Moon (P)
Devil Woman (R)
Hands of Love (P)
≈ Have You Seen My Baby (R)
≈ Miss O'Dell (G)
≈ Nutopian... Anthem (J)
Oh My My (R)
≈ Rock 'N' Roll People (J)
≈ Six O'Clock (R)
≈ Tragedy (P)
≈ When the Night (P)
≈ You're Sixteen (R)

Now the sequencing begins in earnest with placement of George's track. Does it open the album? Close the album? Go at some high-visibility spot somewhere else? Well, our Assembler would have to consider all three, and will find it complicated, but full of possibilities.

The full track does not work well as either an album opener or closer, being slow and possibly seeming overlong in either of those positions. In many ways, it doesn't resemble a typical pole track at all. But the fact that it is basically modular in nature allows a somewhat non-traditional approach. A shortened introduction of the theme — a careful edit — could serve as a prologue to the album, allowing a different track to become the de facto album opener. Similarly, reprising it in edited form at the very end serves as a coda rather than the hard album closer.

The full track obviously must appear somewhere, and the natural spot may very well be at the end of a side, rather than either the beginning or buried in the middle. Indeed, only the end of side two — and thus the end of disc one — really works, placing the song centrally, as a fulcrum for everything else.

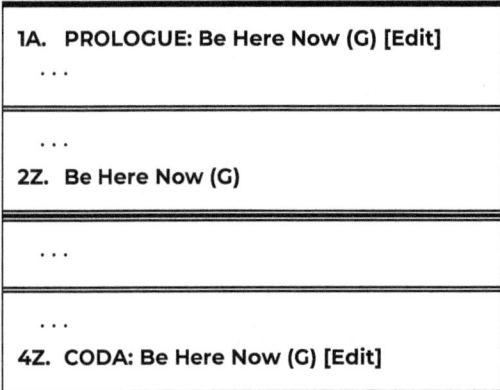

1A.	PROLOGUE: Be Here Now (G) [Edit]
...	
...	
2Z.	Be Here Now (G)
...	
...	
4Z.	CODA: Be Here Now (G) [Edit]

Bluebird (P)
≈ Bring on the Lucie... (J)
≈ Day the World...'Round (G)
Don't Let Me Wait Too Long (G)
Down and Out (R)
Give Me Love (Give Me... (G)
Helen Wheels (P)
Hi, Hi, Hi (P)
I Know (I Know) (J)
I'm the Greatest (R)
Intuition (J)
≈ Let Me Roll It (P)
Live and Let Die (P)
≈ Living...Material World (G)
Mama's Little Girl (P)
Meat City (J)
Mess I'm In, The (P)
Mind Games (J)
My Love (P)
Night Out (P)
One Day (At a Time) (J)
One More Kiss (P)
Only People (J)
Out the Blue (J)
Photograph (R)
Step Lightly (R)
≈ Sue Me, Sue You Blues (G)
Sunshine Life for Me... (R)
≈ That Is All (G)
≈ Tight A$ (J)
Try Some, Buy Some (G)
You and Me (Babe) (R)
You Are Here (J)

From here our Assembler would be looking for the actual opener and closer, to sit inside the prologue and coda, plus something to properly set up the title track in the middle. In this instance, these three spots seem even more important than usual.

The list of available tracks contains an unusually large number that could fit in the pole positions. To refresh: Side openers must have strong first sounds, be among the best in the set, and create the right tone for the music which will follow. Side closers should be (or at least sound) summative in some way, hard to follow, and leave an impression which will stay with the listener.

All four former Beatles made less than optimal choices for their solo album openers during this period. "Mind Games" is too sleepy to open an album. "Big Barn Bed" is too cloying. "Give Me Love (Give Me Peace on Earth)," though a fine track, is too self-contained to start an album. It would work better to open side two, yielding the opener to the album's title track. As mentioned above, *Ringo* began with the most provocative track, despite something better being right there.

After extensive listening for this position, the answer for the opener turns out to be an ad lib by Lennon buried in the middle of *Mind Games*: "Alright boys. This is it…over the hill." John's playful tone offsets George's serious lines, making sure that they do not cast a pall over the album, while also addressing directly the subject on everybody's mind: Will the Beatles still be relevant? The song which follows, "Bring on the Lucie (Freda Peeple)," bounces nicely off of George's prologue, without erasing it. The uptempo track makes a great opener, albeit with slightly political content, that at least doesn't contain even a whiff of the stridency heard on John's earlier solo album.

Though we do not need to extend the opening right now, the tracks which come next seem so obvious in the listening that they basically self-select into the next positions. "Hi, Hi, Hi" extends the party, while allowing Paul's voice an early feature. Though it was a modest hit as a single, the track feels much more anchored when heard in sequence with John's song. It also provides the perfect setup for Ringo's first appearance (with George) on "Sunshine Life for Me (Sail Away Raymond)," which modifies the tone by a small measure, while keeping the party going. In this opening sequence, the Beatles sound like they are having fun, and also much more vital than just *relevant*.

1A.	PROLOGUE: Be Here Now (G) [Edit]
1B.	**Bring on the Lucie (Freda Peeple) (J)**
1C.	**Hi, Hi, Hi (P)**
1D.	**Sunshine Life for Me… (R)**

There may be equally good options that would fit into this sequence, but it flows so smoothly, and seems so obvious, that there is no reason to look further.

The close of the album must build to George's coda. While we would typically be looking for a strong statement here, in this case we also need one that is not entirely definitive, and can be followed — if only by a quick reprise of the album's main theme. Rather than a summative statement like "You and Me (Babe)," something more energetic will create a better bed for George's closing philosophizing. The goal here would be to embody the album's theme: We aren't looking back. We are looking forward. Forget all that. Come along with us. Whatever comes next is going to be fun. You need to be here now.

Given these goals, there may be no better way to end this album than in a place where "people were dancing like there's no tomorrow." There is hardly a more "now" track on the eligible list than "Meat City," and hardly a better lyric to set up George's fundamental idea. As a closer, it works perfectly — the one track that John's running order got right on *Mind Games*. It's also perhaps the most fresh and contemporary track that any Beatle created during this era. In its 2003 remixed incarnation, the lyrics pop out, the band sounds great, and John's simple and quirky imagery and singing create genuine excitement. Its ending, again with fun ad libs from John, yields perfectly to George's coda. A great case can be made that this should have been a single all on its own, rather than wasted as a B-side. It might then have been recognized and remembered as a classic.[1]

Assigning "Meat City" to close the album does raise an important issue which can't wait. That track must be preceded by something just as strong so that it doesn't appear to come out of nowhere. A quick look for possibilities yields Paul's "Night Out," which ends on the same chord that begins John's song. A segue turns out to be not only possible, but essentially seamless.

Still, "Night Out" is mostly instrumental, which might feel like a waste of vinyl at the end of side four. So, to add heft, another Paul track in the same key, "Helen Wheels," is used to create a suite of a very different kind. The word "suite" actually sounds a little too precious, as does "medley." Call it instead a *power sequence* — unlike anything the Beatles have done before, and unlike anything on any of the solo albums. The effect of putting these three tracks together is of the Beatles rocking in a very 1973 way — sounding wholly contemporary, incredibly vital, and fully confident at having dispelled all of the ghosts and all of the doubts.

> . . .
> 4W. Helen Wheels (P)
> 4X. Night Out (P)
> 4Y. Meat City (J) [Edit]
> 4Z. CODA: Be Here Now (G) [Edit]

The matter of setting up the title track comes next, with the search again going out for a track which can create the perfect space in which George's full song can be

---

[1] One reason it was not a single may be the opening bar, in which someone — likely John — miscounted. This should have been fixed in the session, but everyone just drops a beat somewhere to get things back together. Unfortunately, it weakens what would otherwise be an incredibly powerful opening. A better producer would have insisted on a quick redo of *just* the opening, which could have been edited onto the front of the track with no loss of intensity or change in "vibe." Luckily, for our purposes, modern digital editing makes a proper fix relatively easy.

heard and appreciated. The answer is easy: "I'm the Greatest" ends with Ringo basking in the old applause, albeit somewhat ironically. As the most openly self-referential and pseudo-nostalgic track in the collection, as well as the one most likely to elicit excitement from the fanbase, it seems a natural thematic fit with "Be Here Now." It is a one-two(-three) punch of, "Hey, remember how great we were? Well, now, get over it already."

Moreover, as Ringo shout-sings the closing line, "I'm gonna be the greatest in this world, in the *next* world, and in *any* world!" we cannot help but notice that he can't really mean this. He doesn't really believe that. It isn't a boast. It's a nod toward what fans might believe, and might *think* he believes, which in the singing sounds a cautionary note of self-reflection — a note that is then taken up immediately by George. The two tracks could not fit more perfectly together in temperament, music, and theme.

Where "I'm the Greatest" really excels, however, is in how it builds. From a simple set of verses with an obvious chronology, the song and track builds to a climax befitting the best tracks of the solo years. Its ending is significantly more effective than its beginning, the latter actually in service to the former. With a bigger beginning, the track would be less effective. But that very component is what makes it a lousy opener. It will sound markedly better with something before it.

What that something is will have to come later, but since the ending of "I'm the Greatest" works perfectly with the opening of "Be Here Now," and the duo makes a very strong thematic pairing, the Assembler will put them together as a unit at the end of the first disc.

```
. . .
2Y.  I'm the Greatest (R)
2Z.  Be Here Now (G)
```

Three of the eight pole tracks required for a double album have now been placed. The next step is to seek the rest. Perhaps most obvious are the three songs which became big hits, and could easily have been recognized as such in advance. "Live and Let Die," the familiar recording simply recast as a Beatle track, becomes the opener of side two. "Photograph," the Harrison/Starr collaboration which surprised many but would not have surprised our Assembler, leads off side three. And Harrison's "Give Me Love (Give Me Peace on Earth)" can be paired with "Mind Games" to start side four with big ideas before the record wraps up with rock.

Pole tracks to end sides one and three are somewhat more difficult to identify, though knowing what will follow them after the flip of the disc is helpful. Among other things, it eliminates some options for parity reasons. Thus, to precede Paul's side two opener, options from John, George and Ringo include "Try Some, Buy Some," which looks like a possibility by virtue of its long fadeout. But "Don't Let Me

Wait Too Long" gets the nod as a stronger, more upbeat way to end side one. And to precede George's side four opener, in John, Paul, and Ringo's remaining tracks we find, "Let Me Roll It," which looks plausible, but is bested by "Step Lightly" as the best way to end side three. Unfortunately, neither of these comes with a natural pairing to set it up, though having tried "Try Some, Buy Some" to end side three, it turns out that it works just as well right before Ringo's side closer.

1A. PROLOGUE: Be Here Now (G) [Edit]	Bluebird (P)
1B. Bring on the Lucie (Freda Peeple) (J)	≈ Day the World...'Round (G)
1C. Hi, Hi, Hi (P)	Down and Out (R)
1D. Sunshine Life for Me... (R)	I Know (I Know) (J)
. . .	Intuition (J)
1Z. Don't Let Me Wait Too Long (G)	≈ Let Me Roll It (P)
	≈ Living...Material World (G)
2A. Live and Let Die (P)	Mama's Little Girl (P)
. . .	Mess I'm In, The (P)
2Y. I'm the Greatest (R)	My Love (P)
2Z. Be Here Now (G)	One Day (At a Time) (J)
	One More Kiss (P)
3A. Photograph (R)	Only People (J)
. . .	Out the Blue (J)
3Y. Try Some, Buy Some (G)	≈ Sue Me, Sue You Blues (G)
3Z. Step Lightly (R)	≈ That Is All (G)
	≈ Tight A$ (J)
4A. Give Me Love... (G)	You and Me (Babe) (R)
4B. Mind Games (J)	You Are Here (J)
. . .	
4W. Helen Wheels (P)	
4X. Night Out (P)	
4Y. Meat City (J) [Edit]	
4Z. CODA: Be Here Now (G) [Edit]	

At this point, the list of available tracks still contains a couple of very strong songs that haven't been programmed. Two of Paul's slower tracks will need careful placement and context. "My Love" will need to be sandwiched between songs which are at least modestly more energetic, but not too much so. Similarly, "Bluebird" will need something to bounce off of.

To the former, "My Love" would be wrong on side four, and somehow feels like it needs to be forward in the line-up, and likely on side one since the Assembler would see it as a potential hit. Though such a track wouldn't typically go in the middle of a side, the closer it gets to an edge, the harder it is to give the proper bed. The first try at placing it would therefore be after "Sunshine Life for Me (Sail Away Raymond)" — a pseudo-novelty, which creates a space into which something more serious can slide. When that turns out to work just fine, the question becomes about coming out of its big finish and bridging the space to George's closer. In some ways it comes down to how the following track opens, and after trying a couple of possibilities, the lazy smoothness of John's "You Are Here" (complete with a "nine" to gently puncture Paul's heightened mood) creates both the perfect release for "My Love" and setup for "Don't Let Me Wait Too Long." Side one is complete.

1A.	PROLOGUE: Be Here Now (G) [Edit]	
1B.	Bring on the Lucie (Freda Peeple) (J)	
1C.	Hi, Hi, Hi (P)	
1D.	Sunshine Life for Me... (R)	
1M.	**My Love (P)**	
1N.	**You Are Here (J)**	
1Z.	Don't Let Me Wait Too Long (G)	

"Bluebird," being a more complex song, provides more of a challenge. It definitely seems something of a kindred spirit to Lennon's "One Day (At a Time)," perhaps because of very simpatico saxophone solos, though the atrocious backup vocals on the latter would have to be cleaned up before it could be truly declared as Beatle-worthy. Because "Bluebird" ends cold, and "One Day (At a Time)" opens cold, it makes sense to program them in that order, with the sax solo tag at the end nicely summing up the sequence. This then can bump comfortably against George's opening to "Try Some, Buy Some" near the end of side three.

The gap before "Bluebird" then becomes the next natural object of attention. Whatever comes out of the majestic fade to Ringo and George's "Photograph" will have to change the mood, preferably with its first sound. Though "Tight A$" jumps off the list as a possibility, the chunky opening of "The Mess I'm In" actually works better. Happily, however, the chaotic end of that song actually provides the perfect bed for "Tight A$," with the drum sounds at the transition matching nicely.

Though not actually intentional, the resulting move from John back to Paul, that is from "Tight A$" to "Bluebird," is completely smooth, allowing side three to be declared complete and, counting "Photograph" also in George's column, with all of the Beatles represented twice.

3A.	Photograph (R)
3F.	**The Mess I'm In (P)**
3G.	**Tight A$ (J)**
3M.	**Bluebird (P)**
3N	**One Day (At a Time) (J)**
3Y.	Try Some, Buy Some (G)
3Z.	Step Lightly (R)

With side two looking somewhat daunting, the hole in side four seems like the easiest thing to fill next. Since Ringo is noticeably missing from this line-up, we will look to his remaining availables for a solution. Of those, his original song, "Down and Out" fits the best. It opens with a Harrison guitar lick, and its cold close creates the perfect spot for McCartney to step in with his Land Rover. Side four is thus complete and well-formed.

1A. PROLOGUE: Be Here Now (G) [Edit]	≈ Day the World...'Round (G)
1B. Bring on the Lucie (Freda Peeple) (J)	I Know (I Know) (J)
1C. Hi, Hi, Hi (P)	Intuition (J)
1D. Sunshine Life for Me... (R)	≈ Let Me Roll It (P)
1M. My Love (P)	≈ Living...Material World (G)
1N. You Are Here (J)	Mama's Little Girl (P)
1Z. Don't Let Me Wait Too Long (G)	One More Kiss (P)
	Only People (J)
	Out the Blue (J)
2A. Live and Let Die (P)	≈ Sue Me, Sue You Blues (G)
...	≈ That Is All (G)
2Y. I'm the Greatest (R)	You and Me (Babe) (R)
2Z. Be Here Now (G)	

- 3A. Photograph (R)
- **3F. The Mess I'm In (P)**
- **3G. Tight A$ (J)**
- **3M. Bluebird (P)**
- **3N One Day (At a Time) (J)**
- 3Y. Try Some, Buy Some (G)
- 3Z. Step Lightly (R)

- 4A. Give Me Love... (G)
- 4B. Mind Games (J)
- **4M. Down and Out (R)**
- 4W. Helen Wheels (P)
- 4X. Night Out (P)
- 4Y. Meat City (J) [Edit]
- 4Z. CODA: Be Here Now (G) [Edit]

The last gap, that on side two, is difficult in part because of its significance. We know that it begins with Paul's very large soundtrack song, and ends with our Big Themes. In between, the songs must bring the two ends together organically, without overwhelming them. In other words, it's not that these tracks have to be big or intense in any specific way, but they must act as glue to fill a critical crack.

Two tracks remain which also speak to the history of the group, albeit in very different ways. George's "Sue Me, Sue You Blues" has lyrics which might not have been written in exactly that way if the group had still been collaborating. But it is so catchy, and the subject matter now so familiar to all involved, that it feels like a natural to include. Likewise, "Let Me Roll It" remains, and we are assuming that John would have had no interest in using his veto, especially since Paul has always insisted that it isn't about what everyone thinks it's about. Together, these two tracks make a complex of *acknowledgment*, a subtle clearing of the air before getting to the Big Stuff.

Using those two songs along with what is already there leaves us a bit too light on John's voice. The tracks of his that remain on our list, however, are starting to look rather slight against everything else. "Intuition" is the best of them, and a quick listen next to the songs already selected demonstrates that it gets a new lease on life when following "Live and Let Die." John's pop music sounds great next to Paul's drama music, like two sides of a coin. Following it with "Let Me Roll It" also works surprisingly well, demonstrating yet again the versatility of these two songwriters, and how proximity lifts them both.

"Sue Me, Sue You Blues" then follows Paul, leaving one hole to fill: between that and John and Ringo's big track. We start with the idea that, for balance purposes, this should probably be a John track. That's not hard and fast, of course, but using any other voice would leave the side lopsided. Of John's four available songs, two are pure pop, and this seems like the right tone for the spot.

Unfortunately, the lyrics to the bouncy, clap-along "Only People" read like a cliché, especially when compared to everything else on this side:

> *Only people know just how to talk to people*
> *Only people know just how to change the world*
> *Only people realize the power of people*
> *Well, a million heads are better than one*
> *So come on*

On the other hand, the sentiments of the straight pop "I Know (I Know)" make the song seem like it was tailor-made for this spot:

> *The years have passed so quickly*
> *One thing I've understood*
> *I am only learning*
> *To tell the trees from the wood*

In a happy accident, "I Know (I Know)" ends cold, on the lyric, "no more cryin'," with its final chord sort of just hanging in the air. Into that moment, the opening piano chord of "I'm the Greatest" slides perfectly, and even in a relative key.[2] Both the chord and the first lyric, "When I was a little boy…" sound entirely like an intentional connection. The two songs, indeed their two central ideas, sound as if they belong together.

Thus, the assembly is capped with serendipity, while balance is maintained, and the flow from song to song is exceptionally smooth. All Beatles get their due, and two of John's lesser songs are offered distinct elevation by the other Beatles. Side two, and the album, are now complete.

1A. PROLOGUE: Be Here Now (G) [Edit]	≈ C Moon (P)
1B. Bring on the Lucie (Freda Peeple) (J)	≈ Day the World…'Round (G)
1C. Hi, Hi, Hi (P)	Devil Woman (R)
1D. Sunshine Life for Me… (R)	Hands of Love (P)
1M. My Love (P)	≈ Have You Seen My Baby (R)
1N. You Are Here (J)	≈ Living…Material World (G)
1Z. Don't Let Me Wait Too Long (G)	Mama's Little Girl (P)
	≈ Miss O'Dell (G)
	≈ Nutopian… Anthem (J)
2A. Live and Let Die (P)	Oh My My (R)
2C. Intuition (J)	One More Kiss (P)
2M. ≈ Let Me Roll It (P)	Only People (J)
2N. ≈ Sue Me, Sue You Blues (G)	Out the Blue (J)
2T. I Know (I Know) (J)	≈ Rock 'N' Roll People (J)
2Y. I'm the Greatest (R)	≈ Six O'Clock (R)
2Z. Be Here Now (G)	≈ That Is All (G)
	≈ Tragedy (P)
	≈ When the Night (P)
3A. Photograph (R)	You and Me (Babe) (R)
3F. The Mess I'm In (P)	≈ You're Sixteen (R)
3G. Tight A$ (J)	
3M. Bluebird (P)	
3N One Day (At a Time) (J)	
3Y. Try Some, Buy Some (G)	
3Z. Step Lightly (R)	

4A. Give Me Love… (G)
4B. Mind Games (J)
4M. Down and Out (R)
4W. Helen Wheels (P)
4X. Night Out (P)
4Y. Meat City (J) [Edit]
4Z. CODA: Be Here Now (G) [Edit]

---

[2] The movement is from F# minor (in the key of A) to B Major, which John then outlines by playing an F# as his second note in the left hand.

Be Here Now

(Double album)
Principal Recording: September 1972 - November 1973
Release: December 1973

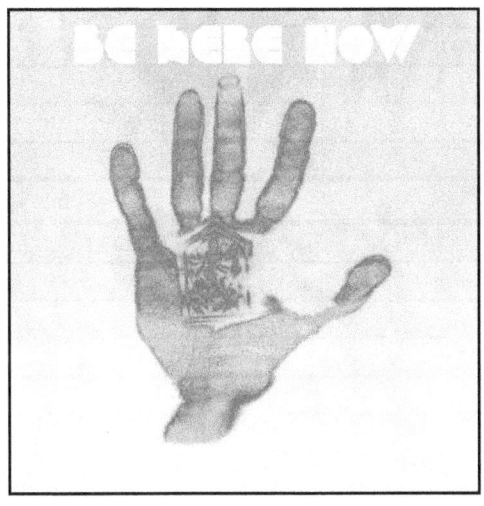 

Side One
1. PROLOGUE: Be Here Now (Harrison)
2. Bring on the Lucie (Freda Peeple) (Lennon)
3. Hi, Hi, Hi (McCartney*)
4. Sunshine Life for Me
   (Sail Away Raymond) (Harrison)
5. My Love (McCartney*)
6. You Are Here (Lennon)
7. Don't Let Me Wait Too Long (Harrison)

Side Two
1. Live and Let Die (McCartney*)
2. Intuition (Lennon)
3. Let Me Roll It (McCartney*)
4. Sue Me, Sue You Blues (Harrison)
5. I Know (I Know) (Lennon)
6. I'm the Greatest (Lennon)
7. Be Here Now (Harrison)

Side Three
1. Photograph (Starkey/Harrison)
2. The Mess I'm In (McCartney*)
3. Tight A$ (Lennon)
4. Bluebird (McCartney*)
5. One Day (At a Time) (Lennon)
6. Try Some, Buy Some (Harrison)
7. Step Lightly (Starkey)

Side Four
1. Give Me Love
   (Give Me Peace on Earth) (Harrison)
2. Mind Games (Lennon)
3. Down and Out (Starkey)
4. Helen Wheels (McCartney*)
5. Night Out (McCartney)
6. Meat City (Lennon)
7. CODA: Be Here Now (Harrison)

* Originally "McCartney/McCartney"

Make It Yourself

Total Running Time: 1:33:50

Tk	Rill	Title	Source	Dur
F3-A1	—	Prologue: Be Here Now [Edit]	[1]	1:10
F3-A2	0	Bring on the Lucie (Freda People)	[2]	4:10
F3-A3	(2.0)	Hi, Hi, Hi	[3, bonus]	3:05
F3-A4	0	Sunshine Life for Me (Sail Away Raymond)	[4]	2:41
F3-A5	(1.2)	My Love	[3]	4:05
F3-A6	0	You Are Here	[2]	4:07
F3-A7	0	Don't Let Me Wait Too Long	[1]	2:58
			Total:	22:20
F3-B1	—	Live and Let Die	[3, bonus]	3:08
F3-B2	(2.0)	Intuition	[2]	3:06
F3-B3	(1.0)	Let Me Roll It [Edit]	[5]	3:49
F3-B4	0	Sue Me, Sue You Blues [Edit]	[1]	3:19
F3-B5	0	I Know (I Know)	[2]	3:44
F3-B6	(2.4)	I'm the Greatest	[4]	3:19
F3-B7	(3.5)	Be Here Now	[1]	4:12
			Total:	24:40
F3-C1	—	Photograph	[4]	3:55
F3-C2	0	Mess I'm In, The [Studio version, edit]	[3, bonus]	4:36
F3-C3	0	Tight A$	[2]	3:39
F3-C4	2.5	Bluebird	[5]	3:19
F3-C5	(1.5)	One Day (At a Time)	[2]	3:06
F3-C6	0	Try Some, Buy Some	[1]	3:57
F3-C7	(7.0)	Step Lightly	[4]	3:17
			Total:	25:53
F3-D1	—	Give Me Love (Give Me Peace on Earth)	[1]	3:31
F3-D2	(3.0)	Mind Games [Edit]	[2]	4:10
F3-D3	(1.0)	Down and Out	[4, bonus]	3:00
F3-D4	0	Helen Wheels	[5]	3:37
F3-D5	(6.0)	Night Out	[3, bonus]	2:28
F3-D6	(4.5)	Meat City [Edit]	[2]	2:47
F3-D7	0	Coda: Be Here Now [Edit]	[1]	1:22
			Total:	23:56

[1] *Living in the Material World*
[2] *Mind Games* (seek the 2003 remix versions)
[3] *Red Rose Speedway*
[4] *Ringo*
[5] *Band on the Run*

NOTE: Descriptions of edits and crossfades, with sample audio, are available at: **SaveTheBeatles.com**

Release
December 1973

Most Popular Albums
November 1971 - November 1973

US		UK	
Allman Brothers Band	*Brothers and Sisters*	The Beatles	*The Beatles 1962-1966*
The Beatles	*The Beatles 1967-1970*	The Beatles	*The Beatles 1967-1970*
Bread	*The Best of Bread*	Carpenters	*Now & Then*
Cat Stevens	*Teaser and the Firecat*	Cat Stevens	*Teaser and the Firecat*
Chicago	*Chicago V*	David Bowie	*Aladdin Sane*
Curtis Mayfield	*Superfly*	David Bowie	*Hunky Dory*
Don McLean	*American Pie*	David Bowie	*...Ziggy Stardust and...*
Elton John	*Goodbye Yellow Brick...*	David Cassidy	*Cherish*
Elton John	*Honky Chateau*	Don McLean	*American Pie*
Led Zeppelin	*Houses of the Holy*	Elton John	*Don't Shoot Me I'm...*
Led Zeppelin	*Led Zeppelin IV*	Elton John	*Goodbye Yellow Brick...*
Pink Floyd	***Dark Side of the Moon***	Gilbert O'Sullivan	*Back to Front*
Roberta Flack	*First Take*	Gilbert O'Sullivan	*Himself*
The Rolling Stones	*Hot Rocks 1964-1971*	Lindisfarne	*Fog on the Tyne*
Seals & Crofts	*Diamond Girl*	Peters and Lee	*We Can Make It*
Seals & Crofts	*Summer Breeze*	Pink Floyd	*Dark Side of the Moon*
Soundtrack	*Shaft*	Rod Stewart	*Never a Dull Moment*
Stevie Wonder	*Innervisions*	**Simon and Garfunkel**	***Greatest Hits***
Stevie Wonder	*Talking Book*	Slade	*Slade Alive!*
War	*The World Is a Ghetto*	T. Rex	*Electric Warrior*

Most popular album in bold

Two years have passed, and a great many significant releases have come and gone and begun to change the pop music landscape. It is hard to measure the absence of the Beatles, but their reentry as a source of nostalgia definitely had an impact, occupying three slots here. Likewise, the presence of records like Simon and Garfunkel's compilation, the Rolling Stones' compilation, *American Pie*, and two of Gilbert O'Sullivan's 60's pastiche albums, adds fuel to the nostalgia fire. Also just off this list is the King himself, with *Aloha from Hawaii*.

Another round of mature singer/songwriters (Cat Stevens, Elton, Stevie Wonder) has blossomed. Neil Diamond, Neil Young, Harry Nilsson and Paul Simon all have albums just below the cutoff for this list. Likewise, art-rock (Bowie, Pink Floyd) and soft rock (Seals & Crofts, Bread, Roberta Flack) are coming into their own.

In all, this is a landscape perfectly ripe for the anti-nostalgia message at the heart of *Be Here Now*. Had the music been not quite as good, one can imagine that lesson falling on deaf ears. As it is, however, the Beatles might even have lapped this field, throwing all the aforementioned categories into a bit of self-reflection.

Topping the Charts
December 1973

US			UK	
Elton John	*Goodbye Yellow...*	1	Roxy Music	*Stranded*
Ringo Starr	*Ringo*	2	David Bowie	*Pin Ups*
The Who	*Quadrophenia*	3	David Cassidy	*Dreams Are...*
Neil Diamond	*Jonathan Livingston...*	4	Black Sabbath	*Sabbath Bloody...*
Jim Croce	*You Don't Mess...*	5	Perry Como	*And I Love You So*
Rolling Stones	*Goats Head Soup*	6	Gilbert O'sullivan	*I'm a Writer Not...*
Steve Miller Band	*The Joker*	7	David Essex	*Rock On*
Allman Brothers Band	*Brothers And Sisters*	8	The Who	*Quadrophenia*
Jim Croce	*Life And Times*	9	Ringo Starr	*Ringo*
Cheech & Chong	*Los Cochinos*	10	Nazareth	*Loud 'n' Proud*

At what would have been the moment of release for *Be Here Now*, Ringo was already a presence near the top of the album charts — the one and only time he ever had that distinction. This success plays directly into the narrative that the public still clamored for Beatles, even after several years, and all the clamoring may have been the fuel for this particularly nostalgic moment.

In our slightly altered narrative, his album does not exist, but is subsumed into the group project. This suggests that the Beatles could have again debuted very near the top of the charts. But in this instance, it seems very possible that success by the Beatles might have come at the expense of another artist.

How might the career of Elton John been affected if the Beatles were still releasing throughout the 70s? Though a very hard thing to quantify, it's almost certain that he would have been hurt. The void left by the Beatles clearly aided Elton's emergence as super-charged singer-songwriter, and he slipped neatly into the space vacated by the group. Obviously, he was not the only act to do that, but at his peak — which begins here — he was very nearly as big as they had ever been. Conversely, his synergy with the cultural moment might have stepped on some of the Beatles' remaining momentum. Despite not being able to quantify either scenario, it seems clear that there would have been uncomfortable overlap.

That overlap is not 100%, but it is significant. It's not our purpose here to calculate that percentage, but it's definitely worth noting that this is the moment when acts like Elton, ELO and more soft-rock acts like the Allman Brothers, America, Seals & Crofts, Harry Nilsson, and Bread began to emerge, potentially as a direct result of the vacuum left by the Beatles breakup. The continuation of the group might have closed the loophole into which they fit, or at least modified what they could and could not do. Then again, all of these artists were highly talented, and may have been able to ride along right next to the biggest group the world had ever known, perhaps even eclipsing it at times.

In other words, it's not that these acts wouldn't have landed without that vacuum, but merely to acknowledge that a significant subset of recording artists were certainly aided by the Beatles breakup as the market began to look for something to fill a very large unguarded slice of the audience, one the solo Beatles could not capture reliably on their own. Of course, had they still been releasing, the aging Beatles might not have looked quite as vital as we might want to imagine — which merely has to be allowed as a possibility.

This moment on the charts is very typical of that phenomenon, and dropping a Beatles album into this market would have caused significant ripples on the careers of these artists, and through popular music in general — which we have to admit was one of their strongest abilities from the very start.

Discussion

After two years without any new music, what a treat it would have been to find a new Beatles double album in stores at Christmas of 1973. In addition to filling a whole lot of Christmas stockings, it might have changed the shape of 70s popular music for several years.

In our imagined narrative, this would have been the third Beatles double album, and reviewers would have noticed right away how little resemblence it bears to the other two. In retrospect, *The White Album* would have seemed somewhat embryonic, perhaps even naïve by comparison. *Dream*, which would have been three years old at this point, would have now looked much more fraught, more tense, much more emotional in many ways.

In context with those, *Be Here Now* looks and sounds almost serene, at least until it starts to wind up on side four, sending the listener back out into the world with a shot of newly urgent Beatle energy. That final burst, when coupled with the other rockers, would have reminded everyone of just how powerful the Beatles could be, even as the presence of plenty of pop would have kept them squarely in the mainstream.

Keep in mind that all of this new music would have been heard in context of the Beatles' 10-year anniversary, and the retrospective albums which, in our altered narrative, would have been issued a few months earlier than they actually were to cover the absence of anything new in 1972. Thus the comparison between "old" and "new" Beatles would have been stark, even surprising. What we hear by compiling all of this music into one album is that the Beatles still have a distinct style all their own, and it has continued to evolve at a steady pace. This is considerably less noticeable when hearing this music spread across multiple solo albums which are filled out with other, lesser music.

Harrison, especially, sounds like not just the sage of the group, but also an accomplished pop master. His work is every bit as strong as Lennon's or McCartney's, and he clearly has earned his place as their equal in terms of balance. Likewise, Ringo sounds great, getting only features that highlight his special abilities. No doubt many of the tracks which were singles — and hits — in the real world, would have experienced the same result with the Beatles name attached. This album would have had long legs.

Some of the criticisms which might have applied have been deftly sidestepped. Though relevance was an increasing issue in the real world, and would have been a question before anyone heard this album, no such question remains after hearing it. This music sounds like it belongs squarely in the decade it is found, if slightly ahead of where the market will ultimately move.

Complaints which dogged the solo work — Paul's slightness, George's preachiness, John's politics, Ringo's awkwardness — have no analogues here. This shows how the use of an Assembler might have edited out those qualities most likely to detract from the finished product, without watering it down at all.

If there is a criticism to be leveled, it may be that the production values are less interesting that listeners expected from the Beatles. The Assembler would certainly have had to remix some tracks, and fix some obvious deficiencies, but the fundamentals of the recordings — studios, acoustics, microphones, etc. — likely could not have been mitigated completely. The credits on a project like this probably would have read, "Produced by The Beatles. Executive Producer: The Assembler." In this way some of the vagaries in sound are explained away.

Still, the lack of studio innovation would have caught the ears of reviewers. Some might have lamented this loss, while others would have seen, correctly, that the Beatles now transcended the idea that the studio could make up for things missing from their own songwriting and performing. By this point, it would have been recognized that the group was much more concerned with the songs themselves, and the performances, rather than the recording techniques — a shift that would have been in progress since 1970 at this point, and here reaches its first fruition.

Importantly, however, the leaps in fidelity which began driving popular music at about this time essentially eluded the solo Beatles. Nothing any of them ever recorded sounds as deeply polished as, say, *Fleetwood Mac* or *Dark Side of the Moon*. At this point, however it doesn't represent much of a problem for the group. To their audience, it would have been irrelevant.

Indeed, the mere fact that you could have a Beatles double album in your hands at this point would have delighted many. That alone justifies the project, and allows the Beatles to spread their simple message about the need to be here, in this moment, now, and not in some faded past.

Fusion Era #4

December 1973-May 1975

Vienna

15 / VIENNA

"[The Beatles] might do bits together again, we don't know yet... I don't think we'll get together as a band again. I just don't think it'll work actually. It might not be as good."

— Paul McCartney, March 1974

"How can we get together if George won't play with Paul?"

— Ringo Starr, November 1974

"For us to do that, we'd have to do it more than just to resurrect what went on in the 60s. So...whatever format we did together, it would have to be interesting to us musically...otherwise there'd be no point. We don't want to just do it for the old time's sake. We do it because we want to."

— John Lennon, December 1974

"We all grew up, lived in a room together for years and years, and it's a natural thing for each one of us to develop individually."

— George Harrison, December 1974

Chronology

1973

Band on the Run released	DEC	Phil Spector steals *Rock 'n' Roll* tapes

1974

Patti Boyd moves in with Eric Clapton	JAN	Recording *McGear* with brother Michael
Producing Harry Nilsson (*Pussy Cats*) Famously heckles Smothers Brothers	MAR	Paul and John, "A Toot and a Snore in '74" Announces intention to tour
Holds auditions for Wings	APR	Returns to NY with May Pang Producing Mick Jagger
Launches Dark Horse Records with A&M	MAY	Strong reunion rumors floating around
Travels to Nashville for recording sessions	JUN	Recovers *Rock 'n' Roll* tapes
Recording *Walls and Bridges*	JUL	First ever Beatles convention held in Boston
Recording *Goodnight Vienna* Working on *One Hand Clapping* (TV)	AUG	Recording with Elton John Reports seeing a UFO
Launches Ring O' Records with Polydor	SEP	*Walls and Bridges* released
Announces Wings world tour "Junior's Farm" released	OCT	Resumes recording *Rock 'n' Roll* Meets Olivia Arias
Dark Horse North America Tour (25 shows) Begins recording *Venus and Mars* Guests on stage with Rod Stewart	NOV	*Goodnight Vienna* released Guests on stage with Elton John Meets Ono backstage at Elton concert
Dark Horse North America Tour (19 shows) Meets US President Gerald Ford *Dark Horse* released	DEC	Agree to dissolve Beatles partnership *The Today Show* (TV) Signs dissolution papers at Disneyworld

1975

Recording with David Bowie Reconciles with Ono, end of "Lost Weekend"	**JAN**	Recording *Venus and Mars* in New Orleans
Making *Lizstomania* (film)	**FEB**	*Roots* bootleg LP released *Rock 'n' Roll* rush-released
Presenter at *17th Annual Grammys* (TV)	**MAR**	Wins Grammy for *Band on the Run*
Salute to Lew Grade (TV, last performance) *The Tomorrow Show* (TV)	**APR**	*The Smothers Brothers Show* (TV)
Apple Studio closes	**MAY**	*Venus and Mars* released

Introduction

In the real world of 1974, the former Beatles were riding the twin highs of the four-disc retrospective, and four separately successful solo albums. No one was in much of a hurry to make a new album. In fact, the first six months of the year passed with hardly a single recording session among them, as they enjoyed watching multiple singles and albums march, one after another, up the charts.

This is obviously a moment when we might pause to wonder whether continuing the group would even have been necessary. Maybe the Beatles did better for themselves by breaking up. Chart numbers, sales numbers and profit numbers aren't the same thing, of course, but success is success, right?

In support of that idea, remember that those four particular solo albums were arguably the best, most consistent overall, quartet of vinyl the former Beatles would ever produce simultaneously. *Ringo* and *Band on the Run* are often hailed as the best albums made by their respective artists, while *Mind Games* and *Living in the Material World*, though not as highly regarded, still rank near the top for each artist.

We will not ask these questions, however — or ask and answer them, if you prefer — because it is entirely self-evident that *Be Here Now* (or some other group project like it) would likely have been orders of magnitude more satisfying than three of these solo albums, even if it were made from their parts. And that fourth album, *Band on the Run*, which is left nearly unchanged in our slightly altered narrative, would presumably have experienced a similar level of success regardless of what the group did.

Further, with the Beatle mystique firmly reanimated by the oldies, and refreshed by a new, imagined, fused album, the public would have clamored for more Beatles product, something which didn't really ever happen with the solo albums — *clamoring*, that is. Though they were technically hits, the chart appearances for three of the four were relatively fleeting, and contemporary reviews were all over the board. Such would not have been the case with the group project. Any concerns about the group's relevance would have been allayed, and the "Beatle moment" which happened with the release of "blue" and "red" would have been happily extended and amplified.

So, we will move forward with the group resolving to continue using the meta-Beatles model indefinitely. The leftovers from *Be Here Now* might have made their way out as reconfigured solo albums, the relative success of which is essentially irrelevant. And the assumption would have been that they could hastily assemble a follow-up group album in time for Christmas of 1974.

That, however, would have turned out to be surprisingly difficult, and for an unexpected reason: This is the era when John, George and Ringo all split from their spouses. Despite the reprieve in musical stressors, the personal situations became increasingly complicated and difficult, with twists and turns right out of a soap opera. Coupled with the ingestion of copious controlled substances, this set the stage for John's infamous "lost weekend" — heartily joined at times by Ringo — and George's "naughty period." Paul, though stable with Linda, was still stinging from the breakup of Wings before Lagos. All four Beatles were in an unsettled state, and this had a noticeable impact on their productivity.

When recording sessions resumed in July, our Assembler would have been wary. Stories of wild behavior were all over the tabloids, and very little of the music would have sounded up to BQ requirements — at least at first. Harrison was going on tour, and his sessions in Los Angeles (which eventually became *Dark Horse*) were producing dreadful results. Reviews of the tour did not have buoy anyone's hopes.

Sometime during the fall, it would have become necessary to push the next release out at least six months, giving all of the artists more time to produce material up to the usual standards. The ongoing success of the previous album would actually have made this a rather easy decision, as *Be Here Now* likely would have remained on the charts for many months.

By the end of 1974, all but George would finally have filled their quotas, and the Assembler would have had to make a tough call: Go with the best of George's bad lot? Change the balance between songwriters and absorb the fallout? Or hold out hope that something better from him would come along? We will have the Assembler wait, unwilling to tarnish the Beatle brand in any way, and that will turn out to be sufficient — though it will be a close call.

The solo albums that actually came out of this cycle, the ones from which *Vienna* would have been created, were another mixed bag — mixed enough that, in the real world of 1975, the relevance of three of the former Beatles was openly in question. The diehard fans were satisfied, but their numbers were fading. Even the music that made a splash disappeared quickly, leaving barely a ripple on the sea of pop music. Only Paul had successfully found his second act, and in the real world, only he was now carrying the banner of undeniable relevance, and therefore, Beatlemania.

Such would not have been the case had there been a group album. As we will see, relevance would have been far from anyone's mind as the Beatles did again what they had already done so many times. They would have pushed the goal out once again, and once again exceeded it. Such is the power of the Beatle Magic, even when animated from this great distance.

15 / VIENNA

Recording
June 1974 – May 1975

ⓐ Studio recording   ◉ Single release   ✈ Touring

The first half of 1974 saw almost no recording at all from the former Fabs — at least for themselves. Paul produced his brother's album, and John produced Harry Nilsson's. George and Ringo each launched record labels, Dark Horse Records and Ring O'Records respectively, leading them to focus more on other artists.

But in truth, the priority was much more on partying than making music, although the two activities coincided more often than they probably should have. Among the resulting oddities was a jam session in California which included both John and Paul, along with a host of other famous faces. Known today as "A Toot and a Snore in '74," the session produced no listenable music, but the surviving recording offers a peak into what it was like to be a rock and roll icon, potentially past prime, in the mid 1970s. It was also the last time the two musicians would ever play together.

Not long after, McCartney held auditions to fill out the gaps in the Wings lineup, then recorded briefly in Nashville, went back home and made a TV special that was never released, then traveled to New Orleans to begin work on *Venus and Mars*. Anecdotes from this time say that Paul invited John to join him in New Orleans to write some new songs, and that John planned to accept, but it never came to pass.

Ultimately, *Venus and Mars* was viewed as a worthy follow-up to *Band on the Run*, despite not having the same transcendent quality. It yielded multiple hits that were perfect for playing in front of an arena crowd, which set the table for Paul to tour again — a highly successful world tour which spanned more than a year, and encompassed the recording and release of yet another studio album along the way, while also eventually yielding a hit three-disc live album.

In the fall of 1974, George announced his own tour and then made a record so he would have something to promote on the road. The resulting album, called *Dark Horse* like his new record label, documented his personal upheaval, but did not connect well with listeners, who complained about the quality of the songs and George's voice. Similarly, the tour performances disappointed audiences for the same reasons — plus the incongruous presence of Ravi Shankar as opening act. Audiences also bristled at George's decision to alter certain sacrosanct lyrics. Any goodwill remaining from his early solo success and charitable activities was finally and fully exhausted.

With all of that baggage, George resumed recording, picking up right about where he left off and eventually assembling *Extra Texture (Read All About It)*. If anything, it was received even more harshly than its predecessor, and sold even fewer copies, which would hardly have been thought possible.

Ringo decided to take no chances — well, no *musical* chances — on his next album, and followed something akin to the formula used for *Ringo*. Only one former Beatle agreed to participate, reducing the interest among fans, but John Lennon's song became the title track. Other famous names on the album included Billy Preston, Harry Nilsson and Elton John. The one chance he took was with the artwork, which was based inexplicably on the classic sci-fi B-movie from the 1950s, *The Day the Earth Stood Still*. This seemingly random connection was never fully explained (more on this below). Though the album made a fleeting appearance on the US charts, it had no impact whatsoever in the UK, and most reviewers saw *Goodnight Vienna* as a pale shadow of its predecessor.

It was John who had two full-scale recording projects in this era. First came the May Pang-inspired *Walls and Bridges*, which featured an immensely successful collaboration with Elton John that provided Lennon with his first solo number one single. Reviews of the album were generally positive, but with reservations. Despite considering it an improvement over *Mind Games*, it was still seen as uneven, and only partially satisfying.

Lennon's other project was to finally finish *Rock 'n' Roll* and clear the decks of the "Come Together" copyright infringement lawsuit. The tapes that Phil Spector had confiscated were recovered, but pretty quickly proved discouraging since most ears could tell there had been a bit too much partying involved in the sessions. The best tracks were retained and repaired, while a new batch of songs were recorded

15 / VIENNA

very quickly in New York. The resulting album initially saw release in an unauthorized version sold through mail order, the result of Lennon passing a rough assembly tape to exactly the wrong person — the unscrupulous Morris Levy, initiator of the lawsuit. Even in its authorized version, the album sold only modestly. It would assume a curious place in John's catalog as a project which should have worked, despite its genesis out of contractual obligation, but never found its voice. The single "Stand By Me" remains its most lasting impact.

After that, John reunited with Yoko, disappeared into the Dakota, had a baby and, beyond a quick cameo on Ringo's next album, would not be heard from again until 1980. By then, much water would have passed under the bridges of the other former Beatles' solo careers.

Materials

Overview
87 tracks: 23 eligible, 18 provisional

The imagery in the art of this era includes all sorts of allusions to travel. Two of the former Beatles, Ringo and Paul, appeared headed into space, while the other two were either riding a dark horse or hopping a wall to cross a bridge. Maybe more to the point, all four seem to be considering whether the moment had come to step off the stage. Still, collectively they are not so much saying "goodnight" to Vienna, as something more like, "Let's try somewhere else for a while — maybe Vienna!"

Within that restless envelope, McCartney tells stories about "Lonely Old People," Lennon wanders an "Old Dirt Road," and Harrison finds himself "So Sad" that his guitar "can't keep from crying." All of this makes it more stark that Starkey protests too much, with a happy sheen that we know now was artificial.

Indeed, superficialities abound. To a degree, all four appear to be punching in the rock-n-roll clock. Was John really happier? Was George really so disillusioned? Was Paul really a pop star again? Was Ringo really going to get into that spacecraft and fly away? (Anwer: Yes. See the commercial…)

In collecting their best bits into a single album, we find a previously concealed lightness, and a whole lot of fun. These Beatles may be "Scared" and "Tired…" and "Soily," but they know how to deal with it: It turns out that whatever gets you through the night is alright.

SAVE THE BEATLES!

John Lennon
32 tracks: 6 eligible, 6 provisional

Sources

L10	*Walls and Bridges* R: Jul-Aug 74 P: Lennon S: Record Plant (NY)	74-Sep
L11	*Rock 'n' Roll* R: Oct 73 - Oct 74 P: Lennon/Spector S: A&M (LA), Record Plant (NY)	75-Feb
L12	"~~Stand by Me~~" / "Move Over Ms. L" R: Jul-Oct 74 P: Lennon S: Record Plant (NY)	75-Mar
	(Unreleased)	

Tracks

#9 Dream (Lennon)   L10-07, 74-Aug
✓ A late masterwork, with distinctive music, lyrics, feel. Descended from psychedelia, matured.

Ain't That a Shame (Domino/Bartholomew)   L11-05, 74-Oct
⊘ (Style/Content) Very heavy, busy arrangement. Sounds like work, not fun.

Angel Baby (Hamlin)   L11, 73-Dec
⊘ (Style/Content) Pure wall of sound, Lennon's vocal pretty buried. Just spins aimlessly until it ends.

Be My Baby (Barry/Greenwich/Spector)   L11, 73-Dec
⊘ (Style/Content) Unlike others in the collection in that it at least has shape. JL vocal is compromised.

Be-Bop-A-Lula (Davis/Vincent)   L11-01, 74-Oct
⊘ (Style/Content) Among the better RnR tracks, but still without much shape. JL vocal is nothing special.

Beef Jerky (Lennon)   L10-10, 74-Aug
⊘ (Filler) Fun riff, and nice quote of Macca. Lots of details. Great track, but has no place on an album.

Bless You (Lennon)   L10-05, 74-Aug
✓ Beautiful writing. Soft emotions. Nothing else like it in JL's catalog. Another late masterwork.

Bony Moronie (Williams)   L11-11, 74-Oct
⊘ (Style/Content) Chunky beat. Way overdone. Never quite gets off the ground. Vocal sounds strained.

Bring It on Home to Me/Send Me Some Lovin' (Cooke/Marascalco/Price)   L11-10, 74-Oct
⊘ (Style/Content) Weird reading, with stretched out verses. Like the rest, too much going on. Hiccups.

Do You Wanna Dance? (Freeman)   L11-06, 74-Oct
⊘ (Style/Content) Another vocal shouted over a too-busy, yet somehow shapeless, arrangement

Going Down on Love (Lennon)   L10-01, 74-Aug
≈ (Quality) Weepy self-pity

Here We Go Again (Lennon/Spector)   L11, 73-Dec
≈ (Quality) Very large production, good sounding record, but the song is basically a jot.

Just Because (Price)   L11-13, 74-Oct
⊘ (Style/Content) Closing time sentiment. End-of-the-set vocal. You don't have to go home, but don't stay here.

Just Because (Reprise) (Price)   L11, 73-Dec
⊘ (Style/Content) Shout out to the other Beatles is the only thing of value here.

15 / VIENNA

Move Over Ms. L (Lennon) — L12-02, 74-Oct
≈ (Style/Quality) RnR treatment for a new song is more interesting than the rest of the project.

Nobody Loves You (When You're Down and Out) (Lennon) — L10-11, 74-Aug
≈ (Quality) Weepy, overlong and painfully self-pitying. A low point.

Old Dirt Road (Lennon/Nilsson) — L10-03, 74-Aug
≈ (Quality) Boring

Peggy Sue (Allison/Petty/Holly) — L11-09, 74-Oct
○ (Style/Content) Pure mush. Chiming guitars in the break have potential, but this car has no wheels.

Rip It Up/Ready Teddy (Blackwell/Marascalco) — L11-03, 74-Oct
○ (Style/Content) Among the cleaner tracks on RnR, but still pointless. Workmanlike all around.

Scared (Lennon) — L10-06, 74-Aug
✓ Lives up to its title, and does not go over the top. Fantastic arrangement. Borderline classic.

Since My Baby Left Me (Crudup) — L11, 73-Dec
○ (Style/Content) More fun than most of RnR. JL sounds smooth, playful. Call/response is great, crazy fun.

Slippin' and Slidin' (Bocage/Collins/Penniman/Smith) — L11-08, 74-Oct
○ (Style/Content) Fine, but like the rest, without any sense of fun or joy. Straight reading. Boring.

Stand by Me (Leiber/Stoller/King) — L11-02, 74-Oct
○ (Style/Content) Cleanest track on RnR, and with imaginative arrangement. Still, JL shouts and strains.

Steel and Glass (Lennon) — L10-09, 74-Aug
≈ (Content) All Beatles would have liked the idea

Surprise, Surprise (Sweet Bird of Paradox) (Lennon) — L10-08, 74-Aug
✓ Clean and fresh sound. Great song, fine lyrics, happy sound.

Sweet Little Sixteen (Berry) — L11-07, 74-Oct
○ (Style/Content) The band plods and plods. Sounds like mud in music form. Lousy arrangement, too.

To Know Her Is to Love Her (Spector) — L11, 73-Dec
○ (Style/Content) What the hell were they thinking? Slow ... and long ... and drawn out ... terribly. Awful.

What You Got (Lennon) — L10-04, 74-Aug
✓ Firey, funky, powerful. A late masterwork. Great horns. A total success.

Whatever Gets You thru the Night (Lennon) — L10-02, 74-Aug
✓ Such a good vibe that it's easy to forgive the shallow, me-decade sentiment.

Ya Ya (Dorsey/Levy/Lewis/Robinson) — L10-12, 74-Aug
○ (Filler) Novelty only.

Ya Ya (Dorsey/Levy/Lewis/Robinson) — L11-12, 74-Oct
○ (Style/Content) Among the lighter arrangements. More sprightly. Still, JL sleepwalks through the vocal.

You Can't Catch Me (Berry) — L11-04, 74-Oct
○ (Style/Content) Despite the lawsuit, no malice heard here. Still, the bloated band chugs unhelpfully.

Without anyone knowing it, in this period John Lennon produced his last studio recordings for quite some time. They are a very mixed bag. On the one hand, he revisits some of his favorite music in what should be a triumphant victory lap. Instead, it is a nonevent, filled with recordings that are frustrating and unsatisfying on many levels. On the other hand, he produces a batch of new songs that are a distinct step up from his other recent work, yet still swing wildly in tone and quality, resulting in an album that is roughly equal parts satisfying and disappointing.

Beatle orthodoxy has it that *Walls and Bridges* was a return to form for John, but to latter day ears it sounds more like flashes of form surrounded by the same old wheel-spinning. For every "Whatever Gets You through the Night" there is a "Going Down on Love." For every "What You Got" there is a corresponding "Nobody Loves You (When You're Down and Out)." There is the old vitriol, but now it is even more cringe-inducing. And the project requires an instrumental — certainly great but ultimately better suited to a B-side — to fill out the length.

Had there been an immediate follow-up, it's easy to imagine this album as the bridge to a resurgence of bold creativity, in the same way that *Thirty Three & 1/3* presaged *George Harrison*. Indeed, some of the demos which would later emerge as potential songs for John's intended follow-up suggest that very thing. But it did not happen, so *Walls and Bridges* stands as a sort of ellipsis at the end of John's main body of solo work.

To be clear, the quality of both writing and recording here is a considerable notch up from *Mind Games*. Having a single that went to number one obviously testifies to that fact. Moreover, when John trades in sadness and regret on this disc, it's in the form of tight and highly listenable records. As an example, the album opener, "Going Down on Love," has a bright and punchy horn arrangement which attempts to paper over rather morose lyrics, including a truly desperate-sounding paraphrase of his younger self ("Somebody please, please help me…").

John's trek with Harry Nilsson out onto an "Old Dirt Road" contains a clever reference to Sons of the Pioneers, but only to distract from imagery that is downright desolate. The closer, "Nobody Loves You (When You're Down and Out)," is lyrically right from the self-pitying pit John has mined many times, but its elegant production and elaborate arrangement make it considerably more palatable. In all three cases, however, the tone and content of the songs cannot be overcome by pure studio layering. At their core, songs like this make for a discomfiting listen.

The album's greatest transgression, "Steel and Glass," scars side two. John didn't pull any punches, and it would have been a better track if he had. The song is nearly a direct rewrite of his earlier misstep, "How Do You Sleep?" He would later try to dismiss both songs by claiming that he was talking about himself as much as the apparent targets (Allen Klein and Paul McCartney, respectively), or that he was expressing a strong but fleeting emotion, but John's catalog would be better without either of these tracks. "Steel and Glass" remains provisionally eligible for the group album only because it might have tickled all four Beatle hearts at that particular moment. Our Assembler will let them have a laugh at the expense of their former associate, but leave the track in the archives where it should have stayed.

15 / VIENNA

John tucks a much better, and more sly, acknowledgement of a personal feud into "Beef Jerky," where the unmistakable riff from McCartney's "Let Me Roll It" is plainly heard. It comes off as a very gentle, "Yeah, I heard what you did there," message to Paul, which has much more impact than the full-on attacks of the other songs. Lennon did not often traffic in subtlety, but when he did, he showed complete mastery. Unfortunately, his direct attacks were more visible, and either drew listeners into a hateful (and decidedly non-Beatle-y) space, or caused them to turn away. Neither outcome has any place on a Beatle record.

The greatness of *Walls and Bridges* is found, therefore, in the cracks between these semi-mitigated downers, and could be increased by diminishing their prominence even further. For example, in the context of the album, "What You Got" comes across as surprisingly forgettable, its strengths muted by placement in the dead zone at the middle of side one. This powerful track, which contains Lennon's most fierce vocal performance in years, clearly belongs in a pole position. Indeed, it would be the last time he would ever offer such a passionate performance on an original song. The first line even includes a clear statement of his goal, perhaps trying to get ahead of the inevitable complaints he expected about some of the album's other material: "Don't want to be a drag..." The track is anything but a drag, and would have served especially well on a Beatles project.

"Scared" is another track which disappears into the mists of the album but sounds positively like a masterwork when extracted. The lyrics read like a descendant of "Hold On" from *John Lennon/Plastic Ono Band*, coming down as they do on the side of self-encouragement rather than self-pity, which is most welcome. He turns in another vocal filled with conviction, and the brilliant arrangement by Ken Ascher adds to the power of the track.

The obligatory Yoko track, "Bless You," thankfully does not use her name, which leaves it eligible for inclusion on a group album. Not only does the song avoid apologizing, it actually represents Lennon at his most tender-hearted and open. Music and lyrics are seamlessly interwoven, and the track features a fine vocal over the most satisfying instrumental work on any Lennon album. Though not exactly a classic, at least in its original context, the song actually embodies the unfulfilled potential of John's solo years, being simple, imaginative, emotional, and ultimately relatable to many in the audience. Here he writes both for himself, and for anyone who ever said goodbye to love. The universality of the emotion makes it ideal for a Beatles project, and it's a great shame that the song did not feature more prominently on his solo release.

The obvious "May Pang" track, "Surprise, Surprise (Sweet Bird of Paradox)," also earns the right to be brought forward, at least provisionally. Not as satisfying as "Bless You," it nonetheless has a breeziness and originality that has been missing from much of John's solo work. Those same qualities pervade "#9 Dream," and what might have been a throwaway (John described it as such) becomes a welcome piece of pure pop — the sort that no one but John Lennon could ever create, which makes it a track to treasure.

Still, *Walls and Bridges* feels largely like another missed opportunity. In pulling it apart, however, we find enough good music that it does feel like better assembly would have resulted in a significantly more satisfying album. If we retroactively apply our received assembly techniques, we might get something more like this:

1A.	What You Got
1B.	Surprise, Surprise (Sweet Bird of Paradox)
1C.	Bless You
1Y.	Old Dirt Road
1Z.	Scared
2A.	#9 Dream
2B.	Nobody Loves You (When You're Down...
2X.	Going Down on Love
2Y.	Whatever Gets You Through the Night
2Z.	Ya Ya (Rock 'n' Roll version)

Gone are the worst tracks, and the best are shifted into the most visible positions. Weaker tracks are better disguised. The album is shorter, but still long enough at roughly 40 minutes — a much stronger 40 than the original's 46.

Rock 'n' Roll is the album that every John Lennon fan *wants* to love. Conceptually speaking, what could be more exciting than hearing Lennon revisit the favorite songs of his youth? Only, it isn't exciting, really. It's also not bad, exactly. It just sort of *is*.

Perhaps the biggest problem is that these records do not recapture anything approaching the spirit of the originals, which were uniformly exciting, spare in instrumentation, with electricity provided mainly through distinctive vocal performances. This is what Lennon loved about them originally, and what he was good at himself, so it seems obvious that he could have provided such electricity.

But these records don't even capture Lennon at his best singing. His vocals sound forced, shouted, strained, and bothered by lousy effects. Further, the persistently overblown arrangements tend to bury his voice among the painfully overactive saxophones, emphasizing the least attractive feature of his voice. At every turn, his singing has to compete with other instrumentation instead of being the primary focus, and his performance often sounds pained as a result.

15 / VIENNA

    This is all descended from the same old "wall of sound" problems. Phil Spector's incessant overproduction, which Lennon retained even after Spector was gone, may have sounded fine at one time — I say, *may* — but it definitely sounded terrible in the higher stereo fidelity of the mid-70s, no doubt explaining Spector's famous "Back to Mono" obsession. Not only do the instruments sound like mush, the frenetic over-arranging and over-playing obscures any interesting details. There are simply too many ideas fighting with each other, and every crack in the sound is filled. As a result, there is a sameness to all of these records, as if each is just a new iteration of the same old thing.

    At times the band positively lumbers, barely able to move to the next beat under its own weight. Of all of Lennon's post-Beatles efforts, *Rock 'n' Roll* is the one which cries out most for a radical "stripped down" remix. Even then, I fear the result would be disappointing because of what the cacophony inside the studio forced John and the instrumentalists to do. My further hunch is that the effects were baked into the recordings (versus added in the mix) and the individual source tracks are also mush.

    For our purposes, there is certainly nothing on *Rock 'n' Roll* that merits bringing forward to a fused Beatles album. It may be enough to say that no covers would really be allowed on such a project anyway, and that touches on another reason why the album misfires: Lennon is primarily a *songwriter*. And, more to the point, the songs he wrote are among those which put the old ones out to pasture, adding complexity back into a genre that had valued relatively simple blues-based songs. When considering the material he selected, we find that all of the original *records* were classics, but the *songs* themselves don't have very much to chew on. They are much more like gum than steak, and *Rock 'n' Roll* dramatizes that fact all too well.

    After slogging through the album, one longs for the stripped down intensity of the oldies outtakes from *John Lennon/Plastic Ono Band* and *Imagine*. There John played with nothing to prove, and with a stripped down band. The resulting outtakes are always lively, if also sloppy and generally incomplete. An album of that stuff might not have been much better than this, but I'm inclined to think that it just might have.

    The album would still have been made, of course, even if the Beatles were still collaborating. It was famously part of the settlement for cribbing a single line of Chuck Berry's "You Can't Catch Me" for "Come Together." Perhaps John would have tried to talk the other Beatles into contributing, but they would have wisely declined. Though each former Beatle did eventually revisit oldies from the same era, this was not the right moment. Even if the group was still collaborating from a distance, John would have been left to resolve this himself, which is just as well.

SAVE THE BEATLES!

Paul McCartney
24 tracks: 11 eligible (7 withheld), 5 provisional (4 withheld)
Bracketed tracks are considered in a different era

Sources

M14		"Junior's Farm" / "Sally G" R: Jul 74 P: McCartney	S: Sound Shop (Nashville)	74-Oct
M15		*Venus and Mars* R: Nov 74 - Feb 75 P: McCartney	S: Various (3)	75-May
M21		["Wonderful Christmastime"] / "Rudolph the Red-Nosed Reggae" R: Jun-Jul 79 P: McCartney	S: Various (2)	79-Nov
M22		~~"Coming Up"~~ / ["Coming Up (Live)"] & "Lunchbox/Odd Sox" R: Jan 75 - Jul 79 P: McCartney	S: Various (3)	80-Apr
M28		~~"Take It Away"~~ / "I'll Give You a Ring" R: Jan 74 - Dec 80 P: Martin	S: AIR (London)	82-Jun
		(Unreleased)		

Tracks

◆ *Eligible or provisional but withheld for solo project*

Baby Face (Akst/Davis) ⊘ (Filler) More fun in New Orleans, but just a jot. Best left on a private reel.		M15, 74-Aug
Call Me Back Again (McCartney/McCartney) ✓◆ Overdone, but serves the musical sequence as a setup for the hit.		M15-10, 75-Feb
Crossroads Theme (Hatch) ≈◆ (Content) This clears some of the sweetness of the ending. The band is obviously good.		M15-13, 75-Feb
Going to New Orleans (My Carnival) (McCartney/McCartney) ⊘ (Filler) Really just a 12-bar goof. Light, but not interesting.		M15, 75-Feb
I'll Give You a Ring (McCartney) ≈ (Quality) Music hall. Paul had the good sense not to release this earlier.		M28-02, 73-Dec
Junior's Farm (McCartney/McCartney) ✓ Amazing that Paul could still write songs this good this late. Meaningless fun.		M14-01, 74-Jul
Let's Love (McCartney) ✓ Music hall sad song, but not too twee. Brevity and simplicity are assets here.		M15, 74-Jun
Letting Go (McCartney/McCartney) ✓◆ There is some arena rock heft here, but overwrought. Still, bring on the weed.		M15-06, 74-Nov
Listen to What the Man Said (McCartney/McCartney) ✓ Great radio music, filled with confidence that sells its odd chorus-with-no-words.		M15-11, 75-Feb
Love in Song (McCartney/McCartney) ✓◆ A good SLS, with the two preceding, forms the essence of Wings sound.		M15-03, 74-Nov
Love My Baby (McCartney) ⊘ (Style) Novelty only. Releasable if recorded properly, but probably not worth it.		M15, 74-Aug
Lunchbox/Odd Sox (McCartney) ⊘ (Filler) Just another long "link." A total throwaway.		M22-03, 75-Feb
Magneto and Titanium Man (McCartney/McCartney) ≈◆ (Content) Very weird song and track, but light and catchy mid-70s pop.		M15-05, 75-Feb

15 / VIENNA

●	My Carnival (McCartney/McCartney) ⊘ (Filler) 12-bar fun, sort of New Orleans-style.		M, 75-Feb
●	Rock Show (McCartney/McCartney) ✓◆ Great rock song. Tone hasn't aged well, but it caught a moment.		M15-02, 75-Feb
●	Rudolph the Red-Nosed Reggae (Marks) ⊘ (Content/Filler) Silly track. Barely worthy of a B-side. Should have stayed on a private reel.		M21-02, 74-Dec
●	Sally G (McCartney/McCartney) ⊘ (Style/Quality) Nothing likeable about this one at all. "Rocky Raccoon" on weed.		M14-02, 74-Jul
●	Send Me the Heart (McCartney/Laine) ⊘ (Style) Paul and Denny do country pastiche. Inoffensive, but beyond pointless.		M14, 74-Jul
●	Soily (McCartney) ✓ Solid rocker with fine hook. Weird lyrics, but just a carrier wave for the music. Works.		M15, 74-Aug
●	Spirits of Ancient Egypt (McCartney/McCartney) ≈◆ (Content) Another quirky misfit that somehow works with this album's mood.		M15-08, 75-Feb
●	Treat Her Gently / Lonely Old People (McCartney/McCartney) ✓◆ Isolated, this would be too much. In context, it completes the album's thought.		M15-12, 75-Feb
●	Venus and Mars (McCartney/McCartney) ✓◆ Coded messages never sounded so good. A win, if odd.		M15-01, 75-Mar
●	Venus and Mars (Reprise) (McCartney/McCartney) ✓◆ Reprise to start the side actually works, and the variation is welcome.		M15-07, 75-Feb
●	You Gave Me the Answer (McCartney/McCartney) ≈◆ (Style) A least 10 years late, it's still not hard to listen to.		M15-04, 75-Feb

Note: "Walking in the Park with Eloise" is not considered because it was neither written, co-written, or sung by Paul.

It is entirely possible that a Beatles album made at this particular moment would have sounded a lot like *Venus and Mars* — at least if Paul were leading things. But that notion highlights exactly the problems solved by recording separately. Paul had a ton of new material, knew exactly what he wanted, and would have allowed precious little room for collaboration. Would George Harrison have wanted to play guitar — painstakingly dictated by Paul — on "Magneto and Titanium Man"?

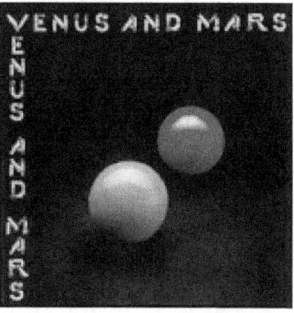

Would John Lennon have been willing to sing and play on songs he probably hated, like "Lonely Old People" or "You Gave Me the Answer"? Unlikely.

To restate something which seems quite obvious in retrospect: The moment they actually broke up was essentially the same moment they became too big for one another, a very natural thing given their wide-ranging talents and extensive success. Not that we need it, but this album is powerful confirmation of the wisdom of abandoning their original recording practices. No one but Paul would have wanted to work on this material, and no one but Paul would have wanted an album like this going out under the Beatle brand in 1974.

Simultaneously, though, *Venus and Mars* demonstrates just as clearly that McCartney could easily have had his solo career *and* contributed heartily to group projects. He wrote a lot of songs, of a wide variety of styles and quality, and could have spread them around freely. This stands in contrast to his former bandmates. Though the amount of music made by former Beatles in this period is surprisingly similar, the differences in outcome are stark. McCartney had multiple singles that were hits, where Lennon, Harrison and Starkey sometimes sounded like they were writing/recording on fumes.

This concept is important in understanding how we must treat *Venus and Mars* when it comes to the group project. In short: Paul wouldn't have wanted to give it up, and the Assembler wouldn't have really needed it.

This album has a unified sound, and a highly successful structure. Even though individual pieces are weak in isolation, the assembly clearly grants the album greater-than-the-sum-of-its-parts status. Paul has again applied his formula for a "concept" album — the *lite* version — and again it works. Disrupting this in the interest of the Beatles would have been incredibly difficult.

A major piece of the album's success is the nearly flawless opening sequence. The title track has a hypnotic quality that continues to build until it breaks flawlessly into "Rock Show," which itself eventually gracefully steps aside to reveal "Love in Song." Each part is great on its own, and yet they manage to bring each other to a higher level. (If some of this is, as some suspect, coded language aimed at John Lennon, it is of no consequence to the perception of the album.)

Similarly, the closing sequence is also masterful, if somewhat harder to take. From the spoken intro before "Listen to What the Man Said" to the closing notes of the wildcard track, "Crossroads Theme," the final nine minutes offer 1) a hit for the road, 2) a little sentimentality, and 3) something unexpected. Your reaction to "Treat Her Gently/Lonely Old People" will depend on your tolerance for this side of Paul, but at this point in his solo career it was still welcomed by many fans as an echo of his Beatle days. There is an argument to be made that this very song was the tipping point, but again, opinions will differ.

The album contains two tracks which simply must be regarded as "pot boilers" — i.e. 70s pop/rock at its best, or worst, depending on your tastes. Both "Letting Go" and "Call Me Back Again" simmer and eventually boil. It takes a willing listener to enjoy these, given the need to look past the overwrought and achingly slight lyrical content. Considered as *product* — i.e. commercial creatures — and not *art*, both of these would have to be considered clear successes. You are forgiven, however, if you find them skippable.

Two novelty tracks are present, cleverly disguised as sort of supernatural wonderings that dovetail with the central concept of "reading the stars." Heard in isolation, and outside of that weird cultural moment, both "Spirits of Ancient Egypt" and "Magneto and Titanium Man" sound rather silly. But both tracks move nicely, apparently telling stories, although don't ask me to explain them. As a noncontiguous trio with McCulloch's "Medicine Jar" they somehow seem like variations on a theme, and manage to convince a listener that this theme, whatever it is, is in some way worthy. Pull them apart and that evaporates, and each seems very slight indeed. McCartney's assembly triumphs over questionable material once again.

Perhaps it could go without saying that the central "concept" and subject matter on *Venus and Mars* is typically mystifying. Where Lennon and Harrison were, to a degree, baring their souls, McCartney is closer to Starkey in simply pounding out material — except with unmatchable songwriting abilities. Even McCartney's misfires are tuneful and well-constructed. After a few spins, most listeners will sing along with these songs comfortably, and happily oblivious to the nonsense of the lyrics — something that cannot be said for much of the repertoire generated by the other former Beatles in this period.

Tunefulness is certainly not the best or only measure of quality, of course, but the ability to write songs that draw in their audiences certainly is. Paul captures his audience quite skillfully throughout this album, beginning with the pure candy of the opening "suite," and reinforcing that capture with more of the same to begin side two. This is world-class artistic manipulation, thankfully benign.

Regardless of the quality of the music, the presence of Paul's lite concept ingredients makes *Venus and Mars* much more successful as a complete artistic statement than the albums by the other former Beatles in this era. Recall that this formula is built on an evocative title and cover image (gatefold sleeve preferred), a memorable title track with reprise, a broad enough concept to promote interpretation, good enough music, and painstaking assembly. Lennon's *Rock 'n' Roll* probably comes the closest, with a central concept and a great cover image, but it lacks the rest. For our purposes, Lennon's album would be easy to borrow from (if we wanted to), but McCartney's is difficult to draw on without breaking up the album's strengths, which include a highly unified sound.

Central to that sound is the use — indeed, subsuming overuse — of compression on the masters. Without getting too deep into technical weeds, compression is a process by which the loudest and softest sounds in a recording are brought closer together in volume, creating a smaller dynamic range, but a more integrated and powerful overall sound.

A certain degree of compression is applied to all recordings, both when they are created in the studio and when they are mixed and mastered later.[1] In the early days this was to prevent the needle from jumping out of the groove on a phonograph record, and was something of an art form in itself.[2] Eventually, it became standard

---

[1] Even more is added by radio stations.
[2] A man named Harry Moss provided this service for almost all of the Beatles records, and a meaningful portion of their post-*Rubber Soul* success is owed to his great skills.

practice because it provides a finishing "sheen" of smoothness to the sound, a technique which really came of age in the 70s.

In the case of *Venus and Mars*, compression brings all of this very disparate music into roughly the same sonic space. Despite the wide variety in instrumentation and styles — the album really is a tour-de-force in this regard — there is a sameness to the sound on all of the tracks, and this is due largely, though not entirely, to its mastering and the over-application of compression. Everything on the album sounds controlled and unified, though also somewhat tamped-down, even when it ventures into elaborate horn or string arrangements.

The unity created by this process is something of a secret sauce, and often tied to individual engineers and/or studios. Though it's tempting to think this may have been related to the New Orleans sessions, it is much more likely a product of the final mixing at Wally Heider Studios in Hollywood. Paul never allowed such a heavy hand with compression either before or after this album. To hear the difference explicitly, compare the openness of "Let Me Roll It" to the squeezed-down sound of "Call Me Back Again." (Listen especially to the snare drum.)

To a degree, therefore, the unified nature of this album is an illusion, much like that of *Band on the Run* or even *Sgt. Pepper* itself, yet it is a similarly *effective* illusion. Simply put, and from the perspective of our Assembler, this means that these tracks sound much better together than apart. When the sonic component is combined with masterful sequencing, *Venus and Mars* defies the deconstruction necessary to repurpose the music.

As you can see in the BQ scoring, many of these tracks are good enough to transfer to a group project — individually — if we could extract them. In fact, beyond the Jimmy McCulloch track and the TV theme song, basically anything on this album — running the whole spectrum from music hall to sold out arena — *could* be brought forward. But even the best of these tracks doesn't sound quite as good outside the context of the album, and hardly anything here sounds very good next to the work of the other Beatles.

Of course, even if the Assembler wanted to, there is a hard limit to how much could have been lifted, based on the meta-Beatles rules. But the bigger problem may be with the album itself. If you try to remove four tracks from *Venus and Mars*, the album falls apart. Such is the level of care with which Paul has conceived, finished and assembled these tracks to sound like a set. For that reason, most of these tracks, though eligible, are unavailable to the Beatles.

The Assembler will extract exactly one song, the one which is the least like the rest on the album, and also happens to be the most appropriate to program on a group project. "Listen to What the Man Said" is classic McCartney, updated for its era, and will sit quite well next to the best of John, George and Ringo.

15 / VIENNA

Were this all the material McCartney had available, it would have been a much bigger problem for the group project. But he also offers a batch of very strong non-album singles, and some worthy outtakes. Notably, none of this material could have replaced tracks cleaved from the album since they are in a very different tone. But luckily for our project, if you collect the singles and put them together with the best outtakes and the one outlier from the album, you have a suite of McCartney music that is the perfect size and quality for what the Beatles needed. Thus, even in our slightly altered narrative, *Venus and Mars* would have been released in a form very close to what we know.

Considered as a whole, *Venus and Mars* is totally a mid-70s classic. With just the right tone and mood for that moment in pop music, plus a Beatle-like diversity in its repertoire, and gobs of success, the album encapsulates an entire era in a way not unlike *Sgt. Pepper*. Though it certainly didn't reach as deeply into the culture, this batch of songs went on to populate Paul's highly successful world tour, and thus reanimated Beatlemania to a surprising degree, effectively mounting a wholesale takeover of the Beatle brand. This is the album which cemented McCartney as a big star once again.

So it may seem like nitpicking to say that the songs are collectively a touch thin, and the concept rather silly. It may seem unkind to point out that it sold nowhere near as many copies as its predecessor. But that leads right to the important takeaway: No one cared. This album was still a success, and kept the Wings ball rolling in a healthy fashion. It led to the tour, and stands as a testament to Paul's versatility, perseverance, and expertise, which he came by through relentless trial and error. Though *Band on the Run* was clearly the better album, *Venus and Mars* succeeds by being plenty good enough, providing proof that McCartney's musical reinvention as a pseudo-solo artist was no fluke. That is all he could have hoped for at this moment.

The outtakes from this period are alternately useful and dismissable. They include an elaborate but unbearable reading of the Tin Pan Alley standard, "Baby Face," which was rejected along with the insufferable, "I'll Give You a Ring," several pointless versions of "My Carnival," and a handful of other instrumentals and sketches not really worth mentioning. In reality, only "Let's Love," something of a torch song that manages to avoid going over the top, is worthy of consideration. Alone, it has the potential for unwelcome pathos, but it can be put to fine use on the group project, and sounds like it deserves to wear the Beatles name.

The unreleased rocker, "Soily," is of a piece with "Rock Show," meaning that there wasn't really a need to include it on *Venus and Mars* (though it would become part of the *Wings Over America* tour and album). This will be to the benefit of the Beatles album. Along with the fantastic single, "Junior's Farm," it might have

demonstrated to the world that, while McCartney was something of a diffuse impresario in his solo work, he could still focus when it came to the group. The saddest thing about "Junior's Farm" is that, in not being included on any album, it tends to be forgotten, when it really should be remembered among the best of what a solo McCartney could do. The Assembler has the power to change that.

Ringo Starr
11 tracks: 3 eligible, 3 provisional

Sources

S08	*Goodnight Vienna* R: Aug 74 P: Perry S: Sunset (LA), Workshop (LA)	74-Nov

Tracks

(It's All Down to) Goodnight Vienna (Lennon)	S08-01, +J, 74-Aug
✓ Just the right amount of quirky, this feels like a true "Ringo" song deep down inside.	

All by Myself (Starkey/Poncia)	S08-06, 74-Aug
⊘ (Quality) Feels pointless, like product. Somebody else's record with RS vocal.	

Call Me (Starkey)	S08-07, 74-Aug
⊘ (Quality) Low quality song. Like "Don't Pass Me By," but with generic, boring session backing.	

Easy for Me (Nilsson)	S08-10, 74-Aug
✓ A fine song and nice choice for RS. Vocal wavers, but somehow works.	

Goodnight Vienna (Reprise) (Lennon)	S08-11, +J, 74-Aug
✓ With gusto, indeed! Lennon provides the energy, and that's why it works.	

Husbands and Wives (Miller)	S08-04, 74-Aug
⊘ (Filler) An earnest vocal, but RS is in over his head. He is not a song stylist, by any means.	

No No Song (Axton/Jackson)	S08-08, 74-Aug
⊘ (Style/Quality) Irresistibly catchy. Would have been a hit with any vocalist. RS adds nothing unique.	

Occapella (Toussaint)	S08-02, 74-Aug
≈ (Style) Nice riff, and a happy sound overall. Slight, but inoffensive.	

Only You (And You Alone) (Ram/Rand)	S08-09, +J, 74-Aug
≈ (Filler) Classic song. Competent vocal. But nothing particularly distinctive about the record.	

Oo-Wee (Starkey/Poncia)	S08-03, 74-Aug
≈ (Quality) Attempting to follow "Oh My My," this isn't quite as successful, but still catchy and nice.	

Snookeroo (John/Taupin)	S08-05, 74-Aug
⊘ (Quality) Lousy song, sketchy vocal performance. Pseudo-autobio crap lyric. Forced.	

15 / VIENNA

Richard Starkey had only one release in the period we are considering for this rescued album. The first sound on *Goodnight Vienna*, a count-off by none other than John Lennon, sets us up for a repeat of the good feelings of *Ringo*, but ultimately lightning doesn't quite strike twice. Though not a bad album, exactly, this is something of a near miss. The high points are pleasant, even enjoyable, but the low points feel ominous, a hint of what is to come.

We will pluck the title track for use on the Beatles project, along with its reprise, but not just because of Lennon's presence or authorship. It is truly the only track on the album which gets the most out of what Ringo has to offer as a vocalist and frontman. It's also the only one with any "Beatle" flavor at all. Others come close, but tend to rely on factors beyond Ringo himself for their success, using slick production to work around his liabilities rather than finding a way to harness them. As was the case throughout his solo career, it appears that only another former Beatle really knows how to channel Ringo's uniqueness.

Harry Nilsson, perhaps something of an "honorary former Beatle" in those days, is the only other artist who comes close. His "Easy for Me" nicely evokes both Lennon and McCartney in tone and content, coming close to catching what Ringo can do best. Indeed, Ringo's version is eminently more listenable than Nilsson's own recording. The song itself is a little too weepy, and the vocal a little too sloppy, conjuring memories of *Beaucoups of Blues*, though not quite descending to that level. The track certainly must be considered a candidate for the group project, but will ultimately not make the cut.

Elton John and Bernie Taupin, on the other hand, prove themselves utterly unable to tap anything of Ringo's charm. Not only is their song, "Snookeroo," poorly-conceived and ill-fitted to the artist, but the attempts by producer Richard Perry to force it into life only highlight how lousy it is. Contemporary reviews often singled this out as among the better tracks, but that's more likely due to Elton's superstardom than the actual quality of the record itself. The finished product comes across as forced merriment, with a false sense of autobiography, almost the exact opposite of the title track's ease.

Both of the covers, "Only You (And You Alone)" and "Husbands and Wives," are essentially filler here, and would have been regarded as such on a Beatles project as well. Neither of Starkey's vocals find anything new in these songs, though Lennon's presence on the former certainly causes Ringo to raise his game, and it is among the album's better sung selections. Again, Lennon has found a song which suits Ringo well, but the reading is a little too sleepy to carry forward unless nothing better can be found.

Three tracks feature Starkey as songwriter. Two songs written with Vini Poncia attempt to extend the charms of their collaborations on *Ringo*, with only modest success. "Oo-Wee" is the more memorable of the two, being catchy and nicely commercial. "All by Myself" is inoffensive, but ultimately rather forgettable. Ringo's solo composition, "Call Me," only highlights his need for a collaborator to smooth out the rough edges of his ideas. It comes off as a kid brother to "Don't Pass Me By," but without anything distinctive in the backing track to lift the amateurish writing. All three originals have the generic quality which we will come to know well on Ringo's next few albums.

"Occapella" is a great sounding track, worthy of consideration in the provisional category. With a catchy riff and a breezy feel, this is among the best of what Ringo would do in the class we might call "international playboy pop." Also in that category would be "No No Song," which was justifiably selected as a single due to its inherent catchiness. Unfortunately, it's not Ringo's performance that really made this a hit. The song is infectious enough that it would likely have been just as big a hit if it had been recorded by someone else — say, Jimmy Buffett.

If there were any outtakes from these sessions, they have not surfaced, and it is perhaps just as well. Ringo's contribution to the group project is pretty easy to spot, and when you remove the filler from this project, the little that is left could have gone in the can for use on some later solo project (or not).

It's worth noting that the overall concept for the album, though distinctive, was also somewhat incoherent. The title apparently references an old Liverpool expression, certainly unknown to any Americans, for when the time has come to pack up and go. With that little bit of information, the cover photo seems to suggest that Ringo is about to board a spaceship and fly away forever. Oh, no! But the visual reference to *The Day the Earth Stood Still*, which was carried through to promotional stunts and other materials, would not help sell this record. It mostly benefited a Canadian group known as Klaatu, indirectly sparking a frenzy about a stealth Beatles reunion that never happened. Incoherence has its price.

Beyond the title track, there appears to be no connection between the album's packaging concept and its music. Though that's hardly a requirement, especially in the 70s, it adds to the sense that this project wasn't fully baked, or at least not as carefully prepared as its predecessor. That trend would continue, and this would be the last Ringo project which could reasonably be called "palatable."

George Harrison
20 tracks: 3 eligible, 4 provisional

Sources

H05	"~~Dark Horse~~" / "I Don't Care Anymore" R: Oct 74 P: Harrison S: A&M (LA)			74-Nov
H06	*Dark Horse* R: Nov 73 - Oct 74 P: Harrison S: FPSHOT, A&M (LA)			74-Dec
H07	*Extra Texture (Read All About It)* R: Aug 74 - Jun 75 P: Harrison S: EMI, FPSHOT, A&M (LA)			75-Sep

Tracks

Answer's at the End, The (Harrison) — H07-02, 75-Apr
⊘ (Quality) Ponderous, heavy, sluggish. Loops around without shape.

Bit More of You, A (Harrison) — H07-06, 75-May
⊘ (Filler) Embarrassing filler. Emphasizes how little of value there is here.

Bye Bye, Love (Bryant/Bryant/Harrison) — H06-04, 74-Oct
⊘ (Filler) Halting, shrill, desolate deconstruction and rewrite. Painful.

Can't Stop Thinking About You (Harrison) — H07-07, 75-Jun
⊘ (Quality) A germ of a good idea, but doesn't work. Feels forced, unnatural.

Dark Horse (Harrison) — H06-07, 74-Oct
⊘ (Quality) Forced song, with annoying "gallop." Painful all around.

Ding Dong, Ding Dong (Harrison) — H06-06, +R, 74-Oct
⊘ (Content/Quality) Clunky chord progression and rhythms. Not a good song.

Far East Man (Harrison/Wood) — H06-08, 74-Jun
✓ Very cool, comfortable sound. Nice saxes. Best vocal on the album.

Grey Cloudy Lies (Harrison) — H07-09, 75-Jun
⊘ (Quality) Another looper, without any payoff. It twirls inoffensively, but bores.

Hari's on Tour (Express) (Harrison) — H06-01, 74-Oct
⊘ (Filler) Sounds like the theme to "The GH Variety Hour." Better suited to a B-side. Poor opener.

His Name Is Legs (Ladies and Gentlemen) (Harrison) — H07-10, 75-Jun
⊘ (Quality) Annoying shuffle beat and seemingly random chord changes. Inexplicable.

I Don't Care Anymore (Harrison) — H05-02, 74-Oct
⊘ (Quality) Demo quality

It Is 'He' (Jai Sri Krishna) (Harrison) — H06-09, 74-Oct
⊘ (Quality/Content) Terrible tuning problems. Annoying "shuffle" chorus. Sloppy.

Māya Love (Harrison) — H06-05, 74-Oct
✓ Positive, up beat, confident. Leading edge of GH's ultimate sound.

Ooh Baby (You Know That I Love You) (Harrison) — H07-04, 75-Jun
≈ (Quality) Nice but unrealized idea. Salvaged when rewritten as "Pure Smokey."

Simply Shady (Harrison) — H06-02, 74-Oct
⊘ (Quality) Lopes along without much point, and a grating vocal.

![]	**So Sad** (Harrison)	H06-03, +R, 74-Oct
	≈ (Quality) Nice guitars, but weepy/reedy/shaky vocal. Song might be better than the recording.	
![]	**This Guitar (Can't Keep from Crying)** (Harrison)	H07-03, 75-May
	≈ (Quality) Bad singing sinks a serviceable, if not quite stellar, song.	
![]	**Tired of Midnight Blue** (Harrison)	H07-08, 75-Apr
	✓ A surprising success. GH sounds good, and the idea is fully realized.	
![]	**World of Stone** (Harrison)	H07-05, 75-Jun
	⊘ (Content/Quality) Tortured, messy melody, and GH is not up to it. Nice piano and guitars.	
![]	**You** (Harrison)	H07-01, 75-May
	≈ (Quality) Catchy pop riff, but painfully thin lyric. Parody of Macca?	

George Harrison's contributions to this group project come from his least artistically satisfying period. Indeed, as you can see from the track list, clearing out all of the unusable material on *Dark Horse* leaves almost nothing, and we have to look to the music of *Extra Texture (Read All About It)*, just being worked on as *Vienna* would have been assembled, to make up George's expected quota on the Beatles album. Some songs on *Extra Texture* go way back, and had been rejected before, but the best of it — the little which could be used by the group — was very fresh, and that is what our Assembler would have been after.

Indeed, our slightly altered narrative would have had to include a call to George by the Assembler sometime in the spring, noting that there were rumors of better material being written, and beseeching him to get to the recording done as quickly as possible. We will assume that Harrison would have complied, providing rough mixes from which the Assembler would select the tracks to prioritize, and then finishing those first. That process would have run right up to the album due date. A close call, that, but well worth it in the final analysis. (For these reasons, the actual historical available dates are not used for some of these tracks. In the real world, portions of *Extra Texture* were finished slightly after the fantasy release date for *Vienna*.)

The problems with these two albums, created in a somewhat overlapping fashion, are actually pretty simple. George's voice is in rough shape, likely due to health issues and rampant drug use. His singing, always somewhat reedy, has descended completely into his throat and nose, sounding thin and pulled and nasal and forced. As a result, on *Dark Horse* it was generally smothered in "room" (reverb effects) during mixing, and then pulled way back into the instrumental background. This leaves the vocals sounding more like a bad George Harrison impersonator singing with his head in a metal tube. Thankfully, the same technique was avoided on *Extra*

15 / VIENNA

Texture, but the overall result is not much better. The sound of his voice is simply painful to listen to in this era.

The songs do his voice no favors either. They lurch in strange directions structurally and rhythmically, while also being lyrically unsatisfying.[3] His melodies are ill-conceived, and often beyond his diminished vocal abilities. Most of these songs sound horribly forced — as if there was no inspiration behind them, but the need to generate product.

Worst among these may be "Ding Dong, Ding Dong," an astonishingly bad song that somehow made its way onto a single.[4] In it, George covers Big Ben(!), likely with tongue in cheek, but with a hard edge, and without employing the songwriter's craft to soften the mischievous idea into something palatable. The result is a novelty song which grates almost from the first note.

But calling out this one track as the worst of the set leaves multiple candidates on the table. On *Dark Horse*, both the annoying title track and disastrous pseudo-cover of "Bye, Bye Love" speak to the depths of Harrison's creative nadir. Even the recording craft is called into question by "It Is 'He' (Jai Sri Krishna)," which features blatantly out-of-tune singing and playing, especially from the guest instrumentalists. Ultimately, the album sounds like a bad day at work.

On *Extra Texture*, songs with potential like "The Answer's at the End," "Can't Stop Thinking About You," and "Grey Cloudy Lies," loop endlessly through odd chord progressions until they just stop. They lack the coherent structure of verse-chorus-bridge that we know Harrison can harness creatively, and offer nothing innovative or even palatable in its place. Each song begs for a rewrite — a full realization of the underlying idea. A fourth song which could go on this list, "Ooh Baby (You Know That I Love You)," demonstrates this principle clearly. It would be rewritten as "Pure Smokey," with its potential nicely realized, and make a sterling addition to Harrison's next (and the next meta-Beatles) album.

Harrison's diminished vocals mar the recordings of otherwise serviceable songs like "Māya Love," "Far East Man," and "This Guitar (Can't Keep from Crying)." We will still be able to find a place for two of these on the Beatles project, but assume that our Assembler would have taken George into a vocal booth and gently coaxed a

---

[3] I want to note the possibility that Harrison's structural choices in songwriting were influenced by the Indian music with which he surrounded himself. I have spent some time trying to find an overlap which might explain, or at least hint at reasons for his strange choices, but have been unsuccessful. Still, not being an expert on Indian music, I cannot rule it out either. It will have to remain a subject beyond the scope of this project. Therefore, when I talk of structure in this context, I am referring to western pop song structures specifically.

[4] With an equally bad, but fascinating video. Interestingly, however, the song appears to have inspired a very subtle and generally overlooked response from McCartney (see the next chapter for more).

better performance out of him. Of the music in these two albums, only the fantastic "Tired of Midnight Blue" has a high enough BQ to make it through to the group project with no alterations.

"This Guitar (Can't Keep from Crying)" provides an interesting study in the risks of evoking the past in Beatle solo work. With sound and content superficially similar to "While My Guitar Gently Weeps," critics felt free to dismiss this song as a weak echo of its predecessor. The truth is, as always, considerably more complex. The two songs have chord progressions which, though similar, have some marked differences, and they actually diverge in lyrical theme right from the beginning. Where the earlier track was a guitar-based lament for the state of the world, the newer one is all about the songwriter, who sounds almost perplexed that what comes out of his guitar does not match his feelings or circumstance.

Where the guitar of the first song cries for external things which are not, the new one cries from the inside for how it has been misunderstood and mistreated. As such, the second song is very much a sequel to, and extension of the first — in the best sense. In something of an early meta moment, the fact that reviewers and fans might miss this key aspect of the lyrics is actually what the lyrics are about. George laid a subtle trap, and pretty much the whole world fell into it.

It does not help that the newer song has been recorded with a sheen of California polish that undermines its keening nature. When listening to the two tracks back to back, one is struck first by the rawness captured at EMI in 1968, versus the silky smooth edgelessness of the mid-70s A&M sound. It is a clear case of how the advance of recording technology has had consequences for the art.

The second thing, however, is the sharply contrasting presence/absence of Paul McCartney as supporting voice, and Ringo Starr as supporting propulsion.[5] On *The White Album*, McCartney's intensity encourages George's lead vocal and underlines the thematic material. Harrison cannot provide himself with the same level of encouragement on "This Guitar." Likewise, studio pro Jim Keltner chooses minimalism, focusing on his toms, and is mixed way back with reverb, where Ringo adopted a driving beat that dominates the right channel of the stereo mix, and is nearly bone dry. Though it's tempting to argue that this is comparing apples and oranges, it highlights some of what the Beatles brought to each other that they could not get as solo artists from session musicians. (Comparing lead guitarists between the tracks really is apples to oranges, and is far too subjective to declare a winner.)

The comparison obviously undermines the notion that fusing the solo Beatle recordings together for group projects could have been anywhere near as satisfying as the group working together in the same studio. But our Assembler was the

---

[5] A less obvious difference, though certainly a factor, would be Lennon's rhythm guitar, which is indistinct enough, and has been mixed back far enough, to somewhat disappear in the Beatles record. What factor it played in the session is therefore difficult to estimate.

gatekeeper, and would have been charged with shaping records like this into a form befitting the group and the brand. That George's version of this song on *Extra Texture (Read All About It)* is disappointing hides the strength and potential of the song itself. Perhaps the Assembler could have talked all four Beatles into the same studio to realize this fine song in the best way possible. Add that to your list of post-breakup fantasy scenarios!

Whatever the overall merits of "This Guitar (Can't Keep from Crying)" as a song, they are further obscured by its placement on the album in a spot where George Martin would typically have placed songs that were meant to be glossed over. In that spot, the song sounds extra weak and whiny and underbaked. Yet it is strong enough, and important enough, to bring forward to the group project, if only to see whether it gains anything by being heard in a different way. (Spoiler alert: It will.)

Two questionable songs beg for further examination. Each has serious problems, but one became a minor hit, while the other stunk up the end of an album, leaving many listeners shaking their heads.

"You" has a very catchy hook, and a reasonably coherent structure, but perhaps the most vapid and underwritten lyrics ever set to vinyl by a Beatle. Were it not for its provenance (it was written for Ronnie Spector in 1971), one might think it a parody of Macca's "silly love songs." That cannot be completely ruled out, of course, given George's slyness and oscillating disdain/tolerance for his former bandmate, but I know of no documentation which would support the idea.

"His Name Is Legs (Ladies and Gentlemen)" most clearly typifies George's artistic problems in this era by containing A) a tortured melody, B) seemingly random chord changes, C) a terrible vocal performance, D) an inscrutable lyric, E) questionable production values, and F) the wrong placement on the album. Ostensibly a comedy/novelty record, whatever humor it might have held for contemporary audiences has not survived — a typical problem with comedy records, and the antithesis of the Beatles' knack for embodying timelessness. Though George likely couldn't have cared less, the net effect is a piece of elaborate and perplexing filler on an album that already contains obvious filler ("A Bit More of You"). That it gets the last word just adds to the indignity.

It's unlikely that either of these albums could have been improved by better sequencing, but there is little question that the order of the songs made things worse, not better. On *Dark Horse*, the opener, "Hari's on Tour (Express)," is an inoffensive instrumental, with an interesting pedigree, but much more suited to a B-side than featured album track. It makes a rather lousy first impression. Likewise, the closer, "It Is 'He' (Jai Sri Krishna)," is completely forgettable — except for its lousy sound. On *Extra Texture (Read All About It)*, "You" may very well be the best choice for opener, but given what follows, it sets a bar that simply cannot be met. And, as mentioned, "His Name is Legs (Ladies and Gentlemen)" makes a pretty lousy closer for a number of reasons. On each album, it's hard to see any sequence that could mitigate the unfortunate songwriting and recording.

The good songs here, the ones with high enough BQ to move forward to a group project, are not really all that special, but they at least have the potential of sounding better next to better music. "Tired of Midnight Blue" is the lone standout on either of these albums, being sophisticated and very smooth. Indeed, smoothness is also the key factor for the others, including "Far East Man" and "Māya Love." All three of these tracks, along with some of the also rans like "Can't Stop Thinking About You" and "Ooh Baby (You Know That I Love You)" suggest the direction that Harrison's impending redemption will take.

Starting on his next release he will sand the edges off, and finally find his true songwriting voice. In that way, these two albums can be optimistically regarded as preludes. Unfortunately, without that foreknowledge, they simply disappoint.

No outtakes are available here, and only one lone non-album track exists for consideration. Unfortunately, "I Don't Care Anymore" may be the literal nadir of Harrison's recording career. Sounding more like a sloppy demo, it gives the distinct impression that it was tossed off without any consideration for quality. We can forgive George because we know things got better, but trying to sell this to fans, even as a B-side, represents unacceptable contempt for the fan base.

15 / VIENNA

Assembly
30 tracks: 16 eligible, 14 provisional

✓	#9 Dream	L10-07, 74-Aug
✓	Bless You	L10-05, 74-Aug
≈	Going Down on Love	L10-01, 74-Aug
≈	Here We Go Again	L11, 73-Dec
≈	Move Over Ms. L	L12-02, 74-Oct
≈	Nobody Loves You (When You're…	L10-11, 74-Aug
≈	Old Dirt Road	L10-03, 74-Aug
✓	Scared	L10-06, 74-Aug
≈	Steel and Glass	L10-09, 74-Aug
✓	Surprise, Surprise (Sweet Bird…	L10-08, 74-Aug
✓	What You Got	L10-04, 74-Aug
✓	Whatever Gets You thru the Night	L10-02, 74-Aug
≈	I'll Give You a Ring	M28-02, 73-Dec
✓	Junior's Farm	M14-01, 74-Jul
✓	Let's Love	M15, 74-Jun
✓	Listen to What the Man Said	M15-11, 75-Feb
✓	Soily	M15, 74-Aug
✓	(It's All Down to) Goodnight Vienna	S08-01, +J, 74-Aug
✓	Easy for Me	S08-10, 74-Aug
✓	Goodnight Vienna (Reprise)	S08-11, +J, 74-Aug
≈	Occapella (Toussaint)	S08-02, 74-Aug
≈	Only You (And You Alone)	S08-09, +J, 74-Aug
≈	Oo-Wee	S08-03, 74-Aug
✓	Far East Man	H06-08, 74-Jun
✓	Māya Love	H06-05, 74-Oct
≈	Ooh Baby (You Know That I Love You)	H07-04, 75-Jun
≈	So Sad	H06-03, +R, 74-Oct
≈	This Guitar (Can't Keep from Crying)	H07-03, 75-May
✓	Tired of Midnight Blue	H07-08, 75-Apr
≈	You	H07-01, 75-May

The list of available tracks is quite reasonable, giving options for each Beatle, without the need to leave very much behind. The exception is John Lennon, with twice as many as each of the others, and not much to do with them if they don't make this album. Again, he has created enough for his album, and nothing extra.

A few tracks are eliminated right away as not quite fitting in with this collection:

- ≈ Going Down on Love (J)
- ≈ Here We Go Again (J)
- ≈ I'll Give You a Ring (P)
- ≈ Move Over Ms. L (J)
- ≈ Nobody Loves You... (J)
- ≈ Only You (And You Alone) (R)
- ≈ Ooh Baby (You Know... (G)
- ≈ Oo-Wee (R)
- ≈ So Sad (G)
- ≈ Steel and Glass (J)

Even thinned in this way, Lennon's collection is formidable in this context. As discussed above, *Walls and Bridges* hides its strengths very well. When it came time to look for pole tracks for this group album, "What You Got" somewhat surprisingly jumped out from the entire collection of eligible tracks as perhaps the most forceful and infectious statement a Beatle had made in years. Lennon's opening exclamation of "One!" makes the perfect first sound for this album. Removed from the vagaries of the solo project, the track stands out as an overlooked classic, with John turning in a great lick and a raucous vocal. With this as an opener, the Beatles would have sounded positively modern in 1975, with no traces of the 60s beat group from Liverpool — except for the continued commitment to excellence.

From that powerful opener, it felt almost mandatory to place Paul's great rocker, "Junior's Farm," next to extend the vibe, then follow that with Ringo and John's collaboration to keep the party going. Paul had issued his track as a single, and it sounded just fine in isolation, but it gains strength between two examples of John's strength. As has happened so many times with these two great writers, they feed off one another, even if it is us forcing them to do so. Also, in this context "Goodnight Vienna" avoids the somewhat neutered feel it had as an opener on Ringo's album. Here it becomes a quirky party extender, which is just as its creators clearly wanted but did not achieve in the original context.

After that trio of strong, nearly incendiary, masterworks (yes, they sound like that when heard together), George's "Far East Man" retains the excellence while cooling down the vibe in a most welcome way. The track's lights-down-low smoothness makes the perfect counterbalance to what has gone before. The invitation to Sinatra, which felt like something of a mocking dare on George's album, feels more like a genuine tribute in the context of a group project — where "we" now refers to the Beatles instead of George's anonymous (to Sinatra, at least) studio players. In this quartet of conjoined openers, the four Beatle voices have once again contributed to a sequence that is completely unexpected, immensely satisfying, and wholly *Beatles*.

15 / VIENNA

1A. **What You Got (J)**	#9 Dream (J)
1B. **Junior's Farm (P)**	Bless You (J)
1C. **Goodnight Vienna (R)**	Easy for Me (R)
1D. **Far East Man (G)**	Goodnight Vienna (Reprise) (R)
. . .	Let's Love (P)
	Listen to What the Man... (P)
	Māya Love (G)
. . .	≈ Occapella (R)
	≈ Old Dirt Road (J)
	Scared (J)
	Soily (P)
	Surprise, Surprise... (J)
	≈ This Guitar (Can't Keep... (G)
	Tired of Midnight Blue (G)
	Whatever Gets You thru... (J)
	≈ You (G)

At this point, we've done over half of side one without even considering the other three pole positions — a sure sign of how strong the material is. This comes as a bit of a surprise given the reputations of the source albums, as is the fact that we still haven't found spots for all of the great music. "Junior's Farm" certainly could have been a pole track, possibly opening side two, but we have other options for that spot, and nothing else that could have extended John's opener quite as effectively. It will stay where it is.

It turns out that there's really only one candidate to close the album, anyway: the collaboration between Lennon and Elton. "Whatever Gets You through the Night" is arguably the strongest song available for this album, which would typically make it a candidate for opener, but it has the feeling of a summation deep down in its bones, and is relatively self-contained. On *Walls and Bridges* it comes second on side one, sandwiched between the clunky opener, "Going Down on Love," and the desolate ballad, "Old Dirt Road," sapped of its strength by its placement and surroundings. This is why the song sounded so much better as a single (i.e. on the radio), and virtually disappears on the album. Since it is designed to stand alone, it's unexpectedly tough to follow — the key criteria used to identify closers. If it opened this album, finding a suitable extender would be tough, and using it anywhere but the very end would squander its strengths.

Though the fade out at the track's end works for radio, and for a mid-side entry on John's essentially structureless album, it would seem like a rather banal exit for a Beatles album. Luckily, an immediate opportunity to improve the ending presents itself in Ringo's reprise of "Goodnight Vienna." With a quick edit for length, and a crossfade which retains John's comment about "gusto," it adds a touch of whimsy while also providing a much cleaner and more satisfying album close than a simple fade out. Again, this is what its creators had hoped for on the solo album, but it didn't have the desired effect. There, it felt tacked on and somewhat forced. Here, it is most natural, and even suggests the album title.

1A. What You Got (J)	#9 Dream (J)
1B. Junior's Farm (P)	Bless You (J)
1C. Goodnight Vienna (R)	Easy for Me (R)
1D. Far East Man (G)	Let's Love (P)
...	Listen to What the Man... (P)
	Māya Love (G)
	≈ Occapella (R)
...	≈ Old Dirt Road (J)
2Y. Whatever Gets You thru the Night (J)	Scared (J)
2Z. CODA: Goodnight Vienna (Reprise) (R)	Soily (P)
	Surprise, Surprise... (J)
	≈ This Guitar (Can't Keep... (G)
	Tired of Midnight Blue (G)
	≈ You (G)

To that point, in keeping with the desire to avoid confusion by not using names of actual albums, Ringo's album title will be shortened to a single, clean word, which intentionally does not match the cover photo of the newly-abandoned, but not yet derelict, Apple headquarters.[1] This idea is borrowed from *Ringo's Rotogravure*, moved up in time a bit to match the moment's sentiments. The mismatch between title and image also throws sand into attempts to scrutinize the cover, while tapping an occasional Beatles practice of name-checking iconic locations.

As with the beginning of the album, the end leads to a natural and almost inevitable progression of music. With Paul's piano ballad "Let's Love" on the eligible list, we can see an obvious way to properly set up John's hit. Paul's quiet song becomes an "11 o'clock" ballad (in showbiz terms), allowing John's response to be properly emphasized as an exciting closing number. This idea is affirmed when Paul, in a move that would have sounded twee in just about any other context, slips in a major chord to end a song which has otherwise been in a minor key.[2] Luckily, this chord also happens to match perfectly the opening of "Whatever Gets You through the Night," and the connection is completely seamless. Paul's worst instincts are mitigated, and John's already strong song is made stronger by becoming a musical answer to Paul — yet another example of elevation from a distance.

Continuing to extend the sequence from its end toward the beginning, we find only one really good option to set up "Let's Love," which also lets us meet the ever-

---

[1] From *The Beatles Day By Day*, pg. 168: "2 May[, 1975] - Apple Records' office closes down forever."

[2] This well-known and well-worn technique is called a "Picardy third," which explains Paul's spoken ad lib on the end, "...[from] tears to Picardy."

15 / VIENNA

present parity requirements. In a stroke of luck, George's "Tired of Midnight Blue" creates the right context for Paul's ballad, allowing the album to close like it opened, with the four voices in close proximity. Thematically, George brings us to midnight, Paul croons into the wee hours, and John gets us through the night — at which point Ringo assures everyone (somewhere around dawn, no doubt) that the band will be back very soon. It's a subtle set of connections, which is why it works. The theme is in the cracks, and completely ignorable, if you like. Indeed, the idea is barely a whiff, and only present at all when the four voices are rescued from their solo vagaries.

1A. What You Got (J)	#9 Dream (J)
1B. Junior's Farm (P)	Bless You (J)
1C. Goodnight Vienna (R)	Easy for Me (R)
1D. Far East Man (G)	Listen to What the Man... (P)
...	Māya Love (G)
	≈ Occapella (R)
	≈ Old Dirt Road (J)
...	Scared (J)
2W. Tired of Midnight Blue (G)	Soily (P)
2X. Let's Love (P)	Surprise, Surprise... (J)
2Y. Whatever Gets You thru the Night (J)	≈ This Guitar (Can't Keep... (G)
2Z. CODA: Goodnight Vienna (Reprise) (R)	≈ You (G)

The remaining pole positions are now relatively easy to fill. Of the remaining tracks, Paul's certain hit, "Listen to What the Man Said" is, as usual, highly flexible. It could easily open or close a side (but not the album), and it can be used for setup, extension or reaction. In that way, it recalls "Got to Get You Into My Life," which, as we saw earlier, was an important factor in giving George Martin complete flexibility to structure *Revolver* for maximum impact.

Assuming that track can fill in wherever needed, other possibilities present themselves for the poles. The studio recording of "Soily," though nowhere near as flexible, definitely sounds like an opener.[3] It offers nothing to connect to either of the sequences already in place, so it will be slotted to open side two, assuming other parts can be fit around it.

One such part actually jumps out in the listening as the perfect contrast to the extended cacophony which ends "Soily." John's "#9 Dream" provides a fantastic counterpoint, while also keeping things moving. In putting these together, we hear the two Beatles in non-traditional roles. Paul, the master of pop, provides a solid

---

[3] A point driven home by its inclusion as the closer on *Wings Over America*, where it fairly lays an egg. Not only is it an overlong encore song that nobody has ever heard before, but it begs to be followed by something which would close the show with triumphant familiarity. It is a rare case of a misstep in assembly by Paul.

rocker, while John, old school rocker that we know he can be, provides a delicious piece of pure pop. Once again, the two songs work together, each making the other sound better.

1A. What You Got (J) 1B. Junior's Farm (P) 1C. Goodnight Vienna (R) 1D. Far East Man (G) ...	Bless You (J) Easy for Me (R) Listen to What the Man... (P) Māya Love (G) ≈ Occapella (R) ≈ Old Dirt Road (J) Scared (J)
2A. Soily (P) **2B. #9 Dream (J)** ... 2W. Tired of Midnight Blue (G) 2X. Let's Love (P) 2Y. Whatever Gets You thru the Night (J) 2Z. CODA: Goodnight Vienna (Reprise) (R)	Surprise, Surprise... (J) ≈ This Guitar (Can't Keep... (G) ≈ You (G)

Returning to the end of side one, none of the remaining tracks in the "eligible" list have quite the right quality. A look at the alternates offers a couple of potential Ringo tracks, such as the cover, "Only You (And You Alone)." But the Beatles are probably not interested in covers at this point when there are so many solid originals. Instead, George's sequel to a Beatles classic, which would have been brought to this project at the very last moment, begins to look like a possibility.

The question becomes whether George's "This Guitar (Can't Keep from Crying)" can be elevated into something at least approaching the grandeur of its more familiar older brother, "While My Guitar Gently Weeps." Its long, slow fade might be just the thing to end a side, assuming that whatever comes next (in this case, "Soily") clears out any lingering desolation — which is exactly what happens.

As heard in the middle of side one on *Extra Texture (Read All About It)*, that song has always been perceived as something of a throwaway, or at least a comedown from its predecessor. Indeed, George does appear to just toss it into the miscellany on his album, hiding it amid a collection of tracks which do not resonate in any way with the song's aspirations. Most contemporary reviews dismissed it as a pale descendant of his classic track from *The White Album*, and this is certainly understandable. It is built on a stock chord sequence, and George's lead guitar, though formidable, neither matches nor invokes Clapton's earlier, angst-ridden playing — not particularly better or worse, just very different.

But, as noted above, there is still some heft there. George has written a confessional statement that really does advance from the earlier song, if properly contextualized. Just shifting it from a forgettable solo album to a group project takes it part of the way. Placing it at the end of a side, with its long fade out, also elevates its standing. The final component of its reclamation would be to properly set it up, and this turns out to be where Paul's hit can make the most impact.

On *Venus and Mars*, Paul's song ends with an orchestral segue to "Treat Her Gently (Lonely Old People)," and it was carefully scored to be this way. As a suite, on a solo album, it is at least reasonably palatable, if containing an unfortunate amount of pathos. If transplanted whole to a Beatles album, however, the sequence would likely take the air out of everything else. It could not end the album, unless all four Beatles had decided to record it together, and that is completely out of the question. Even Paul found the need to dispel some of the melodrama by tacking on "Crossroads Theme." Thus, the second half of that suite simply must be left on Paul's solo album.

But a simple edit, at the point before the segue begins, reveals that Paul and George are in relative keys, G and G minor, respectively. The orchestral tag to "Listen to What the Man Said" leads to a long-held cello note which is in both chords (D), and creates both the proper musical context and the right emotional context for George. The seriousness in George's song is foreshadowed, and the buoyancy of "…the wonder of it all, baby…" becomes the first salvo in a conversation between two Beatles who mostly were not speaking to one another at this time. The combination is still a suite, but of a different kind, in which two Beatle voices seem pleasantly synchronous. Frankly, it's not that often that Paul and George can elevate each other in this way, but the moment really works.

The sequence also makes a fine bracket for the flip of the disc:

1A. What You Got (J)
1B. Junior's Farm (P)
1C. Goodnight Vienna (R)
1D. Far East Man (G)
 …
1Y. Listen to What the Man… (P)
1Z. ≈ This Guitar (Can't Keep from… (G)

Bless You (J)
Easy for Me (R)
Māya Love (G)
≈ Occapella (R)
≈ Old Dirt Road (J)
Scared (J)
Surprise, Surprise… (J)
≈ You (G)

2A. Soily (P)
2B. #9 Dream (J)
 …
2W. Tired of Midnight Blue (G)
2X. Let's Love (P)
2Y. Whatever Gets You thru the Night (J)
2Z. CODA: Goodnight Vienna (Reprise) (R)

With the most important slots filled, we have two small gaps left in order to complete the sides. There remain only a handful of tracks on the eligible list.

A perfectly good Ringo track, "Easy for Me," remains, but it becomes clear that there is no good place for it in the lineup. Side two would effectively come to a halt if that bridged the gap. Having two Ringo songs on this album is hardly a necessity. It's really only best to do if it is the perfect fit, and this definitely is not.

John's "Surprise, Surprise (Sweet Bird of Paradox)" also seems somehow out of step with the rest of the album content as it has developed in this assembly. Adding it in either of these gaps would come perilously close to transplanting some of the banality of his solo album. The same is not true with "Bless You," which actually feels like it adds to the breadth of this album.

"Scared" is probably the most complex of the remaining tracks. It begins with a wolf's howl, which we could certainly excise with a simple edit. But somehow that feels of a piece with the rest of the "night music" which will occupy the end of side two. It's tempting to place that immediately before "Tired of Midnight Blue" — if only because of the similar subject matter. The Beatles had done that before, but here it feels too spot on. This is a case where neither song would benefit from having an association with the other, despite the surface connection in the titles ("scared" and "tired"). Additionally, it would force "Bless You" onto side one, where it really is not welcome between "Far East Man" and "Listen to What the Man Said." Fortunately, "Scared" works very well in that side one slot, foreshadowing from a safe distance what is to come, if you choose to see it that way. The howling wolf emerges naturally from the guitar figure at the end of "Far East Man," and the fade out dovetails nicely with the spoken intro to "Listen to What the Man Said" — something which also could be easily excised with an edit, but has a role to play in making that a smooth transition.

That leaves "Māya Love" and "Bless You" to fill the gap on side two. In truth, they drop right in, George first — to avoid two songs in a row by the same Beatle — which also allows John's spoken outro to connect directly to the beginning of "Tired of Midnight Blue." Again, this is a case of avoiding something that is simply too spot on. If placed on side one, John's ad lib, "We take a listen," would bump up against the start of a song with the word "listen" in the title. You may think this would be a natural thing to do, but it is simply too obvious. The principles of assembly hold that such connections can only be made if there is a strong reason to do it *and* they do not appear too cute or obvious. Those criteria cannot be met here, putting songs in the wrong places for their best hearing.

15 / VIENNA

1A. What You Got (J)	Easy for Me (R)
1B. Junior's Farm (P)	≈ ~~Going Down on Love (J)~~
1C. Goodnight Vienna (R)	≈ ~~Here We Go Again (J)~~
1D. Far East Man (G)	≈ ~~I'll Give You a Ring (P)~~
1M. Scared (J)	≈ ~~Move Over Ms. L (J)~~
1Y. Listen to What the Man... (P)	≈ ~~Nobody Loves You... (J)~~
1Z. ≈ This Guitar (Can't Keep from... (G)	≈ Occapella (R)
	≈ Old Dirt Road (J)
	≈ ~~Only You (And You Alone) (R)~~
2A. Soily (P)	≈ ~~Ooh Baby (You Know... (G)~~
2B. #9 Dream (J)	≈ ~~Oo-Wee (R)~~
2M. Māya Love (G)	≈ ~~So Sad (G)~~
2N. Bless You (J)	≈ ~~Steel and Glass (J)~~
2W. Tired of Midnight Blue (G)	Surprise, Surprise... (J)
2X. Let's Love (P)	≈ You (G)
2Y. Whatever Gets You thru the Night (J)	
2Z. CODA: Goodnight Vienna (Reprise) (R)	

When you look at the list of eligible and alternate tracks, and acknowledge that not all eligible tracks were used, and that digging into the alternates was necessary to solve an important sequencing dilemma, you may be tempted to think this could have been a double album. After all, there is just the right amount of music, with nothing extra. But that fact alone suggests caution.

The balance between the voices would have been upset significantly, requiring either a deeper dive into Paul's outtakes, or a further raiding of *Venus and Mars*. Neither of those options is satisfactory because the dropoff in quality is precipitous. The same can be said for John's and George's remaining tracks. In truth, about the only track on the list that hasn't been mentioned, and feels like it might have a chance to contribute, is Ringo's "Occapella." Trying to squeeze that into the existing assembly yields no good options because it is so stylistically different from everything else. There is no real way to justify the Beatles moving in that musical direction, especially because even Ringo doesn't ever enter that same space again. To fit it into this album as a one-off, you would have to drop something that is a better match temperamentally, and disrupt the natural sequencing as a result.

It brings home a point that must always be held close: The essential problem with the solo years is *dilution*. As such, the essential solution is *concentration*. As soon as the process is opened up to lesser material, the finished product starts to sound like a hodge-podge, and it becomes incrementally more difficult to cover up all of the warts which get introduced.

As a single album, this lineup works, and works well. As a double, it immediately inherits multiple weaknesses from the source projects which are more or less impossible to paper over. In reality, making the right choices on what to cut may be the hardest — but most important — part of the Assembler's job. That occasionally will mean that some personal favorites (like "Easy for Me" and "Occapella") fall away, but that is the price we must pay for allowing the meta-Beatles to elevate each other once again.

Indeed, that was a price they paid in the late 60s by excluding George's lesser material, even as it became more formidable. But a key piece of Beatle Magic was editing each other, and you can argue that their rare missteps all involved letting things through which might have been better edited out. In the fused albums we are imagining, this aspect would have moved even more to the fore.

Fortunately, the outlets of B-sides for group singles, as well as solo albums, would have been readily available, so the music might not have been lost entirely. Both of Ringo's potentially "lost" tracks could have served well on Beatles singles of the era, or formed the seeds of more satisfying solo projects.

As an aside, at 15 tracks and 56 minutes the Beatles would have been providing quite a good value for the dollar on this one-disc album. By this point in the real world, a 10-song album was standard, and with an increasing prevalence of long songs, less tracks was not a problem. In other words, as long as an artist had *either* 10 songs or about 40 minutes, the standard was met. The Beatles would have bested both of these standards here.

Consider this quick sampling of classic albums from around the same time:

Album	Artist	Tracks	Minutes
Born To Run	Bruce Springsteen	8	39
Blood On The Tracks	Bob Dylan	10	52
A Night At The Opera	Queen	12	43
Wish You Were Here	Pink Floyd	5	44
Fleetwood Mac	Fleetwood Mac	11	42
Still Crazy After All These Years	Paul Simon	10	36
One Of These Nights	The Eagles	9	43
Young Americans	David Bowie	8	40
Darryl Hall & John Oates	Hall & Oates	10	35
The Who By Numbers	The Who	10	37
Averages		**9.3**	**41.1**

Working to these standards, a single album of Beatles music would have required relatively little of each songwriter — less than has been used on *Vienna*. John, Paul and George would have each needed to skim only three tracks from whatever solo project they were pursuing at the time, leaving one spot open for Ringo. Given the quantity of music they were still producing, this would seem, from a distance, incredibly easy to accomplish.

The reality would have been more complicated, of course, with internal competitive forces still fully functioning. In this period, for example, Lennon would have been left in the uncomfortable position of having produced more than enough

15 / VIENNA

for his quota on a group album, but not quite enough for a solid solo album. Once again, he would find some of his music excluded, which could have been a new source of band conflict, while also potentially leading to solo albums even more diluted than those we know.

Our assumption in these pages is that the Beatles would have wanted to hold to their original standard of providing exceptional value and exceptional quality, and would have done so even if it meant overcoming internal strife and diverging from industry standards — which they could not have cared less about.

S A V E   T H E   B E A T L E S !

Vienna

Principal Recording: June 1974 - May 1975
Release: June 1975

Side One
1. What You Got (Lennon)
2. Junior's Farm (McCartney*)
3. Goodnight Vienna (Lennon)
4. Far East Man (Harrison)
5. Scared (Lennon)
6. Listen to What the Man Said (McCartney*)
7. This Guitar (Can't Keep from Crying) (Harrison)

Side Two
1. Soily (McCartney)
2. #9 Dream (Lennon)
3. Māya Love (Harrison)
4. Bless You (Lennon)
5. Tired of Midnight Blue (Harrison)
6. Let's Love (McCartney)
7. Whatever Gets You thru the Night (Lennon)
8. Goodnight Vienna (Reprise) (Lennon)

* Originally "McCartney/McCartney"

15 / Vienna

Make It Yourself

Total Running Time: 56:24

Tk	Rill	Title	Source	Dur
F4-A1	—	What You Got	[1]	3:03
F4-A2	(3.0)	Junior's Farm	[2, bonus]	4:15
F4-A3	(2.5)	(It's All Down to) Goodnight Vienna	[3]	2:32
F4-A4	0	Far East Man	[4]	5:46
F4-A5	0	Scared	[1]	4:27
F4-A6	(9.5)	Listen to What the Man Said [Edit]	[2]	3:34
F4-A7	*	This Guitar (Can't Keep from Crying)	[5]	4:13

Total: 27:53

Tk	Rill	Title	Source	Dur
F4-B1	—	Soily [Studio version]	[2, bonus]	3:54
F4-B2	(1.1)	#9 Dream	[1]	4:39
F4-B3	(4.5)	Māya Love	[4]	4:18
F4-B4	0	Bless You	[1]	4:37
F4-B5	0	Tired of Midnight Blue	[5]	4:50
F4-B6	0	Let's Love	[2, bonus]	1:57
F4-B7	(4.0)	Whatever Gets You thru the Night	[1]	3:14
F4-B8	(11.0)	Goodnight Vienna (Reprise) [Edit]	[3]	1:00

Total: 28:31

[1] *Walls and Bridges*
[2] *Venus and Mars*
[3] *Goodnight Vienna*
[4] *Dark Horse*
[5] *Extra Texture (Read All about It)*

* NOTE: Descriptions of edits and crossfades, with sample audio, are available at:

SaveTheBeatles.com

Release
June 1975

Most Popular Albums
December 1973 - May 1975

US		UK	
BTO	*BTO II*	10cc	*Original Soundtrack*
BTO	*Not Fragile*	Barry White	*Can't Get Enough*
Charlie Rich	*Behind Closed Doors*	Bay City Rollers	*Once Upon a Star*
Chicago	*Chicago VII*	Bay City Rollers	*Rollin'*
The Doobie Brothers	*What Were Once Vices...*	Carpenters	*The Singles 1969-1973*
Earth, Wind & Fire	*...the Way of the World*	Ross/Gaye	*Diana and Marvin*
Elton John	*Caribou*	Elton John	*Greatest Hits*
Elton John	*Greatest Hits*	Engelbert Humperdinck	*His Greatest Hits*
Jim Croce	*Life and Times*	**Mike Oldfield**	***Tubular Bells***
Jim Croce	*You Don't Mess...*	Original Soundtrack	*The Sting*
John Denver	*Back Home Again*	Paul McCartney/Wings	*Band on the Run*
John Denver	***Greatest Hits***	Perry Como	*And I Love You So*
Joni Mitchell	*Court and Spark*	Queen	*Sheer Heart Attack*
Paul McCartney/Wings	*Band on the Run*	Rick Wakeman	*Journey to the Centre...*
Soundtrack	*The Sting*	The Stylistics	*The Best of the Stylistics*

Most popular album in bold

It is hard to look at this list without noting that it represents the doldrums of the 70s. And it is these doldrums which would eventually metastisize into synth-rock, and along the way lead directly to the rise of both disco and punk as responses. Indeed, the most artistically satisfying release on either of these lists may very well be by a former Beatle: *Band on the Run*. Only Queen, Joni Mitchell and Barry White even make a run in the direction of art over product.

Interestingly, greatest hits albums have now come to dominate, as record companies figured out that old music could be sold over and over in a variety of packages, while new music would always be speculative, a lesson learned from — who else? — the Beatles. The same dynamic led to the rise of soundtrack albums as primary releases instead of afterthoughts.

All of this means there is at least still room for the Beatles. There is nothing like *Vienna* on this list anywhere. You might argue that this is because the times have passed the Beatles by, or that they might have sounded like neither fish nor fowl. I am more inclined to say that there is a *void* in this list of music that only the Beatles could have filled. Perhaps there would not have been shockwaves, but their collective voice would have been heard loud and clear, and their album would have been a substantial hit. In a way, the Beatles would once again have truly stood alone.

15 / VIENNA

Topping the Charts
June 1975

US			UK	
Elton John	*Captain Fantastic...*	1	The Stylistics	*Best Of The Stylistics*
Earth, Wind & Fire	*That's The Way...*	2	Elton John	*Captain Fantastic...*
Soundtrack	*Tommy*	3	Bay City Rollers	*Once Upon a Star*
Jeff Beck	*Blow By Blow*	4	Kraftwerk	*Autobahn*
America	*Hearts*	5	Tammy Wynette	*Best of Tammy...*
Alice Cooper	*Welcome to My...*	6	The Three Degrees	*Take Good Care of...*
Chicago	*Chicago VIII*	7	Judy Collins	*Judith*
Bad Company	*Straight Shooter*	8	Tom Jones	*20 Greatest Hits*
Lynyrd Skynyrd	*Nuthin'fancy*	9	The Carpenters	*The Singles 1969 1973*
Carly Simon	*Playing Possum*	10	Mike Oldfield	*Tubular Bells*

Again we find Elton John at the top of the charts when *Vienna* would have been released. The question remains whether the two acts would have coexisted, or whether the Beatles would have squeezed Elton out — or vice versa. Unlike earlier eras, given how established Elton was by this point, it feels like the two acts would have most likely nodded at each other, and danced around at the top of the charts. Either way, once again there is nothing here to truly stand in the way of the Beatles juggernaut. The only real question is whether the public would have come along for the ride.

Of course, we might also ask if *Vienna* could have saved us from the inexplicable juggernaut *Tubular Bells*. That service alone might have justified the Beatles staying together for as long as it took.

Discussion

Without giving too much away, *Vienna* represents the last moment that the Beatles could be really current — that is, finding a niche somewhere in the contemporary canon of popular music, and therefore fully relevant. After this, they would clearly be a "legacy" act whose releases, though greeted with great fanfare and sales, would have had little impact on the rest of the music scene. In this way, the Beatles are likely to have followed that same path taken in the real world by the Rolling Stones, The Who, and other contemporaries.

That would not necessarily have been predictable at the time, because here they have forged a modern sound, and created some fantastic records individually, which could have made a formidable and entirely contemporary group album. Though the voices continue to veer apart in style and tone, the album does still sound remarkably unified, even if nothing like the old days.

As usual, critics would have heard what they expected to hear, though it would have been hard to dismiss any of the music as either passé or sub-standard. The sound of these tracks, when taken together, is vibrant and alive — indeed, much more so than either the other music on the charts, or the solo efforts from which they have been culled.

The group actually sounds more alive than the aforementioned members of the same British Invasion cohort. Where The Who (*Who Are You*) and the Rolling Stones (*It's Only Rock 'n Roll*) had continued making group records uninterrupted, and essentially unchanged in process, they trade more in continuity with what has gone before than innovation or even evolution. This is not to imply anything about the quality of the music, but more that each band's brand relied to a degree on them sounding by and large like they always had, rather than either matching the times or being somehow in front of them. In this way, they could retain the same core following, and not have to rely on recruiting from a new generation of fans.

Vienna is not, of course, an example of what we now would call "70s rock," nor is it exactly "70s pop." The Beatles sound relatively oblivious to other developments in popular music, continuing to inhabit their own distinctive style, which itself continues to evolve in interesting ways. It now diverges from much of the market, which is evolving in multiple different directions at once, while not becoming entirely disconnected. This is both the last time a Beatles album will be completely captivating, and the last time that the market will yield to them for reasons beyond loyalty and nostalgia. Put more plainly, this album would have appealed not only to the already-converted, but also to young listeners who had never heard of the band before, much in the way that Wings developed a following who had never heard of the Beatles (this author among that group).

Start with the likelihood that this album would likely have sold very well. Paul McCartney's growing stature as a solo artist would have served to keep the market warm for Beatles product, and his critics would have noticed that Paul continued to raise his game for group projects. By virtue of removing the dross, John Lennon would have sounded very much like the group's soul, as well as its fiery engine. George Harrison would have neatly skimmed over the pitfalls that plagued his solo recordings, while continuing to provide a sense of the mystical which, by now, would have been baked into the Beatles brand. Ringo Starr's contribution would likely have sounded a bit lonely to critics who, upon receiving only "Goodnight Vienna," may have commented about the need for the drummer to revive his own solo career. They would have had no way of knowing the depths Ringo was avoiding by limiting himself mostly to group projects.

A scant eight years removed from *Sgt. Pepper*, there would no doubt have been critics who wondered whether the world still needed Beatles albums. But all in all, that question would probably have seemed a little mean-spirited, given the good vibes this album projects. This might have been the moment when some fans and critics longed for those old days of studio experimentation and audible togetherness, but the times had clearly changed, and the Beatles, as the music on this album plainly demonstrates, had also changed, albeit not exactly as might have been expected. No longer style or innovation leaders, they would still have been seen as the most formidable supergroup on the planet.

And that may well have been the overarching theme of the reactions. The previous fused albums still had enough unity to mask some of the disparate production and musicianship, but this one would have fallen clearly into "supergroup" territory. Though the individual artists do still elevate one another (as they always will), each also clearly displays superstar chops. Like the reaction to Ringo's scant presence, many might have wondered why Lennon and Harrison weren't out there making more (or better) solo records, since they would have been perceived as clearly capable of thriving in any context — which, as we know, wouldn't have been as true as it seemed.

But this is where a fantasy intersects with reality. We know what Lennon, Harrison and Starr actually produced during this period, and in some cases, the world would not be much worse off without it. Anyone longing for more solo work from the individual Beatles would have been imagining things very different from what we know the world actually got. It's a cautionary tale to remember when wishing the world had turned out differently — one worth reflecting on even in our own imaginings. It's always better to leave the audience wanting more.

It puts me in mind of two specific instances where solo albums were eagerly anticipated but ultimately disappointing. The first would be Fleetwood Mac, whose members produced a smattering of solo albums while the group continued recording together. Stevie Nicks had the greatest success, albeit well after the group's prime, but multiple albums by Lindsey Buckingham, Christine McVie, and Mick Fleetwood fared poorly. In each case, the value of the collaborative energy became all too apparent by pulling the pieces apart. McVie's first solo album, specifically, was widely anticipated, given how essential her contributions had been to the group albums. But more than one critic noted a "sameness" pervading her work when not interspersed with the songs/voices of Buckingham and Nicks. (I hear that John McVie also made a solo album.)

Back in our slightly altered reality, Lennon would have released a handful of singles, and only two or three solo albums, but the work of his which made the Beatles albums would have kept him in very high regard among critics and fans. This is, arguably, a better outcome for him in the 70s. It might very well have led to him discovering a different, better solo voice along the way.

The other example worth considering is the four solo albums by Kiss, recorded and released concurrently at the very peak of their popularity. The idea, actually quite interesting and artistically noble in its own away (if less noble in marketing terms), was for each member to be himself and make the kind of album he would like to make. Individual personalities would be on display, and the result would strengthen the band's image once they returned to working together (and sell a lot of records in the meantime). Famously, that is not what happened. Instead, the weaknesses of each member were brutally laid bare, and the project began a downward spiral for the band, all but destroying their franchise.

As we know, this highlighting of weaknesses is a primary narrative of the solo Beatles. Thankfully, their solo efforts did not take down the Beatle brand, but they did deal it a blow. Perhaps, had the Beatles decided to keep collaborating from afar, they could have passed their wisdom to Gene, Paul, Ace and Chris.

With *Vienna*, as with all of the rescued albums, we find that the strengths of the individual artists continue to complement one another, and sufficiently mitigate their weaknesses. That they were no longer leading the music industry is beside the point because they were making great — and distinctive — music which could stand with its head up next to their classics.

Fusion Era #5

June 1975 - September 1977

Flight

16 / FLIGHT

"We're all very good friends. John is keeping very quiet at the moment..."

– Paul McCartney, September 1975

"We didn't start doing it for the money, and we ain't going to end it that way. The Beatles formed because four guys wanted to get together and play. Now those four guys are going their separate ways."

– Ringo Starr, September 1976

"Am invisible."

– John Lennon, January 1977

"We'd have to get to know each other again. Everyone's into their own lives. It seems very difficult, the idea of trying to get together."

– George Harrison, February 1977

Chronology

1975

Divorce from Maureen becomes final	**JUL**	
Wings Over the World (Europe, 13 shows)	**SEP**	*Extra Texture (Read All About It)* released
Sean Lennon born *Shaved Fish* released	**OCT**	*Lizstomania* premieres
Wings Over the World (Australia, 9 shows)	**NOV**	*Blast From Your Past* released

1976

Mal Evans dies Recording contract with EMI expires	**JAN**	Recording *Wings at the Speed of Sound* Signs with A&M Records
Father, James McCartney, dies *Wings Over the World* (Europe, 5 shows) *Wings at the Speed of Sound* released	**MAR**	Signs with Polydor/Atlantic
Father, Alfred Lennon, dies	**APR**	*Saturday Night Live* (TV) offers $3000 for Beatles reunion, John and Paul watching
Wings Over the World (North America, 19 shows)	**MAY**	George and Ringo attend Wings show in Toronto
Wings Over the World (North America, 12 shows)	**JUN**	Records "Cookin' (In the Kitchen of Love)" with John
Officially receives "Green card"	**JUL**	Misses album deadline due to hepatitis
Court declares "subconscious plagiarism" of "He's So Fine" Sued by A&M, moves to Warner Brothers	**SEP**	*Wings Over the World* (Europe, 4 shows) *Ringo's Rotogravure* released
Wings Over the World (England, 3 shows)	**OCT**	Sell the former Apple headquarters on Saville Row
The Best of George Harrison released *Thirty Three & 1/3* released *Saturday Night Live* (TV)	**NOV**	Appears on stage with The Band, filming *The Last Waltz* (film)
Wings Over America released	**DEC**	The Rutles have appeared

16 / FLIGHT

1977

Settle outstanding disputes with Allen Klein	JAN		Attends inaugural gala for Jimmy Carter
Allen Klein indicted for tax evasion	APR		*Thrillington* released
Live! At the Star Club... released *The Beatles at the Hollywood Bowl* released	MAY		Recording on *Fair Carol* in Virgin Islands "Seaside Woman" released
Divorce from Patti finalized	JUN		
James McCartney born	SEP		*Ringo the 4th* released

Introduction

Just before the beginning of this period, the nine-year recording contract the Beatles had signed with EMI in 1967 expired. The last ties to Beatle obligations, at least in an artistic sense, were finally broken.

But if the group had still been collaborating up to this point, there is no reason to think they would have stopped. This certainly would have been a moment for taking stock, and perhaps a chance to renegotiate all of those rules set up for the first fused release. But we will assume that all of that could have been worked out, and the albums would have kept coming.

Though Paul would still have emerged by this point as a superstar in his own right, he always had enough material left over to throw a few tracks at a group project without impacting his own. Both Harrison and Starkey still had something to prove, and might have appreciated having the relative safety of a meta Beatles album to buffer their ongoing attempts at credibility — or redemption.

Lennon's reaction, the hardest to guess at, almost certainly would have been more complex. He might have been relieved that the pressure for solo albums was off, or frustrated that a new solo recording contract did not materialize. His reaction would have set the tone for his approach to new group projects. He might have been willing to come out of the Dakota every once in a while to work on a track (or four) for a group album, or he might have sequestered himself and shot demo tapes toward the others with the promise of coming out to record vocals if someone else made the backing tracks. He might have simply stonewalled. There are certainly many other possibilities. We will simply assume that he would agree to be part of the occasional group project, and leave it at that.

Looking at the creative calendar, it does appear that an era effectively came to an end with the release of *Vienna* in 1975. In that way, the next group album, whatever it would have been, would have ushered in what might best be called, at least in retrospect, a lean phase for the Beatles. Sessions now happened even more sporadically, with considerably less overlap among the artists. Likewise, album releases were far more scattered.

Though the working method could have remained similar, with each passing year the individual artists would have shown less interest in the group releases and more in their own, and this moment appears to be some sort of tipping point. There would have begun much more premeditative balancing between releasing music on group vs. solo projects, and a greater reluctance to have an otherwise good track withheld under the assumption that it eventually might become part of a group project. From here on out, the group projects would have been the tail rather than the dog.

It seems likely that someone would have challenged the almighty control which had been ceded to the Assembler all these years — even if the results had been as positive as we imagine. Perhaps one or more of the Fabs might have wanted a shot at the role, or at least a more powerful say. Perhaps the Assembler might have made demands after dealing with many frustrations trying to stitch together such disparate styles into coherent releases. It's possible to imagine the Assembler fed up and ready to walk out, and the Beatles sensing (or not) the risks that would pose. We will have to assume that some sort of equilibrium was maintained, and the Assembler stayed and retained a strong creative role, with ultimate responsibility for the releases.

So, as 1976 began, there would have been a shudder of negotiation, followed by the restoration of peace with only minor changes to the working methods, and the assumption that another group album could be assembled late in the year. Each member would have agreed, and also been contractually obligated, to contribute.

As McCartney raced through sessions for *Wings at the Speed of Sound* in early 1976, he would also have kept a group project in the back of his mind. And with touring expected to fill the rest of the year, he would have used those sessions as his best chance to put something in the can to give to the group later.

Harrison and Starkey also recorded albums in 1976 that would have placed them in the same position. Recognizing at least some level of obligation to the band, but wondering just what that amounted to, each would have been obliged to hold some music in reserve, eventually waiting on Lennon to provide his quota of new material. All three would likely have wondered, however, just whether Lennon would provide anything at all, and with good reason. After the session for "Cookin' (In the Kitchen of Love)" in May, John went silent. Paul, George and Ringo would have started wondering if maybe things were changing more than anyone had guessed, given the birth of Sean Lennon the previous fall.

Indeed, Lennon's home recordings in 1976 are few, and there is simply no way to assemble an album with all four members in proper balance late in 1976. As a result, even if the Beatles were still theoretically collaborating at that point, the solo releases likely would have looked very much like what we know — perhaps with a few tweaks of schedule and content. There would have been no choice but to hold over the group project into 1977. Eventually, someone would have had to convince Lennon that he needed to provide some new music — a position he had been in many times in Beatle history, and an occasion to which he always rose.

Fortunately for our slightly altered narrative, Lennon did begin writing again in 1977, and we will assume that he would have been willing to do a limited amount of studio recording to provide material for the group project. For some fans, it may be hard to imagine this diversion from the real world. But keep in mind that Lennon's retreat was partly due to a lack of sufficient offers from record companies.[1] Given that his restlessness and desire to write new material apparently returned in 1977,

---

[1] *You Never Give Me Your Money*, pg 237

and there would have been at least some limited level of obligation to the band, it becomes possible to imagine him doing a few quick sessions in the summer of 1977 in order to make a group album possible in the fall. His demos do show an enthusiasm for what he was writing, which adds fuel to our imagined fire.

All of this would have put the Assembler in a complicated position. Tracks would have stacked up, and potentially been plucked away, throughout 1976. Once a revised release date in the fall of 1977 had been agreed upon, there likely would have been a flurry of activity to provide additional material, with various Beatles in various states of grumpiness about it. Harrison would likely have just walked away, having already provided enough material for his quota. McCartney would probably have relished the opportunity to have an outlet for his new material, given that his next solo album was still a year off. Starkey would have been happy to bend to the circumstances, and his marketing team would have had no choice but to work around the group requirements.

Flight would therefore have been assembled from the tracks withheld from 1976 projects, and new tracks created in 1977 specifically to fill it out. There would have been a span of almost 18 months between the first and last recorded tracks, both of which are by McCartney ("Warm and Beautiful" and "Girls' School," respectively), and we will assume that he would have accepted the delay and had no issue filling whatever gaps the removal of these tracks would have created in his solo catalog.

One side note. Given that Lennon did not actually do any studio recording in 1976 or 1977, we are forced to use recordings from 1980, with posthumous overdubs in 1983, to get a feel for how the songs would sound next to those of the other Beatles. Thankfully, in terms of recording technology and style, not that much changed between 1977 and 1980. It's imperfect, but unavoidable, and it turns out that they sound reasonably contemporary.

Similarly, and with some trepidation, there is little choice but to use the 1994 Threetles version of "Free as a Bird" rather than John's demo, to get a feel for how it would have fit. This raises the idea that something like that could have happened in 1977, with John providing basic tracks only, perhaps recorded at home, and handing them to the others to finish — a task McCartney and Starr might have relished even then. In fact, by this point in the real world, such recording "from a distance" had already been done a number of times by the Beatles, including tracks for *Ringo*. As such, perhaps it's not as crazy as it first sounds to bring the Threetles to 1977.

That also makes it not entirely crazy to think that, had this worked, yet another method of collaboration between the bandmates might have opened up. And that idea, in turn, leads to new ways to wonder about potential reunions, the thought of which always raises a sigh.

Recording
April 1976 - September 1977

⚙ Studio recording   ◯ Single release   ✈ Touring

	JAN	FEB	MAR	APR	MAY	JUN	JUL	AUG	SEP	OCT	NOV	DEC
76	👤	⚙	⚙	WINGS AT THE SPEED OF SOUND	✈	✈			✈	✈		
	👤					⚙	⚙			⚙		🖼	
	👤				⚙	⚙	⚙	⚙		🖼		
77	👤		⚙	⚙		⚙			⚙		March '78: 🖼
	👤			⚙			⚙		◯	🖼		

Paul McCartney, on a break from his *Wings Over the World* tour, hastily recorded the fifth Wings studio album, *Wings at the Speed of Sound*, during the early part of 1976. Despite lukewarm reviews, it sold very well, on the strength of two smash hit singles. The band then resumed their tour, including a wildly successful swing through the United States which would be packaged into yet another hit record, *Wings Over America*. The triple album — take that, George, John, and Yoko! — featured a cross section of hits from both the Wings and Beatles eras of Paul's career, and about this time spawned the half-joking wonderment among younger fans that Paul had ever been in a band before Wings. Unbeknownst to all involved, this would be the absolute apex of popularity and success for the band.

After the Wings tour came to an end, McCartney began recording the follow-up to *Speed of Sound*, sessions which included time on a makeshift yacht studio in the Carribean. Throughout 1977, the band laid down basic tracks for the new album, eventually recording what would become one of the biggest selling UK singles of all time. "Mull of Kintyre," written with Denny Laine and featuring a group of bagpipers known as the Campbeltown Pipe Band, became a cultural phenomenon in England, while making nearly no impact anywhere else, due largely to severe mishandling by Capitol Records in the US.

The success of "Mull of Kintyre" was bittersweet, however, because it came after two members of Wings had quit the band. When sessions resumed to complete *London Town*, only a three-piece band would partake. Though this followed the rough outline of the working methods used for *Band on the Run*, the finished product was significantly less successful artistically. The album received mostly tepid reviews for general inconsistency, though it did yield a number one single in the US in "With a Little Luck," and sold relatively well. (Note: Tracks for *London Town* are considered here despite not being completely finished until later in 1977 or early 1978. The presumption is that Paul's recording process would have been less leisurely if there were a Beatles project being prepared during the summer of 1977.)

Richard Starkey continued to try one more time to mine the formula which had resulted in success three years earlier. This time he made sure that all of the other three former Beatles were either present or represented, even coaxing John Lennon out of the Dakota for a final recording session before he became totally invisible. Paul McCartney contributed a song and some backing vocals. George Harrison's schedule made it impossible for him to participate in person, so Ringo opted to record an old song George had written, creating an involuntary presence on the album that actually resulted in George suing Ringo.

In some ways, the music on *Ringo's Rotogravure*, which critics universally panned and the public virtually ignored, was in some ways overshadowed by a compelling photo on the back of the sleeve, showing the old front door of Apple headquarters, now derelict and covered with graffiti. The Beatles would shortly dispose of the property once and for all.

Through the summer of 1976, Harrison recorded sporadically, but was quite pleased with the results. The finished album, *Thirty Three & 1/3*, received more critical love than George had known since his first solo album, with many critics acknowledging that the worst tendencies of his earlier recordings (preaching and whining) seemed to be gone altogether. Unfortunately, something had changed in the marketplace and the album had no impact either culturally or on the sales charts. This is essentially the moment when former Beatles not named McCartney became largely irrelevant to popular music.

As if to prove that very point, Ringo abandoned the old formula on his next album, and instead allowed producers to pitch him as a potential star of the latest fad: disco. Embarrassing as this was, it yielded no lasting consequences because very few people ever even heard of *Ringo the 4th*, let alone purchased a copy. Among the worst-reviewed albums in solo Beatle history, it is also among the poorest sellers, not even making an appearance on any chart.

Meanwhile, Lennon settled in to the Dakota. Contrary to his later characterizations, he did not exactly stop writing, but this period contains only a few confirmed demos — a gain for him, loss for the fans, and critical turning point in the narrative of the solo Beatles.

Materials

Overview
69 tracks: 33 eligible, 5 provisional

In the recordings from this era, we see two Beatles sounding comfortable and confident, and two sounding tentative and unsettled. George turns in the best record, but Paul's is the biggest seller. Ringo turns in finished product, but John's unfinished demos are considerably more interesting.

Perhaps coincidentally, John and Ringo each used imagery of birds in flight, even as a band called Wings flew around the world generating flights of hysteria among second generation Beatles fans. Nothing in George's music adds to this yearning to release the surly bonds and float upward, primarily because he seems to be looking down from up there already.

The fracturing of their respective sounds has continued apace. George has found something smooth and new, where Paul has gone full into MOR pop-n-roll, and Ringo rents his soul to disco. We can fairly wonder where John might have come down if he had been recording, but it's hard to imagine him sounding much different than he had right before he disappeared.

There still feels like an opportunity for the best work by all four men to be collected and push everyone higher into that imagined sky. Paul's first album of the era is really a near-miss, but its peripherals have some lift. His second is more churlish waves than carefree winds. And though George's album is a direct hit in terms of quality, it ultimately flew too far under the public's radar to make much of a dent. Despite his aspirations, Ringo's feet are planted firmly on the ground, while both quality and relevance have flown the coop. And John? Well, as he would have told you, he was "free as a bird," though his very next lyric tells us it's only the "*next best* thing to be," leaving all to wonder what he might have considered "best."

Paul McCartney
29 tracks: 16 eligible (9 withheld), 1 provisional (1 withheld)

Sources

M16	*Wings at the Speed of Sound* R: Sep 75 - Feb 76 P: McCartney		S: EMI	76-Mar
M17	"Girls' School" & "Mull of Kintyre" R: Feb-Aug 77 P: McCartney		S: Rude, Ranachan; EMI	77-Nov
M18	*London Town* R: Feb 77 - Jan 78 P: McCartney		S: Various (3)	78-Mar

16 / FLIGHT

	(Pseudonymous release)
	(Unreleased)

Tracks
◆ *Eligible or provisional but withheld for solo project*

😎	**B-Side to Seaside** (McCartney) (Issued as "Suzy and the Red Stripes") ⊘ (Quality) Total throwaway. Clunky, pointless, built from typical Macca "links."	M, 77-Mar
	Backwards Traveller (McCartney) ✓◆ More coded messages, but not quite a complete song, Potential missed.	M18-04, 77-Dec
	Beware My Love (McCartney/McCartney) ≈◆ (Quality) Catchy but lightweight. It fills a spot, but doesn't stick in the mind.	M16-04, 76-Feb
	Boil Crisis (McCartney) ⊘ (Quality) Not sure what Macca was thinking. Maybe trying to be someone else?	M18, 77-Oct
	Cafe on the Left Bank (McCartney) ✓◆ Another terrific song which evokes the early days while not sounding passé.	M18-02, 77-Nov
	Children Children (McCartney/Laine) ⊘ (Quality) Written for children, this might work in another context. Here it tanks.	M18-06, 77-Mar
	Cook of the House (McCartney/McCartney) ⊘ (Quality) Crummy song, and no sound effects can save it.	M16-07, 76-Feb
	Cuff Link (McCartney) ⊘ (Filler) Bad instrumental. Kills the album dead.	M18-05, 77-Dec
	Deliver Your Children (McCartney/Laine) ⊘ (Quality) A morality tale that is way out of place. Well-intentioned, but simplistic and dumb.	M18-11, 77-Nov
	Don't Let It Bring You Down (McCartney/Laine) ✓ A nice thought, and well-formed, this succeeds where much of the album fails.	M18-13, 77-Nov
	Don't You Wanna Dance (McCartney) ⊘ (Unfinished) Just a jot, this falls into "link" territory.	M18, 76-Jul
	Famous Groupies (McCartney) ⊘ (Quality) Not exactly a bad idea, but the music hall approach really grates.	M18-10, 77-Nov
	Girlfriend (McCartney) ⊘ (Quality) Way too cute, without much to redeem it. Automatic writing.	M18-07, 77-Dec
	Girls' School (McCartney) ✓ Great rocker, with weird (non-PC) lyrics. But overshadowed on this 45.	M17-01, 77-Aug
	I'm Carrying (McCartney) ✓◆ A SLS that completes a trifecta of greatness at the start of the album.	M18-03, 77-Dec
	I've Had Enough (McCartney) ⊘ (Quality) Not credible as a song or a track. It pretends to bite, but has no teeth.	M18-08, 78-Jan
	Let 'Em In (McCartney/McCartney) ✓◆ Macca finds a new type of quirky — again. Irresistible sing-along. Coded message?	M16-01, 76-Feb
	London Town (McCartney/Laine) ✓◆ JPM at his best, but sets a standard that the album just can't live up to.	M18-01, 77-Aug

	Morse Moose and the Grey Goose (McCartney/Laine)	M18-14, 77-Dec
	⊘ (Quality) Painfully long, painfully weird, painfully pointless. This is one to hate.	
	Mull of Kintyre (McCartney/Laine)	M17-02, 77-Aug
	✓ A classic that sounded silly to US ears at the time. Wasn't marketed well.	
	Must Do Something About It (McCartney/McCartney)	M16-09, 76-Feb
	✓◆ A simple song with a great feel. Seek the version with Paul's vocal.	
	Name and Address (McCartney)	M18-12, 77-Mar
	✓ The parade of styles continues. Nice sound. Nice song. But kind of alone.	
	Note You Never Wrote, The (McCartney/McCartney)	M16-02, 75-Oct
	✓◆ Moody, and maybe silly, but somehow mesmerizing. This works.	
	San Ferry Anne (McCartney/McCartney)	M16-10, 76-Feb
	✓◆ Another that slips away without leaving an impression. Skillful writing, but...yawn.	
	She's My Baby (McCartney/McCartney)	M16-03, 76-Feb
	⊘ (Quality) Falling off the wagon, this one is dumb filler. Would have fit on RRS.	
	Silly Love Songs (McCartney/McCartney)	M16-06, 76-Feb
	✓◆ Writing with full confidence, but dinging his own brand. Still, it has aged well.	
	Warm and Beautiful (McCartney/McCartney)	M16-11, 76-Feb
	✓ An overlooked classic, but leaves a too sweet taste as an album closer.	
	Waterspout (McCartney)	M18, 77-Jun
	✓ Very catchy. Typically incoherent lyric seems like it MIGHT mean something.	
	With a Little Luck (McCartney)	M18-09, 77-Nov
	✓ Nice 70s pop. Slinky synths and a great vibe. Smart writing.	

Paul McCartney's music from this period comes at the absolute peak of Wings. He would have his biggest 70s hits here, and maintain the hold he recently gained as the undisputed sole heir to Beatlemania.

Before you recoil too much from that characterization, consider that it was by choice, and wouldn't have had to be that way. When John Lennon stepped out onto the stage with Elton John in 1974, the crowd erupted in an unexpected frenzy, considerably greater than anything Elton had received during the show, and much like the old days. Similarly, when George Harrison began his *Dark Horse* tour around that same time, crowds screamed and were over the moon — until they realized they weren't exactly getting the former Beatle they had hoped for. In other words, either John or George could have also inherited Beatlemania, but made intentional decisions not to. Even Ringo could certainly have claimed part of that inheritance, but made no such moves toward live performance until forming his All-Starr Band many years later. By then, however, too much time had passed and his crowds, while very warm, did not scream in a manner descended from Beatlemania.

McCartney, in contrast, went full bore into the old act, albeit with different bandmates and at least some different songs. That this worked as well as it did is a testament not just to the excellence of the musicians in Wings, which is beyond question, but almost more to the staying power of the Beatles' fame. McCartney's willingness to embrace it rather than turn his back on it — as his former bandmates had done, and as he himself had done in the earliest Wings tours — meant that the audiences got the chance to relive something, even if most of them had probably not lived it in the first place.

McCartney's recorded music from this period was designed to enhance this dynamic, with Paul making very Beatle-compatible records, and putting on the very show audiences would have loved to see from the Fabs themselves. *Wings at the Speed of Sound*, for example, is built around two massive hits that sound as if they might actually be the Fabs in disguise. If "Silly Love Songs" seems a little too cute for that description, remember that "cuteness" was always Paul's corner of the Beatles' group personality. And if "Let 'Em In" feels a little too  formulaic, consider that it sounded like nothing else on the radio at that time, being a merging of multiple influences into something new and remarkably simple — a description which might be applied to any number of Beatle tracks.

It is tempting to conclude, therefore, that Paul had been in some way the soul of the Beatles — which all too many second generation fans did. Obviously, this has always been a terrible mistake. More accurate would be to say that Paul, at this point in his solo career, had figured out which things to distill from his Beatles years, and how to build his brand and its products around those things. Fans will probably disagree on whether it was a good or bad thing that he did this, when he might have taken a very different course, as did the others.

As a follow-up to *Venus and Mars*, all that was needed from *Speed of Sound* was compatibility and marketability. Thus, it is a very *safe* record, and sounded very familiar and comfortable right from the first moment of release. This is neither a compliment nor a criticism. *Speed of Sound* clearly does not aspire to be anything as complex as either *Venus and Mars* or *Band on the Run*. Unlike those albums, this is a mere collection of tracks, in service to no bigger idea of any kind. It contains neither a compelling title nor cover photograph, and there's no hint of a "reprise" of any kind, or even a surface concept. There really isn't anything connecting the tracks beyond their appearance on the same disc — a rarity, if not exactly a first, for McCartney as a solo artist.

In a sign of intentional democracy, all band members get features. This even includes using their original songs, as on Linda's novelty track, "Cook of the House" (co-written by Paul, according to the credits), Jimmy McCulloch's "Wino Junko," and Denny Laine's "Time to Hide." Of these, the latter two are ineligible for consideration to a Beatles project because Paul neither wrote nor sang on them. Linda's track stays on the list, but would likely be nothing but a novelty even with Paul singing lead.

Two other tracks, written by Paul, get lead vocals from another band member. Denny takes lead on "The Note You Never Wrote," a moody, mysterious, and engaging song that is surprisingly effective. With a Paul vocal, it might have fit well into a Beatles album. "Must Do Something About It" gives drummer Joe English a chance to sing, but this is really just a throwaway song and track, reminiscent of the *Red Rose Speedway* era. The same can be said for much of the remainder of the album, including "San Ferry Anne," "She's My Baby," and "Beware My Love." Only the first of this mostly forgettable trio has anything approaching memorability.

The album closes, however, with the instant classic, "Warm and Beautiful." The song has been maligned in some corners as too sweet, but that is mostly due to its divergence from the rest of the material and its placement in the running order. As the album closer, it has nothing following it to offset the admitted sweetness and clear the air, such as "Yellow Submarine" did after "Here, There and Everywhere." The reality is that Paul has written yet another standard, one that belongs in the canon of great songs, but will likely never be found there because of how it was initially contextualized.

We will assume that Paul allowed the Assembler to snatch up this track, which clearly belongs on a group project, and have him find something else to end his album. Given that there are no real leftovers from the sessions, it's hard to know how that might have worked out, but we will assume that Paul would have agreed, given the substantial increase in visibility and better contextualization the song would have received.

Clearly, Paul did not give the same amount of effort to *Speed of Sound* as he had to its predecessors — neither in writing, recording or assembly. At this point, he may have realized that it didn't matter, or simply not had enough time given the requirements of the concurrent touring. The album was received coolly by critics, but enthusiastically by fans, aided by substantial airplay for the two big hits, and the visibility of the tour. It spent seven weeks at number one in the US.

But both the airplay and the sales would be dwarfed in the UK a few months later by the release of "Mull of Kintyre" — a single for the ages. From a distance, the attraction seems quite clear. Via simplicity and just the right instrumentation, Paul and co-author Laine evoke a whole countryside, perhaps a whole country, or even a whole way of life. Until then, Paul's love of his farm and the attendant simple life often felt somewhat artificial, as if a carefully curated piece of his public persona, designed to separate him psychologically and geographically from his Beatle years. All that was wiped away by this ode to an obscure place that quickly came to represent a bucolic sense of perfection.

The record did not catch on in the US, and the reason is hardly a mystery: The record company did not believe it would, and did nothing for it, even as it continued to float at or near the top of the UK charts. The conventional wisdom that it was somehow wrong for the American market just doesn't ring true, especially considering the song's long tail. With such simplicity, and judging by the number of times it has been heard since in coffee houses everywhere, it is likely among the most covered McCartney songs of all time. That Capitol could make nothing of it may be perhaps the single biggest missed opportunity in McCartney's solo catalog — and it cost them dearly when the time came for Paul to consider where he would sign next.

"Girls' School," though designated as a double A-side, made no impact on either side of the Atlantic. This is a shame because not only is it a solid rocker, but it tells a quirky story in a quirky setting filled with what latter day listeners would certainly consider "politically incorrect" imagery. Paul is probably content that this track isn't well remembered, but its provocations were pretty tame, and somewhat obscured. It will make a fine addition to the group project, where it will better get its due.

Those two tracks, cleaved into a non-album single, were recorded along with most of the material which became *London Town*. For our purposes, even though the album was not formally mixed until the following January, we will assume that the Assembler had access to rough mixes during the summer of 1977, when most of the recording took place, and could have made requests of McCartney regarding the group album. Unfortunately, there might not been much in the way of requests forthcoming.

The finished album shows some aspirations of moving back to McCartney's tried-and-true formula. It definitely features a compelling cover image, and a simple and malleable "concept," but it can't meet the additional criteria of good enough music and careful assembly. Paul doesn't even *try* to reprise the title track, perhaps recognizing that it outclassed everything else on the album.

Indeed, the first 11 minutes of *London Town* has every bit as much potential as any other album Macca made in the 70s. It rivals the first 13 minutes of *Band on the Run*, and the first 12 minutes of *Venus and Mars* in the building of a musical world. It sets a careful stage, a distinct tone, and brings us into the expectation of something like a story.

Then it tanks, big time. From the moment "Backwards Traveler" segues into "Cuff Link," we emerge from the compelling and carefully-woven setup, into a world of annoying pastiche, blatant banality and utter incomprehensibility. Unfortunately, like too many of the other solo Beatle projects, the culprit is not exclusively the sequencing. It's the material, which is largely substandard, sounding even more so after expectations get raised by the beginning. Perhaps if those first four fantastic tracks hadn't been clustered so well the dropoff in quality wouldn't be so noticeable, but it is, and no amount of care in sequencing could have saved the material.

As a source of potential Beatles music, therefore, those first four tracks are all the Assembler might have even been interested in. Indeed, there is a reasonable case to be made that any group album assembled in this period could have used that opening unchanged — provided the other Beatles were actually playing on it. That would have violated the rule of no more than two consecutive tracks by the same songwriter, but perhaps a Lennon response might have contributed to or extended the sequence, and brought in a response from Harrison.

In the world of fused Beatles albums, however, the sequence would simply have overwhelmed any group project, which neither the Assembler nor the other Beatles would have allowed. These tracks will remain eligible, but withheld by Paul once he realizes that the group album is moving in a different direction.

Of the rest of the album, only "With a Little Luck" and "Don't Let It Bring You Down" might appeal to the Assembler. The former is brimming with Beatle optimism, while the latter offers a gentle reassurance for when things don't turn out. Of the two, the first sits the least comfortably with the rest of the available material in this era, sounding a little too self-contained. The same problem afflicts "Name and Address," the homage to the Sun sound. Though it feels strong enough for consideration, its status as something of a unicorn will keep it off the group album.

The rest of *London Town* is sadly disposable. Dreck like "I've Had Enough" and "Girlfriend" — grating even in Michael Jackson's squishy cover — might have better stayed in the can. The same squishiness applies to the two "children" collaborations with Laine, "Children Children" and "Deliver Your Children." No one would argue with the sentiments, but the songs are slight in the extreme. Similarly, the incoherence and bloatedness of "Morse Moose and the Grey Goose" feels like it is primarily filling space.

"Famous Groupies" can't really be thrown in with the others. Though certainly annoying, it also feels like some sort of coded message, making it at least marginally more interesting — though still not interesting enough to be eligible for a group album. Like the rest, even in our slightly altered world, it would have been released on a version of *London Town* almost identical to what the world actually heard.

Given the timing of these session, we might imagine a controversy in which Paul sees the assembly of the group album in progress, decides to write and record the very Beatle-y "London Town" to give it some shape, but finds it left behind by the Assembler because it does not fit the theme which is developing. Indeed, as we will see, it will be tracks by two other Beatles which suggest the album's theme, and Paul's latest magnum opus, fantastic as it is, would have hijacked that.

There is a degree to which this is the point where we can imagine Paul's confidence at such a high level that he no longer feels bound to what the Assembler wants for the group projects. Part of our exercise in this book has to be the realization that the 70s would have eventually led to all four Beatles asserting their independence — only *without* all the acrimony which surrounded the actual breakup. They would have tested the solo waters, retreated back to the group, then repeated the cycle until all felt confident enough to go it alone in perpetuity. This would have been the better way to ease into the solo era for everyone, either allowing mistakes to have a lower profile, or avoiding them altogether.

That comes with the assumption that eventually they would all break out of that pattern and come to see the group projects as secondary, and perhaps even unnecessary. The benefit of this "soft" breakup is that it allows everyone to adjust to the new demands, and only gradually set the group aside, resulting in more successful solo careers. The cost — the group's inevitable breakup — would still have had to be paid, but that could have happened in a much less painful fashion, while also leaving behind a group catalog almost twice as large.

Indeed, the inevitability of solo works dominating the group's output, and the greater chance for solo success by working up to that, is what our project here is all about. By definition, we've always known, or should have, that this process would bring about its own end, which Paul's work at this juncture suggests might have come by now, at least for him.

One final note on this era. In a largely overlooked connection, after George covered Big Ben for "Ding Dong, Ding Dong" in late 1974, and relations between the former Beatles thawed during 1975, we find Paul tacking a sly reference to George's hit onto the beginning of his own. As Paul told the story, the opening of "Let 'Em In" was something of a serendipitous thing, but we would be wise to look beyond. In context, the doorbell chimes which open the track (and the album) feel more like a smiling nod in George's direction — and an "I saw what you did there" wink to George's semi-nostalgic video. The chimes are immediately followed by a lyric which sounds different once the connection has been recognized: "Someone's knockin' at the door / Somebody's ringing the bell ... Do me a favor, open the door, and let 'em in." It's as if Paul has heard what he thought was an invitation — a knock on the door, if you will — from another former Beatle, and is answering it. Can it be mere coincidence that the track also ends with a modern version of the quintessential Beatles fadeout fakeout?

Yes, it could all be innocent and coincidence and unrelated, but Paul has been a well-known purveyor of misdirection before. The fraternal connections between John, Paul, Geoge and Ringo ran very deep, and they loved nothing more than to play such games, tucking little secrets into tracks at every point in their careers.

Alas, if this was indeed a coded message of some sort, it did not bear fruit. But how must it have sounded to the other Beatles to hear Paul's message, whatever it was, coming from every radio for months in the summer of 1976?

Ringo Starr
22 tracks: 5 eligible, 2 provisional

Sources

S09	*Ringo's Rotogravure* R: Apr-Jul 76 P: Mardin		S: Cherokee (LA), Atlantic (NY)	76-Sep
S10	"Wings" / "Just a Dream" R: Feb-Jun 77 P: Mardin		S: Atlantic (LA)	77-Aug
S11	*Ringo the 4th* R: Feb-Jun 77 P: Mardin		S: Cherokee (LA), Atlantic (NY)	77-Sep

Tracks

Can She Do It Like She Dances (Duboff/Robinson) — S11-06, 77-Jun
∅ (Quality) "Honky-tonk-ish" boom-chicka meets disco. Just a terrible song/record.

Cookin' (In the Kitchen of Love) (Lennon) — S09-06, +J, 76-Jun
✓ Not JL's best, but authentic, unlike everything else here. A flicker of Beatle magic.

Cryin' (Starkey/Poncia) — S09-04, 76-Jul
∅ (Style/Quality) Quirky beat adds/drops cannot disguise clichéd tripe. Also on the wrong album.

Dose of Rock 'n' Roll, A (Groszman) — S09-01, +J, 76-Jul
✓ Happy, pseudo-throwback, straight pop. Catchy, if a little clichéd, rewrite of "Hey! Baby."

Drowning in the Sea of Love (Gamble/Huff) — S11-01, 77-Jun
∅ (Style) Disco hell. Even a spirited vocal (mixed way back) cannot redeem this.

Gave It All Up (Gallagher/Lyle) — S11-04, 77-Jun
∅ (Quality) Weepy, lousy story song, bad for Ringo. Contrived product.

Gypsies in Flight (Starkey/Poncia) — S11-09, 77-Jun
∅ (Quality) Pedal steel, slow shuffle, lousy vocal, on the wrong album — still in no way good.

Hey! Baby (Channel) — S09-02, 76-Jul
≈ (Filler) Feelgood sing-along, nicely done. Simple and fits Ringo nicely.

I'll Still Love You (Harrison) — S09-07, 76-Jul
✓ Risky to try without GH, but Ringo (with Lon Van Eaton) pulls it off. Works well.

It's No Secret (Starkey/Poncia) — S11-08, 77-Jun
∅ (Style) Wants to be 70s California soft rock, but fails. Disco-ish, cold, cheap, imitative, boring.

Just a Dream (Starkey/Poncia) — S10-02, 76-Jun
∅ (Style) Not a bad song, but a TERRIBLE record. Worst. Disco. Ever.

Lady Gaye (Starkey/Poncia/Ward) — S09-10, 76-Jul
∅ (Style/Quality) International playboy. Relaxed beat, with some swagger, but no real point.

Las Brisas (Starkey/Andrews) — S09-09, 76-Jul
∅ (Style) International playboy. Mariachi. Harmless, but not catchy enough to hang with RS's big hits.

Out on the Streets (Starkey/Poncia) — S11-05, 77-Jun
∅ (Style) An unholy disco-ish four-in-the-bar song with terrible lyrics. Ringo gives it his all.

Pure Gold (McCartney) — S09-03, +P, 76-Jul
✓ Weak song from Macca mines familiar tropes, goes nowhere. Ringo phones it in. Dull.

	Simple Love Song (Starkey/Poncia) ⊘ (Style/Quality) Inoffensive but banal. Not quite disco, not quite pop, nothing much here.	S11-10, 77-Jun
	Sneaking Sally Through the Alley (Toussaint) ⊘ (Style/Quality) Embarassing, dumb song, wasting a host of great musicians. Nothing redeeming.	S11-07, 77-Jun
	Spooky Weirdness (uncredited) ≈ (Filler) Not especially compelling, but definitely lives up to its name.	S09-11, 76-Jul
	Tango All Night (Hague/Seufert) ⊘ (Style) International playboy. Pseudo-latin beat performed completely square. Bad.	S11-02, 77-Jun
	This Be Called a Song (Clapton) ⊘ (Quality/Filler) Weird mish-mash of styles. Not a good choice for RS, very awkward.	S09-08, 76-Jul
	Wings (Starkey/Poncia) ✓ Palatable, even fitting, for Ringo. Straight pop, and not bad at all.	S11-03, 77-Jun
	You Don't Know Me at All (Jordan) ⊘ (Style) Pre-disco, formulaic, cheesy. Inoffensive, but would set Ringo on a very bad path.	S09-05, 76-Jul

At this point in our slightly altered narrative, Richard Starkey would probably still have been making the same sorts of albums he actually made, and just hoping that his fellow Beatles and the Assembler would find something worthy of advancing under the group's name. They would have, but just barely.

The essential problem, as it always has been, is that Ringo has very little emotional range to his singing. This simultaneously means there are limits, and no limits. The limits are that the music can't ask him to do too much. He just doesn't have that. But it also means that he is not necessarily restricted to some particular style. His voice can be applied across many different styles with the *potential* for success. That's why Ringo's catalog contains country ... next to mariachi ... next to pop ... next to rock ... next to (God help us) disco.

Unfortunately, quality matters. While Ringo can make the most of a *good* song, and theoretically could thrive next to a mariachi band, he cannot lift a *bad* song. Unlike McCartney, who has a bag of tricks which can turn the fluffiest idea into a satisfying record, Starkey is only ever as good as his material.

Further, good material isn't quite enough. At the risk of sounding like a broken record, there are "Ringo" songs, and "non-Ringo" songs, and producers needed to recognize and work within this important principle. Unfortunately, during this era his collaborators started in earnest to sell him out — quite literally. The assumption appears to have been that his distinctive style of singing was a salesman that could sell anything. That approach was misguided and disrespectful, and essentially torpedoed his career.

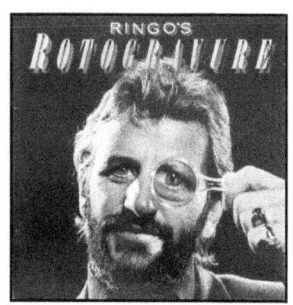

Ringo's Rotogravure attempts to pick up where we left him on *Goodnight Vienna*. Two former Beatles are heard, with the third present in songwriting only. Plenty of famous names are also present,[2] but the result is an undeniable mess.

There seems to be the embryo of a throwback theme at the beginning of the album, with three songs in a row that suggest a bygone era. Two of those, "A Dose of Rock 'n' Roll" and "Hey! Baby" are pleasant enough evocations of the 50s, despite feeling generally irrelevant to pop music in 1976. Since they are sufficiently charming, however, both will be brought forward for consideration by the Assembler. The third track, McCartney's "Pure Gold," sounds entirely phoned in, but will remain eligible due exclusively to provenance. Starkey's own "Cryin'" seems to want to follow these in structure and content, but its production sounds entirely too modern, rendering the song itself an empty anachronism.

From there, the album veers through an obstacle course of styles, never again hitting on anything related to the opening, with mostly forgettable results.

Both Harrison's song, "I'll Still Love You," and Lennon's "Cookin' (In the Kitchen of Love)" stand out from the background by being neither half-assed pastiche, nor forgettable. While Lennon's is the lesser song, his presence on the track makes a significant difference, lifting the energy of the recording well above everything that surrounds it. Though Harrison was not present to record his song, and ultimately would sue Ringo over the recording, Starkey enlisted Lon Van Eaton to play some Harrison-esque guitar, and the track sounds more like the Beatles than anything he's done since "I'm the Greatest." Both of these tracks will translate easily to the group project, and nothing else on this album comes even remotely close. "Spooky Weirdness" stays on the provisional list because it has the potential to be a wild card, faintly recalling the studio hijinks of "You Know My Name (Look Up the Number)."

It's a bit of false advertising to put Ringo's name on the travesty known as *Ringo the 4th*. It really should be credited directly to the marketeers who conceived and realized this. Ringo's voice is used as a prop, mixed so far back on most of these tracks that he might as well be Johnny Bravo. In front of him are some of the best session musicians (and future stars) of the era,[3] but they shouldn't have to take the blame for this either.

The clear intent is to position Ringo as a purveyor of disco, with the obvious goal of cashing in on a fad before it flames out. But even with that in mind, the album fails. It contains only one pure disc track, "Drowning in the Sea of Love," and two that are close but don't quite get there, "Out on the Streets," and "She Can Do It Like She Dances." Another, 'Simple Love Song," leans that direction but cannot commit. Still two other tracks purport to be something else, but find themselves nearly subsumed into disco-esque

---

[2] Peter Frampton, Eric Clapton, Dr. John, Melissa Manchester, and Harry Nilsson.
[3] Bette Midler, Melissa Manchester, Richard Tee, Luther Vandross, and David Foster.

instrumentation and arrangements. "Tango All Night" wants to be Latin, but the band can't keep a straight face all the way through, while "It's No Secret" wants to be Glen Campbell or Eagles, while almost breaking into full disco toward the end.

The only redeeming song, "Wings," is straight pop/rock, fits Ringo well, and does not sound either like a cliché or a fad. It's the only track the group might have considered, and because it picks up a theme floating among the former Beatles, might have provided the group project with a title song if not for McCartney's ubiquitous use of the word.

These sessions famously also produced one of the worst ever Ringo tracks, "Just a Dream," which was used only as a B-side — but inexplicably *twice*. The song itself has a couple of nice turns, and is not really the problem. Regrettably, the recording takes Ringo completely down the disco rabbit hole. Every element is stereotypical, from the beat, to the back-up vocals, to the high strings, to the overactive bass — just everything. The track is like a time machine to a very unfortunate moment in pop.

Weirdly, this particular record might not be so unbearable if it were sung by anyone but a former Beatle. Maybe it could even have been a hit for someone with the right look and lack of dignity. For anyone with the stage name Ringo Starr it's a rather degrading exercise. The style does not suit Ringo, and his performance is so square that a listener can almost see him self-consciously tapping his foot on every beat throughout. Maybe more to the point, if Ringo ever had his own "style," this is about as far away from it as a record could be. In that way, it is an oddly fascinating, if simultaneously repulsive, listen. Needless to say, it would have been completely irrelevant to any Beatles project.

Beyond the released tracks, there is not a thing known to be left in the archives for either of these albums, and thus nothing else to mine. Thankfully, we have enough tracks to make up Ringo's quota on the album, some of which will also help satisfy parity requirements among the Beatles along the way.

George Harrison
11 tracks: 9 eligible (6 withheld), 2 provisional (2 withheld)

Sources

H08	*Thirty Three & 1/3* R: May-Sep 76 P: Harrison/Scott	S: FPSHOT	76-Nov
	(Unreleased)		

Tracks

◆ = *Eligible, but withheld*

Beautiful Girl (Harrison)		H08-03, 76-Sep
✓◆ GH sounds relaxed, confident. Very fine song, and sweet, warm record.		
Crackerbox Palace (Harrison)		H08-09, 76-Sep
✓◆ Uptempo, happy sound. Very playful, and gently meaningful.		
Dear One (Harrison)		H08-02, 76-Sep
✓◆ Boldly drumless and smooth as silk. Beatle-y arrangement exudes health and warmth.		
It's What You Value (Harrison)		H08-06, 76-Sep
✓ Confident and catchy, underrated straight pop. Great chorus. Refreshing from GH.		
Learning How to Love You (Harrison)		H08-10, 76-Sep
✓◆ With GH maturing as a songwriter and vocalist, this rewrite is beautifully crafted. Great track.		
Mo (Harrison)		H, 77-Mar
✓ Great song. Leading edge of the excellence of the GH album. Similarities to "Faster."		
Pure Smokey (Harrison)		H08-08, 76-Sep
✓ GH rewrites himself, with significant improvement. Smooth, late night sound. Pure FM.		
See Yourself (Harrison)		H08-05, 76-Sep
✓◆ Pointed, but not harsh. Purposeful pop, with Beatle-y mixed meter. Works.		
This Song (Harrison)		H08-04, 76-Sep
✓◆ Solid hit potential, unfortunately unrealized — but nothing wrong here. Great track.		
True Love (Porter)		H08-07, 76-Sep
≈◆ (Filler) Something of a misfire, but it could be that listening to Porter made GH a better songwriter.		
Woman Don't You Cry for Me (Harrison)		H08-01, 76-Sep
≈◆ (Style) Echoes his ponderous writing, but mostly sounds like turning a corner to something new.		

In this period, George Harrison made a critical turn in the nature and quality of his recorded works. The growing presence of Olivia Arias is only the most obvious external change. He also resolved the "My Sweet Lord" litigation, finalized his divorce from Patti, suffered a life-threatening bout of hepatitis, began recovery from various addictions, switched record labels — twice — and anticipated the birth of Dhani. More directly to the music, he engaged Tom Scott to co-produce his next batch of recordings.

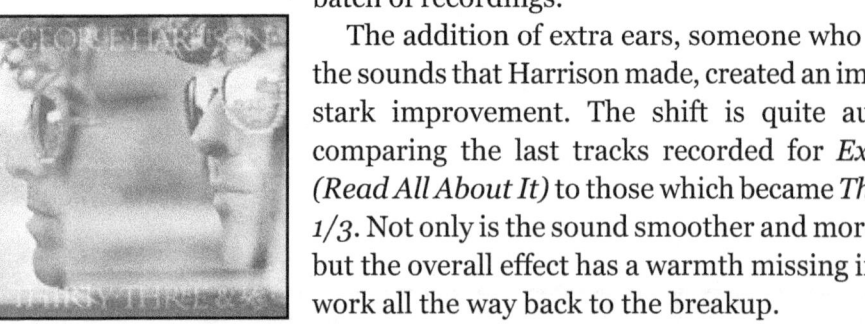

The addition of extra ears, someone who could shape the sounds that Harrison made, created an immediate and stark improvement. The shift is quite audible when comparing the last tracks recorded for *Extra Texture (Read All About It)* to those which became *Thirty Three & 1/3*. Not only is the sound smoother and more integrated, but the overall effect has a warmth missing in Harrison's work all the way back to the breakup.

A great way to hear this is to listen to "Ooh Baby (You Know That I Love You)" followed immediately by "Pure Smokey." The latter, clearly a rewrite of the former, builds on the same riff, now beautifully accentuated by the horns in a way only suggested in the earlier track. Likewise, the lyrics moved from a rambling, somewhat muttered banality, to an idea with form, shape and direction.

Once you've completed that listening experiment, move next to "Learning How to Love You," a somewhat overlooked classic cast in roughly the same mold, but nudging the idea in a slightly different direction. Though similar in feel, both song and track now mellow into soft 70s mood lighting, courtesy of the Fender Rhodes piano which, though present on the earlier record, comes here into a warm glory. The Fender is a classic 70s instrument, and especially so when played by the incomparable Richard Tee — as it is on both of the newer tracks.

Perhaps the best way to characterize the shift is as a release of tension. Harrison's two previous albums are filled with tension — in his singing, writing, playing and recording. It is a subtle thing, amplified slightly at every step of the recording process. Likewise, the release of that tension on *Thirty Three & 1/3* is amplified by every part of the process. Harrison's voice, which in earlier moments had sounded at odds with the backing track, now integrates seamlessly. His guitar-playing, which had fallen into sliding sameness, now sings again — a voice rather than a fixture.

So stark is the difference in quality that basically anything on this album is good enough for the Beatles, and could have served both to elevate and be elevated. When considering this new material, the Assembler would have found more than enough to love and work with, while also recognizing the need to give Harrison a solo moment. So even though there are many tracks on *Thirty Three & 1/3* that would have been eligible for a Beatles album, the smallest number possible will be extracted. We will have the Assembler request that a couple of tracks to be brought forward, and allow Harrison to withhold the rest. This is clearly a moment when George will be reluctant to give too much to the group anyway, and with good reason. Thus, *Thirty Three & 1/3* could have been released nearly unchanged.

Separate from George's solo album, a famously orphaned track might have made its way to the group project. "Mo" is a great piece of pop writing recorded as a gift for Mo Ostin's 50th birthday, and apparently never considered for release on any Harrison project. The Assembler will grab it because this is clearly a harbinger of even greater warmth to come, effectively a bridge between the warmth of *Thirty Three & 1/3* and the maturity and mastery which will be found on George's next record. It also has a great, Beatle-y feel, and will sit well next to tracks of the same era by the other Beatles.

John Lennon
7 tracks: 3 eligible, no provisional

Sources

L14	**Milk and Honey** (2 tracks) R: Aug-Sep 80 P: Lennon/Ono (Douglas) S: Hit Factory (NY)			84-Jan
	(Unreleased)			

Tracks

Free as a Bird (Lennon) ✓ JL's ode to being out of contract is built on melancholy. The Threetles made it pop.	L, +PGR, 77-Sep
I Don't Wanna Face It (Lennon) ✓ Not quite realized, but still a substantial piece. Overly familiar territory.	L14-03, 77-Sep
Mirror, Mirror (On The Wall) (Lennon) ⊘ (Unfinished) Sad waltz with some interesting turns, but not complete enough to consider.	L, 77-Sep
Nobody Told Me (Lennon) ✓ Jaunty vibe. Classic JL lyric — if a little lite. Pointed toward good things to come.	L14-05, 76-Dec
Now and Then (Lennon) ⊘ (Unfinished) Another sad song, and sadly unfinished. Hardly any hit potential. Deep album only.	L, 77-Sep
One of the Boys (Lennon) ⊘ (Unfinished) Up tempo and breezy, but overly self-conscious, even for JL.	L, 77-Sep
She's a Friend of Dorothy's (Lennon) ⊘ (Unfinished) So much potential here, both as a hit and with artistic value.	L, 76-Dec

As John begins his self-imposed exile at the Dakota, the process of evaluating his songs for an imagined Beatles album must change, at least slightly. We now have a patchwork of demos: some for complete songs, some for songs that will never be finished, and some that will morph over time or be cannibalized into different songs. Of these, some will never emerge from demo state, while others will be taken up in studios later — in two cases, *much* later.

One thing to note that is very important, however, is that all of John's later claims about not touching his guitar for years at a time are patently false. Indeed, just when you think you've heard every demo he did during his four years away, another one surfaces. Knowing what we do about John's temperament, it is frankly impossible to imagine him musically dormant, while entirely possible to imagine him making hyperbolic statements later, for image-building purposes, which may have felt true to him, but were not even half-truths.

While the abundance of demoed material may seem at first like a potential boon to the process of rescuing Beatle albums, that is not really the case. As we have come to know, John's working methods involved generating ideas on a more or less constant basis, and then only curating them when it came time to go into the studio. Had there been recording sessions in 1977, say for a follow-up to *Walls and Bridges*, it seems likely that John would have taken any number of these song fragments and pounded them into usable material, either right before the session or during it. When you look at the list of songs above, the nature of his follow-up can be imagined, at least a little.

Of course, during this period, he thought he might be writing songs for an autobiographical Broadway show, an idea which appears never to have advanced beyond the inevitable title, *The Ballad of John and Yoko*, and a couple of song ideas. We will treat all of these as if they might have been available to our Assembler, though we will find him generally uninterested in unfinished ideas.

Since part of our goal with this project is to get a sense for how the rescued Beatles albums might have *sounded*, just like the Assembler we will be forced to prioritize songs which were actually finished enough to get some studio time in 1980, while placing them in our timeline where they first appeared as demos, and just ignoring the interval between writing and recording. Admittedly, this pulls some sounds from 1980 and 1994 back to 1977, but it's the best avenue available.

One alternative would be to have the Assembler accept these tracks in demo form and place them in the group album anyway — similar to John's inclusion of "My Mummy's Dead" on *Plastic Ono Band*. Unfortunately, the ever-increasing proficiency and success of the other former Beatles in the studio makes this an unattractive option. A demo of "I Don't Wanna Face It" would not have sat on an album comfortably next to Paul's lushly finished recording of "Mull of Kintyre."

We are fortunate, however, that there is enough here to scrape together a contribution from John that will roughly balance his other bandmates. This is possible because the songs on our list are, for the most part, finished, and entirely of a quality sufficient for the project. That will not be the case again until 1980, bringing about the hiatus discussed in the next chapter. But there is much to be liked in this truncated collection.

Indeed, in the intervening decades, skilled artists have demonstrated the strength of at least two of these songs, taking up the cause that Lennon did not. Amid the vast ephemera on YouTube can be found a Threetles-like treatment of "Now and Then" by an anonymous author which is good enough to be mistaken for the rumored real thing. It clearly demonstrates the strength of the song idea, and how it might have become a moody masterpiece. Similarly, a very skilled group known as Estefy Lennon Band has created a fully-realized reading of "She's a Friend of Dorothy" which reveals the song as a lost pop masterpiece.

We cannot use these recordings in our rescue, of course, but they provide tantalizing glimpses of what might have been possible had the Beatles been collaborating, and John willing enough to contribute a track or two from his self-imposed exile.

"Free as a Bird" may very well have been one of those contributions. Though not Lennon's most substantial composition ever, it made for a nice pop record with the later contributions for the *Anthology* project. Had there only been the demo of "Free as a Bird," we would not have been able to consider it for this particular rescue. The Assembler would have likely rejected it with the other nascent ideas. Since we know what the Threetles would do later with this demo, we will pull their recording back in time and consider it here. This is not to suggest that such a dynamic would have happened at the time. It's rather difficult to gauge the level of interest the others might have had in gussying up a demo by one member who refused to do the work himself, but the dynamic would have been markedly different in 1977 than it would eventually be in 1994.

The "finished" recording from *Anthology* clearly represents an instance of the Beatles using pure craft to lift a lesser idea, though it hardly results in a great piece of art. Perhaps most interesting is that while George and Ringo contribute distinctive, instantly recognizable playing, Paul's contributions — beyond his lead vocal during the break — are largely anonymous. We know it is Paul playing bass and singing back-up, and probably doing a hundred other things, but all the edges are sanded off. It doesn't sound like Beatle-Paul at all, highlighting that there was a very real distinction, and line of demarcation in Paul's career as a whole. His contributions here do not rise to the emotional level he and George once created behind John's voice. Surely Lennon's absence is part of this, but so is Jeff Lynne's skilled but overly controlled production. The Threetles sound way too much like the Traveling Wilburys or Tom Petty. George Martin wisely begged off the project, but that just becomes another lost potential, another *what if...?*

As it turns out, "Free as a Bird" will form the spine of a theme for the album when balanced against a track with similar imagery by Ringo. John's lyric appears to refer, at least partly, to his freedom from a recording contract. Considered in that light, however, John sounds less like someone relishing that freedom than someone trying to convince himself that he should. Indeed, this notion dovetails with the presence of so many songs in at least close to finished form. Overall, in this era, John sounds like he is preparing for a reentry even as he sings lyrics that would suggest the opposite path — the one we know he ultimately took. With Lennon, as always, multiple possibilities for his next step sat shoulder-to-shoulder, and anything could happen.

The two songs lifted from the later *Milk and Honey* are justified to include in this era by their presence on demos, though there is some ambiguity there. Different sources report different dates, and such discrepancies can be difficult to resolve. This is really of only minor consequence because neither of these songs forms the foundation for anything distinctive about this rescue project. They are, in essence, avatars of John to the group rather than representations of his full presence in the project — just a somewhat thinner version of the dynamic we have been engaged in all along. It still results in the four voices lifting each other in a unique way, even if John is almost literally phoning it in. If a demo of another song were to surface from this era, there is a reasonable likelihood that a place could be found for it among the other contents which will make up this rescue, displacing either of these.

Thankfully, despite being lesser compositions, both "Nobody Told Me" and "I Don't Wanna Face It" are of a quality which is compatible with the rescue project. Neither song has complex lyrical content, but both come off as sort of happy, jaunty blowing off of steam. "Nobody Told Me" is the better song, as was borne out by it becoming a surprise hit single in 1984.

John's output would continue to be sporadic, but never stop completely, and that works to our advantage here, giving us and our Assembler the chance to contextualize these songs and bring out their strengths, even as we admit that they are distant echoes of what we know John can do.

Assembly
20 tracks: 18 eligible, 2 provisional

	✓ Don't Let It Bring You Down	M18-13, 77-Nov
	✓ Girls' School	M17-01, 77-Aug
	✓ Mull of Kintyre	M17-02, 77-Aug
👤	✓ Name and Address	M18-12, 77-Mar
	✓ Warm and Beautiful	M16-11, 76-Feb
	✓ Waterspout	M18, 77-Jun
	✓ With a Little Luck	M18-09, 77-Nov
	✓ Cookin' (In the Kitchen of Love)	S09-06, +J, 76-Jun
	✓ Dose of Rock 'n' Roll, A	S09-01, +J, 76-Jul
	≈ Hey! Baby	S09-02, 76-Jul
	✓ I'll Still Love You	S09-07, 76-Jul
	✓ Pure Gold	S09-03, +P, 76-Jul
	≈ Spooky Weirdness	S09-11, 76-Jul
	✓ Wings	S11-03, 77-Jun
	✓ It's What You Value	H08-06, 76-Sep
👤	✓ Mo	H, 77-Mar
	✓ Pure Smokey	H08-08, 76-Sep
	✓ Free as a Bird	L, +PGR, 77-Sep
👤	✓ I Don't Wanna Face It	L14-03, 77-Sep
	✓ Nobody Told Me	L14-05, 76-Dec

A first look at the track list yields a few songs with not much chance of making the album. These just don't look quite as good in context with everything else, so they can be set aside, while still remaining available in case the Assembler gets stuck anywhere along the way:

Dose of Rock 'n' Roll, A (R)   Pure Gold (R)
≈ Hey! Baby (R)   ≈ Spooky Weirdness (R)

The assembly proper then begins with the realization that escapism is a thread which runs through these tracks. John doesn't want to "face it," and rejoices in being "free as a bird." A somewhat lonely Paul retreats to his favorite mull, to mull. George, the least interested in escape, still can be heard finding deep comfort and retreat in his spirituality. Even Ringo starts his otherwise by-the-book love song with this sad, and somehow personal, couplet:

> *If I had the wings of an eagle,*
> *Over these broken dreams I would fly.*

It's hard to spot any obvious pole tracks on the list, but there is a clear connection via imagery between Ringo and John. If Ringo is seen as wanting to fly over trouble and to his one true love, John is a bird who has already flown. With that skimpy idea as a starting point, the Assembler will make a provisional call to place these two tracks at opposite ends of the project, and see if the middle can make them work.

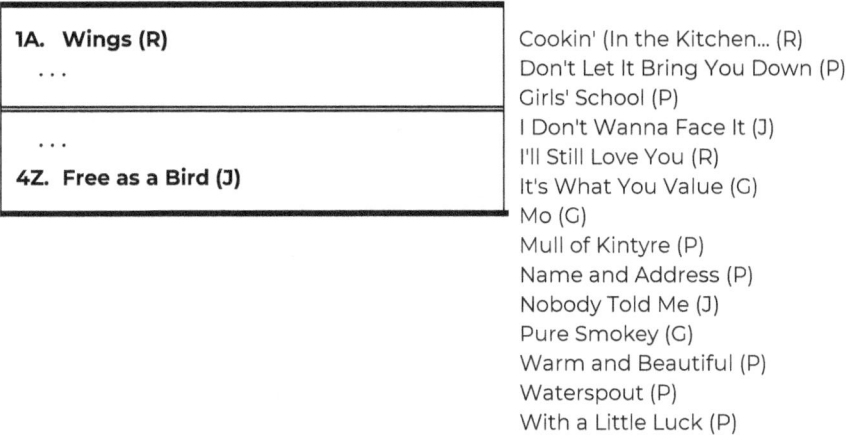

1A. Wings (R)
...
...
4Z. Free as a Bird (J)

Cookin' (In the Kitchen... (R)
Don't Let It Bring You Down (P)
Girls' School (P)
I Don't Wanna Face It (J)
I'll Still Love You (R)
It's What You Value (G)
Mo (G)
Mull of Kintyre (P)
Name and Address (P)
Nobody Told Me (J)
Pure Smokey (G)
Warm and Beautiful (P)
Waterspout (P)
With a Little Luck (P)

The idea isn't really to create a "concept" album, per se — which the Beatles certainly wouldn't have been caught dead doing at this point. Rather it is to have some thin framework and fill in around the edges. Indeed, not every track needs to contribute directly, and at least some will have no link whatsoever.

Without any obvious way to proceed, which is to say no obvious connections or placements beyond that first step, the Assembler reverts to the old formula, working from the outside toward the middle.

Thus, feature tracks are the next to identify — one at the beginning to extend the opener, and one penultimate track to set up the closer. The latter is the easier to identify, with George's "Pure Smokey" almost jumping off the list as a late-in-the-album title, the end of which allows for many possible followers, including Lennon's track. In the absence of something more perfect, it gets that penultimate slot.

Extending Ringo's MOR love song, itself something of a non-traditional opener, requires a track just a little more uptempo, and perhaps with a different tone. Paul's "Let 'Em In" would certainly fit this spot, but we don't have that option since Paul withheld it for his solo album. There is simply no way that a track that good could have been withheld long enough to be considered for this album. The Assembler was lucky to get "Warm and Beautiful" withheld as it is.

"Crackerbox Palace" seems like another possibility, sounding something like a second opener, though the same exact thing can be said about John's "Nobody Told Me." Decisions like this look tough at first, but Lennon's track is clearly more in keeping with the thread being explored, while George's track veers off into its own quirky territory, and would be much harder to follow.

Admittedly, this is something of a false equivalence. A quick look at the available tracks shows any number of uptempo songs which might fill this spot, including at least one other each by John ("I Don't Wanna Face It") and George ("This Song"). In the end, there may be no perfect track for the spot, but "Nobody Told Me" is sufficient for now. If another one appears, or a better place for that track becomes available, the Assembler can always change direction later.

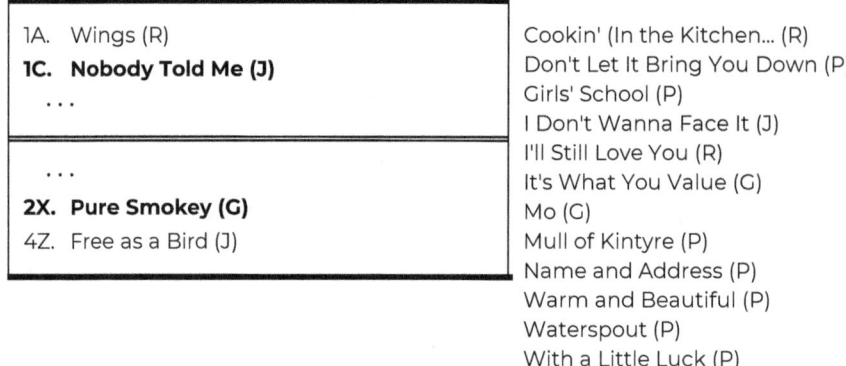

Indeed, the sprightly reset provided by "Nobody Told Me" would probably have to be considered to open side two. But it gets bumped by another track which must go there since it will not fit anywhere else.

McCartney's "Girls' School" is strong enough for use as a pole track, self-contained enough so as to not fit comfortably in the middle of a sequence, and different enough from the rest that it doesn't have much role to play in either setting up or interpreting something else. That leaves the opening of side two as more or less the only spot it will fit. It's a classic case of a McCartney story song in which the story is barely a sketch, but the track is nonetheless a solid rocker, and provocative in its own way. Moreover, its opening cheers signal the beginning of something new, a resetting of the show after intermission.

Such separateness means that "Girls' School" doesn't provide much, if any, guidance on what to put before it at the end of side one. Again the Assembler must turn to the old principles and try and find something reasonably difficult to follow, but compelling enough to encourage a flip of the disc. Truthfully, at this point in their career, that latter criteria seems a bit anachronistic. Nobody was getting so bored by Beatles albums that they failed to flip the disc — something which cannot be said for some of the sad solo albums...

When looking for something to fill this spot, McCartney is eliminated to avoid two of his songs in a row. This blessedly narrows things down. Though there are possibilities among Harrison's tracks, the recording which bubbles to the surface is Starr singing Lennon in "Cookin' (In the Kitchen of Love)." Not only is it an uptempo way to end the side, it has a spot where it comes to a grand pause, is revived by Lennon's count-off, and then settles into a vamp which eventually fades out with some curious ad libs. It seems to serve as a guarantee that the album will not get too serious, and that there's more party to come on side two. This then turns out to be true when the next track is Paul's rocker.

It probably would have felt a little bit like pulling teeth at this point to the Assembler. Nothing has locked in immediately as perfectly placed, beyond perhaps "Girls' School." Nevertheless, a form is starting to appear.

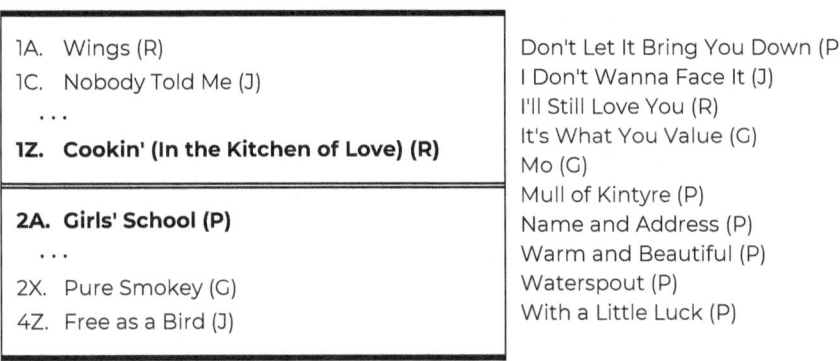

It's important to note that these decisions can always be undone, and they only are not undone if nothing better comes along. With Ringo's "Wings" as an unconventional opener, it is potentially ripe for replacement. But if nothing else comes along — and nothing really has or will — it starts to settle into that position, and all of the other sequencing decisions descend from that, providing support to it, making it seem more and more like it's in the right place. If everything is firing properly, the decision begins to look stronger with each new slot being filled. If not, starting over is always a possibility.

But moving along as if this is going to work, the Assembler would have known that "Warm and Beautiful" would have to make the album, given that he had to talk Paul into leaving it off *Speed of Sound*. It would certainly be a side two song, and turns out to sit comfortably next to "Pure Smokey" as part of the closing sequence. This might also have led to the realization that "Warm and Beautiful" in C major is in a relative key to "I'll Still Love You" in C minor. Suddenly a complex of love songs — different enough not to be boring — has been created. A piece of the puzzle fills in.

Likewise, "Mull of Kintyre" will obviously have to make the album, but would now be too big to fit on side two. Not quite right to follow "Nobody Told Me" in the third slot, it also isn't quite right to set up "Cookin'" and thus must be connected to each if it is to sit in the middle of the side.

So the task becomes blessedly specific, and therefore much easier. Only one track on the list can sufficiently set up "Mull." "It's What You Value" is in the same key, with an entirely different tone, and leaves the perfect space at the end for Paul's lazy, waltzing guitar to enter. The album now looks like this:

1A. Wings (R)	Don't Let It Bring You Down (P)
1C. Nobody Told Me (J)	I Don't Wanna Face It (J)
. . .	Mo (G)
1M. It's What You Value (G)	Name and Address (P)
1N. Mull of Kintyre (P)	Waterspout (P)
. . .	With a Little Luck (P)
1Z. Cookin' (In the Kitchen of Love) (R)	
2A. Girls' School (P)	
. . .	
2V. I'll Still Love You (R)	
2W. Warm and Beautiful (P)	
2X. Pure Smokey (G)	
4Z. Free as a Bird (J)	

Assuming that the goal remains 14 tracks total — though it certainly wouldn't have to — each side is now missing two titles. Also, we have only one Lennon track left to place, likely on side two because, including Ringo's track, John is already represented twice on side one. We knew going into this, however, that Lennon's contribution would be limited, and having four tracks from him at this point is actually something of a major achievement, even if one is sung by someone else.

With those things in mind, the two remaining spots on side one will have to go to Paul and George, in that order, while side two will be completed with John's other track, and something by either Paul or George, who will have to duke it out. Though our Assembler's rules do allow two songs in a row by the same Beatle (but no more), at this point in the narrative even string two together begins to look untenable. The variety brought by alternating voices has turned out to be one of the strengths of this type of assembly — that is, a critical component of the "fusion" method. It would take extraordinary circumstances to program two songs in a row by the same Beatle at this late date.

Ideally, filling the gap on side one between "Mull" and "Cookin'" would involve something of more substance than either of those tracks. But nothing matching this description is left on the list. Though side one does not yet have a proper ballad ("Mull" ultimately being much too large for that designation), this doesn't really feel like the moment for one either. George has some fine tracks left to choose from, including one that also has the advantage of not needing to be lifted from a solo album. "Mo" is uptempo pop, arguably among George's most plainly commercial solo tracks ever, and sits unexpectedly well between "Mull" and "Cookin'."

McCartney's spot is considerably tougher to fill. "Waterspout" remains on the list, and feels like a possibility. Two songs remain from *London Town*, though "London Town" itself is a title track if ever there was one, and also a pole track — more specifically, an *opener* — which would be wasted in any other position. And despite its obvious Beatle-y qualities, as mentioned above, the track would simply have overwhelmed everything else in this collection. Indeed, the songs Paul will put next to it on his own album will have no chance at living up to the potential it suggests. The other available track, "Name and Address," comes across as more of a novelty, and is just not right for the project.

"Pure Gold," McCartney's song sung by Ringo, hovers on the provisional list but represents something of a problem. Ringo already sings a song by John, and another by George on this album. Paul would certainly have wanted to join that party, but "Pure Gold" is not really good enough for a Beatles album. Indeed, having three songs by Ringo on one album may be overdoing it a bit anyway. The Assembler would have had to explain this to McCartney, who would not have liked it one bit, and would have extracted an agreement for an extra song on the album in exchange, settling the question of who gets the extra slot on side two.

At that point, however, the Assembler would have to tell Paul that he needed to provide another track if he really wanted both of those slots now reserved for him. "Waterspout" can take one of them, but nothing else on the list will work for the other. The question then would be whether Paul would come up with something new or dip into his archive to fill it.

Since we cannot work with the idea of Paul writing something specifically for an open spot, we take a look into his archive and find a song languishing that does indeed fill the spot well enough. "Mama's Little Girl" goes all the way back to *Red Rose Speedway*, and would have been released on that album had it been a double as planned. In this context, the song provides contrast to the dual openers by Ringo and John, and completes the quadrifecta of Beatle voices to open the album.

Side one is thus finally complete, albeit with numbering that clearly indicates its patchwork nature.

To complete side two, the first question is whether John's "I Don't Wanna Face It" fits better coming out of "Girls' School," or leading into "I'll Still Love You." With just a little listening, it becomes quite obvious that the first option prevails.

This leaves the spot promised to McCartney, which will go, somewhat unceremoniously, to "Waterspout" — the only track left of Paul's to be considered, and one which fits well enough into that slot — at least as well as it would ever fit anywhere, given its quirkiness. Thus both sides bear marks of being pulled together in painstaking fashion.

1A.	Wings (R)	~~Dose of Rock 'n' Roll, A (R)~~
1C.	Nobody Told Me (J)	≈ ~~Hey! Baby (R)~~
1H.	**Mama's Little Girl**	Name and Address (P)
1M.	It's What You Value (G)	~~Pure Gold (R)~~
1N.	Mull of Kintyre (P)	≈ ~~Spooky Weirdness (R)~~
1S.	**Mo (G)**	Waterspout (P)
1Z.	Cookin' (In the Kitchen of Love) (R)	With a Little Luck (P)

2A.	Girls' School (P)
2C.	**I Don't Wanna Face It (J)**
2E.	**Don't Let It Bring You Down (P)**
2V.	I'll Still Love You (R)
2W.	Warm and Beautiful (P)
2X.	Pure Smokey (G)
4Z.	Free as a Bird (J)

Given the amount of work and compromise associated with this assembly, it's fair to wonder whether something better was available. If such an option exists, however, it is not apparent. Simply put, no Beatle brought very much substance to the table in this era, which harks back to the notion of escapism. Every track here seems to want to be somewhere else, just as its composer does.

Looking back at the eligible tracks, it is still impossible to identify anything which would be obviously better for the pole positions. Likewise, no additional connections between tracks appear even after everything has been considered and reconsidered and twisted and turned. Therefore an argument can be made that even the meta-Beatles shouldn't have tried to make an album of these tracks.

But that conclusion forgets the purpose of these albums in the first place. Regardless of how much work it took to assemble these disparate tracks into an album, the end result is a piece of work in which every track sounds better — significantly so — than it either did or would have on the solo project from which it was extracted. Even when the connections are imperfect, the voices lift one another. In fact, when listening to this collection without knowing the effort needed to pull it together, it sounds remarkably unified, as we will get to below.

Flight

Principal Recording: April 1976 - September 1977
Release: September 1977

Side One
1. Wings (Starkey/Poncia)
2. Nobody Told Me (Lennon)
3. Mama's Little Girl (McCartney*)
4. It's What You Value (Harrison)
5. Mull of Kintyre (McCartney/Laine)
6. Mo (Harrison)
7. Cookin' (In the Kitchen of Love) (Lennon)

Side Two
1. Girls' School (McCartney)
2. I Don't Wanna Face It (Lennon)
3. Don't Let It Bring You Down (McCartney/Laine)
4. I'll Still Love You (Harrison)
5. Warm and Beautiful (McCartney*)
6. Pure Smokey (Harrison)
7. Free as a Bird (Lennon)

* Originally "McCartney/McCartney"

Make It Yourself

Total Running Time: 55:06

Tk	Rill	Title	Source	Dur
F5-A1	—	Wings	[1]	3:22
F5-A2	(1.0)	Nobody Told Me	[2]	3:29
F5-A3	0	Mama's Little Girl	[3, bonus]	3:41
F5-A4	0	It's What You Value	[4]	5:05
F5-A5	0	Mull of Kintyre	[5, bonus]	4:36
F5-A6	(3.5)	Mo	[U]	4:49
F5-A7	(1.0)	Cookin' (In the Kitchen of Love)	[6]	3:40

Total: 28:46

Tk	Rill	Title	Source	Dur
F5-B1	—	Girls' School	[5, bonus]	4:30
F5-B2	(2.3)	I Don't Wanna Face It	[2]	3:18
F5-B3	(3.0)	Don't Let It Bring You Down [Edit]	[5]	4:12
F5-B4	2.5	I'll Still Love You	[6]	2:53
F5-B5	0.5	Warm and Beautiful	[7]	3:08
F5-B6	0	Pure Smokey	[4]	3:51
F5-B7	0	Free as a Bird	[8]	4:24

Total: 26:20

[U] Unreleased (Seek on YouTube)
[1] *Ringo the 4th*
[2] *Milk and Honey*
[3] *Wild Life* or *Red Rose Speedway*
[4] *Thirty Three & 1/3*
[5] *London Town*
[6] *Ringo's Rotogravure*
[7] *Wings at the Speed of Sound*
[8] *Anthology 1*

NOTE: Descriptions of edits and crossfades, with sample audio, are available at:

SaveTheBeatles.com

Release
September 1977

Most Popular Albums
June 1975 - August 1977

US		UK	
Streisand/Kristofferson	*A Star Is Born*	ABBA	*Arrival*
Barry Manilow	*Barry Manilow Live*	ABBA	*Greatest Hits*
Boston	*Boston*	The Beach Boys	*20 Golden Greats*
Boz Scaggs	*Silk Degrees*	Bob Marley/Wailers	*Exodus*
Chicago	*Chicago X*	Carpenters	*Horizon*
Commodores	*Commodores*	Demis Roussos	*Forever and Ever*
Eagles	*One of These Nights*	Eagles	*One of These Nights*
Eagles	*Hotel California*	Eagles	*Hotel California*
Eagles	*Greatest Hits 1971-1975*	Eagles	*Greatest Hits 1971 75*
Electric Light Orchestra	*A New World Record*	Electric Light Orchestra	*A New World Record*
Elton John	*Captain Fantastic and...*	**Fleetwood Mac**	***Rumours***
Fleetwood Mac	***Rumours***	Leo Sayer	*Endless Flight*
Gary Wright	*The Dream Weaver*	Original Soundtrack	*A Star Is Born*
George Benson	*Breezin'*	Paul McCartney/Wings	*...at the Speed of Sound*
Jefferson Starship	*Red Octopus*	Pink Floyd	*Wish You Were Here*
Paul McCartney/Wings	*...at the Speed of Sound*	Queen	*A Night at the Opera*
Paul Simon	*Still Crazy After All...*	Rod Stewart	*Atlantic Crossing*
Peter Frampton	*Frampton Comes Alive*	Rod Stewart	*A Night on the Town*
The Steve Miller Band	*Fly Like an Eagle*	The Shadows	*20 Golden Greats*
Stevie Wonder	*Songs in the Key of Life*	Stevie Wonder	*Songs in the Key of Life*

Most popular album in bold

Clearly, easy listening California soft rock was dominating this cycle, having arisen as a provisional answer to the mid-70s doldrums, joined by vestiges of the old times. Elton John, still present, has begun to fade, so Fleetwood Mac and Eagles have stepped in to set the pace here, as they would for the next few years — even without new releases. Peter Frampton also gets his 15 minutes.

Only one former Beatle is present, with an album that even our slightly altered world would have left primarily intact. This makes it hard to project how a group album might have sounded in this market. Thematically, *Flight* would have fit right in, even if the music ran somewhat counter to the prevailing winds. The album might have found itself lumped together with other remains of the 60s, including wily chart veterans Rod Stewart, Steve Miller, and the reconstituted Jefferson Starship. Still, with the Beatles name, a certain level of visibility would have been guaranteed.

It is difficult, however, to see the Beatles having much cultural impact at this point. Fleetwood Mac's magnum opus was so dominant that it's almost easier to imagine the Fabs moving toward that direction, rather than anyone else moving toward them. Indeed, the same might be said about the Beatles entering a space dominated by Henley and Frey. The only significant argument against either of these musical possibilities is that none of the solo Fabs actually moved in either of those directions. Thus we can only guess what sort of pressures this shift would have placed on the Fabs if they had been working together at all.

This is, however, the point at which a fused Beatles album begins to look a little out of step with the mainstream, which has found its way around the legacy they left, even as many of these acts owe them a great debt. It remains possible that the previous fused albums had cracked open a space that would only ever be occupied by the Beatles, but that gets harder to imagine the farther we move from the breakup.

Topping the Charts
September 1977

US			UK	
Fleetwood Mac	*Rumours*	1	Elvis Presley	*40 Greatest*
Crosby, Stills & Nash	*CSN*	2	Connie Francis	*20 All Time Greats*
Soundtrack	*Star Wars*	3	Jean Michel Jarre	*Oxygene*
James Taylor	*JT*	4	Elvis Presley	*Moody Blue*
Elvis Presley	*Moody Blue*	5	Original Soundtrack	*A Star Is Born*
Commodores	*Commodores*	6	Fleetwood Mac	*Rumours*
The Emotions	*Rejoice*	7	Elvis Presley	*Welcome To My World*
Peter Frampton	*I'm In You*	8	Johnny Mathis	*...Collection*
The Steve Miller Band	*Book Of Dreams*	9	Yes	*Going For The One*
Shaun Cassidy	*Shaun Cassidy*	10	The Stranglers	*Stranglers IV...*

Rumours was released in February of 1977, and thus was still at the beginning of its remarkable chart run when *Flight* would have been released. For the first time, it feels like either Fleetwood Mac or Crosby, Stills and Nash, with their masterpiece *CSN*, might have dampened the Beatles' release party, at least in the US. In the UK, the Fabs would have been much more likely to grab the number one spot quickly.

The success of *CSN* does provide an interesting analogy. It had been seven years since *Déjà Vu*, and the foursome had reverted to a threesome. Their strife as a band was legendary, and there was a fair amount of surprise that they had managed to put together a new album at all. But the public was primed for their return, and bought the album in great numbers. It is certified at 4x platinum, second only to its predecessor in their catalog.

The Beatles would not have been away quite as long, but the public would have become well aware of their fractured recording process, and might have continued to be surprised by each new release. This is the best argument that *Flight* would have seen results at least somewhat comparable to *CSN*.

In short, this is the point where it gets harder to make the argument that the fans would have still been there when the record hit stores, though this market certainly had room for another resurrected juggernaut.

16 / Flight

Discussion

Perhaps the most important thing to notice about *Flight* is the sense that the post-Beatles era would have begun here, even as they kept releasing. This isn't a commentary on the music, but rather the changing of the guard. The Beatles have become skilled elder statesmen — a pop group emeritus, as it were.

By this point, that label had already been hung on pretty much any band remaining from the 60s. Though the music was accomplished and appreciated, an air of quiet awe would have been the more likely response than enthusiastic screams. The hardcore fans would still have been there, and even the second generation fans, but they would have found themselves explaining to younger folks just what was so great about the group. It happened to the Rolling Stones, The Who, etc. Here it happens to the Beatles.

Perhaps you imagined that such a day would never come for the greatest band the world has ever known, but all things must pass, right? We'd be lying to ourselves if we tried to claim that this Beatles album — or *any* Beatles album released at this point — would have been the dominant force in popular music. To be sure, it would have been revered by some, but also nitpicked by some, dismissed by some, sighed over by some, and ignored by some.

Critics would probably have fallen into two main camps. The first would have acknowledged that these Beatles albums were still really good, and deserved their inevitable success. The second would have been more circumspect, wondering what all the hubbub was about, and trying to pop the reverence bubble. Some would have compared them favorably to the classic albums, while others would have said things like, "I'll take *Abbey Road* over this shit every time."

Truthfully, we may all straddle that line somewhat. No one would probably have claimed that *Flight* was somehow a return to past glories. It would have been foolish to do so. The smarter marketing would have played into the idea that, "...here is some new music by the people who all but invented pop music as we know it. Take a listen, you'll probably like it."

Indeed, there is much to like on this album. All of the tracks have great life baked into them, and together form a picture of people aging — but *gracefully*. Bothersome existential questions aren't really the Beatles' stock in trade anymore. This album is really about just making great music, and hoping it elevates everyone who hears it.

None of the old issues are here, and whatever new issues we heard in the solo releases aren't really here either. John's domesticity is hinted at, but not overdone. His familiar melancholy is remarkably tamed, and found in uptempo songs that might actually have been hits. Paul's flights of pop fancy are likewise restrained, and his sense of the bucolic finds its most pleasant expression. George certainly touches on his typical big themes, but for the most part inhabits a mellow space where we find his company warm and welcoming. Ringo, as always, provides just the right counterbalance to everything else.

On side two, John and Paul talk to one another again, as do George and Ringo. In perhaps the album's best moment, Paul offers a surprisingly intimate consolation to John's woes, the likes of which has never been heard before in the Beatles canon. Throughout the album, all four Beatles are heard in conversations of one sort or another. It comes to a warm fruition in the closing track, where all four voices comingle (albeit by a little time-shifting magic), and the freedom John expresses manages to feel real for that time and place, where in isolation many years later it would feel somewhat forced.

Though some might have been scrutinizing this Beatles album for signs and themes — as always has and always will happen — nothing new really emerges. The images of flight are freeing, not confining, and they do not lend themselves to very much scrutiny. Fans would have had to appreciate this album for what it is on the surface, itself something very special.

Critics might have noticed John's diminished presence, but would have given great notices to his tracks. Assuming that he found the finished product palatable, and read mostly the positive reviews, it's possible to imagine John accepting the inevitability of another Beatles project, and coming to it with a bit more vigor the next time.

Then again, if they started to feel like they had overstayed their welcome — an undercurrent likely still to be hovering around after their previous album — any or all of the Beatles might have decided this was the right moment to step away. We won't let them do that quite yet, because the most experienced artists often have the most interesting and important things to say, and the experiences still to come for the Beatles have so much potential.

This album would certainly have been engaging enough to keep fans alert for something more, though it would be a long while. Fearing that each new release might also have been the last, some would inevitably have regarded it only in that context. As a swan song, *Flight* may be a little thin, however. As a statement of who the Beatles were and were not at this moment in time, it is just right.

They are, in some ways, who we have always known them to be. In others, they demonstrate the results of growth and change and maturity. If nothing else, *Flight* is a mature album by four men who appeared long before reaching that personal milestone. It is polished, and handsome, and beautiful. It is surprisingly sentimental, but dry-eyed. It asks questions that it does not try to answer.

These are the Beatles we always imagined they might have become if they had stayed together. Even from a distance, their voices resonate, and we who listen are engaged and lifted by their wings.

Intermission

October 1977–February 1980

[. . . Hiatus . . .]

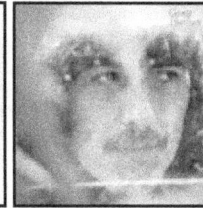

17 / HIATUS

"Someone pointed out, that since we broke up, the only way we can all go is downhill 'cuz individually none of us will attain what we attained together. And I think that's a very nice statement. And it wasn't derogatory or anything, but it's a fact of life, you know."

— Ringo Starr, August 1977

"Everybody's sued each other to their hearts' content, and now we're all good friends."

— George Harrison, April 1979

"Remember our silence is a silence of love and not indifference… P.S. We noticed that three angels were looking over our shoulders when we wrote this!"

— John Lennon (with Yoko), May 1979

"Having come all this way, I can remember only the good stuff.."

— Paul McCartney, July 1979

Chronology

1977

"Mull of Kintyre" released	NOV/DEC	*Scouse the Mouse* released

1978

Ends one year sabbatical Writing for George Harrison	JAN/FEB	Shooting *Ringo* (TV)
All You Need is Cash (TV) airs	MAR	*London Town* released
Ringo (TV) airs in US, w/ cameo by George *Bad Boy* released	APR/MAY	Father, Harold Harrison, dies
Cynthia's *A Twist of Lennon* (book) released	JUN/JUL	Agrees to finance *The Life of Brian* (film)
Dhani Harrison born Marries Olivia Arias	AUG/SEP	Bee Gees/Frampton *Pepper* film premieres
"Rockestra" sessions *Wings Greatest* released	OCT-DEC	*Rarities* (UK) released

1979

George Harrison released	FEB/MAR	"Goodnight Tonight" released *Wings Over the World* (TV) airs
Survives serious health scare Allan Klein convicted of tax evasion, jailed PGR jam at Clapton/Boyd wedding	APR/MAY	*Wings Over the World* (TV) airs in UK *Back to the Egg* released *New York Times* ad: "What, When, Why"
"Wonderful Christmastime" released Wings UK Tour (20 shows)	NOV/DEC	*Back to the Egg* (TV) airs Performs at *Concerts for Kampuchea*

1980

Arrested, jailed for 10 days in Japan Wins Grammy for "Rockestra Theme"	JAN/FEB	Shooting *Caveman* (film) Meets Barbara Bach

17 / HIATUS

Introduction

We come to a moment when we simply must declare a *grand pause* in the narrative of fused Beatles albums. This derives, quite simply, from a lack of available material by John Lennon, without which we cannot have any type of group album. Only a couple of his songs, in varying states of completion, can be definitively dated to this period, and assembling a Threetles album from the tracks available would not have satisfied anyone.

This would have meant a choice. One possibility would be to tuck some new material away and use it to gently pressure John into emerging for a short time. It's basically impossible to imagine Lennon succumbing to such pressure, and almost as impossible to imagine the other Beatles going along with the strategy for more than a few months. Paul would have continued to write profusely, and likely not been willing to let great — or even just *finished* — songs languish. Likewise, George would still have had the creative outburst found in his most consistently satisfying album. No one would have wanted to wait for Lennon.

So the other option would be to pause the group — *without* announcing any sort of permanent split, of course — and dive headlong into the solo waters. Up to this point in our slightly altered narrative, we've seen only Paul establish himself as a truly successful solo artist, while projects by the others have been almost uniformly disappointing. But confidence would have been high, and with the waters already tested, it might have been time for full submergence. In our best case scenario, the fused Beatles have provided a cushion for the solo Beatles, letting them return safely to the fold no matter how a venture into sololand turned out. Now would have been the time for that process to bear fruit.

With the second of these options as the only viable one, our Assembler would not have tried to stand in the way of any solo albums made by the other Beatles while John was on sabbatical. It's reasonable to assume that all of the music still would have been reviewed as it was created, with earmarks placed on a track here or there which sounded like the germ of a new group album. And though it's possible that, with creativity in the air, John might have been lured back and produced enough tracks for an album, we can't work with songs he didn't write.

In truth, it's not exactly fair to blame John exclusively. Unlike Paul and George, Ringo produced an album in this era containing nothing whatsoever that the other Beatles would have accepted. His output is nearly as big a black hole as John's. Had there been a group project here, a suitable feature for Ringo would have had to be pulled out of someone's hat.

Having stepped off the treadmill before, there would likely have been no reservations among the group about allowing such a fallow period. It's certainly possible that they would even have *wanted* this, and done it regardless of what material was being produced. For example, from a marketing standpoint, a layoff of a couple of years might have served to increase anticipation in the fanbase.

A three-year gap between albums for a supergroup isn't really all that unusual, of course. The Rolling Stones had two years between albums from '74 to '80. The Who had two to three years between albums after 1967. Even Fleetwood Mac, at the height of their intense popularity, allowed two to three years between albums after 1975. Besting all of these would have to be Crosby, Stills & Nash (& Young), with five to seven years between albums after 1970.

As bands age, it seems sort of like a natural progression. The Beatles were all certainly aging, and not necessarily gracefully — at least from a creative standpoint. Disco had sucked up much of the energy in popular music, and the stage was set for the backlash which punk rock and its variants provided. In a sign of things to come, Prince released his debut album in 1978, and Michael Jackson released *Off the Wall* in 1979. Traditional pop music still had a place, but it was not seen as a genre with very much growth potential. As such, there is an argument to be made that nothing the Beatles could have released at this moment would have sounded relevant anyway, and that a hiatus was perfectly natural to make way for a later triumphant return. Since that is how most of the solo releases in this period were actually regarded — as irrelevant — we will go with that to further justify the time away.

One can imagine Paul McCartney trying to rally the others at some point along the way, but he probably would have been rebuffed — short of invoking contractual obligation. It all means that the three solo albums from these two years can be left unaltered, with nothing from them meaningfully contextualized by putting it with the contemporary work of the others.

Considering all of this, we will simply let this time pass without a new release. At the very least, we know we will hear very different Beatles when they return.

17 / HIATUS

Recording
October 1977 – February 1980

🎛 Studio recording   ⬤ Single release   ✈ Touring

		JAN	FEB	MAR	APR	MAY	JUN	JUL	AUG	SEP	OCT	NOV	DEC
77	J											⬤	
	P											🎛	
78	J	🎛		[img]			🎛	🎛	🎛	🎛	🎛	←[img]
	P			🎛	🎛	🎛	🎛	🎛	🎛	🎛	🎛		
	G				🎛	[img]							
79	J	🎛	🎛	🎛⬤		[img]	🎛 (F6)	🎛 (F6)			⬤✈	✈
	P			[img]									
80													

John Lennon's retreat from the public eye preceded by only a few months a similar, but less well-known retreat by George Harrison, who would later claim that he did not so much as touch a guitar for all of 1977. This appears supported by the utter lack of any known recordings by George during this year.

When he next picked up a guitar, Harrison also resumed writing and recording, though in very low-key sessions at his home studio. Throughout 1978, with Olivia now pregnant, George created a set of recordings which would ultimately redeem him with critics, even as it made almost no chart impact. *George Harrison* garnered near-universal positive reviews, and spawned a hit single in "Blow Away." But album sales were tepid, and came nowhere near matching the uptick in quality. Discouraged by the response, when George next resumed recording, it would be only out of contractual obligation.

With only a short break after completing *London Town*, Paul McCartney dove back in, recasting two players in Wings, engaging Chris Thomas to produce, and giving extensive effort to what would become *Back to the Egg*, and an accompanying stand-alone single, "Goodnight Tonight." Among the recordings he made in this era were two by an entity christened "Rockestra," which featured a who's who list of famous rock musicians. When the album appeared, however, the critics were harsh, and the public also showed very little interest.

As that album came and went, McCartney put the band on hold and retreated to his farm to return to his solo roots. He rented recording equipment, worked by himself, and assembled a sprawling collection of demos, experiments, and stress-relievers which would be trimmed into *McCartney II*. It would be nearly a year from the time these recordings were made to when they were released, and this would be a critical period which saw the final dissolution of Wings after an infamous drug bust and nine days of incarceration for Paul in Japan.

Where McCartney's two albums represented over a year of painstaking work, Ringo Starr, working with Vini Poncia, generated *Bad Boy* in a mere 10 days. The haste showed and, predictably, it was all but ignored by critics and the public, after which it would be over two years before Ringo recorded again.

Far away, behind thick stone walls in New York, John Lennon continued making demos, methodically putting song ideas through multiple iterations, recording some over and over. Many of these would never be finished, but his persistence makes it clear that, even if he didn't realize it, his days as a pop musician were not quite over, just waiting for some spark to wake them up again.

Materials

Overview
43 tracks: 17 eligible, 9 provisional

The simplest way to sum up the recordings by the Threetles during this long but sparsely-filled period is to say that Paul and Ringo continued churning out product, while George led with his musical heart. For Paul, the result was a mixed bag of hits and misses, a few cringe-inducing videos, and long layoff. For Ringo, the result was desolate and unpleasant, and nearly fatal. For George, the result was less dire, but still something akin to a broken musical heart.

We cannot look to either Paul or Ringo for any substance. There are no personal lyrics, no investigations of large issues, not even much in the way of Beatle echoes. For George, it was a new voice, like some sort of bridge had been crossed, even when he was singing material he wrote back in those old days.

As usual, there were tracks from Paul and George which were of sufficient BQ to be considered for a group album, but nothing here that would really compel the creation of such a thing. In truth, Paul's output would not have sat very well next to George's, and Ringo's doesn't even get considered. These were definitely the dog days of the solo 70s.

17 / HIATUS

Ringo Starr

12 tracks: none eligible, 1 provisional

Sources

S12	*Bad Boy* R: Nov 77	P: Poncia		S: Elite (Bahamas) +1	78-Apr

 (Unreleased)

Tracks

Bad Boy (Armstrong/Long) — S12-02, 77-Nov
⊘ (Style/Quality) Oh, boy-oy-oy-oy-oy. A doo-wop song, and a very unpleasant one at that.

Hard Times (Skellern) — S12-06, 77-Nov
⊘ (Style/Quality) Generic in every way. Nothing interesting in any way. Really.

Heart on My Sleeve (Gallagher/Lyle) — S12-04, 77-Nov
⊘ (Style/Quality) Sounds like a David Cassidy reject — 5 years too late!

Lipstick Traces (On a Cigarette) (Neville) — S12-03, 77-Nov
⊘ (Style/Quality) Echoes of the 50s, but filtered through the 70s, in a bad way.

Man Like Me, A (O'Lochlainn) — S12-10, 77-Nov
⊘ (Style/Quality) Ringo steps into a pool of light for his solo turn, but it's very cringey.

Monkey See – Monkey Do (Franks) — S12-08, 77-Nov
⊘ (Style/Quality) Routine song, not customized to Ringo. Pure product.

Old Time Relovin' (Starkey/Poncia) — S12-09, 77-Nov
⊘ (Style/Quality) Lopes along, with all of the edges sanded off. Disappears from memory instantly.

One Way Love Affair (Ballard) — S, 78-Jul
⊘ (Quality) Terrible song, terrible vocal, terrible production.

She's So in Love (Ballard) — S, 78-Jul
⊘ (Quality) Terrible song, terrible vocal, terrible production.

Tonight (McLagan/Pidgeon) — S12-07, 77-Nov
⊘ (Style/Quality) Uninteresting song. Bad arrangement. Empty-sounding record.

Where Did Our Love Go (Holland/Dozier/Holland) — S12-05, 77-Nov
⊘ (Style/Quality) Best of the 60s as channeled through the worst of the 80s. Unholy, truly terrible mash-up.

Who Needs a Heart (Starkey/Poncia) — S12-01, 77-Nov
≈ (Style) Straight pop rock. Inoffensive, if also not very memorable. RS wisely yields vocal in spots.

The cover image on *Bad Boy* is a sad reminder of the depths Richard Starkey sank to at this point in his career. The music reflects this, with only one track on this album even provisionally available if the group had needed it. Most of these tracks are pure product: conventional, interchangeable, unmemorable.

We might wonder just who they thought would buy this album — which made only an incredibly fleeting appearance on the charts, and resulted in Ringo being dropped by his record company. The album was accompanied by a TV special which falls among former Beatle projects best completely forgotten. Who was Ringo's potential audience a this point? Certainly not aging Beatlefans.

If there had been a group album at this time, the Assembler would probably have had to plead with one of the other Beatles to produce something usable for Ringo. In that way we can imagine that a group project might have lifted Ringo himself, perhaps even helping him avoid the personal lows we know he had during this era.

George Harrison
10 tracks: 8 eligible, 2 provisional

Sources

H09	*George Harrison* R: Mar-Nov 78	P: Harrison/Titelman	S: FPSHOT, AIR	79-Feb

Tracks

Blow Away (Harrison) ✓ As good as GH gets. Maybe the best pure pop song he ever wrote. Fantastic record.		H09-05, 78-Nov
Dark Sweet Lady (Harrison) ✓ GH shows mature songwriting chops. This is well-conceived and perfectly executed.		H09-07, 78-Nov
Faster (Harrison) ✓ Shades of "Mo." Not entirely engaging to non-car people, but filled with happy enthusiasm.		H09-06, 78-Nov
Here Comes the Moon (Harrison) ✓ Not to be thought of as a sequel, this is a gem which has been dismissed. Very nice.		H09-03, 78-Nov
If You Believe (Harrison/Wright) ✓ A little uneasy in structure, aspiring to something beyond where it reaches.		H09-10, 78-Nov
Love Comes to Everyone (Harrison) ✓ Straight pop, and very successful. Great song and a gem of a recording.		H09-01, 78-Nov
Not Guilty (Harrison) ≈ (Content) Ten years later, this song still sounded contemporary. A better reading than in 1968.		H09-02, 78-Nov
Soft Touch (Harrison) ✓ Built around two — count 'em TWO — solid riffs. Fully-formed and really great.		H09-09, 78-Nov
Soft-Hearted Hana (Harrison) ≈ (Content) A fine "get high" song. Loopy but well-written, with a recording made while sober!		H09-04, 78-Nov
Your Love Is Forever (Harrison) ✓ Another in a group of just sweet, complete, beautiful songs. Like candy.		H09-08, 78-Nov

17 / HIATUS

After all that has come and gone since George Harrison stepped onto the stage with the Beatles, on this eponymous album we finally have the George Harrison we always imagined. On the one hand, it's a great shame that none of this music can be used on a group project. On the other, it would have been a great shame to remove any of this music and weaken this album.

Further, it's a great shame that this album did not come just a little earlier — say two years earlier — when it might have meant a little more in the world of popular music. By the time *George Harrison* was released, too much water had flowed under the bridge, and former Beatles had been relegated to a niche in popular music. As a result, though people heard the one big hit, they didn't really buy or hear the album.[1]

That big hit, "Blow Away," may be the most commercial song George ever wrote, and also the happiest. Indeed, commerciality and happiness infuse this entire album. From one track to the next, George sounds relaxed, at ease, confident, smiley, and fully mature as an artist. There is no question that this album contains the most consistently mature songwriting of his career.

To its credit, the album has no central concept other than that suggested by its title. George's life path is on display, including a remake of a sore spot from 1968 ("Not Guilty"), and a worthy sequel to another career high point ("Here Comes the Moon"). He fully acknowledges the effect of love ("Love Comes to Everyone," "Soft Touch," "Dark Sweet Lady" and "Your Love is Forever"), and indulges in a new passion ("Faster"). His foray into spirituality ("If You Believe") is gentle and open, if perhaps a little simplistic — which beats his former stridency any day. Even a loopy "get high" song ("Soft-Hearted Hana") seems of a piece with the rest of this music.

The Assembler, trying to stay up on what everyone was doing, would probably have tried to talk George into holding out a track or two for the next group project, but George would have demurred, gently and firmly. Though hardly a concept album in any way, there is a unity among the ideas and the sound that gives strength to the whole beyond just the strength of each individual track.

Combined with the timing, there really is no way to find out what this music might have been able to do next to songs by other Beatles. Nothing here needs elevation, but everything here might have provided elevation to something else. Then again, none of this really feels like group material anyway. It really does feel like the work of a confident *solo* artist, and there is a reasonable possibility that these songs might have been diminished through repurposing.

---

[1] I bought my copy for $1 in the cutout bin, where there were maybe 10 more copies languishing there at the time. Somebody somewhere thought this would sell big.

We must simply be content to let this album be the great album that it is — arguably the best, most whole and satisfying artistic statement George Harrison would ever make.

Paul McCartney
21 tracks: 9 eligible, 6 provisional
Bracketed tracks are considered in a different era

Sources

M19	["Goodnight Tonight"] / "Daytime Nighttime Suffering" R: Oct 78 - Jan 79 P: A/McCartney; B/McCartney/Thomas S: Various (2)	79-Mar
M20	*Back to the Egg* R: Jun 78 - Feb 79 P: McCartney/Thomas S: Various (4)	79-May
M21	"Wonderful Christmastime" / ["Rudolph the Red-Nosed Reggae"] R: Jun-Jul 79 P: McCartney S: Various (2)	79-Nov
	(Unreleased)	

Tracks

After the Ball / Million Miles (McCartney) — M20-10, 78-Sep
✓ Pure craftsmanship. We could ask why, but there is no why. Just two notions made into songs.

Arrow Through Me (McCartney) — M20-07, 78-Jul
✓ One of a kind. Sophisticated easy listening. Smoothness obscures its complexity.

Baby's Request (McCartney) — M20-14, 78-Nov
✓ Underappreciated, very fine song.

Broadcast, The (McCartney) — M20-12, 79-Feb
≈ (Filler) Perhaps a little overly serious for the album, but a good use of a nice musical idea.

Daytime Nighttime Suffering (McCartney) — M19-02, 79-Feb
✓ A B-side that belonged on the album. This is good writing.

Did We Meet Somewhere Before (McCartney) — M18, 78-Mar
⊘ (Quality/Style) Music hall song, but recording mixes styles uncomfortably. Not a good song. Horse hooves.

Getting Closer (McCartney) — M20-02, 78-Nov
✓ Great, late rocker. Doesn't try to hard, just rocks the way Paul should at that point.

I Can't Write Another Song (McCartney) — M, 78-Dec
≈ (Demo) A germ of a good idea, and a full song. Could be coded messages.

Old Siam, Sir (McCartney) — M20-06, 78-Jul
≈ (Quality) In the "meaningless lyrics" category, it nonetheless manages a bit of mystery. Nice guitars.

Praying Mantis Heart (McCartney) — M, 78-Dec
⊘ (Demo) Not realized, but with potential.

Reception (McCartney) — M20-01, 78-Sep
≈ (Filler) Really just a link. Not much to it. Synths may be a little over the top.

17 / HIATUS

Reggae Moon (McCartney) ⊘ (Demo) An extended "link."		M, 78-Dec
Rockestra Theme (McCartney) ≈ (Filler) Not Paul's best instrumental, or song idea, but a compelling project nonetheless. Fun.		M20-08, 78-Oct
Same Time Next year (McCartney) ⊘ (Quality) Macca writing to task, sounds forced. Unusually clunky melody and chords.		M, 78-May
Seems Like Old Times (McCartney) ⊘ (Quality) Echoes of the music hall, but not as smooth. Forced tune and lyric.		M, 78-Dec
So Glad to See You Here (McCartney) ✓ The better of the Rockestra tracks, and actually a good song. Somewhat overlooked.		M20-13, 78-Sep
Spin It On (McCartney) ✓ Definitely trying too hard. Not exactly bad, but feels undeniably inauthentic.		M20-04, 78-Jul
To You (McCartney) ≈ (Quality) Not a bad song, but Macca's vocal just tries too hard. Wrong tone in the recording.		M20-09, 78-Jul
We're Open Tonight (McCartney) ✓ An overgrown link, but might have been thrown away too hastily. Maybe a good song there.		M20-03, 78-Sep
Winter Rose / Love Awake (McCartney) ✓ More "parts" being linked. Somewhat misfitted to the project, but where else would they fit?		M20-11, 78-Jul
Wonderful Christmastime (McCartney) ⊘ (Content) Certainly enduring, though barely a sketch. Sufficiently merry for most.		M21-01, 79-Jul

If you need evidence that Paul McCartney's work can be maddening, look no further. Here he has created a project which is frustrating for exactly the opposite reason as the previous album. Where *London Town* was a potentially interesting concept populated with lousy music, *Back to the Egg* is a perfectly fine collection of music wrapped in an utterly sabotaging concept.

Start with the acknowledgement that Paul was returning to his old formula, as evidenced by the great care which went into the cover photography, and other details like the elaborate egg-themed labels, and the assembly of scraps into a "medley" on side two. These provide the skinny framework on which Paul attempts to hang the project. There is a solid opening to the album, and even a reprise on side two to create the impression that things were tied together. All of the usual elements were attempted — and all fell completely flat.

From these elements we might guess — correctly, as it turns out — that the album was provisionally titled *We're Open Tonight*. This leads us to wonder, with jaws dropped, how the envelope for the music went so completely, horribly wrong. Indeed, the silliness of the cover image is enough to render the music inside completely irrelevant. *Back to the Egg* was doomed before anyone took off its shrink-wrapping. In fairness, Paul was once again latching onto a cultural theme —

the same one used for *Venus and Mars* — for his imagery. But by 1979, fascination with space and aliens and all of that had begun to wane. The idea of Wings returning from some interstellar adventure (tour?) in a spaceship is completely ridiculous, and seemed so at the time.

What is so frustrating is that the framing concept is completely inorganic and imposed on the music, which does not reference it at all. Paul's comments in interviews at that time suggest that the underlying concept was really about returning to rock-n-roll — "the egg" — after forays out into the universe of pop, an idea supported by the album's harder sound. He was heard professing appreciation for burgeoning punk, New Wave, and related trends. His goal with the recording sessions was obviously to find a more raw sound for the group, and he accomplished this admirably and with integrity. Unfortunately, he then wrapped the whole thing in an idea which more than offset his advances.

When you listen to the music separate from the title and artwork, as our Assembler would have, a very different theme emerges, suggested by multiple references to radio and broadcasting. A flip of the radio dial provides a segue between one radio reference, "Reception" and the strong opening track, "Getting Closer," which contains its own radio lyrics. Side two features the elegant, if mystifying, "The Broadcast," and the album ends with a plea to the DJ to play "my baby's request...one more time." It sounds like this project might have started out being about late night FM radio — a far superior idea. One might also imagine that "open tonight" could suggest a mythical late night music club at which the band is performing a radio show, as seen in the video for "Goodnight Tonight" But a spaceship? Fried eggs?

By all rights, this *maybe* could have worked. As we've seen, all McCartney needs is the whiff of a theme, good assembly and good artwork to create something which seems greater than the sum of its parts — even if it might not otherwise be. On *Back to the Egg*, it flops in spectacular fashion.

Truthfully, the Assembler might not have been able to help Paul avoid these problems. There just isn't much here that might have sounded better on a Beatles project. The best track is actually just off the edge of the album, and we will assume that the Assembler could have talked Paul into withholding "Goodnight Tonight" until a new group album materialized (the track will be discussed further in the next chapter). Its B-side, "Daytime Nighttime Suffering," likewise could have made that jump, but might have been better used to brighten a reconceived album, perhaps replacing "Rockestra Theme," which really belongs on a B-side itself.

One other track, "Cage" would also become available for the group project, and we will assume that McCartney would have offered it to the Assembler after deciding not to use it on his album. A structured song, built on some silly sounds, with equally silly lyrics, it nonetheless has a much more Beatle-y quality than the rest of the

17 / HIATUS

Paul's tracks from this era. It would have sounded quite out of place on *Back to the Egg*, but will fit right in on the next, delayed group album.

When all is said and done, from the standpoint of the Beatles, not much is lost by allowing this project to move forward during the group's hiatus. With the possible exception of "Arrow Through Me," a true gem of a song and record, none of these songs really sound like Beatles material. Even if the "medley" which makes up a chunk of side two has echoes of the Fabs, it takes up way more room that Paul would have been allotted on a fused album. As was typically the case, he created way more material than the Beatles could ever have used, and solo albums really make a lot of sense for releasing such things. It's just unfortunate that, every once in a while, such projects go bad for reasons unrelated to the actual music.

FUSION ERA #6
───────────────────────────────
MARCH 1980-NOVEMBER 1980

Wheels, Walls and Waterfalls

"You can't reheat a soufflé."
> *– Paul McCartney, July 1980*

"To say that somebody thinks we, the ex-Beatles, are removed from reality is their personal concept."
> *– George Harrison, August 1980*

"The Beatles only exist on film and on record and in people's minds."
> *– John Lennon, September 1980*

"I'm going crazy with this record business, I wanna stop it, you want me to stop it, Everybody wants it to stop."
> *– Ringo Starr, November 1980*

Chronology

1980

Rarities (US) released	**MAR-MAY**	*McCartney II* released
Writing for *Double Fantasy* in Bermuda	**JUN/JUL**	*I, Me, Mine* (book) released, limited edition
Recording *Double Fantasy* Signs with Geffen Records	**AUG-OCT**	Final Wings recording session
Double Fantasy released Deposition: "I and the three other former Beatles have plans to stage a reunion concert."	**NOV**	*Rockshow* (film) released

18 / Wheels, Walls and Waterfalls

Introduction

When *Wheels, Walls and Waterfalls* would have finally appeared in the fall of 1980, it would have been three long years since the release of *Flight*. As mentioned, this drought was largely — but not entirely — driven by the difficulty in getting music from John Lennon.

Everything changed in 1980. Suddenly three Beatles were back in the studio, but it was a different trio. Lennon, Harrison and Starr were all recording again, while McCartney stayed away — sort of. He had retreated again to his farm with a rented multitrack recorder after *Back to the Egg* was released in 1979, and produced a sprawling collection of doodles in various states of realization, all of which could have been available to a group project. By the fall of 1980, there was plenty of new material from all of the former Beatles, and a solid sense, in retrospect at least, that the recordings would be much more powerful as a group project than as separate solo albums.

Could this have provided the impetus for some group sessions? It seems likely. McCartney was certainly in the mood, as suggested by his inclusion of Beatle caricature photos within the gatefold sleeve of *McCartney II*. The images seem altogether like a gentle invitation, as does his donning of a Beatle suit for the video of "Coming Up." While Lennon publicly professed that his desire had been to make his comeback album with Yoko, he may have felt otherwise if a group opportunity were available, especially given Jack Douglas's reports of great stress between the couple while recording *Double Fantasy*. Harrison had grown tired of recording, was doing so only out of contractual obligation, and might have seen camaraderie as a relief from the pressure. Or not.

Starkey, more than any of the others, was already working behind the scenes to reunite the group — at least approximately — on his next album. Ultimately, McCartney and Harrison did contribute to *Stop and Smell the Roses*, and Lennon had agreed to contribute. Ringo's efforts might have given special momentum to a reunion if the fusion framework were still on the table, as we are assuming it would have been.

Barring a full-fledged studio reunion, a fused album could have been easily assembled using the old tried-and-true techniques — potentially with enough left over for solo albums by all four artists. The Assembler would have found a bounty of material to listen through, although questions of quality, combined with solo ambitions, would have limited the project to a single vinyl disc. In acknowledging this, it must also be admitted that not everything in the pile was worthy of the Beatles name. By 1980, some of the tanks seemed to be nearly empty.

Still, a group album at this moment would certainly have been greeted with enthusiasm by all, much as Lennon's return was — the best source of an appropriate comparison. Then reviewers and the public, as always, would have determined whether the album had any legs. At the cusp of a new decade, there would certainly have been open wondering if the group would be relevant to the 80s. Still, it seems likely that someone somewhere would have written that the world should just rejoice whenever the four Beatles come together on vinyl, recognizing that it is always a happy occasion, and that the world becomes a better place.

Recording
March 1980 – November 1980

⊛ Studio recording ◯ Single release

		JAN	FEB	MAR	APR	MAY	JUN	JUL	AUG	SEP	OCT	NOV	DEC
79	👤						⊛	⊛					
80	👤								⊛	⊛		🖼	
	👤				◯	👤	◯			◯	⊛	⊛	
	👤				⊛	⊛	⊛	⊛	⊛	⊛	⊛	⊛	
	👤							⊛	⊛	⊛	⊛	⊛	

Paul McCartney's contribution to a group album at this point would have come from solo sessions he held the previous year. Somewhat stung by the critical drubbing of *Back to the Egg*, he had retreated to Scotland, much like when the Beatles broke up, and worked solo. Never short of ideas, the sessions produced way more music than would fit on a single album, but only a single album was released as *McCartney II*. It was generally received with puzzlement by critics, though it did spawn a hit in "Coming Up," and the fans had fun with the accompanying video, which cast Paul and Linda as the entire band. Ultimately, the album had disappointing sales, and would remain a unique curiosity in McCartney's catalog.

Roughly a year and a half after finishing sessions for *George Harrison*, the artist found himself with an obligation to provide a new album to his record label. Once again, he did only low key sessions in his home studio, and eventually presented Warner Brothers with *Somewhere in England*. To his surprise, the record company declared it insufficiently commercial and wanted changes. The album release, scheduled for late 1980, was scrapped, and George went back to the studio, eventually replacing four songs and the artwork before the label was satisfied.

18 / Wheels, Walls and Waterfalls

When finally released in 1981, the revised *Somewhere in England* was buoyed somewhat by George's tribute to John Lennon, "All Those Years Ago," which was a substantial hit, if only because it contained all three surviving Beatles. But even with that publicity, the album made only a brief appearance on the charts, and left barely a ripple, either with reviewers or the public. It disappeared quickly, almost as if it had never existed.

Ringo changed course yet again, being dissatisfied with everything about his most recent recording project. He jettisoned those collaborators and decided on a full scale return to the strategy which had resulted in his biggest solo hit album. As such, he obtained agreements from all three of his fellow former Beatles to contribute, then began working with many other famous guest songwriters, producers and musicians on an album provisionally titled *Can't Fight Lightning*.

Lennon died before he could make his contribution, but McCartney worked on four tracks, while Harrison contributed two. Harry Nilsson produced three others, with Stephen Stills and Ron Wood rounding out the producer list. Even with all of that star power, the album, eventually retitled *Stop and Smell the Roses*, was a disappointment, being poorly reviewed and selling very few copies. It also resulted in Ringo being dropped by his record label.

Lennon's return to the studio after four years away was famously handled with utter secrecy, and begun without a record deal. His muse had returned in full force during a trip to Bermuda, and it was clear to all participants that both his songwriting and guitar chops were in fine shape. Counting tracks by Yoko, nearly two album's worth of material was recorded in about two months, with those tracks deemed best being polished for release as *Double Fantasy*.

Predictably, anticipation for the album could not have been higher, and the teaser single, "(Just Like) Starting Over," made a generally favorable first impression. Initial reviews of the album, however, were typically hedged, and often favored Ono's tracks over Lennon's. The initial chart profile looked disheartening, and it appeared as if the album might have stalled outside the top ten. This is hardly a foregone conclusion, however, because in his last days, Lennon embarked on a promotional blitz the like of which no solo Beatle had done for years. He sat for numerous interviews, some of which were quite long and in-depth, and even began talking about a tour.

With his death, of course, everything changed. The album, and its subsequent singles, were immensely successful, ultimately coming in a close second behind *Band on the Run* in terms of chart popularity in the solo era. In some cases, negative reviews which had been scheduled to run were recalled and replaced by more sympathetic takes. As a result, *Double Fantasy*, despite the early critical misgivings, is now widely considered a classic.

When Lennon died, McCartney was already at work on a follow-up to *McCartney II*, which had been received with lousy reviews but respectable sales. His big decision was to resume work with George Martin, which eventually led to the official disbanding of Wings. The sessions were barely underway when Lennon was killed, and it changed the nature of the project, though McCartney and Martin continued working in their grief. It would be quite some time before *Tug of War* surfaced.

Materials

Overview
55 tracks: 18 eligible, 11 provisional

After a decade of divergence, all four former Beatles had settled into mature solo sounds. Remarkably, those sounds remained compatible, if somewhat hammered into conventionality by the music industry. Only Paul retained any sense of studio playfulness, and the sounds he made wound up seeming too odd for the mainstream, despite containing significant harbingers of what was to come in the next decade.

Thus, we look to these recordings more for their content than style. Even there, we would find only modest divergence and a shift toward conventionality. John sings of domestic bliss, while George sings of spirituality, and Paul and Ringo merely sing. In some ways, everything is in its place. In others, everything is *too much* in its place. If the Beatles still had the ability to surprise and delight, it is not exactly on display in this collection of works — at least not separately.

Taken together, however, we can find threads and some distinct whiffs of the old magic. Not only have Paul and John written two very different versions of the same song, but the trio of songs which give this rescued album its name come from a place of maturity which is new, welcome, and amplified by collecting them in one place. They offer a summation of the hiatus now ended, while also containing a painful foreshadowing of what lay ahead.

As always, however, a type of strength emerges which is not found on any of the disparate solo releases. Ringo and Paul sounded a bit lost on their respective records, but nothing like that remains after their best has made the transfer to a group project. Likewise, both George and John sound compromised alone, and strong together.

Perhaps they would have approached this project suspecting it would be their last — a suggestion based not on foreknowledge of what came next, but on the music. Much of what is here is in some way summative. In its own gentle way, this collection of recordings might have made a fine swan song, despite our undeniable desire that such an occasion would never have come.

Paul McCartney

26 tracks: 6 eligible, 6 provisional

Bracketed tracks are considered in a different era

Sources

M19	"Goodnight Tonight" / ["Daytime Nighttime Suffering"] R: Oct 78 - Jan 79 P: A/McCartney; B/McCartney/Thomas S: Various (2)	79-Mar
M22	"Coming Up" / "Coming Up (Live)" & ["Lunchbox/Odd Sox"] R: Jan 75 - Jul 79 P: McCartney S: Various (3)	80-Apr
M23	*McCartney II* R: Jun-Jul 79 P: McCartney S: Home, Spirit of Ranachan	80-May
M24	"Waterfalls" / "Check My Machine" R: Jun-Jul 79 P: McCartney S: Home, Spirit of Ranachan	80-Jun
M25	"Temporary Secretary" / "Secret Friend" R: Jun-Jul 79 P: McCartney S: Home, Spirit of Ranachan	80-Sep
	(Unreleased)	

Tracks

All You Horse Riders / Blue Sway (McCartney) — M23, 79-Jul
○ (Filler) Pt 1: Thin 12-bar synths. Pt 2: Not quite electronica. Not very interesting. What vaults are for.

Blue Sway (McCartney) — M23, 79-Jul
○ (Filler) Nice groove, but that's all.

Bogey Music (McCartney) — M23-09, 79-Jul
○ (Style) A complete throwaway with just enough style to make it (slightly) interesting.

Bogey Wobble (McCartney) — M23, 79-Jul
○ (Filler) Annoying.

Cage (McCartney) — M20, 78-Sep
✓ Wrong for the album, but still has merit. Structured, catchy, quirky. Weird mash-up of ideas.

Check My Machine (McCartney) — M24-02, 79-Jul
○ (Filler) Annoying, but perfect for a B-side. Not worth a second listen, and barely a first.

Coming Up (McCartney) — M23-01, 79-Jul
✓ Infectious, if pretty silly. Macca does nicely all on his ownsome.

Coming Up (Live at Glasgow) (McCartney) — M22-02, 79-Dec
○ (Filler) Live performance adds nothing, and reveals the song to be as lightweight as imagined.

Darkroom (McCartney) — M23-10, 79-Jul
≈ (Quality) So fluffy. So silly. So meaningless. Not as annoying as others, but still annoying.

Front Parlour (McCartney) — M23-06, 79-Jul
○ (Filler) Of a piece with all of the other instrumentals on this project. Interchangeably silly.

Frozen Jap (McCartney) — M23-08, 79-Jul
○ (Filler) Four-in-the-bar, with a more interesting melody than most of these sketches. Still disposable.

Goodnight Tonight (McCartney) — M19-01, 79-Feb
✓ Disco? Who cares! This is a great track in every way — if you skip the video.

Mr. H Atom (McCartney)		M23, 79-Jul
⊘ (Filler) Catchier than most such sketches, though of dubious value. Vaultable.		
Nobody Knows (McCartney)		M23-05, 79-Jul
≈ (Quality) Probably fun to make — a quick something out of nothing. But don't think too hard.		
On the Way (McCartney)		M23-03, 79-Jul
≈ (Quality) Sketchy recording, but a real song. Not saying great, but might have made a fine Wings track.		
One of These Days (McCartney)		M23-11, 79-Jul
✓ Apology? Maybe. There is some vulnerability which lifts this above many other tracks.		
Robber's Ball (McCartney)		M, 79-Jun
≈ (Style/Quality) Odd and at least slightly annoying, but sufficiently original, and interesting.		
Secret Friend (McCartney)		M25-02, 79-Jul
⊘ (Filler) Give Macca credit for early electronica. This one is at least interesting, if still annoying.		
Simple as That (McCartney)		M, 80-Aug
≈ (Demo) Unusual groove. Interesting lyric. Something there worth listening to.		
Stop, You Don't Know Where She Came From (McCartney)		M, 80-Aug
⊘ (Quality) Clean demo of a throwaway jot. Not about anything.		
Summer's Day Song (McCartney)		M23-07, 79-Jul
✓ Perhaps too twee for most, but at least clean and well-formed. Nice harmonies.		
Temporary Secretary (McCartney)		M23-02, 79-Jul
≈ (Style) Despite much hatred, this opened doors for future artists. Unique in the catalog. Interesting.		
Waterfalls (McCartney)		M23-04, 79-Jul
✓ The most beautiful of the collection, it shows a genuinely pensive Macca. Fine song.		
We All Stand Together (McCartney)		M, 80-Aug
⊘ (Style) Fine for children. Even so, not very interesting.		
We All Stand Together (Humming Version) (McCartney)		M, 80-Aug
⊘ (Filler) More interesting and palatable than the vocal version, but still too twee.		
You Know I'll Get You Baby (McCartney)		M23, 79-Jul
⊘ (Filler) Minimalist 12-bar, clearly just for fun. But it's not really. Nothing to hear here.		

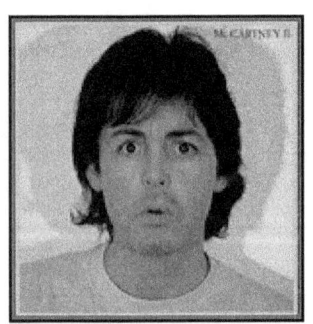

With Wings on hold, in this era we touch base with *pure McCartney*. We find him in a cocoon similar to that which he inhabited after the Beatles breakup, and take the temperature of his solo decade. Some things have definitely changed in the 10 years between eponymous albums.

First, some similarities. Like the earlier solo album, almost everything he recorded falls into the category of "elaborate demo" rather than finely polished studio master. Also similar is the fact that much of *McCartney II* is at least passingly engaging, and what strengths the album has come largely from its almost perfect assembly. Indeed, when listening through all of the B-sides and outtakes from this project — of which there are painfully many — it becomes very clear that Paul made exactly the right choices for what to include and exclude on the album, and assembled everything carefully enough to make it seem like there is a lightness and a sort of progression at work. That's about where the similarities end.

Unlike *McCartney*, even the most polished songs in this collection are hardly masterworks. Only "Coming Up," "Waterfalls," and "One of These Days" could be considered even fully ripe, and it is only this trio, plus the engaging — if very slight — "Summer's Day Song" which could have been considered for a Beatles project. If the instrumentals on his first album were the prototypes for what we would come to call "links," here the idea of the "link" explodes into its full glory. When considered as a whole body of work, the tracks recorded during the sessions for *McCartney II* are overwhelmingly small musical ideas, extended for the amusement of their creator, without much to offer those of us who were not at the sessions.

Much has been made about "Temporary Secretary" as a progenitor of later sample- and loop-based music, and this may well be the case. But the track works *despite* its pulsating loop and not *because* of it. McCartney has slyly used his loop sample as a carrier wave for a very traditional song which, alas, is something of a likeable throwaway. Still, we must give him credit for finding the perfect spot on the album for such a creation. It extends the strength of the album's opener, "Coming Up," and makes the most of a "feature" spot. That it might have spawned imitators in some places is really more nicety than revolution.

A handful of tracks have been marked as provisional because, as instrumentals and song sketches go, they are good enough, roughly interchangeable, and could have served a purpose on a group album if the situation called for it. This is not to suggest much value, but merely to acknowledge that having a big box of parts is a good way to start creating a hypothetical Beatles album. Presumably the Assembler would have listened to everything, made a few notes, and only returned to these tracks if they happened to fill exactly the right need.

Perhaps the most noticeable difference between Paul's bookend one-man-band albums, separated as they were by a tumultuous decade, is how at ease he sounds in his later sketching. Where everything on the first album was filled with angst, frustration and disorientation, everything in the later period is free of such strong emotions — beyond perhaps a puff of regret. To that point, the inset photos on the album's gatefold sleeve may be the most significant aspect of the project. By including such obvious references to his former bandmates, Paul seems to be saying, "Hey, we've done the solo thing, now let's get back to it," seeking a reconciliation and renewal which, as it turned out, could never come.

A couple of other songs from the era, not associated with the solo sessions, bear brief discussion. "Cage" was a leftover from *Back to the Egg* which, being a structured and engaging track, sounds like it really does belong on a group project. The early demo of "Simple as That" from this period, despite being not much more than a sketch, is far superior to the finished track as heard on *The Anti-Heroin*

Project: It's A Live-In World. Had Macca maintained the feel of this demo as he moved forward, rather than slipping to a semi-reggae, pop-ish variation, the song would not have attained the fluffy, hollow, preachy feel it ultimately did. His demo sounds much more like the warning he intended, and avoided the worst pitfalls of such songs. It is interesting enough to consider next to material by the other Fabs.

"Goodnight Tonight" has been held over from the preceding interval by our Assembler, who we will say suspected that it might sound better on a fused Beatles album than as a solo single. This polarizing dance track, often dismissively tagged as "disco," is undoubtedly a style departure for McCartney, but an entirely successful one. He resists the urge to go all the way down the rabbit hole which enveloped popular music (including Ringo) during the disco craze, and meets it roughly halfway, using a less modified latin beat as his foundation. (Listen to the claves.) Couple that with an irresistible hook in the bass, and a crazily accessible, repetitive-but-not-grating (YMMV) lyric, and you have something actually memorable from this point in Paul's career. Regrettably, the video undermines almost all of the track's strengths, another reason why it is a pleasant fantasy that the Assembler might have intervened to make things better.

Paul's contributions to the group project will thus be quite varied, and augmented by an unexpected reunion with Lennon as the album's wild card closing double-reprise.

John Lennon
9 tracks: 7 eligible, no provisional

Sources

| L13 | *Double Fantasy*
R: Aug-Sep 80 | P: Lennon/Ono/Douglas | S: Hit Factory (NY) | 80-Nov |

(Unreleased)

Tracks

(Just Like) Starting Over (Lennon) ✓ Straight confection, but just enough auto-bio to be true to Lennon. Simple, but sweet.	L13-01, 80-Sep
Beautiful Boy (Darling Boy) (Lennon) ✓ A gem. Grown-up ideas couched as lullaby. A sentimental masterwork.	L13-07, 80-Sep
Cleanup Time (Lennon) ✓ Feels more like dusting off the chops than using them. Still, catchy and well-formed.	L13-03, 80-Sep

18 / Wheels, Walls and Waterfalls

	Dear Yoko (Lennon) ⊘ (Content) Good vibe, but simplistic song. Band is tight, but ultimately the whole thing is sort of cringey.	L13-12, 80-Sep
	I'm Losing You (Lennon) ✓ Open diary writing, but dull. Quote of "Long Lost John" is the most compelling aspect.	L13-05, 80-Sep
	Not For Love Nor Money (Illusions) (Lennon) ⊘ (Unfinished) A minor composition, work in progress. Writing like GH, but hardly a hidden classic.	L, 79-Oct
	Real Love (Lennon) ✓ A lesser composition, gussied into an "event." With JL's edges sanded, not much here.	L, +PGR, 80-Jun
	Watching the Wheels (Lennon) ✓ All about its lyrics, and thus not much musically. Perhaps protesting a bit too much...	L13-08, 80-Sep
	Woman (Lennon) ✓ A sentimental favorite. Fantastic arrangement and vocal.	L13-10, 80-Sep

Of all the solo albums, *Double Fantasy* is the most difficult to separate from the emotions of its era. In John's writing, playing and singing there is a contentedness and hopefulness which is all anyone could hear after his death. It is all anyone can hear to this very day. In its entirety, as a symbolic artistic statement and talisman of an unspeakable painful moment, the album is widely considered a classic.

So it is with trepidation and care that we must approach the music critically. The bare truth is that this album was not well received in its first weeks of release, before John's murder. Further, this reaction seems borne out on detailed listening. Optimists argue that the album would have eventually caught fire and reached the top of the charts even without the events of December 8, perhaps goosed by additional singles, public appearances, or even an imagined world tour. Perhaps. Apologists argue that it is exactly what John said it was — a peek into his new, domestic and settled life — and should be accepted at face value. Fair enough.

Outside of their provenance, however, these tracks are a very mixed bag. They range from the simple and sweet "(Just Like) Starting Over" and "Beautiful Boy (Darling Boy)," to the virtually forgettable "Cleanup Time" and "Dear Yoko."

When the album was released, "I'm Losing You" was called out by reviewers as perhaps the most substantial new Lennon song, but there is not much to recommend it to a latter day listener — except, perhaps, John's only vocal performance on the album with any intensity. Famously, an early take of the song had featured members of Cheap Trick and drawn an even more intense vocal from John. The toned-down remake actually suggests that he was intentionally trying to downplay his intensity — perhaps being encouraged to do so — on the project. This decision, though a valid artistic choice, ultimately worked to his disadvantage.

Likewise, "Watching the Wheels," which garnered much comment at the time, seems like an intentionally wan descendent of "The Ballad of John and Yoko" or, God help us, "New York City." Lennon's straightforward style of personal narrative lyrics seemed somewhat passé upon release in 1980, but comes across more as mildly disingenuous self-justification — or even self-deception — today. Even without knowledge of the complications behind the walls of the Dakota, the song seems to be protesting too much. More than a report of facts, the lyrics border on magical thinking. The overall effect is not helped by unimaginative music.

What does help throughout the album, however, is the exceptional production work by Jack Douglas, and the fine group of studio musicians. *Double Fantasy* sounds absolutely nothing like any other John Lennon record, and is the only one of his solo releases with a production sheen comparable to what the Beatles had achieved. The effect is like a window being opened and the staleness of John's past production techniques dissipating. If the overall sound is a touch too conventional for a former Beatle, it triumphs by being blessedly transparent, allowing the artist to be clearly heard.

That John participated in this degree of polish after publicly disdaining such things for so long is especially telling. Despite all of his pronouncements otherwise, Lennon clearly liked what could be achieved in a recording studio, and took full advantage of it — at least when he was willing to put in the time. All of this was driven home by the puzzling release of *Double Fantasy Stripped Down* in 2010, which unwittingly revealed the massive benefits that Douglas's careful mixing had brought to a rather underwhelming collection of songs.

The most provocative track would be "Woman," which John described in multiple interviews as the most Beatle-y track on the album, written as something of a "grown-up version" of "Girl" from *Rubber Soul*. Though potentially cloying in both lyric and music, the production and John's vocal performance give the song a sense of timelessness, lifting it above all other material recorded in these sessions. It is the only song on the album which clearly and distinctly transcends the moment, thus sadly recalling the old Beatle magic.

The Assembler will run with it, partly because "Woman" also features an unexpected symbiosis with McCartney's earlier "Goodnight Tonight," in that the two choruses follow the same musical progression — at the end, even in the same key. Though the progression is rather common, one cannot help but wonder if Paul's hit, which went to number five on the US charts in the months before John wrote his song, might have wormed its way into John's subconscious. The Assembler will utilize this overlap to reunite the two songwriters for a brief double-reprise on the rescued album.

It is important to note that Ono's tracks on *Double Fantasy*, though irrelevant to a Beatles project, got much more positive critical reaction than Lennon's in the early days of the album's life. There is certainly a harder edge to her material, and John's guitar playing forms a significant part of the foundation for that. Her tracks clearly got the more energetic treatment in recording, ceding to her, and withholding from him, a critical piece of his instrument: intensity. It's truly regrettable that John pulled punches on his own tracks, while offering so much energy and revitalized chops to Ono's songs. Though her songs here are a step above much of her earlier material, they still plainly resemble amateur efforts compared to John's application of songwriting craft. His songs may not be great, but at least they are all sufficiently imaginative and exceedingly well put together.

Notable among the demos from this period is "Real Love," which the Threetles would famously enhance many years later. Though it remains on the eligible list, it is of a piece with the other songs, and will make no impact on the rescue project.

Ultimately, despite some disappointment and trepidation, our Assembler would have had no choice but to consider all of John's tracks for the group album — except "Dear Yoko," which the other Beatles would still have rejected for its use of a specific name. The question would become how to slot these tracks on the album to find and accentuate the strong bits. In a true rarity, and a sign of the weakness of the material, nothing that Lennon brings to this project would go on the short list for any of the pole track positions.

Perhaps, upon realizing this, John would have relished the turnabout, but it is more likely that he would have steeled himself and come up with something to beat the best anyone else had offered. It's a reminder that our rescued albums can only ever be a glimpse of what might have happened, because the stars could have aligned very differently if the old Beatle competition of egos was still functioning.

George Harrison
10 tracks: 4 eligible, 1 provisional

Sources

H10	*Somewhere in England* (6 tracks) R: Mar 80 - Feb 81 P: Harrison/Cooper	S: FPSHOT	81-Jun
	(Unreleased)		

Tracks

	Baltimore Oriole (Carmichael)	H10-05, 80-Sep
	⊘ (Filler) Nice enough, but GH doesn't offer the song much as a stylist. It just pads along. A non-event.	
	Flying Hour (Harrison)	H10, 80-Sep
	✓ Hardly a classic, but competent and likeable enough. Clear of GH's worst instincts.	

SAVE THE BEATLES!

Hong Kong Blues (Carmichael)		H10-09, 80-Sep
⊘ (Filler) GH has obviously learned things from covering songs like this, but the records are dull.		
Lay His Head (Harrison)		H10, 80-Sep
⊘ (Quality) Not bad but structurally deficient. Lacks hook and chorus to finish a good idea. Boring.		
Life Itself (Harrison)		H10-03, 80-Sep
✓ One of George's gems. Gorgeous guitars. Filled with gentility plus movement. Sounds like joy.		
Sat Singing (Harrison)		H10, 80-Sep
⊘ (Quality) Competent but completely forgettable. Feels like product.		
Save the World (Harrison)		H10-10, 80-Sep
⊘ (Quality) Classic GH chord progression that wanders untamed. Very thin sound. A cliché all around.		
Tears of the World (Harrison)		H10, 80-Sep
✓ Best of the album rejects, with solid music and a point. Definitely usable.		
Unconsciousness Rules (Harrison)		H10-02, 80-Sep
≈ (Quality) Pleasantly poppy, but feels very "formula." Nothing special.		
Writing's on the Wall (Harrison)		H10-08, 80-Sep
✓ Pensive, prescient without being maudlin. GH writes plainly and avoids his worst tendencies.		

Perhaps the short half-life of *George Harrison* best explains the "contractual obligation" nature of this follow-up. The record company rejected the first version of *Somewhere in England*, though pinpointing any improvements brought about by the resulting revisions is difficult at best. Four songs were excised and four were added, but the overall difference in the finished product is minimal. Though not a bad album, exactly, it is most certainly a *pointless* album — in both incarnations.

Here we consider only those tracks which were in the original line-up, since George's enforced refinements would not have made the deadline for this rescued Beatles album. Two of the tracks which were later dropped are actually better than what replaced them: "Flying Hour" and "Tears of the World." The former is a catchy version of ideas George has explored before about the value of *now*. The latter, despite being a "bad things are bad" list song, manages to avoid complete despair and sound, if not exactly hopeful, at least resolute that there are potential answers, and some spiritual justice. Both tracks would certainly have been considered by the group, despite being rejected by a record executive. We will assume that the Beatles would not have tolerated such interventions.

That idea illustrates clearly, however, just how little clout individual former Beatles sometimes had. If anything, *Somewhere in England* sounds like the music made by an artist who has all but given up the ideals he once held, recognizing how little ideals have to do — in the assessment of the music industry — with creating a salable commodity. This is not to say that the album, either version, is bad. It is not. But it also isn't good. For the most part, it just *is*. Some moments are more interesting, and some are less, but the range in quality is rather small, and as a listener, your mileage may vary from track to track.

From the point of view of the Assembler, however, "Life Itself" is a sure standout track, with the potential to be heard as a masterwork if properly contextualized. Within George's solo album, unfortunately, it is just another track, which is a great pity. Here is another case of the rescued Beatles projects finding a diamond that all but disappeared amid the many rhinestones of the solo years.

Ringo Starr
10 tracks: 1 eligible, 4 provisional

Sources

S13	*Stop and Smell the Roses* (8 tracks) R: Jul 80 – Feb 81 P: Various (6)		S: Various (Undetermined)	81-Oct
	(Unreleased)			

Tracks

Attention (McCartney) ≈ (Quality) Not Macca's best song, but right for Ringo. Very happy-sounding record.	S13-04, +P, 80-Jul
Drumming is My Madness (Nilsson) ⊘ (Quality) Sort of sleepy for such a big statement. Ultimately, a lousy song.	S13-03, 80-Nov
Private Property (McCartney) ⊘ (Quality) Lousy Macca castoff song, weird horns. Mish mash of sounds, styles. Not successful.	S13-01, +P, 80-Jul
Red and Black Blues (Tietgen) ⊘ (Quality) Boring song, terrible vocal	S13, 80-Aug
Stop and Take the Time to Smell the Roses (Starkey/Nilsson) ⊘ (Style/Quality) A cliché from its conception. Someone should have said no.	S13-05, 80-Nov
Sure to Fall (Perkins/Claunch/Cantrell) ≈ (Style) A sweet Perkins cover, even if a little overdone. Ringo's singing is strained at the top.	S13-08, +P, 80-Jul
Wrack My Brain (Harrison) ≈ (Quality) A rare misfire for GH/RS. Mostly a failure of the arrangement. Good song. Bad record.	S13-02, +G, 80-Nov
You Belong to Me (King/Stewart/Price) ≈ (Filler) Sure it's a cliché, but the arrangement is spirited, simple. Doesn't pretend to be anything more.	S13-07, +G, 80-Nov
You Can't Fight Lightning (Starkey) ⊘ (Quality/Filler) Essentially a jam, but utterly uninteresting until Linda starts singing. Even then…	S13, +P, 80-Jul
You've Got a Nice Way (Stills/Stergis) ✓ Credit Stills for writing a song that really fits Ringo's strengths, and making a great record.	S13-09, 80-Aug

After years making automatic product, Ringo decided to try and recapture the old magic by inviting back a host of famous friends to help him make records. The result is tepid and almost completely forgettable. And, no, a contribution from John Lennon likely would not have made things much better.

The best track from the sessions, bar none, is provided not by a former Beatle, but by another familiar name of the same age. Stephen Stills contributed "You've Got a Nice Way," the only track here which actually matches Ringo's style, abilities, and essentially unchanged persona. The track sounds complete in a way that most of the others do not — as if its creators worked it until they got it just right. Because of this, it will find a welcome place in the virtuous circle of the group album.

Six tracks recorded for *Stop and Smell the Roses* feature Paul or George, but they are thin at best, embarrassing at worst. Paul's "Private Property" and "You Can't Fight Lightning" won't even get the dignity of being considered for the group project. Moreover, retaining George's tuba-based "Wrack My Brain" on the provisional list is a mere courtesy since it is perhaps the least distinguished Harrison/Starkey collaboration of the solo era. Of the covers, only "You Belong to Me" finds some spirit in its pedestrian arrangement.

A couple of stray tracks which did not quite make the deadline will be considered with the next rescue project, but even if they had been included here, would not have challenged the long-established reality that Ringo is best enjoyed in small doses. His contributions to this rescued album will benefit simply from not being held down by the sandbags of lesser material. This is, after all, the whole idea of our rescue process, and once again it works wonders of addition by subtraction.

Assembly
29 tracks: 18 eligible, 11 provisional

	✓ Cage	M20, 78-Sep
	✓ Coming Up	M23-01, 79-Jul
	≈ Darkroom	M23-10, 79-Jul
	✓ Goodnight Tonight	M19-01, 79-Feb
	≈ Nobody Knows	M23-05, 79-Jul
🎧	≈ On the Way	M23-03, 79-Jul
	✓ One of These Days	M23-11, 79-Jul
	≈ Robber's Ball	M, 79-Jun
	≈ Simple as That	M, 80-Aug
	✓ Summer's Day Song	M23-07, 79-Jul
	≈ Temporary Secretary	M23-02, 79-Jul
	✓ Waterfalls	M23-04, 79-Jul
	✓ (Just Like) Starting Over	L13-01, 80-Sep
	✓ Beautiful Boy (Darling Boy)	L13-07, 80-Sep
	✓ Cleanup Time	L13-03, 80-Sep
🎧	✓ I'm Losing You	L13-05, 80-Sep
	✓ Real Love	L, +PGR, 80-Jun
	✓ Watching the Wheels	L13-08, 80-Sep
	✓ Woman	L13-10, 80-Sep
	✓ Flying Hour	H10, 80-Sep
	✓ Life Itself	H10-03, 80-Sep
🎧	✓ Tears of the World	H10, 80-Sep
	≈ Unconsciousness Rules	H10-02, 80-Sep
	✓ Writing's on the Wall	H10-08, 80-Sep
	≈ Attention	S13-04, +P, 80-Jul
	≈ Sure to Fall	S13-08, +P, 80-Jul
🎧	≈ Wrack My Brain	S13-02, +G, 80-Nov
	≈ You Belong to Me	S13-07, +G, 80-Nov
	✓ You've Got a Nice Way	S13-09, 80-Aug

As always, once the eligible and provisional tracks have been collected, a few just look less attractive, and will be set aside:

≈ Darkroom (P)
≈ Nobody Knows (P)
≈ On the Way (P)
≈ Robber's Ball (P)
≈ Sure to Fall (R)
≈ Temporary Secretary (P)
≈ Wrack My Brain (G)

The assembly then starts with two sets of tracks pulled together to form sequences which will give the album its shape, tone and theme. As we start, however, keep in mind that this album would have been made without knowledge of what was to come on December 8. The project would have begun in earnest when John began the recording sessions which produced *Double Fantasy*, and completed on roughly the same schedule as that album.

The first of these multi-song complexes is the "W" songs, one each from John, George and Paul, which have a distinct resonance together — beyond their titles, music or even lyrics. Each is a reflection on life, emotions, and the current state of things for the adult Beatles. (Alas, Ringo's "W" song, "Wrack My Brain" is not of a high enough quality to become part of the sequence.)

Famously, John's lyric for "Watching the Wheels" is an explainer for his time away, climaxing in its chorus with the memorable lyric:

> *No longer riding on the merry-go-round*
> *I just had to let it go*

Less famously, George's song "Writing's on the Wall" treads on similar ground:

> *The writing's on the wall brother,*
> *Your life is in your hands*

Further, in an astonishing twist, George's bridge eerily foreshadows events:

> *Strange we hold on to things that have no grace or power*
> *While death holds on to us much more with every passing hour*
> *And all the time you thought it would last*
> *Your life, your friends would always be*
> *'Til they're drunk away or shot away or die away from you.*

Lest you think this is some sort of retcon, multiple sources confirm that the song was recorded well before Lennon was killed. In fact, it was on the version of *Somewhere in England* that Warner Brothers rejected in September of 1980.

McCartney's "Waterfalls" was even older, having been written in the summer of 1979. Its relatively simple lyric and plaintive tone suggests loneliness — more specifically, the feeling of missing something or someone essential. In the context of Paul's album, it reads like a sort of sad love song, with more personal overtones than usual. This is amplified by putting the song next to the other Beatles.

Importantly, if these songs were all of the same musical temperament, putting them together might not have been possible. But as it is, they really complement

18 / Wheels, Walls and Waterfalls

each other almost perfectly. The Assembler will be able to recast them as a set, and use their key words to title the album. It's clear from the beginning that none of these songs is really right to either begin or end a side. There are no pole tracks here, despite the fact that John used his as one.

Though the exact order might need to be changed depending on what is placed around them, John's soundscape at the end of "Watching the Wheels" matches nicely with the opening of George's track, and the end of that song creates a nice space into which Paul's opening sounds can appear. With the idea that these will collectively be the title tracks for the album, they get assigned to side one, and their assembly comes down to this:

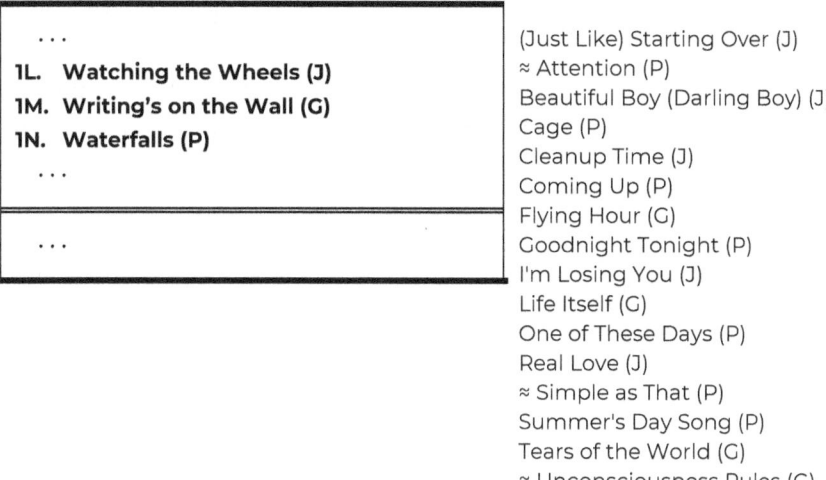

The second complex comes as the result of a fortuitous, or perhaps dubious, overlap in songs by John and Paul.

Perhaps the first thing to get out of the way is that "Goodnight Tonight" and "Woman" are very definitely *not* the same song. But their choruses, Paul's "Don't say it…say anything, but don't say goodnight tonight," and John's "Oo oo, well, well…do do do," start with the same musical idea and follow the same chord structure. Late in the song, as John begins his final verse, the arrangement moves up half a step, putting his chorus into the same key as Paul's. That's where the fun really begins. With only a slight change of tempo for each, and a little careful aligning, a seamless virtual duet emerges, with the singing even alternating perfectly between the voices.

Since Paul's song was written and released first, we might wonder if John was referencing his former partner's hit. That seems unlikely. Also unlikely is that he used the same structure intentionally to somehow align the songs. Most likely is that the two songs were written completely independent of one another, and it is mere coincidence that both songwriters settled on that chord progression at the same time. Also possible is that John heard Paul's hit on the radio — it spent six weeks on the Billboard top ten in the spring and early summer of 1979 — and his subconscious took over from there — for which we would not fault him.

Setting their origins aside, the Assembler would have recognized the overlap and realized that the best thing to do is put the songs with each other on the album. This works in part because the tracks are so different. Paul's is a dance record, while John's, for a change, is the "silly" love song. Contrasting styles is perfectly allowed — even encouraged — by the assembly rules, and the idea that theses two very different tracks could sit next to one another on the album without anyone noticing the similarities in songwriting until they were pointed out, might have been irresistible to all involved.

Though Paul's track is a potential album closer, it seems a little too obvious. For now, these will be placed somewhere in the middle of side two on the album:

... 1L. Watching the Wheels (J) 1M. Writing's on the Wall (G) 1N. Waterfalls (P) ...	(Just Like) Starting Over (J) ≈ Attention (P) Beautiful Boy (Darling Boy) (J) Cage (P) Cleanup Time (J) Coming Up (P)
... **2M. Woman (J)** **2N. Goodnight Tonight (P)** ...	Flying Hour (G) I'm Losing You (J) Life Itself (G) One of These Days (P) Real Love (J) ≈ Simple as That (P) Summer's Day Song (P) Tears of the World (G) ≈ Unconsciousness Rules (G) ≈ You Belong to Me (R) You've Got a Nice Way (R)

With five tracks already used, and only one of them even potentially a pole track, the Assembler must now dig a little harder for how to open and close this album.

Paul used "Coming Up" to open his album, and it definitely has the character of an opener. John used "(Just Like) Starting Over," and it, too, has some qualities associated with that spot. Of George's eligible tracks, only "Flying Hour" has any real potential for this purpose, but it is a little too stark lyrically to make a good first impression. Somehow, none of these is quite right to begin this album.

One of the songs Paul wrote for Ringo, however, seems to set a better tone for what will follow, and even includes an invitation to the listener: "Give me your attention for awhile." Maybe more to the point, there is no better spot on the album for "Attention." It would be wrong in any of the other pole positions, and might simply disappear if placed anywhere else. Though slight, it becomes the opener basically by virtue of the fact that it's good enough, and that's the only spot where it can totally thrive on the album. It makes a happy first sound.

What may have been only a provisional track when first evaluated actually makes so much more sense when used this way. Lightweight though it is, "Attention" has an optimism about it which is important to establish from the beginning, especially given what we know is coming from the three W's. Though they are not pessimistic, necessarily, they are all introspective, and the listener will need to have been somewhere else first in order to hear those songs properly.

That suggests using "Coming Up" as an extender to the opener. Again, it is lightweight but optimistic, catchy and energetic. It also has the advantage of being able to bump comfortably against "Watching the Wheels" at the beginning of the title complex. The beginning therefore looks like this:

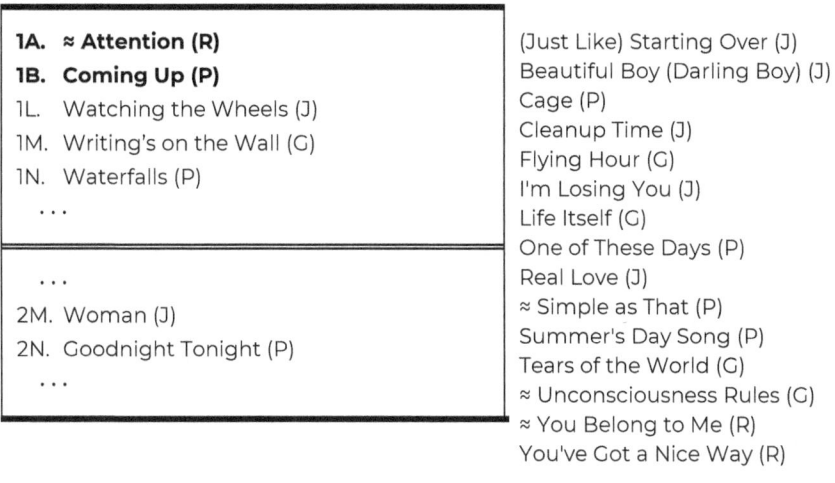

To close the album, we really must set aside "Goodnight Tonight" as both too obvious, and too slight. It has no big idea, and not even much reason to exist beyond its beat (and regrettable video, perhaps). It's just a little slice of fun, and must really be answered by something more substantial in order to clear its liabilities — a classic and recurring issue with Paul's songs which plagued him as a solo artist. That said, it actually is a pretty good candidate for a feature position, such as the penultimate track. Feature tracks do not need to be substantial, as long as they are paired with something that is.

So we search the available tracks for something which answers Paul's frivolity, sums up the themes of the W's, and leaves the listener with a feeling that something has been said. Fishing through the list of eligible and provisional tracks, "Flying

Hour" presents itself again, but once again doesn't quite fit the need, its music not entirely aligned closely enough with its lyric to work as a final statement. The only track on the eligible list which seems to have enough heft is George's anthemic "Life Itself." The immediate questions are whether it sits well next to "Goodnight Tonight," and whether it makes a good enough final sound.

To the first question, it appears to sit fairly well, coming off as a return to meaningful form after a modest diversion. To the second question, with its long fadeout through optimistic music, again the answer would have to be yes. And yet... (We will return to this caveat.)

1A. ≈ Attention (R)	(Just Like) Starting Over (J)
1B. Coming Up (P)	Beautiful Boy (Darling Boy) (J)
1L. Watching the Wheels (J)	Cage (P)
1M. Writing's on the Wall (G)	Cleanup Time (J)
1N. Waterfalls (P)	Flying Hour (G)
...	I'm Losing You (J)
	One of These Days (P)
	Real Love (J)
...	≈ Simple as That (P)
2M. Woman (J)	Summer's Day Song (P)
2N. Goodnight Tonight (P)	Tears of the World (G)
2Z. Life Itself (G)	≈ Unconsciousness Rules (G)
	≈ You Belong to Me (R)
	You've Got a Nice Way (R)

Returning to the end of side one, whatever track goes there, it will have to emerge from McCartney's "Waterfalls." An obvious possibility, therefore, is Lennon's "Beautiful Boy (Darling Boy)" — which opens with the sound of ocean. But the connection is not quite right.

It will probably sound blasphemous to say this, but in the summer of 1980, the Beatles and the Assembler might have hesitated to put something like John's lullaby on their album, especially given the very visible presence of ballads like "Waterfalls" and "Woman" and "Life Itself." Though obviously a potential pole track (which John used as such on *Double Fantasy*), it feels almost *too* personal to sit comfortably next to the rest of these tracks. It feels especially soloistic, and is somehow different from the tone which is being developed with the rest of these tracks. Unlike the earlier "Good Night" from *The White Album*, this song could not close the collection, and does not have an obvious role in any other place. Also, in the context of the macho group dynamics, even after all this time John may have been more reticent to offer the song in the first place.

Given the iconic nature of this track, and its crushing lyrics, and the fact that it truly is one of John's masterworks, it might seem impossible that it would not have been included here. But the Assembler's job is to create a virtuous circle from the parts available, and this amazing song might have simply been the odd one out. With an apology and promise that it would appear on the next album, the Assembler would have had to put the assembly ahead of any sentimentality at this point. Obviously, the circumstances of the next album would be decidedly different, but the Assembler's promise would be kept.

Instead, John's homage to 50s doo-wop, "(Just Like) Starting Over" emerges much better from Paul's solitary song, doing as its title suggests and restarting the optimistic vibe. With its false ending and long fadeout, it might very well serve as the capstone to side one. But where there's one homage, why not another?

As mentioned above, most of the contributions to Ringo's album by Paul and George did not impress. But what they could not find on "Wrack My Brain," George and Ringo did find on "You Belong to Me." Though a very straight reading of this chestnut, Ringo is in fine voice, and the positive energy is infectious. Best of all, clocking in at a scant 2:08, it is almost gone before a listener would have time to register it as filler. Perhaps the Assembler would waffle at whether to include this or not, but ultimately leave it in as a nod to balance, given that Lennon and McCartney again appear to be dominating this assembly.

1A.	≈ Attention (R)	Beautiful Boy (Darling Boy) (J)
1B.	Coming Up (P)	Cage (P)
1L.	Watching the Wheels (J)	Cleanup Time (J)
1M.	Writing's on the Wall (G)	Flying Hour (G)
1N.	Waterfalls (P)	I'm Losing You (J)
1Y.	**(Just Like) Starting Over (J)**	One of These Days (P)
1Z.	**≈ You Belong to Me (R)**	Real Love (J)
		≈ Simple as That (P)
	...	Summer's Day Song (P)
2M.	Woman (J)	Tears of the World (G)
2N.	Goodnight Tonight (P)	≈ Unconsciousness Rules (G)
2Z.	Life Itself (G)	You've Got a Nice Way (R)

Side two now presents a challenge, namely to set up the trio which have surfaced to end the album.

Potential openers for side two are surprisingly numerous. From John, either "Cleanup Time" or "I'm Losing You" might work. From Paul, "Cage" seems worth considering. From Ringo, "You've Got a Nice Way," his best in this era, is obviously good enough and might fit. Even George's "Unconsciousness Rules," found on the provisional list, seems a possibility given the way this album has developed.

A few titles are clearly eliminated. "Wrack My Brain" and "Tears of the World" never stood much of a chance of being included here, and neither did "Summer's Day Song," "One of These Days," or anything from Paul on the provisional list. Paul's tracks were retained as eligible just in case something specific might fill a hole, and no such holes have appeared. Since the album is fairly well balanced between the voices at this point, one of John's two possible tracks won't be needed, so "Cleanup Time" is jettisoned without really a second thought.

The best four tracks to complete the collection are therefore: "Cage," "I'm Losing You," "Unconsciousness Rules," and "You've Got a Nice Way." Since any could open the side, the ordering of these tracks will depend entirely on flow — which is to say, how they best flow from one to another.

Considering how each track ends, therefore, is essential. Ringo has a clean fade, while John has a fade into guitar sound effects that brought about a segue into a Yoko track. The tracks by Paul and George each end cold. There are probably multiple satisfying ways to arrange these four tracks.

But the Assembler will consider the end of the sequence first, finding that the fade out of "You've Got a Nice Way" is the best to set up "Woman." John's crazy guitar sounds actually can be bumped up against the scream which opens "Cage," creating yet another John/Paul sequence. The cold end of "Cage" works best with the beginning of Ringo's track, especially if Paul's last note overlaps with its first drum sound. This leaves "Unconsciousness Rules" to begin the sequence and open the side. Luckily, the drum opening of "I'm Losing You" fits right up against George's cold ending, and side two is complete.

1A.	≈ Attention (R)	Beautiful Boy (Darling Boy) (J)
1B.	Coming Up (P)	Cleanup Time (J)
1L.	Watching the Wheels (J)	Flying Hour (G)
1M.	Writing's on the Wall (G)	One of These Days (P)
1N.	Waterfalls (P)	Real Love (J)
1Y.	(Just Like) Starting Over (J)	≈ Simple as That (P)
1Z.	≈ You Belong to Me (R)	Summer's Day Song (P)
		Tears of the World (G)

2A.	**≈ Unconsciousness Rules (G)**
2B.	**I'm Losing You (J)**
2C.	**Cage (P)**
2D.	**You've Got a Nice Way (R)**
2M.	Woman (J)
2N.	Goodnight Tonight (P)
2Z.	Life Itself (G)

Well, not quite. Though "Life Itself" makes a meaningful end to the collection, it's been a while since the Beatles used the old hidden track trick. In this case, the superimposition of the choruses of "Woman" and "Goodnight Tonight" makes an interesting and — at 38 seconds — very brief topper. Paul pleads, "Don't say

18 / Wheels, Walls and Waterfalls

goodnight," while John tosses in with "I love you, now and forever…" The effect is not unlike a latter day "I've Got a Feeling."

Would the meta-Beatles and their Assembler have actually done something like this? Let's just say that there's no way to know, and do it anyway.

1A. ≈ Attention (R)	Beautiful Boy (Darling Boy) (J)
1B. Coming Up (P)	Cleanup Time (J)
1L. Watching the Wheels (J)	≈ ~~Darkroom (P)~~
1M. Writing's on the Wall (G)	Flying Hour (G)
1N. Waterfalls (P)	≈ ~~Nobody Knows (P)~~
1Y. (Just Like) Starting Over (J)	≈ ~~On the Way (P)~~
1Z. ≈ You Belong to Me (R)	One of These Days (P)
	Real Love (J)
	≈ ~~Robber's Ball (P)~~
2A. ≈ Unconsciousness Rules (G)	≈ Simple as That (P)
2B. I'm Losing You (J)	Summer's Day Song (P)
2C. Cage (P)	≈ ~~Sure to Fall (R)~~
2D. You've Got a Nice Way (R)	Tears of the World (G)
2M. Woman (J)	≈ ~~Temporary Secretary (P)~~
2N. Goodnight Tonight (P)	≈ ~~Wrack My Brain (G)~~
2Y. Life Itself (G)	
2Z. Woman/Goodnight Tonight (Reprise) (J/P)	

SAVE THE BEATLES!

Wheels, Walls and Waterfalls

Principal Recording: March 1980 - November 1980
Release: November 1980

Side One
1. Attention (McCartney)
2. Coming Up (McCartney)
3. Watching the Wheels (Lennon)
4. Writing's on the Wall (Harrison)
5. Waterfalls (McCartney)
6. (Just Like) Starting Over (Lennon)
7. You Belong to Me (King/Stewart/Price)

Side Two
1. Unconsciousness Rules (Harrison)
2. I'm Losing You (Lennon)
3. Cage (McCartney)
4. You've Got a Nice Way (Stills/Stergis)
5. Woman (Lennon)
6. Goodnight Tonight (McCartney)
7. Life Itself (Harrison)
8. Reprise: Woman/Goodnight Tonight (Lennon/McCartney)

Make It Yourself

Total Running Time: 53:24

Tk	Rill	Title	Source	Dur
F6-A1	—	Attention	[1]	3:41
F6-A2	0	Coming Up	[2]	3:50
F6-A3	0.5	Watching the Wheels [Edit]	[3]	4:14
F6-A4	*	Writing's on the Wall	[4]	3:57
F6-A5	1.0	Waterfalls	[2]	4:41
F6-A6	0	(Just Like) Starting Over	[3]	3:54
F6-A7	1.0	You Belong to Me	[1]	2:12

Total: 26:31

Tk	Rill	Title	Source	Dur
F6-B1	—	Unconsciousness Rules	[4]	3:33
F6-B2	0	I'm Losing You [Edit]	[3]	3:57
F6-B3	*	Cage	[U]	3:06
F6-B4	(1.0)	You've Got a Nice Way	[1]	3:31
F6-B5	1.0	Woman	[3]	3:28
F6-B6	0	Goodnight Tonight	[5]	4:12
F6-B7	(1.8)	Life Itself	[4]	4:23
F6-B8	*	Woman/Goodnight Tonight (Reprise)	—	0:38

Total: 26:53

[U] Unreleased (Seek on YouTube)
[1] *Stop and Smell the Roses*
[2] *McCartney II*
[3] *Double Fantasy*
[4] *Somewhere in England*
[5] *Back to the Egg*

* NOTE: Descriptions of edits and crossfades, with sample audio, are available at:

SaveTheBeatles.com

Release
November 1980

Most Popular Albums
September 1977 - October 1980

US		UK	
Barbra Streisand	*Guilty*	ABBA	*The Album*
Bee Gees	*Spirits Having Flown*	ABBA	*Voulez-Vous*
Billy Joel	*52nd Street*	Boney M	*Night Flight to Venus*
Billy Joel	*Glass Houses*	Barbra Streisand	*Guilty*
Billy Joel	*The Stranger*	Barry Manilow	*Manilow Magic*
Bob Seger	*Against the Wind*	Blondie	*Parallel Lines*
Bob Seger	*Stranger in Town*	Bread	*The Sound of Bread*
Christopher Cross	*Christopher Cross*	Diana Ross/Supremes	*20 Golden Greats*
Diana Ross	*Diana*	Dire Straits	*Dire Straits*
Donna Summer	*Bad Girls*	Electric Light Orchestra	*Discovery*
The Doobie Brothers	*Minute by Minute*	Electric Light Orchestra	*Out of the Blue*
Eagles	*The Long Run*	Ian Dury/Blockheads	*New Boots & Panties*
Foreigner	*Double Vision*	**Jeff Wayne**	***War of the Worlds***
Foreigner	*Foreigner*	Kate Bush	*The Kick Inside*
Led Zeppelin	*In Through the Out...*	Madness	*One Step Beyond*
Michael Jackson	*Off the Wall*	Michael Jackson	*Off the Wall*
Pink Floyd	*The Wall*	Original Soundtrack	*Grease*
Queen	*The Game*	Original Soundtrack	*Saturday Night Fever*
The Rolling Stones	*Some Girls*	The Police	*Outlandos D'amour*
Soundtrack	*Grease*	The Police	*Regatta De Blanc*
Soundtrack	***Saturday Night Fever***	Rod Stewart	*Greatest Hits*
Steely Dan	*Aja*	Roxy Music	*Flesh and Blood*
Styx	*The Grand Illusion*	Sky	*Sky 2*
Supertramp	*Breakfast in America*	Supertramp	*Breakfast in America*
Tom Petty and...	*Damn the Torpedoes*	UB40	*Signing Off*

Most popular album in bold

In our imagined narrative, this period would have been a long hiatus for the group, and that is supported by the utter lack of solo Beatles on either of these lists. Viewed collectively, they were releasing less frequently, with John now in hiding, and George also skipping a year. Whatever relevance they may have been able to retain as a group is unknown, but as solo artists, they were now rapidly descending into niche status.

The biggest shift since the last era may actually be in a form of homogenization. In looking at these lists, the distinct categories, though still vaguely present, are somewhat harder to draw out. Instead, a period of consolidation has led to a "pop" sheen over everything, which has subsumed all of the typical distinctions. Though Pink Floyd, Kate Bush and Steely Dan still represent the "art" end, each also has pop tendencies, and such crossover is widely prevalent. From the other side, though Queen has shed some of their more esoteric instincts, there is still an "artsy" aspect to their pop. The singer/songwriters are no longer writing as introspectively, but generating pure pop like *52nd Street*, *Christopher Cross* and *Damn the Torpedoes*.

In a clear sign of the erasure of lines between categories, groups like Styx, Supertramp, Foreigner, Madness and Roxy Music are leading the way into something best termed as simply "pop rock" — its biggest quality being that it can be almost anything at any time. Ironically, this hearkens back to the variety that the Beatles originally brought to pop music. An argument can be made that the Fabs would have returned to a music industry doing their schtick better than they could.

Into this, other styles had arisen, but essentially as overlarge niches. The punk movement bubbles beneath the foam of general popularity, peaking out only with watered-down New Wave variants like the Police, Blondie, and Ian Dury. The Sex Pistols, the Pretenders, and Elvis Costello sit just off the bottom of these lists. Likewise, disco — which had a bigger footprint in the world of singles — is only represented here by Michael Jackson's *Off the Wall*, and the soundtrack to *Saturday Night Fever*, only the latter of which is a quintessential disco release. The Village People are also dancing just out of sight.

Since we are assuming that the Beatles were off the stage during this time, their return would have been subject to all of the forces which shaped pop music while they were away. This makes for a precarious picture, and no certainty that their return would have garnered the same sort of overwhelming success they had always known. Though *Wheels, Walls and Waterfalls* would have been comfortable on these lists, it might also have been *too* comfortable. Blending in is something the Beatles had never done before, but there is the distinct possibility that it could have happened here.

Their album would certainly have been a big event, and gotten a great deal of early publicity, but it might not have had the tail that so many of their other releases had — if only due to the sort of commoditization demonstrated by the popular titles. To a post-*Rumours* world, the Beatles might very well have sounded like just another product.

Topping the Charts
November 1980

US			UK	
Barbra Streisand	*Guilty*	1	Barbra Streisand	*Guilty*
Queen	*The Game*	2	Stevie Wonder	*Hotter Than July*
The Doobie Brothers	*One Step Closer*	3	The Police	*Zenyatta Mondatta*
Bruce Springsteen	*The River*	4	Motorhead	*Ace of Spades*
Pat Benatar	*Crimes Of Passion*	5	Whitesnake	*Live In The Heart of...*
Kenny Rogers	*Greatest Hits*	6	OMD	*Organisation*
Diana Ross	*Diana*	7	Status Quo	*Just Supposin'*
Supertramp	*Paris*	8	Bruce Springsteen	*The River*
AC/DC	*Back In Black*	9	The Three Degrees	*Gold*
ELO	*Xanadu*	10	Kate Bush	*Never for Ever*

The moment of release for *Wheels, Walls and Waterfalls* would have been a pretty good one. There are no recent solo albums whose sales we can inspect to get an idea of how the group might have been received, but nothing on either of these lists looks so dominant that the Beatles could not have jumped in front. Paul's most recent effort, *McCartney II*, had done well enough based on low expectations, but was a very niche product in many ways and isn't a very good indicator. The next release, *Double Fantasy*, would be the closest available, and as we know, its sales were impacted by events outside of the music.

Since we must subsume Lennon's death into our altered narrative, it feels right to look at the performance of *Double Fantasy* for clues on how a group album would have done in the same context. It started slow, with great hopes, and strong initial orders, and then was tempered by lackluster reviews. A Beatles release, by contrast, would have started with even higher hopes, even greater trepidations, even stronger initial orders, and even more uncertainty about what reviewers would think. Looking at these charts, a strong opening would have been reasonably likely, but from there, it's very difficult to project.

Without a doubt, however, the death of a Beatle would then have shaken the world no less under our altered circumstances, and all that actually happened to the group catalog would have happened likewise around the imagined album. Similarly, though we might expect a group effort to have debuted higher than *Double Fantasy*, we can also expect that, wherever it was on the charts when John was killed, sales would have spiked.

Discussion

Do Beatles albums need to be *profound* to be *great*? That seems to be the big question that *Wheels, Walls and Waterfalls* asks. There are certainly passing references to big subjects — love, death, loss, priorities — but they occupy niches on this album, rather than the central corridor. This probably would have even surprised the Assembler, given how carefully the three big "W" songs were knit into a sequence of Big Ideas.

Indeed, the first thing reviewers might have noticed is that this album breaks no new ground, either musically, lyrically, or sonically. While not exactly workmanlike, it has the sound of well-seasoned recording artists going through their paces. In the case of the Beatles, these paces are still interesting, but the cultural places they once occupied have all but closed in the time they were away.

So maybe there is a question behind the question: Just who would the Beatles have been in 1980? In some ways, this album shows them occupying new spaces, but in other ways, they appear as if coming full circle. Listening to this music, you can reasonably wonder what, if anything, this album is about, or if it is even "about" anything — or more importantly, whether it needs to be.

Six of the 14 songs are essentially pure pop, and several others might be categorized as just on the edge of pop, albeit with slightly more personal undertones. Though Paul and John each place a toe in the pool of profundity, only George seems to be contemplating the deep end. And yet his moves in that direction come with his most pleasant and accessible music in years. If "Life Itself" seems a bit too thick for George's skinny solo album, here it feels more like an inevitable and welcome bit of the old Beatle transcendence.

It's possible to imagine critics complaining that the Beatles had said this all before, and that the audience for any amount of introspection in pop music had completely dried up. That is hard to argue with, given what the pop landscape looked like when this album would have appeared. A critical issue with the reception of *Double Fantasy* may have been that the audience it tried to reach had stopped believing that pop music still had any meaning. The market lane that John and Yoko actually occupied, though no one could say this at the time, was the nostalgia zone.

Thus, it is possible to imagine that same fate for a group album. Though the Beatles do not *sound* like dinosaurs on this album, the world might not have been able to hear anything else. Yet, in a strangely prescient way, the Beatles of *Wheels, Walls and Waterfalls* actually seem to know this somehow, and have turned in an album that is as much *dessert* as it is *main course*.

Recognizing they they would never again be able to make an album completely devoid of complex issues or introspection — because of who they were and how they got there — but that the role of their work would have shifted, they simply treat these subjects as part of the course of everything, and not as life's show-stoppers. Anyone who has ever turned 40 knows exactly how that goes. This may be the lesson learned by the now mature Beatles. It is certainly at least part of what John was trying to sell through his return to the limelight in 1980.

Because of their maturity, there is a central ease to everything heard from the Beatles here, and it only becomes more noticeable as this album gets absorbed. It's almost as if John's sheen of contentedness, which the others seem to share when their songs are placed in the same vicinity, has radiated outward. Frankly, the Beatles all sound *happy* on this album, even as they occasionally ruminate. In short, this is, by far, the lightest and happiest of the fused Beatles albums, and their overall happiest-sounding LP since, well, pick your favorite early album.

The question remains about what market there would have been for this music, especially in the long term. The album is certainly packed with catchy music, and almost any of these tracks might have become the next hit single. Theoretically, with the right timing, singles from this album could have been dropped every few months for a couple of years, a level of commerciality they had not displayed for some time.

Though we often think about the great commercial success the Beatles enjoyed, we rarely would apply the adjective "commercial" to their work. That word suggests pandering, or simplicity, or even just plain fashion. Of these, only the third ever actually applied to the Beatles, but does not seem to be what's at work here.

To figure out what is at work, we must return to the notion of craftsmanship, a much less cynical characterization that acknowledges their status as music royalty, and affirms their freedom to turn out whatever they like. In our experiment of rescuing Beatles albums, we certainly imagine that they would have had such latitude, and that no matter what they released, the public would have taken notice, wondered what they had to say, bought it, listened to it, and actually cared about what they found there. That the Beatles were not breaking new ground would have been entirely irrelevant by this point.

Perhaps the salient answer to the question we started with is that a Beatles album absolutely did not need to be *profound* to be *great*. Truthfully, it would hardly seem like the Beatles without at least at little ruminating on big issues, but as long as the music was *respectable* and *imaginative* and *intentional* and *rewarding* and *beautiful* and *timeless*, there would have been somebody who cared. These are some of the key attributes which always made a Beatles album great, and they are not adjectives we can typically apply to the solo releases of this era. Happily, they all seem to apply to *Wheels, Walls and Waterfalls*.

This album sounds like a fully home-cooked meal. In an era of increasingly fast food music, this album would have delighted the palates of listeners, while also sticking to their ribs, if not in a very heavy way. One might feel satisfied, not over full, and ready for an after dinner drink. More importantly, it would have shown again the undeniable power of the Beatles to give the world exactly what it needed, when it needed it.

FUSION ERA #7
───────────────────────────────

DECEMBER 1980-OCTOBER 1982

In Spite of All

19 / In Spite of All

"It's still up to us to make what we can of it."

—*John Lennon, December 8, 1980*

"The music was always more important than anything else."

—*Ringo Starr, March 1981*

"I think the kind of anchor that had held us together was still there."

—*Paul McCartney, April 1982*

"It was like reaching the top of a wall and then looking over and seeing that there's so much more on the other side."

—*George Harrison, September, 1982*

Chronology

1980

Killed by crazed gunman	**DEC**		Record sales spike

1981

Recording in Montserrat with Stanley Clarke, Carl Perkins, Stevie Wonder	**FEB/MAR**		Philip Norman's *Shout!* (book) released
Leaves CBS Records Palimony suit filed by Nancy Andrews *Caveman* (film) premieres Marries Barbara Bach	**APR**		PGR jam at Ringo's wedding reception Announces that Wings has disbanded
"All Those Years Ago" released *Somewhere in England* released	**MAY/JUN**		Yoko's *Season of Glass* released Killer pleads guilty to second degree murder
Jack Douglas sues over unpaid royalties	**JUL**		*Time Bandits* (film) released
Release of "That'll Be the Day" preempted	**SEP/OCT**		*Stop and Smell the Roses* released (RCA)
Recording with Michael Jackson Attempts/fails to buy back Northern Songs	**NOV**		*I, Me, Mine* (book) released, hardcover

1982

Wins Grammy for *Double Fantasy*	**FEB**		
Recording with Michael Jackson *Tug of War* released	**APR/MAY**		*The Beatles at the Beeb* (radio) airs
The Complete Silver Beatles (Decca audition) released *The Compleat Beatles* (film) released	**SEP/OCT**		"The Girl Is Mine" (duet with Michael Jackson) released *Gone Troppo* released

19 / In Spite of All

Introduction

We can do many things with our slightly altered reality, but the sad fact is that there would be no new John Lennon music after December 8, 1980. We have no choice but to write the tragic events of that day into our narrative.

Had the Beatles still been collaborating from a distance, the impact obviously would have been profound, though not necessarily any more profound than it actually was on the three solo artists in the real world. Perhaps the primary difference is that the group would have had a new album in stores when it happened. Obviously, however, the success or failure of that album would have been no one's primary concern. It's reasonable to think that it might have followed the same trajectory as *Double Fantasy*, which jumped to number one in the weeks after Lennon died, and subsequently seared itself into cultural memory as a talisman of the tragedy.

Soon enough, questions would have arisen about the group's plans, and they would have publicly deflected those questions as much as possible. But privately, they likely would have been throwing themselves back into the work of making music, which is exactly what they did in the real world. Eventually, however, they would have had to make some very difficult choices about what to do next.

For our purposes here, we will assume that, after a period of shock and grief, the surviving Beatles would likely have started to wonder whether *Wheels, Walls and Waterfalls* was a sufficient swan song for the band. With some sketches of new Lennon songs remaining in the can, and a strong desire to honor their fallen brother, we will further assume that they would have reconvened after a year or so to begin assembly of one last fused album for a more proper final curtain. This process would have been longer and more involved than any of the previous fused albums, and would take them on a wistful journey, reacquainted them with some old friends, while also keeping their heads and hearts very much in the present.

This creates the opportunity to rescue tracks that, in the real world, mostly languished on ever more disappointing solo albums. John's contributions are hereby protected from the deeply unpleasant duet album, *Milk and Honey*. Paul would still have made *Tug of War*, but some surprisingly strong outtakes would be spared the humiliation of *Pipes of Peace*. George and Ringo's tracks are plucked from albums that almost no one heard — and which would not be missed had they never existed.

The Assembler would have had an especially delicate task. First, there would have been the matter of finishing — or intentionally leaving unfinished — Lennon's final batch of songs. Again the prospect of a Threetles-like solution appears. It's possible to imagine them hitting upon the same framing which would serve them later: namely, imagining that Lennon had merely gone out for a break while they finished up things he had left open. If such a process had happened then, at least they would have started with studio tracks that were not quite as difficult to wrangle as the cassette demos used later. But with such fresh emotions, it is hard to know whether such a thing would even have been possible.

There would have been the usual pressures of parity, compounded by trying to channel John's point of view — and tempering Yoko's — while also keeping Paul and George happy about their representations on the album. If they had avoided being together in the studio for all of those years, they may have been forced into joint studio work now, if only because it was the right thing to do.

Next, there would be difficult choices about the overall tone to be set with the album. In later years, especially on the *Anthology* discs, the surviving Beatles (along with their studio collaborators) have demonstrated a surprisingly sentimental approach to their seminal works. Questionable moments like "A Beginning" and the cloying crossfades between demos and finished masters would need to be avoided. It would have been up to the Assembler to enforce some discipline. All would have wanted to avoid a maudlin approach, but there might have been friction about how best to achieve that. Emotions would have been at an all-time high.

It's tempting to suggest that the Assembler should simply step aside and let the Beatles do this one themselves. But as we have seen, they were not always the best arbiters of their material. An independent set of ears would have been crucial, same as always, and we will assume that there were no challenges to a process which would have served them well for a decade at that point — even as we also accept that the musicians might have been more involved in the assembly on this occasion than on anything since *Abbey Road*.

Along the way, there might have been objections to augmenting tracks that John had left unfinished, or arguments about which solo tracks best served the album's charter, or whether they should even continue with the project at all. It's just as likely, however, that the parties would have put aside any lingering differences in the interest of creating a proper memorial and capstone for a 20-year career. Either way, the necessary production and assembly would likely have taken the better part of a year, with all agreeing that a release in late 1982 — roughly two years after John's death, and almost exactly 20 years after the release of "Love Me Do" — would be the best possible option.

Once the album was assembled, however, it would have been clear to all involved that the group synergy had remained intact, even after losing its founder and most provocative voice. The synergy was heightened by the strong emotions of loss, while remaining largely dry-eyed. Overt sentimentality, while essentially unavoidable, would have been at least somewhat muted in favor of sketched reminiscences. And a final side would mourn Lennon's death, say goodbye to the band, and, through a serendipitous acquisition, poignantly recall the very reason it all began.

19/In Spite of All

Recording
December 1980 – October 1982

⊙ Studio recording   ○ Single release

John Lennon's murder came while all three of his former partners were hard at work on solo projects. Indeed, there hadn't been this much simultaneous former Beatle recording activity since 1974. Unsurprisingly, all three surviving Beatles went forward with their projects even as they grieved, and took only short amounts of time away to process what had happened. As a matter of course, each resumed work quickly and with renewed energy. Harrison finished the revisions to *Somewhere in England*, while Starkey finished *Stop and Smell the Roses*.

McCartney dug in on *Tug of War* with a fervor not seen since his Beatle days — which is saying something, considering his ever-present perfectionist ways. The sprawling sessions, produced by George Martin, which took place over the course of more than a year, ultimately featured a parade of famous guests, including Stanley Clarke, Stevie Wonder, Carl Perkins, and Ringo Starr. Denny Laine was present at the beginning, but ultimately left and was replaced by Eric Stewart.

The release of Paul's album was delayed multiple times, and when *Tug of War* finally emerged many critics hailed it as McCartney's new masterwork. A single with Stevie Wonder, "Ebony and Ivory" was a worldwide hit, and the album's side one closer, "Here Today," Paul's emotional tribute to John Lennon, was recognized as an instant classic, inevitably — and appropriately — compared favorably to "Yesterday." The album also sold better than any solo Beatle album other than *Double Fantasy* had in many years.

Enough material was left over from *Tug of War* that McCartney and Martin immediately planned a follow-up. Though it took nearly a year of tweaking, and included Paul working on new tracks with Michael Jackson, *Pipes of Peace* was nowhere near as successful either critically or commercially. Indeed, critics savaged it in a way which had become familiar throughout McCartney's post-Beatles work. The public ignored the album, even as they lapped up the Jackson collaborations on singles and in videos. It would be the start of a long creative slide for McCartney, which did not ebb until he began working with Elvis Costello several years later.

Despite the failure of *Stop and Smell the Roses*, and his lack of a recording contract, Ringo trudged on. Next he began what would be a very long and fruitful collaboration with former Eagle Joe Walsh. The album they created, *Old Wave*, despite being a notch up in quality for Ringo, was not even released in either the US or UK, and only found a willing label in Canada. It received no publicity to speak of, and sold only a tiny number of copies — which have since become collectors items!

Harrison still owed music to Warner Brothers, and so in 1982 he recorded another lackluster, contractually obligated album. *Gone Troppo*, which followed the pattern of being ignored by critics and all but the most die-hard fans, would be the last music from George until *Cloud Nine* and the Traveling Wilburys brought him out of semi-retirement late in the 80s.

John Lennon's final recording sessions had left behind enough music for a follow-up to *Double Fantasy* which he and Yoko had already titled *Milk and Honey*. The unpolished tracks languished for a time, and Yoko eventually had a falling out with producer Jack Douglas. Sometime in 1983 she resolved to polish John's tracks, write some new songs herself, and complete the final duet album. Though it did spawn a surprise hit in "Nobody Told Me," the underwhelming album came and went very quickly, leaving no meaningful lasting impression.

Eventually, the radio program *Lost Lennon Tapes* would provide fans with legitimate, official access to numerous recordings made during John's Dakota days. It would become clear that, though he denied it, he had remained very active creatively during those years, even as he stepped back from fame and insulated himself from much of the outside world.

In an odd, perhaps fitting twist, those demos provided the means for a virtual Beatles "reunion" during the *Anthology* project. Though the result was hardly a reanimation of Beatle Magic, it was still a clear case of technology and imagination fusing the Beatles back together, if only for a moment, and allowing them to elevate one another again across a great distance of time, much as we have been attempting to do in this project.

Materials

Overview
72 tracks: 25 eligible, 14 alternates

The solo Beatle recordings of this era were made, for the most part, in response to the death of John Lennon. Yet, surprisingly, the overt references and influences are relatively muted. Paul and George each made one overt tribute track, but there is a sense in these recordings that life — like the music itself — simply had to go on.

We know, for example, that many of the songs recorded in the aftermath of John's death had been written before the tragedy, and it's not always possible to tell which were from before or after. In those days, after so many years of being pummeled by media and the fans, all three surviving Beatles were inclined to play their cards very close to the vest.

So when these projects are viewed individually, the few responses which exist are spread far and wide. Were it not seared into every Beatle fan's experience, it might be possible to listen to these solo albums and not gain a sense that anything major had happened since the last time around. In Ringo's work of this era, for example, there is essentially no mention at all.

Gathering the most relevant bits onto a fused group album cannot alter that fact. It can result in some concentration of the grief, but the Beatles all seem wary of too much concentration in that regard. So rather than plucking everything smacking of having been influenced by John's death and gluing it together to make the album, our Assembler will have to be a bit more surgical. Despite the relatively small amount of material affected, there is still enough to create a seminal statement by the group, and do so with a slightly different form of concentration than would have been used previously.

To a degree, the whole thing would have to be built around the tracks John left behind unfinished. These would have had to be finessed somehow, but then could have formed the scaffolding on which the emotions could play out. There are wonderful opportunities for voices to elevate one another scattered throughout these recordings, even if they sometimes don't directly address the elephant in the room. That will have to happen, as always, in between the voices.

SAVE THE BEATLES!

George Harrison
14 tracks: 5 eligible, 4 provisional

Sources

H10	*Somewhere in England* (4 tracks) R: Mar 80 - Feb 81 P: Harrison/Cooper	S: FPSHOT	81-Jun
H11	*Gone Troppo* R: May-Aug 82 P: Harrison/Cooper/McDonald	S: FPSHOT	82-Nov

Tracks

All Those Years Ago (Harrison)	H10-04, +PR, 81-Feb
✓ Somewhat jaunty for its subject matter, but probably not hit material without the subtext.	
Baby Don't Run Away (Harrison)	H11-08, 82-Aug
⊘ (Quality) Unattractive vocal arrangement and too many vocoders/synths. Slow, boxy sound.	
Blood from a Clone (Harrison)	H10-01, 81-Feb
⊘ (Quality) Odd combination of instruments, quirky beat, pointed lyrics, all add up to not much.	
Circles (Harrison)	H11-10, 82-Aug
≈ (Content) Pre-maturity songwriting. Still clunky even with a smoother arrangement. Weepy, overlong.	
Dream Away (Harrison)	H11-09, 82-Aug
✓ Awesome Lennon-esque nonsense chorus. Positive, jaunty and infectious. A complete success.	
Gone Troppo (Harrison)	H11-05, 82-Aug
≈ (Quality) Leisure life incarnate. Uncomplicated, but about as memorable as a happy hour drink.	
Greece (Harrison)	H11-04, 82-Aug
⊘ (Filler) A pleasant, guitar-based lark, but it mostly just takes up space. Nothing especially "grecian."	
I Really Love You (Swearingen)	H11-03, 82-Aug
⊘ (Filler) Sounds like they had fun making this, but it's hard to see a point. Almost parody of doo-wop.	
Mystical One (Harrison)	H11-06, 82-Aug
≈ (Quality) Lyrically, George's "Watching the Wheels." Poppy tune sounds detached from the ideas.	
Teardrops (Harrison)	H10-06, 81-Feb
≈ (Quality) Ridiculously up-tempo sad song. Very catchy, if you can let the lyrics go.	
That Which I Have Lost (Harrison)	H10-07, 81-Feb
⊘ (Quality) Simplistic, twangy, skippy, clunky, square song. Unpleasant. But don't blame the tuba player.	
That's the Way It Goes (Harrison)	H11-02, 82-Aug
✓ Really nice song. Easy and flowing. Great arrangement. One that got lost amid the lousiness.	
Unknown Delight (Harrison)	H11-07, 82-Aug
✓ Beautiful pop ballad. Fully formed and warm. BVs suspect. Cribs his "Something" solo!	
Wake Up My Love (Harrison)	H11-01, 82-Aug
✓ Synth-heavy pure pop. Quirky rhythm in verse is disorienting or this might have been a hit.	

For George, this era began with finding four replacement tracks to finish *Somewhere in England*. He clearly did not relish the task, as the lyrics of "Blood from a Clone" attest, and the results don't exactly improve the album. If anything, the more whimsical cover art probably did more to lift the tone, which is basically all the record company wanted.

The most notable replacement, of course, is the original Threetles reunion, "All Those Years Ago." The track, recycled after being rejected by Ringo, and still featuring his rather anonymous drumming, only became an event when Paul, Linda and Denny added nearly inaudible backup vocals, and the lyrics were changed just enough to become a tribute to John.

Ringo's argument that it didn't fit his vocal range rings false because the song he took instead, "Wrack My Brain" is actually even less of a fit. But his mention of not liking the lyrics, coupled with George's statement that the original had featured the same chorus but been "a bit more uptight," suggest that the song may have had a much different intent in its initial incarnation.

Harrison never revealed the original lyrics, but consider how a small pronoun tweak might have changed things: "*You were* shouting all about love / while *you* treated *me* like a dog." Given the fact that George and John were famously estranged in that period, it feels at least possible that this tribute originated as something with more bite.

Even not knowing what revisions went into the finished version, it makes for something of a paper tribute to John. The incongruously uptempo feel and "bop she waddy waddy" backup vocals seem detached from the lyric and subject matter. Of course, it was a huge hit, and the mere presence of three Beatles makes it a shoo-in for the tribute album that this rescue would become.

The replacement parts created for *Somewhere in England* have one thing in common with *Gone Troppo*, namely a sense that none of it really matters. Though the latter is the marginally better album, if ever there was a blank collection of tracks called an "album" during the solo era, *Gone Troppo* is it.

Wisely, George included "Dream Away," which is far and away the most successful track here, being the sort of catchy hit that someone like Paul McCartney might have written, and with a lyric entirely congruent with its tone. Its only potential rival for best song on the album is "Unknown Delight," a fine song which suffers from intonation problems in the background vocals, and contains a curious (at least in this context) quoting of a lick from "Something." Perhaps — and this is only speculation — it was meant to connect the two songs for a sentimental reason.

Two other tracks merit consideration by the Assembler. "Wake Up My Love" is pure pop, fresh and listenable, and "That's the Way It Goes" is another jaunty gem that might have shone more brightly in better surroundings. Unfortunately, despite the higher quality, neither of these will fit the tone of the rescued Beatles album, and can remain as happy additions to George's solo catalog.

Nothing else here generates much in the way of discernible emotions in the listener — which includes "Circles," one of the songs famously demoed for, but not used on, *The White Album*. Though this version is more palatable than the Beatles-era demo, the weaknesses of the song remain clear. It falls squarely into the category with George's other "spinning" songs that turn and turn until they simply stop. Given its title and provenance, this may very well be the prototype for such tracks in Harrison's catalog. George matured massively as a songwriter during this decade, and hauling out this less mature oldie makes his advances all the more apparent.

Ringo Starr
14 tracks: 1 eligible, 4 provisional

Sources

S13	*Stop and Smell the Roses* (2 tracks) R: Jul 80 - Feb 81 P: Various (6)		S: Various (Undetermined)	81-Oct
S14	*Old Wave* R: Feb-Jul 82 P: Ballard/Walsh		S: Startling +1	83-Jun
	(Unreleased)			

Tracks

	Alibi (Starkey/Walsh) ⊘ (Style/Quality) Not so much a song as a bunch of chords strung together. Just terrible.	S14-03, 82-Jul
	As Far as We Can Go (Ballard) ⊘ (Style/Quality) A clunky piano ballad. Poor song. Incredibly banal.	S14-08, 82-Jul
	Back Off Boogaloo (Starkey) ⊘ (Filler) Imaginative remake of one of Ringo's best songs. Still, why?	S13-10, 80-Dec
	Be My Baby (Walsh) ⊘ (Style/Quality) More interesting than most. Verse makes a nice setup. Chorus can't carry it through.	S14-04, 82-Jul
	Brandy (Jefferson/Simmons) ⊘ (Quality) Story song, but a very boring story. Routine production. Lousy vocal.	S13, 81-Feb
	Dead Giveaway (Starkey/Wood) ⊘ (Style/Quality) Song is just too boring. High in RS's vocal range, and he sounds strained.	S13-06, 81-Feb
	Everybody's in a Hurry But Me (Starkey/Walsh/Entwistle/Clapton/Stainton) ⊘ (Filler) Rockabilly wanna be. Workout for everybody but RS, who plays the same beat all the way.	S14-09, 82-Jul
	Going Down (Starkey/Walsh) ≈ (Filler) Another instrumental, but a pretty meager feature for Ringo. Songwriters didn't finish it.	S14-10, 82-Jul
	Hopeless (Starkey/Walsh) ⊘ (Style/Quality) Incredibly square reading of a dreadful song. Just, yuk.	S14-02, 82-Jul
	I Keep Forgettin' (Leiber/Stoller) ⊘ (Style/Quality) Reaching for ideas in the arrangement leads to Ringo growling his vocal. Howling. Bad.	S14-06, 82-Jul

19/In Spite of All

	In My Car (Starkey/Walsh/Foster/Goody)	S14-01, 82-Jul
	≈ (Style/Quality) What passed for pop at that moment, but not the least bit credible.	
	Picture Show Life (Reid/Slate)	S14-07, 82-Jul
	≈ (Content) Song is at least not terrible, but kind of random for Ringo. Something of a vocal stretch.	
	She's About a Mover (Sahm)	S14-05, 82-Jul
	≈ (Quality) Up tempo, with nice energy, but ends up repeating title over and over. Rewrite of "Tight A$"?	
	Wake Up (Starkey)	S13, 81-Feb
	✓ Best track recorded for the album. Lively, catchy, makes Ringo sound good.	

Old Wave was never released in the US or UK, and would be Ringo's last studio album for almost a decade. The best that can be said is that it represents an earnest attempt at making a modern pop record. Full of synthesizers and Joe Walsh's guitar, it sounds like it was made in good fun, but it is by no means *good*. Though a couple of tracks might have been considered by the Assembler, we will assume that this album would have been left untouched in the process of creating the tribute album. And much like actually happened, it would have made no impact even in a wider release.

So Ringo's lone contribution to the group album will have to be one of the outtakes from *Stop and Smell the Roses*. The mistitled "Wake Up" (which clearly should have been called "You Gotta Know") may very well be better than anything which actually made that album. The straight pop song matches Ringo well vocally and temperamentally, and though devoid of weight, allows Ringo to serve the role he always had, as a nice distraction, and a voice critical to making any album sound like the Beatles.

Paul McCartney
29 tracks: 15 eligible (8 withheld), 4 provisional (2 withheld)

Sources

M26		"~~Ebony and Ivory~~" / "Rainclouds" R: Dec 80 - Dec 81 P: Martin	S: AIR (London), AIR (Montserrat)	82-Mar
M27		*Tug of War* R: Dec 80 - Dec 81 P: Martin	S: AIR (London), AIR (Montserrat)	82-Apr
M29		"~~Say Say Say~~" / "Ode to a Koala Bear" R: Dec 80 - Apr 82 P: Martin	S: AIR (London), Cherokee (LA)	83-Oct
M30		*Pipes of Peace* R: Oct 80 - Jul 83 P: Martin	S: Various (7)	83-Oct
		(Unreleased)		

S A V E T H E B E A T L E S !

Tracks
◆ *Eligible or provisional but withheld for solo project*

Average Person (McCartney) — M30-08, +R, 81-Mar
⊘ (Quality) Unwelcome echoes of "Penny Lane," lousy by comparison. Mostly fluff.

Ballroom Dancing (McCartney) — M27-06, 81-Dec
✓◆ A bigger track than it has any right to be. The very slight idea is gussied up nicely.

Be What You See (Link) (McCartney) — M27-10, 81-Dec
≈◆ (Filler) Fills a hole, and that's all it's supposed to do.

Christian Bop (McCartney) — M, 82-Jan
⊘ (Filler) A rare extended link that appears to have not been a very good idea in the first place.

Dress Me Up as a Robber (McCartney) — M27-11, 81-Mar
✓◆ Great riff, slick guitars, and a cool vocal performance. Unique in the Macca catalog.

Ebony and Ivory (McCartney) — M27-12, 81-Mar
⊘ (Content) Really unfortunate. Simplistic, and instantly dated. Embarrassing for all involved.

Get It (McCartney) — M27-09, 81-Mar
✓◆ Macca can make any kind of record you can imagine. Proved again here. Perkins sounds great.

Here Today (McCartney) — M27-05, 81-Dec
✓ A true masterwork, even without the subtext. One for the ages.

Hey Hey (McCartney/Clarke) — M30-09, 81-Mar
⊘ (Filler) Fine riff, but not worthy of an album. Belongs on a B-side.

It's Not On (McCartney) — M, 82-Feb
✓ Truly odd. Compelling. Structured. More interesting than most Macca of the era.

Keep Under Cover (McCartney) — M30-04, 80-Dec
✓ Energetic and well-formed pop.

Man, The (McCartney/Jackson) — M30-06, 81-Dec
⊘ (Style) Best of the MJ duets. Solid song. Nice energy. Great vox and arrangement. But, just, no.

My Old Friend (feat. Carl Perkins) (Perkins) — M, 81-Mar
✓ Perkins sings with genuine sweetness, and the song succeeds because of that. Beautiful.

Ode to a Koala Bear (McCartney) — M29-02, 80-Dec
⊘ (Quality) Very late Wings sound, and like others, given more energy than the song deserves.

Other Me, The (McCartney) — M30-03, 82-Oct
⊘ (Quality) Dreadful, cheap apology. "I acted like a dustbin lid." Indeed. Bad idea, and lousy recording.

Pipes of Peace (McCartney) — M30-01, 82-Oct
≈ (Quality) The world did not need this tripe. It manages to take away from its brother song.

Pound Is Sinking, The (McCartney) — M27-07, 81-Mar
✓◆ Fun with words/guitars. Imaginative. Structured. Meaningless, but somehow says something.

Rainclouds (McCartney/Laine) — M26-02, 80-Dec
✓ Famous for provenance, but basically filler. BVs are really great, incl LM! No bass. Complex.

Say Say Say (McCartney/Jackson) — M30-02, 82-Apr
⊘ (Style) Despite being a megahit, it had no legs. Dated immediately, and pretty cringey now.

So Bad (McCartney) — M30-05, +R, 82-Oct
≈ (Quality) Totally SLS, without much to redeem it. Routine words and music.

Somebody Who Cares (McCartney) — M27-03, 81-Mar
✓◆ A very fine piece of work. Beautiful song and recording. Sounds earnest and warm.

Sweetest Little Show (McCartney)		M30-07, 81-Dec
✓ Mannered but warmly reminiscent. Works despite some cuteness.		
Take It Away (McCartney)		M27-02, +R, 81-Mar
✓◆ A great, confident track, and definitely worth the work that went into it. A real pleasure.		
Through Our Love (McCartney)		M30-11, 82-Oct
✓ Considered a SLS, but a significant work. Stylish and appropriately large in scale.		
Tug of Peace (McCartney)		M30-10, 82-Oct
⊘ (Filler) Worst kind of filler, it taints the song it follows after.		
Tug of War (McCartney)		M27-01, 81-Dec
✓◆ Perfect to open the album, it sets a clear tone. Maybe not a great song, but a great record.		
Twice in a Lifetime (McCartney)		M, 82-Nov
⊘ (Quality) Oddly ponderous. Never finds a stable idea. Tone is full MOR.		
Wanderlust (McCartney)		M27-08, 81-Dec
✓◆ Ever the craftsman, this succeeds despite being somewhat precious. Semi-anthemic.		
What's That You're Doing? (McCartney/Wonder)		M27-04, 81-Mar
≈◆ (Style) Stevie provides the meat, and Paul the plate. Not a bad combo, if a little artificial.		

Paul McCartney's work in this period is among the most complex, varied, and ultimately satisfying of his entire solo career. He shakes off the artificialities of Wings, applies maximum effort when much less might have sufficed, and holds himself once again to the old standards. His musical and lyrical imagination is operating on high gear. Significantly, the genesis of the shift coincides with his decision to invite George Martin to produce, which results in the first truly Beatle-scale recordings by any solo Beatle since "Live and Let Die."

Such is the increase in quality that one imagines Paul, having found his entreaties to his former bandmates unfruitful, deciding to simply have a go at the old way of working, just without the other Beatles. To that end, he branched out on studios, musicians, techniques, and songwriting. He also branched out emotionally, no doubt as reaction to the loss of Lennon.

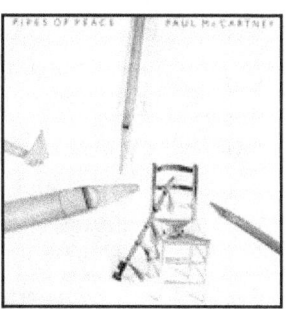

The shift does not come without issues, of course, and there are some whoppers. Namely, collaborations with Stevie Wonder, Stanley Clarke, and Michael Jackson all fall somewhere between underwhelming and cringe-inducing. Wonder alternately leads Paul into success ("What's That You're Doing?"), and follows him into morass ("Ebony and Ivory"). Clarke is severely underutilized as a mere session musician ("Somebody Who Cares" and "Hey Hey"), essentially missing a fantastic opportunity. Jackson proves a game compadre, but he and McCartney bring out the most indulgent aspects of each other, and the resulting records are painfully syrupy pop ("Say Say Say" and "The Man," plus "The Girl is Mine" from *Thriller*). The work with Carl Perkins was different, as we will see below.

In other words, it is not the collaborations which fuel or define Paul's success in this era, as he may have intended when hatching the plan. Rather, it is Paul himself who digs deep, pushes hard, refreshes working methods, listens to outside voices, and once again polishes tracks until they are the very best they can be. Though the bulk of music on these two albums was recorded in 1981, periodic polishing sessions continued right up until the release date for each, stretching well into 1983 for the second album. The old Beatle energy infuses much of Paul's work in this era, and credit goes squarely to both McCartney and Martin, with a nod to Starkey.

Notably, there really isn't enough great material here for two full albums, but more like an album and a half. George Martin's famous restraint appears to have prevailed, and *Tug of War* is a single album filled to the brim with the absolute best material, while *Pipes of Peace* gets the leftovers, and still must be padded out significantly. The obvious solution, in a world where the surviving Beatles are preparing a tribute album, is to skip the follow-up solo project, and give the best remaining tracks to the group. That is what we will assume the Assembler proposes.

Thus, *Tug of War* will remain largely unchanged, beyond the shift of "Here Today" to the tribute project — not as big a loss as it may at first appear.

The one glaring and rather uncharacteristic error in the assembly of *Tug of War* is ending with "Ebony and Ivory," perhaps the least satisfying track on the album. Though it sounds on the surface like a summation, it is really the introduction of a new idea to an album which contains nothing else like it. If the intention was to resolve the "tug of war" with some sort of "perfect harmony," it is a stretch, to say the least. The well-intentioned lyric is too syrupy for that, and as a result, an otherwise great album fizzles mightily just before it can stick the landing.

The better place for that track, if it must be heard at all, is at the end of the first side, where it's stickiness can be cleared by the flip of the disc, followed by the deep dive into better music on side two. It could still have been a single — perhaps better as a stand-alone — either way mitigating its negative effect on the album.

Admittedly, solving that problem by moving "Ebony and Ivory" pushes "Here Today" out of a very good spot. Paul's tribute wouldn't work at the end of the album, but sounds great at the end of side one, especially right after something so stylistically separate as "What's That You're Doing?" Standing stark and alone to end a side genuinely does give it strength.

The only other spot where "Here Today" might also work would be as the penultimate track on the album, saving its strength until as close to the end as possible, then following it with a sensitive final statement. Unfortunately, there is nothing on either *Tug of War* or *Pipes of Peace* which could serve that role. It seems that Paul is one song short of being able to use that option.

In our slightly altered narrative, shifting "Here Today" to the group album makes eminent sense, as you will see below, and we will simply say that Paul would have solved the resulting sequencing problem . . . somehow.

There isn't much more to say about *Tug of War*. The wide variety of music is of exceptionally high quality, and there is a sense of unity among the tracks — even though there really is no central theme or concept. Paul ventures into overt references to his Beatle days, and this is as clear-eyed as such remembrances will ever be throughout the entire solo canon. Sentimentality, though present, is kept at bay, and a sense of fun is reanimated.

In a welcome surprise, Carl Perkins joins in on that fun via "Get It," a rare McCartney pastiche that is offered without irony. It just sounds great, as if Perkins had somehow been flash frozen at his peak, and his style remained relevant until scientists could thaw him out. We know this isn't the case, but something must have clicked between him and McCartney, and "Get It" accomplishes what "Name and Address" had not several years earlier.

Likewise, when Perkins wrote a new song for McCartney during the sessions, the result was pure magic — almost literally. The story has become well known that Perkins's "My Old Friend" contains as its chorus the last thing John Lennon ever said to Paul. Whether truly a message from the beyond is irrelevant, but Paul's emotional reaction is not. He sings a sweet, sad, and emotion-filled harmony behind Perkins, and lends his playing to round out the simple and beautiful arrangement.

The recording stayed in the can until Perkins released it on his own album, *Go Cat Go!*, in 1996. The Assembler would have recognized that a guest lead vocalist was firmly against the original rules of fusion (from chapter 11), but would have remembered this track well, even after only one hearing. Knowing that the Beatles were all big Perkins fans, this would have stayed on the eligible list, perhaps even surreptitiously.

Pipes of Peace, being something of a trainwreck, took some fine records down with it. You are forgiven if you have written it all off, but I would commend three tracks which show the same effort as those on *Tug of War*, but were effectively swallowed up by the dreck surrounding them.

"Keep Under Cover" is pure pop, but in a crisp and buoyant way that is the utter opposite of the tracks with Jackson. It moves smoothly across a non-stick percussion surface, and deftly builds in synthesizers and a rewarding structure.

"Sweetest Little Show" verges on being just too cute, and gets no redemption when followed by the true clunker, "Average Person." Separate the two, however, and "Sweetest Little Show" sounds more like one of the overt Beatles references that snuck in under cover. The little show in the middle — complete with polite applause — actually paints a picture that the rest of the song comments upon. Though perhaps an acquired taste, it actually pays off.

"Through Our Love" is large enough that it was obviously built to end an album. But that doesn't work on *Pipes of Peace* because it is preceded by two instrumentals, and the whole audience has tuned out before it even starts. Then, being a classic SLS, its opening turns off anyone who has stuck around, telescoping just another interchangeable Macca ballad — which it is not. (That would be "So Bad.") Perhaps the production gets a tad too big, but the song is worth it, and when removed from the pressure of closing the album, it becomes more than serviceable — it really sings.

In terms of other stray tracks, it's a mixed bag. "Rainclouds," despite being a B-side throwaway, is quite a piece of craftsmanship. As a song, it isn't much. But the production — and especially the vocal arrangement — turns it into an infectious piece of pop engineering. Contrast this with another throwaway, "The Other Me," which no amount of pop engineering could save from its own exasperating dumbness.

One outtake bears special note, along with a lament that it is so different from anything else that a contemporary release was essentially impossible. "It's Not On" may be one of McCartney's quirkiest ever tracks — at least among those that are quirky in a good way. It's a story song, with a compelling but opaque plot, and a unique mixture of speaking and singing. Most fans would probably love to hear the album that this might have become.

When considered as one big project, which *Tug of War* and *Pipes of Peace* essentially were, the creative whiplash is astounding. But the upshot is that the great music is truly *great*, and the bad music, while truly *bad*, was sequestered, and the damage limited. If only restraint had remained the word after the success of volume one of the set.

Our Assembler would likely have had access only to the leftovers from *Tug of War*, and it would have been released in a fashion very similar to the one we know. We will assume, however, that Paul was willing to have "Here Today" placed where it could be even more powerful, namely on the final fused Beatles album.

John Lennon
15 tracks: 4 eligible, 2 alternates

Sources

L14	*Milk and Honey* (4 tracks) R: Aug-Sep 80 P: Lennon/Ono (Douglas) S: Hit Factory (NY)	84-Jan
	(Unreleased)	

19 / In Spite of All

Tracks

	(Forgive Me) My Little Flower Princess (Lennon)	L14-09, 80-Nov
	✓ A good idea not quite formed, displays again JL's wide musical range.	
	Across the River (Lennon)	L, 80-Nov
	⊘ (Demo) Fast country, but has the feeling of cleaning the musical house.	
	Borrowed Time (Lennon)	L14-07, 80-Nov
	✓ The pastiche is unfortunate given the weight of the lyric. Not quite great.	
	Dear John (Lennon)	L, 80-Nov
	≈ (Demo) Solid idea, musically and lyrically. One to really wish could have been finished.	
	Gone from This Place (Lennon)	L, 80-Nov
	⊘ (Demo) Terribly sad song, probably never would have made it out of demo form.	
	Grow Old with Me (Lennon)	L14-11, 80-Nov
	✓ Better in conception than realization. A bit cloying and clichéd. Martin's strings help.	
	Happy Rishikesh Song, The (Lennon)	L, 80-Nov
	⊘ (Demo/Content) Feels like a GH parody, then turns darkly introspective. Hard to know what to make of it.	
	Help Me To Help Myself (Lennon)	L, 80-Nov
	⊘ (Demo) Indistinct ballad, interchangeable with many others.	
	I'm Stepping Out (Lennon)	L14-01, 80-Nov
	✓ A little too pat, as if more wish than reality. Not a bad song, but not genuine.	
	India (Lennon)	L, 80-Nov
	⊘ (Demo) One of many iterations of this melody. Might have settled into something nice.	
	Life Begins At 40 (Lennon)	L, 80-Nov
	⊘ (Demo) Country, without much potential. Just a very sad jot.	
	Memories / Howling At The Moon (Lennon)	L, 80-Nov
	⊘ (Demo) Derivative, of himself and others. Like Macca, JL generating short ideas then combining.	
	Mr. Hyde's Gone (Don't Be Afraid) (Lennon)	L, 80-Nov
	≈ (Demo) Rare JL writing music hall. Unusual feel, a welcome variation.	
	Serve Yourself (Lennon)	L, 80-Nov
	⊘ (Demo/Content) Provocative, but also cold. Feels harsh in demo form. Might have come out that way.	
	You Saved My Soul (With Your True Love) (Lennon)	L, 80-Nov
	⊘ (Demo) 50s-inspired, but a carbon copy rather than something new. "...you saved me from suicide..."	

After considering and using most of the polished tracks from *Double Fantasy* on the previous fused Beatles album, here we consider only the echoes of the last work of John Lennon's life. Much of it remained in demo form, forcing us to imagine what might have been, if circumstances had been different. Given John's efficiency with ideas, it seems possible that most of this would have made it out eventually, perhaps not for years, and perhaps not in a form resembling where it started. Alternately, he was well known for bursts of creativity which resulted in abandoning — or at least postponing — work on songs that did not come quickly. Both possibilities are real, and there is no way to choose.

Though we can imagine a Threetles-like approach to some of these demos, there is not much here which would warrant such treatment. As interesting as some of these snippets are, none are obviously better than the tracks Lennon worked on in the studio during *Double Fantasy*, and all would have required a fair amount of creative work to turn into reasonable records. For our purposes, we will therefore have to assume that the Assembler would have prioritized tracks John had at least started in the studio over those which were merely unfinished ideas on cassette.

As with the finished songs (discussed in the previous chapter), much the same problems haunt the four tracks that were left over. For starters, they are not his best work, sounding at least a little bit rusty even when the instincts are good and the songwriter's craft on clear display. Additionally, without Jack Douglas's polishing, a fair amount of work would have had to go into them to make them releasable. This work might have been done by the other Beatles in our slightly altered world, of course, but nothing like that actually happened, so we must work with what is there.

Regrettably, there are no masterworks here. The only one that we still have in our back pocket is "Beautiful Boy (Darling Boy)," held over from the previous project. There is nothing that powerful in any of the other leftovers, nothing to either open or close a Beatles album. The most compelling track, "Grow Old With Me," is itself only a demo, albeit a complete one, and something of a sweet cliché from its first note. It bears the imprint of John's missing intensity, just as with everything else recorded in this era. We cannot fault John for this approach, of course, but we would be remiss if we did not at least notice and lament what seems like a loss.

This thought leads right to the acknowledgement that John Lennon owed us *nothing*. Like the others, he gave what in George Harrison's words amounted to his "nervous system" with the Beatles. We are not within our rights to expect anything more from him. Even as we lament the fact that the *Double Fantasy/Milk and Honey* tracks are not in the same class as most of his Beatles work, or even his better solo work, in this particular summative moment we must step back and pay tribute to the *totality* of his work, and even acknowledge that his fame, which we perpetuated, is what cost him his life.

None of this is in John's final music, of course, but music is fundamentally a set of relationships — between notes, chords, rhythms, lyrics, songwriter, musician, audience, critic, and many tangential others. Like all art, music is not complete until it meets an audience, and what the audience brings to the art is every bit as important as what the artist offers. Thus, this final collection of Lennon tracks cannot be about what he brought to the table, but rather our response.

Acting as our proxy, therefore, the Assembler's response will have to be to latch onto everything that is good enough to be massaged into something Beatle-worthy. There is definitely enough here to do that, and the gauntlet is thrown down once again to find the right tracks from the other Beatles to place next to this music, and lift John's final work into the light it actually deserves.

19 / In Spite of All

Assembly
29 tracks: 17 eligible, 12 provisional

	✓ All Those Years Ago	H10-04, +PR, 81-Feb
	≈ Circles	H11-10, 82-Aug
	✓ Dream Away	H11-09, 82-Aug
	≈ Gone Troppo	H11-05, 82-Aug
	≈ Mystical One	H11-06, 82-Aug
	≈ Teardrops	H10-06, 81-Feb
	✓ That's the Way It Goes	H11-02, 82-Aug
	✓ Unknown Delight	H11-07, 82-Aug
	✓ Wake Up My Love	H11-01, 82-Aug
	≈ Going Down	S14-10, 82-Jul
	≈ In My Car	S14-01, 82-Jul
	≈ Picture Show Life	S14-07, 82-Jul
	≈ She's About a Mover	S14-05, 82-Jul
	✓ Wake Up	S13, 81-Feb
	✓ Here Today	M27-05, 81-Dec
	✓ It's Not On	M, 82-Feb
	✓ Keep Under Cover	M30-04, 80-Dec
	✓ My Old Friend	M, 81-Mar
	≈ Pipes of Peace	M30-01, 82-Oct
	✓ Rainclouds	M26-02, 80-Dec
	≈ So Bad	M30-05, +R, 82-Oct
	✓ Sweetest Little Show	M30-07, 81-Dec
	✓ Through Our Love	M30-11, 82-Oct
	✓ (Forgive Me) My Little Flower Princess	L14-09, 80-Nov
	✓ Borrowed Time	L14-07, 80-Nov
	≈ Dear John	L, 80-Nov
	✓ Grow Old with Me	L14-11, 80-Nov
	✓ I'm Stepping Out	L14-01, 80-Nov
	≈ Mr. Hyde's Gone (Don't Be Afraid)	L, 80-Nov

This delicate assembly begins by acknowledging that the album will be different from all the others in important ways. All of the rescued albums have had their own unique personalities, of course, but this one will have multiple *purposes*, and may have to break some rules in order to accomplish them.

In tone, this album will have to split the difference between contemporary pop and emotional tribute. It cannot be weepy or maudlin, but it also cannot be coldly dry-eyed. It will have to include John's voice, while acknowledging his very large absence. It will have to retain as much balance as possible between the songwriters, while especially celebrating the conversation between their voices, which has long been central to the Beatles' success. While actively exploring the dialogue between John and Paul, it must not disrespect or minimize the significant contributions from Ringo and George.

A few tracks stand out as not particularly useful to the task at hand, and are set aside with the proviso that they can be recalled at any point, if necessary:

- ≈ Circles (G)
- ≈ Dear John (J)
- ≈ Going Down (R)
- ≈ Gone Troppo (G)
- ≈ Mr. Hyde's Gone... (J)
- ≈ Pipes of Peace (P)
- ≈ She's About a Mover (R)
- ≈ So Bad (P)
- ≈ Teardrops (G)

Early on, a decision might have come down that any tribute to John should not be too overt, which he would have rejected, and should not be the whole subject of the project. Perhaps it could occupy, say, half of the album, if that. So the assembly might have started with the specific idea that side one would be a collection of modern pop — the current (and final) state of the Beatles — while side two could become a more focused, if still loose, tribute. With that in mind, a famous bit of serendipity would have helped set the proper tone.

At the time that this album would have been assembled, Paul McCartney actually re-acquired the disc from the first ever Beatles recording session in 1958. On one side, a cover: Buddy Holly's "That'll Be the Day." On the other, an original, the only McCartney/Harrison composition the Beatles ever recorded: "In Spite of All the Danger." Technically speaking, the music was performed by proto-Beatles: Lennon, McCartney and Harrison, with Colin Hanton on drums and John Lowe on piano. Thankfully, the voices and playing and attitude are easily recognizable as precursors of the band's early sound.

In the real world, Paul had the recording cleaned up, and made 50 copies to give to friends. Then he tucked the disc away for years before eventually releasing an edit as part of *Anthology*. In our imagined world, we will assume he saw opportunity to end the band's catalog as it began. The Assembler would have agreed and immediately placed "In Spite of All the Danger" as the album's emotional closer, and eventual namesake.

19/In Spite of All

Everything else on the album will build to this moment, frame it, and create the proper bed in which it can be heard. Doing that the Beatles way, however, will prove surprisingly complicated. For now, the Assembler begins by creating some pairings.

The most obvious coupling is made possible by the extended final sound of "Sweetest Little Show." On *Pipes of Peace*, Paul uses the chord to create a clunky segue to "Average Person," a song decidedly unfit for a Beatles album. The connection is one of the reasons that the virtues of the first song are very difficult to hear, since they are stolen by the lousiness of the connected song.

The same final chord turns out to perfectly match the opening of John's "(Forgive Me) My Little Flower Princess." A different segue is created, both songs are elevated, and John and Paul are reunited, if only by segue.

A second pairing comes almost out of necessity. With John's tragically optimistic "Borrowed Time" among the tracks available for the album, two things become clear: The song must be included, and it must be handled with the utmost care. The best way to do this is to find something simpatico to follow it, a song which neither comments on John's track, nor upstages it, and especially does not taint its pathos. Basically, "Borrowed Time" needs an indirect, but compatible response.

After trying a handful of possibilities, Paul's "Through Our Love" turns out to have just the right combination of respect and movement away. Sounding much like the Beatles of old, the song grows in intensity gradually, with a lyric just ambiguous enough to be worth parsing in that context. John's playfulness and spontaneity are properly balanced by Paul's trademark polish and extravagance, which in this case includes a lush orchestration by George Martin. It even seems as if Paul's opening lyrics, "We wasted time and again / On things, things we already knew…" are answering John's patter about "all that crap." Meanwhile, Paul's excesses, so cloying in this track's original presentation at the end of *Pipes of Peace*, now seem purposeful and are thus held in check. Again, the pairing lifts each artist.

A third pairing is almost too obvious. The Assembler might have tried to avoid it, but ultimately given in because the connection is so strong, and the sequence incredibly powerful.

At the time this album would have been pulled together, John's "Grow Old With Me" was still an unadorned demo, and that is essentially how it was first heard on *Milk and Honey*. But many years later, Yoko Ono commissioned George Martin to add an orchestration. He produced a sensitive and lush score, and married it seamlessly to the cleaned up demo. We will modify that history somewhat, and assume that, had there been a Beatles album in 1982, the commission might have taken place then, which allows Martin's enhanced version to be brought forward to this assembly.

That extremely emotional track will be paired with another, also featuring a Martin score for strings. Paul's "Here Today" is actually in the same key, and when following John's track, appears to be almost a continuation, or at least an extension. As happened so often with the two songwriters, their own bits and pieces can be fit together into something bigger than either could have imagined. That is exactly what happens with this pairing.

These three pairings, which do not appear to contain obvious pole tracks, could then have been spread across the two sides of the disc, sequenced roughly by level of drama, and adhering to the idea that anything approaching an overt tribute should be part of side two.

. . .	(All Those Years Ago (G)
1M. Sweetest Little Show (P)	Dream Away (G)
1N. (Forgive Me) My Little Flower Princess (J)	I'm Stepping Out (J)
. . .	≈ In My Car (R)
	It's Not On (P)
. . .	Keep Under Cover (P)
2E. Borrowed Time (J)	My Old Friend (P)
2F. Through Our Love (P)	≈ Mystical One (G)
. . .	≈ Picture Show Life (R)
2M. Grow Old with Me (J)	Rainclouds (P)
2N. Here Today (P)	That's the Way It Goes (G)
. . .	Unknown Delight (G)
2Z. In Spite of All the Danger (B)	Wake Up (R)
	Wake Up My Love (G)

With these designations, and the album closer in place, the next spot to fill is the album's opening. Based on the list of tracks, there are several possible approaches. The first sound could certainly be uptempo pure pop, such as George's "Wake Up My

Love." But that might have been jarring to a fan dropping the needle with some trepidation to begin with. Another possible opener in the pop category would be Ringo's sole contribution, "Wake Up" — if only it did not taste so much like empty calories. It's just too lightweight to be an opener in this context, and, given the scarcity of Ringo tracks available, we also probably don't want his voice to be the first thing heard and then disappear forever.

Instead, we might consider John's lightweight "I'm Steppin' Out," complete with count-off, as a way to ease the listener into the pathos of the project right from the beginning. Unfortunately, starting with John's voice in this way seems like just too much, and renders everything after it as so much piffle. Frankly, opening the album with *any* of John's available tracks would probably sound disrespectful or overly opportunistic, which could damage the perception of everything else. Something akin to this actually happened with *Milk and Honey*.

As we have seen, however, this project must be built on connections between tracks even more than on the prior hypothetical albums. George Martin's principles, which we have used all along, of a pole track opener followed by a feature piece, followed by a change of mood, will need to be suspended somewhat to accommodate multiple tracks pulled together as a multi-part opener.

An old and very effective trick, which goes all the way back to *With the Beatles*, is to open the album with a cold vocal. Paul provides us with that opportunity in "Keep Under Cover," in which the first sound is the word "love," followed by a lyric that can be heard in multiple ways:

> *Love, I'm going to pick you up in the morning*
> *Love, I'm going to take you out on a journey*
> *I don't know where I'm going to*
> *But I know what I've been going through*
> *Without you by my side*

Paul's lyrics are an invitation, while also an acknowledgement of loss, and a fitting proxy for the trepidation that all of the artists would have felt as this project got underway. His music is dry-eyed while also flecked with fear and sadness. In an unexpected way, "Keep Under Cover" welcomes the listener into the emotional world of this project through uptempo pop which hides reservations, uncertainty and hope.

The ending of the track also provides a seamless setup for "I'm Steppin' Out." This gets John into the project early, but also mitigates whatever discomfort fans might have felt about hearing his voice. John's playfulness is immediately contagious even if the song is somewhat slight. The overall effect is to extend the opener, but with a conscious lightening of mood. John sounds funny and happy, and that is what matters most in this spot.

Through this process, John effectively reassures the listener that everything's going to be alright, and that they should just sit back and have some fun. The idea is emphasized through his patter at the end of "I'm Steppin' Out":

> *I'm steppin' out, just for a while, ain't been out for days gotta do it tonight, gimme a break, gimme a break, gotta get out, gotta get out, just for a while, just for the night, I'll be in before one...or two...or three...Goodbye!*

The Assembler would have certainly remixed the track to make sure John's ad libs didn't disappear into the fade out, and then would have recognized that all of John's busking makes the perfect setup for Ringo's feature, "Wake Up."

After three pieces of pure pop, we come to a point where a change in tone is necessary. For balance purposes, it will have to be George who provides the shift, and the best track to do that is "Unknown Delight." Not only a beautiful love song, it also contains that brief but sweet reference to *Abbey Road* in the guitar solo, subtly touching the past while laying a soft bed on which to meditate in the present. The fact that it stands alone, without any real connection to some bigger album "concept" is actually one of its strengths relative to this occasion. It serves to cleanse the palette, and keep the album grounded in the present.

The assembly is off and running, avoiding all of the obvious pitfalls, and bringing the fans a by-now-familiar dose of the meta-Beatle magic. The effect is one of almost pure joy which, in the hearing, would have been tinged with that ongoing sadness all fans can remember from the era. Most importantly, it creates a great context for hearing everything which will follow. So after basic setup, the album looks like this:

1A. Keep Under Cover (P)	All Those Years Ago (G)
1B. I'm Stepping Out (J)	Dream Away (G)
1C. Wake Up (R)	≈ In My Car (R)
1D. Unknown Delight (G)	It's Not On (P)
...	My Old Friend (P)
1M. Sweetest Little Show (P)	≈ Mystical One (G)
1N. (Forgive Me) My Little Flower Princess (J)	≈ Picture Show Life (R)
...	Rainclouds (P)
	That's the Way It Goes (G)
	Wake Up My Love (G)

...
2E. Borrowed Time (J)
2F. Through Our Love (P)
...
2M. Grow Old with Me (J)
2N. Here Today (P)
...
2Z. In Spite of All the Danger (B)

Two important parts, the inner pole tracks, are not yet in place, and now rise to the surface for solutions. Thankfully, neither spot is hard to fill.

George will provide the opener to side two in the form of his tribute song, "All Those Years Ago." Despite its considerable caveats, it is definitely strong enough to be a pole track, and also does a good job of creating a frame in which the rest of the tribute can take place. It would be weakened further by placement in the middle of a side. Indeed, it seems likely that "All Those Years Ago" would have been selected as the leadoff single for the album, and been just as big a hit. Fortunately, it also turns out that no further bridge is necessary between that track and "Borrowed Time." They work well enough together.

The end of side one is also rather easy to fill, and it will be a rare case of the Assembler using a track in exactly the same way it was used in the real world by the solo artist. John's "Beautiful Boy (Darling Boy)," withheld from *Wheels, Walls and Waterfalls* because it didn't quite fit the tone of the project, here finds the perfect context at the end of a side, just as it did on *Double Fantasy*. The opening sound of the ocean emerges naturally from the jazzy guitars at the end of "(Forgive Me) My Little Flower Princess," and the fact that this means two tracks in a row by the same Beatle — a semi-break with the evolved fusion rules — will simply have to be accepted. There is no better way, and this way is beyond beautiful.

This is the moment, in this hypothetical album, when the mood turns from pop toward tribute, and a better fulcrum could not be found. John's crushing final masterwork lays a path for us to leave the safety of side one and venture into uncertainty — in this case it will become a meditation on the "other plans" which would have so deeply impacted the band, just as they did the real world. As such, it provides perfect context for the tribute which will follow after the flip of the disc.

Closing in on the finished running order, it now looks like this:

1A. Keep Under Cover (P)	Dream Away (G)
1B. I'm Stepping Out (J)	≈ In My Car (R)
1C. Wake Up (R)	It's Not On (P)
1D. Unknown Delight (G)	My Old Friend (P)
...	≈ Mystical One (G)
	≈ Picture Show Life (R)
1M. Sweetest Little Show (P)	Rainclouds (P)
1N. (Forgive Me) My Little Flower Princess (J)	That's the Way It Goes (G)
1Z. Beautiful Boy (Darling Boy) (J)	Wake Up My Love (G)
	Wake Up My Love (G)
2A. All Those Years Ago (G)	
2E. Borrowed Time (J)	
2F. Through Our Love (P)	
...	
2M. Grow Old with Me (J)	
2N. Here Today (P)	
...	
2Z. In Spite of All the Danger (B)	

Three gaps remain to be closed, and there is plenty of music left to consider. Two of these are relatively easy. A quick listen reveals that "Here Today," as suspected earlier, works quite well as the penultimate track on the album, so the space between it and the final track can simply be removed. Similarly, with seven tracks already on side one, and the end of "Unknown Delight" sounding perfectly fine next to the beginning of "Sweetest Little Show," that gap can also disappear.

The remaining gap on side two is at the heart of the tribute portion of the album, and will have to be handled with great care. For balance purposes, it seems that we must look at George's tracks first. The most obvious possibility would have to be "Flying Hour," the fantastic outtake from *Somewhere in England* held over from the previous project A piece of effective pop, George's lyric is all about reacting to the past, which he says, in trademark fashion, must be set aside without sentiment. On the heels of the highly sentimental "Through Our Love," George's track could provide a nice contrast, offset, and clearing of the decks before the final sequence.

But it doesn't work. When placed in that spot, "Flying Hour" seems to yield no room for what the album must do next — namely: dream, remember, celebrate and grieve. Indeed, George's chorus, repeated multiple times, would seem to dismiss the whole idea of doing any of that:

> *The past it is gone,*
> *The future may not be at all,*
> *The present improve the flying hour.*

The Beatles obviously believed what George was saying. Similar ideas are sprinkled throughout their solo catalogs and interviews, enough so that even one of our hypothetical albums, *Be Here Now*, had to address the principle directly. But such things are relative, and this album must be at least partly about acknowledging John's lost dreams, remembering and celebrating the best of what has gone before, and grieving, *before* moving on. The best way to do that is to welcome the sentiments even while acknowledging that they, like all things, must pass.

None of this is to criticize George's track in any way. In fact, it's a great track, and a real shame to have been left unreleased for so long. But as much as it looks on the surface like the obvious choice to fill this spot on the album, it just does not fit. Perhaps it could have surfaced as a B-side, maybe even for the inevitable "Borrowed Time" single.

With balance problems still in mind, the Assembler would have had to look more closely at the available George tracks, but trying to find something else there proves fruitless. "Dream Away," "Wake Up My Love" and "Mystical One" all break too much with the mood being built, and "That's the Way It Goes" seems heartlessly dismissive in this context. Looking back at those George tracks set aside at the beginning of the assembly process also yields nothing. "Circles" might fit in concept, but it just isn't a high enough quality song for the occasion. It would grind in a spot which needs simplicity, clarity and a classic form.

So the linchpin of side two will ultimately be the most unexpected. Perhaps it's hard to imagine the Beatles allowing a guest artist to occupy so much space on one of their conjoined albums, but in this case, the story alone might make it worthwhile. It is now well known that, while Carl Perkins was on Montserrat recording *Tug of War*, he wrote a song to thank Paul for his hospitality — a song which, in an extraordinary twist, contained the final words that John Lennon had ever spoken to Paul McCartney the last time they saw each other.

If the idea of mystical lyrics from beyond the grave seems like too much, or at least not a good enough reason to program *any* piece of music in such a high profile spot, you can take heart that the song, "My Old Friend," is actually wonderful. It's possible to set aside anything about messages from Beyond, and simply include the song for its purity and exceptional quality. The rest is gravy.

Frankly, it's hard to imagine a simpler, more heartfelt song between friends. Indeed, "My Old Friend" seems to capture, from a distance, the essential nature of the relationships between the four Beatles. That it is sung by a voice they all knew and loved — one of their early heroes rather than one of them — makes it that much more special, and easier to absorb.

Paul augmented Carl's singing and guitar with tasteful — and for the most part minimal — instruments and voices. We can imagine that, had the surviving Beatles been working together on this album, they might have reformed to add the harmonies and instruments together. Regardless, the feel, especially in the context of a hypothetical fused Beatles album, is one of tribute going multiple directions. Carl honors Paul. Paul honors Carl. The Beatles honor Carl. The inclusion of words attributed to John honors his memory, and the song's treatment of friendship honors the long and winding road traveled together by John, Paul, George and Ringo. Miraculously, it all happens at the same time.

Recall that our Assembler might have snuck the song onto the short list for inclusion after only one listening, but been dubious about finding a spot for it on the album. But as side two developed, and the hole remained unfilled after multiple rounds of experimentation, it would have become clear that "My Old Friend" could be dropped like a capstone into the middle of the side. Perkins's plaintive but crystal clear singing would become the perfect and simple antidote to any sense of the maudlin, setting up beautifully what comes next.

"My Old Friend" is a great song, plain and simple, and that it was written, sung, and contributed to this project by one the Beatles' heroes makes it as inevitable as it would have been surprising.

1A.	Keep Under Cover (P)	≈ ~~Circles (G)~~
1B.	I'm Stepping Out (J)	≈ ~~Dear John (J)~~
1C.	Wake Up (R)	Dream Away (G)
1D.	Unknown Delight (G)	≈ ~~Going Down (R)~~
1M.	Sweetest Little Show (P)	≈ ~~Gone Troppo (G)~~
1N.	(Forgive Me) My Little Flower Princess (J)	≈ In My Car (R)
1Z.	Beautiful Boy (Darling Boy) (J)	It's Not On (P)
		≈ ~~Mr. Hyde's Gone... (J)~~
		≈ Mystical One (G)
2A.	All Those Years Ago (G)	Rainclouds (P)
2E.	Borrowed Time (J)	≈ Picture Show Life (R)
2F.	Through Our Love (P)	≈ ~~Pipes of Peace (P)~~
2J.	**My Old Friend (P)**	≈ ~~She's About a Mover (R)~~
2M.	Grow Old with Me (J)	≈ ~~So Bad (P)~~
2N.	Here Today (P)	That's the Way It Goes (G)
2Z.	In Spite of All the Danger (B)	Wake Up My Love (G)
		≈ ~~Teardrops (G)~~

This assembly remains slightly off our preferred balance, with John leading with five tracks, Paul following with four, Ringo with his customary one, and George with only two — unless you count the title track, for which George gets songwriting credit. This suggests trying to squeeze in another track for George, but that turns out to be overly difficult.

With 14 tracks already, the album runs to a full length of 47 minutes. Adding a track would require either editing other tracks, or a bit of advanced mastering.

One idea might have been to place "Flying Hour" at the very end of the album, after the archival Beatles track. Tempting as this is, it dilutes the undeniable power of the Beatles ending their collective recording career with the sweet sounds from their earliest days. When heard after that, "Flying Hour" sounds too dismissive, even as it certainly embodies an emotion the group endorsed. The long and short of it is that the album is not lacking something that another track — *any* track — can add. The imbalance will simply have to remain.

As always, the album assembly must include selection of artwork, and this one is particularly dicey. Photographs of the band remain out of the question, but it seems likely this decision could have been made in conjunction with Yoko. Thus, it seems possible that she might have offered photos from the time after John's death, including the ones which wound up on her own album, *Season of Glass*. The famously dramatic cover photo of that album would have been too much for the Beatles, just as it all but overwhelmed the music on hers. The photo on the back cover, however, seems just about right. (Perhaps there were others, but we cannot work with that possibility.)

19 / In Spite of All

The view is of Central Park and the city beyond, a view now closely identified with John Lennon. Yoko's presence in the photo does not seem like a reason not to use it, but rather a signal to fans that she was in support of the final group project. This is an assumption we will make, admittedly without really any reason to believe one way or the other on the subject. It just seems likely that, if there had been fused Beatles albums in the 70s, Yoko would have approved of and cooperated with the creation of a final one to honor John's memory, even if she would later make such an album herself. Of course, there are also reasons to think exactly the opposite.

The stark image may seem too emotional, and perhaps something that would have cast a pall over the project in terms of marketing. No doubt the marketeers would have preferred something lighter in color and more upbeat. In the end, a stark photo seems to be the right way to set the mood for the album, while also not condemning it to any sort of funereal feel, a la *Let It Be*. The back cover might have been pure white, with a track listing, perhaps with inset photos of the individual Beatles, an Apple logo, and not much else. Inside, lyrics and maybe some individual images also drawn from Yoko, or maybe nothing more.

In the end, that particular photo seems to demonstrate the great distances that the Beatles had traveled in what would have been a 20-year career at that point. Indeed, this album would likely have been released on or near the 20th anniversary of their first single, "Love Me Do." The distances since then were not just physical, but also musical and commercial and emotional and spiritual. Acknowledging this on the cover of the group's final album, even indirectly, seems entirely appropriate.

S A V E T H E B E A T L E S !

In Spite of All

Principal Recording: December 1980 - October 1982
Release: November 1982

Side One

1. Keep Under Cover (McCartney)
2. I'm Stepping Out (Lennon)
3. Wake Up (Starkey)
4. Unknown Delight (Harrison)
5. Sweetest Little Show (McCartney)
6. (Forgive Me) My Little Flower Princess (Lennon)
7. Beautiful Boy (Darling Boy) (Lennon)

Side Two

1. All Those Years Ago (Harrison)
2. Borrowed Time (Lennon)
3. Through Our Love (McCartney)
4. My Old Friend (feat. Carl Perkins) (Perkins)
5. Grow Old with Me (Lennon)
6. Here Today (McCartney)
7. In Spite of All the Danger (McCartney/Harrison)

19 / In Spite of All

Make It Yourself

Total Running Time: 47:15

Tk	Rill	Title	Source	Dur
F7-A1	—	Keep Under Cover	[1]	3:01
F7-A2	0	I'm Stepping Out [Edit]	[2]	4:03
F7-A3	(2.0)	Wake Up	[3]	3:38
F7-A4	0	Unknown Delight	[4]	4:13
F7-A5	0	Sweetest Little Show [Edit]	[1]	2:48
F7-A6	*	(Forgive Me) My Little Flower Princess	[2]	2:22
F7-A7	(5.0)	Beautiful Boy (Darling Boy)	[5]	4:00

Total: 24:08

Tk	Rill	Title	Source	Dur
F7-B1	—	All Those Years Ago	[6]	3:37
F7-B2	(2.0)	Borrowed Time	[2]	4:27
F7-B3	(2.0)	Through Our Love	[1]	3:24
F7-B4	0	My Old Friend	[7]	3:19
F7-B5	0	Grow Old with Me [Edit]	[8]	3:05
F7-B6	0	Here Today	[9]	2:28
F7-B7	3.0	In Spite of All the Danger	[10]	2:44

Total: 23:07

[1] *Pipes of Peace*
[2] *Milk and Honey*
[3] *Stop and Smell the Roses*
[4] *Gone Troppo*
[5] *Double Fantasy*
[6] *Somewhere in England*
[7] *Go Cat Go!* (Carl Perkins album)
[8] *John Lennon Anthology* (and others)
[9] *Tug of War*
[10] *Anthology 1*

* NOTE: Descriptions of edits and crossfades, with sample audio, are available at:

SaveTheBeatles.com

SAVE THE BEATLES!

Release
November 1982

Most Popular Albums
November 1980 - October 1982

US		UK	
AC/DC	*Back in Black*	ABC	*The Lexicon of Love*
Asia	*Asia*	Adam And The Ants	*Kings of the Wild...*
Foreigner	*4*	Barbra Streisand	*Love Songs*
Go-Go's	*Beauty and the Beat*	Cliff Richard	*Love Songs*
The J. Geils Band	*Freeze-frame*	Dire Straits	*Love Over Gold*
John Cougar	*American Fool*	Dire Straits	*Makin' Movies*
John Lennon/Yoko Ono	*Double Fantasy*	Duran Duran	*Duran Duran*
Journey	***Escape***	**Duran Duran**	***Rio***
Kenny Rogers	*Greatest Hits*	Elkie Brooks	*Pearls*
Loverboy	*Get Lucky*	The Human League	*Dare*
Men At Work	*Business as Usual*	The Kids From Fame	*The Kids from "Fame"*
Neil Diamond	*The Jazz Singer*	Madness	*Complete Madness*
Pat Benatar	*Crimes of Passion*	Neil Diamond	*The Jazz Singer*
The Police	*Ghost in the Machine*	Phil Collins	*Face Value*
The Police	*Zenyatta Mondatta*	Phil Collins	*Hello, I Must Be Going!*
REO Speedwagon	*Hi Infidelity*	Queen	*Greatest Hits*
The Rolling Stones	*Tattoo You*	Randy Crawford	*Secret Combination*
Stevie Nicks	*Bella Donna*	Stevie Wonder	*Hotter Than July*
Styx	*Paradise Theater*	Ultravox	*Vienna*
Toto	*Toto IV*	Vangelis	*Chariots of Fire*

Most popular album in bold

Let's admit that the Beatles would have sounded like an anachronism in this group of music. "Pop rock" has flourished, buoyed by the rapidly-expanding variant, "synth rock." It's not that guitar-based bands are gone — witness the rise of Dire Straits, the Go-Gos, John Cougar (Mellancamp), and the reemergence of the Stones — but so much of what is here relies on the fast-maturing world of synthesizer technology. It is barely an exaggeration to say that anyone with fingers and big hair could become a star once synths began to dominate.

So we don't really look at this list in order to figure out how the Beatles would have been regarded by contemporary music fans. They would have sounded a bit out of sync — which is a nice way of saying *irrelevant*. Nothing they could have made or released at this point would have returned them to their roots as trend-setters and studio innovators. The best they could do would be to exit gracefully, which is the extent of what *In Spite of All* aspires to do.

19 / In Spite of All

Topping the Charts
November 1982

US			UK	
John Cougar	*American Fool*	1	Kids from Fame	*The Kids from "Fame"*
Fleetwood Mac	*Mirage*	2	Phil Collins	*Hello I Must Be Going!*
Bruce Springsteen	*Nebraska*	3	Squeeze	*Singles 45's and Under*
Men At Work	*Business As Usual*	4	Kids from Fame	*Kids from Fame Again*
Billy Squier	*Emotions In Motion*	5	Dionne Warwick	*Heartbreaker*
Michael McDonald	*If That's What It Takes*	6	Dire Straits	*Love Over Gold*
Alan Parsons Project	*Eye In The Sky*	7	Supertramp	*Famous Last Words*
The Who	*It's Hard*	8	Various Artists	*Reflections*
Billy Joel	*The Nylon Curtain*	9	Culture Club	*Kissing To Be Clever*
A Flock Of Seagulls	*A Flock Of Seagulls*	10	Status Quo	*From the Makers Of*

This final fused Beatles album would have been released almost simultaneously with two of the most influential albums of the early 80s, not yet visible on these charts: Michael Jackson's *Thriller* and Prince's *1999*. In the real world, the solo Beatles did not sound very much like these records, and on occasions that they tried to, the results were most unfortunate.

Still, the Beatles always carved their own space within popular music, and it seems inevitable that any Beatles album released after the death of John Lennon would have immediately jumped to the top of the charts regardless of style, tone or quality. But the quality of *In Spite of All* is high enough to suggest that it would have displaced any of these records for quite some time.

An anachronism at the top of the charts isn't really all that unusual. In the eras of earlier fused Beatles albums, there were occasions of crooners besting the rockers, and novelties outstripping everything else. So it would have been here, only now with the Beatles — as legacy act — displacing the younger set.

McCartney's *Tug of War* may be the best analogue. He was no longer viewed as the vital pop star he had been during the heyday of Wings, but the market took a pause to acknowledge a master in their midst. Buoyed by excellent reviews and a hit single, *Tug of War* demonstrated that the public was eager for a reaction to Lennon's death, and looked to McCartney to provide one.

In our slightly altered narrative, it would have been the surviving Beatles creating that reaction, and it seems reasonable that the public's response would have been exponentially greater. Thus we will assume that *In Spite of All* would have garnered significant commercial success.

Discussion

It probably could go without saying that the musical world would have almost completely stopped, if only for a short time, for this album. One part of that would have been mere astonishment at the arrival of a new Beatles album two years after the death of a Beatle. Another part of that would have been a foreboding sense that this would be the last music from the group ever. Still another part would have been a collective holding of breath to see if the group could stick the landing.

Once on turntables, however, that breath would have been released, along with a torrent of emotions. It would not be difficult to cry while listening, but it would also not be difficult to simply lean back and enjoy the wash of music, as John would certainly have preferred. There may have been no outpouring of astonishment in what had been accomplished, but only because the product sounds so seamless. The world was accustomed to the Beatles getting it right, and would not have been surprised that it had happened again.

Critics would have recognized this as a modestly better outing than its predecessor, but probably lamented the somewhat artificial nature of embellishments to John's songs — much as happened with both *Milk and Honey* and *Anthology*. But the criticisms would have been muted in deference to the sheer scale of the project. No one would have expected the Beatles to top themselves again, but this album would have been perceived as orders of magnitude better than any band, 20 years after its first appearance on the music scene, and missing a critical member due to tragedy, had any right to create.

The focus would certainly have been on John's fiv songs. There would have been acknowledgment that they were not his best, but that would have been accompanied by appreciation of their simplicity, seeming spontaneity, and utter freedom from artifice. Listeners would have experienced the palpable loss in "Borrowed Time" and "Beautiful Boy (Darling Boy)" — in some ways the same as we all first heard them, but in some ways more deeply. They would have heard the lightness in "I'm Steppin' Out." Extracted from the context of frustrating duet albums, and placed once again next to his most robust collaborators, John's songs are free to soar — both emerging from, and yielding to, the voices of his old colleagues, his old friends, his brothers.

Paul's songs, meanwhile, would have been recognized as comparable in quality to those on his recent magnum opus, *Tug of War*. He might have been accused of cuteness, especially for a track like "Sweetest Little Show," despite that fact that even its somewhat precious show-within-a-show comes off as an homage to the Beatles in this context — for which John immediately asks forgiveness in the following track!

But that very dynamic would have certainly been noticed. With Paul and John's voices interspersed in that way, the old equilibrium is recreated and sustained. Even more than in recent years, on this album when John is simple and straightforward,

19 / In Spite of All

Paul answers with structure and imagery. When Paul is ambiguous, John answers with a clear mind and feet on the ground. On this album, critics might have been inclined to recognize that the interplay between their voices still sounds vital in meta form, even if not quite as visceral as it did when they were in the same studio.

There would have been notes about George's relative under-representation, especially given his renaissance of quality. And Ringo's track might have gone largely unnoticed. But both of these would have been offset by the presence of Carl Perkins, and the archival proto-Beatles that close the album.

Side two of this album may not have challenged *Abbey Road*, or even some of the better sides of the fusion years, but it makes a fitting tribute to a fallen musician, made from his own sounds, set in a bed of musical friendship and love. This would have been, at least, the goal of all involved, and it seems self-evident upon listening.

In this slightly altered reality, there would have been no *Pipes of Peace* to drain away the goodwill from Paul's previous solo album. The tiredness of George's solo outings might have been set aside. And the world might have actually noticed Ringo's solo work again — especially if the presence of a new Beatles album took the place of his making one or more of those bad solo efforts.

In fairness, we must also consider the opposing views. Though the actual pop music of 1982 was hardly going to change the world, the Beatles still would have sounded old-fashioned to many ears — even, or perhaps *especially*, in an elaborate production like this album. Detractors would certainly have emerged, perhaps wondering what all the shouting was about for a band that had long ago peaked. The presence of strings and massive production numbers might have been dismissed as relics with no place in a new, synthesizer-based and video-based world. Given Paul's decidedly mixed results in making videos, it seems at least possible that an errant video might have sucked some life out of the album's reception.

But all would have had to accept that a Beatles album — *any* Beatles album — would always be a major event, and that this would likely be the last, something that was not widely known at the time of *Abbey Road*. We might even assume that there was some grand announcement of this ending when the album was released. The world that cried over John's death in 1980 would have had a chance to grieve again through this album, while also getting a memento which summed up the entire Beatles era. Talk about a complex set of emotions!

Maybe more importantly, the album would surely have sold in vast quantities around the world, perhaps even rivalling the sales of Beatles albums back in the old days. As event albums go, this would have been the ultimate, and its appeal would have stretched to all corners of recorded music. There would have been a "Beatle moment" the likes of which the world had not seen in a very long time, and would never see again. The Beatles would have gone out the way they came in, and the way they had always been, and the way they would always be: on top.

Coda

Imagine an alternative script. The McCartney *album is released, and its creator merely issues a cryptic comment about the Beatles, along the lines of 'Who knows what will happen?' Lennon is isolated in his room of primal screams at the Inn on the Park and says nothing. Later in 1970, with the 'split' still not made public, Lennon undertakes one of the frequent changes of heart that litter his career, and invites the Beatles to help him record the songs inspired by his experience with Janov. The Beatles stumble, or stride, into a new decade, and then . . . ?*

— Peter Doggett, *You Never Give Me Your Money*

The central idea of this book is, of course, preposterous. Once disputes arose between the Beatles over management, money, and music, the die was cast. Working together, even as imagined here, simply could never have happened. We know that because, well, it didn't.

But therein lies the joy of the fantasy. If we turn off our minds, relax and float downstream, we find that the dying might have been, well, *optional* after all. We can animate that impossible world and walk around in it a little bit. Maybe a slightly altered reality might have been better than the one we got. Or not. Who knows?

Worst

In the worst case, by the time a decade of fused albums had passed, the spell might have been broken. Not only might the Beatles have become just as irrelevant as their solo careers, but that descent into irrelevance might have taken the classic albums along with, tarnishing their memory and blunting their legacy. Through waning cultural impact, a decade of meta-Beatles music, while good in the short term, might have tainted the entire catalog – all the way back to "Love Me Do."

The still-current-meta-Beatles, though not being asked frequently about potential reunions, would still have found themselves answering a static and relentless set of questions about the state of the band. Is this the last album? Did you play together in the studio? Will you ever do that again? Have you broken up? Do you think this music is as good as in the old days?

They would no doubt have still had disagreements among themselves, and maybe those would have been kept from the public, or not. Solo projects might have been rarer, slighter and less successful, further undermining the group's long reputation. One spectacularly failed group project could have sunk the whole myth – as John Lennon always said he wanted. Perhaps the shadow of the Beatles would have grown and darkened as the years passed, and metastisized in devastating ways.

Best

In the best case, the world gets another decade of Beatles music, perhaps even a real studio reunion at some point. The music is vibrant, and maturing, and still thrilling on some level, even as other styles rise around it. A second generation of fans gets firsthand exposure to the group, and the breadth of the group's catalog continues to grow. Their records remain influential, and many of the sub-genres of popular music that they midwifed become infused with ideas that allow them to mature and prosper rather than flame out. The shallowness which dogged the decade's pop music might have been mitigated, while the straight pop excellence which flourished was nudged into something even more meaningful.

In this scenario, the Beatles get a respite from the onslaught they faced in the 60s, and are able to have meaningful lives, even separate careers – flourishing both inside and outside of the group. Instead of being regarded for what they lacked as solo artists, or what they were *not* doing together, their reputation would have mellowed into that of genial elders, who surfaced every couple of years to show the world what true excellence really means. The luster on the group's image would have shown brighter even if, in retrospect, the music didn't quite shatter expectations like it once had. Maturity would still have looked good on the men and the music.

Push

In between these two extremes is a scenario which seems perhaps the most likely. In this middle world, the albums would have sold well, but waned in influence just as the solo Beatles did. A second generation of fans would have found the group, but viewed them as a little out of touch with newer music, unaware of the role the Beatles had played in expanding the pop music landscape. Eventually, however, their status as standard bearers of creative excellence would have been the same.

Everyone would have been happy to still have the Beatles around, but would look back wistfully at *Abbey Road*, and *Sgt. Pepper*, just as we do now. The lives of the individual Beatles would have followed paths similar to what actually happened, with the questions changing only slightly, despite being asked with the same frequency: Will you ever tour again? Will you ever break up for good? How often do you all play together in the studio now? Do you still talk to each other? Do you still like each other?

The fade into reduced relevance would have followed the same curve for the group as it did for three of its members, with Paul still emerging as the most successful solo Beatle, perhaps even the eventual – because he was *willing* – standard-bearer for the brand as the other three retreated from the limelight. Some missteps would have been avoided, and others would have inevitably popped up. Releases would have come less frequently, but there would have been flashes of the old excitement with every one. Over time, those flashes wouldn't last quite as long or be quite as intense, much as happened with so many bands of the 60s.

In truth, this most likely scenario looks a whole lot like what actually happened. Maybe it wasn't the breakup which changed how the world saw the Beatles, but merely the passage of time – the aging, the growing up, the moving on of the former screaming teenagers. Maybe, even in a slightly altered universe, the ultimate outcome would have been surprisingly similar.

So what should we wish?

On balance, it seems like **the risks are greater than the rewards**. Despite having another decade's worth of music, the real possibility of the group's image being tarnished beyond repair is too great a price to pay. The risk within the risk is that the world might forget those halcyon early days: "Can you believe that people in the 60s went crazy for new albums by *The Beatles*?!? What were they thinking?"

The Beatles' own desire to dismiss their early years might have taken root in the fans. The world might have been convinced that anything but what the Beatles were doing *right now* should be ignored as if it never happened. But everything new – far removed from their earliest sounds – would have been less compelling. The world would have begun to tune out.

On balance, it seems that **the rewards outweigh the risks**. With another decade's worth of music, the band's collective output virtually doubles, and all of it very high quality. The reward within the reward is that, in extending their relevance, they continue to raise the bar. The fans hear everything as echoes of the halcyon early days: "Can you believe that the Beatle are still so great after all these years?"

The Beatles' own desire to distance themselves from their early years would have failed to take root. Even as the band kept moving, the fans would keep one ear in the present and one in the past. Everything new, though far removed from their earliest sounds, would have evoked that old glow of Beatle Magic, and the world would have continued to tune in.

You will decide how you feel. For me, I wish two mutually exclusive things at the same time. I wish they had done at least this, and I'm really glad they didn't. I wish they had stayed together, in whatever capacity, and I'm glad they broke up when and how they did.

Alas, we are not George Bailey. No guardian angel can show us what that different world would have looked like to help make the choice. In our Capra-esque fantasies, we tend to only imagine a *better* world if the Beatles had not gone their separate ways in 1970. But when you really think about it, the line between the possible outcomes is surprisingly thin. A tiny detail here or there, a small action or inaction, might have changed things dramatically – as is always true in life itself.

I decided to embark on this thought experiment to see if it was possible to get a little glimpse of what that world might have been like, and I hope that has been accomplished. Obviously, nothing can be *known*. We cannot *know* how the music would have been received. We cannot *know* how the act of assembling the music into fused albums might have changed the next round. We cannot *know* what sorts of adjustments the Beatles would have made along the way based on how their collective work was being received. We cannot *know* how fans would have reacted, or how the next generation might have regarded the group, especially without the drama associated with their disintegration.

We cannot *know* how the Beatles would have changed as people, and what those changes might have brought to the music. The further away we get from the breakup, the greater the differences in the men and the music – both in the real and imagined worlds – though some things are probably fundamental. John Lennon likely would have remained unpredictable, passionate, impatient, impulsive. Paul McCartney would have remained a consummate entertainer and craftsman, while also guarded and inscrutable. George Harrison would still have sought truth, fed his spirit, become a gardener, and seen through the veils. Ringo Starr would have stayed a gentle giant, flexible, loyal, and with one hell of a solid beat.

If things did change, it might have been in spurring each other on to even greater heights than imagined here, whether sitting next to one another in the same studio, or merely by listening closely to what the others had done somewhere far away, and reacting. Maybe they could have collectively found a new voice for their generation, even as the idealistic 60s morphed into the self-centered 70s. No matter what else happened, we can certainly wish that a simple change of circumstance would have put John Lennon somewhere else on December 8, 1980, and allowed George Harrison's cancer to be detected earlier.

Having now imagined that slightly altered narrative, let us take away what we can. Three powerful conclusions can be drawn from the experiment.

First, it works! It's not the same, but it works, and it's great. The Beatles do indeed elevate one another simply by virtue of proximity. Putting their best solo music together with George Martin's principles yields something special. A new sort of Beatle Magic is created which is unexpected, welcome, and has been waiting many years to be revealed. The examples of assemblies found here are just that: examples. Many other great fused albums can probably be made, and the search is worth our time. There is still more to be mined in the solo careers of the former Beatles. Their music is not yet fully appreciated, and considering all they have given of themselves, we own them the attempt to do it.

Second, the altered narrative is not without risks. Though we imagine the best, reality has a pesky way of intervening. The Beatles were people, moving about in the world, and there are scenarios in which staying together in any capacity is worse for their legacy – and the music – than breaking up. This is a cautionary thought.

Third, by lurching apart as they did, the Beatles essentially cauterized their narrative into just the type of story we love to ponder over and over: that of unfulfilled potential. Beyond just leaving the audience wanting more, the Beatles walked off the stage and gave us the gift of unexplored possibilities. By not going on, they gave us a chance to *imagine* them going on, which we will be doing forever. And through exploring those possibilities, we come to fully realize that in breaking up when and how they did, they assured themselves immortality, for better or worse.

During the course of this project, *Egypt Station* appeared on my phone, free through one of the music services. Though it bears signs of dilution and familiar self-indulgence, there were several moments when the music took my breath away, much as McCartney records have always been able to do – utterly without warning. It reminded me of why I started this project. So much great music by the former Beatles is unknown by those who might appreciate it. If this thought experiment leads even one person to a new appreciation of the solo Beatles, I will be satisfied.

Any time we look closely, listen with intention, and deeply consider the art of the Beatles, we find again what we have always known about John, Paul, George and Ringo: There exist many universes to explore within the music.

Rick Prescott
Minneapolis, Minnesota
April 10, 2020

Appendix

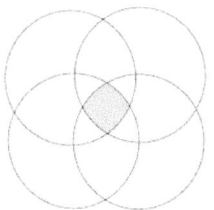

We shall not cease from exploration
And the end of all our exploring
Will be to arrive where we started
And know the place for the first time.
Through the unknown, unremembered gate
When the last of earth left to discover
Is that which was the beginning...

Appendix I
Creative Calendar

In their early years, the Beatles went in to the studio whenever cracks in their hectic schedule allowed. Brian Epstein and George Martin famously established the goal of releasing "a single every three months, and a long-playing record every year."[1] High demand eventually forced them to modify it slightly to, "four singles and two albums a year,"[2] though it would always remain a moving target. In the UK, the only year in which the Beatles released four singles and two albums was 1963.

When they stopped touring, the recording schedule changed. They established blocks of time for recording, and released new music whenever they deemed it ready, albeit always trying to have something to sell at Christmas.

After the breakup, the former Beatles did not coordinate recording sessions in any way. Each solo Beatle recorded whenever, wherever, and with whomever he pleased. Likewise, their solo releases were not timed to avoid collisions in the marketplace. There were, in fact, plenty of times when albums and singles by various solo Beatles competed head-to-head, especially because everyone still wanted to have something in stores during the holidays.

The calendar which follows summarizes recording sessions, releases, and various other activities, beginning with their first group sessions in 1962, and continuing through *Milk and Honey* in 1984, which represents the end of the survey period for this project.

Among the patterns which become visible are eras during the solo years in which all four Beatles recorded and released more or less concurrently. From this it becomes possible to designate "eras" in which contemporaneous solo recordings can be collected and reviewed, with the intent of assembling the best tracks into a fused Beatles album.

Importantly, each era is defined based on recording activities, not releases. Cutoff lines are inserted to indicate the beginning and end of what might be called the period of "principle recording" for each rescued album. In practice, the borders between eras are not quite as clean as indicated here. Incidental overlap is discussed as necessary in the album chapters.

At the end, a table of the resulting "fusion eras" summarizes both the recording periods and any breaks between, along with the presumed timing of the meta-Beatles releases. (Another overview of these eras, which focuses on groupings of solo albums, can be found in chapter 11, *Fusion*.)

---

[1] *All You Need is Ears*, pg. 136
[2] *Summer of Love*, pg. 25

Notes

- In the group era, sessions are only listed if they include at least one Beatle.

- In the solo era, session listings are approximations based on the best available documentation.

- The timing of demo recordings is not represented on the grid.

- The earliest release date is used, whether in the US or UK.

- In some (4) limited cases — times of especially high activity — there was not enough room on the calendar for all icons which belong in a particular box. For visual clarity, an icon sometimes had to be placed in an adjacent box with a small arrow indicating where it actually belongs.

- All *distilled core studio releases* are documented. (See the next section of this appendix for more on this concept.) In addition, selected *extended catalog releases* which are of general relevance are included.

- Empty rows are omitted. If a solo Beatle did not record or release in a given year, he is not shown on the grid.

Appendix 1/Creative Calendar

The following movie posters, which might be difficult to identify in icon form, are included in the calendar:

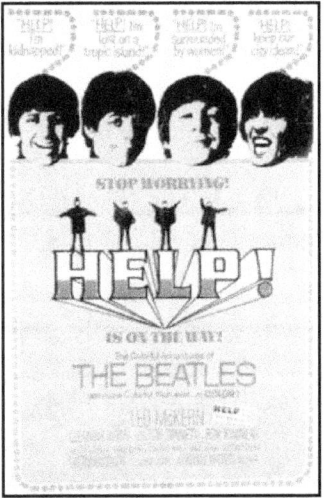

The following multimedia projects are noted here, but not included in the calendar due to space constraints:

- *Imagine* (TV film, December 1972)
- *James Paul McCartney* (TV film, April 1973)
- *Ringo* (TV film, April 1978)
- *Rockshow* (Film, November 1980)
- *Concert for Kampuchea* (Film, August 1980; Album, March 1981)

SAVE THE BEATLES!

Creative Calendar

- 🎛 Studio recording
- 🔊 Local/regional concerts
- ✈ International tour
- 🎬 Filming
- 💿 Single release
- 🏝 Vacation

Appendix I / Creative Calendar

		JAN	FEB	MAR	APR	MAY	JUN	JUL	AUG	SEP	OCT	NOV	DEC
69	👥	🎬	🎞		🎞	🎞		🎞	🎞				
	👩						🎞	💿		🎞🔊	💿		🔊
	👧										🎞	🎞	🎞
	👶										🎞	🎞	🎞
	ERA										**F1 - *Dream***		
70	👥	🎞			🎞								
	👩	🎞	💿							🎞	🎞		
	👧	🎞	🎞							🎞 (F2)	🎞		
	👶					🎞	🎞	🎞	🎞	🎞			
	👶	🎞	🎞				🎞				🎞💿		
	ERA		**F1 - *Dream***										
71	👩		🎞	💿		🎞	🎞🔊	🎞💿		🎞		🎞💿
	👧	🎞	🎞💿				🎞						
	👶		🎞				🎞	🎞💿	🔊			🎞	
	👶				💿				🔊	🎞			
	ERA		**F2 - *Beggars in a Gold Mine***								💿		
72	👩	🎞	🎞	🎞			🎞	🔊					
	👧		🎞💿🔊	🎞		💿		✈	✈	🎞	🎞	🎞	🎞💿
	👶			🎞							🎞	🎞	
	👶			💿								🎞	
	ERA										**F3 - *Be Here Now***		

Save the Beatles!

Appendix I / Creative Calendar

Year		JAN	FEB	MAR	APR	MAY	JUN	JUL	AUG	SEP	OCT	NOV	DEC
77	👥				■	■					■		
	👤		⊚	⊚		⊚			⊚			○	
	👤		⊚				⊚		○	■		⊚	
	ERA				*F5 - Flight*					●		*Hiatus*	
78	👥												■
	👤	⊚		■				⊚	⊚	⊚	⊚	⊚ ←	■
	👤			⊚	⊚	⊚	⊚	⊚	⊚	⊚			
	👤			⊚	■								
	ERA					*Hiatus*							
79	👤	⊚	⊚	⊚○		■	⊚ (F6)	⊚ (F6)			○ ✈	✈	
	👤		■										
	ERA					*Hiatus*							
80	👥				■						■		
	👤								⊚	⊚	■		
	👤				○	■	○			○	⊚	⊚	⊚
	👤				⊚	⊚	⊚	⊚	⊚	⊚		⊚	⊚
	👤								⊚	⊚	⊚	⊚	⊚
	ERA	*Hiatus*			*F6 - Wheels Walls Waterfalls*						●		F7
81	👤		⊚	⊚		⊚			⊚	⊚	⊚	⊚	⊚
	👤		⊚	⊚			■						
	👤		⊚	⊚							■		
	ERA					*F7 - In Spite of All*							

S A V E   T H E   B E A T L E S !

Summary of Fusion Eras

ERA	TITLE	BEGIN	END	ACTIVITY	RELEASE
F1	*Dream*	69-Oct	70-Oct	Principal recording	70-Dec
F2	*Beggars in a Gold Mine*	70-Nov	71-Sep	Principal recording	71-Nov
F3	*Be Here Now*	71-Oct	72-Aug	Break	73-Dec
		72-Sep	73-Nov	Principal recording	
F4	*Vienna*	73-Dec	74-May	Break	75-Jun
		74-Jun	75-May	Principal recording	
F5	*Flight*	75-Jun	76-Mar	Break	77-Sep
		76-Apr	77-Sep	Principal recording	
		77-Oct	80-Feb	Hiatus	
F6	*Wheels, Walls and Waterfalls*	80-Mar	80-Nov	Principal recording	80-Nov
F7	*In Spite of All*	80-Dec	82-Oct	Principal recording	82-Nov

Appendix II
Distilled Core Studio Releases

A traditional discography focuses on collecting and detailing all commercial releases under an artist's name. In the context of the Beatles and this project, such a list would contain way too much information. The lists in these pages use specific filters to provide exactly what is needed and nothing more.

Therefore, and importantly, the lists contained here are not to be confused with discographies. They do not attempt to be comprehensive lists of commercial releases. Rather, recognizing that a release of new music is both a commercial and artistic act, an act that it is fundamentally different from later reissues, these lists make it possible to see in stark relief the activities, progressions, and rhythms of an artist's recording career. What the marketers did with the music later — i.e. after it was first released — is of no interest to this project.

As such, these are relatively short lists. But if you were to listen to everything on the list, you would hear the totality of the artist's *distinct core studio works* — the primary body of recordings that the artist made during the survey period.

IMPORTANT: The survey period for this book ends with the release of *Milk and Honey* in January 1984. Thus, no recordings made or released after that date are included in the catalogs below.

Overview

Distilled vs. Comprehensive

> To *distill* an artist's catalog is to list only releases which contain previously unreleased music. This eliminates compilations, reissues, reconfigurations, and anything else without new music. A definition of "new" music in this context can be found below. By contrast, a *comprehensive* listing shows all releases, regardless of music contained.

Core vs. Extended

> *Core* releases are those which define an artist's career. In the case of a recording artist, these are the principle albums and singles which are considered to be central to the artist's body of work, and mass marketed to a mainstream audience. By contrast, recordings which are not central in some way, such as demos, experimental or archival recordings, limited release,

pseudonymous or promotional items, etc. represent part of the artist's *extended* catalog.

Studio vs. Live

Studio recordings are defined as those made by an artist within a professional recording studio or equivalent, without the presence of an audience, in which the artist has complete artistic control over conditions and the final output.

About Distillation

In general, the first release to contain a piece of new music makes the list. If a track appears on an album, and later on a single, the single is considered a reissue for the purposes of these lists, even if it is not *exactly* the same as the album cut — for example, if it has been edited for radio. Conversely, if a track appears first on a single, and later on an album, the single will generally be listed, and the album track is considered a reissue, subject to criteria detailed here.

The key exception is the "teaser" single, which typically is released immediately prior to, or concurrent with, an album release. In most cases, the tracks used as teaser singles are best considered with the music on the album, especially if the single is released less than about 30 days prior to its parent album. In such a case, the single is not listed (unless it also contains a non-album B-side), and the track is counted with the parent album.

Distinguishing between a "teaser" and a stand-alone single is important, and somewhat subjective. 30 days is a rough criteria, but context must also be considered. The Beatles released "Ticket to Ride" as a single a full four months before it appeared on the *Help!* album. Indeed, they still had two months of work left on the album when the single came out. In such a case, the single release clearly is not a "teaser" in the typical sense, and therefore the track is counted with the single, which is included on the list. Such decisions have been made on a case-by-case basis.

Core Period

The *core period* for an artist is that time in which they did their most significant, compelling, and "classic" work. It begins with the first widespread, mainstream release of new music, and ends with the last contemporary, non-archival release of new music. Music outside of these time constraints is more properly considered with the artist's *extended* catalog.

Appendix II / Releases

For a group like the Beatles, the core period begins with the first mainstream mass market release, and ends with the group's breakup. Importantly, the core period cannot be reopened even if the group were to reform to some degree later. This acknowledges that such reunions necessarily represent a separate period in the group's career, and not an extension of the original "classic" period which had already ended. Thus, for a group, once the core period closes, it cannot be reopened.

For a solo artist, posthumous releases are considered individually, and can extend the core period if they were in process at the time of death, and subsequently received wide release.

For the Beatles and the individual members, the core periods are as follows:

- **Beatles:**
  - Began on October 5, 1962 ("Love Me Do")
  - Ended on May 8, 1970 (*Let It Be*)

- **John Lennon:**
  - Began on July 4, 1969 ("Give Peace a Chance")
  - Ended on January 9, 1984 (*Milk and Honey*)

- **Ringo Starr:**
  - Began on March 27, 1970 (*Sentimental Journey*)
  - Continues as of this writing (April 2020)

- **Paul McCartney:**
  - Began on April 17, 1970 (*McCartney*)
  - Continues as of this writing (April 2020)

- **George Harrison:**
  - Began on November 23, 1970 (US release of "My Sweet Lord")
  - Ended on November 18, 2002 (*Brainwashed*)

New Music, Variations, Distinct Works

Much has been made of the many variations in which each Beatles track can be heard. Many tracks have mono and stereo mixes which diverge to varying degrees. Some variations arose in mastering, such as the early Capitol releases in the US. Sometimes tracks were intentionally edited or mixed differently for different occasions. Such variations are less common in the solo era, but they do still exist. And in recent years, newly remastered and/or remixed versions of everything have become *de rigueur*.

Even so, "Come Together" is still "Come Together," no matter how it is tweaked, mixed or edited. It is one *distinct work*, with variations.

Most variations will be ignored by the lists below since they provide little beyond minutia in terms of understanding the art. This is not to say that they are uninteresting, but rather that this project deals with the music at a different level.

To be considered for these lists, the variation must be significant enough that a separate *distinct work* is created. For example, the two versions of "Revolution" are clearly separate and distinct works. In this case, the band made two completely different recordings of the same song, which is obviously a sufficient variation, as such remakes always are.

Not all situations are quite so clear. One less obvious and lesser-known example is "Please Please Me." When the time came to include the track on their debut album, the tape used for the single had gone missing. George Martin was forced to use a different take for the album, and do some fancy editing to pull together all of the parts, since the harmonica had been added as an overdub. The result, while still "Please Please Me," contains differences which must be considered significant, such as the muff of the lyrics which causes a passing giggle in John's vocal. The two versions are best viewed as separate *distinct works*.

Such issues continue, to a lesser degree, into the solo era. The radio edit of "With a Little Luck" is two and a half minutes shorter than the album version, but that difference is not sufficient to create a separate *distinct work*. On the other hand, the two versions of "Isn't a Pity" are definitely different enough to warrant separate consideration. Many instances can be found of tracks having longer or shorter fades across various releases, and the so-called "extended remix" brought about a new type of variation which may or may not need to be considered as a *distinct work*.

Since the goal of these catalogs is not to be exhaustive about such variations, but rather to catalog only the underlying *distinct works*, the decision on what constitutes a significant variation has been made on a case-by-case basis.

Finally, all bootlegs are considered with the artist's extended catalog, despite being far too numerous and varied in quality to catalog in any serious way (though some have tried). Bootlegs are a blessing and a curse to a project like this. On the one hand, there are widely-known unreleased recordings which really must be considered when reviewing an artist's work for a given period. On the other, there is practically no way to review *everything* that an artist recorded because there is simply no way to know that you've reached the end of what is available. There is always *one more* unreleased nugget.

By definition, the lists of releases which follow do not include any unreleased music. Since it was necessary to consider some unreleased recordings for this project, they have been included in the next appendix, *Distinct Works Catalogs*.

Appendix II / Releases

Notes

- On the following lists, the recording dates, producers and studios listed with each entry pertain to only the *new* tracks on the release.

- Release dates are truncated to year and month for better readability.

- Whenever possible, the first release date is used, regardless of whether it was in the UK or US. Release dates for other markets are not considered.

- In the handful of cases where Beatle tracks were released early in the US, the UK releases and dates are still used, as they are the only ones which were approved by the Beatles directly.

- In five cases, the same album title was used on UK and US releases, while the contents differed significantly. Once again, only the UK versions approved directly by the Beatles are considered.

The Beatles
Distilled Core Studio Releases

ID		TITLE / Recorded	Producer	Studio(s)	RELEASE	NEW
B01		"Love Me Do" / "P.S. I Love You" Sep 62	Martin	EMI	62-Oct	2
B02		"Please Please Me" / "Ask Me Why" Nov 62	Martin	EMI	63-Jan	2
B03		*Please Please Me* Feb 63	Martin	EMI	63-Mar	12[a]
B04		"From Me to You" / "Thank You Girl" Mar 63	Martin	EMI	63-Apr	2
B05		"She Loves You" / "I'll Get You" Jul 63	Martin	EMI	63-Aug	2
B06		*With the Beatles* Jul-Oct 63	Martin	EMI	63-Nov	14
B07		"I Want to Hold Your Hand" / "This Boy" Oct 63	Martin	EMI	63-Nov	2
B08		"Komm, gib mir deine Hand" / "Sie liebt dich" (GER) Oct 63 - Jan 64	Martin/Demmler	EMI, Pathé Marconi (Paris)	64-Feb	2
B09		"Can't Buy Me Love" / "You Can't Do That" Jan-Mar 64	Martin	EMI, Pathé Marconi (Paris)	64-Mar	2
B10		*Long Tall Sally* Mar-Jun 64	Martin	EMI	64-Jun	4
B11		*A Hard Day's Night* (UK) Jan-Jun 64	Martin	EMI, Pathé Marconi (Paris)	64-Jul	11[b]
B12		"I Feel Fine" / "She's a Woman" Oct 64	Martin	EMI	64-Nov	2
B13		*Beatles for Sale* Aug-Oct 64	Martin	EMI	64-Dec	14
B14		"Ticket to Ride" / "Yes It Is" Feb 65	Martin	EMI	65-Apr	2
B15		"Help!" / "I'm Down" Jun 65	Martin	EMI	65-Jul	2
B16		*Help!* (UK) Feb-Jun 65	Martin	EMI	65-Aug	12[c]
B17		"Day Tripper" & "We Can Work It Out" Oct 65	Martin	EMI	65-Dec	2
B18		*Rubber Soul* (UK) Jun-Nov 65	Martin	EMI	65-Dec	14
B19		"Paperback Writer" / "Rain" Apr 66	Martin	EMI	66-May	2

Appendix II / Releases

B20		*Revolver* (UK) Apr-Jun 66 Martin		EMI	66-Aug	14
B21		*A Collection of Beatles Oldies* May 65 Martin		EMI	66-Dec	1
B22		"Penny Lane" & "Strawberry Fields Forever" Nov 66 - Jan 67 Martin		EMI	67-Feb	2
B23		*Sgt. Pepper's Lonely Hearts Club Band* Nov 66 - Apr 67 Martin		EMI, Regent	67-May	13
B24		"All You Need Is Love" / "Baby, You're a Rich Man" May-Jun 67 Martin		EMI, Olympic	67-Jul	2
B25		"Hello, Goodbye" / "I Am the Walrus" Oct-Nov 67 Martin		EMI	67-Nov	2
B26		*Magical Mystery Tour* (UK) Apr-Nov 67 Martin		EMI, Olympic, Chappell	67-Dec	5[d]
B27		"Lady Madonna" / "The Inner Light" Jan-Feb 68 Martin		EMI, EMI (Bombay)	68-Mar	2
B28		"Hey Jude" / "Revolution" Jul-Aug 68 Martin		EMI, Trident	68-Aug	2
B29		*The Beatles* ["The White Album"] May-Oct 68 Martin		EMI, Trident	68-Nov	30
B30		*Yellow Submarine* May 66 - Feb 68 Martin		EMI, De Lane Lea	69-Jan	4
B31		"Get Back" / "Don't Let Me Down" Jan 69 (uncredited)		Apple, Olympic	69-Apr	2
B32		"The Ballad of John and Yoko" / "Old Brown Shoe" Feb-Apr 69 Martin		EMI	69-May	2
B33		*Abbey Road* Feb-Aug 69 Martin		EMI, Olympic, Trident	69-Sep	14[e]
B34		*No One's Gonna Change Our World* Feb 68 - Oct 69 Martin		EMI	69-Dec	1
B35		"Let It Be" / "You Know My Name (Look Up the Number)" May 67 - Jan 70 Martin		EMI, Apple	70-Mar	2
B36		*Let It Be* Feb 68 - Apr 70 Spector		EMI, Apple, Olympic	70-May	12[f]
						215

a. Does not count two tracks that had been previously released on single "P.S. I Love You" and "Ask Me Why"; Does count two tracks with significant variations from the single releases: "Love Me Do" (drummer) and "Please Please Me" (alt take/edit)

b. Does not count two tracks that had been previously released on singles: "Can't Buy Me Love" and "You Can't Do That"

c. Does not count two tracks that had been previously released on singles: "Ticket to Ride" and "Help!"

d. Does not count one track that had been previously released on a single: "I Am the Walrus"

e. In three instances, counts two songs as one because they were recorded together: "Sun King/Mean Mr Mustard," "Polythene Pam/She Came In Through the Bathroom Window," and "Golden Slumbers/Carry That Weight."

f. Does count three significant remixes: "Across the Universe," "Let It Be," and "Get Back"

Selected items from The Beatles' Extended Releases

62-Jan	*My Bonnie (with Tony Sheridan)*
70-Feb	*Hey Jude*
70-Dec	*From Then to You (Christmas Record Compilation)*
73-Apr	*The Beatles (1962-1966)* ["red"]
73-Apr	*The Beatles (1967-1970)* ["blue"]
76-Jun	*Rock 'n' Roll Music*
77-Apr	*Live! at the Star-Club in Hamburg, Germany; 1962*
77-May	*The Beatles at the Hollywood Bowl*
77-Oct	*Love Songs*
78-Dec	*Rarities* [UK]
80-Mar	*Rarities* [US]
80-Oct	*The Beatles Ballads*
82-Mar	*Reel Music*
82-Oct	*20 Greatest Hits*
88-Mar	*Past Masters (Volumes One and Two)*
94-Nov	*Live at the BBC*
95-Nov	*Anthology 1*
96-Mar	*Anthology 2*
96-Oct	*Anthology 3*
03-Nov	*Let It Be... Naked*
13-Nov	*On Air — Live at the BBC Volume 2*

APPENDIX II / RELEASES

John Lennon
Distilled Core Studio Releases
Strikethrough indicates re-released tracks, or those not counted for another reason.

Note: No distinction is made here between releases credited to "John Lennon," "Plastic Ono Band," "John Lennon and Yoko Ono," or other such variations.

ID	TITLE / Recorded	Producer	Studio(s)	RELEASE	NEW
L01	"Give Peace a Chance" / ~~"Remember Love"~~ Jun 69	Lennon/Ono	Perry (Montreal)	69-Jul	1
L02	"Cold Turkey" / ~~"Don't Worry Kyoko..."~~ Sep 69	Lennon/Ono	EMI	69-Oct	1
L03	"Instant Karma!" / ~~"Who Has Seen the Wind?"~~ Jan 70	Spector	EMI	70-Feb	1
L04	*John Lennon/Plastic Ono Band* Sep-Oct 70	Lennon/Ono/Spector	EMI, Ascot Sound	70-Dec	11
L05	"Power to the People" / ~~"Open Your Box"~~; ~~"Touch Me"~~ Jan-Feb 71	Lennon/Ono/Spector	Ascot Sound	71-Mar	1
L06	*Imagine* Feb-Jul 71	Lennon/Ono/Spector	EMI, Ascot +1	71-Sep	10
L07	"Happy Xmas (War Is Over)" / ~~"Listen, the Snow is Falling"~~ Oct 71	Lennon/Ono/Spector	Record Plant (NY)	71-Dec	1
L08	*Some Time in New York City* Feb-Mar 72	Lennon/Ono/Spector	Record Plant (NY)	72-Jun	12
L09	*Mind Games* Jul-Aug 73	Lennon	Record Plant (NY)	73-Oct	12
L10	*Walls and Bridges* Jul-Aug 74	Lennon	Record Plant (NY)	74-Sep	12
L11	*Rock 'n' Roll* Oct 73 - Oct 74	Lennon/Spector	A&M (LA), Record Plant (NY)	75-Feb	13
L12	~~"Stand by Me"~~ / "Move Over Ms. L" Jul-Oct 74	Lennon	Record Plant (NY)	75-Mar	1
L13	*Double Fantasy* Aug-Sep 80	Lennon/Ono/Douglas	Hit Factory (NY)	80-Nov	7
L14	*Milk and Honey* Aug-Sep 80	Lennon/Ono (Douglas)	Hit Factory (NY)	84-Jan	6

89

Selected items from John Lennon's Extended Releases
68-Nov *Unfinished Music No. 1: Two Virgins*
69-May *Unfinished Music No. 2: Life with the Lions*
69-Nov *Wedding Album*
69-Dec *Live Peace in Toronto 1969*
71-Jul "~~God Save Us~~" / "Do the Oz" (as "Elastic Oz Band")
75-Oct *Shaved Fish*
82-Nov *The John Lennon Collection*

APPENDIX II / RELEASES

Paul McCartney

Distilled Core Studio Releases (through 1983)
Strikethrough indicates re-released tracks, or those not counted for another reason.

Note: No distinction is made here between releases credited to "Paul McCartney," "Paul and Linda McCartney," "Wings," "Paul McCartney and Wings," or other such variations.

ID	TITLE / Recorded	Producer	Studio(s)	RELEASE	NEW
M01	*McCartney* Dec 69 - Feb 70	McCartney	Home, Morgan, EMI	70-Apr	13
M02	"Another Day" / "Oh Woman, Oh Why" Oct-Nov 70	McCartney	Columbia (NY)	71-Feb	2
M03	*Ram* Oct 70 - Mar 71	McCartney/McCartney	Columbia (NY) +2	71-May	12
M04	*Wild Life* Jul-Aug 71	McCartney/McCartney	EMI	71-Dec	10
M05	"Give Ireland Back to the Irish" / "Give Ireland... (Version)" Feb 72	McCartney/McCartney	EMI	72-Feb	2
M06	"Mary Had a Little Lamb" / "Little Woman Love" Nov 71 - Mar 72	McCartney/McCartney	Columbia (NY)	72-May	2
M07	"C Moon" & "Hi, Hi, Hi" Nov 72	McCartney	Various	72-Dec	2
M08	"~~My Love~~" / "The Mess (live)" Mar 72 - Aug 73	McCartney	A: EMI, B: The Hague	73-Mar	1
M09	*Red Rose Speedway* Mar-Dec 72	McCartney	Various (6)	73-Apr	12
M10	"Live and Let Die" / "I Lie Around" Oct 72	A: Martin; B: McCartney	A: AIR; B: Various	73-Jun	2
M11	"Helen Wheels" / "Country Dreamer" Aug-Sep 73	McCartney	EMI (Lagos), ARC (Lagos)	73-Oct	2
M12	*Band on the Run* Aug-Oct 73	McCartney	EMI (Lagos), ARC (Lagos) +2	73-Dec	9
M13	"~~Band on the Run~~" / "Zoo Gang" Apr 73	McCartney	EMI	74-Jun	1
M14	"Junior's Farm" / "Sally G" Jul 74	McCartney	Sound Shop (Nashville)	74-Oct	2
M15	*Venus and Mars* Nov 74 - Feb 75	McCartney	Various (3)	75-May	12
M16	*Wings at the Speed of Sound* Sep 75 - Feb 76	McCartney	EMI	76-Mar	9
M17	"Girls' School" & "Mull of Kintyre" Feb-Aug 77	McCartney	Rude, Ranachan; EMI	77-Nov	2

		Title	Dates	Producer	Studio	Released	Chart
M18		*London Town*	Feb 77 - Jan 78	McCartney	Various (3)	78-Mar	14
M19		"Goodnight Tonight" / "Daytime Nighttime Suffering"	Oct 78 - Jan 79	A/McCartney; B/McCartney/Thomas	Various (2)	79-Mar	2
M20		*Back to the Egg*	Jun 78 - Feb 79	McCartney/Thomas	Various (4)	79-May	13
M21		"Wonderful Christmastime" / "Rudolph the Red-Nosed Reggae"	Jun-Jul 79	McCartney	Various (2)	79-Nov	2
M22		~~"Coming Up"~~ / "Coming Up (Live)" & "Lunchbox/Odd Sox"	Jan 75 - Jul 79	McCartney	Various (3)	80-Apr	2
M23		*McCartney II*	Jun-Jul 79	McCartney	Home, Spirit of Ranachan	80-May	11
M24		~~"Waterfalls"~~ / "Check My Machine"	Jun-Jul 79	McCartney	Home, Spirit of Ranachan	80-Jun	1
M25		~~"Temporary Secretary"~~ / "Secret Friend"	Jun-Jul 79	McCartney	Home, Spirit of Ranachan	80-Sep	1
M26		~~"Ebony and Ivory"~~ / "Rainclouds"	Dec 80 - Dec 81	Martin	AIR (London), AIR (Montserrat)	82-Mar	1
M27		*Tug of War*	Dec 80 - Dec 81	Martin	AIR (London), AIR (Montserrat)	82-Apr	12
M28		~~"Take It Away"~~ / "I'll Give You a Ring"	Jan 74 - Dec 80	Martin	AIR (London)	82-Jun	1
M29		~~"Say Say Say"~~ / "Ode to a Koala Bear"	Dec 80 - Apr 82	Martin	AIR (London), Cherokee (LA)	83-Oct	1
M30		*Pipes of Peace*	Oct 80 - Jul 83	Martin	Various (7)	83-Oct	11

167

Selected items from Paul McCartney's Extended Releases

74-Oct "Walking in the Park with Eloise" / "Bridge Over the River Suite"
(as "The Country Hams")
76-Dec *Wings Over America*
77-Apr *Thrillington* (As "Percy 'Thrills' Thrillington")
77-May "Seaside Woman" / "B-side to Seaside"
(as "Suzy and the Red Stripes")
78-Nov *Wings Greatest*

APPENDIX II/RELEASES

George Harrison
Distilled Core Studio Releases (through 1983)
Strikethrough indicates re-released tracks, or those not counted for another reason.

ID	TITLE / Recorded	Producer	Studio(s)	RELEASE	NEW
H01	All Things Must Pass May-Oct 70	Harrison/Spector	EMI, Trident, Apple	70-Nov	23
H02	"Bangla Desh" / "Deep Blue" Jul 71	Harrison/Spector	Record Plant West (LA)	71-Jul	2
H03	"~~Give Me Love (Give Me Peace on Earth)~~" / "Miss O'Dell" Oct 72 - Mar 73	Harrison	Apple, FPSHOT	73-May	1
H04	Living in the Material World Oct 72 - Mar 73	Harrison (Spector)	EMI, Apple, FPSHOT	73-May	11
H05	"~~Dark Horse~~" / "I Don't Care Anymore" Oct 74	Harrison	A&M (LA)	74-Nov	1
H06	Dark Horse Nov 73 - Oct 74	Harrison	FPSHOT, A&M (LA)	74-Dec	9
H07	Extra Texture (Read All About It) Aug 74 - Jun 75	Harrison	EMI, FPSHOT, A&M (LA)	75-Sep	10
H08	Thirty Three & 1/3 May-Sep 76	Harrison/Scott	FPSHOT	76-Nov	10
H09	George Harrison Mar-Nov 78	Harrison/Titelman	FPSHOT, AIR	79-Feb	10
H10	Somewhere in England Mar 80 - Feb 81	Harrison/Cooper	FPSHOT	81-Jun	10
H11	Gone Troppo May-Aug 82	Harrison/Cooper/McDonald	FPSHOT	82-Nov	10
					97

Selected items from George Harrison's Extended Releases

68-Nov   *Wonderwall Music*
69-May   *Electronic Sound*
71-Dec   *The Concert for Bangladesh*
76-Nov   *The Best of George Harrison*

Ringo Starr

Distilled Core Studio Releases (through 1983)
Strikethrough indicates re-released tracks, or those not counted for another reason.

ID	TITLE / Recorded	Producer	Studio(s)	RELEASE	NEW
S01	*Sentimental Journey* Oct 69 - Mar 70	Martin	Various (7)	70-Mar	12
S02	*Beaucoups of Blues* Jun 70	Drake	Music City (Nashville)	70-Sep	12
S03	"~~Beaucoups of Blues~~" / "Coochy Coochy" Jun 70	Drake	Music City (Nashville)	70-Oct	1
S04	"It Don't Come Easy" / "Early 1970" Mar-Oct 70 — A: Harrison, B: Starr		Trident, EMI	71-Apr	2
S05	"Back Off Boogaloo" / "Blindman" Aug-Sep 71 — A: Harrison, B: Starr/Voorman		Apple	72-Mar	2
S06	"~~Photograph~~" / "Down and Out" Oct 72 - Jul 73	Harrison/Perry	B: Apple or FPSHOT	73-Sep	1
S07	*Ringo* Mar-Jul 73	Perry	Various (7)	73-Nov	10
S08	*Goodnight Vienna* Aug 74	Perry	Sunset (LA), Workshop (LA)	74-Nov	11
S09	*Ringo's Rotogravure* Apr-Jul 76	Mardin	Cherokee (LA), Atlantic (NY)	76-Sep	11
S10	"~~Wings~~" / "Just a Dream" Feb-Jun 77	Mardin	Atlantic (LA)	77-Aug	1
S11	*Ringo the 4th* Feb-Jun 77	Mardin	Cherokee (LA), Atlantic (NY)	77-Sep	10
S12	*Bad Boy* Nov 77	Poncia	Elite (Bahamas) +1	78-Apr	10
S13	*Stop and Smell the Roses* Jul 80 - Feb 81	Various (6)	Various (Undetermined)	81-Oct	10
S14	*Old Wave* Feb-Jul 82	Ballard/Walsh	Startling +1	83-Jun	10

103

Selected items from Ringo Starr's Extended Releases

71-Dec *The Concert for Bangladesh*
75-Nov *Blast from Your Past*
77-Dec *Scouse the Mouse*

APPENDIX II / RELEASES

Solo Release Summary

Distilled Core Studio Releases (through 1984)
Strikethrough indicates re-released tracks, or those not counted for another reason.

REL	ID	TITLE
69-Jul	L01	"Give Peace a Chance" / ~~"Remember Love"~~
69-Oct	L02	"Cold Turkey" / ~~"Don't Worry Kyoko…"~~
70-Feb	L03	"Instant Karma!" / ~~"Who Has Seen the Wind?"~~
70-Mar	S01	*Sentimental Journey*
70-Apr	M01	*McCartney*
70-Sep	S02	*Beaucoups of Blues*
70-Oct	S03	~~"Beaucoups of Blues"~~ / "Coochy Coochy"
70-Nov	H01	*All Things Must Pass*
70-Dec	L04	*John Lennon/Plastic Ono Band*
71-Feb	M02	"Another Day" / "Oh Woman, Oh Why"
71-Mar	L05	"Power to the People" / ~~"Open Your Box"; "Touch Me"~~
71-Apr	S04	"It Don't Come Easy" / "Early 1970"
71-May	M03	*Ram*
71-Jul	H02	"Bangla Desh" / "Deep Blue"
71-Sep	L06	*Imagine*
71-Dec	L07	"Happy Xmas (War Is Over)" / ~~"Listen, the Snow is Falling"~~
71-Dec	M04	*Wild Life*
72-Feb	M05	"Give Ireland Back to the Irish" / "Give Ireland… (Version)"
72-Mar	S05	"Back Off Boogaloo" / "Blindman"
72-May	M06	"Mary Had a Little Lamb" / "Little Woman Love"
72-Jun	L08	*Some Time in New York City*
72-Dec	M07	"C Moon" & "Hi, Hi, Hi"
73-Mar	M08	~~"My Love"~~ / "The Mess (live)"
73-Apr	M09	*Red Rose Speedway*
73-May	H03	~~"Give Me Love (Give Me Peace on Earth)"~~ / "Miss O'Dell"
73-May	H04	*Living in the Material World*
73-Jun	M10	"Live and Let Die" / "I Lie Around"
73-Sep	S06	~~"Photograph"~~ / "Down and Out"
73-Oct	M11	"Helen Wheels" / "Country Dreamer"
73-Oct	L09	*Mind Games*
73-Nov	S07	*Ringo*
73-Dec	M12	*Band on the Run*

74-Jun	M13	~~"Band on the Run"~~ / "Zoo Gang"
74-Sep	L10	*Walls and Bridges*
74-Oct	M14	"Junior's Farm" / "Sally G"
74-Nov	S08	*Goodnight Vienna*
74-Nov	H05	~~"Dark Horse"~~ / "I Don't Care Anymore"
74-Dec	H06	*Dark Horse*
75-Feb	L11	*Rock 'n' Roll*
75-Mar	L12	~~"Stand by Me"~~ / "Move Over Ms. L"
75-May	M15	*Venus and Mars*
75-Sep	H07	*Extra Texture (Read All About It)*
76-Mar	M16	*Wings at the Speed of Sound*
76-Sep	S09	*Ringo's Rotogravure*
76-Nov	H08	*Thirty Three & 1/3*
77-Aug	S10	~~"Wings"~~ / "Just a Dream"
77-Sep	S11	*Ringo the 4th*
77-Nov	M17	"Girls' School" & "Mull of Kintyre"
78-Mar	M18	*London Town*
78-Apr	S12	*Bad Boy*
79-Feb	H09	*George Harrison*
79-Mar	M19	"Goodnight Tonight" / "Daytime Nighttime Suffering"
79-May	M20	*Back to the Egg*
79-Nov	M21	"Wonderful Christmastime" / "Rudolph the Red-Nosed Reggae"
80-Apr	M22	~~"Coming Up"~~ / "Coming Up (Live at Glasgow)" & "Lunchbox/Odd Sox"
80-May	M23	*McCartney II*
80-Jun	M24	~~"Waterfalls"~~ / "Check My Machine"
80-Sep	M25	~~"Temporary Secretary"~~ / "Secret Friend"
80-Nov	L13	*Double Fantasy*
81-Jun	H10	*Somewhere in England*
81-Oct	S13	*Stop and Smell the Roses*
82-Mar	M26	~~"Ebony and Ivory"~~ / "Rainclouds"
82-Apr	M27	*Tug of War*
82-Jun	M28	~~"Take It Away"~~ / "I'll Give You a Ring"
82-Nov	H11	*Gone Troppo*
83-Jun	S14	*Old Wave*
83-Oct	M29	~~"Say Say Say"~~ / "Ode to a Koala Bear"
83-Oct	M30	*Pipes of Peace*
84-Jan	L14	*Milk and Honey*

Appendix III
Catalog of Solo Recordings
1969-1982

This section contains an alphabetical listing of all recordings by the former Beatles which are relevant to this project. Since relevance is subjective, the first thing to note is that this is not, and does not attempt to be, a comprehensive list of either songs written or recordings made.

It does include all tracks from official, mainstream commercial releases under the artist's name from the start of the solo era in June 1969 ("Give Peace a Chance") until the last non-archival release by John Lennon in January 1984 (*Milk and Honey*). Effectively, this means only recordings through the end of 1982, since 1983 saw only the polishing of a few McCartney tracks for *Pipes of Peace*, and sessions for music which would not be released until later. For more information on which releases are included and why, see Appendix II, *Distilled Core Studio Releases*.

Beyond the official releases, this list also contains selected tracks which went unreleased originally, but were subsequently included as bonus tracks on archival rereleases. Selected tracks from the artist's extended catalog are also included if they are deemed to contain material which might have been considered for a Beatles project. Similarly, selected unreleased tracks are included based on timing, quality, and releasability. A small set of songs, mostly by McCartney, are listed which were officially released outside of the given timeframe despite being recorded within it (such as "My Carnival"). In all of these cases, to be included, the track had to be a studio recording of a song which did not already appear on the list.

Demo recordings are included only when they are of significant songs not otherwise on the list, and they might have been developed by the group or solo artist if the Beatles had still been releasing together. This facilitates the inclusion of Harrison's voluminous *All Things Must Pass* demos, and the demos made by Lennon during his Dakota Days. With McCartney, there is often a fine line between a demo and a releasable track. In general, his "demos" are included only if they were of completed songs that were not officially recorded, and which might have been considered for development under slightly altered circumstances.

Songswhich were neither written nor sung by a former Beatle are not included, even if they appeared on an official release. Examples of this class would be tracks by Ono which Lennon did not write, co-write, or sing lead vocal on — even if they appear on an album under his name ("Kiss, Kiss, Kiss"). Similarly, tracks written and sung by other members of Wings are not included since they would have had no relevance to a Beatles project ("Again and Again and Again"). If a former Beatle is singing lead on a song he did not write, which describes large portions of Ringo's catalog, that would still have been considered and is included below. Conversely, if he *wrote* the song but did not sing lead on it ("Must Do Something About It"), it is also included — provided it was on a release under his name. In these cases we will presume that, had there been a Beatles project, he might very well have recorded the vocal himself. Songs which were truly given away ("Let's Love" and "God Save Us") are included on a selected basis, and generally only if there is a suitable demo available in the artist's voice for consideration.

The list does not include music which would have had no chance of commercial release. This eliminates all tracks from John and George's early experimental releases. The list also excludes guest appearances, such as Starr's performances on the London Symphony Recording of *Tommy*, or McCartney's contribution to Michael Jackson's *Thriller*.

Each listing is accompanied by the songwriter's name, a reference to the official release, if any, and the availability date of the song/track. These dates are gleaned from a wide variety of sources and attempt to represent the earliest that the song might have been available for consideration.[1] They must be regarded as approximate dates only, even in cases when specific dates are thought to be well known. Approximations work well enough for most parts of this project, and in truth, much conflicting information has been published about many tracks. It can be difficult to know what to believe. Thus, special attention was paid only in cases where the suggested date fell near the cutoff between two different rescue projects. Even there, some guesswork was necessary from time to time.

Each listing also includes a one-line thumbnail review, written from the perspective of our mythical Assembler. These reviews only attempt to assess the suitability of the track for inclusion on a group project, had there been one — in other words, to determine the *Beatle Quality* of the song/track. See chapter 1, *Circles*, for more information on BQ.

A searchable and sortable version of the data is available at:

SaveTheBeatles.com

---

[1] The ultimate source has to be *Eight Arms To Hold You: The Solo Beatles Compendium* by Chip Madinger and Mark Easter, which is indeed exhaustive — but sometimes also *exhausting*. The book, though exceptional, cannot penetrate entirely into the recesses of home studio recording, and sometimes must resort to approximations or omissions of dates. Still, the recordings catalogs presented here use Maginder and Easter's documentation to settle matters which cannot be otherwise settled.

APPENDIX III / SOLO RECORDINGS

Catalog of Solo Recordings
1969-1982

Key

(1)	(2)	Song Title (Songwriter)	ID, Availability Date
		(3) (4) Thumbnail review	

(1) Beatle (2) Related Release (3) BQ (Beatle Quality) (4) BQ concerns
Songs are listed alphabetically by title

(Forgive Me) My Little Flower Princess (Lennon) — L14-09, 80-Nov
✓ A good idea not quite formed, displays again JL's wide musical range.

(It's All Down to) Goodnight Vienna (Lennon) — S08-01, 74-Aug
✓ Just the right amount of quirky, this feels like a true "Ringo" song deep down inside.

(Just Like) Starting Over (Lennon) — L13-01, 80-Sep
✓ Straight confection, but just enough auto-bio to be true to Lennon. Simple, but sweet.

#9 Dream (Lennon) — L10-07, 74-Aug
✓ A late masterwork, with distinctive music, lyrics, feel. Descended from psychedelia, matured.

$15 Draw (Pickard) — S02-07, 70-Jun
⊘ (Style/Quality) Story song. Ringo's a guitar player now? Vocal deep in reverb. Cheap product.

1882 (McCartney) — M09, 70-Dec
≈ (Style) Long, elaborate, dark story song. Equally fascinating and tedious. Studio version best.

3 Legs (McCartney) — M03-02, 70-Oct
⊘ (Content) Sending a message, music and lyrics are pointed, good.

4th of July (McCartney/McCartney) — M, 73-Mar
⊘ (Quality) Forced writing. Vaguely incoherent lyric. Chord progression and melody sound tortured.

Across the River (Lennon) — L, 80-Nov
⊘ (Demo) Fast country, but has the feeling of cleaning the musical house.

African Yeah Yeah (McCartney/McCartney) — M04, 71-Aug
⊘ (Filler) Weed-fueled nonsense. Is this fun? You decide.

After the Ball / Million Miles (McCartney) — M20-10, 78-Sep
✓ Pure craftsmanship. We could ask why, but there is no why. Just two notions made into songs.

Ain't That a Shame (Domino/Bartholomew) — L11-05, 74-Oct
⊘ (Style/Content) Very heavy, busy arrangement. Sounds like work, not fun.

Aisumasen (I'm Sorry) (Lennon) — L09-03, 73-Aug
⊘ (Quality) Impossibly boring.

Alibi (Starkey/Walsh) — S14-03, 82-Jul
⊘ (Style/Quality) Not so much a song as a bunch of chords strung together. Just terrible.

All by Myself (Starkey/Poncia) — S08-06, 74-Aug
⊘ (Quality) Feels pointless, like product. Somebody else's record with RS vocal.

All Things Must Pass (Harrison) — H01-14, 70-Oct
✓ Sloppy recording of a great song. The feel sells it, as did the news around it.

All Those Years Ago (Harrison) — H10-04, 81-Feb
✓ Somewhat jaunty for its subject matter, but probably not hit material without the subtext.

All You Horse Riders / Blue Sway (McCartney) — M23, 79-Jul
⊘ (Filler) Pt 1: Thin 12-bar synths. Pt 2: Not quite electronica. Not very interesting. What vaults are for.

Save the Beatles!

Angel Baby (Hamlin) — L11, 73-Dec
⊘ (Style/Content) Pure wall of sound, Lennon's vocal pretty buried. Just spins aimlessly until it ends.

Angela (Lennon/Ono) — L08-09, 72-Mar
⊘ (Quality) Another duet that really shows how poorly these voices go together.

Another Day (McCartney/McCartney) — M02-01, 70-Oct
✓ One of Paul's "lonely" characters. Slight but catchy. Successful pop.

Answer's at the End, The (Harrison) — H07-02, 75-Apr
⊘ (Quality) Ponderous, heavy, sluggish. Loops around without shape.

Apple Scruffs (Harrison) — H01-11, 70-Oct
⊘ (Quality) Respectful? Possibly. Its simplicity is both vice and virtue. What's hidden matters.

Arrow Through Me (McCartney) — M20-07, 78-Jul
✓ One of a kind. Sophisticated easy listening. Smoothness obscures its complexity.

Art of Dying (Harrison) — H01-16, 70-Oct
✓ Great riff, and part of the real power of this era. Confident and inspired writing.

As Far as We Can Go (Ballard) — S14-08, 82-Jul
⊘ (Style/Quality) A clunky piano ballad. Poor song. Incredibly banal.

Attention (McCartney) — S13-04, 80-Jul
≈ (Quality) Not Macca's best song, but right for Ringo. Very happy-sounding record.

Attica State (Lennon/Ono) — L08-03, 72-Mar
⊘ (Quality) Heartfelt garbage. Song and track are terrible.

Aü (live) (Lennon/Ono) — L08-14, 71-Jun
⊘ (Filler) Raise your hand if you listened to this all the way through at least once... Liar!

Average Person (McCartney) — M30-08, 81-Mar
⊘ (Quality) Unwelcome echoes of "Penny Lane," lousy by comparison. Mostly fluff.

Awaiting on You All (Harrison) — H01-13, 70-Oct
⊘ (Content) Really joy-filled track. Another statement of what GH has in the tank — i.e. a lot.

B-Side to Seaside (McCartney) — M, 77-Mar
⊘ (Quality) Total throwaway. Clunky, pointless, built from typical Macca "links."

Baby Don't Run Away (Harrison) — H11-08, 82-Aug
⊘ (Quality) Unattractive vocal arrangement and too many vocoders/synths. Slow, boxy sound.

Baby Face (Akst/Davis) — M15, 74-Aug
⊘ (Filler) More fun in New Orleans, but just a jot. Best left on a private reel.

Baby's Request (McCartney) — M20-14, 78-Nov
✓ Underappreciated, very fine song.

Back Off Boogaloo (Starkey) — S05-01, 71-Sep
≈ (Content) A great song. The recording is likewise fantastic, just the right level of density.

Back Off Boogaloo (Starkey) — S13-10, 80-Dec
⊘ (Filler) Imaginative remake of one of Ringo's best songs. Still, why?

Back Seat of My Car, The (McCartney) — M03-12, 71-Jan
✓ Structured and significant, sounds like act two of a movie. Very good.

Backwards Traveller (McCartney) — M18-04, 77-Dec
✓ More coded messages, but not quite a complete song. Potential missed.

Bad Boy (Armstrong/Long) — S12-02, 77-Nov
⊘ (Style/Quality) Oh, boy-oy-oy-oy-oy. A doo-wop song, and a very unpleasant one at that.

Ballad of Sir Frankie Crisp (Let It Roll) (Harrison) — H01-12, 70-Oct
⊘ (Quality) Good idea for a song, but not fully realized. Structural problems get in the way.

Ballroom Dancing (McCartney) — M27-06, 81-Dec
✓ A bigger track than it has any right to be. The very slight idea is gussied up nicely.

Baltimore Oriole (Carmichael) — H10-05, 80-Sep
⊘ (Filler) Nice enough, but GH doesn't offer the song much as a stylist. It just pads along. A non-event.

Appendix III / Solo Recordings

Band on the Run (McCartney/McCartney) — M12-01, 73-Oct
✓ Another three-parter. Great imaginary landscape. Sounds wide and worthy.

Bangla Desh (Harrison) — H02-01, 71-Jul
⊘ (Quality) Unfortunately a truly lousy song, with its heart in the right place.

Be Here Now (Harrison) — H04-08, 73-Mar
✓ A gem. Gentle, introspective, calm, pointed, beautiful.

Be My Baby (Barry/Greenwich/Spector) — L11, 73-Dec
⊘ (Style/Content) Unlike others in the collection in that it at least has shape. JL vocal is compromised.

Be My Baby (Walsh) — S14-04, 82-Jul
⊘ (Style/Quality) More interesting than most. Verse makes a nice setup. Chorus can't carry it through.

Be What You See (Link) (McCartney) — M27-10, 81-Dec
≈ (Filler) Fills a hole, and that's all it's supposed to do.

Be-Bop-A-Lula (Davis/Vincent) — L11-01, 74-Oct
⊘ (Style/Content) Among the better *RnR* tracks, but still without much shape. JL vocal is nothing special.

Beaucoups of Blues (Rabin) — S02-01, 70-Jun
⊘ (Style/Quality) Straining at the top of his range, uncharacteristic, BVs and dobro are hardcore country.

Beautiful Boy (Darling Boy) (Lennon) — L13-07, 80-Sep
✓ A gem. Grown-up ideas couched as lullaby. A sentimental masterwork.

Beautiful Girl (Harrison) — H08-03, 76-Sep
✓ GH sounds relaxed, confident. Very fine song, and sweet, warm record.

Beef Jerky (Lennon) — L10-10, 74-Aug
⊘ (Filler) Fun riff, and nice quote of Macca. Lots of details. Great track, but has no place on an album.

Behind That Locked Door (Harrison) — H01-07, 70-Oct
✓ Country, but in a sweet way. Nice lazy feel has a warmth in its lyric and arrangement.

Best Friend (McCartney) — M09, 72-Aug
⊘ (Quality) Somewhat generic blues. Skates along without much character or shape. A throwback.

Beware My Love (McCartney/McCartney) — M16-04, 76-Feb
≈ (Quality) Catchy but lightweight. It fills a spot, but doesn't stick in the mind.

Beware of Darkness (Harrison) — H01-10, 70-Oct
⊘ (Quality) Unfortunately eery in sound and structure. This is simply a misfire.

Big Barn Bed (McCartney/McCartney) — M09-01, 71-Mar
✓ Catchy, uptempo pop. Builds nicely, but settles into annoying repetition.

Bip Bop (McCartney/McCartney) — M04-02, 71-Aug
⊘ (Quality) A hopelessly cutesy "baby" song.

Bip Bop (Link) (McCartney/McCartney) — M04-07, 71-Aug
⊘ (Filler) Unnecessary, but harmless — even though it "reprises" a lousy song.

Bit More of You, A (Harrison) — H07-06, 75-May
⊘ (Filler) Embarrassing filler. Emphasizes how little of value there is here.

Blackpool (McCartney) — M03, 71-Aug
≈ (Filler/Quality) Blues, with a back-to-roots feel, but the lyric is pretty lousy.

Bless You (Lennon) — L10-05, 74-Aug
✓ Beautiful writing. Soft emotions. Nothing else like it in JL's catalog. Another late masterwork.

Blindman (Starkey) — S05-02, 71-Aug
≈ (Quality) A true oddity, but very Ringo. The record really captures his unique quality. A quirky gem.

Blood from a Clone (Harrison) — H10-01, 81-Feb
⊘ (Quality) Odd combination of instruments, quirky beat, pointed lyrics, all add up to not much.

Blow Away (Harrison) — H09-05, 78-Nov
✓ As good as GH gets. Maybe the best pure pop song he ever wrote. Fantastic record.

Blue Sway (McCartney) — M23, 79-Jul
⊘ (Filler) Nice groove, but that's all.

SAVE THE BEATLES!

Blue, Turning Grey Over You (Razaf/Waller) — S01-07, 70-Feb
○ (Style) Big band really swings. RS double-tracked vocal can't keep up. Not right for him.

Bluebird (McCartney/McCartney) — M12-03, 73-Oct
✓ Non-silly love song. Mysterious and well-formed. Perfect instrumentation.

Bogey Music (McCartney) — M23-09, 79-Jul
○ (Style) A complete throwaway with just enough style to make it (slightly) interesting.

Bogey Wobble (McCartney) — M23, 79-Jul
○ (Filler) Annoying.

Boil Crisis (McCartney) — M18, 77-Oct
○ (Quality) Not sure what Macca was thinking. Maybe trying to be someone else?

Bony Moronie (Williams) — L11-11, 74-Oct
○ (Style/Content) Chunky beat. Way overdone. Never quite gets off the ground. Vocal sounds strained.

Borrowed Time (Lennon) — L14-07, 80-Nov
✓ The pastiche is unfortunate given the weight of the lyric. Not quite great.

Brandy (Jefferson/Simmons) — S13, 81-Feb
○ (Quality) Story song, but a very boring story. Routine production. Lousy vocal.

Bridge on the River Suite (McCartney/McCartney) — M, 72-Oct
○ (Filler) Soundtrack-like, this sounds mostly like the lost B-side of "Live and Let Die"

Bring It on Home to Me/Send Me Some Lovin' (Cooke/Marascalco/Price) — L11-10, 74-Oct
○ (Style/Content) Weird reading, with stretched out verses. Like the rest, too much going on. Hiccups.

Bring on the Lucie (Freda Peeple) (Lennon) — L09-05, 73-Aug
≈ (Content) Simple, almost simplistic. Passing lyric issues, but overall positive vibe.

Broadcast, The (McCartney) — M20-12, 79-Feb
≈ (Filler) Perhaps a little overly serious for the album, but a good use of a nice musical idea.

Bye Bye Blackbird (Dixon/Henderson) — S01-04, 70-Mar
○ (Quality/Style) Back porch banjo. Awkward segue to big band. RS is probably dancing. Also awkward.

Bye Bye, Love (Bryant/Bryant/Harrison) — H06-04, 74-Oct
○ (Filler) Halting, shrill, desolate deconstruction and rewrite. Painful.

C Moon (McCartney/McCartney) — M07-01, 72-Nov
≈ (Quality) Likable enough, but slight in the extreme.

Cafe on the Left Bank (McCartney) — M18-02, 77-Nov
✓ Another terrific song which evokes the early days while not sounding passé.

Cage (McCartney) — M20, 78-Sep
✓ Wrong for the album, but still has merit. Structured, catchy, quirky. Weird mash-up of ideas.

Call Me (Starkey) — S08-07, 74-Aug
○ (Quality) Low quality song. Like "Don't Pass Me By," but with generic, boring session backing.

Call Me Back Again (McCartney/McCartney) — M15-10, 75-Feb
✓ Overdone, but serves the musical sequence as a setup for the hit.

Can She Do It Like She Dances (Duboff/Robinson) — S11-06, 77-Jun
○ (Quality) "Honky-tonk-ish" boom-chicka meets disco. Just a terrible song/record.

Can't Stop Thinking About You (Harrison) — H07-07, 75-Jun
○ (Quality) A germ of a good idea, but doesn't work. Feels forced, unnatural.

Check My Machine (McCartney) — M24-02, 79-Jul
○ (Filler) Annoying, but perfect for a B-side. Not worth a second listen, and barely a first.

Children Children (McCartney/Laine) — M18-06, 77-Mar
○ (Quality) Written for children, this might work in another context. Here it tanks.

Christian Bop (McCartney) — M, 82-Jan
○ (Filler) A rare extended link that appears to have not been a very good idea in the first place.

Circles (Harrison) — H11-10, 82-Aug
≈ (Content) Pre-maturity songwriting. Still clunky even with a smoother arrangement. Weepy, overlong.

APPENDIX III / SOLO RECORDINGS

Cleanup Time (Lennon) — L13-03, 80-Sep
✓ Feels more like dusting off the chops than using them. Still, catchy and well-formed.

Cold Turkey (Lennon) — L02-01, 69-Sep
✓ (Early) Chilling and powerful, this is an overlooked masterwork. One of JL's best ever.

Cold Turkey (live) (Lennon) — L08-10, 69-Dec
⊘ (Filler) Lousy recording of a lousy, sluggish, overlong performance. Mushy jam.

Coming Up (McCartney) — M23-01, 79-Jul
✓ Infectious, if pretty silly. Macca does nicely all on his ownsome.

Coming Up (Live at Glasgow) (McCartney) — M22-02, 79-Dec
⊘ (Filler) Live performance adds nothing, and reveals the song to be as lightweight as imagined.

Coochy-Coochy (Starkey) — S03-02, 70-Jun
✓ A one-chord jam, but sounds like they were having fun. It's Ringo-quirky in many ways.

Cook of the House (McCartney/McCartney) — M16-07, 76-Feb
⊘ (Quality) Crummy song, and no sound effects can save it.

Cookin' (In the Kitchen of Love) (Lennon) — S09-06, 76-Jun
✓ Not JL's best, but authentic, unlike everything else here. A flicker of Beatle magic.

Cosmic Empire (Harrison) — H01, 70-May
≈ (Demo) A great, catchy, upbeat, lost song. Would definitely be considered if completed.

Country Dreamer (McCartney/McCartney) — M11-02, 72-Sep
⊘ (Style/Quality) Lazy writing. Clichéd words and music. Nice steel playing, but very misplaced.

Crackerbox Palace (Harrison) — H08-09, 76-Sep
✓ Uptempo, happy sound. Very playful, and gently meaningful.

Crippled Inside (Lennon) — L06-02, 71-Jul
≈ (Quality/Content) Clichéd and flip, this is a blunt JL working in tired folk forms.

Crossroads Theme (Hatch) — M15-13, 75-Feb
≈ (Content) This clears some of the sweetness of the ending. The band is obviously good.

Cryin' (Starkey/Poncia) — S09-04, 76-Jul
⊘ (Style/Quality) Quirky beat adds/drops cannot disguise clichéd tripe. Also on the wrong album.

Cuff Link (McCartney) — M18-05, 77-Dec
⊘ (Filler) Bad instrumental. Kills the album dead.

Dark Horse (Harrison) — H06-07, 74-Oct
⊘ (Quality) Forced song, with annoying "gallop." Painful all around.

Dark Sweet Lady (Harrison) — H09-07, 78-Nov
✓ GH shows mature songwriting chops. This is well-conceived and perfectly executed.

Darkroom (McCartney) — M23-10, 79-Jul
≈ (Quality) So fluffy. So silly. So meaningless. Not as annoying as others, but still annoying.

Day the World Gets 'Round, The (Harrison) — H04-10, 73-Mar
≈ (Content/Quality) Not a bad idea, but something missing. Preachy.

Daytime Nighttime Suffering (McCartney) — M19-02, 79-Feb
✓ A B-side that belonged on the album. This is good writing.

Dead Giveaway (Starkey/Wood) — S13-06, 81-Feb
⊘ (Style/Quality) Song is just too boring. High in RS's vocal range, and he sounds strained.

Dear Boy (McCartney/McCartney) — M03-04, 71-Mar
⊘ (Content) Ambitious, and well-formed. Vocal work is all excellent.

Dear Friend (McCartney/McCartney) — M04-09, 71-Aug
⊘ (Content/Quality) Weepy. Repetitive. Needs a good edit. Should have been a B-side.

Dear John (Lennon) — L, 80-Nov
≈ (Demo) Solid idea, musically and lyrically. One to really wish could have been finished.

Dear One (Harrison) — H08-02, 76-Sep
✓ Boldly drumless and smooth as silk. Beatle-y arrangement exudes health and warmth.

Dear Yoko (Lennon) — L13-12, 80-Sep
⊘ (Content) Good vibe, but simplistic song. Band is tight, but ultimately the whole thing is sort of cringey.

Deep Blue (Harrison) — H02-02, 71-Jul
✓ GH mourns his mother with grace and dignity. A hidden gem.

Dehradun (Harrison) — H01, 70-May
✓ Anthemic in feel, it would have been great to hear this fully realized.

Deliver Your Children (McCartney/Laine) — M18-11, 77-Nov
⊘ (Quality) A morality tale that is way out of place. Well-intentioned, but simplistic and dumb.

Devil Woman (Starkey/Poncia) — S07-09, 73-Jul
✓ Well suited to Ringo's style, voice, and drumming. Just having a fun time.

Did We Meet Somewhere Before (McCartney) — M18, 78-Mar
⊘ (Quality/Style) Music hall song, but recording mixes styles uncomfortably. Not a good song. Horse hooves.

Ding Dong, Ding Dong (Harrison) — H06-06, 74-Oct
⊘ (Content/Quality) Clunky chord progression and rhythms. Not a good song.

Do the Oz (Lennon/Ono) — L, 71-May
⊘ (Filler) Serviceable instrumental, but Yoko's vocals will drive away most ears.

Do You Wanna Dance? (Freeman) — L11-06, 74-Oct
⊘ (Style/Content) Another vocal shouted over a too-busy, yet somehow shapeless, arrangement

Don't Cry Baby (McCartney) — M01, 70-Jan
⊘ (Filler) Instrumental of "Oo You"

Don't Let It Bring You Down (McCartney/Laine) — M18-13, 77-Nov
✓ A nice thought, and well-formed, this succeeds where much of the album fails.

Don't Let Me Wait Too Long (Harrison) — H04-04, 73-Mar
✓ Great record. Should have been a single. One idea short of classic.

Don't You Wanna Dance (McCartney) — M18, 76-Jul
⊘ (Unfinished) Just a jot, this falls into "link" territory.

Dose of Rock 'n' Roll, A (Groszman) — S09-01, 76-Jul
✓ Happy, pseudo-throwback, straight pop. Catchy, if a little clichéd, rewrite of "Hey! Baby."

Down and Out (Starkey) — S06-02, 72-Nov
✓ Great song, wasted on a B-side. GH guitar is most welcome. Nice production, too.

Down to the River (Harrison) — H01, 70-Jun
⊘ (Quality) Blues just for fun — and it is fun. No doubt meant for a private reel, and best left there.

Dream (Mercer) — S01-09, 70-Feb
✓ A standard that actually fits Ringo's voice and emotional range, in a very nice arrangement.

Dream Away (Harrison) — H11-09, 82-Aug
✓ Awesome Lennon-esque nonsense chorus. Positive, jaunty and infectious. A complete success.

Dress Me Up as a Robber (McCartney) — M27-11, 81-Mar
✓ Great riff, slick guitars, and a cool vocal performance. Unique in the Macca catalog.

Drowning in the Sea of Love (Gamble/Huff) — S11-01, 77-Jun
⊘ (Style) Disco hell. Even a spirited vocal (mixed way back) cannot redeem this.

Drumming is My Madness (Nilsson) — S13-03, 80-Nov
⊘ (Quality) Sort of sleepy for such a big statement. Ultimately, a lousy song.

Early 1970 (Starkey) — S04-02, 70-Oct
≈ (Content/Quality) Sweet sentiments, and simple. Hopeful. But not "Beatle quality" writing.

Easy for Me (Nilsson) — S08-10, 74-Aug
✓ A fine song and nice choice for RS. Vocal wavers, but somehow works.

Eat at Home (McCartney/McCartney) — M03-09, 70-Oct
≈ (Content) Inoffensive, but borders on filler. Built on simple pleasures, but not one.

Ebony and Ivory (McCartney) — M27-12, 81-Mar
⊘ (Content) Really unfortunate. Simplistic, and instantly dated. Embarrassing for all involved.

Appendix III / Solo Recordings

Every Night (McCartney) — M01-04, 70-Feb
✓ An instant classic. Great musical idea, and nice lyric.

Everybody, Nobody (Harrison) — H01, 70-May
≈ (Demo) Ballad with great potential, might be used as is.

Everybody's in a Hurry But Me (Starkey/Walsh/Entwistle/Clapton/Stainton) — S14-09, 82-Jul
○ (Filler) Rockabilly wanna be. Workout for everybody but RS, who plays the same beat all the way.

Famous Groupies (McCartney) — M18-10, 77-Nov
○ (Quality) Not exactly a bad idea, but the music hall approach really grates.

Far East Man (Harrison/Wood) — H06-08, 74-Jun
✓ Very cool, comfortable sound. Nice saxes. Best vocal on the album.

Faster (Harrison) — H09-06, 78-Nov
✓ Shades of "Mo." Not entirely engaging to non-car people, but filled with happy enthusiasm.

Fastest Growing Heartache in the West (Kingston/Dycus) — S02-03, 70-Jun
○ (Style/Quality) Fiddle and steel, but set very high for Ringo's voice.

Flying Hour (Harrison) — H10, 80-Sep
✓ Hardly a classic, but competent and likeable enough. Clear of GH's worst instincts.

Free as a Bird (Lennon) — L, 77-Sep
✓ JL's ode to being out of contract is built on melancholy. The Threetles made it pop.

Front Parlour (McCartney) — M23-06, 79-Jul
○ (Filler) Of a piece with all of the other instrumentals on this project. Interchangeably silly.

Frozen Jap (McCartney) — M23-08, 79-Jul
○ (Filler) Four-in-the-bar, with a more interesting melody than most of these sketches. Still disposable.

Gave It All Up (Gallagher/Lyle) — S11-04, 77-Jun
○ (Quality) Weepy, lousy story song, bad for Ringo. Contrived product.

Get It (McCartney) — M27-09, 81-Mar
✓ Macca can make any kind of record you can imagine. Proved again here. Perkins sounds great.

Get on the Right Thing (McCartney/McCartney) — M09-03, 70-Oct
✓ Nice structured pop, but labored. Takes a long time to get to not much point.

Getting Closer (McCartney) — M20-02, 78-Nov
✓ Great, late rocker. Doesn't try to hard, just rocks the way Paul should at that point.

Gimme Some Truth (Lennon) — L06-06, 71-Jul
✓ A successful blend of anger and cleverness.

Girlfriend (McCartney) — M18-07, 77-Dec
○ (Quality) Way too cute, without much to redeem it. Automatic writing.

Girls' School (McCartney) — M17-01, 77-Aug
✓ Great rocker, with weird (non-PC) lyrics. But overshadowed on this 45.

Give Ireland Back to the Irish (McCartney/McCartney) — M05-01, 72-Feb
○ (Content/Quality) Politics aside, this is a terrible record.

Give Ireland Back to the Irish (Version) (McCartney/McCartney) — M05-02, 72-Feb
○ (Filler) The instrumental version is better because no bad lyrics.

Give Me Love (Give Me Peace on Earth) (Harrison) — H04-01, 73-Mar
✓ A plaintive plea, but hopeful. Catchy and welcoming.

Give Peace a Chance (Lennon/McCartney) — L01-01, 69-Jun
≈ (Early) A catchy jot, using repetition as its main tool. The universal central thought saves it.

God (Lennon) — L04-10, 70-Oct
≈ (Content) Big ideas, big emotions, big words, big music. It doesn't get much bigger than this one.

God Save Us (Lennon/Ono) — L, 71-May
○ (Quality/Content) Thin politics over thin music. It made no political or artistic impact.

Going Down (Starkey/Walsh) — S14-10, 82-Jul
≈ (Filler) Another instrumental, but a pretty meager feature for Ringo. Songwriters didn't finish it.

Save the Beatles!

Going Down on Love (Lennon) — L10-01, 74-Aug
≈ (Quality) Weepy self-pity

Going Down to Golders Green (Harrison) — H01, 70-May
✓ Whimsical, if derivative, 8-bar fun. Fully realized and worth considering. GH sounds good.

Going to New Orleans (My Carnival) (McCartney/McCartney) — M15, 75-Feb
⊘ (Filler) Really just a 12-bar goof. Light, but not interesting.

Gone from This Place (Lennon) — L, 80-Nov
⊘ (Demo) Terribly sad song, probably never would have made it out of demo form.

Gone Troppo (Harrison) — H11-05, 82-Aug
≈ (Quality) Leisure life incarnate. Uncomplicated, but about as memorable as a happy hour drink.

Goodnight Tonight (McCartney) — M19-01, 79-Feb
✓ Disco? Who cares! This is a great track in every way — if you skip the video.

Goodnight Vienna (Reprise) (Lennon) — S08-11, 74-Aug
✓ With gusto, indeed! Lennon provides the energy, and that's why it works.

Great Cock and Seagull Race (McCartney) — M03, 71-Feb
⊘ (Filler) 12-bar fun. Instrumental excellence, to be sure, but really nothing to see here.

Greece (Harrison) — H11-04, 82-Aug
⊘ (Filler) A pleasant, guitar-based lark, but it mostly just takes up space. Nothing especially "grecian."

Grey Cloudy Lies (Harrison) — H07-09, 75-Jun
⊘ (Quality) Another looper, without any payoff. It twirls inoffensively, but bores.

Grow Old with Me (Lennon) — L14-11, 80-Nov
✓ Better in conception than realization. A bit cloying and clichéd. Martin's strings help.

Gypsies in Flight (Starkey/Poncia) — S11-09, 77-Jun
⊘ (Quality) Pedal steel, slow shuffle, lousy vocal, on the wrong album — still in no way good.

Hands of Love (McCartney/McCartney) — M09-11, 72-Oct
✓ The only good part of the medley. A nice pure pop song. Linda BVs out of tune.

Happy Rishikesh Song, The (Lennon) — L, 80-Nov
⊘ (Demo/Content) Feels like a GH parody, then turns darkly introspective. Hard to know what to make of it.

Happy Xmas (War Is Over) (Lennon/Ono) — L07-01, 71-Oct
⊘ (Content) Timeless — in a good way. The only duet with Yoko that actually works.

Hard Times (Skellern) — S12-06, 77-Nov
⊘ (Style/Quality) Generic in every way. Nothing interesting in any way. Really.

Hari's on Tour (Express) (Harrison) — H06-01, 74-Oct
⊘ (Filler) Sounds like the theme to "The GH Variety Hour." Better suited to a B-side. Poor opener.

Have I Told You Lately That I Love You? (Wiseman) — S01-11, 70-Feb
⊘ (Style/Quality) Just add go-go dancers and comic takes for the camera. Dreadful.

Have You Seen My Baby (Newman) — S07-02, 73-Jul
≈ (Quality) Spirited arrangement and playing lifts a pretty plain song.

Hear Me Lord (Harrison) — H01-18, 70-Oct
⊘ (Quality) "Lord" language notwithstanding, this track feels preachy from its bones. Unattractive.

Heart of the Country (McCartney/McCartney) — M03-07, 70-Nov
✓ Earnest but cloying. In context, feels derivative and twee. Still a pretty good song.

Heart on My Sleeve (Gallagher/Lyle) — S12-04, 77-Nov
⊘ (Style/Quality) Sounds like a David Cassidy reject — 5 years too late!

Helen Wheels (McCartney/McCartney) — M11-01, 73-Sep
✓ Another great post-Beatles rocker. Quirky but rock solid.

Help Me To Help Myself (Lennon) — L, 80-Nov
⊘ (Demo) Indistinct ballad, interchangeable with many others.

Here Comes the Moon (Harrison) — H09-03, 78-Nov
✓ Not to be thought of as a sequel, this is a gem which has been dismissed. Very nice.

APPENDIX III / SOLO RECORDINGS

Here Today (McCartney) — M27-05, 81-Dec
✓ A true masterwork, even without the subtext. One for the ages.

Here We Go Again (Lennon/Spector) — L11, 73-Dec
≈ (Quality) Very large production, good sounding record, but the song is basically a jot.

Hey Diddle (McCartney/McCartney) — M03, 70-Oct
✓ Walks a fine line between catchy and annoying, but the craft is strong and this works.

Hey Hey (McCartney/Clarke) — M30-09, 81-Mar
⊘ (Filler) Fine riff, but not worthy of an album. Belongs on a B-side.

Hey! Baby (Channel) — S09-02, 76-Jul
≈ (Filler) Feelgood sing-along, nicely done. Simple and fits Ringo nicely.

Hi, Hi, Hi (McCartney/McCartney) — M07-02, 72-Nov
✓ Cheeky and catchy. A very slight confection.

His Name Is Legs (Ladies and Gentlemen) (Harrison) — H07-10, 75-Jun
⊘ (Quality) Annoying shuffle beat and seemingly random chord changes. Inexplicable.

Hold Me Tight (McCartney/McCartney) — M09-09, 72-Sep
⊘ (Quality) Pure purgatory SLS. Terrible lyric. Goes around in circles to nowhere.

Hold On (Lennon) — L04-02, 70-Oct
✓ A warm blanket of self-comfort, wrapped in simple and beautiful music. Cookie.

Hong Kong Blues (Carmichael) — H10-09, 80-Sep
⊘ (Filler) GH has obviously learned things from covering songs like this, but the records are dull.

Hopeless (Starkey/Walsh) — S14-02, 82-Jul
⊘ (Style/Quality) Incredibly square reading of a dreadful song. Just, yuk.

Hot as Sun/Glasses (McCartney) — M01-05, 70-Jan
⊘ (Filler) A doodle.

How Do You Sleep? (Lennon) — L06-08, 71-Jul
⊘ (Content) Cheap shots and overplayed insults result in a blood stain on JL's catalog.

How? (Lennon) — L06-09, 71-Jul
✓ Fantastic original music with a heartfelt, searching lyric. Best in show.

Husbands and Wives (Miller) — S08-04, 74-Aug
⊘ (Filler) An earnest vocal, but RS is in over his head. He is not a song stylist, by any means.

I Am Your Singer (McCartney/McCartney) — M04-06, 71-Aug
⊘ (Quality) Weak idea. Tortured melody. Rough duet. Weird arrangement.

I Can't Write Another Song (McCartney) — M, 78-Dec
≈ (Demo) A germ of a good idea, and a full song. Could be coded messages.

I Dig Love (Harrison) — H01-15, 70-Oct
✓ Flawed but fixable. Needs an edit to tame it, which is not a small thing. Playful at least.

I Don't Care Anymore (Harrison) — H05-02, 74-Oct
⊘ (Quality) Demo quality

I Don't Wanna Face It (Lennon) — L14-03, 77-Sep
✓ Not quite realized, but still a substantial piece. Overly familiar territory.

I Don't Want to Be a Soldier (Lennon) — L06-05, 71-Jul
⊘ (Quality/Content) Sloppy and unfinished, it is loved more for what a listener imagines it to be.

I Don't Want to Do It (Dylan) — H01, 70-May
≈ (Demo) A catchy lament. Another lost potential classic.

I Found Out (Lennon) — L04-03, 70-Oct
≈ (Content) Primal pain channeled into guitar licks, this really works. Music is original, significant.

I Keep Forgettin' (Leiber/Stoller) — S14-06, 82-Jul
⊘ (Style/Quality) Reaching for ideas in the arrangement leads to Ringo growling his vocal. Howling. Bad.

I Know (I Know) (Lennon) — L09-10, 73-Aug
✓ Rather plain song. The recording is clean, if conventional.

Save the Beatles!

I Lie Around (McCartney/McCartney) — M10-02, 71-Mar
✓ Goofy but fun. Designed to sound lazy, but isn't. Deserves an album slot.

I Live for You (Harrison) — H01, 70-Jun
✓ Very simple, straightforward, fully formed, with a solid lyric. Nice song and track.

I Really Love You (Swearingen) — H11-03, 82-Aug
⊘ (Filler) Sounds like they had fun making this, but it's hard to see a point. Almost parody of doo-wop.

I Remember Jeep (Harrison) — H01-22, 70-Oct
⊘ (Filler) A jam which can be safely ignored, unless you are among the few who are totally into that.

I Wouldn't Have You Any Other Way (Howard) — S02-09, 70-Jun
⊘ (Style/Quality) Slow dance, complete with tickled ivories and female duet voice. Un-Ringo.

I'd Be Talkin All the Time (Howard/Kingston) — S02-06, 70-Jun
⊘ (Style/Quality) "Ringo'd be talkin' all the time"

I'd Have You Anytime (Harrison/Dylan) — H01-01, 70-Oct
≈ (Style/Quality) Lousy song, and GH does nothing to improve it. Ponderous and boring.

I'll Give You a Ring (McCartney) — M28-02, 73-Dec
≈ (Quality) Music hall. Paul had the good sense not to release this earlier.

I'll Still Love You (Harrison) — H01, 70-Oct
✓ Great song, but no complete GH recording to use. We will use Ringo's version later.

I'll Still Love You (Harrison) — S09-07, 76-Jul
✓ Risky to try without GH, but Ringo (with Lon Van Eaton) pulls it off. Works well.

I'm a Fool to Care (Daffan) — S01-05, 70-Feb
✓ Voorman has disavowed it, but this is a very nice arrangement, and RS sounds great.

I'm Carrying (McCartney) — M18-03, 77-Dec
✓ A SLS that completes a trifecta of greatness at the start of the album.

I'm Losing You (Lennon) — L13-05, 80-Sep
✓ Open diary writing, but dull. Quote of "Long Lost John" is the most compelling aspect.

I'm Stepping Out (Lennon) — L14-01, 80-Nov
✓ A little too pat, as if more wish than reality. Not a bad song, but not genuine.

I'm the Greatest (Lennon) — S07-01, 73-Jul
✓ Ringo sings this better than John could have. May be his best-ever track — says something.

I've Had Enough (McCartney) — M18-08, 78-Jan
⊘ (Quality) Not credible as a song or a track. It pretends to bite, but has no teeth.

If Not for You (Dylan) — H01-06, 70-Oct
⊘ (Style/Quality) Sticks out as a mismatch of song and artist. Comes off as wimpy pop-rock.

If You Believe (Harrison/Wright) — H09-10, 78-Nov
✓ A little uneasy in structure, aspiring to something beyond where it reaches.

Imagine (Lennon) — L06-01, 71-Jul
✓ A triumph of inspiration over craft. Great ideas render an otherwise dull track timeless.

In My Car (Starkey/Walsh/Foster/Goody) — S14-01, 82-Jul
≈ (Style/Quality) What passed for pop at that moment, but not the least bit credible.

Indeed I Do (McCartney/McCartney) — M04, 71-Aug
⊘ (Unfinished) Simple enough jot with potential unrealized. Similar to "On the Wings of a Nightingale"

India (Lennon) — L, 80-Nov
⊘ (Demo) One of many iterations of this melody. Might have settled into something nice.

Instant Karma! (Lennon) — L03-01, 70-Jan
✓ Jaunty and catchy but overrated. The lyric is cynical, cold, and the music nothing special.

Intuition (Lennon) — L09-07, 73-Aug
✓ Uncharacteristically jaunty. Pure pop, but covering well-worn territory. Fine for what it is.

Isn't It a Pity (Version One) (Harrison) — H01-04, 70-Oct
⊘ (Content) GH rewrites "Hey Jude," but the impact is muted by overlong and over-dramatic reading.

Appendix III / Solo Recordings

Isn't It a Pity (Version Two) (Harrison) — H01-17, 70-Oct
⊘ (Filler) One version was more than enough. This is regrettable filler.

Isolation (Lennon) — L04-05, 70-Oct
✓ A "primal" track, it brings its title emotion to life. Effective painting in words and sound.

It Don't Come Easy (Starkey) — S04-01, 70-Mar
✓ Among Ringo's best ever. A great start that regrettably didn't set the pattern.

It Is 'He' (Jai Sri Krishna) (Harrison) — H06-09, 74-Oct
⊘ (Quality/Content) Terrible tuning problems. Annoying "shuffle" chorus. Sloppy.

It's Johnny's Birthday (Martin/Coulter/Harrison) — H01-20, 70-Oct
✓ Whimsical and full of good energy.

It's No Secret (Starkey/Poncia) — S11-08, 77-Jun
⊘ (Style) Wants to be 70s California soft rock, but fails. Disco-ish, cold, cheap, imitative, boring.

It's Not On (McCartney) — M, 82-Feb
✓ Truly odd. Compelling. Structured. More interesting than most Macca of the era.

It's So Hard (Lennon) — L06-04, 71-Jul
✓ Bluesy feel, unusual vocal, distinct sound. Underrated and very successful.

It's What You Value (Harrison) — H08-06, 76-Sep
✓ Confident and catchy, underrated straight pop. Great chorus. Refreshing from GH.

Jamrag (live) (Lennon/Ono) — L08-12, 71-Jun
⊘ (Filler) Out of tune. Wandering. Boring. Noisy. Yoko. Seriously: I want these five minutes back.

Jazz Street (McCartney) — M09, 72-Nov
⊘ (Filler) Another typical "link" track.

Jealous Guy (Lennon) — L06-03, 71-Jul
✓ Protesting too much, this reads like an excuse, and fails to convince. Whistling.

Jet (McCartney/McCartney) — M12-02, 73-Oct
✓ Great pop with rock echoes. Paul's vox and guitars are fantastic.

John Sinclair (Lennon) — L08-08, 72-Mar
⊘ (Quality) From the back porch somewhere. Poor lyrics, instantly dated. "Got ta, got ta, got ta, got ta…"

Junior's Farm (McCartney/McCartney) — M14-01, 74-Jul
✓ Amazing that Paul could still write songs this good this late. Meaningless fun.

Junk (McCartney) — M01-06, 70-Jan
✓ Cloying, but simple — in a generally good way.

Just a Dream (Starkey/Poncia) — S10-02, 76-Jun
⊘ (Style) Not a bad song, but a TERRIBLE record. Worst. Disco. Ever.

Just Because (Price) — L11-13, 74-Oct
⊘ (Style/Content) Closing time sentiment. End-of-the-set vocal. You don't have to go home, but don't stay here.

Just Because (Reprise) (Price) — L11, 73-Dec
⊘ (Style/Content) Shout out to the other Beatles is the only thing of value here.

Keep Under Cover (McCartney) — M30-04, 80-Dec
✓ Energetic and well-formed pop.

Kreen - Akrore (McCartney) — M01-13, 70-Feb
⊘ (Filler) Paul can drum. He can really drum. Questionable way to end the album.

Lady Gaye (Starkey/Poncia/Ward) — S09-10, 76-Jul
⊘ (Style/Quality) International playboy. Relaxed beat, with some swagger, but no real point.

Las Brisas (Starkey/Andrews) — S09-09, 76-Jul
⊘ (Style) International playboy. Mariachi. Harmless, but not catchy enough to hang with RS's big hits.

Lay His Head (Harrison) — H10, 80-Sep
⊘ (Quality) Not bad but structurally deficient. Lacks hook and chorus to finish a good idea. Boring.

Lazy Dynamite (McCartney/McCartney) — M09-10, 72-Sep
⊘ (Filler) Turn of phrase becomes lousy stub of a song. Harmonica? Really?

Save the Beatles!

Learning How to Love You (Harrison) — H08-10, 76-Sep
✓ With GH maturing as a songwriter and vocalist, this rewrite is beautifully crafted. Great track.

Let 'Em In (McCartney/McCartney) — M16-01, 76-Feb
✓ Macca finds a new type of quirky — again. Irresistible sing-along. Coded message?

Let It Down (Harrison) — H01-08, 70-Oct
✓ As powerful as GH ever got, this is a cry and a shout and a deep breath. On fire.

Let Me Roll It (McCartney/McCartney) — M12-05, 73-Oct
≈ (Content) With or without subtext, a solid song, great riff, strong vocal, nice arrangement.

Let the Rest of the World Go By (Ball/Brennan) — S01-12, 70-Feb
⊘ (Quality) Likable in some ways, but sounds horribly dated. RS sings harmony!

Let's Love (McCartney) — M15, 74-Jun
✓ Music hall sad song, but not too twee. Brevity and simplicity are assets here.

Letting Go (McCartney/McCartney) — M15-06, 74-Nov
✓ There is some arena rock heft here, but overwrought. Still, bring on the weed.

Life Begins At 40 (Lennon) — L, 80-Nov
⊘ (Demo) Country, without much potential. Just a very sad jot.

Life Itself (Harrison) — H10-03, 80-Sep
✓ One of George's gems. Gorgeous guitars. Filled with gentility plus movement. Sounds like joy.

Light That Has Lighted the World, The (Harrison) — H04-03, 73-Mar
⊘ (Content/Quality) Heartfelt, but grating. Palpably sad, but not a great song.

Lipstick Traces (On a Cigarette) (Neville) — S12-03, 77-Nov
⊘ (Style/Quality) Echoes of the 50s, but filtered through the 70s, in a bad way.

Listen to What the Man Said (McCartney/McCartney) — M15-11, 75-Feb
✓ Great radio music, filled with confidence that sells its odd chorus-with-no-words.

Little Lamb Dragonfly (McCartney/McCartney) — M09-05, 71-Mar
✓ Quirky, structured, interesting. Inscrutable lyric, but nice payoff.

Little Woman Love (McCartney/McCartney) — M06-02, 70-Nov
✓ This is McCartney firing on all cylinders. A great, lost track.

Live and Let Die (McCartney/McCartney) — M10-01, 72-Oct
✓ Forceful and confident. Large scale. The first real portent of hope.

Living in the Material World (Harrison) — H04-06, 73-Mar
≈ (Quality/Content) Galloping beat quickly gets annoying. Strident vocal.

London Town (McCartney/Laine) — M18-01, 77-Aug
✓ JPM at his best, but sets a standard that the album just can't live up to.

Long Haired Lady (McCartney/McCartney) — M03-10, 70-Oct
✓ A "big" song, but not fully realized. Alternates between moody and silly.

Long Lost John (Lennon) — L04, 70-Oct
⊘ (Style/Demo) Rockabilly, and not without potential. Something of a cliché in its unfinished form.

Look at Me (Lennon) — L04-09, 70-Oct
✓ Feels like a rerun somehow, and the least successful track on the album.

Lord Loves the One (That Loves the Lord), The (Harrison) — H04-07, 73-Mar
⊘ (Content) Music is a mixed bag, but lyrics really kill the potential good vibe.

Loser's Lounge (Pierce) — S02-10, 70-Jun
⊘ (Style/Quality) Very straight country song, and very wrong for Ringo. He has nothing for it.

Loup (1st Indian on the Moon) (McCartney/McCartney) — M09-08, 72-Mar
⊘ (Filler) Pointless filler. Kills the album dead. Belongs on a B-side, not as album track.

Love (Lennon) — L04-07, 70-Oct
✓ Fantastic ballad, in which a small sound creates a big emotional space.

Love Comes to Everyone (Harrison) — H09-01, 78-Nov
✓ Straight pop, and very successful. Great song and a gem of a recording.

APPENDIX III / SOLO RECORDINGS

Love Don't Last Long (Howard) — S02-02, 70-Jun
🚫 (Style/Quality) Vocal tremolo, sad story, formulaic, key change.

Love for You, A (McCartney) — M03, 70-Oct
✓ Unusual vocal probably doomed release, but it's a poppy, catchy song. Very slight.

Love in Song (McCartney/McCartney) — M15-03, 74-Nov
✓ A good SLS, with the two preceding, forms the essence of Wings sound.

Love Is a Many Splendoured Thing (Fain/Webster) — S01-08, 70-Mar
🚫 (Style) A nice arrangement for just about anyone else. RS is buried in a chorus of 60s clichés.

Love Is Strange (Baker/Vanderpool/Smith) — M04-03, 71-Aug
🚫 (Filler) Weird choice for a cover, and not interesting at all. Straight reading.

Love My Baby (McCartney) — M15, 74-Aug
🚫 (Style) Novelty only. Releasable if recorded properly, but probably not worth it.

Lovely Linda, The (McCartney) — M01-01, 70-Jan
🚫 (Filler) A pleasant stub. Appropriate way to transition from group to solo.

Luck of the Irish, The (Lennon/Ono) — L08-07, 72-Mar
🚫 (Quality) Sounds like a jot that filled a hole. Lyrics are trite and unpleasant.

Lunchbox/Odd Sox (McCartney) — M22-03, 75-Feb
🚫 (Filler) Just another long "link." A total throwaway.

Magneto and Titanium Man (McCartney/McCartney) — M15-05, 75-Feb
≈ (Content) Very weird song and track, but light and catchy mid-70s pop.

Mama's Little Girl (McCartney/McCartney) — M09, 72-Mar
✓ A bit too cute, but simple, classic Macca.

Mamunia (McCartney/McCartney) — M12-06, 73-Sep
≈ (Quality) Somehow overcomes its leaning toward vapidness.

Man Like Me, A (O'Lochlainn) — S12-10, 77-Nov
🚫 (Style/Quality) Ringo steps into a pool of light for his solo turn, but it's very cringey.

Man We Was Lonely (McCartney) — M01-07, 70-Feb
✓ Alternately cheesy and profound. Bad chorus spoils good verses.

Man, The (McCartney/Jackson) — M30-06, 81-Dec
🚫 (Style) Best of the MJ duets. Solid song. Nice energy. Great vox and arrangement. But, just, no.

Mary Had a Little Lamb (McCartney/McCartney) — M06-01, 72-Mar
🚫 (Content/Style) Intentions aside, this is a terrible record.

Māya Love (Harrison) — H06-05, 74-Oct
✓ Positive, up beat, confident. Leading edge of GH's ultimate sound.

Maybe I'm Amazed (McCartney) — M01-12, 70-Feb
✓ One of Paul's all-time great love songs. And this recording is definitive.

Meat City (Lennon) — L09-12, 73-Aug
✓ An overlooked classic. Slick and cool, in the best way. Seek the remix, which clears things up.

Memories / Howling At The Moon (Lennon) — L, 80-Nov
🚫 (Demo) Derivative, of himself and others. Like Macca, JL generating short ideas then combining.

Mess I'm In, The (McCartney/McCartney) — M09, 72-Mar
✓ One of Paul's great post-Beatles rockers. Wasted in live version on a B-side.

Mess, The (live) (McCartney/McCartney) — M08-02, 72-Aug
≈ (Live) A staple of the live show, this rocker sounds fine live, but better in the studio.

Mind Games (Lennon) — L09-01, 73-Aug
✓ Repetitive, circular, somewhat thin, but somehow a classic. A place you want to spend time.

Mirror, Mirror (On The Wall) (Lennon) — L, 77-Sep
🚫 (Unfinished) Sad waltz with some interesting turns, but not complete enough to consider.

Miss O'Dell (Harrison) — H03-02, 73-Feb
≈ (Quality) Mostly inside jokes and laughter. Sloppy, but has some charm.

Save the Beatles!

Mo (Harrison) — H, 77-Mar
✓ Great song. Leading edge of the excellence of the GH album. Similarities to "Faster."

Momma Miss America (McCartney) — M01-09, 70-Jan
⊘ (Filler) Template for many forgettable B-sides to come.

Monkberry Moon Delight (McCartney/McCartney) — M03-08, 70-Nov
⊘ (Quality) Pushing for something new, but this is not it. Bad song. Bad record.

Monkey See – Monkey Do (Franks) — S12-08, 77-Nov
⊘ (Style/Quality) Routine song, not customized to Ringo. Pure product.

Morse Moose and the Grey Goose (McCartney/Laine) — M18-14, 77-Dec
⊘ (Quality) Painfully long, painfully weird, painfully pointless. This is one to hate.

Mother (Lennon) — L04-01, 70-Oct
≈ (Content) JL bares it all. Among his most powerful art ever. Pain felt, transmitted, but not dispelled.

Mother Divine (Harrison) — H01, 70-May
≈ (Demo) Potential anthemic qualities, but not much more than a sketch.

Move Over Ms. L (Lennon) — L12-02, 74-Oct
≈ (Style/Quality) RnR treatment for a new song is more interesting than the rest of the project.

Mr. H Atom (McCartney) — M23, 79-Jul
⊘ (Filler) Catchier than most such sketches, though of dubious value. Vaultable.

Mr. Hyde's Gone (Don't Be Afraid) (Lennon) — L, 80-Nov
≈ (Demo) Rare JL writing music hall. Unusual feel, a welcome variation.

Mrs. Vandebilt (McCartney/McCartney) — M12-04, 73-Oct
≈ (Quality) Slight but manages to sound important through strong structure.

Mull of Kintyre (McCartney/Laine) — M17-02, 77-Aug
✓ A classic that sounded silly to US ears at the time. Wasn't marketed well.

Mumbo (McCartney/McCartney) — M04-01, 71-Aug
⊘ (Quality) Brutal vocal. Everything forced. Unlistenable.

Mumbo (Link) (McCartney/McCartney) — M04-10, 71-Aug
⊘ (Filler) Another pointless "reprise." Not bad, but not helpful.

Must Do Something About It (McCartney/McCartney) — M16-09, 76-Feb
✓ A simple song with a great feel. Seek the version with Paul's vocal.

My Carnival (McCartney/McCartney) — M, 75-Feb
⊘ (Filler) 12-bar fun, sort of New Orleans-style.

My Love (McCartney/McCartney) — M09-02, 73-Jan
✓ Sappy MOR, but catchy, if template driven. Skilled writing. The original SLS.

My Mummy's Dead (Lennon) — L04-11, 70-Oct
⊘ (Content/Style) The instinct is understandable, but as codas go, this is too melodramatic. TMI.

My Old Friend (Perkins) — M, 81-Mar
✓ Perkins sings with genuine sweetness, and the song succeeds because of that. Beautiful.

My Sweet Lord (Harrison) — H01-02, 70-Oct
⊘ (Content) Derivative but infectious. The chanted Hare Krishna language can be off putting.

Mystical One (Harrison) — H11-06, 82-Aug
≈ (Quality) Lyrically, George's "Watching the Wheels." Poppy tune sounds detached from the ideas.

Name and Address (McCartney) — M18-12, 77-Mar
✓ The parade of styles continues. Nice sound. Nice song. But kind of alone.

Nashville Freakout (Drake/Starkey/et. al. (+15)) — S02, 70-Jun
⊘ (Filler) Probably was fun to record, but nothing really to it.

New York City (Lennon) — L08-05, 72-Mar
⊘ (Quality) As homages to a favorite city go, this sucks. Banal in the worst possible way.

Night and Day (Porter) — S01-02, 69-Oct
≈ (Quality) Starts with promise, but vocal limitations are evident immediately. Band is fantastic.

Appendix III / Solo Recordings

Night Out (McCartney) — M09, 72-Sep
✓ A rare sketch with real force, probably due to the guitars and driving beat. A good one.

Nineteen Hundred and Eighty-Five (McCartney/McCartney) — M12-09, 73-Oct
≈ (Quality) Very odd song. Lyric is weak, but the intensity saves it. It rolls well.

No No Song (Axton/Jackson) — S08-08, 74-Aug
⊘ (Style/Quality) Irresistibly catchy. Would have been a hit with any vocalist. RS adds nothing unique.

No Words (McCartney/Laine) — M12-07, 73-Oct
≈ (Quality) Forgettable, but not unlikeable. Feels like part of the "story."

Nobody Knows (McCartney) — M23-05, 79-Jul
≈ (Quality) Probably fun to make — a quick something out of nothing. But don't think too hard.

Nobody Loves You (When You're Down and Out) (Lennon) — L10-11, 74-Aug
≈ (Quality) Weepy, overlong and painfully self-pitying. A low point.

Nobody Told Me (Lennon) — L14-05, 76-Dec
✓ Jaunty vibe. Classic JL lyric — if a little lite. Pointed toward good things to come.

Not For Love Nor Money (Illusions) (Lennon) — L, 79-Oct
⊘ (Unfinished) A minor composition, work in progress. Writing like GH, but hardly a hidden classic.

Not Guilty (Harrison) — H09-02, 78-Nov
≈ (Content) Ten years later, this song still sounded contemporary. A better reading than in 1968.

Note You Never Wrote, The (McCartney/McCartney) — M16-02, 75-Oct
✓ Moody, and maybe silly, but somehow mesmerizing. This works.

Now and Then (Lennon) — L, 77-Sep
⊘ (Unfinished) Another sad song, and sadly unfinished. Hardly any hit potential. Deep album only.

Now Hear This Song of Mine (McCartney) — M03, 71-Feb
⊘ (Filler) Likely no more than sung refrains, there's nothing here.

Nowhere to Go (Dylan/Harrison) — H01, 70-May
≈ (Demo/Content) Tortured chord progression. Embodies its title, and goes nowhere. "Beatle Jeff/Ted"

Nutopian International Anthem (Lennon) — L09-06, 73-Aug
≈ (Content) Silly, but maybe he could have talked the others into it.

Occapella (Toussaint) — S08-02, 74-Aug
≈ (Style) Nice riff, and a happy sound overall. Slight, but inoffensive.

Ode to a Koala Bear (McCartney) — M29-02, 80-Dec
⊘ (Quality) Very late Wings sound, and like others, given more energy than the song deserves.

Oh My Love (Lennon/Ono) — L06-07, 71-Jul
✓ A weepy love song that's just the right amount of weepy. GH guitar is beautiful.

Oh My My (Starkey/Poncia) — S07-06, 73-Jul
✓ One of Ringo's likeable, classic novelties. Not a viable, long-term career strategy, though.

Oh Woman, Oh Why (McCartney) — M02-02, 70-Nov
⊘ (Content) Truly unfortunate. One of Paul's "stains."

Oh Yoko! (Lennon) — L06-10, 71-Jul
⊘ (Content) Light and fun, but built around a lyric that is far too specific. Ultimately, it annoys.

Old Dirt Road (Lennon/Nilsson) — L10-03, 74-Aug
≈ (Quality) Boring

Old Siam, Sir (McCartney) — M20-06, 78-Jul
≈ (Quality) In the "meaningless lyrics" category, it nonetheless manages a bit of mystery. Nice guitars.

Old Time Relovin' (Starkey/Poncia) — S12-09, 77-Nov
⊘ (Style/Quality) Lopes along, with all of the edges sanded off. Disappears from memory instantly.

Om Hare Om (Gopala Krishna) (Harrison) — H01, 70-Jun
⊘ (Style) Not usable by the group, but good enough (with a better vocal) for a GH solo album.

On the Way (McCartney) — M23-03, 79-Jul
≈ (Quality) Sketchy recording, but a real song. Not saying great, but might have made a fine Wings track.

Save the Beatles!

One Day (At a Time) (Lennon) — L09-04, 73-Aug
✓ Original, but so wifty that it all but floats away. Musical cotton candy — sticky.

One More Kiss (McCartney/McCartney) — M09-04, 72-Dec
✓ Music hall. Quaint and skilled writing. Has a place, but maybe not here.

One of the Boys (Lennon) — L, 77-Sep
◯ (Unfinished) Up tempo and breezy, but overly self-conscious, even for JL.

One of These Days (McCartney) — M23-11, 79-Jul
✓ Apology? Maybe. There is some vulnerability which lifts this above many other tracks.

One Way Love Affair (Ballard) — S, 78-Jul
◯ (Quality) Terrible song, terrible vocal, terrible production.

Only People (Lennon) — L09-09, 73-Aug
✓ Would-be anthem has virtually no heft. Routinized passion.

Only You (And You Alone) (Ram/Rand) — S08-09, 74-Aug
≈ (Filler) Classic song. Competent vocal. But nothing particularly distinctive about the record.

Oo You (McCartney) — M01-08, 70-Jan
✓ Template for the "solo rocker." Nice riff, but feels somehow hollow.

Oo-Wee (Starkey/Poncia) — S08-03, 74-Aug
≈ (Quality) Attempting to follow "Oh My My," this isn't quite as successful, but still catchy and nice.

Ooh Baby (You Know That I Love You) (Harrison) — H07-04, 75-Jun
≈ (Quality) Nice but unrealized idea. Salvaged when rewritten as "Pure Smokey."

Other Me, The (McCartney) — M30-03, 82-Oct
◯ (Quality) Dreadful, cheap apology. "I acted like a dustbin lid." Indeed. Bad idea, and lousy recording.

Out of the Blue (Harrison) — H01-19, 70-Oct
◯ (Filler) Jams are generally boring, and this is no exception.

Out on the Streets (Starkey/Poncia) — S11-05, 77-Jun
◯ (Style) An unholy disco-ish four-in-the-bar song with terrible lyrics. Ringo gives it his all.

Out the Blue (Lennon) — L09-08, 73-Aug
✓ Not bad, exactly, but rewriting himself. Harrison-esque chord wandering.

Peggy Sue (Allison/Petty/Holly) — L11-09, 74-Oct
◯ (Style/Content) Pure mush. Chiming guitars in the break have potential, but this car has no wheels.

Photograph (Starkey/Harrison) — S07-03, 73-Jul
✓ Other candidate for "best Ringo track ever." Catchy, upbeat, well-formed.

Picasso's Last Words (Drink to Me) (McCartney/McCartney) — M12-08, 73-Oct
✓ Not the greatest song, but the legend elevates it. Works well with reprise.

Picture Show Life (Reid/Slate) — S14-07, 82-Jul
≈ (Content) Song is at least not terrible, but kind of random for Ringo. Something of a vocal stretch.

Pipes of Peace (McCartney) — M30-01, 82-Oct
≈ (Quality) The world did not need this tripe. It manages to take away from its brother song.

Plug Me In (Harrison) — H01-21, 70-Oct
◯ (Filler) Another boring jam. Pure filler.

Pound Is Sinking, The (McCartney) — M27-07, 81-Mar
✓ Fun with words/guitars. Imaginative. Structured. Meaningless, but somehow says something.

Power Cut (McCartney/McCartney) — M09-12, 72-Oct
◯ (Quality) Forced writing. Not entirely bad, but not a whole idea. Forgettable.

Power to the People (Lennon) — L05-01, 71-Feb
✓ Tough political statement. Politics aside, it is a powerful, funky, very big track.

Praying Mantis Heart (McCartney) — M, 78-Dec
◯ (Demo) Not realized, but with potential.

Private Property (McCartney) — S13-01, 80-Jul
◯ (Quality) Lousy Macca castoff song, weird horns. Mish mash of sounds, styles. Not successful.

Appendix III / Solo Recordings

Pure Gold (McCartney) — S09-03, 76-Jul
✓ Weak song from Macca mines familiar tropes, goes nowhere. Ringo phones it in. Dull.

Pure Smokey (Harrison) — H08-08, 76-Sep
✓ GH rewrites himself, with significant improvement. Smooth, late night sound. Pure FM.

Rainclouds (McCartney/Laine) — M26-02, 80-Dec
✓ Famous for provenance, but basically filler. BVs are really great, incl LM! No bass. Complex.

Ram On (McCartney) — M03-03, 71-Feb
✓ (Quality) A stub. Pleasant enough, but insufficient for the "concept" of an album.

Ram On (Reprise) (McCartney) — M03-11, 71-Feb
≈ (Filler) No new ideas. A reprise of nothingness.

Real Love (Lennon) — L, 80-Jun
✓ A lesser composition, gussied into an "event." With JL's edges sanded, not much here.

Reception (McCartney) — M20-01, 78-Sep
≈ (Filler) Really just a link. Not much to it. Synths may be a little over the top.

Red and Black Blues (Tietgen) — S13, 80-Aug
⊘ (Quality) Boring song, terrible vocal

Reggae Moon (McCartney) — M, 78-Dec
⊘ (Demo) An extended "link."

Remember (Lennon) — L04-06, 70-Oct
✓ Sloppy track, and the song is not quite tamed. But who cares?

Rip It Up/Ready Teddy (Blackwell/Marascalco) — L11-03, 74-Oct
⊘ (Style/Content) Among the cleaner tracks on RnR, but still pointless. Workmanlike all around.

Robber's Ball (McCartney) — M, 79-Jun
≈ (Style/Quality) Odd and at least slightly annoying, but sufficiently original, and interesting.

Rock 'N' Roll People (Lennon) — L09, 73-Aug
≈ (Quality) Not inherently a bad song, but JL has troubles with the melody. Can't commit. A rare problem.

Rock Show (McCartney/McCartney) — M15-02, 75-Feb
✓ Great rock song. Tone hasn't aged well, but it caught a moment.

Rockestra Theme (McCartney) — M20-08, 78-Oct
≈ (Filler) Not Paul's best instrumental, or song idea, but a compelling project nonetheless. Fun.

Rode All Night (McCartney) — M03, 70-Oct
≈ (Filler) Raucous drum and guitar jam, occasional vocal improv. Potentially useful with edit.

Rudolph the Red-Nosed Reggae (Marks) — M21-02, 74-Dec
⊘ (Content/Filler) Silly track. Barely worthy of a B-side. Should have stayed on a private reel.

Run of the Mill (Harrison) — H01-09, 70-Oct
⊘ (Quality) A song which never settled. Not bad, exactly, but always feels unfinished.

Sally and Billy (Lennon) — L, 70-Nov
⊘ (Demo) Intriguing, with potential, but not usable as is.

Sally G (McCartney/McCartney) — M14-02, 74-Jul
⊘ (Style/Quality) Nothing likeable about this one at all. "Rocky Raccoon" on weed.

Same Time Next year (McCartney) — M, 78-May
⊘ (Quality) Macca writing to task, sounds forced. Unusually clunky melody and chords.

San Ferry Anne (McCartney/McCartney) — M16-10, 76-Feb
✓ Another that slips away without leaving an impression. Skillful writing, but...yawn.

San Francisco Bay Blues (Fuller) — L06, 71-Jul
⊘ (Demo) A lark, just for fun.

Sat Singing (Harrison) — H10, 80-Sep
⊘ (Quality) Competent but completely forgettable. Feels like product.

Save the World (Harrison) — H10-10, 80-Sep
⊘ (Quality) Classic GH chord progression that wanders untamed. Very thin sound. A cliché all around.

Say Say Say (McCartney/Jackson) — M30-02, 82-Apr
⊘ (Style) Despite being a megahit, it had no legs. Dated immediately, and pretty cringey now.

Scared (Lennon) — L10-06, 74-Aug
✓ Lives up to its title, and does not go over the top. Fantastic arrangement. Borderline classic.

Scumbag (live) (Lennon/Ono/Zappa) — L08-13, 71-Jun
⊘ (Filler) I think you had to be in the band to appreciate this one.

Secret Friend (McCartney) — M25-02, 79-Jul
⊘ (Filler) Give Macca credit for early electronica. This one is at least interesting, if still annoying.

See Yourself (Harrison) — H08-05, 76-Sep
✓ Pointed, but not harsh. Purposeful pop, with Beatle-y mixed meter. Works.

Seems Like Old Times (McCartney) — M, 78-Dec
⊘ (Quality) Echoes of the music hall, but not as smooth. Forced tune and lyric.

Send Me the Heart (McCartney/Laine) — M14, 74-Jul
⊘ (Style) Paul and Denny do country pastiche. Inoffensive, but beyond pointless.

Sentimental Journey (Green/Brown/Homer) — S01-01, 70-Mar
⊘ (Quality) Sounds like a joke, like it might break into something cool at any second. Doesn't. A total mess.

Serve Yourself (Lennon) — L, 80-Nov
⊘ (Demo/Content) Provocative, but also cold. Feels harsh in demo form. Might have come out that way.

She's a Friend of Dorothy's (Lennon) — L, 76-Dec
⊘ (Unfinished) So much potential here, both as a hit and with artistic value.

She's About a Mover (Sahm) — S14-05, 82-Jul
≈ (Quality) Up tempo, with nice energy, but ends up repeating title over and over. Rewrite of "Tight A$"?

She's So in Love (Ballard) — S, 78-Jul
⊘ (Quality) Terrible song, terrible vocal, terrible production.

She's My Baby (McCartney/McCartney) — M16-03, 76-Feb
⊘ (Quality) Falling off the wagon, this one is dumb filler. Would have fit on RRS.

Silent Homecoming (Pickard) — S02-12, 70-Jun
⊘ (Style/Quality) Another sad story song. Timely, but has aged poorly. Melody is too much for RS.

Silly Love Songs (McCartney/McCartney) — M16-06, 76-Feb
✓ Writing with full confidence, but dinging his own brand. Still, it has aged well.

Simple as That (McCartney) — M, 80-Aug
≈ (Demo) Unusual groove. Interesting lyric. Something there worth listening to.

Simple Love Song (Starkey/Poncia) — S11-10, 77-Jun
⊘ (Style/Quality) Inoffensive but banal. Not quite disco, not quite pop, nothing much here.

Simply Shady (Harrison) — H06-02, 74-Oct
⊘ (Quality) Lopes along without much point, and a grating vocal.

Since My Baby Left Me (Crudup) — L11, 73-Dec
⊘ (Style/Content) More fun than most of RnR. JL sounds smooth, playful. Call/response is great, crazy fun.

Singalong Junk (McCartney) — M01-11, 70-Feb
⊘ (Filler) Pleasant filler. Less cloying without lyrics, but aimless.

Single Pigeon (McCartney/McCartney) — M09-06, 72-Mar
⊘ (Quality) Forced writing. Weak idea padded. Very slight for the amount of effort.

Six O'Clock (McCartney/McCartney) — S07-08, 73-Jul
≈ (Quality) Nice when Beatles work together again, but this is a non-event. Song is lousy.

Slippin' and Slidin' (Bocage/Collins/Penniman/Smith) — L11-08, 74-Oct
⊘ (Style/Content) Fine, but like the rest, without any sense of fun or joy. Straight reading. Boring.

Smile Away (McCartney) — M03-06, 70-Nov
⊘ (Quality) Forced. Bad lyrics. Cliché. Another "stain."

Sneaking Sally Through the Alley (Toussaint) — S11-07, 77-Jun
⊘ (Style/Quality) Embarassing, dumb song, wasting a host of great musicians. Nothing redeeming.

Appendix III / Solo Recordings

Snookeroo (John/Taupin) — S08-05, 74-Aug
⊘ (Quality) Lousy song, sketchy vocal performance. Pseudo-autobio crap lyric. Forced.

So Bad (McCartney) — M30-05, 82-Oct
≈ (Quality) Totally SLS, without much to redeem it. Routine words and music.

So Glad to See You Here (McCartney) — M20-13, 78-Sep
✓ The better of the Rockestra tracks, and actually a good song. Somewhat overlooked.

So Sad (Harrison) — H06-03, 74-Oct
≈ (Quality) Nice guitars, but weepy/reedy/shaky vocal. Song might be better than the recording.

Soft Touch (Harrison) — H09-09, 78-Nov
✓ Built around two — count 'em TWO — solid riffs. Fully-formed and really great.

Soft-Hearted Hana (Harrison) — H09-04, 78-Nov
≈ (Content) A fine "get high" song. Loopy but well-written, with a recording made while sober!

Soily (McCartney) — M15, 74-Aug
✓ Solid rocker with fine hook. Weird lyrics, but just a carrier wave for the music. Works.

Some People Never Know (McCartney/McCartney) — M04-05, 71-Aug
✓ Simple idea, but ineffective. Obvious, automatic, banal. LM vocal distracts.

Somebody Who Cares (McCartney) — M27-03, 81-Mar
✓ A very fine piece of work. Beautiful song and recording. Sounds earnest and warm.

Spin It On (McCartney) — M20-04, 78-Jul
✓ Definitely trying too hard. Not exactly bad, but feels undeniably inauthentic.

Spirits of Ancient Egypt (McCartney/McCartney) — M15-08, 75-Feb
≈ (Content) Another quirky misfit that somehow works with this album's mood.

Spooky Weirdness (uncredited) — S09-11, 76-Jul
≈ (Filler) Not especially compelling, but definitely lives up to its name.

Stand by Me (Leiber/Stoller/King) — L11-02, 74-Oct
⊘ (Style/Content) Cleanest track on RnR, and with imaginative arrangement. Still, JL shouts and strains.

Stardust (Carmichael/Parish) — S01-06, 69-Nov
⊘ (Quality) RS strains to tame the melody. Instrumental flourishes tend to go over the top. Too much.

Steel and Glass (Lennon) — L10-09, 74-Aug
≈ (Content) All Beatles would have liked the idea

Step Lightly (Starkey) — S07-07, 73-Jul
✓ Great low-key groove. Perfect fit — voice, tone, content. A straight success. Ugh, tap dancing.

Stop and Take the Time to Smell the Roses (Starkey/Nilsson) — S13-05, 80-Nov
⊘ (Style/Quality) A cliché from its conception. Someone should have said no.

Stop, You Don't Know Where She Came From (McCartney) — M, 80-Aug
⊘ (Quality) Clean demo of a throwaway jot. Not about anything.

Sue Me, Sue You Blues (Harrison) — H04-02, 73-Mar
≈ (Content) Inventive and jaunty. Bad vibes transmuted without anger.

Suicide (McCartney) — M01, 70-Jan
⊘ (Style/Quality) Music hall, with strange lyric, diffuse melody, weird word accents, a curiosity only.

Summer's Day Song (McCartney) — M23-07, 79-Jul
✓ Perhaps too twee for most, but at least clean and well-formed. Nice harmonies.

Sunday Bloody Sunday (Lennon/Ono) — L08-06, 72-Mar
⊘ (Quality) Strident, and well-intentioned, but over the top. Two notches too big.

Sunshine Life for Me (Sail Away Raymond) (Harrison) — S07-04, 73-Jul
✓ A great track. Simple and fun. GH and RS always make a great team.

Sunshine Sometime (McCartney) — M03, 70-Oct
✓ Simply and lovely, giving the impression of a morning in Scotland.

Sure to Fall (Perkins/Claunch/Cantrell) — S13-08, 80-Jul
≈ (Style) A sweet Perkins cover, even if a little overdone. Ringo's singing is strained at the top.

Save the Beatles!

Surprise, Surprise (Sweet Bird of Paradox) (Lennon) — L10-08, 74-Aug
✓ Clean and fresh sound. Great song, fine lyrics, happy sound.

Sweet Little Sixteen (Berry) — L11-07, 74-Oct
⊘ (Style/Content) The band plods and plods. Sounds like mud in music form. Lousy arrangement, too.

Sweetest Little Show (McCartney) — M30-07, 81-Dec
✓ Mannered but warmly reminiscent. Works despite some cuteness.

Take It Away (McCartney) — M27-02, 81-Mar
✓ A great, confident track, and definitely worth the work that went into it. A real pleasure.

Tango All Night (Hague/Seufert) — S11-02, 77-Jun
⊘ (Style) International playboy. Pseudo-latin beat performed completely square. Bad.

Teardrops (Harrison) — H10-06, 81-Feb
≈ (Quality) Ridiculously up-tempo sad song. Very catchy, if you can let the lyrics go.

Tears of the World (Harrison) — H10, 80-Sep
✓ Best of the album rejects, with solid music and a point. Definitely usable.

Teddy Boy (McCartney) — M01-10, 70-Jan
✓ Classic or misfire? A story song with only sketchy story. Carefully written.

Tell Me What Has Happened to You (Harrison) — H01, 70-May
≈ (Demo/Quality) A sketch with some potential, but not fully formed.

Temporary Secretary (McCartney) — M23-02, 79-Jul
≈ (Style) Despite much hatred, this opened doors for future artists. Unique in the catalog. Interesting.

Thank You Darling (McCartney) — M09, 72-Dec
⊘ (Quality/Filler) Weak rewrite of "Heart and Soul" — with kazoos.

Thanks for the Pepperoni (Harrison) — H01-23, 70-Oct
⊘ (Filler) Great chops, but who cares? This is a waste of vinyl.

That Is All (Harrison) — H04-11, 73-Mar
≈ (Quality) Weepy. Preachy. Reedy. GH voice set badly.

That Which I Have Lost (Harrison) — H10-07, 81-Feb
⊘ (Quality) Simplistic, twangy, skippy, clunky, square song. Unpleasant. But don't blame the tuba player.

That Would Be Something (McCartney) — M01-02, 70-Jan
✓ Only a one-line lyric, yet it's enough. The simple riff works.

That's the Way It Goes (Harrison) — H11-02, 82-Aug
✓ Really nice song. Easy and flowing. Great arrangement. One that got lost amid the lousiness.

This Be Called a Song (Clapton) — S09-08, 76-Jul
⊘ (Quality/Filler) Weird mish-mash of styles. Not a good choice for RS, very awkward.

This Guitar (Can't Keep from Crying) (Harrison) — H07-03, 75-May
≈ (Quality) Bad singing sinks a serviceable, if not quite stellar, song.

This Song (Harrison) — H08-04, 76-Sep
✓ Solid hit potential, unfortunately unrealized — but nothing wrong here. Great track.

Through Our Love (McCartney) — M30-11, 82-Oct
✓ Considered a SLS, but a significant work. Stylish and appropriately large in scale.

Tight A$ (Lennon) — L09-02, 73-Aug
≈ (Quality) Spicy enough, if a bit repetitive.

Tired of Midnight Blue (Harrison) — H07-08, 75-Apr
✓ A surprising success. GH sounds good, and the idea is fully realized.

To Know Her Is to Love Her (Spector) — L11, 73-Dec
⊘ (Style/Content) What the hell were they thinking? Slow . . . and long . . . and drawn out ... terribly. Awful.

To You (McCartney) — M20-09, 78-Jul
≈ (Quality) Not a bad song, but Macca's vocal just tries too hard. Wrong tone in the recording.

Tomorrow (McCartney/McCartney) — M04-08, 71-Aug
⊘ (Quality) Shoddy song. Never mention in the same breath with precursor. Sketchy vox.

APPENDIX III / SOLO RECORDINGS

Tonight (McLagan/Pidgeon) — S12-07, 77-Nov
⊘ (Style/Quality) Uninteresting song. Bad arrangement. Empty-sounding record.

Too Many People (McCartney) — M03-01, 70-Nov
⊘ (Content) Feud-starter, but structured, and actually a fine song.

Tragedy (Nelson/Burch) — M09, 72-Mar
≈ (Filler) Casual cover. Nice enough, but improved when rewritten as "Band on the Run."

Treat Her Gently / Lonely Old People (McCartney/McCartney) — M15-12, 75-Feb
✓ Isolated, this would be too much. In context, it completes the album's thought.

True Love (Porter) — H08-07, 76-Sep
≈ (Filler) Something of a misfire, but it could be that listening to Porter made GH a better songwriter.

Try Some, Buy Some (Harrison) — H04-09, 73-Mar
✓ Ambitious (Beatle-y) scale. Mostly works, despite reedy vocal.

Tug of Peace (McCartney) — M30-10, 82-Oct
⊘ (Filler) Worst kind of filler, it taints the song it follows after.

Tug of War (McCartney) — M27-01, 81-Dec
✓ Perfect to open the album, it sets a clear tone. Maybe not a great song, but a great record.

Twice in a Lifetime (McCartney) — M, 82-Nov
⊘ (Quality) Oddly ponderous. Never finds a stable idea. Tone is full MOR.

Uncle Albert/Admiral Halsey (McCartney/McCartney) — M03-05, 71-Jan
✓ Three-parter. Cinematic, but plot-free. Quirky but catchy. Playful, fun.

Unconsciousness Rules (Harrison) — H10-02, 80-Sep
≈ (Quality) Pleasantly poppy, but feels very "formula." Nothing special.

Unknown Delight (Harrison) — H11-07, 82-Aug
✓ Beautiful pop ballad. Fully formed and warm. BVs suspect. Cribs his "Something" solo!

Valentine Day (McCartney) — M01-03, 70-Jan
⊘ (Filler) A fine instrumental, but probably could have been a nice song.

Venus and Mars (McCartney/McCartney) — M15-01, 75-Mar
✓ Coded messages never sounded so good. A win, if odd.

Venus and Mars (Reprise) (McCartney/McCartney) — M15-07, 75-Feb
✓ Reprise to start the side actually works, and the variation is welcome.

Wah-Wah (Harrison) — H01-03, 70-Oct
⊘ (Content) Powerful guitar image. Full arrangement, yet not cluttered. A fine piece of work.

Waiting (Howard) — S02-11, 70-Jun
⊘ (Style/Quality) Why is Ringo singing this? Wrong for his voice, image, talents, persona. Bad idea.

Wake Up (Starkey) — S13, 81-Feb
✓ Best track recorded for the album. Lively, catchy, makes Ringo sound good.

Wake Up My Love (Harrison) — H11-01, 82-Aug
✓ Synth-heavy pure pop. Quirky rhythm in verse is disorienting or this might have been a hit.

Walking in the Park with Eloise (J. McCartney) — M, 74-Jul
⊘ (Style/Quality) Sweet tribute to Paul's dad, but of little interest beyond that.

Wanderlust (McCartney) — M27-08, 81-Dec
✓ Ever the craftsman, this succeeds despite being somewhat precious. Semi-anthemic.

Warm and Beautiful (McCartney/McCartney) — M16-11, 76-Feb
✓ An overlooked classic, but leaves a too sweet taste as an album closer.

Watching the Wheels (Lennon) — L13-08, 80-Sep
✓ All about its lyrics, and thus not much musically. Perhaps protesting a bit too much...

Waterfalls (McCartney) — M23-04, 79-Jul
✓ The most beautiful of the collection, it shows a genuinely pensive Macca. Fine song.

Waterspout (McCartney) — M18, 77-Jun
✓ Very catchy. Typically incoherent lyric seems like it MIGHT mean something.

SAVE THE BEATLES!

We All Stand Together (McCartney) — M, 80-Aug
⊘ (Style) Fine for children. Even so, not very interesting.

We All Stand Together (Humming Version) (McCartney) — M, 80-Aug
⊘ (Filler) More interesting and palatable than the vocal version, but still too twee.

We're Open Tonight (McCartney) — M20-03, 78-Sep
✓ An overgrown link, but might have been thrown away too hastily. Maybe a good song there.

Well (Baby Please Don't Go) (Traditional) — L06, 71-Feb
⊘ (Quality) Heavy and slow, this really lumbers. Great take — vocal and band — but just for fun.

Well (Baby Please Don't Go) (live) (Ward) — L08-11, 71-Jun
⊘ (Filler) Sounds mean-spirited, angry. Very chunky beat, slow. Band takes time to figure it out...

Well Well Well (Lennon) — L04-08, 70-Oct
✓ Primal screams run amok. Not bad, but could have used an edit.

What Is Life (Harrison) — H01-05, 70-Oct
✓ Clearly a "statement" song, and one of GH's masterworks.

What You Got (Lennon) — L10-04, 74-Aug
✓ Firey, funky, powerful. A late masterwork. Great horns. A total success.

What's That You're Doing? (McCartney/Wonder) — M27-04, 81-Mar
≈ (Style) Stevie provides the meat, and Paul the plate. Not a bad combo, if a little artificial.

Whatever Gets You thru the Night (Lennon) — L10-02, 74-Aug
✓ Such a good vibe that it's easy to forgive the shallow, me-decade sentiment.

When the Night (McCartney/McCartney) — M09-07, 72-Mar
≈ (Quality) Germ of a good song, but never pays off. Endless call-response very annoying.

When the Wind Is Blowing (McCartney/McCartney) — M04, 70-Dec
≈ (Unfinished) Quiet, gentle vibe, but largely wordless vocal leaves it incomplete.

Where Did Our Love Go (Holland/Dozier/Holland) — S12-05, 77-Nov
⊘ (Style/Quality) Best of the 60s as channeled through the worst of the 80s. Unholy, truly terrible mash-up.

Whispering Grass (Don't Tell the Trees) (Fisher/Fisher) — S01-03, 70-Mar
⊘ (Quality) RS vocal is actually charming, but the busy string arrangement piles on the sap.

Who Can See It (Harrison) — H04-05, 73-Mar
⊘ (Quality/Content) Almost great, but awkward. GH vocal is weak in upper range.

Who Needs a Heart (Starkey/Poncia) — S12-01, 77-Nov
≈ (Style) Straight pop rock. Inoffensive, if also not very memorable. RS wisely yields vocal in spots.

Wild Life (McCartney/McCartney) — M04-04, 71-Aug
⊘ (Quality) Plodding, overlong, nothing to catch or hold the ear. Dumb lyric. Bad vocal.

Window, Window (Harrison) — H01, 70-May
≈ (Demo/Quality) Jaunty waltz. Lyric isn't quite refined. Imagery is a little diffuse.

Wine, Women and Loud Happy Songs (Kingston) — S02-08, 70-Jun
⊘ (Style/Quality) Might work if Ringo were some sort of loser. But he's not, and this song is just bad for him.

Wings (Starkey/Poncia) — S11-03, 77-Jun
✓ Palatable, even fitting, for Ringo. Straight pop, and not bad at all.

Winter Rose / Love Awake (McCartney) — M20-11, 78-Jul
✓ More "parts" being linked. Somewhat misfitted to the project, but where else would they fit?

Wishing Book, The (Adcock) — S02, 70-Jun
⊘ (Style/Quality) Much like the rest of the album, it's just wrong for Ringo.

With a Little Luck (McCartney) — M18-09, 77-Nov
✓ Nice 70s pop. Slinky synths and a great vibe. Smart writing.

Without Her (Pickard) — S02-04, 70-Jun
⊘ (Style/Quality) Kind of sounds like The Monkees

Woman (Lennon) — L13-10, 80-Sep
✓ A sentimental favorite. Fantastic arrangement and vocal.

Appendix III / Solo Recordings

Woman Don't You Cry for Me (Harrison) — H08-01, 76-Sep
≈ (Style) Echoes his ponderous writing, but mostly sounds like turning a corner to something new.

Woman Is the Nigger of the World (Lennon/Ono) — L08-01, 72-Mar
⊘ (Content) Powerful, but built on a squishy metaphor. The idea does not outweigh the offensive term.

Woman of the Night (Pickard) — S02-05, 70-Jun
⊘ (Style/Quality) Again very high, story song.

Wonderful Christmastime (McCartney) — M21-01, 79-Jul
⊘ (Content) Certainly enduring, though barely a sketch. Sufficiently merry for most.

Working Class Hero (Lennon) — L04-04, 70-Oct
✓ Chilling and pointed, efficient and honest, this is Lennon at his absolute best.

World of Stone (Harrison) — H07-05, 75-Jun
⊘ (Content/Quality) Tortured, messy melody, and GH is not up to it. Nice piano and guitars.

Wrack My Brain (Harrison) — S13-02, 80-Nov
≈ (Quality) A rare misfire for GH/RS. Mostly a failure of the arrangement. Good song. Bad record.

Writing's on the Wall (Harrison) — H10-08, 80-Sep
✓ Pensive, prescient without being maudlin. GH writes plainly and avoids his worst tendencies.

Ya Ya (Dorsey/Levy/Lewis/Robinson) — L10-12, 74-Aug
⊘ (Filler) Novelty only.

Ya Ya (Dorsey/Levy/Lewis/Robinson) — L11-12, 74-Oct
⊘ (Style/Content) Among the lighter arrangements. More sprightly. Still, JL sleepwalks through the vocal.

You (Harrison) — H07-01, 75-May
≈ (Quality) Catchy pop riff, but painfully thin lyric. Parody of Macca?

You Always Hurt the One You Love (Roberts/Fisher) — S01-10, 70-Mar
⊘ (Style) Great potential disappears into a pure cheese arrangement. But don't blame the great band!

You and Me (Babe) (Harrison/Evans) — S07-10, 73-Jul
✓ In context, this really works. Outside, it sounds a little dumb. Still, likeable all around.

You Are Here (Lennon) — L09-11, 73-Aug
✓ Gentle, sweet, and new musical territory for John. Simplicity is an asset here. Nice steelwork.

You Belong to Me (King/Stewart/Price) — S13-07, 80-Nov
≈ (Filler) Sure it's a cliché, but the arrangement is spirited, simple. Doesn't pretend to be anything more.

You Can't Catch Me (Berry) — L11-04, 74-Oct
⊘ (Style/Content) Despite the lawsuit, no malice heard here. Still, the bloated band chugs unhelpfully.

You Can't Fight Lightning (Starkey) — S13, 80-Jul
⊘ (Quality/Filler) Essentially a jam, but utterly uninteresting until Linda starts singing. Even then...

You Don't Know Me at All (Jordan) — S09-05, 76-Jul
⊘ (Style) Pre-disco, formulaic, cheesy. Inoffensive, but would set Ringo on a very bad path.

You Gave Me the Answer (McCartney/McCartney) — M15-04, 75-Feb
≈ (Style) A least 10 years late, it's still not hard to listen to.

You Know I'll Get You Baby (McCartney) — M23, 79-Jul
⊘ (Filler) Minimalist 12-bar, clearly just for fun. But it's not really. Nothing to hear here.

You Saved My Soul (With Your True Love) (Lennon) — L, 80-Nov
⊘ (Demo) 50s-inspired, but a carbon copy rather than something new. "...you saved me from suicide..."

You're Sixteen (Sherman/Sherman) — S07-05, 73-Jul
≈ (Filler) A simple and fun cover. Nobody is trying too hard, and it just works.

You've Got a Nice Way (Stills/Stergis) — S13-09, 80-Aug
✓ Credit Stills for writing a song that really fits Ringo's strengths, and making a great record.

Your Love Is Forever (Harrison) — H09-08, 78-Nov
✓ Another in a group of just sweet, complete, beautiful songs. Like candy.

Zoo Gang (McCartney/McCartney) — M13-02, 73-Apr
⊘ (Filler) Just a sketch, and not very interesting.

Summary of Solo Recordings
1969-1982, By Availability Date, then Alphabetical

69-Jun	Give Peace a Chance (L01-01)		70-Oct	Beware of Darkness (H01-10)
69-Sep	Cold Turkey (L02-01)		70-Oct	Early 1970 (S04-02)
69-Oct	Night and Day (S01-02)		70-Oct	Eat at Home (M03-09)
69-Nov	Stardust (S01-06)		70-Oct	Get on the Right Thing (M09-03)
69-Dec	Cold Turkey (live) (L08-10)		70-Oct	God (L04-10)
70-Jan	Don't Cry Baby (M01)		70-Oct	Hear Me Lord (H01-18)
70-Jan	Hot as Sun/Glasses (M01-05)		70-Oct	Hey Diddle (M03)
70-Jan	Instant Karma! (L03-01)		70-Oct	Hold On (L04-02)
70-Jan	Junk (M01-06)		70-Oct	I Dig Love (H01-15)
70-Jan	Lovely Linda, The (M01-01)		70-Oct	I Found Out (L04-03)
70-Jan	Momma Miss America (M01-09)		70-Oct	I Remember Jeep (H01-22)
70-Jan	Oo You (M01-08)		70-Oct	I'd Have You Anytime (H01-01)
70-Jan	Suicide (M01)		70-Oct	I'll Still Love You (H01)
70-Jan	Teddy Boy (M01-10)		70-Oct	If Not for You (H01-06)
70-Jan	That Would Be Something (M01-02)		70-Oct	Isn't It a Pity (Version One) (H01-04)
70-Jan	Valentine Day (M01-03)		70-Oct	Isn't It a Pity (Version Two) (H01-17)
70-Feb	Blue, Turning Grey Over You (S01-07)		70-Oct	Isolation (L04-05)
70-Feb	Dream (S01-09)		70-Oct	It's Johnny's Birthday (H01-20)
70-Feb	Every Night (M01-04)		70-Oct	Let It Down (H01-08)
70-Feb	Have I Told You Lately That I Love You? (S01-11)		70-Oct	Long Haired Lady (M03-10)
70-Feb	I'm a Fool to Care (S01-05)		70-Oct	Long Lost John (L04)
70-Feb	Kreen - Akrore (M01-13)		70-Oct	Look at Me (L04-09)
70-Feb	Let the Rest of the World Go By (S01-12)		70-Oct	Love (L04-07)
70-Feb	Man We Was Lonely (M01-07)		70-Oct	Love for You, A (M03)
70-Feb	Maybe I'm Amazed (M01-12)		70-Oct	Mother (L04-01)
70-Feb	Singalong Junk (M01-11)		70-Oct	My Mummy's Dead (L04-11)
70-Mar	Bye Bye Blackbird (S01-04)		70-Oct	My Sweet Lord (H01-02)
70-Mar	It Don't Come Easy (S04-01)		70-Oct	Out of the Blue (H01-19)
70-Mar	Love Is a Many Splendoured Thing (S01-08)		70-Oct	Plug Me In (H01-21)
70-Mar	Sentimental Journey (S01-01)		70-Oct	Remember (L04-06)
70-Mar	Whispering Grass (Don't Tell the Trees) (S01-03)		70-Oct	Rode All Night (M03)
70-Mar	You Always Hurt the One You Love (S01-10)		70-Oct	Run of the Mill (H01-09)
70-May	Cosmic Empire (H01)		70-Oct	Sunshine Sometime (M03)
70-May	Dehradun (H01)		70-Oct	Thanks for the Pepperoni (H01-23)
70-May	Everybody, Nobody (H01)		70-Oct	Wah-Wah (H01-03)
70-May	Going Down to Golders Green (H01)		70-Oct	Well Well Well (L04-08)
70-May	I Don't Want to Do It (H01)		70-Oct	What Is Life (H01-05)
70-May	Mother Divine (H01)		70-Oct	Working Class Hero (L04-04)
70-May	Nowhere to Go (H01)		70-Nov	Heart of the Country (M03-07)
70-May	Tell Me What Has Happened to You (H01)		70-Nov	Little Woman Love (M06-02)
70-May	Window, Window (H01)		70-Nov	Monkberry Moon Delight (M03-08)
70-Jun	$15 Draw (S02-07)		70-Nov	Oh Woman, Oh Why (M02-02)
70-Jun	Beaucoups of Blues (S02-01)		70-Nov	Sally and Billy (L)
70-Jun	Coochy-Coochy (S03-02)		70-Nov	Smile Away (M03-06)
70-Jun	Down to the River (H01)		70-Nov	Too Many People (M03-01)
70-Jun	Fastest Growing Heartache in the West (S02-03)		70-Dec	1882 (M09)
70-Jun	I Live for You (H01)		70-Dec	When the Wind Is Blowing (M04)
70-Jun	I Wouldn't Have You Any Other Way (S02-09)		71-Jan	Back Seat of My Car, The (M03-12)
70-Jun	I'd Be Talking All the Time (S02-06)		71-Jan	Uncle Albert/Admiral Halsey (M03-05)
70-Jun	Loser's Lounge (S02-10)		71-Feb	Great Cock and Seagull Race (M03)
70-Jun	Love Don't Last Long (S02-02)		71-Feb	Now Hear This Song of Mine (M03)
70-Jun	Nashville Freakout (S02)		71-Feb	Power to the People (L05-01)
70-Jun	Om Hare Om (Gopala Krishna) (H01)		71-Feb	Ram On (M03-03)
70-Jun	Silent Homecoming (S02-12)		71-Feb	Ram On (Reprise) (M03-11)
70-Jun	Waiting (S02-11)		71-Feb	Well (Baby Please Don't Go) (L06)
70-Jun	Wine, Women and Loud Happy Songs (S02-08)		71-Mar	Big Barn Bed (M09-01)
70-Jun	Wishing Book, The (S02)		71-Mar	Dear Boy (M03-04)
70-Jun	Without Her (S02-04)		71-Mar	I Lie Around (M10-02)
70-Jun	Woman of the Night (S02-05)		71-Mar	Little Lamb Dragonfly (M09-05)
70-Oct	3 Legs (M03-02)		71-May	Do the Oz (L)
70-Oct	All Things Must Pass (H01-14)		71-May	God Save Us (L)
70-Oct	Another Day (M02-01)		71-Jun	Aü (live) (L08-14)
70-Oct	Apple Scruffs (H01-11)		71-Jun	Jamrag (live) (L08-12)
70-Oct	Art of Dying (H01-16)		71-Jun	Scumbag (live) (L08-13)
70-Oct	Awaiting on You All (H01-13)		71-Jun	Well (Baby Please Don't Go) (live) (L08-11)
70-Oct	Ballad of Sir Frankie Crisp (Let It Roll) (H01-12)		71-Jul	Bangla Desh (H02-01)
70-Oct	Behind That Locked Door (H01-07)		71-Jul	Crippled Inside (L06-02)

Appendix III / Solo Recordings

71-Jul	Deep Blue (H02-02)	73-Apr	Zoo Gang (M13-02)
71-Jul	Gimme Some Truth (L06-06)	73-Jul	Devil Woman (S07-09)
71-Jul	How Do You Sleep? (L06-08)	73-Jul	Have You Seen My Baby (S07-02)
71-Jul	How? (L06-09)	73-Jul	I'm the Greatest (S07-01)
71-Jul	I Don't Want to Be a Soldier (L06-05)	73-Jul	Oh My My (S07-06)
71-Jul	Imagine (L06-01)	73-Jul	Photograph (S07-03)
71-Jul	It's So Hard (L06-04)	73-Jul	Six O'Clock (S07-08)
71-Jul	Jealous Guy (L06-03)	73-Jul	Step Lightly (S07-07)
71-Jul	Oh My Love (L06-07)	73-Jul	Sunshine Life for Me (Sail Away Raymond) (S07-04)
71-Jul	Oh Yoko! (L06-10)	73-Jul	You and Me (Babe) (S07-10)
71-Jul	San Francisco Bay Blues (L06)	73-Jul	You're Sixteen (S07-05)
71-Aug	African Yeah Yeah (M04)	73-Aug	Aisumasen (I'm Sorry) (L09-03)
71-Aug	Bip Bop (Link) (M04-07)	73-Aug	Bring on the Lucie (Freda Peeple) (L09-05)
71-Aug	Bip Bop (M04-02)	73-Aug	I Know (I Know) (L09-10)
71-Aug	Blackpool (M03)	73-Aug	Intuition (L09-07)
71-Aug	Blindman (S05-02)	73-Aug	Meat City (L09-12)
71-Aug	Dear Friend (M04-09)	73-Aug	Mind Games (L09-01)
71-Aug	I Am Your Singer (M04-06)	73-Aug	Nutopian International Anthem (L09-06)
71-Aug	Indeed I Do (M04)	73-Aug	One Day (At a Time) (L09-04)
71-Aug	Love Is Strange (M04-03)	73-Aug	Only People (L09-09)
71-Aug	Mumbo (Link) (M04-10)	73-Aug	Out the Blue (L09-08)
71-Aug	Mumbo (M04-01)	73-Aug	Rock 'N' Roll People (L09)
71-Aug	Some People Never Know (M04-05)	73-Aug	Tight A$ (L09-02)
71-Aug	Tomorrow (M04-08)	73-Aug	You Are Here (L09-11)
71-Aug	Wild Life (M04-04)	73-Sep	Helen Wheels (M11-01)
71-Sep	Back Off Boogaloo (S05-01)	73-Sep	Mamunia (M12-06)
71-Oct	Happy Xmas (War Is Over) (L07-01)	73-Oct	Band on the Run (M12-01)
72-Feb	Give Ireland Back to the Irish (M05-01)	73-Oct	Bluebird (M12-03)
72-Feb	Give Ireland Back to the Irish (Version) (M05-02)	73-Oct	Jet (M12-02)
72-Mar	Angela (L08-09)	73-Oct	Let Me Roll It (M12-05)
72-Mar	Attica State (L08-03)	73-Oct	Mrs. Vandebilt (M12-04)
72-Mar	John Sinclair (L08-08)	73-Oct	Nineteen Hundred and Eighty-Five (M12-09)
72-Mar	Loup (1st Indian on the Moon) (M09-08)	73-Oct	No Words (M12-07)
72-Mar	Luck of the Irish, The (L08-07)	73-Oct	Picasso's Last Words (Drink to Me) (M12-08)
72-Mar	Mama's Little Girl (M09)	73-Dec	Angel Baby (L11)
72-Mar	Mary Had a Little Lamb (M06-01)	73-Dec	Be My Baby (L11)
72-Mar	Mess I'm In, The (M09)	73-Dec	Here We Go Again (L11)
72-Mar	New York City (L08-05)	73-Dec	I'll Give You a Ring (M28-02)
72-Mar	Single Pigeon (M09-06)	73-Dec	Just Because (Reprise) (L11)
72-Mar	Sunday Bloody Sunday (L08-06)	73-Dec	Since My Baby Left Me (L11)
72-Mar	Tragedy (M09)	73-Dec	To Know Her Is to Love Her (L11)
72-Mar	When the Night (M09-07)	74-Jun	Far East Man (H06-08)
72-Mar	Woman Is the Nigger of the World (L08-01)	74-Jun	Let's Love (M15)
72-Aug	Best Friend (M09)	74-Jul	Junior's Farm (M14-01)
72-Aug	Mess, The (live) (M08-02)	74-Jul	Sally G (M14-02)
72-Sep	Country Dreamer (M11-02)	74-Jul	Send Me the Heart (M14)
72-Sep	Hold Me Tight (M09-09)	74-Jul	Walking in the Park with Eloise (M)
72-Sep	Lazy Dynamite (M09-10)	74-Aug	(It's All Down to) Goodnight Vienna (S08-01)
72-Sep	Night Out (M09)	74-Aug	#9 Dream (L10-07)
72-Oct	Bridge on the River Suite (M)	74-Aug	All by Myself (S08-06)
72-Oct	Hands of Love (M09-11)	74-Aug	Baby Face (M15)
72-Oct	Live and Let Die (M10-01)	74-Aug	Beef Jerky (L10-10)
72-Oct	Power Cut (M09-12)	74-Aug	Bless You (L10-05)
72-Nov	C Moon (M07-01)	74-Aug	Call Me (S08-07)
72-Nov	Down and Out (S06-02)	74-Aug	Easy for Me (S08-10)
72-Nov	Hi, Hi, Hi (M07-02)	74-Aug	Going Down on Love (L10-01)
72-Nov	Jazz Street (M09)	74-Aug	Goodnight Vienna (Reprise) (S08-11)
72-Dec	One More Kiss (M09-04)	74-Aug	Husbands and Wives (S08-04)
72-Dec	Thank You Darling (M09)	74-Aug	Love My Baby (M15)
73-Jan	My Love (M09-02)	74-Aug	No No Song (S08-08)
73-Feb	Miss O'Dell (H03-02)	74-Aug	Nobody Loves You (When You're Down...) (L10-11)
73-Mar	4th of July (M)	74-Aug	Occapella (S08-02)
73-Mar	Be Here Now (H04-08)	74-Aug	Old Dirt Road (L10-03)
73-Mar	Day the World Gets 'Round, The (H04-10)	74-Aug	Only You (And You Alone) (S08-09)
73-Mar	Don't Let Me Wait Too Long (H04-04)	74-Aug	Oo-Wee (S08-03)
73-Mar	Give Me Love (Give Me Peace on Earth) (H04-01)	74-Aug	Scared (L10-06)
73-Mar	Light That Has Lighted the World, The (H04-03)	74-Aug	Snookeroo (S08-05)
73-Mar	Living in the Material World (H04-06)	74-Aug	Soily (M15)
73-Mar	Lord Loves the One (That Loves the Lord) (H04-07)	74-Aug	Steel and Glass (L10-09)
73-Mar	Sue Me, Sue You Blues (H04-02)	74-Aug	Surprise, Surprise (Sweet Bird of Paradox) (L10-08)
73-Mar	That Is All (H04-11)	74-Aug	What You Got (L10-04)
73-Mar	Try Some, Buy Some (H04-09)	74-Aug	Whatever Gets You thru the Night (L10-02)
73-Mar	Who Can See It (H04-05)	74-Aug	Ya Ya (L10-12)

SAVE THE BEATLES!

74-Oct	Ain't That a Shame (L11-05)		76-Sep	Dear One (H08-02)
74-Oct	Be-Bop-A-Lula (L11-01)		76-Sep	It's What You Value (H08-06)
74-Oct	Bony Moronie (L11-11)		76-Sep	Learning How to Love You (H08-10)
74-Oct	Bring It on Home/Send Me Some Lovin' (L11-10)		76-Sep	Pure Smokey (H08-08)
74-Oct	Bye Bye, Love (H06-04)		76-Sep	See Yourself (H08-05)
74-Oct	Dark Horse (H06-07)		76-Sep	This Song (H08-04)
74-Oct	Ding Dong, Ding Dong (H06-06)		76-Sep	True Love (H08-07)
74-Oct	Do You Wanna Dance? (L11-06)		76-Sep	Woman Don't You Cry for Me (H08-01)
74-Oct	Hari's on Tour (Express) (H06-01)		76-Dec	Nobody Told Me (L14-05)
74-Oct	I Don't Care Anymore (H05-02)		76-Dec	She's a Friend of Dorothy's (L)
74-Oct	It Is 'He' (Jai Sri Krishna) (H06-09)		77-Mar	B-Side to Seaside (M)
74-Oct	Just Because (L11-13)		77-Mar	Children Children (M18-06)
74-Oct	Maya Love (H06-05)		77-Mar	Mo (H)
74-Oct	Move Over Ms. L (L12-02)		77-Mar	Name and Address (M18-12)
74-Oct	Peggy Sue (L11-09)		77-Jun	Can She Do It Like She Dances (S11-06)
74-Oct	Rip It Up/Ready Teddy (L11-03)		77-Jun	Drowning in the Sea of Love (S11-01)
74-Oct	Simply Shady (H06-02)		77-Jun	Gave It All Up (S11-04)
74-Oct	Slippin' and Slidin' (L11-08)		77-Jun	Gypsies in Flight (S11-09)
74-Oct	So Sad (H06-03)		77-Jun	It's No Secret (S11-08)
74-Oct	Stand by Me (L11-02)		77-Jun	Out on the Streets (S11-05)
74-Oct	Sweet Little Sixteen (L11-07)		77-Jun	Simple Love Song (S11-10)
74-Oct	Ya Ya (L11-12)		77-Jun	Sneaking Sally Through the Alley (S11-07)
74-Oct	You Can't Catch Me (L11-04)		77-Jun	Tango All Night (S11-02)
74-Nov	Letting Go (M15-06)		77-Jun	Waterspout (M18)
74-Nov	Love in Song (M15-03)		77-Jun	Wings (S11-03)
74-Dec	Rudolph the Red-Nosed Reggae (M21-02)		77-Aug	Girls' School (M17-01)
75-Feb	Call Me Back Again (M15-10)		77-Aug	London Town (M18-01)
75-Feb	Crossroads Theme (M15-13)		77-Aug	Mull of Kintyre (M17-02)
75-Feb	Going to New Orleans (My Carnival) (M15)		77-Sep	Free as a Bird (L)
75-Feb	Listen to What the Man Said (M15-11)		77-Sep	I Don't Wanna Face It (L14-03)
75-Feb	Lunchbox/Odd Sox (M22-03)		77-Sep	Mirror, Mirror (On The Wall) (L)
75-Feb	Magneto and Titanium Man (M15-05)		77-Sep	Now and Then (L)
75-Feb	My Carnival (M)		77-Sep	One of the Boys (L)
75-Feb	Rock Show (M15-02)		77-Oct	Boil Crisis (M18)
75-Feb	Spirits of Ancient Egypt (M15-08)		77-Nov	Bad Boy (S12-02)
75-Feb	Treat Her Gently / Lonely Old People (M15-12)		77-Nov	Cafe on the Left Bank (M18-02)
75-Feb	Venus and Mars (Reprise) (M15-07)		77-Nov	Deliver Your Children (M18-11)
75-Feb	You Gave Me the Answer (M15-04)		77-Nov	Don't Let It Bring You Down (M18-13)
75-Mar	Venus and Mars (M15-01)		77-Nov	Famous Groupies (M18-10)
75-Apr	Answer's at the End, The (H07-02)		77-Nov	Hard Times (S12-06)
75-Apr	Tired of Midnight Blue (H07-08)		77-Nov	Heart on My Sleeve (S12-04)
75-May	Bit More of You, A (H07-06)		77-Nov	Lipstick Traces (On a Cigarette) (S12-03)
75-May	This Guitar (Can't Keep from Crying) (H07-03)		77-Nov	Man Like Me, A (S12-10)
75-May	You (H07-01)		77-Nov	Monkey See – Monkey Do (S12-08)
75-Jun	Can't Stop Thinking About You (H07-07)		77-Nov	Old Time Relovin' (S12-09)
75-Jun	Grey Cloudy Lies (H07-09)		77-Nov	Tonight (S12-07)
75-Jun	His Name Is Legs (Ladies and Gentlemen) (H07-10)		77-Nov	Where Did Our Love Go (S12-05)
75-Jun	Ooh Baby (You Know That I Love You) (H07-04)		77-Nov	Who Needs a Heart (S12-01)
75-Jun	World of Stone (H07-05)		77-Nov	With a Little Luck (M18-09)
75-Oct	Note You Never Wrote, The (M16-02)		77-Dec	Backwards Traveller (M18-04)
76-Feb	Beware My Love (M16-04)		77-Dec	Cuff Link (M18-05)
76-Feb	Cook of the House (M16-07)		77-Dec	Girlfriend (M18-07)
76-Feb	Let 'Em In (M16-01)		77-Dec	I'm Carrying (M18-03)
76-Feb	Must Do Something About It (M16-09)		77-Dec	Morse Moose and the Grey Goose (M18-14)
76-Feb	San Ferry Anne (M16-10)		78-Jan	I've Had Enough (M18-08)
76-Feb	She's My Baby (M16-03)		78-Mar	Did We Meet Somewhere Before (M18)
76-Feb	Silly Love Songs (M16-06)		78-May	Same Time Next year (M)
76-Feb	Warm and Beautiful (M16-11)		78-Jul	Arrow Through Me (M20-05)
76-Jun	Cookin' (In the Kitchen of Love) (S09-06)		78-Jul	Old Siam, Sir (M20-06)
76-Jun	Just a Dream (S10-02)		78-Jul	One Way Love Affair (S)
76-Jul	Cryin' (S09-04)		78-Jul	She's So in Love (S)
76-Jul	Don't You Wanna Dance (M18)		78-Jul	Spin It On (M20-04)
76-Jul	Dose of Rock 'n' Roll, A (S09-01)		78-Jul	To You (M20-09)
76-Jul	Hey! Baby (S09-02)		78-Jul	Winter Rose / Love Awake (M20-11)
76-Jul	I'll Still Love You (S09-07)		78-Sep	After the Ball / Million Miles (M20-10)
76-Jul	Lady Gaye (S09-10)		78-Sep	Cage (M20)
76-Jul	Las Brisas (S09-09)		78-Sep	Reception (M20-01)
76-Jul	Pure Gold (S09-03)		78-Sep	So Glad to See You Here (M20-13)
76-Jul	Spooky Weirdness (S09-11)		78-Sep	We're Open Tonight (M20-03)
76-Jul	This Be Called a Song (S09-08)		78-Oct	Rockestra Theme (M20-08)
76-Jul	You Don't Know Me at All (S09-05)		78-Nov	Baby's Request (M20-14)
76-Sep	Beautiful Girl (H08-03)		78-Nov	Blow Away (H09-05)
76-Sep	Crackerbox Palace (H08-09)		78-Nov	Dark Sweet Lady (H09-07)

Appendix III / Solo Recordings

78-Nov	Faster (H09-06)
78-Nov	Getting Closer (M20-02)
78-Nov	Here Comes the Moon (H09-03)
78-Nov	If You Believe (H09-10)
78-Nov	Love Comes to Everyone (H09-01)
78-Nov	Not Guilty (H09-02)
78-Nov	Soft Touch (H09-09)
78-Nov	Soft-Hearted Hana (H09-04)
78-Nov	Your Love Is Forever (H09-08)
78-Dec	I Can't Write Another Song (M)
78-Dec	Praying Mantis Heart (M)
78-Dec	Reggae Moon (M)
78-Dec	Seems Like Old Times (M)
79-Feb	Broadcast, The (M20-12)
79-Feb	Daytime Nighttime Suffering (M19-02)
79-Feb	Goodnight Tonight (M19-01)
79-Jun	Robber's Ball (M)
79-Jul	All You Horse Riders / Blue Sway (M23)
79-Jul	Blue Sway (M23)
79-Jul	Bogey Music (M23-09)
79-Jul	Bogey Wobble (M23)
79-Jul	Check My Machine (M24-02)
79-Jul	Coming Up (M23-01)
79-Jul	Darkroom (M23-10)
79-Jul	Front Parlour (M23-06)
79-Jul	Frozen Jap (M23-08)
79-Jul	Mr. H Atom (M23)
79-Jul	Nobody Knows (M23-05)
79-Jul	On the Way (M23-03)
79-Jul	One of These Days (M23-11)
79-Jul	Secret Friend (M25-02)
79-Jul	Summer's Day Song (M23-07)
79-Jul	Temporary Secretary (M23-02)
79-Jul	Waterfalls (M23-04)
79-Jul	Wonderful Christmastime (M21-01)
79-Jul	You Know I'll Get You Baby (M23)
79-Oct	Not For Love Nor Money (Illusions) (L)
79-Dec	Coming Up (Live at Glasgow) (M22-02)
80-Jun	Real Love (L)
80-Jul	Attention (S13-04)
80-Jul	Private Property (S13-01)
80-Jul	Sure to Fall (S13-08)
80-Jul	You Can't Fight Lightning (S13)
80-Aug	Red and Black Blues (S13)
80-Aug	Simple as That (M)
80-Aug	Stop, You Don't Know Where She Came From (M)
80-Aug	We All Stand Together (Humming Version) (M)
80-Aug	We All Stand Together (M)
80-Aug	You've Got a Nice Way (S13-09)
80-Sep	(Just Like) Starting Over (L13-01)
80-Sep	Baltimore Oriole (H10-05)
80-Sep	Beautiful Boy (Darling Boy) (L13-07)
80-Sep	Cleanup Time (L13-03)
80-Sep	Dear Yoko (L13-12)
80-Sep	Flying Hour (H10)
80-Sep	Hong Kong Blues (H10-09)
80-Sep	I'm Losing You (L13-05)
80-Sep	Lay His Head (H10)
80-Sep	Life Itself (H10-03)
80-Sep	Sat Singing (H10)
80-Sep	Save the World (H10-10)
80-Sep	Tears of the World (H10)
80-Sep	Unconsciousness Rules (H10-02)
80-Sep	Watching the Wheels (L13-08)
80-Sep	Woman (L13-10)
80-Sep	Writing's on the Wall (H10-08)
80-Nov	(Forgive Me) My Little Flower Princess (L14-09)
80-Nov	Across the River (L)
80-Nov	Borrowed Time (L14-07)
80-Nov	Dear John (L)
80-Nov	Drumming is My Madness (S13-03)
80-Nov	Gone from This Place (L)
80-Nov	Grow Old with Me (L14-11)
80-Nov	Happy Rishikesh Song, The (L)
80-Nov	Help Me To Help Myself (L)
80-Nov	I'm Stepping Out (L14-01)
80-Nov	India (L)
80-Nov	Life Begins At 40 (L)
80-Nov	Memories / Howling At The Moon (L)
80-Nov	Mr. Hyde's Gone (Don't Be Afraid) (L)
80-Nov	Serve Yourself (L)
80-Nov	Stop and Take the Time to Smell the Roses (S13-05)
80-Nov	Wrack My Brain (S13-02)
80-Nov	You Belong to Me (S13-07)
80-Nov	You Saved My Soul (With Your True Love) (L)
80-Dec	Back Off Boogaloo (S13-10)
80-Dec	Keep Under Cover (M30-04)
80-Dec	Ode to a Koala Bear (M29-02)
80-Dec	Rainclouds (M26-02)
81-Feb	All Those Years Ago (H10-04)
81-Feb	Blood from a Clone (H10-01)
81-Feb	Brandy (S13)
81-Feb	Dead Giveaway (S13-06)
81-Feb	Teardrops (H10-06)
81-Feb	That Which I Have Lost (H10-07)
81-Feb	Wake Up (S13)
81-Mar	Average Person (M30-08)
81-Mar	Dress Me Up as a Robber (M27-11)
81-Mar	Ebony and Ivory (M27-12)
81-Mar	Get It (M27-09)
81-Mar	Hey Hey (M30-09)
81-Mar	My Old Friend (M)
81-Mar	Pound Is Sinking, The (M27-07)
81-Mar	Somebody Who Cares (M27-03)
81-Mar	Take It Away (M27-02)
81-Mar	What's That You're Doing? (M27-04)
81-Dec	Ballroom Dancing (M27-06)
81-Dec	Be What You See (Link) (M27-10)
81-Dec	Here Today (M27-05)
81-Dec	Man, The (M30-06)
81-Dec	Sweetest Little Show (M30-07)
81-Dec	Tug of War (M27-01)
81-Dec	Wanderlust (M27-08)
82-Jan	Christian Bop (M)
82-Feb	It's Not On (M)
82-Apr	Say Say Say (M30-02)
82-Jul	Alibi (S14-03)
82-Jul	As Far as We Can Go (S14-08)
82-Jul	Be My Baby (S14-04)
82-Jul	Everybody's in a Hurry But Me (S14-09)
82-Jul	Going Down (S14-10)
82-Jul	Hopeless (S14-02)
82-Jul	I Keep Forgettin' (S14-06)
82-Jul	In My Car (S14-01)
82-Jul	Picture Show Life (S14-07)
82-Jul	She's About a Mover (S14-05)
82-Aug	Baby Don't Run Away (H11-08)
82-Aug	Circles (H11-10)
82-Aug	Dream Away (H11-09)
82-Aug	Gone Troppo (H11-05)
82-Aug	Greece (H11-04)
82-Aug	I Really Love You (H11-03)
82-Aug	Mystical One (H11-06)
82-Aug	That's the Way It Goes (H11-02)
82-Aug	Unknown Delight (H11-07)
82-Aug	Wake Up My Love (H11-01)
82-Oct	Other Me, The (M30-03)
82-Oct	Pipes of Peace (M30-01)
82-Oct	So Bad (M30-05)
82-Oct	Through Our Love (M30-11)
82-Oct	Tug of Peace (M30-10)
82-Nov	Twice in a Lifetime (M)

Appendix IV
Certified Sales

Many sources list anecdotal record sales information. Almost every Beatles book you read will throw out some seemingly authentic number for a particular album, without any supporting documentation. There is often no way to know the source of the information. Such numbers tend to be difficult or impossible to verify. I have yet to see a case where the chain of references led to an entirely trustworthy source.

Sometimes these numbers are drawn from industry trade reports, press releases, or verbal statements by someone associated with an artist or label. Sometimes they come from reference books, whose own sources are nebulous or dubious. Indeed, sales figures without documentation may very well be nothing more than *wishful guesses*, and are inherently unreliable. They should be considered as *marketing materials*, and taken with a grain of salt.

The reality is that actual sales numbers for recordings are notoriously hard to come by. There is great incentive within the recording industry to keep them secret. When they are high, they might be reason to boast, but when they are low, they can be embarrassing and damaging to an artist's brand. Further, record companies and recording artists often spar over royalty payments, and the winner of the tussle tends to be the party with the most persistent (i.e. ruthless) accountant. This is one of the bitter lessons we all learned from Allen Klein.

Perhaps the only way to get anything approaching reliable sales numbers is to use the official certifications from the Recording Industry Association of America (RIAA) and the British Phonographic Industry (BRIT).

Certifications are at least a significant step up from anecdotes, though even they have some inherent problems. The same incentives toward secrecy apply, and record companies can schedule certifications to best manipulate royalty payments. Additionally, the calculation methods have changed substantially over time, complicating head-to-head comparisons from different eras. Even reissues can cause problems because they may or may not be counted with the numbers from the original release.

But certifications are at least based on *audited sales data*, making them theoretically the most reliable numbers available to the public. Though not exact sales figures, they represent milestones which a release has achieved. An album certified as "Platinum" by the RIAA has sold *at least* one million units — but it is likely to have sold more, perhaps many more. How many more will not be known until the next certification, and may well never be known. But the certification at least says something meaningful about the sales, and we can be certain that the number of actual sales is not *lower* than its certification.

Thus, sales figures quoted in this book are taken from RIAA and BRIT certifications as much as possible. The following amounts are used for the certification levels:

RIAA		BRIT	
Platinum	1,000,000 units	**Platinum**	300,000 sales
Gold	500,000 units	Gold	100,000 sales
Silver	60,000 sales		

The difference between "units" and "sales" is significant, and complicated, and somewhat beyond the scope of this appendix, but an example gives the basics.

In the BRIT numbers, we know that the "Gold" certification for George Harrison's *All Things Must Pass* means that 100,000 people walked into record stores (back when people actually did that) and bought the album.

But the RIAA numbers count physical discs sold, and consider each disc a separate "unit." George's album is certified 6x Platinum, meaning 6,000,000 units sold, but *All Things Must Pass* is a triple album, so each sale contains three units. To get the number of actual purchases, you have to divide the certification number by the number of discs in the set. This certification tells us, therefore, that there were at least 2 million purchases of the whole album. RIAA numbers have therefore been adjusted as necessary to compare apples to apples. In the chart which follows, multi-disc releases show the number of discs in parentheses. This adjustment is still not perfect, but close enough for our purposes.

These certifications do not include sales in any other countries beyond the US and UK. We will assume that the proportions between the titles are likely to be at least roughly similar throughout the world — even knowing that certain pockets of the world fell harder for certain records. Those differences, however, are not significant to this project.

Beatles albums before *Rubber Soul* are not listed because of the differences between UK and US versions, which make it impossible to compare and combine certification numbers. *Yellow Submarine* is not listed because it contained only four new tracks. Sales of *Magical Mystery Tour* combine both the album and double-EP version, which were certified separately. In the chart, compilations and live albums are shown in *italics*. All figures are current as of April 2020.

Finally, it's worth noting that worldwide sales of albums like *Sgt. Pepper*, *Abbey Road*, and *1* are widely reported in the 30 million range each, more than double the certified numbers shown on this chart, and higher than the totals you would get by adding in certifications from smaller markets. As stated at the outset, it is difficult to find trustworthy sources to back up these numbers, but they do not sound unreasonable.

Appendix IV / Certified Sales

For our purposes, however, it is the relative sales levels between the records that are required, more than hard and fast totals. The Beatles sold a lot of records, both together and apart, and we are left to accept that the actual numbers can never be known for certain, and are largely beside the point. All we really need is to know how they did relative to one another, and this information is sufficient for that.

Certified Sales
US/UK, as of April 2020

Items in *italics* are extended catalog releases.

ARTIST	TITLE	SALES (Millions)
	Sgt. Pepper's Lonely Hearts Club Band	16.10
	1	14.30
	Abbey Road	12.60
	The Beatles [The White Album] (2)	12.60
	The Beatles 1967 - 1970 (2)	9.10
	The Beatles 1962 - 1966 (2)	8.10
	Magical Mystery Tour	6.40
	Rubber Soul	6.30
	Revolver	5.60
	Hard Day's Night	4.30
	Let It Be	4.10
	Band on the Run	3.30
	Double Fantasy	3.30
	All Things Must Pass (3)	2.10
	Imagine	2.10
	McCartney	2.00

Save the Beatles!

	Pipes of Peace	1.30
	Venus and Mars	1.30
	Wings Greatest	*1.30*
	Back to the Egg	1.10
	London Town	1.10
	Ringo	1.10
	Shaved Fish	*1.10*
	Tug of War	1.10
	Wings at the Speed of Sound	1.10
	Ram	1.00
	McCartney II	0.60
	Milk and Honey	0.60
	Mind Games	0.60
	Red Rose Speedway	0.60
	Rock 'n' Roll	0.60
	Dark Horse	0.56
	Goodnight Vienna	0.56
	The Best of George Harrison	*0.56*
	Thirty Three & 1/3	0.56
	Walls and Bridges	0.56
	Extra Texture (Read All About It)	0.50
	George Harrison	0.50
	Living in the Material World	0.50
	John Lennon/Plastic Ono Band	0.50

Appendix IV / Certified Sales

	Wild Life	0.50
	Wings Over America (3)	0.43
	The Concert for Bangladesh (3)	0.17

The following are not certified, indicating sales below 560,000:

Ringo
Bad Boy
Beaucoups of Blues
Old Wave
Ringo the 4th
Ringo's Rotogravure
Sentimental Journey
Stop and Smell the Roses

George
Gone Troppo
Somewhere in England

John
Some Time in New York City (2)

Appendix V
Chart Scoring

The longer a title stays on the charts, and the higher it peaks, the more popular it is relative to all the other titles in the market at that same moment. Chart Scoring aggregates information for each title from multiple weeks and multiple charts to create a single number, attempting to measure its popularity for comparison purposes.

This is a measurement of *relative popularity* only, as there probably is no way to measure *absolute popularity* outside of actual sales numbers. The scoring process means that a 1967 album which was on the charts for 25 weeks, with five weeks at number one, will receive exactly the same score as a 1977 album with the same chart profile — despite the fact that the albums may have sold in very different quantities. It serves as an equalizer between eras, given the significant market shifts which happened between *Please Please Me* and *Milk and Honey*.

In other words, Chart Scoring essentially tries to answer exactly one question: "How big a splash did this record make when it was released, relative to the rest of the market?" The bigger the splash, the more likely that the record would leave a cultural footprint, including influencing other artists of the same era.

This is an *approximate* and *imperfect* measure, to be sure. Some records make a big splash but are forgotten quickly. Others make a smaller splash but resonate over time, becoming cherished classics. Some are perfect for their moment, and quickly sound dated. Others emerge as timeless, defying the shifting currents of fashion. This metric cannot measure such long-term impacts, only the impact at first release.

It also cannot be used to either measure or imply sales. The number one hit this week may have sold many more or less than the number one hit last week. Because of such variance, chart data cannot be used in any way to calculate or even estimate raw sales, and therefore neither can Chart Scoring. For more on sales, see Appendix IV, *Certified Sales*.

Scores are given as follows for each week that a title appears on a chart:

```
#1 = 10 points
#2 to #10 = 6 points
#11 to #40 = 3 points
#41 to #100 = 1 point
```

Points are given separately for appearances on US and UK charts, then an overall score is calculated by weighing the results according to total market size, with the US market roughly four times the size of the UK market.

SAVE THE BEATLES!

There is nothing magic about these point assignments or the weighting. Arguments can be made for all sorts of alternate scoring schemes. But after trying many different versions, and finding the results broadly similar, this model seemed to sufficiently reflect real world popularity.

The underlying data is available for review at:

SaveTheBeatles.com

Chart Scoring
US/UK albums, scores combined

ARTIST	TITLE	SCORE
	Sgt. Pepper's Lonely Hearts Club Band	2113
	Band on the Run	1451
	Abbey Road	1338
	Rubber Soul	1020
	The Beatles [The White Album]	996
	The Beatles 1967-1970	967
	Double Fantasy	898
	Wings at the Speed of Sound	862
	The Beatles 1962-1966	816
	Revolver	797
	Ram	771
	Imagine	758
	Magical Mystery Tour	754
	Let It Be	698
	All Things Must Pass	697

Appendix V / Chart Scoring

	McCartney	628
	Venus and Mars	565
	Tug of War	485
	The Concert for Bangladesh	480
	Wings Over America	455
	Red Rose Speedway	442
	Ringo	439
	Living in the Material World	417
	London Town	398
	McCartney II	310
	Walls and Bridges	292
	Pipes of Peace	264
	Rock 'n' Roll	260
	Back to the Egg	259
	Mind Games	258
	John Lennon/Plastic Ono Band	252
	Goodnight Vienna	240
	Shaved Fish	203
	Wild Life	191
	Dark Horse	184
	Wings Greatest	176
	Milk and Honey	173
	Extra Texture (Read All About It)	156
	Thirty Three & 1/3	150

	George Harrison	131
	Somewhere in England	104
	Sentimental Journey	101
	Ringo's Rotogravure	80
	Blast from Your Past	76
	Best of George Harrison	64
	Some Time in New York City	64
	Beaucoups of Blues	36
	Stop and Smell the Roses	8
	Bad Boy	0
	Gone Troppo	0
	Ringo the 4th	0

Items in *italics* are extended catalog releases.

Appendix VI
Beatles Recordings

Key

Songwriter Information

    Songwriter Credit - Omitted for "Lennon/McCartney"
    Songwriter Class Sequence - Numbered by order of release:

B	Lennon/McCartney/Harrison/Starkey
C	Cover
H	Harrison
LM	Lennon/McCartney
LMS	Lennon/McCartney/Starkey
S	Starkey

    LM Class - For Lennon/McCartney tracks only:

L	Lennon alone
L+	Lennon with some help from McCartney
LM	Lennon with major help from McCartney
≈	Full collaboration
ML	McCartney with major help from Lennon
M+	McCartney with some help from Lennon
M	McCartney alone

    These designations are derived from comments in interviews.

Recording Information

    Recording ID - Numbered by order of completion
    Personnel - Indicates who played on the track:

B	All Beatles
JPGR	Subsets of Beatles
M	George Martin
W	Billy Preston
+	Additional guest musicians

    Phase Number - See chapter 3, *Phases*

Notes *can be found at the end.*

Save the Beatles!

ID	Release	Title (Songwriter)	Recording	Notes
B01-A1	10/5/62	Love Me Do (LM-001, M+)	B-001 (B, 2)	[1]
B01-B1	10/5/62	P.S. I Love You (LM-002, M)	B-002 (B+, 2)	
B02-A1	1/11/63	Please Please Me (LM-003, L)	B-004 (B, 2)	[2]
B02-B1	1/11/63	Ask Me Why (LM-004, L+)	B-005 (B, 2)	
B03-A1	3/22/63	I Saw Her Standing There (LM-005, M+)	B-009 (B, 2)	
B03-A2	3/22/63	Misery (LM-006, ≈)	B-014 (BM, 2)	
B03-A3	3/22/63	Anna (Go to Him) (Alexander, C-01)	B-010 (B, 1)	
B03-A4	3/22/63	Chains (Goffin/King, C-02)	B-012 (B, 1)	
B03-A5	3/22/63	Boys (Dixon/Farrell, C-03)	B-011 (B, 1)	
B03-A7	3/23/63	Please Please Me (2) (LM-003, L)	B-016 (B, 2)	[3]
B03-B1	3/22/63	Love Me Do (2) (LM-001, M+)	B-003 (B+, 2)	[4]
B03-B3	3/22/63	Baby It's You (David/Williams/Bacharach, C-04)	B-015 (BM, 1)	
B03-B4	3/22/63	Do You Want to Know a Secret (LM-007, ≈)	B-007 (B, 2)	[5]
B03-B5	3/22/63	A Taste of Honey (Scott/Marlow, C-05)	B-006 (B, 1)	
B03-B6	3/22/63	There's a Place (LM-008, L+)	B-008 (B, 2)	
B03-B7	3/22/63	Twist and Shout (Medley/Russell, C-06)	B-013 (B, 1)	
B04-A1	4/11/63	From Me to You (LM-009, ≈)	B-017 (B, 2)	
B04-B1	4/11/63	Thank You Girl (LM-010, ≈)	B-018 (B, 2)	
B05-A1	8/23/63	She Loves You (LM-011, ≈)	B-019 (B, 2)	[6]
B05-B1	8/23/63	I'll Get You (LM-012, ≈)	B-020 (B, 2)	
B06-A1	11/22/63	It Won't Be Long (LM-013, L+)	B-027 (B, 2)	
B06-A2	11/22/63	All I've Got to Do (LM-014, L)	B-029 (B, 2)	
B06-A3	11/22/63	All My Loving (LM-015, M)	B-028 (B, 2)	
B06-A4	11/22/63	Don't Bother Me (Harrison, H-01)	B-032 (B, 2)	
B06-A5	11/22/63	Little Child (LM-016, ≈)	B-033 (B, 2)	
B06-A6	11/22/63	Till There Was You (Willson, C-07)	B-025 (B, 1)	
B06-A7	11/22/63	Please Mister Postman (Holland et. al., C-08)	B-023 (B, 1)	
B06-B1	11/22/63	Roll Over Beethoven (Berry, C-09)	B-026 (B, 1)	
B06-B2	11/22/63	Hold Me Tight (LM-017, M)	B-031 (B, 2)	
B06-B3	11/22/63	You Really Got a Hold On Me (Robinson, C-10)	B-021 (BM, 1)	
B06-B4	11/22/63	I Wanna Be Your Man (LM-018, M+)	B-036 (BM, 2)	
B06-B5	11/22/63	Devil in Her Heart (Drapkin, C-11)	B-022 (B, 1)	
B06-B6	11/22/63	Not a Second Time (LM-019, L)	B-030 (BM, 2)	
B06-B7	11/22/63	Money (That's What I Want) (Bradford/Gordy, C-12)	B-024 (BM, 1)	
B07-A1	11/29/63	I Want to Hold Your Hand (LM-020, ≈)	B-034 (B, 2)	[6]
B07-B1	11/29/63	This Boy (LM-021, L)	B-035 (B, 2)	
B08-A1	2/4/64	Komm, gib mir deine Hand (L/M/Nicolas/Hellmer, LM-020)	B-037 (B, 2)	[7]
B08-B1	2/4/64	Sie liebt dich (L/M/Nicolas/Montogue, LM-011)	B-038 (B, 2)	[7]
B09-A1	3/16/64	Can't Buy Me Love (LM-022, M)	B-039 (B+, 2)	
B09-B1	3/16/64	You Can't Do That (LM-023, L)	B-040 (B, 2)	
B10-A1	4/10/64	Long Tall Sally (Johnson/Penniman/Blackwell, C-13)	B-046 (BM, 1)	[8]
B10-A2	4/10/64	I Call Your Name (LM-024, L)	B-047 (B, 2)	[8]
B10-B1	6/19/64	Slow Down (Williams, C-14)	B-055 (BM, 1)	
B10-B2	6/19/64	Matchbox (Perkins, C-15)	B-049 (BM, 1)	
B11-A1	6/26/64	A Hard Day's Night (LM-025, L)	B-048 (B, 2)	[9]
B11-A2	6/26/64	I Should Have Known Better (LM-026, L)	B-041 (B, 2)	[9]
B11-A3	6/26/64	If I Fell (LM-027, L)	B-044 (B, 2)	[9]
B11-A4	6/26/64	I'm Happy Just to Dance with You (LM-028, ≈)	B-045 (B, 2)	[9]
B11-A5	6/26/64	And I Love Her (LM-029, M+)	B-042 (B, 3)	[9]
B11-A6	6/26/64	Tell Me Why (LM-030, L)	B-043 (BM, 2)	[9]
B11-B1	7/10/64	Any Time at All (LM-031, L+)	B-052 (B, 2)	
B11-B2	6/26/64	I'll Cry Instead (LM-032, L)	B-050 (B, 2)	[9]

APPENDIX VI / BEATLES RECORDINGS

B11-B3	7/10/64	Things We Said Today (LM-033, M)	B-053 (B, 2)	
B11-B4	7/10/64	When I Get Home (LM-034, L)	B-054 (B, 2)	
B11-B6	7/10/64	I'll Be Back (LM-035, L+)	B-051 (B, 2)	
B12-A1	11/23/64	I Feel Fine (LM-036, L)	B-065 (B, 3)	
B12-B1	11/23/64	She's a Woman (LM-037, M+)	B-061 (BM, 3)	
B13-A1	12/4/64	No Reply (LM-038, L+)	B-060 (BM, 2)	
B13-A2	12/4/64	I'm a Loser (LM-039, L)	B-057 (B, 2)	
B13-A3	12/4/64	Baby's in Black (LM-040, ≈)	B-056 (B, 2)	
B13-A4	12/4/64	Rock and Roll Music (Berry, C-16)	B-068 (BM, 1)	
B13-A5	12/4/64	I'll Follow the Sun (LM-041, M)	B-066 (B, 3)	
B13-A6	12/4/64	Mr Moonlight (Johnson, C-17)	B-064 (B, 1)	
B13-A7	12/4/64	Kansas City/Hey-Hey-Hey-Hey! (Leiber/Stoller/Penniman, C-18)	B-063 (BM, 1)	
B13-B1	12/4/64	Eight Days a Week (LM-042, ML)	B-062 (B, 2)	
B13-B2	12/4/64	Words of Love (Holly, C-19)	B-069 (B, 1)	
B13-B3	12/4/64	Honey Don't (Perkins, C-20)	B-070 (B, 1)	
B13-B4	12/4/64	Every Little Thing (LM-043, M)	B-059 (B, 2)	
B13-B5	12/4/64	I Don't Want to Spoil the Party (LM-044, L)	B-058 (B, 2)	
B13-B6	12/4/64	What You're Doing (LM-045, M)	B-071 (BM, 2)	
B13-B7	12/4/64	Everybody's Trying to Be My Baby (Perkins, C-21)	B-067 (B, 1)	
B14-A1	4/9/65	Ticket to Ride (LM-046, LM)	B-072 (B, 2)	
B14-B1	4/9/65	Yes It Is (LM-047, L+)	B-075 (B, 2)	
B15-A1	7/19/65	Help! (LM-048, L+)	B-081 (B, 2)	
B15-B1	7/19/65	I'm Down (LM-049, M)	B-085 (B, 2)	
B16-A2	8/6/65	Night Before, The (LM-050, M)	B-076 (B, 2)	
B16-A3	8/6/65	You've Got to Hide Your Love Away (LM-051, L)	B-078 (B+, 3)	
B16-A4	8/6/65	I Need You (Harrison, H-02)	B-073 (B, 3)	
B16-A5	8/6/65	Another Girl (LM-052, M)	B-074 (B, 2)	
B16-A6	8/6/65	You're Going to Lose That Girl (LM-053, L)	B-080 (B, 2)	
B16-B1	8/6/65	Act Naturally (Russell/Morrison, C-22)	B-087 (B, 1)	
B16-B2	8/6/65	It's Only Love (LM-054, L)	B-086 (B, 2)	
B16-B3	6/14/65	You Like Me Too Much (Harrison, H-03)	B-077 (BM, 2)	[10]
B16-B4	6/14/65	Tell Me What You See (LM-055, M)	B-079 (B, 2)	[10]
B16-B5	8/6/65	I've Just Seen a Face (LM-056, M)	B-084 (B, 1)	
B16-B6	8/6/65	Yesterday (LM-057, M)	B-088 (P+, 4)	
B16-B7	6/14/65	Dizzy Miss Lizzy (Williams, C-23)	B-082 (B, 1)	[10]
B17-A1	12/3/65	Day Tripper (LM-058, L+)	B-091 (B, 2)	[11]
B17-A2	12/3/65	We Can Work It Out (LM-059, ML)	B-096 (B, 3)	[11]
B18-A1	12/3/65	Drive My Car (LM-060, ML)	B-090 (B, 3)	
B18-A2	12/3/65	Norwegian Wood (This Bird Has Flown) (LM-061, L+)	B-093 (B, 3)	
B18-A3	12/3/65	You Won't See Me (LM-062, M)	B-101 (B+, 3)	
B18-A4	12/3/65	Nowhere Man (LM-063, L)	B-095 (B, 3)	
B18-A5	12/3/65	Think for Yourself (Harrison, H-04)	B-099 (B, 2)	
B18-A6	12/3/65	Word, The (LM-064, LM)	B-100 (BM, 2)	
B18-A7	12/3/65	Michelle (LM-065, M+)	B-097 (B, 3)	
B18-B1	12/3/65	What Goes On (Lennon/McCartney/Starkey, LMS-1)	B-098 (B, 2)	[12]
B18-B2	12/3/65	Girl (LM-066, L+)	B-102 (B, 3)	
B18-B3	12/3/65	I'm Looking Through You (LM-067, M)	B-104 (B, 3)	
B18-B4	12/3/65	In My Life (LM-068, LM)	B-094 (BM, 3)	[13]
B18-B5	12/3/65	Wait (LM-069, M)	B-103 (B, 2)	
B18-B6	12/3/65	If I Needed Someone (Harrison, H-05)	B-092 (BM, 3)	
B18-B7	12/3/65	Run for Your Life (LM-070, L)	B-089 (B, 2)	
B19-A1	5/30/66	Paperback Writer (LM-071, ML)	B-106 (B, 3)	
B19-B1	5/30/66	Rain (LM-072, L)	B-107 (B, 3)	
B20-A1	8/5/66	Taxman (Harrison, H-06)	B-119 (B, 3)	
B20-A2	8/5/66	Eleanor Rigby (LM-073, ML)	B-115 (JPG+, 3)	[13]

B20-A3	6/20/66	I'm Only Sleeping (LM-074, L+)	B-111 (B, 3)	[14]
B20-A4	8/5/66	Love You To (Harrison, H-07)	B-105 (PGR+, 4)	
B20-A5	8/5/66	Here, There and Everywhere (LM-075, M)	B-117 (B, 3)	
B20-A6	8/5/66	Yellow Submarine (LM-076, M+)	B-113 (BM+, 3)	
B20-A7	8/5/66	She Said She Said (LM-077, L)	B-120 (JGR, 3)	
B20-B1	8/5/66	Good Day Sunshine (LM-078, M+)	B-116 (BM, 3)	
B20-B2	6/20/66	And Your Bird Can Sing (LM-079, L+)	B-110 (B, 3)	[14]
B20-B3	8/5/66	For No One (LM-080, M)	B-112 (PR+, 4)	
B20-B4	6/20/66	Doctor Robert (LM-081, L+)	B-108 (B, 3)	[14]
B20-B5	8/5/66	I Want to Tell You (Harrison, H-08)	B-114 (B, 3)	
B20-B6	8/5/66	Got to Get You into My Life (LM-082, M)	B-118 (B+, 3)	
B20-B7	8/5/66	Tomorrow Never Knows (LM-083, L)	B-109 (BM, 3)	
B21-B2	6/14/65	Bad Boy (Williams, C-24)	B-083 (B, 1)	[15]
B22-A1	2/13/67	Penny Lane (LM-084, M)	B-123 (BM+, 3)	[11]
B22-A2	2/13/67	Strawberry Fields Forever (LM-085, L)	B-122 (B+, 3)	[11]
B23-A1	5/26/67	Sgt Pepper's Lonely Hearts Club Band (LM-086, M)	B-127 (BM+, 3)	[16]
B23-A2	5/26/67	With a Little Help from My Friends (LM-087, ≈)	B-132 (BM, 3)	
B23-A3	5/26/67	Lucy in the Sky with Diamonds (LM-088, L+)	B-126 (BM, 3)	
B23-A4	5/26/67	Getting Better (LM-089, ML)	B-130 (BM, 3)	
B23-A5	5/26/67	Fixing a Hole (LM-090, M)	B-124 (BM, 3)	
B23-A6	5/26/67	She's Leaving Home (LM-091, ≈)	B-128 (JP+, 3)	
B23-A7	5/26/67	Being for the Benefit of Mr Kite! (LM-092, L)	B-133 (BM+, 3)	
B23-B1	5/26/67	Within You Without You (Harrison, H-09)	B-135 (G+, 4)	
B23-B2	5/26/67	When I'm Sixty-Four (LM-093, M)	B-121 (B+, 3)	
B23-B3	5/26/67	Lovely Rita (LM-094, M)	B-129 (BM, 3)	
B23-B4	5/26/67	Good Morning Good Morning (LM-095, L)	B-131 (B+, 3)	
B23-B5	5/26/67	Sgt Pepper's Lonely Hearts Club Band (Reprise) (LM-086, M)	B-134 (B, 3)	[17]
B23-B6	5/26/67	A Day in the Life (LM-096, ≈)	B-125 (BM+, 3)	
B24-A1	7/7/67	All You Need Is Love (LM-097, L)	B-141 (BM+, 3)	
B24-B1	7/7/67	Baby, You're a Rich Man (LM-098, ≈)	B-138 (B+, 3)	
B25-A1	11/24/67	Hello, Goodbye (LM-099, M)	B-147 (B+, 4)	
B25-B1	11/24/67	I Am the Walrus (LM-100, L)	B-143 (B+, 3)	
B26-A1	11/27/67	Magical Mystery Tour (LM-101, M+)	B-137 (B+, 3)	[18]
B26-A2	11/27/67	Your Mother Should Know (LM-102, M)	B-144 (B, 3)	[18]
B26-C1	11/27/67	Fool on the Hill, The (LM-103, M)	B-146 (B+, 4)	[18]
B26-C2	11/27/67	Flying (Lennon/McCartney/Harrison/Starkey, B-1)	B-142 (B, 3)	[18]
B26-D1	11/27/67	Blue Jay Way (Harrison, H-10)	B-145 (B+, 4)	[18]
B27-A1	3/15/68	Lady Madonna (LM-104, M+)	B-148 (B+, 3)	
B27-B1	3/15/68	Inner Light, The (Harrison, H-11)	B-149 (JPG+, 4)	
B28-A1	8/26/68	Hey Jude (LM-105, M)	B-160 (B+, 3)	
B28-B1	8/26/68	Revolution (LM-106, L)	B-154 (B+, 3)	[19]
B29-A1	11/22/68	Back in the USSR (LM-107, M)	B-166 (JPG, 3)	
B29-A2	11/22/68	Dear Prudence (LM-108, L)	B-168 (JPG+, 3)	
B29-A3	11/22/68	Glass Onion (LM-109, L)	B-180 (B+, 3)	
B29-A4	11/22/68	Ob-La-Di, Ob-La-Da (LM-110, M)	B-155 (B+, 3)	
B29-A5	11/22/68	Wild Honey Pie (LM-111, M)	B-164 (P, 4)	
B29-A6	11/22/68	Continuing Story of Bungalow Bill, The (LM-112, L)	B-178 (B+, 4)	
B29-A7	11/22/68	While My Guitar Gently Weeps (Harrison, H-12)	B-169 (B+, 4)	
B29-A8	11/22/68	Happiness Is a Warm Gun (LM-113, L)	B-173 (B, 3)	
B29-B1	11/22/68	Martha My Dear (LM-114, M)	B-175 (PG+, 4)	
B29-B2	11/22/68	I'm So Tired (LM-115, L)	B-177 (B, 4)	
B29-B3	11/22/68	Blackbird (LM-116, M)	B-152 (P, 4)	
B29-B4	11/22/68	Piggies (Harrison, H-13)	B-179 (B+, 4)	
B29-B5	11/22/68	Rocky Raccoon (LM-117, M+)	B-161 (BM, 4)	

Appendix VI/Beatles Recordings

B29-B6	11/22/68	Don't Pass Me By (Starkey, S-1)	B-157 (PR+, 4)	
B29-B7	11/22/68	Why Don't We Do It in the Road? (LM-118, M)	B-181 (PR, 4)	
B29-B8	11/22/68	I Will (LM-119, M)	B-171 (JPR, 4)	
B29-B9	11/22/68	Julia (LM-120, L)	B-182 (J, 4)	
B29-C1	11/22/68	Birthday (LM-121, ≈)	B-172 (B+, 3)	
B29-C2	11/22/68	Yer Blues (LM-122, L)	B-162 (B, 4)	
B29-C3	11/22/68	Mother Nature's Son (LM-123, M)	B-163 (P+, 4)	
B29-C4	11/22/68	Everybody's Got Something...Me and My Monkey (LM-124, L)	B-159 (B, 3)	
B29-C5	11/22/68	Sexy Sadie (LM-125, L)	B-165 (B, 4)	
B29-C6	11/22/68	Helter Skelter (LM-126, M)	B-170 (B+, 3)	
B29-C7	11/22/68	Long, Long, Long (Harrison, H-14)	B-176 (PGR+, 4)	
B29-D1	11/22/68	Revolution 1 (LM-106, L)	B-153 (B+, 3)	[20]
B29-D2	11/22/68	Honey Pie (LM-127, M)	B-174 (B+, 4)	
B29-D3	11/22/68	Savoy Truffle (Harrison, H-15)	B-183 (PGR+, 4)	
B29-D4	11/22/68	Cry Baby Cry (LM-128, L+)	B-156 (BM, 3)	[21]
B29-D5	11/22/68	Revolution 9 (LM-129, L)	B-167 (JG+, 4)	
B29-D6	11/22/68	Good Night (LM-130, L)	B-158 (RM+, 4)	
B30-A2	1/13/69	Only a Northern Song (Harrison, H-16)	B-136 (B, 3)	
B30-A3	1/13/69	All Together Now (LM-131, M)	B-139 (B+, 3)	
B30-A4	1/13/69	Hey Bulldog (LM-132, L+)	B-151 (B, 3)	
B30-A5	1/13/69	It's All Too Much (Harrison, H-17)	B-140 (B+, 4)	
B31-A1	4/11/69	Get Back (1) (LM-133, M)	B-188 (BW, 2)	[22]
B31-B1	4/11/69	Don't Let Me Down (LM-134, L)	B-189 (BW, 2)	
B32-A1	5/30/69	Ballad of John and Yoko, The (LM-135, L)	B-195 (JP, 4)	
B32-B1	5/30/69	Old Brown Shoe (Harrison, H-18)	B-197 (B, 4)	
B33-A1	9/26/69	Come Together (LM-136, L)	B-202 (B, 4)	
B33-A2	9/26/69	Something (Harrison, H-19)	B-209 (BW+, 4)	
B33-A3	9/26/69	Maxwell's Silver Hammer (LM-137, M)	B-205 (PGRM, 4)	
B33-A4	9/26/69	Oh! Darling (LM-138, M)	B-207 (B, 4)	
B33-A5	9/26/69	Octopus's Garden (Starkey, S-2)	B-199 (B, 4)	
B33-A6	9/26/69	I Want You (She's So Heavy) (LM-139, L)	B-206 (BW, 4)	
B33-B1	9/26/69	Here Comes the Sun (Harrison, H-20)	B-211 (PGRM, 4)	
B33-B2	9/26/69	Because (LM-140, L)	B-204 (JPGM, 3)	
B33-B3	9/26/69	You Never Give Me Your Money (LM-141, M)	B-203 (B, 4)	
B33-B4	9/26/69	Sun King/Mean Mr Mustard (LM-142, L)	B-200 (BM, 3)	[23]
B33-B5	9/26/69	Polythene Pam/She Came In...Bathroom Window (LM-143, ≈)	B-201 (B, 3)	[23]
B33-B6	9/26/69	Golden Slumbers/Carry That Weight (LM-144, M)	B-208 (B+, 3)	[23]
B33-B7	9/26/69	End, The (LM-145, M)	B-210 (B+, 3)	
B33-B8	9/26/69	Her Majesty (LM-146, M)	B-198 (P, 4)	
B34-A1	12/12/69	Across the Universe (1) (LM-147, L)	B-150 (B+, 4)	[24]
B35-A1	3/6/70	Let It Be (1) (LM-148, M)	B-193 (BW+, 2)	[24]
B35-B1	3/6/70	You Know My Name (Look Up the Number) (LM-149, L)	B-196 (B+, 3)	
B36-A1	5/8/70	Two of Us (LM-150, M)	B-194 (B, 2)	
B36-A2	5/8/70	Dig a Pony (LM-151, L)	B-192 (BW, 2)	
B36-A3	5/8/70	Across the Universe (2) (LM-147, L)	B-215 (B+, 4)	[25]
B36-A4	5/8/70	I Me Mine (Harrison, H-21)	B-212 (PGR+, 4)	
B36-A5	5/8/70	Dig It (Lennon/McCartney/Harrison/Starkey, B-2)	B-186 (BMW, 1)	[26]
B36-A6	5/8/70	Let It Be (2) (LM-148, M)	B-213 (BW+, 2)	[25]
B36-A7	5/8/70	Maggie Mae (Traditional, C-25)	B-184 (B, 1)	
B36-B1	5/8/70	I've Got a Feeling (LM-152, ≈)	B-190 (BW, 2)	
B36-B2	5/8/70	One After 909 (LM-153, L+)	B-191 (BW, 2)	
B36-B3	5/8/70	Long and Winding Road, The (LM-154, M)	B-187 (BW+, 2)	
B36-B4	5/8/70	For You Blue (Harrison, H-22)	B-185 (B, 2)	
B36-B5	5/8/70	Get Back (2) (LM-133, M)	B-214 (BW, 2)	[25]

Save the Beatles!

[1] Version 1, Ringo drums
[2] Version 1, clean
[3] Version 2, edit/remix, collision/giggles
[4] Version 2, remake, Andy White drums
[5] LM class indeterminate
[6] Version 1, English
[7] Version 2, remake, German
[8] Early release: *The Beatles' Second Album* (US)
[9] Early release: *A Hard Day's Night* (US)
[10] Early release: *Beatles VI* (US)
[11] Double A-side single
[12] Starkey credit a courtesy only
[13] LM class disputed
[14] Early release: *Yesterday and Today* (US)
[15] Released on *Beatles VI* (US), UK: 12/10/66
[16] Version 1
[17] Version 2, remake
[18] Early release: *Magical Mystery Tour* (US)
[19] Version 2, remake, fast
[20] Version 1, slow
[21] Includes "Can you take me back…"
[22] Version 1, Johns/McCartney mix
[23] Recorded as one track
[24] Version 1, Martin mix
[25] Version 2, Spector remix
[26] Improv by Lennon

Appendix VII
Summary of Rescued Albums

TRT - 1:31:06

Dream

Side One
1. What Is Life — 4:18
2. Every Night — 2:27
3. Hold On — 1:47
4. I Dig Love — 3:56
5. Teddy Boy — 2:22
6. Remember — 4:32
7. I'm a Fool to Care — 2:38
TOTAL — 22:02

Side Two
1. Instant Karma! — 3:33
2. I'd Have You Any Time — 2:54
3. Sunshine Sometime — 3:15
4. That Would Be Something — 2:37
5. Well Well Well — 5:56
6. Behind That Locked Door — 3:20
TOTAL — 21:38

Side Three
1. It Don't Come Easy — 2:58
2. Man We Was Lonely — 2:57
3. Isolation — 2:49
4. Oo You — 2:48
5. Coochy Coochy — 4:34
6. Art of Dying — 3:35
7. Working Class Hero — 3:47
TOTAL — 23:30

Side Four
1. All Things Must Pass — 3:38
2. Maybe I'm Amazed — 3:45
3. Love — 2:20
4. Junk — 1:54
5. God — 4:36
6. Dream — 2:40
7. Let It Down — 4:09
8. It's Johnny's Birthday — 0:50
TOTAL — 23:56

Beggars in a Gold Mine

Side One
1. PROLOGUE: Rode All Night — 1:40
2. Back Off Boogaloo — 3:14
3. Gimme Some Truth — 3:10
4. Deep Blue — 3:38
5. Jealous Guy — 4:11
6. Another Day — 3:39
7. How? — 3:39
8. Everybody, Nobody — 2:41
TOTAL — 25:54

Side Two
1. Uncle Albert/Admiral Halsey — 4:54
2. It's So Hard — 2:24
3. Going Down to Golders Green — 2:20
4. Little Woman Love — 2:06
5. Oh My Love — 2:40
6. The Back Seat of My Car — 4:27
7. Imagine — 3:03
8. Dehradun — 3:27
TOTAL — 25:24

TRT - 51:18

TRT - 1:33:50

Be Here Now

Side One
1. PROLOGUE: Be Here Now — 1:10
2. Bring on the Lucie... — 4:09
3. Hi, Hi, Hi — 3:06
4. Sunshine Life for Me... — 2:41
5. My Love — 4:05
6. You Are Here — 4:07
7. Don't Let Me Wait Too Long — 2:58
TOTAL — 22:20

Side Two
1. Live and Let Die — 3:08
2. Intuition — 3:06
3. Let Me Roll It — 3:49
4. Sue Me, Sue You Blues — 3:19
5. I Know (I Know) — 3:44
6. I'm the Greatest — 3:19
7. Be Here Now — 4:12
TOTAL — 24:40

Side Three
1. Photograph — 3:55
2. The Mess — 4:36
3. Tight A$ — 3:39
4. Bluebird — 3:19
5. One Day (At a Time) — 3:06
6. Try Some, Buy Some — 3:57
7. Step Lightly — 3:17
TOTAL — 25:53

Side Four
1. Give Me Love... — 3:31
2. Mind Games — 4:10
3. Down and Out — 3:00
4. Helen Wheels — 3:37
5. Night Out — 2:28
6. Meat City — 2:47
7. CODA: Be Here Now — 1:22
TOTAL — 20:57

Vienna

Side One
1. What You Got — 3:03
2. Junior's Farm — 4:15
3. Goodnight Vienna — 2:32
4. Far East Man — 5:46
5. Scared — 4:27
6. Listen to What the Man Said — 3:34
7. This Guitar (Can't Keep... — 4:13
TOTAL — 27:53

Side Two
1. Soily — 3:54
2. #9 Dream — 4:39
3. Māya Love — 4:18
4. Bless You — 4:37
5. Tired of Midnight Blue — 4:50
6. Let's Love — 1:57
7. Whatever Gets You thru... — 3:14
8. Goodnight Vienna (Reprise) — 1:00
TOTAL — 28:31

TRT - 56:24

Flight

Side One
1. Wings — 3:22
2. Nobody Told Me — 3:29
3. Mama's Little Girl — 3:41
4. It's What You Value — 5:05
5. Mull of Kintyre — 4:36
6. Mo — 4:49
7. Cookin' (In the Kitchen... — 3:40
TOTAL — 28:46

Side Two
1. Girls' School — 4:30
2. I Don't Wanna Face It — 3:18
3. Don't Let It Bring You Down — 4:12
4. I'll Still Love You — 2:53
5. Warm and Beautiful — 3:08
6. Pure Smokey — 3:51
7. Free as a Bird — 4:24
TOTAL — 26:20

TRT - 55:06

Wheels, Walls and Waterfalls

Side One
1. Attention — 3:41
2. Coming Up — 3:50
3. Watching the Wheels — 4:14
4. Writing's on the Wall — 3:57
5. Waterfalls — 4:41
6. (Just Like) Starting Over — 3:54
7. You Belong to Me — 2:12
TOTAL — 26:31

Side Two
1. Unconsciousness Rules — 3:33
2. I'm Losing You — 3:57
3. Cage — 3:06
4. You've Got a Nice Way — 3:31
5. Woman — 3:28
6. Goodnight Tonight — 4:12
7. Life Itself — 4:23
8. Reprise: Woman/Goodnight... — 0:38
TOTAL — 26:53

TRT - 53:24

In Spite of All

Side One
1. Keep Under Cover — 3:01
2. I'm Stepping Out — 4:03
3. Wake Up — 3:38
4. Unknown Delight — 4:13
5. Sweetest Little Show — 2:48
6. (Forgive Me) My Little... — 2:22
7. Beautiful Boy (Darling Boy) — 4:00
TOTAL — 24:08

Side Two
1. All Those Years Ago — 3:37
2. Borrowed Time — 4:27
3. Through Our Love — 3:24
4. My Old Friend — 3:19
5. Grow Old with Me — 3:05
6. Here Today — 2:28
7. In Spite of All the Danger — 2:44
TOTAL — 23:07

TRT - 47:15

Bibliography

It is tempting to list here every resource that I have read or possessed or simply brought up in a browser related to the Beatles. However, the list below contains only those titles actually consulted in the creation of this book.

Print Publications

Badman, Keith
    The Beatles Diary - Volume 2: After The Break-Up 1970-2001
    London: Omnibus Press, 2001

Beatles, The
    Anthology
    San Francisco: Chronicle, 2000

Blake, John
    All You Needed Was Love: The Beatles After the Beatles
    New York: Putnam, 1981

Blaney, John
    Lennon and McCartney Together Alone
    London: Jawbone, 2007

Brocken, Michael and Melissa Davis
    The Beatles Bibliography
    Manitou Springs, Colorado: The Beatle Works Ltd, 2012

    The Beatles Bibliography - Supplement 2013
    Manitou Springs, Colorado: The Beatle Works Ltd, 2014

Brown, Mick
    Tearing Down the Wall of Sound: The Rise and Fall of Phil Spector
    London: Bloomsbury, 2007

Browne, David
    Fire and Rain: The Beatles, Simon & Garfunkel, James Taylor, CSNY,
        and the Lost Story of 1970
    Philadelphia: Da Capo Press, 2011

    "Beatles Art Director on Secrets of the 'Abbey Road' Cover"
    Rolling Stone, August 9, 2019

Carr, Roy and Tony Tyler
>   *The Beatles: An Illustrated Record*
>   New York: Crown, 1981

Castleman, Harry and Walter J. Podrazik
>   *All Together Now: The First Complete Beatles Discography 1961-1975*
>   New York: Ballantine, 1975

Davis, Melissa (see: Brocken, Michael and Melissa Davis)

Doggett, Peter
>   *You Never Give Me Your Money: The Beatles After the Breakup*
>   New York: HarperCollins, 2009

Doyle, Tom
>   *Man on the Run: Paul McCartney in the 1970s*
>   New York: Ballantine, 2013

Easter, Mark (see: Maginder, Chip and Mark Easter)

Emerick, Geoff and Howard Massey
>   *Here, There and Everywhere: My Life Recording the Music of the Beatles*
>   New York: Gotham (Penguin), 2006

Eskow, Gary
>   "Classic Tracks: Paul McCartney's 'Uncle Albert/Admiral Halsey'"
>   *Mix*, August 1, 2004

Goldstein, Richard
>   "We Still Need the Beatles, but ..."
>   *New York Times*, June 18, 1967

Guralnick, Peter
>   *Last Train to Memphis: The Rise of Elvis Presley*
>   Back Bay Books, 1994
>
>   *Careless Love: The Unmaking of Elvis Presley*
>   Back Bay Books, 1999

Harry, Bill
>   *George Harrison Encyclopedia*
>   London: Virgin, 2003

John Lennon Encyclopedia
    London: Virgin, 2000

Hornsby, Jeremy (see: Martin, George)

Jackson, Andrew Grant
    Still the Greatest: The Essential Songs of The Beatles' Solo Careers
    Scarecrow Press, 2012

Johns, Glyn
    Sound Man
    New York: Plume, 2014

Lewisohn, Mark
    The Beatles Recording Sessions
    New York: Harmony, 1988

    The Beatles Day by Day: A Chronology 1962-1989
    New York: Harmony, 1990

    Tune In: The Beatles: All These Years
    New York: Crown Archetype, 2013

Maginder, Chip and Mark Easter
    Eight Arms To Hold You - The Solo Beatles Compendium (Remastered)
    Chesterfield, MO: Open Your Books, 2018

Martin, George
    All You Need is Ears (with Jeremy Hornsby)
    New York: St. Martin's, 1979

    Making Music: The Guide to Writing, Performing & Recording (editor)
    New York: William Morrow, 1983

    Summer of Love: The Making of Sgt Pepper
    London: Pan, 1994

Massey, Howard (see: Emerick, Geoff and Howard Massey)

Mayer, Martin
    "Fifty Thousand Sides Ago: The First Days of the LP"
    High Fidelity Magazine, January 1958

Miles, Barry
    Paul McCartney: Many Years from Now
    New York: Henry Holt and Company, 1997

    The Zapple Diaries. The Rise and Fall of the Last Beatles Label.
    New York: Abrams Image, 2016

Murrells, Joseph
    Million Selling Records from the 1900s to the 1980s
    New York: Arco, 1984

Perry, Rupert (see: Southall, Brian with Rupert Perry)

Podrazik, Walter J. (see: Castleman, Harry and Walter J. Podrazik)

Riley, Tim
    Tell Me Why - A Beatles Commentary (aka: tell me why, The Beatles: album by album, song by song, the sixties and after)
    New York: Da Capo, 2002.

Rodriguez, Robert
    Fab Four FAQ 2.0: The Beatles' Solo Years, 1970-1980
    New York: Hal Leonard, 2010

    Solo in the 70s John, Paul, George, Ringo: 1970-1980
    Chicago: Parading, 2014

Runtagh, Jordan
    "Remembering Beatles' Final Concert"
    Rolling Stone, August 29, 2016

Sawyers, June Skinner
    Read the Beatles
    London: Penguin, 2006

Schaffner, Nicholas (see: Shotton, Pete and Nicholas Schaffner)

Sheff, David
    All We Are Saying: The Last Major Interview with John Lennon
    New York: St Martin's Griffin, 1981

Shotton, Pete and Nicholas Schaffner
    John Lennon In My Life
    New York: Stein and Day, 1983

Smith, Alan
    "At Home With The Lennons, Part 2"
    New Musical Express, August 7, 1971

Smith, Chris
    101 Albums That Changed Popular Music
    Oxford University Press, 2009

Sondheim, Stephen
    Finishing the Hat
    New York: Knopf, 2010

Southall, Brian with Rupert Perry
    Northern Songs: The True Story of the Beatles Song Publishing Empire
    London: Omnibus, 2006

Tyler, Tony (see: Carr, Roy and Tony Tyler)

Weber, Erin Torkelson
    The Beatles and the Historians: An Analysis of Writings About the Fab Four
    Jefferson, North Carolina: McFarland, 2016

Wenner, Jann
    Lennon Remembers - New Edition
    London/New York: Verso, 2000

Westover, Kenneth D.
    The Beatles US LPs: Where They Came From & How They Charted
    Boulder, CO: Cliff Canyon Publishing Company, 1999

White, Richard
    Come Together: Lennon & McCartney in the Seventies
    London: Omnibus, 2016

Williams, Richard
    Phil Spector - Out of His Head
    London: Omnibus, 2003

    "This tape rewrites everything we knew about the Beatles"
    The Guardian, September 11, 2019

Woffinden, Bob
    The Beatles Apart
    London and New York: Proteus, 1981

Womack, Kenneth
> *Maximum Volume: The Life of Beatles Producer George Martin, The Early Years, 1926-1966*
> Chicago Review Press, 2017
>
> *Sound Pictures: The Life of Beatles Producer George Martin: The Later Years, 1966-2016*
> Chicago Review Press, 2018

Internet Resources

Specific Pages

The Beatles Tapes from the David Wigg Interviews (via YouTube)
  youtu.be/db0Y4ul32U8

Classic Tracks: Paul McCartney's "Uncle Albert/Admiral Halsey"
Gary Eskow, August 1, 2004
  mixonline.com/recording/classic-tracks-paul-mccartneys-uncle-albertadmiral-halsey-375127

Columbia Record Catalog 1949 (via Archive.org)
  archive.org/details/columbiarecordca00unse_0

Deconstructing Pop Culture: The Beatles' Contract History with Capitol Records
David Kronemyer, May 15, 2009
  musewire.com/deconstructing-pop-culture-the-beatles-contract-history-with-capitol-records/

The McCartney Recording Sessions (via Archive.org)
Chris Brewer, 2013
  web.archive.org/web/20180629185004/webpages.charter.net/ram71

The Naked Truth About The Beatles' Let It Be Naked
Matt Hurwitz, January 1, 2004
  mixonline.com/news/naked-truth-about-beatles-let-it-benaked-425110

Recording the Imagine Album
  imaginejohnyoko.com/recording-the-imagine-album

Usenet Guide to Beatles Recording Variations, Version 2
Joseph Brennan, May 17, 2000
  columbia.edu/~brennan/beatles

General Resources

BeatlesBible.com
BeatlesInterviews.com
The-PaulMcCartney-Project.com

Live links available at **SaveTheBeatles.com**

Song and Album Index

*These songs and albums are discussed in the text, separate from grid listings. Page ranges in **bold** represent a primary discussion of the title.*

"#9 Dream", 337, 359
"(Forgive Me) My Little Flower Princess", 487, 491
"(It's All Down to) Goodnight Vienna", 7
"(Just Like) Starting Over", 6, 437, 443, 452, 455
1 (compilation album), 8, 566
"1882", 196, 237
"3 Legs", 236
Abbey Road, 5, 8, 16-17, 27, 33, 49, 51, 53, 59-60, 63, 84, 87-88, 144, 148, 150, 166, 169, 174, 185, 196, 205, 210, 219-220, 276, 413, 470, 490, 501, 504, 566
"Across the Universe", 118-120, 123, 128, 134-138, 144
"Act Naturally", 87, 185
"Aisumasen (I'm Sorry)", 14, 288
"All by Myself", 348
"All Things Must Pass", 203, **205-207**, 210
All Things Must Pass, 6, 31, 33, 152, 167, 171, 173, 175, **196-204**, 217, 219-220, 226, 247, 264, 535, 566
"All Those Years Ago", 437, 468, 475, 491
"All Together Now", 117-118, 120
"All You Need Is Love", 118-119
"And I Love Her", 296
"And Your Bird Can Sing", 106-108, 110
"Angela", 284, 286
"Anna (Go to Him)", 68
"Another Day", 196, 226, 231, 233, 240, 254, 257
"Answer's at the End, The", 351
Anthology (project), 169, 400, 470, 472, 486, 497, 500
Anthology 1, 410, 497
Anthology 3, 136, 142
"Any Time at All", 87
"Apple Scruffs", 201
"Arrow Through Me", 7, 429
"Art of Dying", 202, 214
"Ask Me Why", 68
"Attention", 453
"Average Person", 481, 487
"Awaiting on You All", 201
"Baby Face", 345
"Baby It's You", 68, 74
"Baby, You're a Rich Man", 117-118
"Back in the USSR", 16, 87
"Back Off Boogaloo", 226, 232, 249, 254-255, 259-260, 272
"Back Seat of My Car, The", 7, 236, 247, 253, 255-256, 258, 266
Back to the Egg, 15, 26, 153, 418, 421, **426-429**, 435-436, 441, 459
Bad Boy, 7, 35, 153, 418, 422, **423-424**
"Ballad of John and Yoko, The", 63, 135, 139, 284, 444
"Band on the Run", 6, 158, 281, 289, 291-293, 297

Band on the Run, 6, 8, 26, 153, 280, 289, **292-298**, 305, 318, 326-327, 329, 332, 344-345, 368, 382, 387, 389, 437
"Bangla Desh", 226, 230, 246-247
"Be Here Now", 15, 275, 301, 307, 311
Beatles '65, xiii
Beatles at the Beeb, 468
Beatles at the Hollywood Bowl, 377
Beatles for Sale, 58, 63, 87, 185, 208
Beatles' Second Album, The, 580
Beatles VI, 580
Beatles, The, see *White Album, The*
Beatles, The (1962-1966), 279, 319
Beatles, The (1967-1970), 279, 319
"Beaucoups of Blues", 7, 183
Beaucoups of Blues, 7, 35, 152, 167, 171, 174, 180, 183, **187-189**, 190, 217, 347
"Beautiful Boy (Darling Boy)", xi, 443, 454, 484, 491, 500
"Because", 5
"Beef Jerky", 297, 337
"Behind That Locked Door", 202, 211
"Being for the Benefit of Mr Kite!", 84
Best of George Harrison, 376
"Beware My Love", 388
"Beware of Darkness", 180, 200-201
"Big Barn Bed", 254, 261, 292, 309
"Bip Bop", 238
"Birthday", 87
"Bit More of You, A", 353
Blast from Your Past, 376
"Bless You", 337, 362
"Blindman", 249
"Blood from a Clone", 474
"Blow Away", xi, 7, 32, 421, 425
Blue, see *Beatles, The (1967-1970)*
"Blue Jay Way", 116-118, 122, 124
"Blue, Turning Grey Over You", 187
"Bluebird", xi, 292, 297, 312-313
"Borrowed Time", 7, 487, 491-492, 500
"Boys", 68, 74, 185
Brainwashed, 521
"Bring on the Lucie (Freda Peeple)", 309
"Broadcast, The", 428
"C Moon", 279, 289
"Cage", 428, 441, 455-456
"Call Me", 348
"Call Me Back Again", 342, 344
Can't Fight Lightning, see *Stop and Smell the Roses*
"Can't Buy Me Love", 41, 87
"Can't Stop Thinking About You", 351, 354
"Carry That Weight", 5, 185
"Chains", 68
"Check My Machine", 439
"Children Children", 390
"Circles", 476, 493

"Cleanup Time", 443, 455-456
Cloud Nine, 472
"Cold Turkey", 7, 147, 166, 286
"Come Together", 87, 280, 287, 332, 339, 522
"Coming Up", 6, 340, 435-436, 439, 441, 452-453
Complete Silver Beatles, 468
Concert for Bangladesh, The, 226, 228, 232, 272-273, 279
"Continuing Story of Bungalow Bill, The", 258
"Coochy-Coochy", 212-214
"Cook of the House", 181, 387
"Cookin' (In the Kitchen of Love)", 376, 380, 394, 405
"Cosmic Empire", 248
"Country Dreamer", 289
"Crackerbox Palace", 7, 404
"Crippled Inside", 243
"Crossroads Theme", 342, 361
"Cuff Link", 389
"Dark Horse", 7, 349
Dark Horse, 31, 34, 153, 326, 330, 332, **349-354**, 367, 386
"Dark Sweet Lady", 425
"A Day in the Life", 57, 87, 92-93, 95, 100, 119-120, 137, 207
"Day Tripper", 63
"Daytime Nighttime Suffering", 426, 428, 439
"Dear Boy", 236
"Dear Friend", 238
"Dear Prudence", 16
"Dear Yoko", 443, 445
"Deep Blue", 15, 246-247, 255, 257, 259
"Dehradun", 247, 253-254, 266
"Deliver Your Children", 390
"Dig a Pony", 134-136, 139
"Dig It", 28, 134, 136, 138, 181
"Ding Dong, Ding Dong", 7, 351, 391
"Dizzy Miss Lizzy", 87
"Do You Want to Know a Secret", 68-69
"Doctor Robert", 106, 113
"Don't Bother Me", 32
"Don't Let It Bring You Down", 390
"Don't Let Me Down", 63, 134-136, 139, 144
"Don't Let Me Wait Too Long", 300, 312-313
"Don't Pass Me By", 185, 189, 346, 348
"Dose of Rock 'n' Roll, A", 7, 394
Double Fantasy, 6, 21, 153, 434-435, 437, **442-445**, 450, 454, 459, 462-463, 468-469, 472, **483-484**, 491, 497-498
Double Fantasy Stripped Down, 444
"Down and Out", 15, 302, 314
"Dream", 186, 207-208, 214
"Dream Away", 475, 492
"Drive My Car", 87
"Drowning in the Sea of Love", 394
"Early 1970", 167, 183, 189, 213
"Easy for Me", 347, 362, 364
"Eat at Home", 236
"Ebony and Ivory", 6, 471, 479-480
"Eight Days a Week", 87
"Eleanor Rigby", 41, 106, 109, 188, 258
"End, The", 5
"Every Night", 192-193, 205
"Everybody, Nobody", 248, 259, 266

Extra Texture (Read All About It), 31, 153, 332, **349-354**, 360, 376, 396
"Famous Groupies", 390
"Far East Man", 351, 354, 356, 362
"Faster", 396, 425
"Fixing a Hole", 16, 99-101
"Flying", 28, 117-118, 122-123, 128, 185
"Flying Hour", 446, 452, 454, 492, 494
"Fool on the Hill, The", 121-124
"For No One", 41, 106, 109, 113
"For You Blue", 134-136, 139, 248
"Free as a Bird", 381, 400
George Harrison, 7, 31-32, 153, 336, 418, 421, **424-426**, 436, 446
"Get Back", 133-137, 139, 178
Get Back, 27, **131-144**, 148, 151, 173, 192, 305, see also *Let It Be*
"Get It", 481
"Get on the Right Thing", 254, 261, 292
"Getting Better", 16, 93, 96, 99-101
"Getting Closer", 7, 428
"Gimme Some Truth", 243, 255, 259
"Girl", 444
"Girlfriend", 390
"Girls' School", 381, 384, 389, 404-405, 408
"Give Ireland Back to the Irish", 7, 272, 278, 289, 298
"Give Me Love (Give Me Peace on Earth)", 6, 273, 299, 309, 311
"Give Peace a Chance", xx, 11, 147, 181, 521, 535
"Glass Onion", 181
"God", 172, 179-182, 207-209, 214
"God Save Us", 536
"Going Down on Love", 336, 357
"Going Down to Golders Green", 248, 258
Gone Troppo, 7, 31, 153, 468, 472, **474-476**, 497
"Good Day Sunshine", 87, 106-108
"Good Night", 87, 185-187, 454
"Goodnight Tonight", 418, 421, 426, 428, 439, 442, 444, 451, 453-454, 456
Goodnight Vienna, 15, 35, 153, 263, 326, 332, **346-348**, 367, 393
"Got to Get You into My Life", 106-107, 113
"Grey Cloudy Lies", 351
"Grow Old with Me", xi
"Hands of Love", 293, 295
"Happy Xmas (War Is Over)", 272, 282
"A Hard Day's Night", 87
Hard Day's Night, A, 58, 63, 87, 111, 155
Hard Day's Night, A (film), 226
Hard Day's Night, A (US), 580
"Hari's on Tour (Express)", 353
"Have I Told You Lately That I Love You?", 187
"Hear Me Lord", 200-201
"Heart of the Country", 237, 261
"Helen Wheels", 273, 289, 298, 310
"Hello, Goodbye", 117-118, 120-124
"Help!", 87
Help!, 43, 58, 63, 87, 185, 188, 254, 520
Help! (film), 32, 226
"Here Comes the Moon", 425
"Here Comes the Sun", 32, 84, 87, 197
"Here Today", 472, 480-482, 488, 492

Song and Album Index

"Here, There and Everywhere", 106, 111-112, 296, 388
"Hey Bulldog", 118-119, 121-122
"Hey Hey", 479
"Hey Jude", 20, 63, 197, 201
"Hey! Baby", 392, 394
"Hi, Hi, Hi", 272, 279, 289, 298, 309
"His Name Is Legs (Ladies and Gentlemen)", 353
"Hold Me Tight", 69-70
"Hold On", 179, 206, 213, 337
"Honey Don't", 185
"Hot as Sun/Glasses", 193
"How Do You Sleep?", xvi, 229, 232, 244-245, 249, 336
"How?", 243-244, 257, 259, 266
"Husbands and Wives", 347
"I Am the Walrus", 117, 119, 123
"I Am Your Singer", 238
"I Dig Love", 203, 213
"I Don't Care Anymore", 349, 354
"I Don't Wanna Face It", 399, 401, 404, 408
"I Don't Want to Be a Soldier", 243, 245
"I Feel Fine", xiii, 48, 63
"I Found Out", 179
"I Know (I Know)", 288, 315
"I Lie Around", 234, 289
"I Live for You", 204, 247, 261
"I Me Mine", 134-136, 138, 166
"I Saw Her Standing There", 64, 68-69, 71, 87
"I Wanna Be Your Man", 185
"I Want to Hold Your Hand", 63-64
"I Want to Tell You", 106, 113
"I Want You (She's So Heavy)", 84
"I Will", 295-296
"I'd Have You Anytime", 200, 202
"If I Needed Someone", 32
"If Not for You", 202, 204
"If You Believe", 425
"I'll Be Back", 87, 111
"I'll Follow the Sun", 296
"I'll Give You a Ring", 340, 345
"I'll Still Love You", 394, 406, 408
"I'm a Fool to Care", 186, 210
"I'm Down", 63
"I'm Losing You", 443, 455-456
"I'm Only Sleeping", 106, 113
"I'm the Greatest", 182, 273, 281, 303, 311, 316, 394
"Imagine", 20, 145, 247, 252-253, 255-256, 266
Imagine, 6, 21, 152, 226, 232, **241-245**, 263, 265, 280, 283, 289, 305, 339
"Indeed I Do", 195
"Inner Light, The", 121, 123, 127-128
"Instant Karma!", 147, 166, 176, 178, 207, 212
"Intuition", 287-288, 315
"Isolation", 179, 209, 211, 214
"It Don't Come Easy", 166, 171, 183, 189, 209, 211, 226, 232
"It Is 'He' (Jai Sri Krishna)", 351, 353
"It Won't Be Long", 64, 87, 254
"It's All Too Much", 117, 119, 122
"It's Johnny's Birthday", 203, 214
"It's No Secret", 395
"It's Not On", 482

"It's So Hard", 244, 255, 258
"It's What You Value", 406
"I've Got a Feeling", 134-136, 138, 142, 457
"I've Had Enough", 7, 390
"Jealous Guy", 243, 257, 259
"Jet", 292, 297
John Lennon/Plastic Ono Band, 17, 21, 30, 152, 167, 171, **176-183**, 198, 217, 219, 226, 289, 337, 339, 399
"John Sinclair", 284, 286
"Julia", 87, 111, 180
"Junior's Farm", xix, 326, 340, 345-346, 356-357
"Junk", 192-193, 214
"Just a Dream", 392, 395
"Keep Under Cover", 481, 489
"Kreen - Akrore", 193
"Lady Madonna", 43, 51, 118-119, 124, 127
"Lazy Dynamite", 293
"Learning How to Love You", 397
"Let 'Em In", 181, 387, 391, 404
"Let It Be", 133-138
Let It Be, 8, 43, 59, 63, **131-144**, 148, 151, 155, 166-167, 171-174, 178, 201, 218-220, 226, 305, 495, 521, see also *Get Back*
Let It Be (film), 38, 147, 167
Let It Be...Naked, 136-137
"Let It Down", 202, 208
"Let Me Roll It", 292, 297, 312, 315, 337, 344
"Let the Rest of the World Go By", 187
"Let's Love", 345, 358, 536
"Letting Go", 7, 342
"Life Itself", 447, 454, 456, 463
"Light That Has Lighted the World, The", 301
"Listen to What the Man Said", 6, 46, 342, 344, 359, 361-362
"Little Lamb Dragonfly", 261, 292
"Little Woman Love", 233, 240, 258, 289
"Live and Let Die", 234, 273, 280, 289-290, 298, 311, 315, 479
Live Peace in Toronto, 200
Live! At the Star Club..., 377
Living in the Material World, 6, 31, 153, 263, 272-273, 279, **299-302**, 318, 329
"London Town", xi, 7, 390, 407
London Town, 26, 153, 382, 384, **389-392**, 407, 410, 418, 421, 427
"Long and Winding Road, The", 134-135, 137-139, 295-296
"Long Haired Lady", 237, 261
"Long Lost John", 443
"Long Tall Sally", 45, 71
Long Tall Sally (EP), 185
"Long, Long, Long", 84, 87, 111
"Look at Me", 179, 215
"Lord Loves the One (That Loves the Lord), The", 301
"Loup (1st Indian on the Moon)", 292
"Love", 7, 179, 210, 214
"Love Comes to Everyone", 425
"Love for You, A", 230, 240
"Love in Song", 342
"Love Me Do", 41, 45, 68, 71, 87, 470, 495, 503, 521
"Love You To", 41, 106, 110-113

"Lovely Linda, The", 193
"Lovely Rita", 49, 65, 93, 97, 100
"Luck of the Irish, The", 286
"Lucy in the Sky with Diamonds", 92, 96
"Lunchbox/Odd Sox", 340, 439
"Maggie Mae", 134, 136
"Magical Mystery Tour", 117, 119, 121
Magical Mystery Tour (film), 27, 116, 126
Magical Mystery Tour (UK EP), 43, 59, 63, **115-130**, 566
Magical Mystery Tour (US album), **115-130**, 580
"Magneto and Titanium Man", 341-342
"Mama's Little Girl", 298, 407
"Mamunia", 292
"Man We Was Lonely", 180, 192-193, 211
"Man, The", 480
"Martha My Dear", 84, 87
"Mary Had a Little Lamb", 233, 240, 272, 279, 289, 298
"Matchbox", 185
"Maxwell's Silver Hammer", 51
"Maybe I'm Amazed", 192-193, 207, 214, 296
McCartney, 6, 26-27, 152, 166-167, 171, 173, **190-195**, 217-218, 295, 441, 503, 521
McCartney II, 6, 26-27, 153, 422, 434-436, 438, **439-441**, 459, 462
"Meat City", 15, 287-288, 310
"Mess I'm In, The", 298
"Michelle", 49, 87, 111, 296
Milk and Honey, xx, 11, 20-21, 153, 398, 400, 410, 469, 472, **482-484**, 488-489, 497, 500, 511, 519, 521, 535, 571
"Mind Games", 7, 309, 311
Mind Games, 15, 21, 153, 273, 280, 282, **287-289**, 309-310, 318, 329, 332, 336
"Misery", 68-69
"Miss O'Dell", 299
"Mo", 397, 407, 424
"Momma Miss America", 193, 195
"Monkberry Moon Delight", 236
"Morse Moose and the Grey Goose", 145, 390
"Mother", 7, 30, 123, 179-180, 215
"Mother Divine", 248
"Mother Nature's Son", 237
"Move Over Ms. L", 334
"Mrs. Vandebilt", 292
"Mull of Kintyre", 6, 286, 382, 384, 388, 399, 406, 418
"Mumbo", 238
"Must Do Something About It", 388, 536
"My Carnival", 345, 535
"My Love", 6, 145, 273, 289, 295-296, 312-313
"My Mummy's Dead", 179-180, 399
"My Old Friend", 481, 493
"My Sweet Lord", 6, 20, 34, 159, 198, 201, 203, 226, 396, 521
"Mystical One", 492
"Name and Address", 390, 407, 481
"New York City", 284, 444
"Night and Day", 186, 212
"Night Out", 298, 310
"Nineteen Hundred and Eighty-Five", 292
"No No Song", 348
"No Reply", 87, 254
"No Words", 292
"Nobody Loves You (When You're Down and Out)", 336
"Nobody Told Me", 401, 404, 406, 472
"Not Guilty", 425
"Note You Never Wrote, The", 388
"Now and Then", 399
"Nutopian International Anthem", 288
"Occapella", 348, 363-364
"Octopus's Garden", 38, 185, 188
"Ode to a Koala Bear", 477
"Oh My Love", 244, 258
"Oh My My", 305, 346
"Oh Woman, Oh Why", 233, 239
"Oh Yoko!", 244
"Old Brown Shoe", 63, 135, 139
"Old Dirt Road", 333, 336, 357
Old Wave, 7, 35, 153, 472, **476-477**
"One After 909", 44, 134-137, 139
"One Day (At a Time)", 313
"One More Kiss", 295
"One of These Days", 441, 455
"Only a Northern Song", 117, 119, 121, 124
"Only People", 287-288, 315
"Only You (And You Alone)", 347, 360
"Oo You", 190, 193, 214
"Ooh Baby (You Know That I Love You)", 351, 354, 396
"Oo-Wee", 348
"Other Me, The", 482
"Out on the Streets", 394
"Out the Blue", 287
"P.S. I Love You", 68, 73, 296
"Paperback Writer", 63, 106
Past Masters, Volume Two, 126, 130, 142
"Penny Lane", 63-64, 93, 117, 478
"Photograph", 6, 273, 280, 302, 304-305, 311, 313
"Picasso's Last Words (Drink to Me)", 292
"Pipes of Peace", 6
Pipes of Peace, 26, 153, 469, 472, **477-482**, 487-488, 497, 501, 535
"Please Mister Postman", 87
"Please Please Me", 45, 67-68, 71, 87, 522
Please Please Me, 46, 58, 69, 71, 75, 83, 87, 104, 185, 571
"Power to the People", 159, 226, 232, 241, 245, 252-253, 261, 286
"Private Property", 448
"Pure Gold", 394, 407
"Pure Smokey", 349, 351, 396, 403, 405
"Rain", 63, 106
"Rainclouds", 477, 482
Ram, 6, 26, 152, 194, 196, 226, 230-231, **233-238**, 243, 253, 255, 263-265, 294-295
Rarities, 418, 434
"Real Love", 445
"Reception", 428
Red, see *Beatles, The (1962-1966)*
Red Rose Speedway, 6, 26, 153, 196, 233, 237, 254, 272-273, 279, 289, **292-298**, 318, 388, 407, 410
"Remember", 179, 210, 213
"Revolution", 63, 208, 284, 522
"Revolution 1", 84, 87

Song and Album Index

Revolver, 41-42, 50, 59, 63, 75, 87, **105-114**, 117, 185, 297, 359
Ringo, 35, 153, 217, 273, 280, 297, **302-305**, 309, 318, 320, 329, 332, 347-348, 381
Ringo the 4th, 7, 35, 153, 377, 383, 392, **394-395**, 410
Ringo's Rotogravure, 7, 35, 153, 358, 376, 383, **392-394**, 410
"Rock and Roll Music", 45
Rock 'n' Roll, 153, 273, 287, 326-327, 332, 334, 338-339, 343
"Rock Show", 7, 342, 345
"Rockestra Theme", 418, 428
"Rocky Raccoon", 341
"Rode All Night", 237, 240, 260
"Roll Over Beethoven", 87
Rubber Soul, 43, 49, 52, 59, 63-64, 75, 77, 87, 106, 117, 174, 185, 444, 566
"Rudolph the Red-Nosed Reggae", 340, 426
"Run for Your Life", 87
"Run of the Mill", 201
"Sally G", 340
"San Ferry Anne", 388
"Say Say Say", 6, 477, 480
"Scared", 333, 337, 362
"Secret Friend", 439
Sentimental Journey, 20, 35, 152, 166, 170, 173, 175, **183-187**, 190, 217, 521
"Sexy Sadie", 244
Sgt. Pepper's Lonely Hearts Club Band, 8, 27, 36, 49, 57, 59, 63-64, 78-79, 83-84, 87, **89-104**, 111, 116-119, 121, 123, 126, 129, 137, 182, 185, 237, 294, 303, 344-345, 370, 504, 566
Shaved Fish, 376
"She Loves You", 63-64
"She Said She Said", 41, 87, 106, 113
"She's a Woman", 63
"She's Leaving Home", 93, 96, 99-102, 111
"She's My Baby", 388
"Silly Love Songs", 6, 387
"Simple as That", 441
"Singalong Junk", 191, 193
"Single Pigeon", 292
"Smile Away", 236, 255
"Snookeroo", 347
"So Bad", 7, 482
"So Sad", 333
"Soft Touch", 425
"Soft-Hearted Hana", 425
"Soily", 15, 333, 345, 359-360
"Some People Never Know", 239
Some Time in New York City, 7, 21, 152, 201, 272, 278, **282-287**, 289
"Somebody Who Cares", 479
"Something", 32, 197, 474-475
Somewhere in England, 7, 15, 31, 153, 436-437, **445-446**, 450, 459, 468, 471, 474-475, 492, 497
"Spirits of Ancient Egypt", 342
"Spooky Weirdness", 394
Speed of Sound, see *Wings at the Speed of Sound*
"Stand by Me", 334
"Stardust", 166, 187
"Steel and Glass", 336

"Step Lightly", 312
Stop and Smell the Roses, 7, 35, 153, 435, 437, **447-448**, 459, 468, 471-472, 476-477, 497
"Strawberry Fields Forever", 57, 61, 63-64, 93, 117
"Sue Me, Sue You Blues", 315
"Suicide", 195
"Summer's Day Song", 441, 455
"Sunday Bloody Sunday", 286
"Sunshine Life for Me (Sail Away Raymond)", 281, 304, 309, 312
"Sunshine Sometime", 195, 212
"Surprise, Surprise (Sweet Bird of Paradox)", 337, 362
"Sweetest Little Show", 481, 487, 492, 500
"Take It Away", 340
"Tango All Night", 395
"A Taste of Honey", 68, 74, 296
"Taxman", 87, 106-108
"Tears of the World", 446, 455
"Teddy Boy", 134, 136, 192-193, 212-213
"Tell Me What Has Happened to You", 248
"Temporary Secretary", 439, 441
"That Is All", 300
"That Would Be Something", 193, 214
"That's the Way It Goes", 475, 492
"There's a Place", 68-69, 74-75, 98
Thirty Three & 1/3, 7, 31, 153, 336, 376, 383, **395-397**, 410
"This Boy", 63
"This Guitar (Can't Keep from Crying)", 145, 351-353, 360
"This Song", 7, 404
Thrillington, 226, 377
"Through Our Love", 482, 487, 492
"Ticket to Ride", 87, 520
"Tight A$", 287, 313, 477
"Till There Was You", 296
"Tired of Midnight Blue", 352, 354, 359, 362
"Tomorrow", 238
"Tomorrow Never Knows", 106-107, 110, 207
"Too Many People", 236
"Tragedy", 297
"Try Some, Buy Some", 311-313
"Tug of War", 7
Tug of War, 6, 26, 38, 148, 153, 438, 468-469, 471-472, **477-482**, 493, 497, 499-500
"Twist and Shout", 68, 70-75, 87, 207
"Two of Us", 134-136, 139, 144, 237
"Uncle Albert/Admiral Halsey", 6, 231, 236, 253-254, 272
"Unconsciousness Rules", 455-456
"Unknown Delight", 475, 490, 492
"Valentine Day", 193
"Venus and Mars", 7
Venus and Mars, 6, 26, 153, 326-327, 331-332, **340-345**, 361, 363, 367, 387, 389, 428
"Wah-Wah", 201
"Wake Up", 477, 489-490
"Wake Up My Love", 7, 475, 489, 492
"Walking in the Park with Eloise", 341
Walls and Bridges, 6, 21, 153, 326, 332, **334-338**, 356-357, 367, 399
"Warm and Beautiful", 15, 381, 388, 404-405
"Watching the Wheels", 444, 450-451, 453, 474

"Waterfalls", 439, 441, 450, 454
"Waterspout", 407-408
"We Can Work It Out", 63
"Well Well Well", 179, 210, 212
"What Goes On", 28, 49, 87, 156, 185
"What Is Life", 202, 205
"What You Got", xix, 15, 336-337, 356
"Whatever Gets You thru the Night", 6
"What's That You're Doing?", 479-480
"When I'm Sixty-Four", 65, 93, 95, 97
"When the Night", 292
"While My Guitar Gently Weeps", 32, 42, 352, 360
White Album, The, 8, 17, 36, 52, 59, 63, 78, 87, 118, 174, 180, 185, 207, 220, 289, 321, 352, 360, 454, 476
"Who Can See It", 281, 301
"Wild Life", 238
Wild Life, 26, 152, 226, 231, 233, **238-240**, 263, 272, 278, 294-295
"Wings", 15, 231, 392, 395, 405, 529
Wings at the Speed of Sound, 6, 26, 153, 376, 380, 382, **384-388**, 405, 410-411
Wings Greatest, 418
Wings Over America, 345, 376, 382
"With a Little Help from My Friends", 185-186
"With a Little Luck", 6, 383, 390, 522
With the Beatles, 41, 58, 63, 87, 185, 489
"Within You Without You", 65, 83, 87, 93, 95, 97, 100, 103, 110-111, 121
"Woman", 6, 444, 451, 454, 456
"Woman Is the Nigger of the World", 7

"Wonderful Christmastime", 340, 418, 426
"Working Class Hero", 179, 182, 209-210
"Wrack My Brain", 7, 448, 450, 455, 475
"Writing's on the Wall", 450
"Yellow Submarine", 106, 109-110, 112-113, 185, 388
Yellow Submarine, 121, 126, 130, 566
Yellow Submarine (film), 127
Yellow Submarine Songtrack, 126, 130
"Yes It Is", 63
"Yesterday", 41-42, 51, 295-296, 472
Yesterday and Today, 106, 580
"You", 7, 353
"You Always Hurt the One You Love", 187
"You and Me (Babe)", 304, 309
"You Are Here", 281, 287, 313
"You Belong to Me", 448, 455
"You Can't Catch Me", 339
"You Can't Do That", 63
"You Can't Fight Lightning", 448
"You Gave Me the Answer", 341
"You Know My Name (Look Up the Number)", 117, 124, 394
"Your Mother Should Know", 117, 119, 121-122
"You're Sixteen", 6, 304-305
"You've Got a Nice Way", 448, 455-456
"You've Got to Hide Your Love Away", 41
"Zoo Gang", 289

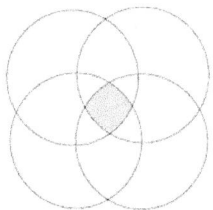

These things have served their purpose: let them be.

What we call the beginning is often the end
And to make an end is to make a beginning.

About the Author

Rick Prescott is a musician and writer living in Minneapolis, Minnesota, USA.
Love and gratitude to Victoria, Noah, Truman, and Kevin.

RickPrescott.com

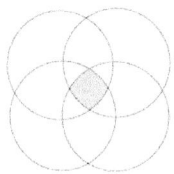

The section quotations are from *Little Gidding* by T. S. Eliot, part of a series known as *Four Quartets*. The poem was written in Great Britain during World War II, and published in 1942, roughly contemporary in time and place with the birth of all four Beatles. Eliot's beautiful words resonate well with the music and careers of the Beatles, being a meditation on age, time, love, beauty, death, redemption, spirituality and the ongoing search for meaning – the things which truly matter.